Learn to Program
with
Visual Basic 6

John Smiley

Active Path Ltd. ®

Learn to Program with Visual Basic 6

© 1998 Active Path

activepath

Published by Active Path Ltd. 30 Lincoln Road, Olton, Birmingham, B27 6PA

Printed in USA

ISBN 1-902745-00-0.

Trademark Acknowledgements

Active Path has endeavoured to provide trademark information about all the companies and products mentioned in this book by the appropriate use of capitals. However, Active Path cannot guarantee the accuracy of this information.

Credits

Author
John Smiley

Development Editor
Gordon Rogers

Technical Editors
Craig Berry
Andy Corsham
Kate Hall
Dev Lunsford
Dominic Shakeshaft

Technical Reviewers
Humberto Abreu
Lindsey Annison
Peter Baker

Antoine Giusti
Dave Jewell
John Kaufmann
Dave Liske
James Spate

Layout and Proof
Sarah Inston

Cover
Andrew Guillaume

Index
Seth Maislin

About the Author

John Smiley is the President of John Smiley and Associates, a computer consulting firm located in South Jersey, serving clients both large and small in the surrounding Philadelphia Metropolitan area. John is also an adjunct professor of computer science at Penn State University in Abington, the Philadelphia College of Textiles and Science, and Holy Family College, and has been teaching computer programming for nearly 20 years. He also teaches a number of very popular online courses at Ziff Davis University (ZDU).

In addition to these pursuits, John has done technical editing on a number of Wrox and Que titles, and has written a Case Study for Beginning Visual Basic 6 by Wrox Press.

He is the author of three ZDU Workbooks.

Feel free to visit John's Web Site at http://www.johnsmiley.com or contact him via email at johnsmiley@johnsmiley.com.

Dedication

This book is dedicated to my wife Linda – believe me, without you, all of this would not be possible.

Acknowledgments

First and foremost, I would like to thank my wife Linda for her unending love and support during the writing of this book. Writing a book at nights and on the weekends requires sacrifices on the part of everyone in the family – particularly Mommy. And you are the greatest Mommy in the world.

Thanks also go to my children Tom, Kevin and Melissa who played a big part of the project, enduring another round of "Be quiet, Daddy's working on his book." Tom, at the time 10 years old, and to my knowledge the youngest Visual Basic programmer in the world, read my draft and completed the exercises. Kevin, now age 10, is the world's youngest authority on the Solar System, and frequently kept me company during late night hours writing the book. And Melissa taught me that it is possible to write a final draft with a 2-year-old on your lap asking you to read Snow White.

Thanks go to the great people at Wrox/Active Path. Dave Maclean gave me the opportunity to pursue my dream of writing my own book on programming. Thanks Dave for your belief in the book and your vision!

I also want to thank Dominic Shakeshaft, Kate Hall and Craig Berry for the great job of editing the book. And to Devin Lunsford, Andy Corsham and Gordon Rogers for the great job of getting the book ready for publication. Special thanks go to Dominic and Kate for their great moral support and encouragement during the book writing process, and for responding so quickly to my numerous emails!

Books aren't produced in a vacuum. Behind the scenes there are reviewers, technical editors, artists, layout specialists, copy editors, indexers, and a group of marketing experts all working towards the goal of making the book a success. My thanks to all of you.

Many thanks also go to the thousands of students I've taught over the years for your tireless dedication to learning the art and science of computer programming. Your great questions and demanding persistence in getting the most out of your learning experience truly inspired me, and contributed greatly to the book. Many of you dragged yourself to class after a long hard day of work, or got up early on your Saturday day off to learn Visual Basic and the other programming languages I have taught. You have my great respect and admiration – and if you read the book carefully, you'll each see yourself somewhere in the persona of the students depicted in this book.

Special thanks go to the ZDU students who participated in a pilot Visual Basic course in April of 1998 using the draft version of this book. Your thorough reading, analysis and feedback about the book was invaluable, and your positive encouragement convinced me and my publisher that the novel approach I took to writing this book could be successful.

I want to thank the many great people I have worked with over the years and who have contributed greatly to my personal and professional growth. To thank you all individually would be impossible – you all know who you are! Thanks also to my friends who have continually asked about the book over the course of the last year.

Finally, I want to thank the members of my family for their great support over the years. Special thanks go to my mother, who has said several hundred novenas for the success of the book, and who is undoubtedly the world's greatest babysitter. Anyone who knows you is inspired by you! Thanks also to Joe and Annette for being Smiley and Associates first paying clients, and for asking about and encouraging my work over the years. Thanks to Bob and Pat for always being there when I needed you. Thanks to my mother, Pat L, Bob and Pat for watching the kids and allowing us to see Paris!

And even though he is not physically here to see this book, thanks to my father for showing me what real heroism is all about. I know somewhere, somehow, someplace, you are already flipping through the pages. And I know that the God who has led me to this moment in time will permit us all to be together again.

John Smiley

Summary of Contents

Table of Contents

Introduction

This book is the key that will open the door to the world of programming. Between these covers is a broad-based introduction to programming using Visual Basic, taught step-by-step, in plain language, and using a host of practical examples. This book will not only teach you the core concepts of programming in Visual Basic, it will also show you how to build a Visual Basic program from the design phase all the way through to delivery. Most books will teach you how to use Visual Basic to make things happen, but they leave you wondering how you start to actually *design* a program. By the end of this book, you'll have a firm foundation for designing and building your own programs, from the ground up.

Who is This Book For?

The book was written for the intrepid beginner, taking those first tentative steps into programming. But if you already know some programming this book will still be useful, as it demystifies and clarifies many concepts that other books skim over. And even if you're a tutor needing background knowledge or examples for teaching programming to beginners, you'll find valuable inspiration here.

What Will You Need?

Not much! Time, patience and, of course, a PC. You get a working copy of Visual Basic on the CD bundled with this book, which also contains the completed code for most of the exercises in the book.

Make sure you install Visual Basic from the enclosed CD before you start – instructions for this are at the end of this section.

To use the Working Model Edition of Visual Basic, you'll need a PC with the following minimum specifications:

- 486 DX/66 processor (Pentium recommended)
- Microsoft Windows 95 or Microsoft NT 4.0
- 24 megabytes of memory (32 megabytes recommended)

What is Covered?

This book will give you a grasp of the important techniques you need to create a 'real world' application. The example application is created stage-by-stage, using a multitude of concepts and materials, and beginning with the essential design phase. Each chapter tackles a different idea or programming concept. Starting with a common task or problem that needs to be overcome, the relevant knowledge is taught and practiced using examples and exercises. The knowledge is then applied to the main project to further reinforce the core techniques and to show how they can be applied to real applications.

How is the Book Structured?

Imagine yourself back at school. OK, so maybe without gym class, mystery meat, and the sweet guy or girl who sat across from you in Chemistry 101 (sigh!). Put yourself in a class of people just like you, who really want to learn about programming. You don't just learn from the teacher; you learn from the questions the other people ask, too.

That's how the Learn to Program (LTP) approach works. Any time the going gets heavy, someone will get confused, and ask the teacher to explain: you'll never get too stuck with difficult concepts. John Smiley's class takes on a challenge – a real application needed by a user. You'll build this project along with them, seeing how the interface and code fit together to make the working program.

The program is taken from the design stage, where the whole application is laid out and planned, through a working prototype, right through to the finished article. Using this approach, you'll get a much more rounded view of the processes involved in programming. Programming doesn't start and end with knowing how code works: you need a direction and a design to start with, and you will probably have to maintain your program, too. With this book, you won't just learn to type code; you'll Learn to Program.

What is 'Learn to Program'?

Learn to Program with Visual Basic 6 is the first in a series of foundation-level books designed to take someone from having no experience with programming up to the level where they can really understand how programming is done. By the end of a 'Learn to Program' book, you might not be a professional programmer yet, but you will have established the beginnings of your programming knowledge. Remember that learning takes time, though, and don't get discouraged. We at Active Path will keep nurturing that skill, all the way up to the professional level.

Do I Get Any Support?

OK, so with a real class you can put your hand up and ask the teacher – what do you do if you get stuck in a book?

You're not alone. Just remember that. The LTP website, on www.activepath.com is there as a resource for you to use. There'll be the opportunity to ask questions and give us feedback (positive or negative – we can take it). The answers to your questions will be posted on the site, so your fellow students can benefit from them, too.

What is Active Path?

Active Path is a new publishing house with a fresh attitude to learning about computer programming. As a publisher, we understand your need to have the most up-to-date, cutting edge information about the computing world around you, but we also understand that the computing world is full of jargon, unintuitive ways of doing things and complex and uninformative software documentation.

So what makes Active Path different? Books from Active Path start at your level. There will always be an entry-level book, for which there's no previous experience required – guaranteed. We're not going to teach you the detailed syntax for every possible command; we'll present the concepts when they become relevant to the problem. We don't believe anything is too complicated to learn; but we do believe that if you can imagine the problem, we should be able to illustrate the solution in terms you can understand.

Future books will take a topic and work you through it, using the foundation we've built at the Learn to Program stage. They'll have detailed examples, and the chance to work out your own solutions to problems designed to get you thinking and apply your knowledge. Most books try to cover everything, but end up leaving you baffled. We think it's more important that you fully understand one topic, and so we'll keep the books to more specific subject matter. If you want to know about the use of databases in Visual Basic, you buy the relevant book. It won't tell you about graphics or anything else – just databases. That way, you won't have to learn anything that's not essential to what you want to know.

Basically, we believe that you should be able to learn what you want, how you want, when you want, and at a pace you feel comfortable with. All we do is write books to enable you to make those choices.

What About Text Styles?

To help you pick out important pieces of information, and distinguish a piece of code from within a paragraph of text, we've used certain fonts and styles throughout the book. We've kept it simple, so we don't distract you from the content, which we believe is the key here. Here are examples of each kind of style we use:

Since this book is about programming, there are quite a few times when we need to point out pieces of code. There are three ways of doing it, but they all look similar, so you can easily pick them out of a crowd. Sometimes we'll just need to refer to a `procedure` or `code-related thing` in the middle of the text.

```
Other times we'll be describing a new chunk of code. If you see an underscore _
it means that you should type the code all as one line, leaving out the
underscore.
```

```
Code that has already been explained won't have the gray background. _
    Quite often it will be a chunk of code you've seen before, but we've _
    changed one line of it, or added something. So the new part looks like this.
```

New **terms** or **new phrases** will be bolded.

Text from a <u>M</u>enu appears like it does on the screen.

Pieces of information that are useful, but not crucial, will look like this.

But if it's really important, it will stand out, like this.

Any time we refer to something on the CD that comes with the book, it will show up like this.

1. There are exercises with numbered steps like this too, in which you'll the steps to see how something works.

2. These are here to help you learn. They'll take you through a concept so you can see the ins and outs of how it all fits together.

3. Some of the exercises build the running project you'll be working on. These are important, because each one builds on the project as you left it after the last exercise.

How to Install Visual Basic

Insert the CD that came with this book into your CD drive. Open up the directory called **'VB6 Working Model Edition'**, and double-click on `setup`.exe. The Working Model Edition will now install.

Alternatively, click on the Windows Start menu, then on Run.... You can then browse to the `setup.exe` file on the CD and run it.

That's all there is to it! The Installation Wizard will guide you through the rest of the process. You'll now be ready to use the book!

We've also included all the files you need to complete the project we build as we go along, as well as finished copies of all the example code. We'll refer to any files you need to copy from the CD as they occur in the text. We've included the finished code as an emergency resource to get you out of a hole if you get stuck - the whole point of this book is that you carry out the practical work for yourself. Refer to our website if you have any queries about using the files on the CD.

OK - let's Learn to Program.

Chapter 1
Where Do I Begin?

"Where do I begin?" is a question I am frequently asked by my students, and this seems like a good question to tackle right at the beginning of this book. In this first chapter, we'll look at the development process of an actual working program through the eyes and ears of my university programming class and you will also be introduced to our 'class project'. By the end of the book, we'll have taken a real-life application through from the concept all the way to the finished product!

Occasionally, my students get disillusioned when they hear that we won't be diving straight in and coding our application. However, when I remind them that programming is much the same as writing a report (or in other words, it is a two stage process of planning and then producing) they tend to settle down.

Where Do We Begin

As part of answering the question, "Where do we begin?" this chapter looks at the **Systems Development Life Cycle**, which is a methodology that has been developed to ensure that systems are developed in a methodical, logical and step-by-step approach. We'll be looking at the Systems Development Life Cycle in quite a bit of detail, since the majority of this book will be spent in developing a real-world application. In this chapter we'll meet with a prospective client and conduct a preliminary interview with him. From that interview (and a subsequent one!) we'll develop a **Requirements Statement**, which provides details as to what the program should do. This Requirements Statement will form the basis of the application that we will develop throughout the rest of the book.

From this point on, you will follow me as I lead a group of my university students in an actual class on Visual Basic. If I do my job right, you will be a part of the class, learning along with them as we complete a fifteen-week course about programming in Visual Basic.

Many books on computer programming have the reader, perhaps as early as the first chapter, code a program which 'cutely' displays a message box that says 'Hello World'. Then the author will point to the fact that within the first few minutes of reading their book, the reader has already written a working program. I'm not so naive as to believe that writing such a program makes you a programmer. Therefore, we'll opt for a slower approach. Simple programs, although great for the ego, are not the programs that are found in the real world. Real-world programs are written to meet someone's needs. These needs are frequently complex and difficult to verbalize. In this book, you and I will embark on a journey together that will see us complete the prototyping stage of a real-world project. I believe that this is the best way to learn programming.

In my university classes, I don't usually introduce the class project until several weeks into the semester. When I finally do introduce the class project, I give the students in my class a Requirements Statement. Since the class project is to develop a Windows application, with an event-driven paradigm (look that one up in the dictionary), I never tell my students exactly *how* the application should look, or how to program it. I tell them only what is required. In other words, I complete the hard part for them - gathering the user requirements.

Programming the Easy Way

When I first began to teach programming, some of my students would tell me that they just didn't know where to start when they first began to work on their programming assignments. They would start to program the application, then stop. Some of them would find themselves re-writing their code and re-designing their application several times. Then they would change it again. Face to face I could usually clear things up for them by giving them a gentle nudge or hint in the right direction. However, their work would show a definite lack of direction. Why the problem? They lacked a plan.

As soon as I realized this, I began to teach them more than just programming. I began to teach them the **Systems Development Life Cycle (SDLC)**, the methodology I mentioned earlier. You see, people need blueprints or maps. They need something tangible, usually in writing, before they can begin a project. Just about all of my students agree that having a blueprint of some kind makes the development process that much easier.

Sometimes I'll meet former students of mine at the university, and I'll ask them how their other programming classes are coming along. Occasionally, they'll tell me that they're working on a great *real-world* assignment of some kind, but they just don't know where to begin. At that point, I'll remind them of what I told them in class - that they should begin with the design of the user interface, observe the default behavior of the design and then add code to fill in the gaps. That's not the problem, they tell me. The problem is that they don't know how to gather the user requirements for the system. They don't really know what the system should do.

Often the real problem is that the client isn't prepared to give the programmers a detailed enough Requirements Statement. In class the professor gives out a well-defined Requirements Statement but in the real world, they need to develop this themselves. Unfortunately, they may not know how to sit down with the prospective user of their system to determine what is required to satisfy the user's needs.

That skill, to listen to the user and determine their needs, is something that I now teach to some extent in all of my computer classes - whether they are programming courses, courses on Systems Analysis and Design, or Database Management.

Planning a Program is Like Planning a House

A friend of mine is a general contractor and home-builder. His job is similar to that of a programmer or system designer. He recently built an addition to a customer's house. He wouldn't think of beginning that work without first meeting with the owner of the house to determine their needs. He couldn't possibly presume to know what the owner wants or needs. The builder's role, in meeting with the owner, is largely to listen and then to advise.

My friend the home builder tells me that certain home owners may want a design that is architecturally unsound - either because their ideas and design are unsafe and would violate accepted building code regulations, or because they would violate local zoning regulations for their neighborhood. In some cases, he tells me, owners ask for features that he is certain they will later regret - and probably hold him responsible for. His role as an advisor demands that he inform the homeowner of these problems.

As soon as my friend believes that he understands what the owner wants, then he prepares a set of blueprints to be reviewed by the homeowner. Frequently the owner, after seeing his own vision on paper, will decide to change something, such as the location of a window or the size of a closet. The *concrete* characteristics of the blueprints make an agreement between the builder and owner easier to arrive at. The same can be said of a concrete plan for the writing of a program or the development of a system.

The big advantage of developing a plan on paper is that, while the project is still on paper, it's relatively painless to change it. Once the house has been assembled and bolted together, it becomes much more of a problem to change something.

The same is true of a computer program. Although it's not physically nailed or bolted together, once a programmer has started to write a program, changing it becomes very labor-intensive. It's much easier to change the design of a system prior to writing the first line of code.

In the world of software development, you would be surprised how many programmers begin work on an application without really having listened to the user. I know some programmers who get a call from a user, take some quick notes over the phone, and deliver an application without ever having met them! It could be that the user's requirements sound *similar* to a something the programmer wrote last year, so the developer feels that will be good enough for the new client.

Other developers go a step further, and may actually meet with the client to discuss the user's needs. Nevertheless, sometimes the developer may not be a good listener, or just as likely, the user may communicate their needs poorly. The result may be that the user receives a program that doesn't come close to doing what they wanted it to do.

In this course, we'll develop a prototype for a real-world application called the **China Shop Project**, and then take it through to the complete product. As we progress through the course together, we will work through one possible solution, but I want you to know that in

Visual Basic programming, the number of solutions are almost infinite. As I tell my students all the time, there are many ways to paint a picture. One of the things I love about teaching Visual Basic is that I have never received the same solution to a project twice. Everyone brings his or her own unique qualities to the project.

I want you to feel free to take the China Shop Project and make your solution different from mine. In fact, I encourage it, but you should stick close to the **Requirements Statement** that we are going to develop in this chapter.

We Receive a Call from the China Shop

One Monday morning I received a call from a prospective client, Mr. Joe Bullina. Having seen my ad in the Western Suburban Times he wanted a computer program. By saying the magic word "program" Mr. Bullina had now got my complete attention.

Mr. Bullina owned a store that sold fine china. The dish variety. I know next to nothing about china. Writing programs about something that you know nothing about is not unusual for a programmer. That's why the Systems Development Life Cycle (SDLC) was introduced many years ago. At a minimum, the SDLC will result in the creation of a Requirements Statement, which will form the basis of an agreement between the programmer and the user as to what the program should do.

Mr. Bullina told me that he had spoken to other software developers in the area, but at their rates ($50 an hour and up), he didn't think he could afford them. Like so many people these days, he was on a tight budget, and I agreed with him, custom software development is not cheap.

"Have you checked out your local computer store for software that might meet your needs?" I asked him.

He told me he had, but with no luck.

"What about trade magazines?" I suggested.

He told me he'd checked them, but the programs advertised seemed too complicated for his needs. He wanted something simple.

"Why computerize?" I asked Mr. Bullina.

He told me it seemed like a good idea. That may sound like a good motive, but it's not usually the best reason to computerize.

We agreed to meet on Tuesday afternoon as I had another client in the area that needed some assistance with a DOS program that I had written. I told Mr. Bullina I'd stop by the China store after I finished up there.

We Meet with Our Client

I arrived at the Bullina China Shop at around 2 p.m. on Tuesday afternoon. Going into the store, a small brick building, I saw that there were around ten or fifteen customers and three neatly dressed sales clerks serving the customers at a counter. A display area took up most of the store. There were glass display counters along the walls and behind the counters were shelves of dishes… I mean fine china. It's always best to try and get into the client's mindset. I got the attention of one of the sales clerks:

"Hi, I'm John Smiley, I'm here to meet with the owner of the store."

"Just a minute Mr. Smiley, Joe is expecting you."

Good, I thought. The sales clerk called the owner by his first name. I prefer an informal atmosphere. It usually makes for better business. A few moments later, Mr. Bullina appeared from behind a curtain separating the front of the store from the back.

"Sorry to keep you waiting," he said, warmly extending his hand. "I was on the phone with one of my overseas china suppliers."

He led me past the counters into the back of store, past shelves of china, and into a small office where we took a seat before getting down to business.

"Mr. Bullina," I said, "in our conversation on the telephone, you said that you were interested in me writing a program for you."

"Please, call me Joe," he said smiling. "Yes, as you probably saw when you came into the shop, I had a number of customers waiting for my sales clerks to serve them. At any given time, I have about ten or more customers in the store, but only three sales clerks to wait on them. Some of those customers will grow impatient and leave. Some of my sales clerks, sensing this, may rush the customers they're helping. The thing about this is that I'm lucky if three out of those ten customers actually purchase something. Most of them are just browsing and checking prices, they have no real intention of buying anything. Still, they're consuming the time and resources of my sales clerks. This is where the program comes in." I was starting to get interested in this. I love projects with a positive payback for my client, and it was obvious that this had one.

"I'd like to place a computer in the middle of the sales floor," he said, "on a table top or counter. Like the kind I've seen in some of the shopping malls. You've probably seen them. They give directions to shoppers, advertise sales, some even print coupons!"

"You mean kiosks," I said.

"Yes, exactly," he continued. "I'd like to place a kiosk computer in the middle of my sales floor, and have it compute a price for a customer based on the selections they make. That way, my sales clerks can concentrate on the customers who actually want to purchase something."

"Do you have any details in your mind as to what you want the program to look like?" I said.

"Not really," Joe said. "I was really hoping you could take care of those details. Don't get me wrong. I know what I want the program to do, that is, calculate a quote for some china. Beyond that, my biggest requirement is that the program be simple. I don't want to intimidate any of my customers. I'm just guessing, but I don't think many of my customers have used a computer before."

"I like my clients to give me as much detail as they can," I said. "That way I can do my best to write a program which really does what they want it to."

"I don't think the program will be very complex," Joe said. "Let me tell you a little bit about the China Shop. Basically, we're a specialty store. We only sell three brands of china, and only one pattern of each brand. Our inventory includes plates, butter plates, soup bowls, cups, saucers and platters. We sell either complete place settings or..."

"Excuse me," I interrupted as I started to take notes. "What's a complete place setting?"

"A complete place setting," he explained, "is one each of a plate, a butter plate, a soup bowl, a cup and a saucer, all of the same brand." He looked at me sensing the confusion on my face. "I guess the business of a software developer is a constant learning process for you," Joe said. "Each new program you write requires that you learn new terms and new rules. It must be difficult."

I nodded in agreement and said, "It's a challenge, but I do enjoy it, almost as much as I enjoy teaching."

"I didn't know you were also a teacher," Joe said. "Where do you teach?"

After I told him, he told me that he would like to take a class with me some day.

"That would be great," I said, "then you'll have an opportunity to learn some of my terms!" We both laughed. "By the way," I said, "what's a butter plate?"

"A butter plate is a 6-inch plate," Joe said. "There are also salad plates and dessert plates, but we don't stock them. Did I tell you that we also sell individual pieces of china?"

"Such as one plate, or two cups?" I replied.

"Yes, exactly," he said. "But we only sell them in quantities of one, two, four or eight."

"Quantities of one, two, four, or eight what?" I asked. "Complete place settings or individual pieces?"

"Both," Joe said. I was beginning to get horribly confused.

"Let me get this straight," I said. "You sell complete place settings in any quantity, but individual pieces only in quantities of one, two, four or eight?"

"No," he said. "The quantity restrictions apply to both complete place settings and individual pieces. Over the years we have found that selling in quantities other than those can really wreak havoc with our inventory."

"I don't know much about china," I said, "but I think my wife and I have an eight piece place setting of Mikasa china at home, plus a platter and some big bowls."

"Yes," he said, "but in my shop, a complete place setting does not include a platter. A complete place setting includes only a plate, a butter plate, a soup bowl, a cup and a saucer. Of course, we do offer platters for sale, although we don't carry the big bowls - most likely those are serving bowls."

"In what quantities," I asked, "do you sell the platters - quantities of one, two, four and eight also?"

"That's a good question," Joe said. "I'm glad you asked that, because I probably would have forgotten to tell you. Because platters are a specialty item, they're very expensive, we only sell platters in quantities of one. In other words, only one to a customer." Joe could see that I was puzzled. "It's confusing I know," he said. "Of course, we can always special order any item in the store if the customer wants it," he said, "but I want the program to restrict the quantity of a platter on the sales quotation to one. Maybe the program could display a message telling the customer they can only purchase one. Is that possible?"

"Sure," I said, "that's possible, that's why I'm here. To give you exactly what you want. You're doing an excellent job of explaining your requirements. A lot of my clients can't express their needs as well as you have. The better you communicate them to me, the closer the program I write for you will come to meeting those needs."

"Let me summarize my understanding of what we have so far," I continued. "The customer can select from three brands of china. You only sell one pattern of each brand. The customer can select either a complete place setting, which consists of one each of a plate, a butter plate, a soup bowl, a cup and a saucer of the same brand. Alternatively, the customer can also select any individual piece they wish. The customer can select complete place settings and individual pieces only in quantities of one, two, four or eight. Platter quantities are limited to one. If the customer attempts to select more than one platter, you want a message displayed telling them that sales of platters are limited to just one."

"That's right so far," Joe said.

"Your china inventory includes plates, butter plates, soup bowls, cups, saucers and platters. A complete place setting is made up of a plate, a butter plate, a soup bowl, a cup and a saucer, all of the same brand," I added and looked up from my notes, somewhat proud of my requirements gathering abilities.

"Yes, that's about it," Joe said, "but did I make it clear that the customer must order the same quantity of everything? In other words, the customer cannot order four cups and two saucers. Again, it wreaks havoc on my inventory."

Fumbling through my notes, I realized I hadn't recorded that. Neither could I remember Joe mentioning this before.

"So," I said, "the customer can't order two cups and four soup bowls, is that correct? Only two cups and two soup bowls, or four cups and four soup bowls?"

Joe nodded approvingly. "Exactly," he said smiling, apparently happy with our progress.

"I just thought of something," I said. "Can the customer order items from different brands? Such as two cups from Brand X, and four saucers from Brand Y?"

Joe thought for a moment. "It's pretty rare for a customer to request a combination like that. If it's OK with you," he continued, "I'd rather restrict the sales quotation to a single brand at one time. If the customer needs to replace pieces from more than one brand, they'll need to get two separate quotes."

That was fine with me, I thought. Ultimately, that one little restriction would make the system easier to program. "One more thing," I said. "In my notes, I've mentioned the word 'order' several times. You want the program to provide only a price quotation, not to initiate an actual sales order. Is that correct?"

"Yes, only a quotation," Joe said. "I want the program to display the price of the customer's selected china pieces. At that point, if they like the price quoted, then they can come to the counter to finalize the sale."

"Can you think of anything else?" I asked.

"No, I don't think so," he said. He hesitated for a moment and then added hopefully. "What do you think? The program doesn't sound too difficult, does it?"

Famous last words, I thought to myself. "Mr. Bullina...Joe," I said, "it's very hard to say at this point. No, it doesn't seem terribly complex. This has just been a preliminary investigation of your requirements though. I still need a few more things from you, in order to get a better idea of the complexity of the project. For instance, we haven't even discussed how the price of the sales quotations should be calculated. I need to know the prices of the individual items."

"Rules," he said obligingly. "Oh yes, that shouldn't be a problem."

"How often do the prices of your china inventory change?" I asked.

"Not very often," he said, but then I detected a look of worry appearing on his face. "But they do change occasionally. If I need to change the price of an item, will you have to rewrite the program?"

"Not if I design it properly," I said. "You could use a software package such as Microsoft Access to maintain the prices of your china inventory, which I could program your system to use. That way, if your inventory prices change, or if you decide to sell a new brand of china, or discontinue an old one, then all you need to do is use Access to update the inventory record."

I could see that I was beginning to lose him.

"I really don't know much about computers," Joe said, "and I don't know what Microsoft Access is. In fact, only one of my sales clerks, Midge, has even used a computer. Incidentally, she was the one who saw your ad. She tells me the only program she knows how to use is something called Notepad."

"That would work," I said. "You, or Midge I should say, could use Notepad to record your inventory prices in a file stored on the computer's hard drive. If the prices change, Midge could then use Notepad to update the prices in the file. We wouldn't need to use Microsoft Access after all."

"That sounds better to me," Joe said. "Would you show Midge how to do that?"

I explained that training is part of my fee. Joe paused for a moment. "How much do you think the program will cost?" he asked.

I hesitated and then said, "Again, Joe, at this point it's difficult for me to say because we're really just in the preliminary investigation phase of what is known as the Systems Development Life Cycle. Every program is different...but I can tell you I have designed and programmed systems, similar in scope to this one, which have cost the client somewhere in the neighborhood of $2,500, not including the price of the computer. With the computer, I would guess somewhere between $3500 and $4000." I was surprised to see a look of disappointment come over his face.

"I really wasn't looking to spend more than a few hundred dollars for the program," he said. "When I was looking through the software aisle at my local computer store, most of those programs were selling for under $50."

I explained to Joe that custom software development is more expensive than purchasing software 'off the shelf'. This is because 'off the shelf' software is sold in large quantities to many people; the development costs can be divided among many purchasers.

I looked up at the clock on his wall and realized that I was nearly late for my Tuesday evening university computer class.

"Joe, I've got to be heading out," I said as I started to gather my notes and place them into my briefcase. "I have a class to get to at 6 p.m."

As I packed up, I explained to Joe that I charged by the hour. With my travel time, and this initial meeting, we were already well over two hours. To design and program the system we had been discussing for just a few hundred dollars would be impossible.

"Here's my card," I said as I took one out of my wallet and handed it to him. "Think it over, and if you're interested, just give me a call."

"How much do you charge per hour?" he asked hesitantly. I told him, and he did some quick mental calculations. "Isn't there anything we could do to cut the cost?" Joe said. "I'm really excited by the possibility of this project, and I would be disappointed not to proceed with it."

I pondered the possibility for a moment, and then an idea hit me. I explained to Joe that on Saturday I would be meeting with my 'Introduction to Programming' Spring Semester class for the first time. I then went on to explain to Joe that for the last year, I'd been thinking about assigning, as a class project, some kind of project just like his, a real-world programming project. I had put out some feelers with some local organizations, but most of them had 'shied' away from having a programming class write a program for them.

"Perhaps," I said, "instead of a formal class project, I can have the class adopt your program as their class project."

Joe looked excited and nervous at the same time. "How would that work?" he asked.

"Well," I said, "each semester I give my programming students a project to develop. Ideally, it's something they can really sink their teeth into. Usually, I just make something up. For instance, last semester, they wrote a program for an imaginary store that sells sneakers. Your project excites me, and I think it will excite them. It's better than anything I could ever dream up, because it's real, with a real customer, you, expecting real results. And your requirements have a few 'quirks' that will make it a little more challenging than anything I could throw at them."

I looked at Joe for a reaction. I saw a look of unease on his face. "I can take these notes," I continued, "distribute them to my students on Saturday, and over the course of our semester, they can program the entire system for you. In eight weeks, you'll have a prototype of the program. Seven weeks after that, you'll have the program running in your store! Unless of course, you're in a huge hurry…"

"No," Joe said, "I can live with fifteen weeks. Of course, I'm guessing that the program won't be as sophisticated as one that you would write. After all, your students are just beginners."

"Not at all," I said. "I'll be working with them every step of the way. You can expect a top-notch program, and I have no doubt that we can do it at a price you can afford."

"What would that be?" Joe said.

"You were willing to pay me a few hundred dollars," I said. "I have eighteen students in my class. How about $450 to be shared equally among the members of the class?"

I must have said the magic words; at this Joe smiled, extended his hand and said, "That sounds like a deal to me."

As I prepared to leave, I warned Joe that what we had done this afternoon merely represented the first step, the tip of the iceberg, so to speak, in a six step process known as the **Systems Development Life Cycle (SDLC)**. The first phase, the **Preliminary Investigation**, had begun and ended with our initial interview. Five phases of the SDLC remained.

As I walked to the door, Joe and I mutually agreed that I would fax him several items within a day or so:

- a letter confirming my agreement to 'take on' the project

- a Requirements Statement that will take shape from the notes I have taken at today's meeting

- the specifications for the computer hardware that he will need to purchase

We agreed that Joe would pay me the sum of $450 for the program, to be equally distributed among the students in my class. For just about all of them, I guessed, this would be their first 'professional' programming job.

I warned Joe that when he read the **Requirements Statement** that I would send him, the possibility existed that he would find some things about his business that I had misinterpreted, and perhaps some things that he was sure he had mentioned that wouldn't appear at all. I told him that the Requirements Statement would act as a starting point for the project. Until I received a signed copy of the Requirements Statement from him, acknowledging his agreement to its terms, neither my student team nor I would proceed with the development of his system.

Joe agreed that he would fax me a letter by the end of the week with details concerning china brands and item prices so that we could begin building a text file of brands and prices for inclusion in his program.

Mr. Bullina told me about a nephew of his who sold computers at a local computer superstore, who, he assured me could get him a deep discount on a new system. I told him that it would be fine with me as long as the system met my minimum systems requirements.

As I walked out the door of the Bullina China Shop, we both said warm 'good byes'. Joe was a genuinely likable man, and I hoped this experience would be a rewarding one for both him and the students in my class. I left Joe attending to a customer in the front of his store, and I headed off to teach my evening class at the university.

The Systems Development Life Cycle (SDLC)

During the drive to my evening class, I gave a lot of thought to Joe's program. The more I thought about it, the more I believed that having my students program the system was a great idea, and I was sure they would think so too. Working on a real-world application would be a great practical assignment for them. Even more so than something I made up, this project would give each of them a chance to become deeply involved in the various aspects of the SDLC. For instance:

- someone in the class would need to work on the user requirements
- someone else would be involved in a detailed analysis of the China Shop
- everyone would be involved in coding the program
- some students would work on installing the software
- some students would be involved in training and implementation

Four days later, on Saturday morning, I met my 'Introductory Programming' class for the first time. For the last few semesters, my university has been using Visual Basic as our introductory programming language.

As is my custom during my first class, I took roll, and asked each of the students to write a brief biography on a sheet of paper. Doing this gives me a chance to get to know them, without the pressure of having to open themselves up to a room full of strangers, although many of them become good friends during the course of the class.

I only called out their first names as I like to personalize the class as much as possible. Usually, I have some duplicated first names, but in this semester, this wasn't a problem.

"Valerie, Peter, Linda, Steve, Katherine Rose."

"If you don't mind, just call me Rose," she said.

"Rhonda, Joe, John."

"Jack, if you don't mind."

"Barbara, Kathy, Dave, Ward, Blaine, Kate, Mary, Chuck, Lou, Bob."

That makes eighteen students.

I began reading over their biographies. A few had some programming experience, using languages that are a bit dated. A number were looking to get into the exciting world of computer programming, either because they had an opportunity at work, or believed one would open up shortly. A couple of them were people looking to get into the work force after years away from it. One of the students, Chuck, was just fifteen, a local high school student. Another student, Lou, was permanently disabled, and although he doesn't look it, he wrote that his disability would probably end up restricting him to a wheelchair.

My classroom is about 40 feet by 20 feet and there are three rows of tables containing PCs. Each student has their own PC, and at the front of the room I have my own, cabled to a projector that enables me to display the contents of my video display.

My first lecture usually involves bringing the class up to a common level so that they feel comfortable with both the terminology and methodology of using the Windows environment. This time, however, instead of waiting a few weeks before introducing the class project, I could hardly wait to tell them. In the first few minutes of class, I introduced the students to the China Shop Project. Just about everyone in the class seemed genuinely excited at the prospect of developing a real-world application. They were even more excited after I offered to split the profits with them. In only their first Visual Basic course, they would all be paid as professionals, with a legitimate project to add to their resumes.

"You mean this course isn't going to be the usual 'read the textbook, and code the examples' course," Ward said.

"Exactly," I said, "we'll be developing a real world application, and getting paid for it!"

"How will we know what to do?" Rose asked nervously.

I explained that in today's class, we'd actually develop a **Requirements Statement**.

"A Requirements Statement," I said, "is just an agreement between the contractor (in this case us) and the customer (in this case Mr. Bullina) that specifies in detail exactly what work will be performed, when it will be completed, and how much it will cost."

I continued by explaining that at this point, all we had were my notes from the initial interview. This was hardly enough to begin anything more than a quick sketch of the program. While we might very well have produced a quick sketch of the user interface in the following hour or so, we still did not know how to write a single line of code in Visual Basic. There was still much to learn! Furthermore, we still did not have the processing rules (e.g., the price of the various items) which Mr. Bullina had promised to fax to me by that day's class.

> *Processing rules are known either as Business Rules or Work Rules.*

And I also pointed out that we still needed to fax him a Requirements Statement and the specifications for the computer itself. I told them that there was the possibility that the Requirements Statement would have some mistakes in it, and even some missing items. I cautioned them not to be too hasty at this point in the project. There was still a lot of planning left to do!

"Such hastiness," I said, "is exactly why the Systems Development Life Cycle was developed."

> *The SDLC was developed because many systems projects were developed which did not satisfy user requirements and the projects that did satisfy user requirements were being developed over budget or over time.*

I saw some puzzled looks. I explained that the Systems Development Life Cycle (SDLC) is a methodology that was developed to ensure that systems are developed in a methodical, logical and step-by-step approach. There are six steps, known as **phases**, in the Systems Development Life Cycle:

> *Different companies may have different 'versions' of the SDLC. The point is that just about everyone who does program development can benefit from one form or other of a structured development process such as this one.*

- The Preliminary Investigation Phase
- The Analysis Phase
- The Design Phase
- The Development Phase

- The Implementation Phase
- The Maintenance Phase

I continued by explaining that out of each phase of the SDLC, a tangible product, or **deliverable,** is produced. This deliverable may consist of a Requirements Statement, or it may be a letter informing the customer that the project cannot be completed within their time and financial constraints. An important component of the SDLC is that at each phase in the SDLC, a conscious decision is made to continue development of the project, or to drop it. In the past, projects developed without the guidance of the SDLC were continued well after 'common sense' dictated that it made no sense to proceed further.

"Many people say that the SDLC is just common sense," I said. "Let's examine the elements of the SDLC here. You can then judge for yourself."

Phase 1: The Preliminary Investigation

I told my class of my meeting with Joe Bullina, which essentially constituted the **Preliminary Investigation Phase** of the SDLC.

"This phase of the SDLC," I said, "may begin with a phone call from a customer, a memorandum from a Vice President to the director of Systems Development, or a letter from a customer to discuss a perceived problem or deficiency, or to express a requirement for something new in an existing system. In the case of the China Shop, it was a desire on the part of Mr. Bullina to develop a 'program' to provide price quotations to customers in his China Shop."

I continued by explaining that the purpose of the **Preliminary Investigation** is not to develop a system, but to verify that a problem or deficiency really exists, or to pass judgment on the new requirement.

The duration of the preliminary investigation is typically very short, usually not more than a day or two for a big project, and in the instance of the China Shop Project, about two hours.

The end result, or deliverable, from the Preliminary Investigation phase is either a willingness to proceed further, or the decision to 'call it quits'. What influences the decision to abandon a potential project at this point? There are three factors, typically called **constraints**, which result in a go or no-go decision.

- **Technical**. The project can't be completed with the technology currently in existence. This constraint is typified by Leonardo Da Vinci's inability to build a helicopter even though he is credited with designing one in the 16th century. Technological constraints made the construction of the helicopter impossible.

- **Time**. The project can be completed, but not in time to satisfy the user's requirements. This is a frequent reason for the abandonment of the project after the Preliminary Investigation phase.

- **Budgetary**. The project can be completed, and completed on time to satisfy the user's requirements, but the cost is prohibitive.

"In the case of the China Shop Project," I told my students, "Mr. Bullina and I came close to dropping the project." I explained that budgetary constraints on the part of Mr. Bullina were the chief reason. Technically, the project was not very complex, and there was no doubt in my mind that together we could easily complete the project. Neither was time a constraint here, as we could easily complete the project during the course of the semester. The limiting factor had been Mr. Bullina's desire to spend no more than a few hundred dollars for the program.

With the assistance of my students, we decided to take on the project, and proceed with the second phase of the SDLC.

Phase 2: Analysis

The second phase of the SDLC, the **Analysis phase**, is sometimes called the **Data Gathering phase**.

I told the students that in this phase we study the problem, deficiency or new requirement in detail. Depending upon the size of the project being undertaken, this phase could be as short as the Preliminary Investigation, or it could take months.

I explained that what this meant for my class was another trip to the China Shop to meet with Mr. Bullina, to spend more time talking with him and observing his operation.

I warned my students that as a developer, you are inclined to believe that you know everything you need to know about the project from your preliminary investigation. However, you would be surprised to find out how much additional information you can glean if you spend just a little more time with the user.

You might be inclined to skip portions of what the SDLC calls for, but it forces you to follow a standardized methodology for developing programs and systems. As we'll see shortly, skipping parts of the SDLC can be a big mistake, whereas adhering to it ensures that you give the project the greatest chance for success.

I told them that while some developers would make the case that we have gathered enough information in Phase 1 of the SDLC to begin programming, the SDLC dictates that Phase 2 should be completed before actual writing of the program begins.

"The biggest mistake we could make at this point would be to begin coding the program. Why is that? As we'll see shortly, we need to gather more information about the business from the owner. There are still some questions that have to be asked."

In discussing the SDLC with the class, I discovered that one of my students, Linda Schwartzer, actually lived about half a mile from the Bullina China Shop. Linda was a full time Network Administrator who was interested in learning to program using Visual Basic. Linda offered to contact Mr. Bullina, and set up an appointment to spend part of the day with him in the China Shop. This meeting would fulfill the data-gathering component of the Analysis Phase. In the short time I had spent with Linda, I sensed a great communicative ability about her, and so I felt very comfortable with Linda tackling the Analysis phase of the SDLC.

Typically, our first class meeting is abbreviated, and since we were basically frozen in time until we could complete Phase 2 of the SDLC, I dismissed the class for the day. Prior to Linda's meeting with Mr. Bullina, I faxed the following letter to him:

Dear Mr. Bullina,

I want to thank you for taking the time to meet with me last Tuesday afternoon. As I discussed with you at that time, it is my desire to work with you in developing a "kiosk" style computer system to be deployed in the middle of your sales floor.

The system will be developed as part of my *Introduction to Programming* computer class at the university. As such, your costs will be $450, payable upon final delivery of the program. In return, you agree to allow me to use your contract to provide my students with a valuable learning experience in developing a real-world application.

Sometime during the coming week, one of my students, Linda Schwartzer, will be contacting you to arrange to spend part of the day observing your business. Although you may not see the necessity in this additional meeting, it will satisfy the next phase of the Systems Development Life Cycle I discussed with you at our meeting. Adhering strictly to the SDLC will result in the best possible system we can develop for you.

I'd like to take this opportunity to highlight the major points we discussed last week. We will develop a Windows-based system for you. Here are the major functions that the developed system will perform:

1. This system will provide a customer with a user-friendly interface for requesting a price quote of fine china.

2. The customer may choose a complete place setting, or may choose individual components for their quotation.

3. The component pieces are: plate, soup bowl, butter plate, cup and saucer.

4. The customer may also select a platter, but the program is to 'assume' a quantity of one whenever the customer selects a platter.

5. The customer may not 'mix and match' brands for the price quote. All of the components must be of the same brand.

6. The customer may only choose a quantity of one, two, four or eight for both place settings and individual components.

7. The customer may not 'mix and match' quantities. For example, the customer may not choose four cups and two saucers.

I think I've covered everything that we discussed last Tuesday. If I have missed anything, please let Linda know when she arrives to observe your operation.

Regards,

John Smiley

This letter, in essence, will become the Requirements Statement that we will formally develop shortly. The next day I received the following fax from Mr. Bullina:

Dear Mr. Smiley,

Here is a price matrix of the prices for the 3 brands of China we sell in our China Shop.

I had a chance to review the fax you sent me yesterday, and everything looks fine. I'm really excited about the project.

One thing I forgot to mention last Tuesday is that we offer a discount for a complete place setting. I hope that this will not complicate the program too much.

BRAND	PLATE	BUTTER PLATE	SOUP BOWL	CUP	SAUCER	PLACE SETTING	PLATTER
CORELLE	$4	$1	$2	$1	$1	$8	$5
FABERWARE	$10	$3	$5	$3	$3	$21	$13
MIKASA	$25	$10	$10	$5	$5	$50	$50

Regards,

Joe Bullina

Complicate the program? Sure, a bit. I was sure Linda would more than likely find other surprises as well. This new 'requirement' was about par for the course. I checked my notes, and Joe was right, he never mentioned it. Of course, a good developer can anticipate requirements such as these. I just missed it.

Linda called me on Monday morning to tell me that she had arranged to meet with Joe Bullina on Thursday morning. That evening Linda called to tell me that the observation had gone well. Contrary to what I expected, she saw nothing in the day-to-day operation that contradicted the notes that I took during my preliminary investigation. For instance, it wouldn't have surprised me to find that someone in the shop was selling china in quantities of three!

However, Linda reported that nothing out of the usual occurred. She did tell me that from her observations, it was obvious that the program would pay for itself in no time. She noticed a number of people who spoke with the sales clerks only to get price quotations, and then immediately left the shop. A 'kiosk' type program would be perfect.

Linda also told me that she assisted Mr. Bullina in developing the computer hardware requirements for his nephew. Because of her background in computer hardware and Network Administration, I had no problem with her doing this. Although ordinarily these specifications aren't developed until Phase 3 of the SDLC, I had promised these specs to Joe, and so I was happy that Linda had assisted him with them.

That Saturday, I again met with our class. After ensuring that I hadn't lost anyone in the intervening week (yes, everyone came back), we began to discuss the third phase of the SDLC.

Phase 3: Design

"Phase 3 of the SDLC is the **Design phase**," I said.

I explained that design in the SDLC encompasses many different elements. Here is a list of the different components that are 'designed' in this phase:

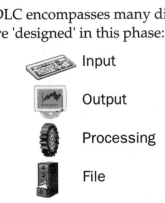

Input

Output

Processing

File

"Typically," I said, "too little time is spent on the design phase. Programmers love to start programming." I continued by saying that you can hardly blame them, with some of the marvelous modern application tools such as Visual Basic to work with. Unfortunately, jumping immediately into coding is a huge mistake.

"After all," I said, "you wouldn't start building a house without a blueprint, would you? You simply cannot and should not start programming without a good solid design."

I pointed out that critics of the SDLC agree that it can take months to complete a house, and making a mistake in the building of a house can be devastating; writing a Visual Basic program, on the other hand, can be accomplished in a matter of hours, if not minutes. If there's a mistake, it can be corrected quickly.

> *Even though at this point the class knew very little about Visual Basic, they were already familiar with Windows programs (a requirement for the course). Designing and developing the 'look' of a Windows program is really independent of the tool that you'll use to program it.*

I should point out here that my role in the Design Phase was to act as a guide for my students. Mr. Bullina had told us what he wanted the program to do. Like any customer, he described his program requirements in functional terms that he understood. My students were familiar with Windows, but at this point in our course, they were not Visual Basic experts. However, knowing Windows was not sufficient for them to know how Mr. Bullina's requirements translated into the terms of a Windows program. Ultimately, it was my job to help them translate those requirements into Visual Basic terms.

Critics of the SDLC further argue that time constraints and deadlines can make taking the 'extra' time necessary to properly complete the Design Phase a luxury that many programmers can't afford.

"I answer in this way," I said, citing a familiar phrase that you have probably heard before. "It seems there is never time to do it right the first time, but there's always time to do it over."

The exceptional (and foolish) programmer can begin coding without a good design. Programmers who do so may find themselves going back to modify pieces of code they've already written as they move through the project. They may discover a technique halfway through the project that they wish they had incorporated in the beginning, and then go back and change code. Worse yet, they may find themselves with a program that 'runs' but doesn't really work, with the result that they must go back and start virtually from the beginning.

"With a good design," I said, "the likelihood of this happening will be reduced dramatically. The end result is a program that will behave in the way it was intended, and generally with a shorter overall program development time."

Armed with our notes from the Preliminary Investigation, Linda's notes from the Detailed Analysis, and Joe Bullina's concurrence of our preliminary Requirements Statement, my students and I began the Design Phase in earnest. By the end of the design phase, we hoped to have a formal Requirements Statement for the program, and perhaps even a rough sketch of what the user interface will look like.

I reminded them that the Requirements Statement would form the basis of our agreement with the Bullina China Shop. For some developers, the Requirements Statement becomes the formal contract to which both they and the customer agree, and sign.

Linda began the design phase by giving the class a summary of the three or four hours she spent in the Bullina China Shop on Thursday. Linda said that she felt comfortable in stating that nothing she had observed that day contradicted the view expressed in my notes, and in my letter to Mr. Bullina.

Not everyone in the class had had the benefit of seeing my notes or the letter, so I distributed to the class copies of my notes, my letter to Mr. Bullina, and his letter to me. I gave them a few minutes to review and digest the material.

We began to discuss the program requirements. I could see there was some hesitation as to where to begin, so I began the process with a question. "Let's begin by making a statement as to what we are trying to accomplish here," I said.

"We need to write a program to display a price quotation," Dave said.

"Excellent," I said. Dave had hit the nail squarely on the head. The primary purpose of the program was to produce a price quotation. To be sure, there would be more to the program than that, but from Mr. Bullina's point of view, all he needed the program to do was to display a price quotation.

Frequently, new programmers are unable to come to grips as to where they should begin in the Design Phase. I suggested to them that most programs are designed by first determining the output of the program. The reasoning here is that if you know what the output of the program should be, you can determine the input needed to produce that output pretty easily. Once you know both the output from, and the input to the program, you can then determine what processing needs to be performed to convert the input to output.

Output Design

I told them that we were fortunate, in that the class's first project was one where the output requirements could be stated so simply: a price quotation.

"Where will the price quotation go?" I asked.

"To a printer?" Jack suggested. "On the computer screen," Rose countered.

"I agree with Rose," I said, "probably to the computer screen."

Some of the students seemed perplexed by my answer. "Probably?" Dave asked.

I explained that Mr. Bullina and I had never formally agreed where the price quotation would be displayed. The issue had never really come up. A kiosk-style program certainly implied the display of the price quotation on a computer screen. However, there was always the chance that Joe would want a price quotation printed to a printer.

"Let's be sure," I said, "to explicitly specify a display of the price quotation in the Requirements Statement. Speaking of which…is there a volunteer to begin to write up the specifications for it?" Dave volunteered to begin writing our Requirements Statement, so he loaded up Microsoft Word and started typing away.

Rhonda made a suggestion for the color and font size for the program's price display, but Peter said that it was probably a bit premature to be talking about colors and font sizes at this point in our design. I agreed, and told them that I never include that amount of detail on a Requirements Statement.

"Is there any other output from the program?" I asked and several moments went by.

"I'd like to suggest that we display the date and time on the computer screen," Valerie suggested. I was pleased with this suggestion, because I knew this would give us a chance to work with a Visual Basic Timer control, which would be good experience. Of course, at this point the students didn't know what a Timer control was, but they would learn about them shortly.

"Good idea," Mary said.

However, Linda disagreed, arguing that the display of the date and time was unnecessary considering the fact that both Windows 95 and Windows NT display the current time on the Windows TaskBar anyway. I countered by saying that in a kiosk-style program like this, Mr. Bullina might choose to turn off the display of the TaskBar. By not displaying the TaskBar, we would lessen the temptation on the part of customers to change important Windows settings that can be accessed via the TaskBar. The majority of the class agreed that this would be our recommendation to Mr. Bullina. Once we decided not to display the TaskBar, we further agreed that displaying the date and time on the program's screen was a good idea.

Taking a moment to summarize, I said, "We now have three output requirements, a price calculation, a displayed date and a displayed time. This is sufficient information to proceed to the next step. Which is?"

Barbara suggested that since we seemed to have the output requirements identified, we should move onto a discussion of processing.

"As I explained earlier, it will be easier for us if we discuss input into the program prior to discussing processing," I said. "It's just about impossible to determine processing requirements if we don't know our input requirements."

Input Design

"So does anyone have any suggestions as to what input requirements we need?" I asked the class.

Dave quickly rattled off several input requirements: a brand of china, one or more component pieces of china and a desired quantity.

"Excellent," I said. "Those certainly appear to be the input to the program. Anything else?"

Kate pointed out that we hadn't yet taken into account the discount for a complete place setting. "The discount for a complete place setting," I said, "is a processing rule, which we will discuss shortly." However, Kate's point about the complete place setting discount was an excellent one. We decided to include a formal definition of a 'complete place setting' in our Requirements Statement.

"Anything else?" I repeated. "How will input be entered into the program? How will the customer let the program know their choice for a china brand, for instance?"

Choosing the Brand

Several students suggested that the user could type the china brand using the computer's keyboard.

"How many brands do we have?" I asked. A quick peek at the handouts revealed that at the present moment, the Bullina China Shop carried only three brands of China. "My motto is to have the user do as little typing as possible," I said. "In fact, I envisioned that absolutely no typing on the part of the user would be necessary."

I could see that some of the students were surprised at my statement. You must remember that a number of them had come from the DOS world, and were accustomed to writing programs where there was a great deal of typing required of the user.

I explained that typically in Windows programs, when there are a finite number of choices, it's best to display a list of choices for the user to choose from.

"Does anyone know of anything they've seen in Windows that displays a list of choices for the user to choose from?" I asked. Mary said she recalled seeing a list of Font names and Font sizes to choose from on the Microsoft Word toolbar:

"That's a list of choices," she said. "Excellent, Mary," I said.

I said this list was actually a Windows **List Box** object. Such a list box would be perfect to display the available china brands in our program. After all, it would be senseless to have the user type the brand name of the china when our program could display it for them in a neat list box.

"Then the user," I said, "need only use their mouse to click on the brand in the list box. No typing required! Let's add that to the Requirements Statements, Dave."

"What else?" I asked.

Choosing the Items

Our discussion then moved on to how the customer would select the individual component china pieces. Some students, obviously liking the idea of a list box, also suggested using one to display the six possible component china pieces. Although this certainly was a workable solution, this situation didn't quite match the previous one for brands.

"If you'll recall my initial meeting with Joe Bullina," I said, "only one brand of china can be selected per quotation. However, more than one item can be selected per quotation." I asked them if they knew of anything in Microsoft Word that displayed a series of choices to the user, where more than one selection could be chosen at a time.

Ward said that he recalled seeing boxes on the Options submenu of the Tools menu that permitted him to specify 'settings' for saving documents in Word. I asked all of the students to take a look at this menu, and sure enough, there were several boxes, which the user can click with their mouse to select settings for saving documents in Word:

> *I pointed out that there was one disadvantage of using the check box that we don't have with the list box. China brands in the list box are displayed as a 'scrollable' list of items. If we need to add more brands, the screen 'real estate' occupied by the list box control doesn't need to change. Check boxes, on the other hand, occupy definite real estate on the screen.*

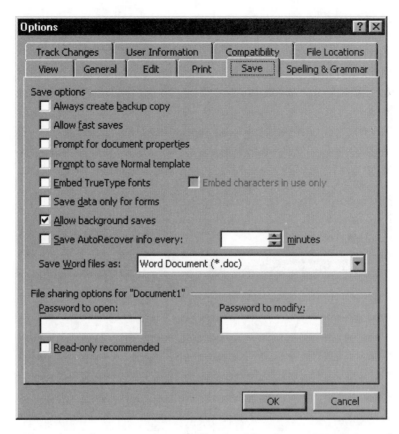

I told the students that these boxes were actually the Windows **Check Box** objects or controls.

"In Windows," I said, "a check box is either selected or not selected. Windows check boxes enable the user to make a selection by clicking on the box with their mouse. The user can then de-select it by clicking on the check box again with their mouse."

We agreed that check boxes would be perfect to permit the customer to make a selection of one or more component china pieces.

"Suppose," I said, "Mr. Bullina calls tomorrow to say that in addition to the six china pieces he is already selling, he wishes to offer salad plates for sale as well. Then our form would need to be redesigned."

It was just about time for a break, and so at break time I called Mr. Bullina at the store and asked him about the likelihood that another component piece might be added to his inventory. He told me it was very unlikely, and so after we returned from break, we decided to use the Check Box to allow the user to specify their china items. Again, I asked Dave to add this to our Requirements Statement.

Quantity

That left us with the quantity to deal with, which caused a great deal of discussion. Several students were in favor of having the user type the quantity into the program somehow. I asked the students to come up with an example in Word where a quantity of some type is specified. Joe immediately cited the Print submenu, where the user can specify the number of copies to be sent to the printer:

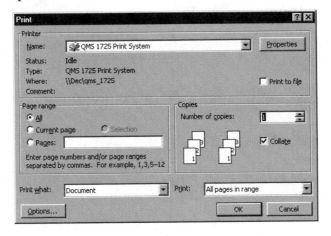

"Excellent, Joe!" I said.

Word uses a combination of something called a **Text Box** and a vertical scrollbar in this Print dialog box. If the user desires, they can type the quantity directly into the text box, or if they wish, they can click on the scrollbar to adjust the quantity. There was only one problem with using this technique in the China Shop Project, and that was the fact that the user could only select quantities of 1,2, 4 or 8.

"That constraint complicates the project a bit," I said.

Several students favored using a list box to display quantities, with the items labeled eight, four, two and one. A list box would be fine for quantity, I thought, but I wanted to give them an opportunity to use another technique. Just then Ward asked about using the 'circles' he saw on the Print submenu to designate Page Range. I told them that those 'circles' were Windows **Option Buttons**...

"Unlike the check box," I said, "where more than one selection can be made at one time, with option buttons, only one selection can be made at any one time." I asked the class to go into the Print menu and the Page Range frame of Word to prove this for themselves. I explained that we could display four buttons representing the four possible permissible quantities, and have the customer make a selection from one of the option buttons to designate their quantity selection.
"Don't we need an option button set for each piece of china that the customer selects?" Bob asked.

Peter reminded everyone that there could only be one choice of quantity. That is, the customer could not ask for two plates and four saucers. The customer could only obtain a price quotation for four saucers and four plates, or two plates and two saucers. In addition, there was a limit of one platter per customer. If the customer selected a platter in their order, then the program would 'assume' a quantity of one. Therefore, Bob's concern over how to allow the customer to select a quantity for each piece was unwarranted. There could be but one quantity selected per price quotation.

Everyone agreed that using option buttons to represent the customer's quantity selection was a good idea, so Dave added this to the Requirements Statement.

The First Screen Design

So far, so good. We had identified all of the input into the system (or so we thought), and had decided how best to input them. During the course of the discussion, Barbara had begun sketching a preliminary form design. She offered to show it to the class, and I displayed it on the classroom projector. This is the preliminary sketch of the input design that she showed to the class:

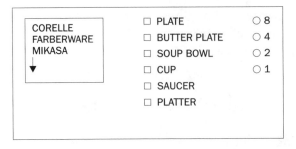

The class was pleased with the sketch, and in general, with all that we had accomplished so far.

Mary, after seeing the sketch, suggested that since we had used Microsoft Word as our guideline up to this point, that our interface should also have a menu, just like Word. Everyone agreed, and this prompted a discussion as to what should appear on our menu:

> *As is usual, I found that a discussion of the menu quite naturally turned into a discussion of processing requirements. I wasn't sure that this was the direction in which I wanted the class to move, but on the other hand, I didn't want to stifle their creativity either. There was no harm in it, since we were under no obligation to include everything in the Requirements Statement.*

- Every Windows application requires a <u>F</u>ile submenu, and a <u>H</u>elp submenu. <u>F</u>ile always contains an E<u>x</u>it command. The <u>F</u>ile menu can be accessed by pressing the *Alt* and *F* combination. The E<u>x</u>it command can be accessed by pressing the *Alt* and *X* combination.

- <u>H</u>elp, which can be accessed by pressing the *Alt* and *H* combination, always contains some basic help, and an <u>A</u>bout command, which can be accessed by pressing the *Alt* and *H* combination and then the letter *A*.

No one in the class was aware of the difficulty and tediousness of writing Visual Basic help files. I cautioned them that creating a <u>H</u>elp menu would complicate our project quite a bit, and that we might want to consider it as a possible enhancement in the future. After some discussion, we decided to drop <u>H</u>elp as a requirement of the menu.

Everyone agreed that there was no need for the typical Windows <u>E</u>dit submenu, since there wouldn't be any editing of any kind occurring.

Blaine suddenly had an idea. He suggested that many users like to customize their environment to some degree or other.

"Customize their environment?" Barbara responded. He explained that he had used other Windows programs where you could specify preferences such as colors, font size, and other options.

"Any ideas on what we should do here?" I asked. "Colors!" was the almost unanimous response. Changing colors seems to hold more of an attraction for beginners than nearly anything else. In practice I don't advise providing a means for the user to change colors. I prefer instead to have the user change colors through the Color settings in the Windows Control Panel. However, the will of the majority prevailed and we agreed to add a menu item to change the background color for the quotation form. I asked Dave to add this to the Requirements Statement as well.

Lou questioned exactly how we would do this. I cautioned him that at this point in the SDLC it wasn't necessary to discuss the 'how' of what the program would do, but to get the requirements on paper.

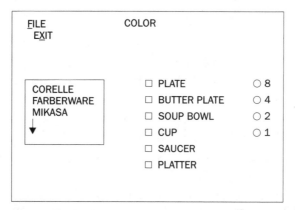

At this point, we agreed on File and Color as menu items for our menu. Dave added these specifications to the Requirements Statement, and Barbara redrew the sketch of the form.

Everyone seemed to notice at the same time that our sketch still didn't show the most important piece of output we had identified! The price quotation. After all, it wasn't like we hadn't discussed it. In fact, we discussed output first. This goes to show you how easy it is to leave something important out.

I have received projects from students in the past where they accepted input into a program, performed processing of some kind, but have forgotten the output!

Having noticed the error of our ways, we had a brief discussion as to where and how to display the price. We finally agreed to place it somewhere toward the bottom of the form, although the exact location wouldn't be determined until we actually began to develop the interface in Visual Basic. Again, Barbara redrew the proposed interface:

Rhonda suggested some changes to the menu layout. We all agreed that these ideas were good ones, so we incorporated them into the project. I particularly liked the changes, because I knew that the programming behind these ideas would prove to be a challenge for them. Here are the changes she proposed:

- Change the name of the Color menu to Preferences menu.
- Add a submenu called Colors, with two choices: Customize and Default (in order to set the colors back to a default color).
- Add two submenu items to the Preferences menu called 'Date and Time On' and 'Date and Time Off'. The idea was to be able to turn the display of the date and time on and off.

After we had added these changes to the Requirements Statement, Ward suggested that we place a border around the check boxes and option buttons, to make them 'stand out'. "Those are called Frames," I said.

We agreed, and Barbara adjusted the sketch of the user interface again:

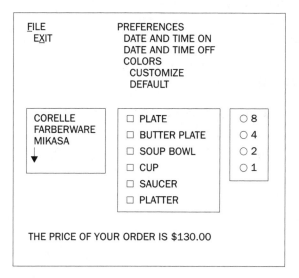

The Requirements Statement

We were working hard, and making excellent progress, and so it was time for another break. Before adjourning, I asked Dave, the student who was developing the Requirements Statement, to let us see what he had developed so far. I made copies of his work, and after break, handed these out to the rest of the class for discussion. Here is the copy of the Requirements Statement I gave to them:

REQUIREMENTS STATEMENT

Bullina China Shop

GENERAL DESCRIPTION

- The program will consist of a main screen, on which there will be:

    A List Box containing china brands.

    6 Check Boxes for china piece components.

    4 Option Buttons representing quantities.

    A menu with submenu items for File and Preferences.

- The File submenu will display only an Exit command. The File menu will be alternatively accessible by pressing the Alt and F combination. The Exit command will be alternatively accessible by pressing the Alt and X combination.
- The Preferences submenu will display a submenu called Colors and a command called Display Date and Time.

- The Colors submenu will consist of two commands called Customize and Default. The Customize command will permit the customer to set the color of the main form to any color they desire through the use of a color dialog box. The Default command will set the color of the main form back to a predetermined color.

- The Display Date and Time command will permit the user to turn the displayed date and time off and on.

OUTPUT FROM THE SYSTEM

- A price quotation displayed on the main form.

- Current Date and Time displayed prominently on the form.

INPUT TO THE SYSTEM

- The customer will specify:

- A single china brand (to be selected using a Visual Basic List Box control).

- One or more component pieces (to be selected using a Visual Basic Check Box control).

- A quantity for the component pieces (to be selected using a Visual Basic Option Button).

BUSINESS RULES

- No more than one platter may be selected.

- Quantities may not be mixed and matched in an order. Only one quantity selection per order.

- Brands may not be mixed and matched in an order. Only one brand per order.

DEFINITIONS

- Complete Place Setting: A user's selection composed of a plate, butter plate, soup bowl, cup and saucer of the same brand.

As you can see, the Requirements Statement can easily form the basis of a contract between the customer and the developer. The Requirements Statement should list all of the major details of the program. You should take care not to paint yourself into any unnecessary programming corners by including any 'window dressing'. These can just get you into trouble later.

For instance, notice here that we didn't specify precisely where we would display the Date and Time. Suppose we had specified the upper right hand corner of the main form, and then later changed our mind and wanted to place it in the lower left-hand corner? Theoretically, deviating from the Requirements Statement could be construed as a violation of contractual terms.

I asked for comments on the Requirements Statement and everyone seemed to think that it was just fine. However, several students turned their attention to the sketch of the user interface, and indicated that they believed there were still some problems with it.

Rhonda apologized for being picky, but pointed out that we had not drawn on where the date and time would be placed. She was right. We had entirely left the date and time display off our latest sketch. Details, details, details! We quickly agreed that we would display it in the upper right hand portion of the form. Because this type of detail was considered 'window dressing', no change to the Requirements Statement was required.

"Anything else?" I asked.

Blaine suggested that our sketch didn't have identifying captions for the check boxes, option buttons, or list box. The rest of the class agreed that the interface would be less confusing to the customer if we provided identifying captions.

"Good point," I said. We decided to place captions on the interface reading Brands, China Pieces and Quantity. Barbara began to make the changes to the sketch.

"Barbara, wait a minute," I said. I told them that displaying a caption with the check boxes and option button frames was easy. However, there was no built-in way of displaying a caption for a list box. "Besides," I said, "the list box items are pretty self-explanatory. Let's drop the caption on the list box."

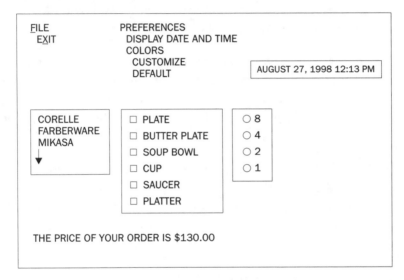

Barbara quickly made the changes to the sketch. Neither one of these changes were detailed enough to warrant mentioning them on the Requirements Statement, so Dave made no changes there.

Everyone thought that the interface was coming along quite nicely, but as they say, 'the proof is in the pudding.' It's only the customer's opinion that counts. With no more comments or suggestions on the user interface or the Requirements Statement, we set about completing the Design Phase of the SDLC by looking at Processing.

Processing Design

"**Processing** is the conversion of inputs to outputs, the conversion of Data to Information," I said. "At this point in the Design phase of the SDLC, we should have now identified all of the output from the program, and all of the input necessary to produce that output."

I explained that just as a good novel will typically have several subplots; a Visual Basic application is no exception. It contains several processing 'subplots' as well.

We have the main 'plot', that is the calculation of the sales quotation, but we also have 'subplots' such as:

- changing the colors of the main form
- turning off and on the display of the date and time
- exiting the application

It's important to note, here, that in Processing Design, we don't write actually write the program. That's done later. In Processing Design, we specify the processes that need to be performed to convert input into output.

Looking at Processing in Detail

"Let's look at a simple example which isn't part of the China Shop Project," I said, "that most of you are probably familiar with, the calculation of your paycheck."

I continued by saying that if you want to calculate your net pay, you need to perform several steps. Here are the steps or functions necessary to calculate your net pay:

1. Calculate gross pay

2. Calculate tax deductions

3. Calculate net pay

Programming is done in the next phase of the SDLC, the Development phase. Specifying how processing is to occur is not as important in this phase as specifying what is to occur. For instance, this sequence identifies the 'what' of processing, not the how. The 'how' is a part of the Development phase.

These functions can be broken down even further. For instance, the calculation of your gross pay will vary depending upon whether you are a salaried employee or an hourly employee. If you are an hourly employee, your gross pay is equal to your hourly pay rate multiplied by the number of hours worked in the pay period. The specification of these functions is exactly what the designer must detail in the Processing Design phase of the SDLC.

When it comes to processing design, documenting the processing rules is crucial because translating processing rules into a narrative form can sometimes result in confusion or misinterpretation. Over the years, systems designers have used various 'tools' to aid them in documenting the design of their systems.

Some designers have used tools called **flowcharts**. Flowcharts use symbols to graphically document the system's processing rules. Here are the net pay processing rules we discussed earlier depicted using a flowchart. (My apologies to any accountants reading this; these calculations have been simplified for illustration purposes.)

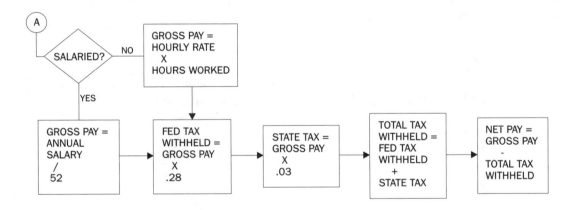

Other designers favor **pseudo-code**. Pseudo-code is an English-like language that describes in non-graphical form how a program should execute. Here are the same net pay processing rules depicted using pseudo-code:

Assumption: Pay is calculated on a weekly basis (52 pay periods per year).

Assumption: Salaried employee pay is Annual Salary divided by 52.

Assumption: Hourly employee pay is Hourly Rate multiplied by hours worked.

1. If employee is salaried, then go to Step 4

2. Employee is hourly, then calculate gross pay equal to hourly wage rate multiplied by hours worked in pay period

3. Go to Step 5

4. Employee is salaried, so calculate Gross Pay equal to Annual Salary divided by 52

5. Calculate Federal Tax withheld equal to Gross Pay multiplied by 0.28

6. Calculate State Tax withheld equal to Gross pay multiplied by 0.03

7. Calculate Total Tax withheld equal to Federal Tax withheld + State Tax withheld

8. Calculate Net Pay equal to Gross Pay less Total Tax withheld

*Both of these techniques found favor in the era of the **procedural program**. A procedural program is one that executes from top to bottom virtually without interruption. A procedural program ordains to the user exactly how they will interact with your program. For instance, in the China Shop Project, the customer will select a brand of china, then select one or more china items, and then select a quantity. I frequently find students who have a strong programming background writing procedural programs. Procedural Programming is like taking a ride on a tour bus, where all of the destination stops are pre-determined, and pre-ordered.*

*Windows programs are **event-driven programs**. Event-driven programs don't force the user to behave in a certain way, but rather react to the user. An event-driven program does not attempt to 'dictate' to the user what they should do in the program, and when they should do it. Instead an event-driven program presents the user with a visual interface that permits them to interact with the program. This is more like choosing the rides at a carnival. Once entry has been gained, the rides they go on and the in order in which they ride them is entirely up to the user. An event-driven program must be able to work and respond to any eventuality.*

"In my classes," I said, "I don't require the use of either flowcharting or pseudo-code. All that I ask from you is that you give careful thought to the processing that is necessary to solve the problem before beginning to code in Visual Basic."

I could see some happy faces and I continued by saying that invariably, this means working out a solution on a piece of paper prior to coding it. Some students are more 'visual' than others, and they prefer to design their solution in graphical terms. Others are less 'visual' and their solutions look very much like the pseudo-code we saw earlier. The point is, without some written plan, the programming process can go awry.

I cited this example. Several years ago, I was teaching a class on another language called COBOL, and I gave my students the following programming problem:

Write a program to calculate the net wage of a laborer who works 40 hours at a pay rate of $5 per hour. Income tax at the rate of 20% of the gross pay will be deducted. What is the net pay?

The correct answer is $160. Forty hours multiplied by $5 per hour results in a gross pay of $200. The income tax deduction is 20% of $200, which is $40. $200 less the $40 income tax deduction results in a net pay of $160.

A number of students calculated the net pay as $240. Instead of deducting the income tax deduction of $40 from the gross pay, they *added* it instead. When I questioned the methodology behind their incorrect answer, most of them told me they thought the problem had been so simple, that they hadn't bothered to work out the solution on a piece of paper ahead of time. They just started coding. Had they taken the time to work out the solution on paper first, they would have known what the answer should be and they wouldn't have submitted a program to me that calculated the results incorrectly.

"This is what I'm suggesting to you," I said. "Take the time to work out the solution on paper. You'll be happy that you did."

Back to the Bullina China Shop

We continued by discussing processing design. I reminded them that, in general, design is an **iterative** process. It's rare that the designer or programmer hits the nail perfectly on the head the first time. It's very possible that after going through processing design, you will discover that you are missing some crucial piece of input necessary to produce a piece of output. In this case, you would need to look at your input processing again. For instance, with the China Project, we could have forgotten to ask the user to specify the quantity of china that they wished to purchase. That omission would make it impossible to calculate a sales quotation.

As a starting point in our processing discussion, we agreed to begin with our primary goal: *To calculate a sales quotation.* We had already determined that in order to calculate a sales quotation, we needed to know the customer's desired brand of china, one or more component china pieces, and the quantity the customer wants.

We started with a hypothetical customer. How would we calculate a sales quotation if the customer selected Mikasa as the brand, a cup and a saucer as the component pieces, and wanted two of each?

"I'd take the price for a Mikasa cup, the price for a Mikasa saucer, add them together, and then multiply by two," Ward said.

"Good," I replied.

Dave suggested, "You could also take the price for a Mikasa cup, multiply it by two, then take the price for a Mikasa saucer, multiply that by two. Then add the two subtotals, and display the result."

"Both would work. What would the sales quotation be?" I asked.

The students turned to the page in their handouts where the prices were written. "Twenty dollars," Joe said. The other students agreed.

"I think we've got a problem here," Chuck said. "We're looking up prices from a sheet of paper. Where is the program going to get these prices?"

"You're right," I said. "So far, we haven't considered how the program will obtain these prices."

Kathy suggested that the prices could be entered every day by one of the sales clerks in the China Shop. I proposed that this would not be very palatable to the China Shop staff. China prices don't change every day. Why force a sales clerk to enter the same prices each day? The system was supposed to permit the sales clerks to have more time serving customers.

Who would want to deal with a system that requires inventory prices to be re-entered each day?

"We'll probably save the prices in a file of some kind," I suggested.

Valerie thought of another problem. "Where will the list of china in the list box come from?" she asked. "We never discussed that either."

Ward said that he felt this process seemed to be 'ego deflating'. We all had thought that our design process was coming along so well, and here were two new problems to contend with. I reminded them that this was exactly what I meant when I said that the design process was an iterative one. We were doing well! Just because we had missed some details, and had to go back and make some changes to our original design, didn't mean that we weren't progressing.

"What data needs to be saved from day to day?" I asked. Mary volunteered; china brands for the list box and china prices for calculations. Blaine suggested that colors, once changed by the user, would also need to be saved from day to day. Nothing frustrates a user more than having to re-select their preferences every time they start up the program.

"What about the other preferences the user can select?" Mary said. "The choice to display the date and time, we should save that as well." I agreed. Anything that alters the user's environment needs to be saved when the program ends, and 'read' when the program starts up again.

"Saved preferences are output, aren't they?" Dave added. "But then when the program starts up again, the preferences are input."

"An excellent observation," I said. "Anything else?"

Ward said, "There's something here I don't understand. How are we going to save these preferences, and then retrieve them later? I understand how the user will interact with our program. But getting prices into our program without the user's interaction … and saving colors … I just don't understand that."

As for prices, I explained that eventually we would create a data file with 'fields' for both brands and prices. When the program starts up, it would 'read' this file, and load up the list box control with the brand names and the prices into something called an **array**.

An array is like a data file on a disk, but it is contained in the computer's RAM. As the file is in the memory it means that any activity relating to the array occurs more quickly. We'll be talking about this in more detail next chapter.

However, for the purposes of the prototype, we would 'hardcode' the information into the program. This would make the information much harder to change, but would get the prototype working as quickly and painlessly as possible.

When the user selects a brand, one or more component pieces, and a quantity, then the program will 'look up' the price of the items in the array, much like we had manually done using a piece of paper earlier.

Once obtained, these prices will be used to calculate a sales quotation.

I further explained that when we advanced the prototype towards the production-ready application, we would save the user's color and date/time preferences to the Windows Registry using a Visual Basic function or command. When the program starts up, it will read these preferences from the Windows Registry, and adjust the color of the form and the visibility of the data/time label accordingly.

One of my students expressed concern about the prospect of working with the Windows Registry. She explained that she heard that 'fooling around' with the Windows registry was dangerous. I explained that Visual Basic's functions for reading from and writing to the Windows Registry was easy and also very safe.

"Why don't we store the prices in the Windows Registry instead of a disk file?" Linda asked.

I explained that this would not be a good idea since the China Shop's sales clerks would be updating inventory prices periodically. Updating a disk file is something the sales staff could easily do using Notepad. However, updating the Windows Registry is not something we could permit them to do.

"Have we missed anything with the price calculation?" I asked. "Suppose," I added, "the customer clicks on a brand, selects a component piece or pieces, but forgets to select a quantity. What should the program do?"

Everyone agreed that we needed to display some sort of error message if we didn't have all of the ingredients necessary to arrive at a valid price calculation. An error message is another form of output.

"How and when should the calculation take place?" I asked.

Mary suggested that we could trigger a price calculation when the user clicked on one of the check boxes to select an item. Barbara said, "Suppose the user clicks on the soup bowl check box, but hasn't yet selected a brand or a quantity. They'll just see an error message telling them to select a brand and a quantity. Aren't you pre-supposing that they've made a selection of brand and quantity first?"

Mary admitted that she was. I agreed. "You've got to be careful not to try to anticipate the order in which you think the user or customer will make their selections," I said. "Brands, Quantity, and Items. That's probably the order that you would make your selections. But that's not going to be the case with every customer."

I explained that expecting customers to perform actions in a particular order sounded very much like procedural programming. Like a trip to the Automated Teller Machine:

- insert card
- enter PIN number
- select withdrawal or deposit
- specify an amount
- deposit your cash or take your cash
- take your receipt
- take your card

I explained that procedural programming is something we want to avoid. Procedural programming often gives the user the feeling that they are being pushed or rushed and that they are not in control. When we write Windows programs, it's a great idea to give the user the impression that they are in control.

I suggested the use of a button captioned Calculate to allow the user to tell the program when they are ready for a price quotation. This way they won't get the impression that the program is waiting for them to do something.

The students thought about this for a moment, and agreed with the notion. We agreed that we would place a button on the form captioned Calculate. We further agreed that we would not perform a price calculation until a brand, a quantity, and at least one component piece had been selected. We added this to the business rules section of our Requirements Statement.

Dave made a great suggestion concerning the selection of a 'complete place setting'. Why not have a check box captioned Complete Place Setting which, when selected, would check off the five component pieces that made up a complete place setting? This would save the customer the trouble of checking off all of the five pieces individually. We added that to the Requirements Statement as well.

Now it seemed as though we were gaining momentum. Another student suggested a Reset button that would set all of the components on the form back to their default values. This was another great idea. Again, we added this to the Requirements Statement.

As I mentioned earlier, during the course of processing design, we may uncover 'holes' in the input or output design. That had been the case here. While it's certain that we eventually would have noticed these holes when we were coding the program, fixing these flaws while you are still in the design phase of the SDLC is easier and cheaper than fixing them in the midst of programming the application.

In large projects particularly, portions of the project may be given to different programmers or even different teams of programmers for coding. It could be some time before flaws in the design are uncovered, in some cases weeks or even months. The longer it takes to discover these flaws, the more likely it is that some coding will have to be scrapped and re-done. A well thought out design phase can eliminate many problems down the line.

We'd plugged the holes in the Price Calculation processing, so now it was time to turn our attention to our 'subplot' processing design. Namely:

- changing the colors of the main form
- turning off and on the display of the date and time
- exiting from the application

We didn't get into a lot of detail with these requirements. You must remember that at this point, I still hadn't taught them anything about Visual Basic. All I could do at this point was to assure them that these requirements were indeed feasible. I reminded them that during the design phase, it's not as important to itemize the 'how' of something, as it is to identify the requirement on paper. We had done that, and in the coming weeks they would learn the Visual Basic 'how' of the requirements.

At this point, one of the students suggested that we couldn't allow the customer to exit the program. Only a sales clerk should be able to exit the program. This presented a dilemma. How could we permit a sales clerk to exit from the program, but not a customer?

Another student suggested prompting for a password before permitting the program to 'end'. Again, the details as to 'how' this would be accomplished we would put off for a bit. We agreed that after the user had selected the Exit submenu, the program would prompt for a password and if it was correct, the program would end. If not, the program would continue to run.

Here is the final sketch of the user interface that the class agreed upon:

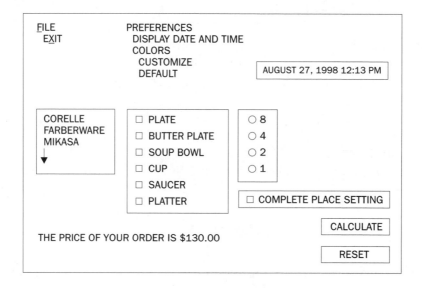

And here is the final Requirements Statement that the class approved:

REQUIREMENTS STATEMENT

Bullina China Shop

GENERAL DESCRIPTION

- The program will consist of a main form, on which there will be:

    A list box containing brands of china

    6 Check Boxes for china piece components

    A single Check Box to permit the customer to select a Complete Place Setting

    4 option buttons representing quantities

    A button, which when clicked, would perform the price calculation

    A button, captioned Reset, which when clicked would clear the selections in the List Box, Check Boxes, and Option Buttons

    A menu with submenu items for File and Preferences

- The File submenu will display only an Exit command. The File menu will be accessible by pressing the Alt and F combination. The Exit command will be accessible by pressing the Alt and X combination.

- The Preferences submenu will display a submenu called Colors and a command called Display Date and Time.

- The Colors submenu will consist of two commands called Customize and Default. The Customize command will permit the customer to set the color of the main form to any color they desire using a color dialog box. The Default command will set the color of the main form back to a predetermined color.

- The Display Date and Time command will permit the user to switch the displayed date and time off and on.

- A password will be required to exit the system via the Exit command of the File submenu.

OUTPUT FROM THE SYSTEM

- A price quotation displayed on the main form

- Current Date and Time displayed prominently on the form

INPUT TO THE SYSTEM

The customer will specify:

- A single china brand (to be selected from a List Box)

- One or more component pieces (to be selected using Check Boxes)

- A quantity for the component pieces (to be selected using an Option Button)

This is not customer input, but:

- The program will read china brands and prices from a text file. The sales clerk using Microsoft Notepad can update the inventory and prices when necessary.

- Any changes made to the user's color preferences will be saved to the Windows Registry and read by the program at startup.

- Any changes made to the user's preference for date and time display will be saved to the Windows Registry and read by the program at startup.

BUSINESS RULES

- No more than one platter may be selected

- Quantities may not be mixed and matched in an order, only one quantity selection per order

- Brands may not be mixed and matched in an order, only one brand per order

DEFINITIONS

- Complete Place Setting: A user's selection composed of a plate, butter plate, soup bowl, cup and saucer of the same brand.

- I checked to see if everyone agreed with the statement, and then revealed that we were now done with the Design Phase of the SDLC. I once again reminded them that the Design Phase of the SDLC tends to be an iterative process, and that we might find ourselves back here at some point. We then moved on to a discussion of the fourth phase of the SDLC.

Phase 4: Development

I told them that we wouldn't spend a great deal of time discussing the **Development Phase** here since the rest of the course would be spent in developing the China Shop Project, in which they would play an active role!

"The Development phase is," I said, "in many ways the most exciting time of the SDLC. During this phase, computer hardware is purchased and the software is developed. Yes, that means we actually start coding the program during the Development phase. We'll be using the standard edition of Visual Basic as our development tool."

I explained that during the Development Phase, we'd constantly examine and re-examine the Requirements Statement to ensure that we were following it to the letter, and I encourage them to do the same. I explained to them that any deviations (and there may be a surprise or two down the road), would have to be approved either by the project leader (me) or by the customer.

I also explained that the Development Phase can be split into two sections, that of Prototyping and Production Ready Application Creation. Prototyping is the stage of the Development Phase that produces a pseudo-complete application, which for all intents and purposes appears to be fully functional.

Developers use this stage to demo the application to the customer as another check that the final software solution answers the problem posed. When they are given the okay from the customer at that point, the final version code is written into this shell to complete the phase.

The class was anxious to begin, but they promised me they would remain patient while I explained the final two phases of the SDLC.

Phase 5: Implementation

The **Implementation Phase** is the phase in the SDLC when the project reaches fruition. I explained to them that after the Development phase of the SDLC is complete, we begin to implement the system. Any hardware that has been purchased will be delivered and installed in the China Shop. In the instance of the China Shop, this means that Mr. Bullina's nephew will deliver and install the PC in the China Shop.

Software, which we designed in Phase 3, and programmed in Phase 4 of the SDLC, will be installed on the PC in the China Shop. Not surprisingly, everyone in the class wanted to be there for that exciting day.

Barbara raised the issue of testing. During the Implementation phase, both hardware and software is tested. Because Mr. Bullina was purchasing the hardware from a reputable computer superstore, the class was fairly certain of hardware integrity. However, the class was confused over the issue of software testing.

We agreed that students in the class would perform most of the testing of the software, as everyone agreed that it would be unreasonable and unfair to expect the customer to test the software we had developed in a 'live' situation. We decided that when the software was installed on the China Shop's PC, the program should be **bug** (problem) free. On the other hand, I cautioned them, almost invariably, the user will uncover problems that the developer has been unable to generate. I told them we would discuss handling these types of problems in more detail in our class on error handling.

I explained that during the Implementation phase, we would also be training the China Shop staff. Again, everyone in the class wanted to participate in user training. One of my students noted that she thought that there needed to be two levels of training performed:

- The first level of training would be aimed directly at the staff of the China Shop. It would involve demonstrating how to turn the computer on each morning and how to shut it down gracefully each night. The staff would also be trained in how to make changes to the two text files necessary to add china brands to the system inventory, and for updating inventory prices. This would require someone training them in the use of Notepad.

- The second level of training would also be aimed at the staff of the China Shop, but this would be more from the customer perspective. Like it or not, the sales staff would be the primary point of contact for customers who were having trouble using the system. Therefore, quite naturally, they would need to know how to operate the system from the customer's perspective.

Several students thought that it would be a good idea to have a student present in the China Shop during the first week of operation, in order to assist customers in the use of the system, and to ease any 'computer' anxiety that the sales staff might have. I thought this was a great idea, and also pointed out that this would provide invaluable feedback on the operation of the system from the most important people in the loop, the end users.

In fact, this feedback led quite naturally into a discussion of the final phase of the SDLC.

Phase 6: Audit and Maintenance

Phase 6 of the SDLC is the **Audit and Maintenance Phase**. In this phase, someone, usually the client, but sometimes a third party such as an auditor, studies the implemented system to ensure that it actually fulfills the Requirements Statement. Most important, the system should have solved the problem or deficiency, or satisfied the desire that was identified in Phase 1 of the SDLC - the preliminary investigation.

More than a few programs and systems have been fully developed that, for one reason or another simply never met the original requirements. The Maintenance portion of this phase deals with any changes that need to be made to the system.

Changes are sometimes the result of the system not completely fulfilling its original requirements, but it could also be the result of customer satisfaction. Sometimes the customer is so happy with what they have got that they want more. Changes can also be forced upon the system because of governmental regulations, such as changing tax laws, while at other times changes come about due to alterations in the business rules of the customer.

As I mentioned in the previous section, we intended to have one or more members of the class in the China Shop during the first week of system operation. That opportunity for the customer to provide direct feedback to a member of the development team would more than satisfy the Audit portion of Phase 6.

In the future, we hoped that Mr. Bullina would be so happy with the program that we had written for him, that he would think of even more challenging requirements to request of the class.

Where To From Here?

It had been a long and productive session for everyone. I said that in our next meeting we would start to discuss how a computer works, and we would actually begin to work with Visual Basic.

Ward asked me how the progression of the project would work, that is, would we finish the project during our last class meeting, or would we be working on it each week? I said that I thought it was important that we develop the program incrementally. Each week we met, we would finish some portion of the project. Developing the project in steps like this would hold everyone's interest, and give us a chance to catch problems before the last week of class.

Summary

The aim of this chapter was to tackle the question "Where do I begin?" We saw that the design of an application is best done systematically, with a definite plan of action. That way, you know that everything has been taken into account.

A good place to begin is with a **requirements statement**, which is a list of what the program has to be able to do. Usually, you get the information for this from whoever is asking you to write the program. It's a good idea to keep in continuous contact with this person, so that any changes they want can be tackled before it becomes too much of a problem.

A good systematic approach is embodied in the **systems development life cycle (SDLC)**, which consists of six phases:

- **The Preliminary Investigation**: Considering the technical, time, and budgetary constraints and deciding on the viability of continuing development of the application.

- **The Analysis Phase**: Gathering the information needed to continue.

- **The Design Phase**: Creating a blueprint of the program's appearance and program structure without actually starting any programming.

- **The Development Phase:** Creating the application, including all interface and code.

- **The Implementation Phase**: Using and testing the program.

- **The Maintenance Phase**: Making refinements to the product to eliminate any problems or to cover new needs that have developed.

Using the SDLC method can make any problems you encounter in your design more obvious, making it easier for you to tackle them at a more favorable point in your design, rather than changing existing code.

As you'll see as we progress, it can also be a good idea to go through a **prototype** stage of the development phase, in which the application contains all the core functionality, but in a more limited fashion. Our China Shop Project prototype (in Chapter 8) will perform the necessary calculations, but have no facility for updating prices or customizing the environment, for example.

Quiz

1. In this chapter, I compare writing a program to what activity?

2. When I enter the store to meet with the China Shop owner for the first time, how many people are in the store?

3. What does SDLC stand for?

4. What are the six phases of the SDLC?

5. What is typically the shortest phase of the SDLC?

6. What is the purpose of the SDLC's Preliminary Investigation phase?

7. After the Preliminary Investigation of the SDLC is completed, a go or no-go decision is made.
   There are three factors, typically called 'constraints', which result in a go or no-go decision. Can you name them?

8. The second phase of the SDLC, the **Analysis Phase**, is sometimes called the...

9. What takes place in the Analysis phase of the SDLC?

10. How many brands of china does the China Shop sell?

11. How many components did my Visual Basic class design during the Design phase of the SDLC?

12. During the Design phase of the SDLC, what component does the analyst or designer typically start with?

13. What is a Requirements Statement?

14. What is the definition of computer processing?

15. What is a computer record?

16. What is the purpose of the Systems Development Life Cycle (SDLC)?

17. Can you name the end result, or deliverable, from the first phase of the SDLC, the Preliminary investigation?

18. Which of the following, a flowchart or pseudo-code, is a graphical depiction of the processing logic of your computer program?

19. What is Joe's biggest requirement for the application we are writing for him?

Extra Credit – The following number is the only one of its kind. What's so special about it? 8,549,176,320

Chapter 2
What is a Computer Program?

In this chapter, we follow my computer class as they learn what a computer program is and what it does. Along the way, you'll learn what happens when you turn your computer on, and we'll de-mystify the 'behind-the-scenes' workings of the computer. Why learn this, you might say? Although you don't need an intimate knowledge of the inner workings of your computer to write Windows programs, the more you know, the better the programs that you write will be.

What is a Computer?

At the conclusion of our last class, I had warned my students that during this class meeting we would need to discuss some of the nitty-gritty of computer hardware and software before we could get on with the fun part of actually looking at and learning Visual Basic.

"Can anyone give me a definition of a computer?" I asked. For whatever reason, everyone seemed to be a little reluctant to volunteer, so I gave my definition:

A computer is a machine, made primarily of metal and plastic. It has few moving parts, and is mostly electrical in nature. It accepts data in some form of input with which it then performs calculations and other types of operations on the data with tremendous speed and accuracy. It then generates information in some form of output.

"We'll look at some of the terms I use here in just a little more detail shortly," I said. I continued by explaining that a computer performs its calculations and operations through instructions that are provided by a human being. Collectively, these instructions are called a computer program, and the person who writes the program is called a programmer.

"You'll be doing exactly that," I said, "when you write programs in Visual Basic."

Data

Linda noted that I had used the word **data** in my definition of a computer, and asked me to clarify exactly what I meant by data. I thought for a moment, and said that data is anything that the computer uses in order to produce information. Data, for example, can be numbers, letters, symbols, names, addresses, student grades, pictures or charts.

"But," I said, "the computer doesn't understand the language of human beings. For that reason, data must first be translated into a language the computer does understand. This, its **native** language, is sometimes known as machine language and takes the form of ones and zeroes. It's also called **binary** language or binary code."

> *It's not only data that must be translated into binary code; programs submitted to the computer to run must also be translated.*

Several students told me they recognized the word binary. I asked if anyone could tell me exactly what binary meant.

"Two," Dave answered.

"Good," I said. Binary means two, and both data and programs are represented in the computer by a series of ones and zeroes.

"Why only ones and zeroes?" Ward asked.

"The reason for that," I said, "is that the computer is electrical. It's relatively easy for the computer to represent data and programs as a series of on or off switches, where 'on' is a one, and 'off' is a zero."

I said that most of my students, at first, are overwhelmed by the notion that the computer uses ones and zeroes to represent data and programs, but it's absolutely true. Because of the miniaturized state of the electronic components in the computer, the computer can contain millions and millions of these on-off switches.

"Each one of these on-off switches has a special name, a **bit**," I said.

Bits

Just about everyone told me they had heard the word **bit** somewhere.

"A bit sounds like something small, and it is," I said. "A bit is the smallest unit of data in the computer. You can think of a bit as the light switch on your wall. It can either be on or off. When a computer bit is **on**, it has a value of 1. When a computer bit is **off**, it has a value of 0."

I displayed the following sketch on the classroom projector:

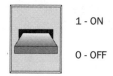

"With one bit, there are only two values that it can represent: 1 or 0. Suppose we add a second bit. With two bits, we can represent four possible values."

- both bits can be off

- both bits can be on

- the first bit can be on and the second off

- the first bit off and the second bit on

I displayed the following sketch on the classroom projector:

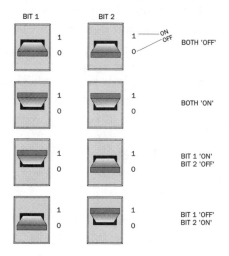

"With 3 bits, there are 8 possible values that we can represent. With 4 bits, 16 values. With 5 bits, 32 values. With 6 bits, 64. With 7 bits, 128 values. And with 8 bits, 256 values."

I displayed the following sketch of 8 light switches on the classroom projector, with some of the switches set to on and some set to off:

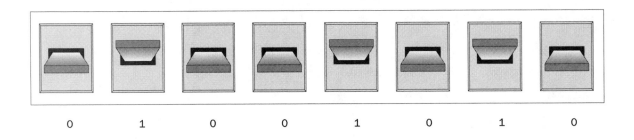

0   1   0   0   1   0   1   0

"This **bit pattern**, as it is called," I said, "is the binary form of the capital letter **J**."

"You're kidding," Ward said. "So my name could be represented in the computer by a pattern of these light switches, I mean ones and zeroes?"

Bytes

"Exactly right," I replied. "There is a unique bit pattern for every letter of the alphabet (both upper and lower case), each number and each punctuation key on the computer's keyboard."

I asked the students to take a quick look at their keyboard. There are 26 letters on the keyboard. Counting both lowercase and uppercase letters, there are 52. Count the numbers and we're up to 62. Now count the punctuation keys.

"On my keyboard, I count another 32," Rose said.

"That gives us a total of 94," Jack said.

I explained that to represent any one of those 94 characters on the keyboard requires 7 bits, because 7 bits can represent 128 characters. To represent the not-printable characters as well requires 8 bits.

"A collection of 8 bits is called a **byte,**" I said, "and the standardized bit pattern is known as the **ASCII Code**. ASCII stands for the American Standard Code for Information Interchange."

"Is there any place where we can find the ASCII Code?" Barbara asked.

"Sure," I said, "when we start up Visual Basic, you'll find that it can easily be found in Visual Basic's On-line Help by searching for the keyword ASCII.

I told them not to be intimidated by all of this talk of bits and bytes. It isn't necessary to memorize the ASCII code in order to be a good programmer. However, knowledge of what goes on behind the scenes can be invaluable.

"A Visual Basic programmer should be aware of binary," I said, "because Visual Basic, like all other programming languages, acts as a translator. The programmer writes in a language, in our case Visual Basic, which is similar to English. Then something known as the Visual Basic compiler converts this English-like writing to binary code which the machine can understand."

Memory

"OK," I said, "we've looked at the most basic form of data in the computer. Let's examine how and where that data is stored in the computer."

I continued by saying that something that always seems to confuse students is the concept of computer memory. I reminded them that in my definition of a computer, I said that it accepts data, and performs calculations and other types of operations on that input in order to generate information.

"These calculations and operations are performed in the computer's memory," I said. "Computer memory is also called **RAM**, which is an abbreviation for **Random Access Memory**. Bits and bytes are recorded electrically in the computer's RAM. The computer uses RAM just like you would use a piece of scratch paper. RAM holds not only data, but every program that is currently running."

I displayed the following sketch on the classroom projector:

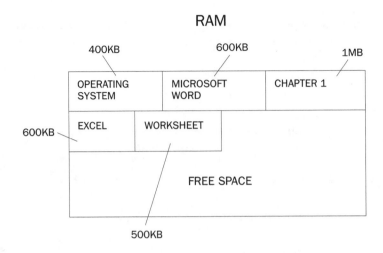

"Here's a sketch of RAM usage in a typical computer," I said.

"Do we need to memorize this?" Rhonda asked.

"Goodness no!" I exclaimed. "I'm not discussing RAM for that reason. What's important here is that you understand how the computer uses it - that's what will make you a better programmer." I continued by explaining that RAM temporarily holds programs that are currently running and any data that these programs require.

"How temporary is temporary?" Mary asked.

"A fraction of a second," I said. "The ones and zeroes stored in RAM are there only as long as the computer is on. When you turn your computer off, the contents of RAM, the bits and bytes, are lost."

"If you are using your computer," I said, "and a thunderstorm suddenly knocks your power out, the contents of RAM are lost in an instant. The term **volatility** is used to describe the temporary and fragile nature of RAM."

"What do KB and MB mean?" asked Rhonda.

"KB is an abbreviation for kilobyte, which is the term for approximately one thousand bytes. A megabyte, which is abbreviated to MB, is approximately a million bytes," I replied. "We'll look more at these terms when we come to talk about computer storage."

"Something that confuses beginners," I said, "is the notion of RAM capacity and the speed at which data can be accessed from it. When you buy a computer, it comes with a certain amount or **capacity** of RAM that is also rated with a length of time. The capacity tells you the total number of bytes that the computer's RAM can hold, and the rating indicates the time it takes the computer to get to or access a particular piece of data in RAM."

"I've taken a look inside my computer at home, and I know that I have 32MB of RAM and it is rated at 60 **nanoseconds**," Peter said.

"Thank you, Peter," I said, "a nanosecond is one billionth of a second. That means that Peter's computer can access a particular piece of data in RAM in 60 billionths of a second."

I continued by saying that in addition to RAM, other devices in the computer also have ratings. For instance, floppy diskettes and hard disk drives are rated in the millisecond range. As there are 1,000,000 nanoseconds in a millisecond, accessing data from a floppy diskette or hard disk drive takes a much longer time than accessing the same data from RAM.

"Relatively speaking then, RAM is very fast," Dave said. "Yes it is," I agreed.

"My computer has 4 gigabytes of RAM," Ward said proudly.

"Actually," I replied, "that'll be the storage capacity of your hard disk drive, which is also measured in bytes. Your hard drive has 4 billion bytes of storage space, as a gigabyte, abbreviated to GB, is approximately one billion bytes. I told you that these terms could be confusing. Your computer has a certain amount of RAM and a certain amount of storage. We'll look at the concept of storage in a minute or so."

Linda observed that RAM capacity is always less than the capacity of the computer's hard drive.

"Excellent observation Linda," I said. "RAM, which as I mentioned uses electricity to store bits and bytes, is much more expensive than disk drives, which use magnetism to permanently store bits and bytes. At home, my computer contains 32MB of RAM, while my hard disk drive contains 3.1GB. Therefore, the capacity of my disk drive is about 100 times as large as my RAM."

I displayed the following slide on the classroom projector:

To summarize then, RAM:

- Uses electricity to store ones and zeroes

- Holds programs and data for execution

- Is temporary in nature, sometimes called volatile

- Has less capacity than a hard disk drive

- Is faster than a hard disk drive

- Is more expensive than a hard disk drive

Computer Storage

"Let's address Ward's confusion concerning RAM and storage," I said. "Beginners frequently confuse the terms memory and storage. This confusion arises because both RAM and hard drive storage capacity is measured in bytes. Here is a chart that shows you some of the common terms of capacity measurement, along with a real world application of the term."

I displayed the following chart on the classroom projector:

Term	Approx.	Other terms used	Real World
Byte	1 character		A letter or number
Kilobyte	1 thousand characters	KB	1 Double-spaced typewritten page
Megabyte	1 million characters	Meg, MB	50 pages of a textbook including graphics and illustrations
Gigabyte	1 billion characters	Gig, Gb	An encyclopedia with graphics, audio and video
Terabyte	1 trillion characters		

"Some of these storage terms," I said, "although they may seem large at first, aren't that big when you consider how much capacity is required to store some common everyday pieces of data. For instance, one chapter of a textbook, including the diagrams and formatting information, may use about 1MB of RAM and storage. An encyclopedia consumes about one-third of the storage capacity of one of our classroom hard disk drives."

"Think of memory as being like a desk. You work with items on your desk, but you store them elsewhere, in a filing cabinet. When you need to work with items, you retrieve them from the cabinet. A computer's filing cabinet is storage. Memory, as we just saw, is RAM, which is electrical and very much a temporary commodity. Sooner or later, you will turn off the computer, but because RAM is temporary, when you do that, any data in the RAM will be lost. The user of the computer must have a way of saving data contained in RAM permanently. Storage, therefore, is where the data which was held temporarily in the RAM is stored permanently."

I continued by saying that computer storage today is either magnetic (hard disk drives and floppy drives) or optical (CD-ROMs and writeable CDs).

"How do disk drives work?" Blaine asked.

"In a nutshell," I said, "whereas RAM uses electricity to record ones and zeroes, disk drives use magnetism to permanently record magnetic ones and zeroes on spinning disks coated with a magnetic oxide. Magnetic oxides can hold information without power. When you switch the computer back on again the information is still there. This is the key idea to storage."

I pointed out that diskette and hard disk drives are actually the slow link in the computer's strong speed chain. Both of these devices introduce us to something we haven't seen yet in the computer - physical movement. Forcing a computer that operates at the speed of electricity to interact with a device that needs to move in order to operate, is like driving a fast sports car in bumper-to-bumper traffic. RAM performs operations on billions of bits in a matter of seconds. By comparison, disk drives are incredibly slow.

Anything that you, the programmer, can do to reduce or eliminate reading or writing data to a disk drive will make the programs you write in Visual Basic much faster.

"The RAM in our classroom computers is rated at 60 nanoseconds," I said. "Our hard disk drive at 9 milliseconds, and our floppy disk drive at 70 milliseconds. If you do some quick math, you'll see that accessing a piece of data in RAM is about 150,000 times faster than accessing that same piece of data on the hard disk drive. Accessing that data on the hard disk drive is about 8 times faster than accessing it from the floppy disk drive."

The operation of floppy and hard disk drives is virtually identical. The main differences are speed of access and storage capacity. Whereas the hard disk drive on my computer holds 3.1GB, the floppy diskette currently sitting in my diskette drive holds a little over 1MB. CD-ROM drives are closer in speed and capacity to a hard disk drive than a floppy diskette drive.

To summarize, then, storage:

- Uses magnetism or optics to store ones and zeroes

- Permanently stores programs and data

- Has more capacity than RAM

- Is slower than RAM

- Is cheaper than RAM

RAM vs. Storage

"Let's summarize our discussion of RAM and storage," I said.

"There are two kinds of information held in a computer," I said. "There are the programs you are using and the documents that you are working on, and the computer treats these bits of data differently. When you have finished with a program, it is simply cleared out of RAM and never gets sent back to storage. After all, you got it from there in the first place, so you can do that again whenever you want to. When you've finished with a document, it's usually saved to the hard disk, so that it can be recovered after the computer is turned off and the RAM is 'flushed'."

Prior to our first break of the day, I displayed the following chart on the classroom projector:

	RAM	**Storage**
How data is recorded	Electricity	Magnetism or Optics
Temporary or Permanent?	Volatile, disappearing when the computer is turned off	Permanent, until you ask the computer to delete file
Cost	More expensive than storage; About $3/MB	Less expensive than RAM; About 10 cents/MB
Time taken to access data	Faster than storage, in the nanosecond range	Slower than RAM, in the millisecond range

What Makes a Computer Program Run?

After break, I asked if anyone could tell me what running a computer program means. There were no anxious volunteers.

"Sometimes," I said, "you'll hear the terms **execute**, **load** or **start** in place of the word **run**. These terms are frequently used interchangeably."

"I've also heard other terms for program," Linda said. "That's right," I agreed. "You'll probably hear me use terms such as **project**, **application**, or **app** quite a bit during this course."

"Did you say 'app'?" Ward asked. "Yes, 'app' is short for application," I said.

I reminded them that most computer programs are written to convert data into information, or indeed to covert information to data, for storage and later processing. The program is written by a programmer and sold or distributed to **end-users**.

"Like the China Shop program," Mary said. "Exactly," I said.

For a program to run on a computer, it must first be written with the aid of an editor (such as Notepad) or a program development tool, such as Visual Basic. After the program is written, the program is either **compiled**, or run in an **interpreted mode**. I displayed the following explanation on the classroom projector:

A compiled program is a program that is translated into machine language instructions (ones and zeroes). The compiled program is saved, usually as a file ending with a file extension of .EXE. The compiled program is then run on a computer, where the ones and zeroes are read directly by the Operating System.

An interpreted program is a program which is not translated ahead of time, but is translated line by line as the program is run. Interpreted programs run more slowly than compiled programs.

I continued by saying that programs that run on a computer are either **Operating Systems** or **Application Programs**. Operating Systems, a term often abbreviated to OS, take care of work within the computer, often very complex and repetitive work, which allows the applications to run. For instance, it is the OS that is responsible for finding the letter you wrote to Aunt Sarah or Uncle Bill last winter.

> *Visual Basic is one programming language among many that can be used to create Application Programs. Most System Programs are written in languages such as Assembler, C and C++, although many apps are written using these languages as well.*

"Few, if any, people would buy a computer just for the Operating System," I said. "It's the apps that you can run that makes the computer a useful tool." I cited word processing, electronic spreadsheet and game programs as common examples of apps.

"Application Programs can't run without the assistance of Operating Systems, can they?" Valerie asked.

"That's right," I said. "Apps couldn't work without an OS to take care of internal chores. On the other hand, an OS would have no purpose if there weren't any applications that people wanted to use."

I displayed this chart illustrating some uses for each type of program:

SYSTEM PROGRAMS	APPLICATION PROGRAMS

READ A FILE FROM DISK
SAVE A FILE TO DISK
FORMAT A DISKETTE
DISPLAY THE LETTER 'K'
   ON THE COMPUTERS
   MONITOR
FIND A FILE ON DISK
	WRITE A LETTER TO COUSIN MOLLY
	CREATE A HOME BUDGET
	PLAY YOUR FAVORITE GAME
	'SURF' THE INTERNET

"Why should we be so concerned about our OS?" Valerie asked. I answered by saying that at this point in their programming careers, the understanding of the OS might not seem very significant. However, in my opinion, you can't be a great programmer without understanding how your programs interact with the OS controlling your computer.

"Is Windows the Operating System?" Ward asked.

"Windows is one of many Operating Systems for the PC," I said. "A PC is capable of running any number of different Operating Systems; you could even run them simultaneously, though frankly you're unlikely to ever want to do that."

"Is an OS written for a specific brand of computer?" Joe asked.

"No," I said, "they are written to work using a specific microprocessor, such as the Intel Pentium microprocessor some of you may have heard of. The Intel family of microprocessors is so popular that many different Operating Systems have been written to run on it, including DOS, UNIX, Windows 95 & 98, and Windows NT."

"The OS is the workhorse of the PC. Virtually from the time the computer is turned on, the OS is in nearly full control. Any app that runs on the PC will run under the control of the OS. It's important to our understanding of programming to know a little bit more about how the OS operates."

"At this point," I said, "our lesson can go in many different directions, because there are many different Operating Systems that can run on a PC. Today we're going to examine two of the most popular Operating Systems, **DOS** and **Windows**."

A Little Computer History

"Why waste time talking about DOS?" Linda asked. "Hasn't that gone by the wayside? I would think everyone here is running Windows at home or at work." However, several students disagreed. Some of them were still running DOS on their PCs at work.

"My purpose here is not to explain how to use DOS," I said. "I want to place Windows in a historical perspective so that you can appreciate it for what it is, an OS that was developed to correct the deficiencies of DOS. For those of you who have never seen DOS in action, today will give you a clearer vision of why Windows was developed."

DOS

"In the next few moments," I continued, "I'll present an overview of DOS, how it boots, how programs run under DOS, RAM usage under DOS, and finally the limitations of DOS that led to the development of Windows."

I noted that DOS (**Disk Operating System**), sometimes known as MS-DOS or PC-DOS, was introduced in 1981 for the original IBM PC.

"The original IBM PC was primitive compared to the computers we're using today in this classroom." I said. "The original version of DOS (Version 1.0) didn't need to be terribly complicated. Today's versions of DOS are much more complicated than their predecessors, reflecting the great advances in hardware that have transformed the computer industry."

Booting DOS

"Most, if not all, PCs sold these days are running a version of Windows," I continued, "which is one of the reasons you're all here. However, worldwide, there are still plenty of PCs still only running DOS." I thought it would help the class if I gave them a historical perspective of Microsoft DOS.

"When DOS was being developed, there were two technological limitations that had to be dealt with:"

- first, the original IBM PC was slow
- second, it didn't have much RAM (64KB)

"We know how important RAM is to the operation of the PC," I said. "Since the size of RAM was restricted to only 64KB, and to run an application, the OS, the application and the data had to be in memory at the same time, you can appreciate why the OS had to be pretty 'lean'.

I continued by explaining that no design could be lean enough. Considering everything that an OS is called upon to do, there was no way to load all of DOS into RAM at the same time and still leave room for anything else. For that reason, DOS was divided into a series of smaller programs. Three programs were designated **intrinsic** programs, and the rest were designated as **extrinsic**.

These three intrinsic programs were designed to permanently remain in RAM (at least while the PC was running). Together, these three files, IO.SYS, MSDOS.SYS, and COMMAND.COM, were small enough (about 45KB) that they could all squeeze into RAM, leaving about 19KB for apps and data.

"But what about those other files," Ward asked, "the extrinsic files you spoke about? What are they used for?"

I explained that the extrinsic files are typically found in a subdirectory of your hard disk drive. Without exception, these files execute commands that are not necessary for the PC to operate. Instead they offered the user some additional tools.

"For instance," I said, "in Windows 95, if you insert an unformatted diskette into your PC's diskette drive, you will be asked if you wish to format the diskette. In DOS, in order to format a diskette, you must run the extrinsic FORMAT program, which is located on the PC's hard disk drive. When you run the FORMAT program, FORMAT.COM is found and then loaded into RAM by the intrinsic portion of DOS, the program is run, and when the diskette is formatted the extrinsic FORMAT program is removed from RAM."

Running Programs in DOS

I then asked the class to consider a computer booting DOS as its Operating System. I had pre-configured a PC to run DOS, and I took a moment to connect it to our classroom projector.

This screenshot is what everyone saw on the classroom projector after the computer had finished booting up:

"What is that?" Rhonda asked. "It looks like a random collection of characters. Did you press the keys by mistake?" Many of the students had never seen a DOS prompt, and it was a shock to them.

"Where is the interface?" Rose asked. "This is it!" I said. "At this point, the computer is now just sitting there waiting for us to give it something to do."

I noticed some obvious grins. "Yes, this is the DOS prompt," I said. "In DOS, this prompt is displayed to let the user know that the computer is ready and willing to do something for them. A flashing underline, called the cursor, blinks to the right of the greater than sign to let the user know that the PC is awaiting instructions."

I continued by saying that at this point, the user can either type in a DOS command, or the name of a program that they want to run.

"In DOS," I said, "only files with extensions ending in .EXE, .COM, or .BAT can be run, although the user doesn't have to type the extension of the file name to run it."

File names in DOS followed an 8.3 naming convention. That is, the name of the file can contain anywhere from 1 to 8 characters, followed by an optional period (.), followed by an optional file extension containing anywhere from 1 to 3 characters. The latest version of DOS, Version 7, supports longer file names.

"After the user enters the name of a command at the DOS prompt," I continued, "DOS takes a quick look in RAM to see if the name of the program the user typed is an intrinsic command, in which case it will be found there. If DOS finds it, the command is executed. If DOS *doesn't* find the name of the command there, DOS continues its search by looking in the current directory, and if that fails, it looks in the directories specified in something called the **DOS Path**."

The DOS Path is a list of directories contained in a special startup file called AUTOEXEC.BAT. The DOS Path tells DOS where to search for the command or program the user wants. If DOS finds the appropriate file, it loads it into RAM and starts the program running. Of course, the program could either be an extrinsic DOS command or an executable program written by someone other than Microsoft.

"That's to keep DOS from having to search the entire hard disk, isn't it?" Linda said. "Exactly," I agreed.

I went on to say that the DOS prompt is an example of a **Character Based Interface**. This means the only way a user can tell the OS what they want to do is to type a command or a file name using the keyboard.

"In other words, there's no mouse," Dave said.

"Right you are," I replied. "The Character Based Interface has some inherent weaknesses. First, typing is slow. Secondly, you need to remember all the commands. And third, it's much easier to make mistakes."

I informed my class that I had installed a copy of WordPerfect for DOS on my PC prior to the beginning of this class this morning. I could tell from their expressions that several of them had never heard of WordPerfect, and so I explained that WordPerfect is a word processing program much like Microsoft Word.

"Unlike the version of Word that we have in the classroom," I said, "the DOS version of WordPerfect does not require Microsoft Windows to run."

I wanted to illustrate how an app runs under DOS. I said that all I needed to do to run the program was to type the name WP at the DOS prompt and then press return. Like this:

```
C:\>WP
```

I did so, and a few seconds later WordPerfect was running on the PC. I quickly exited the program, and we were back to the DOS Prompt.

"How did you know to type WP?" Ward asked. "Good point," I replied. "First, you have to know, and secondly, you have to remember. But suppose instead of typing WP, I type WO instead. Like this:"

```
C:\>WO
```

I did that and this message was displayed on the classroom projector:

BAD COMMAND OR FILE NAME

"What happened?" Bob asked.

I told them that when we had typed the command WP at the DOS prompt, DOS looked in RAM to see if this was an intrinsic DOS command. It wasn't, so it checked the current directory and then each directory in the DOS Path, looking for a file called WP.EXE, WP.COM, or WP.BAT. It finally found a file called WP.EXE in the \WP51 directory that I had placed in the DOS Path of the PC's AUTOEXEC.BAT file.

"And what about WO?" Joe asked.

"DOS," I said, "followed the same procedure looking for a file called WO.EXE, WO.COM or WO.BAT, but couldn't find them anywhere in its path. At that point, it displayed the error message."

"One of those user friendly error messages I've grown to love," Lou said sarcastically.

RAM Usage in DOS

"How much RAM do we have on these PCs?" I asked.

"I believe you said 32MB!" Dave replied.

"That's right," I said, "I bet most of you think that right now, DOS is using this PC's RAM pretty efficiently."

There were a number of affirmative nods. I pointed out that there was a slight problem in our assumption. Back in 1981, when DOS was being written, the programmers working on it were worried about squeezing programs into RAM. Although they anticipated the larger amounts of RAM that would be available in PCs today, they didn't plan for it in their design of DOS. With the 64KB of RAM in the original IBM PC, an upper limit of 1MB of RAM seemed pretty reasonable.

I could see some puzzled looks. "What do you mean an upper limit?" Linda asked.

"I mean that DOS can't load a program into RAM beyond the first megabyte, because it simply can't count beyond one million and that's regardless of the total amount of RAM on the PC. With 32MB of RAM on this PC, by running DOS with only a single program running, we're actually wasting the remaining 31MB of RAM. Only the first megabyte of RAM can be accessed by DOS!"

"Eventually," I said, "third party software vendors and Microsoft itself came up with software to more fully utilize all of the RAM on DOS based PCs, but these attempts were basically a patchwork until Windows came along. Shortly, we'll see that Windows overcame this RAM limitation, which is another reason why it was immediately popular with microcomputer owners."

Valerie noted that the DOS programs she had used in the past seemed rudimentary in comparison to the Windows version of the same program.

"That's an excellent point," I told her. "The RAM limitation severely limits the functionality of DOS programs. To a large degree, the number of bells and whistles that a program has is dependent upon the number of program instructions it contains. In effect, this prevents DOS programs from being as large as their Windows counterparts. For instance, the executable file for the DOS version of WordPerfect is about 300,000 bytes. The executable file for the version of Microsoft Word in our classroom is about 3.5MB."

I explained that as the user begins to use WordPerfect, it makes various requests of DOS (remember, apps work with the OS, not directly with the computer). "For instance," I said, "the user may ask the app to save a document. The app passes the request to the OS which uses one or more of its commands to achieve the required result, using **registers** and **stacks** to process the commands at the right time."

Registers

"Registers and stacks?" Linda said. I explained that registers are high-speed memory devices contained within the microprocessor. Each microprocessor contains varying numbers of registers.

"The microprocessor uses registers to perform calculations" I said, "and to keep track of the next program instruction to be performed. If the OS needs to perform an addition, for example, the microprocessor uses two registers to hold each number, placing the calculated result in a third."

"It sounds like registers are part of RAM," Rhonda said.

"No, that's a common misconception. The registers are contained within the microprocessor."

The Stack

"A stack is a different story," I said. "A stack is a **data structure** contained in RAM that holds information about running applications. Whereas registers are manipulated by the microprocessor, stacks are manipulated either by the app or the OS."

"What's a data structure?" Chuck asked.

I explained that in the world of computer science, data structures are logical entities. They don't physically exist, but are created to aid the OS to do its job.

"We'll be creating data structures of our own later in the course," I said, "when we create files for the China Shop project. Files are data structures."

"I understand the concept of a register," Jack said, "but I'm having trouble understanding stacks."

"Suppose," I said, "you go into your favorite diner or restaurant tonight, and sit at the counter. You're bound to see a pile of dishes placed into a plate 'stack', which is a mechanical device with a cylindrical compartment and a spring on the bottom. The spring pushes upward on the plates, so that when you take one out, the next one pops to the top."

"Yes, I've seen those," Rose said.

"Just like the plate stack is used to store dishes neatly, while providing easy access to the next dish, the data structure stack is used by the OS and app to store program instructions, results of calculations, and other data, ready for when they are needed."

I continued by explaining that when the OS places something onto the stack it is called a **push operation**. Accessing and subsequently removing an entry from the stack is called a **pop operation**. Keeping the details straight as to what on the stack belongs to the OS and what belongs to one or more apps can be complex.

"Fortunately," I said, "that's something we don't really have to worry about because the OS takes care of all of those details. When we discuss Windows, which permits more than one app to run at the same time, we'll see that each Windows application has an internal stack of its own."

Problems with DOS

Ward (obviously a DOS fan) remarked that from his experience, DOS does more than an admirable job of running programs.

"Why do we need Windows?" he said.

In reply, I posed this question, "Suppose the user, while working in WordPerfect, needs to work on their Lotus 1-2-3 spreadsheet file? In DOS, it isn't possible to work on more than one app at the same time unless you use special software. To be on the safe side DOS should only be used for single tasking; this means that the user should work with only one program at a time. The user should finish working in WordPerfect, save whatever document they are working with and exit. DOS clears RAM of WordPerfect and any documents that it was using. The user then stares at the DOS prompt, remembers the command for LOTUS 1-2-3, types it in and waits as DOS locates and loads LOTUS 1-2-3 into RAM."

"So," Ward replied half-heartedly, "what's wrong with that?"

We all agreed that clicking on an icon on your desktop is certainly a lot easier.

"And then suppose," I continued, "that the user needs to incorporate some data from their Lotus 1-2-3 spreadsheet into the WordPerfect document they are working on. In DOS, there's simply no way to take that data and place it in the spreadsheet."

I asked if everyone considered these limitations to be severe or not. Everyone, including my stalwart DOS fans, agreed that these were pretty severe. I pointed out that although there are still many people in the world using DOS, I think most of them would be Windows converts given the choice.

I displayed the following list of DOS limitations on the classroom projector:

DOS uses a Character-based Interface. The user has to type arcane, hard to remember instructions at a DOS prompt to tell the PC what it wants to do. Giving the computer instructions in this way is by nature error-prone. Typing a command at a DOS prompt will never be as easy as clicking on an icon with a mouse.

RAM limitations. DOS cannot take advantage of the modern PC's abundant RAM without the use of additional applications. As we have seen, DOS, even on a PC with 32MB of RAM, will only initially utilize the first megabyte.

DOS is Single Tasking. A DOS user cannot work with more than one application at a time.

DOS lacks a Common User Interface. Every DOS program looks different from the other. A uniform interface greatly reduces training time. In DOS you would have to learn different commands to perform the same function in different applications.

Information Transfer in DOS from one application to another is impossible. In DOS, there is no way to transfer data from one program to another. Windows introduced a 'clipboard' which gives Windows programs a way to easily share data.

I suggested that a die-hard DOS fan might say, "Problem with DOS? There's no problem with DOS. The character-based interface never bothered me. My DOS programs run perfectly fine in 1MB. Besides, who in their right mind would want to run more than one program anyway?"

This statement elicited quite a few chuckles.

"I've heard this argument for years," I said. "To me, this is like saying that airplanes flew better with propellers instead of jet engines. It's time to realize that the five limitations I stated above are the reasons that Microsoft Windows is the Operating System of choice for PCs today."

I continued on with our mini-history lesson. I said that eventually, as PCs became more and more popular, users heard about another microcomputer that had a **graphical user interface** (called a **GUI** - pronounced 'GOO-ey'), which took full advantage of the increasing power of microprocessors, and permitted the user to run more than one program simultaneously.

Just to clear up a few things: 'Windows' is the registered trademark name for the Operating System we are talking about. A 'window' is a rectangular space on the screen in which we do work. And 'Window' is a menu choice that gives the user options about how to arrange the windows (workspaces) on the screen.

"That microcomputer was the Macintosh," I said, " and the users weren't the only ones to see the potential of this. Microsoft did as well and the company began work on Windows."

Microsoft Windows

I could see some relieved looks on the faces of my students. Finally, they were thinking, we're going to look at Windows. Again I emphasized that the reason I had devoted so much time to discussing DOS was because I wanted to place Windows in the correct historical perspective.

"Now I want to move our discussion to Windows, which right now is the dominant GUI interface in the world," I said. "I must warn you, though, that any discussion of Windows is complicated by the fact that there currently are four distinct versions of Windows available: Windows 3.1, Windows 95, Windows 98, and Windows NT. For the most part, I'm going to discuss Windows as if it were a single entity. Where there are differences between the four versions of Windows, I'll point those out."

I started the discussion on Windows by explaining the differences between Windows 3.1, Windows 95, Windows 98 and Windows NT.

"Windows 3.1 evolved from earlier versions of Windows, such as Windows 1.0 and Windows 2.0, which in turn were based on DOS. Windows 95 is based on Windows 3.1 and therefore contains a lot of Windows 3.1 code. Windows NT on the other hand was a brand new OS. Although Windows 95 and Windows NT are two completely different operating systems, they have the same GUI. Windows 98 is the latest operating system that Microsoft has produced, and really replaces Windows 95. For our purposes they can be considered the same; I'll keep mentioning Windows 95 as that's what we're using now."

I continued by saying that Windows 95 continues to be favored for home use, while Windows NT is preferred in the corporate environment. While the hardware requirements for both are pretty stringent, Windows NT requires more RAM than Windows 95.

"Before we get into the nuts and bolts of Windows," I said, "let's take a quick peek at a typical Windows Application, the Windows Calculator. Every Windows program has a similar look and feel, so looking at the Calculator is a great way to discuss the features common to them all.

I instructed everyone in the class to select the Windows Start button, then select Programs-Accessories-Calculator. This screen was displayed on the classroom projector:

"As you can see, the Calculator exemplifies a Windows program," I said. "It's graphical!"

"As you can see, the calculator contains a Title Bar, a Menu Bar, and some of the objects we discussed during our last class. For instance, each of the number keys is a command button. The box at the top of the Calculator, that currently displays the number zero, is a text box."

"Are there any option buttons and check boxes?" Blaine asked.

I asked them to select View-Scientific from the Calculator's menu. When they did, the scientific view of the Calculator was displayed:

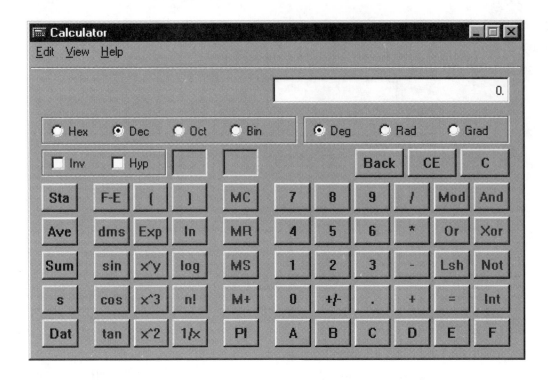

"The scientific view of the Calculator," I said, "has more than its fair share of option buttons and check boxes."

"Notice the option button group with the labels Hex, Dec, Oct and Bin," I said. "Only one option button can be selected at a time. In this case, Dec, an abbreviation of decimal, is selected. With check boxes, more than one check box can be selected in a group, such as Inv and Hyp." I saw a few puzzled looks, but I assured everyone that they would have ample opportunity to experiment with both option buttons and check boxes before the end of the course.

"The Windows Calculator is just a Windows program," I said. "It was written by a programmer using the same types of tools that are available in Visual Basic." I told them that in previous classes, one of the class projects had been for the students to write their own Windows Calculator using Visual Basic.

"Will we be doing that in this class?" Steve asked.

"No," I replied, "all of our energies will be devoted to writing the China Shop Project. But by the end of the course, you will certainly be able to write one if you want to. Let's use the Windows Calculator to discuss the characteristics it shares with every other Windows program, including those we will write ourselves."

The Title Bar

I explained that the Title Bar in a Windows program contains the name of the program. But that's not all it contains. To the left of the program name is an icon that usually represents what the program does. In the case of the Calculator, it's a picture of a calculator.

"The programs that we write," I said, "including the China Shop Project, will contain such an icon. But this icon is more than just window dressing. This icon is called a **Control Menu Bar**."

I asked the class to click their mouse on the icon, and when they did, the Control Menu Bar was revealed:

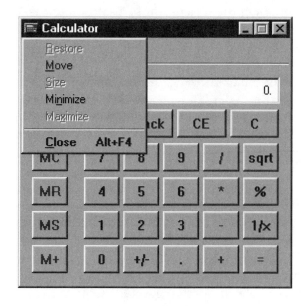

I explained that the Control Menu Bar gives the user options for minimizing, maximizing or closing their window. "When we design the China Shop Project interface," I said, "we'll see that there is a way to tell Visual Basic to either display or not display the Control Menu Bar. As we'll see a little later, we'll choose not to display it."

I asked the students to look to the right hand side of the Title Bar. There are three buttons, the Minimize, Maximize and Close buttons. "In fact, these buttons are shortcuts for the Control Menu Bar. Clicking on the Minimize button reduces the Calculator to an icon on the Windows TaskBar."

"Why is that second button dull?" Rhonda asked.

"That second button is the Maximize button," I replied. "Ordinarily, clicking on it would enlarge the Calculator to the full size of the monitor. However, the designers of the Calculator 'disabled' the Maximize Button, so that the Calculator could not be maximized. We're able to do the same thing for programs we design in Visual Basic."

I also mentioned that you could usually move your mouse pointer to the borders of a Windows program, and click and drag to change the size and shape of the window. However, just as the designers of the Calculator had chosen to disable the Maximize button, they had decided that the user should not be able to resize the window. "Again," I said, "this is something you'll be able to specify for the programs you design in Visual Basic."

I concluded my discussion of the Control Menu Bar by saying that clicking on the Close button closes and then ends the Calculator program.

"When we design the China Shop Project interface," I said "we'll see that in Visual Basic there are options or **properties** that determine which, if any, of these buttons will be displayed when the user runs our program."

I reminded them that we had already decided that the user could only exit the China Shop Program via the menu. "For that reason," I said, "we will disable the Control Menu Bar itself, so that the user won't even see it."

Some people were looking tired after all the things we had covered – from bits and bytes all the way to Windows, and so I asked everyone to take a quick break.

The Menu Bar

When everyone returned from break, we turned our attention to the menu bar of the Calculator. I didn't have to remind the class that we had discussed the China Shop Project's menu at great length during the design phase of the SDLC.

"The Calculator's menu," I said, "deviates slightly from the Windows standard menu in that it does not contain a File command. Aside from that, however, it operates in a typical Windows way. Notice that the Edit command can also be accessed by pressing the *Alt* and *E* keys." I also told them that you can do the same with many menus – just press *Alt* and the underlined letter.

Windows Behavior

"I don't want to leave you with the impression that the main difference between DOS programs and Windows programs is graphical quality," I said. "That's part of it, but not all." I said that there have been some DOS programs with pretty impressive graphical appearances.

"I think though," Linda said, "that to someone coming from the DOS world, the most impressive aspect of a Windows program is the beautiful graphical interface." I agreed. It certainly is startling to view the Calculator for the first time and see that it actually looks like a calculator. The buttons are so lifelike, your first inclination is to reach out and press them with your fingers (in fact, if you had a touch-screen, you could). Without the benefit of a touch-screen, you have to use the next best thing, a mouse.

"A Windows program is also different from a DOS program," I said, "in that it can accept input and responses from a user in lots of ways that a DOS program really can't."

"As an illustration," I said, "I want you to consider exactly what happens when you use your mouse to move the pointer over the number 6 on the calculator, and then click the left mouse button. In fact, several things happen:"

- **First**, the mouse pointer moves in response to the mouse being dragged on the mouse pad.

- **Second**, after the mouse pointer has been placed over the number 6, when the user presses and **holds** the left mouse button, the appearance of the button changes. It appears to have been pressed. I asked them to click on the number 6:

"Notice how the button for the number 6 now looks as if it's being pressed down," I said. "This is the default behavior of the button."

- **Third**, after the user releases the left mouse button, the button reverts to its previous appearance. It no longer appears to be pressed. At the same time the number 6 appears in the box at the top of the window:

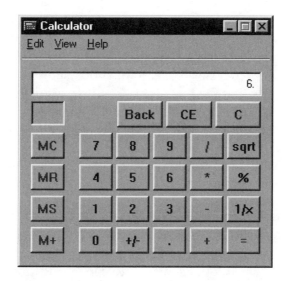

"Will we have to program this kind of behavior into the command buttons we use in the China Shop Project?" Lou asked.

"We won't have to program the button to change its look and feel," I said, "as it's built into the button already. That's one of the things that makes programming in Visual Basic so easy!"

"What's going on behind the scenes here?" Linda asked. "What makes the button change in response to the mouse click?"

"That's a great question," I replied. "Windows is constantly on the alert for **events** taking place in the Windows environment, and has been programmed to react in a pre-determined manner to these events."

"An event?" asked Ward. "I don't exactly know what you mean by that, can you give an example?"

"For instance," I continued, "when the user drags the mouse on their mouse pad, this movement generates a MouseMove event that Windows detects and reacts to. Likewise, when the user presses the left mouse button, that action generates a MouseDown event that Windows detects.

"Most important, Windows has been programmed so that it can detect where on the desktop the mouse has been clicked, in this case over a command button displaying the number 6. It takes this as a cue to change the display of the number to 6 to make it appear as if it's been pressed down. Finally, when the user releases the mouse button, a MouseUp event is generated. Windows detects that the button has been released and that this action took place over the command button displaying the number 6. Windows responds by changing the display of the number 6 back to its original appearance."

"We'll be able to take advantage of these same events," I said, "and pre-determined behavior, when we write the China Shop Project."

I continued by saying that an important feature of Windows is its ability to run more than one program simultaneously. "For instance," I said "while we are running the Calculator, we can also be creating or editing a document in Microsoft Word. Another important feature of Windows is its ability to copy and paste data between applications. For instance, we can use the Calculator to perform a calculation, select Edit-Copy from the Calculator's menu, copy the number in the Calculator's text box into something called the Windows clipboard, then switch to Microsoft Word and select Paste from its menu to copy the result into the document."

A More In-Depth Look at Windows

"Are we going to go behind the scenes of Windows, like we did with DOS?" Dave asked. I asked the rest of the class what they thought and just about everyone agreed we should.

"Ok then, but before we go any further," I said, "I'm afraid we'll have to return back to our discussion of memory because Windows uses something called **Virtual Memory** and I don't want you to become confused."

Virtual Memory

I reminded them that, while they are running, RAM is used to temporarily store the active programs and any data the user is working on. You might think, that for a computer with 32MB of RAM, running out of memory would be next to impossible, but unfortunately, that isn't so. Since Windows allows you to run many programs at the same time, it's actually pretty easy to use it all up.

"Since you can't run a program without first loading it into RAM," I said, "running out of RAM means that you just can't run another program. Windows gets around this problem by using **Virtual Memory**."

I continued by explaining that 'using Virtual Memory' means removing a portion of a running program from RAM, and placing the program, and perhaps some of its data, onto the computer's hard disk drive in something called a **Swap File**. This action frees up some RAM, into which a new program can be loaded. This process, known as swapping or paging, may be repeated every few milliseconds, so enabling the computer to run many more programs than the RAM alone could cope with.

Entire programs are not swapped, just portions of programs or data.

I displayed this illustration of Virtual Memory on the classroom projector:

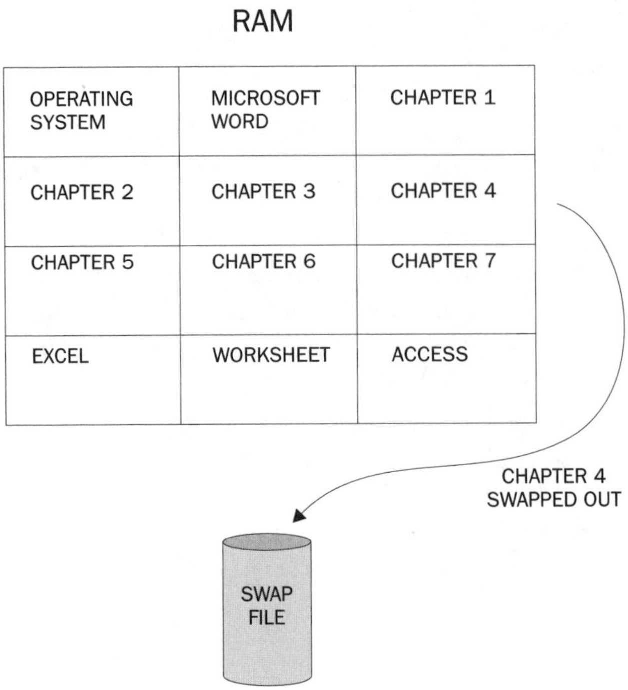

RAM

OPERATING SYSTEM	MICROSOFT WORD	CHAPTER 1
CHAPTER 2	CHAPTER 3	CHAPTER 4
CHAPTER 5	CHAPTER 6	CHAPTER 7
EXCEL	WORKSHEET	ACCESS

CHAPTER 4
SWAPPED OUT

SWAP
FILE

"The big problem with virtual memory is that because you have to use the hard disk drive you are effectively reducing the performance of any paged applications down to that of the storage," I explained.

"Thus the main improvements that Windows makes over DOS are:"

Windows replaced the Character-Based Interface with a Graphical User Interface. The GUI effectively eliminated the user's need to interact with a DOS prompt ever again. Programs are represented by symbols called icons. The user clicks on the icon with the mouse. The program represented by the icon is then run.

The memory constraints of DOS do not effect Windows. Windows uses all the PC's RAM. Not only that, but Windows can simulate more memory than the computer actually contains through the use of Virtual Memory.

<u>**Windows uses Virtual Memory**</u>. Virtual Memory comes in very handy when the user is running their 'umpteenth' simultaneous application, and there's not enough memory to load one more into RAM.

<u>**Windows overcomes the DOS limitation of Single-Tasking**</u>. Windows is multitasking. That means it can run more than one Application Program simultaneously.

Multitasking

"Multitasking," Ward said. "I don't remember discussing that."

"We haven't really," I said. "Although we did discuss that DOS is single-tasking and therefore capable of running only one program at one time. Remember, I said that if we were running WordPerfect for DOS, and needed to run Lotus 1-2-3, we had to first exit WordPerfect since we can't run them simultaneously."

I pointed out that Windows is a multitasking operating system, but the type of multitasking varies with the version of Windows that you are running. Multitasking in Windows 3.1 is vastly different from multitasking in Windows 95 or Windows NT. The differences are significant enough to spend a few moments discussing.

"With a single microprocessor," I said, "it's not really possible for the PC to do anything simultaneously. For instance, when the microprocessor is asked to add a column of 10 numbers, it performs the addition step by step. When the Calculator is running alongside Microsoft Word, multitasking makes it appear as if programs are being executed simultaneously, because computers are so fast these days. The programs will appear to be running uninterrupted, even though the PC is only giving each program a small percentage of its time."

"There are two types of multitasking," I explained, "namely **Pre-emptive Multitasking** and **Non-preemptive Multitasking**."

Non-Preemptive Multitasking

"With non-preemptive multitasking," I said, "it's up to the application to implement the multitasking. In other words, the OS is not in charge." I said that programs running under a non-preemptive multitasking operating system must be specially written to co-operate together, yielding control of the microprocessor every so often. Because the OS can't physically wrestle control away from an application, one program can hog the processor and so the computer can appear to 'lock-up'. "We'll see later that there is a Visual Basic function called DoEvents, which does exactly that, it allows the program to do events while something else is happening" I said.

Worse yet is the case where the unyielding app manages to 'freeze' itself. Since the running program never relinquishes control to the microprocessor, the entire system remains frozen, and the user's only choice is to reboot the PC (or shut down the offending program, using the *CTRL - ALT - DELETE* key combination).

Pre-emptive Multitasking

"With pre-emptive multitasking," I said, "the OS decides when an application no longer has control of the microprocessor and simply takes it away. The program itself has no control over when it gains control of the microprocessor."

"In Visual Basic," I said, "this means that if you forget to code a DoEvents function, the OS will still find a way for other program to get their fair share of the microprocessor's time."

Running Programs in Windows

I told the class that running programs in Windows is vastly different from running them in DOS. The main similarity is in the boot process whereby Windows is loaded into the RAM and the GUI is launched.

"Knowing how a program runs in the Windows environment," I said, "can have an impact on how you code your Visual Basic programs in the future. For that reason, we need to take a close look at how programs run in the Windows environment. Let's divide the process into two parts."

- preparing the Windows program to run
- running the Windows program

Preparing the Windows Program to Run

"Before we can discuss running a Windows program," I said, "I need to introduce you to some new terms. In the world of DOS, programs execute as... well, as programs. In the Windows world, programs are sub-divided into **processes** and **threads**."

> *A process is really nothing more than a program.*
> *A thread is a piece of a Windows program.*

I continued by saying that when a user double-clicks on an icon representing a Windows program, five distinct steps occur:

1. Windows creates a new process and an initial thread for the program

2. The Application Program code is loaded into RAM, just as it is in a DOS program

3. If the application uses any Dynamic Link Libraries, they are also loaded into RAM

4. Space for items such as data and stacks is allocated in RAM

5. The Application Program begins to execute

"Let's discuss each of these in detail," I said.

1. Windows Creates a New Process and an Initial Thread for the Program

In multitasking environments, you frequently see the term 'process' in place of the term 'program'. Under Windows 95 or NT, applications can ask the microprocessor to do work in threads. Theoretically, this can make the entire process run faster.

"That almost sounds like multitasking," Dave said. "That's true," I replied. "Except that this time, it's occurring in the *same* application. However, there is a kicker."

"For instance," I continued, "a program might need three tasks performed in order to accomplish a function, such as updating an inventory record. Task A might take 16 milliseconds. Task B might take 484 milliseconds to complete and Task C 3 seconds. If we ran the tasks on the same process (with one thread), it would take three and a half seconds to accomplish the job."

Then I continued, "However, if we multithreaded the job, allocating one thread to each task, the job would take closer to 4 seconds to complete."

"But that's longer than a single thread. I thought multithreading was supposed to speed things up?" Dave pointed out.

"Good spot, Dave. Unfortunately, multithreading isn't as easy to master as it could be. The extra time is generated directly by the use of the additional threads. You see, when the OS decides that one thread has had enough time to execute, it frees up the processor registers by saving the current contents to RAM and loads in the next thread's data. And that takes some time, and with long threads, that means that the process as a whole takes longer."

"So, why bother with threads at all?" asked Ward.

"Well, there are two occasions when threads can speed up the time required to perform a job. The first is when you have multiple processors. The number of threads allocated to a processor is reduced and so each thread is given more time to execute and so is accomplished quicker. However, most of the time you will be working on a single processor machine, so we really can only rely on the second occasion which is what I call 'down-time'."

I continued, "Down-time is the collection of occasions when the user is (or rather isn't) interacting with the computer. Suppose we have those same three tasks to perform, and this time the long 3 seconds task is user dependent, or in other words, it should be three seconds, but could take longer if the user needs typing practice. Now, instead of the job requiring half a second plus the long task time, the job only takes the long task time as the threads allow the other tasks to complete while the user is messing around. The user also doesn't notice any delay because the swapping between threads is so quick. The moral of the story is that background calculations should always be given their own threads, or at least separate threads to the user interface control tasks."

2. The Application Program Code is Loaded into RAM, just as it is in a DOS Program

"The difference between a Windows and a DOS application is that each process is assigned its own address space in RAM, including its own stack which, if you recall, is a data structure contained in RAM. Stacks are used by the operating system and your applications to store program instructions and other data, so that they can be easily accessed when needed."

"By assigning each process its own address space and stack, Windows isolates each process. This is the reason why (theoretically) one renegade, out-of-control process shouldn't be able to cause the entire PC to crash."

3. If the Application uses any Dynamic Link Libraries, they are also Loaded into RAM

"Dynamic Link Libraries?" Mary said. "I'm checking my notes, but I don't think we've seen those today."

"That's right," I said. "We haven't - yet." I continued by saying that in order to fully explain a **Dynamic Link Library (DLL)**, I needed to go back and explain **Static Link Libraries**. Both types of libraries are special files used to store pre-written and pre-tested program instructions, or **code**. This code has been written so it can be incorporated in someone else's program."

I continued by explaining that the major difference between the two types of library is when they are actually loaded into memory. "Static link libraries are physically combined into each program that uses the instructions they contain," I remarked. "This means that the resulting executable is the size of your code, plus the entire static link library."

"Does that mean," Steve asked, "that if the size of your program is 5 KB and the library code is 3 KB, that the final size of your executable is 8 KB?"

"Yes, but that's not all!" I exclaimed. "If you write two separate programs, the static link library is used twice, but instead of simply being referenced (as you would expect the term 'library' to mean), the whole thing is copied and combined with each separate application."

"So if you have a 5KB program, a 6KB program and a 10KB library, you would generate 31KB of executable in total?" Steve continued.

"That's exactly right, Steve," I said. "A very inefficient process, don't you think?"

"And unfortunately, there is more bad news!" I continued. "Because a copy of the library is made whenever you build an executable out of your program, if you find a mistake in the library and fix it, that's just the beginning of your problems! All of the programs that use that library will be affected and they will all need to be re-built before they will work correctly!"

"Wow, that seems like a lot of hard work," said Rose. "And you have to put up with that inefficient use of hard disk space! Is this where Dynamic Link Libraries come in?" added Jack.

"Yes," I replied, "with Windows and the introduction of DLLs, programmers now had an alternative that retained the benefits of static libraries but cut out most of the drawbacks. Now, programmers didn't have to physically include the library in their code, they just referenced the instructions contained in them."

"I don't understand how this referencing works," said Barbara, "How does the executable get hold of the library's instructions when it needs them?"

"Well, this is the really innovative part and why we needed a new operating system to be invented before the idea of DLLs would work," I said. "You see, when a DLL is created, it is registered with Windows. This means that Windows knows where it is on your hard drive, what information it contains and what name a calling program will use to reference it."

"So when a program is being run in Windows and it gets to a reference to some code held in a DLL, Windows knows exactly what to do. It goes off to the appropriate part of the hard drive, loads up the DLL, looks up the required set of instructions and runs them." I continued.

"That is really clever! And doesn't that mean that you only ever need one copy of the DLL? I mean, once Windows knows where it is, any number of programs can use it, if they know its name, right?" said Steve.

"You're really getting the hang of this, Steve! That's perfectly correct, but there is some more good news!" I replied. "Because Windows is essentially controlling the existence of the DLL in RAM, it knows that once the library has been loaded, the hard disk step can be skipped if another application wants the same DLL. And in fact, if all the applications using the DLL are closed down, Windows will automatically unload the DLL from RAM to save space!"

"Now that is a terrific feature, but what about the bad code problem? Did DLLs solve that as well?" asked Linda.

"Yes they did, Linda!" I said. "If you think about what is happening with a DLL, you will see why! Suppose that you do indeed find a problem with a DLL, fix it and re-construct the library. If you keep the library's appearance (by which I mean its name, location and so on) the same, Windows will simply use the new code whenever a application calls it. You don't have to re-build any of your programs; just use a DLL for any code that might need to change in the first place, and your future maintenance problems will be drastically minimized.

4. Space for Items such as Data and Stacks is Allocated in RAM

In Windows, each process has its own protected area in RAM and its own copy of a stack. When one application 'hangs' it doesn't hang the entire system.

5. The Application Program Begins to Execute

As was the case in the DOS world, the program begins to execute.

"There's certainly a lot more work to get to that stage though," Ward said.

Running the Windows Program

"You're right about that," I said. "Now let's see how running a Windows program is different from running a DOS program."

"Now that the Windows program and everything it requires has been loaded into RAM," I said, "execution can begin. However, you'll see in a moment that running a Windows program is more complicated than executing a DOS program. The reason for that are the windows. I don't mean the OS in this case, but the window objects that occupy the user's desktop."

I asked the students to look at their Windows 95 desktop, as I displayed mine on the classroom projector:

"Virtually everything that you see in Windows is a window," I said. "Let's take a quick look at my desktop:"

- the desktop itself is a window (1 window)
- each icon on the desktop is a window (3 windows)
- the caption underneath each icon is a window (3 windows)
- the Start bar is a window (1 window)
- each button on the Start bar is a window (2 windows)
- each one of the Microsoft Office icons is a window (9 windows)

"By my count, there are 19 windows on my desktop," I said. "Most beginners don't realize that just about everything you see in the Windows environment is a window, and that Windows must maintain visibility of these windows like an air-traffic controller keeps track of planes in the sky. Let's take a look at a Windows application, Microsoft Word:"

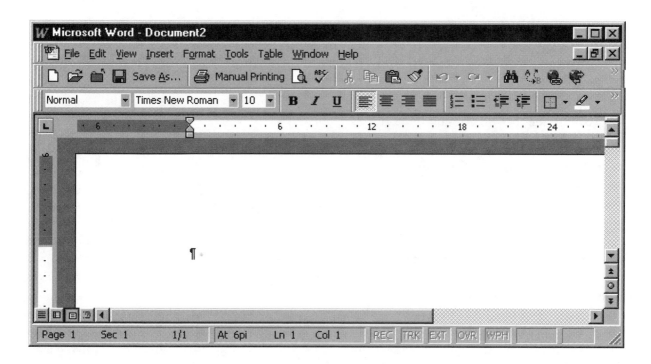

I explained that Microsoft Word is also made up of many windows, but most people don't really think of it in that way. The document window is an obvious window, but what about the menu bar at the top of Word? Or the buttons on the toolbar just beneath that? Or the scroll bars running vertically down the side and horizontally across the bottom? These are all windows.

In Windows, each window has characteristics and behaviors associated with it. For instance, a window has a height and width, it is displayed in a maximized, normal, or minimized state, and it has a location on the screen.

Plus, there are different types of windows. There are windows that we all recognize as windows, and then there are the windows that appear as buttons, icons, lists, scroll bars and even menus. Each of these different types of windows has different behaviors associated with it. For instance, if you click on a menu, the behavior is different to clicking on a scroll bar.

"That all sounds terribly chaotic," Linda said. "How can Windows keep track of all of these windows, and better yet, know what to do with them?"

I told Linda that the answer is through the use of **Windows Handles**, **messages**, and a whole bunch of default behavior that is already built in for you.

"Don't worry," I said. "I'll explain exactly what these items mean and show you how they are used by Windows to make sense out of chaos, just like an air-traffic controller uses radar to co-ordinate the movement and behavior of planes."

The Windows Handle

A Windows handle uniquely identifies each window in the Windows environment. When a window is loaded, the OS assigns it a Windows handle, and each of these numbers is stored in a Windows handle table. This table keeps track of the handle number as well as any other properties that describe the window, such as its height, width, and location on the desktop for later reference.

Without a Windows handle to track each of all the individual windows on the desktop, the OS would become hopelessly confused. Suppose the user moved a window? How would the OS know where the window was located? The very process of moving the window updates the appropriate property of that window in the Windows handle table.

Windows Messages

"I want to compare the Windows environment," I said, "to someone working in front of a very fast conveyor belt that contains boxes and packages bound for delivery all over the world. The person's job is to identify destinations for these packages by markings on them, as the boxes fly by them on the conveyor belt. As soon as the person identifies the destination, they push a button that re-routes the packages to other conveyor belts in the system."

"Now pretend that the person working in front of the conveyor belt is actually the Windows OS. The conveyor belt is the **Windows Message Queue**, and the packages moving along the conveyor belt contain **Windows Messages**, and are marked with a **Windows Handle** number."

"You're not talking about email messages, are you?" Ward asked. "No," I said. "I'm talking about internal Windows messages that are generated when a user clicks on the button of the mouse, or types an entry into a text box, or when a window is resized."

I explained that Windows messages are constantly flowing from apps to Windows, and vice versa. "This process may sound chaotic," I said, "but with the Windows handle, the OS is easily able to determine where the message came from, and where it should go."

"Even more amazing," I continued, "is the fact that in the space of a few seconds, a user can generate hundreds of different events, all of which generate Windows messages. When these messages are generated, they are placed in the Windows Message Queue to await processing. The Message Queue is just a repository where all pending messages, along with their Windows handle numbers, are stored. However, if the system is running well, the messages don't have long to wait before they are processed."

I displayed the following graphic on the classroom projector:

WINDOWS MESSAGE
QUEUE

WINDOWS HANDLER	EVENT
1	CLICK
2	MOUSEDOWN
1	DOUBLE CLICK
2	MOUSEUP
2	GOTFOCUS
2	LOSTFOCUS
1	MOUSEMOVE
1	LOAD

"Windows is constantly checking the Message Queue for pending messages," I said. "In fact, when we discuss the Visual Basic `DoEvents` function, we'll see that Microsoft recommends that we code this function into our program to allow Windows to process pending events on the Windows Message Queue."

"How does Windows know what to do when it reads the Windows message?" Barbara asked.

I explained that since the message contains the Windows handle, Windows knows from which window the message came from. Cross-referencing the Windows handle to the Windows handle table, Windows also knows the type of window the message originated from. Depending upon the type of window, different messages generate different behavior. This behavior is built-in behavior, sometimes known as default behavior. For instance, when you click on an option button, the default behavior for that type of window is different than if you click on a check box.

"Programmers can enhance the default behavior of these windows," I said, "thereby providing additional functionality to their programs."

"I'm confused," Ward said. "Can you give me an example of how Windows uses messages and handles?"

"Sure," I said, "how about this: You have both Word and Excel open on your desktop. You type the number 22. How does Windows know whether to enter the number into Excel, or place it in your Word Document? It all comes down to the Windows handle that accompanies the request to display the number. And that is dependent on something called the focus."

The Focus

I knew it had been an intensive class, and my students were getting a little restless.

"The final subject I wanted to discuss today," I said, "is **the focus**. In Windows, only one window can have the focus at any given time. You cannot have two windows with the focus at the same time."

> *Just because only one object in Windows can have the focus at any one time does not prevent multitasking from happening behind the scenes.*

"Let's take a look at the Excel - Word example I used a minute ago," I said. "Here we have two apps but only one keyboard. How does Windows know which window is to receive the keystrokes you type at the keyboard? Where do the keystrokes go? Do they go to the Excel spreadsheet or to the Word document? The answer is that the keystrokes go to the window that has the focus, the **Active Window**."

"How can you determine the Active Window?" Rhonda asked.

"The title bar of the Active Window will have a different color from the title bars of your other windows," I said. "The exact color depends upon the settings in your Control Panel."

I waited for additional questions, but there were none. I could see the class was getting a little tired after all the material we'd covered, but I wanted to bring together everything we'd learned in this lesson to arrive at a final definition of what a computer program really is.

What is a Computer Program?

I looked around the class: pencils were tapping, heads were down; it had been a tough morning. I took a deep breath, chose my moment carefully, and threw out a simple question: "So what is a computer program?"

Nobody said anything. I could see many furrowed brows.

"Do you mean a DOS program or a Windows program?" asked Steve. "Any type of computer program!" I said.

"How about," Ward said uncertainly, "computer programs are how we make computers do what we want them to do."

"That's a good start, Ward," I said, "but how exactly does a computer perform the tasks we want?"

"By manipulating the data stored inside the computer," Dave offered. I was impressed. The class had obviously understood that everything we see computers do involves the processing of huge amounts of data held inside the computer itself.

"But you haven't told us how we actually write computer programs yet," Linda pointed out.

"I've been waiting for someone to mention that all through the lesson," I said. "The rest of the course is going to explain how to write computer programs in detail, but all you need to know for now is that computer programs are made up of a series of commands and operations that manipulate data. We write specific commands, which we'll learn all about in the coming weeks, to manipulate that data exactly how we want. Is that clear to everyone?"

"So you mean we write out specific commands in a program to tell the computer what to do?" asked Valerie, who had been sitting quietly.

"That's basically it!" I said.

I knew my class wanted to know more about those commands to manipulate data, and how those commands would make up real computer programs, but I cautioned them all to take one step at a time. I explained that this was plenty for them to think about, and that we would be seeing lots of computer programs and how they worked in the lessons to come.

I dismissed class, and told my students that next week, we would start up Visual Basic, and begin to get comfortable with it.

Summary

The aim of this chapter was to help you to understand computers at a fundamental level, to make it easier for you to see how the programs you write fit into the Windows environment. We saw that a computer program is a set of instructions used to control something, or cause something to happen.

During the running of a program, information known as **data** is used or stored. Data, at its lowest level, consists of a series of **bits**, each of which is either on or off. A group of eight bits is called a **byte**. Data exists both in **memory** and **storage**, and these work in different ways. Random Access Memory (RAM) is temporary, and very fast. Storage, on the other hand, is semi-permanent, but has longer access times. That's why programs are loaded into RAM to be run, which speeds up their operation. Both memory and storage have their capacity measured in bytes.

Operating systems include DOS and Windows, and are used to control how the computer interacts with hardware, input devices, output devices, programs, etc.

Windows has a **graphical user interface (GUI)**, which is a user-friendly interface in which the user clicks on buttons, icons, and menus instead of typing commands at a command line. It is also capable of **multitasking**, which is the ability to run more than one program at the same time.

The use of DLL (**Dynamic Link Library**) files reduces the size of programs by keeping procedures that are used by more than one program in separate files. It also means that the procedure can be updated once, without the need to update each program.

Quiz

1. Approximately how many bytes are in a kilobyte?

2. What does the term **volatile** mean when we speak of RAM?

3. How many bits are in a byte?

4. How many possible values can a bit have?

5. Place these terms in order from least to greatest: Megabyte, Kilobyte, Terabyte, Gigabyte.

6. What's the difference between operating systems and application programs?

7. True or False: Visual Basic can be used to create both operating systems and application programs.

8. What does RAM stand for?

9. True or False: Computers are capable of running only one operating system.

10. What does DOS stand for?

11. Where do application programs need to be loaded before they can be run?

12. What are three characteristics of DOS that Windows improved upon?

13. What did Windows replace DOS's character-based interface with?

14. There are two kinds of multi-tasking. Can you name both?

15. True or False: Dynamic Link Libraries (or DLLs) are a characteristic of DOS programs.

16. Each window in the Windows environment is uniquely identified by a Windows _____.

Extra Credit – How many of each animal did Moses take aboard the Ark with him?

Chapter 3
Getting Comfortable with Visual Basic

In this chapter, we follow my computer class as they take their first look at the Visual Basic Integrated Development Environment, or IDE for short. The purpose of the chapter is to give you an overview of the Visual Basic environment.

It is impossible, really, to give you anything more than a 'comfort level' feeling about the IDE. I know that the material in this chapter is a tremendous amount for you to process, but there's no need to memorize it. I just want to introduce you to it. If you ever become confused about any aspect of the IDE, come back to this chapter and refresh your memory. Depending on the version you are using some of the screen shots might differ slightly from yours, but most should match exactly what is displayed on your machine.

The great news about the chapter is that by its end, we'll be ready to start developing the China Shop Project!

The Visual Basic Environment

I began this class by apologizing to my students for making them wait until that point before formally beginning our discussion of Visual Basic. I reminded them that, first and foremost, our class concentrated on good fundamental programming techniques. I told them that a thorough understanding of the Systems Development Life Cycle and what goes on 'behind the scenes' in a computer would provide benefits further down the road, and make them better program writers.

"We'll be examining the Visual Basic **Integrated Development Environment** or **IDE** for short," I said. "It's within this environment that we'll begin to develop the China Shop Project in next week's class. I have often found that the sheer volume of menu items and toolbar buttons in the IDE may be a bit overwhelming for beginners.

Don't worry if you can't remember what all the items do and where they are located. Learning to use the IDE is a gradual process that takes time. I promise you that by the time you finish this course, you'll be feeling much more confident. The IDE is not difficult, or at least, no more so than finding your way around an amusement park for the first time."

Preparing the Way for Programming

"Before we charge into the Visual Basic IDE, we have one last preparation to complete. Beginner programmers sometimes lose their programs because they don't know where they saved them. I want to ensure that once you save your projects, you know where they have been saved and can always find them." I began.

"In order to do that, I'd like you to create the same directory structure on your computer that I have on mine. That way, we will both be 'singing from the same song-sheet'. If the term 'directory' or 'folder' is foreign to you, you probably need to read through your Windows documentation for a refresher."

"I save all of my Visual Basic projects in a directory named **VBFiles**. Underneath this directory, I create subdirectories each appropriately named for the project that I'm working on. Let's create a directory structure for the China Shop Project now."

Exercise

Using Explorer to Make a Home for Our Project

1. Find the Windows Start button and right-click on it. You should see a pop-up menu appear. One of the choices will be the Explore.

2. Select this option and the Explorer window should appear. It should look similar to this screen shot, although since this is a screen shot of my PC, what you are seeing will not be identical. Notice that the Explorer window itself has two windows. The window on the left side is the **directory tree** window, which displays all the directories on your hard drive. The window on the right side is the **files** window, which shows you subdirectories and files contained within the selected directory in the directory tree window:

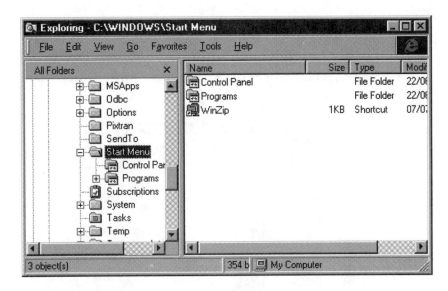

3. Use your mouse to scroll upwards in the directory tree window so that you can see the C: drive of your computer. Your C: drive is your computer's hard drive:

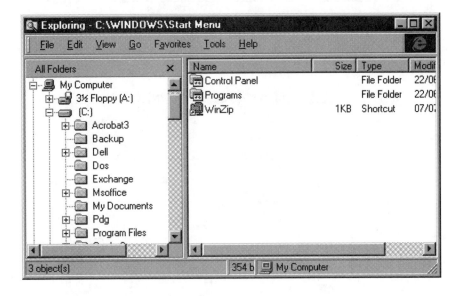

4.   Select the C: drive in the directory tree window by clicking the mouse on it. The files window's content should change to reflect what is contained in the root of your hard drive.

5.   Select File-New-Folder from the menu of the Explorer window. As you can see from the screen shot below, Explorer will create a new folder called New Folder in the right-hand, file window:

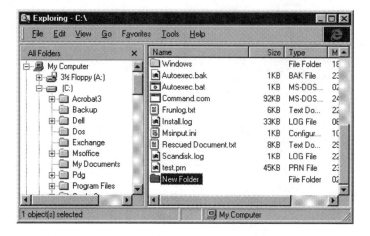

6.   We don't want to name our folder New Folder. Instead we want to name it VBFiles. To give the new folder this name, type the word VBFiles then press the *Enter* key. You should now see a new folder called VBFiles:

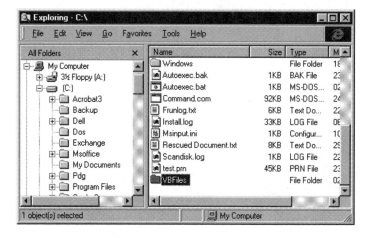

When you press the *Enter* key, you'll see that VBFiles has taken its place in the directory tree of your hard disk drive, while the files window is empty. Remember that a new folder is empty and we haven't saved anything in it yet. We have just a little bit more to do now:

7.   Now we want to create a subdirectory of VBFiles. As I mentioned, I create a subdirectory for each project that I work on in Visual Basic. Since we'll be working on the China Shop Project throughout the rest of the course, let's create a subdirectory called China. We'll need to repeat steps 4, 5 and 6, but with a slight variation. Instead of selecting the C drive as we did in step 4, this time select VBFiles in the directory tree window and then select File-New-Folder from the menu of the Explorer window. As Explorer did the last time, it will create a new folder called New Folder in the right-hand window:

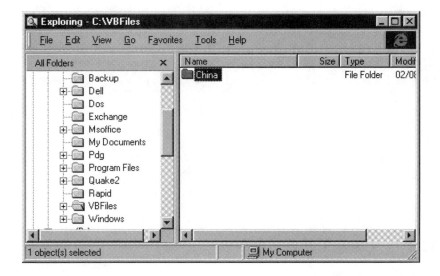

8.   As before, it doesn't make any sense to create a directory called New Folder. We want to name it China instead. As we did in step 6, change the name New Folder by typing over it, this time with the word China. Now press the *Enter* key. You should now see a new folder called China, as a subdirectory of VBFiles.

9. Repeat these steps to create another directory called Practice. It is in this directory that we'll be saving all of our aside examples, just in case we need them later:

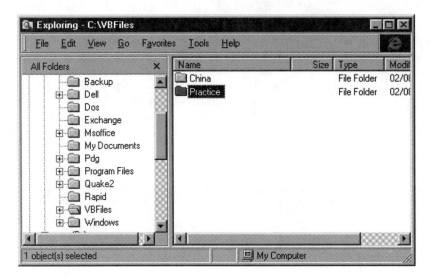

Discussion

That's it! You now have a directory created for your China Shop Project. Make sure that as you build your version of the China Shop Project, that you save all of your work to this directory.

Let's Start Up Visual Basic!

"Visual Basic isn't the only Windows development tool on the market," I said, "but in my opinion, it's the easiest for beginners to use. To start it up, you will find a shortcut on your Start Menu. Try Start–Programs–Microsoft Visual Basic 6.0–Visual Basic 6.0."

Don't worry if your screen doesn't exactly match the screen shots that you see throughout this workbook. As you use Visual Basic more and more, it will "remember" changes you make to the IDE. The more you work in the IDE, the less likely it is that your screen will match mine exactly.

Refer to the Introduction for instructions on how to install the Visual Basic Working Model from the attached CD.

The following window was displayed, indicating that Visual Basic is alive:

"When you first start Visual Basic," I said, "this will most likely be the first screen that you will see. This screen, or dialog as it is called, is part of the Visual Basic IDE. The IDE is where you will write your programs, and where together, we will write the China Shop Project."

The Visual Basic Project

"Take a good look at this initial dialog," I said. "Notice in the lower left hand corner, there is a check box that gives you the option to avoid this dialog in the future. If you select that check box then Visual Basic will skip right by this screen when it starts up. However, if you want, you can have Visual Basic display this dialog again. I'll show you how to do that a little later."

"I call this the **Project** Dialog, because everything on it pertains to a Visual Basic project."

"What's a project?" Steve asked.

"A project is really just a program, that is made up of component pieces," I said. "The China Shop Project that we will create in the coming weeks will be made up of a single form, which makes it pretty simple in Visual Basic terms."

"You've mentioned the term 'form' before, but what exactly do you mean?" asked Dave.

"A form is simply the blank page onto which we place the program's interface. When the program runs, the form becomes the window that you see," I explained.

I pointed out that the Project Dialog contains three tabs labeled New, Existing and Recent. When the Project Dialog is displayed, the New tab is selected, and it shows all the different types of new projects that you can create in Visual Basic.

"However, for the duration of this course, we'll be working exclusively with the Standard EXE project which is the kind of project the China Shop application will be." I continued by saying that when we first start up Visual Basic, it wants to know if we'll be working with a New project or with an Existing project. We indicate our choice by selecting one of these tabs.

"That's pretty similar to other Windows programs," Linda said. "Either create something new, or use an existing one." "That's right," I agreed. "Selecting the New tab indicates that we want to create a new project. Additionally, we must also designate the type of project."

"You said that all of our projects would be Standard EXE Projects, is that right?" Barbara asked. "Exactly," I said. "Selecting the Existing tab indicates that we will be working with an existing project. Now the Recent tab is the one I really love. Selecting it displays a list of recently accessed projects. I use this one all the time."

At this point, I asked everyone to select the New tab by clicking on it. I then asked them to click on the Standard EXE icon, and then to click on the Open Button. I did the same on my PC, and the following screen was displayed on the classroom projector:

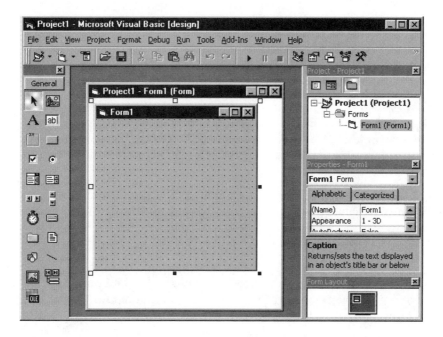

The IDE

"Finally, here we are right in the middle of the IDE!" I exclaimed. "I remember the first time that I saw the IDE, many versions of Visual Basic ago. It can look confusing with so many new menus to get familiar with, but believe me, by the end of our course, you'll feel pretty comfortable navigating through the IDE."

I directed everyone's attention to the window roughly in the middle of the IDE labeled Form1.

"For a new Standard EXE project," I said, "Visual Basic automatically creates a form for you right in the middle of the IDE. Notice that it is labeled Form1, and it is sitting inside of a window labeled Project1."

I explained that we would place the controls that we had discussed during the design phase of the SDLC upon Form1.

"You mean we'll place check boxes and option buttons on that tiny thing?" Joe asked. "That's right Joe," I said. "You'll see a little later that we can enlarge the size of the form within the IDE."

I looked for signs of confusion in their faces but everyone seemed to be hanging in there. "To the left of the form," I said, "is the Visual Basic Tool Box. The icons that you see inside represent the controls that we discussed during the design phase of the SDLC. Labels, check boxes, and option buttons to name a few."

Again, I paused to give them a chance to take this in. "To the right of the form," I said, "are three windows, the Project, Properties and Form Layout Windows. We'll discuss all of these later today."

I continued by saying that the IDE, although unfamiliar to them, is made up of windows and they should be pretty familiar with those. "For instance," I said, "at the top of the IDE is a Title Bar. Right now, its caption reads Project1 Microsoft Visual Basic [design]. This tells us that we're working on a project called Project1, which is the default name assigned to the first new project you create, and that we're in design mode."

The Modes of Visual Basic

"I should explain at his point that there are two distinct modes we'll be using during our programming of Visual Basic," I said. "The first, as I have just mentioned, is Design Mode and the other is Run Mode. Design Mode (or Design Time) is when you are designing the visual interface and writing the code for it while the program is not running. Run Mode (or Run Time) is when you start the program running and the code you have typed in is activated. If you are unsure which mode you are in, the title bar displays either [run] or [design] depending on the mode."

"Is there a way to change the project name?" Rhonda asked. "Project1 isn't very meaningful."

"Yes there is," I said, "and we will do that later in the course."

I continued by directing everyone's attention to the upper left-hand corner of the Title Bar. "Do you see the Control Menu Icon?" I asked, "Clicking on it allows you to move, resize, minimize, maximize and close Visual Basic." I also pointed out that in the upper right hand corner of the IDE are found the Minimize, Maximize/Restore, and Close buttons.

The Visual Basic Menu

Everyone seemed to be pretty comfortable with the notion that the IDE was nothing more than a typical Windows window. I suggested that we now turn our attention to the Menu Bar:

"The Visual Basic menu," I said, "contains the File, Edit, Window, and Help menu options, which appear in virtually all Windows applications, plus some others which are unique to Visual Basic." Some of these menu items such as Query and Diagram we will not discuss. Depending on the version of Visual Basic used, they may not be available.

The File Menu

Before I had a chance to begin discussing the File menu, Rose, jumping ahead of me, remarked that the File menu looked very familiar to her. I agreed with her but also noted that, despite its similarity to the File menus of other Windows programs, there were several submenus that would be foreign to all of us.

"For instance," I said, "since Visual Basic manages everything by project, there are several commands pertaining to projects. In fact, the first six menu items, New Project, Open Project, Add Project, Remove Project, Save Project, and Save Project As..., are all related to project management:"

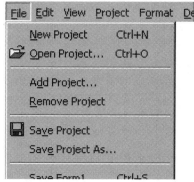

"We'll have an opportunity to work with some of these later in the course," I promised, "and I'll discuss them quickly today."

"The next two items in the File menu I want to discuss are related to printing," I said. "Print and Print Setup."

"What gets printed?" Steve asked. "Good question," I said. "Quite a bit actually. In this case a picture is worth a thousand words. Let's take a closer look at the Print Menu."

The Print Menu

I asked everyone to click on Print from the File menu. I did so and the following dialog was displayed:

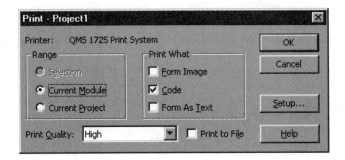

"This looks similar to other Print dialogs," I said, "but there are several Visual Basic unique selections you can make. Take a look at the Print What frame." Several students had trouble locating it, and I assisted them by saying, "It's the frame to the left of the Cancel button."

"Now, to answer Steve's question as to what gets printed." I explained that a Visual Basic program is made up of two parts, the **visual** part, which for the China Shop project will be the form and the controls sitting on it, and the **code** part. The code part is the Visual Basic program instructions that we will learn to write during this course.

"In short," I said, "we have the option to print the visual part by selecting Form Image, or the code we have written by selecting Code, or both."

"What does Form As Text mean?" Dave asked. "In Visual Basic," I said, "when you create a form, it is actually defined by 'behind the scenes' code. Selecting Form As Text allows you to print that 'behind the scenes' code."

I asked everyone to look at the option buttons contained in the Range frame. "There are three options for printing a Visual Basic project," I said. "You can print a Selection, the Current Module, or the Current Project. Selection here refers to code that you have selected in the Visual Basic Code window, which is where you write your program code. Although Visual Basic has several types of module, the only one you need concern yourself with for the duration of this course is the form module."

"Is a form module the same as a form?" Ward asked. "Sorry to confuse you. Yes, it is," I said. "Most programmers use the short version and simply call a form module a form."

"So if your project has more than one module," Dave said, "Current Module designates the module you have currently selected in the IDE?"
"That's exactly right," I said. "By selecting Current Module, you can print all of the code in that module."
"And Current Project," Valerie said, "allows you to print all of the code in the entire project?"
"Great!" I said. "That's correct."
"How often will a programmer actually print the code in a project?" Joe asked.
"Some programmers print the code in their projects pretty often," I said, "and others never do. As for me, I generally print the image of the forms, plus all of the code in the project when I've completed it. It makes great documentation, and I usually file it away with the other vitals of my project, such as my Requirements Statement and my contract."

The Edit Menu

Having finished up with the File Menu, I told my students that I bet they would feel pretty comfortable with the Edit Menu, once they had seen it:

"I hesitate to use the word 'standard' when describing a menu," I said, "but I think I'm pretty safe in describing the Visual Basic Edit menu as fairly standard."

After seeing the Edit menu, just about everyone in the class agreed with me. Included on it were the usual Undo and Redo items, along with Cut, Copy, Paste, Delete and Select All. Also included are Find and Find Next.

I asked the class if I needed to discuss these options in detail. Dave said he was familiar with these Edit menu items from his experience with other Windows programs, and everyone else nodded affirmatively. I continued by saying that the final seven Edit items deserved some additional mention, as they are unique to Visual Basic.

"Indent and Outdent both refer to indentation of Visual Basic program code," I said. "As we'll see when we begin to write our own code, indenting your code can make it easier for you and others to read and understand it. Choosing Indent will indent your program code a tab stop. Outdent undoes the indentation of your code by a tab stop."

"How many characters are in a tab stop?" Barbara asked. "The default is set to 4, but you can alter this via the Tools menu," I replied.

The Insert File option is only active when you are writing code in the Visual Basic Code window. Choosing it allows you to insert a file and the code that it contains, into your Code window.

I cautioned my students that the next four menu items, List Properties/Methods, List Constants, Quick Info, and Parameter Information would make much more sense when we discussed properties, constants, and parameters later on in the course. "For now, suffice to say that selecting these commands provides "hints" to you while writing program code."

The final two menu items, Complete Word and Bookmarks, complete the Edit menu. "Complete Word refers to a wonderful feature of Visual Basic wherein it will attempt to anticipate the code you are typing into the Visual Basic Code Window, and actually complete it for you."

"For instance," I said, "a few weeks from now, you'll be writing code to send data to a printer. You'll use the `Printer` method, which is just a Visual Basic command. After you type the letters `Pr` in the Visual Basic Code window, you can click on this command, and Visual Basic will display a list of everything it knows of that begins with those two letters."

"You could also do the same thing by pressing *Ctrl* and *Space* couldn't you?" Rhonda said.

"That's right, Rhonda," I agreed. "That is the shortcut key combination for that command, as you can see from the menu."

I could see some confusion on a few faces. "Just remember," I said, "I'm just trying to give you an overview here. Don't attempt to memorize anything we're talking about this morning. Next week, when we're coding, you will get lots of opportunities to experiment with these commands."

I asked everyone to click on Bookmark to verify that it does indeed contain four submenus. "The bookmark commands can be extremely useful," I said. "Like so many items in the IDE, sometimes you can forget about them. I know I have to remind myself to use them."

"Bookmarks," Linda said, "do they work pretty much the same way a bookmark in Word would work?"

"Yes," I said. "If you are familiar with bookmarks from using other Windows programs, such as Word, then you know how to use these. If you're not then all you really need to know is that inserting a bookmark is just a helpful way to navigate around a large file without having to scroll through everything."

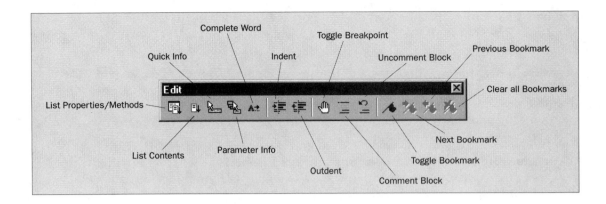

"In order to save you time when you're working, there is a toolbar with icons for many of the commands in this menu," I said. "We'll come to how to display the other toolbars in the next section, but for now, one thing to note is that the Comment Block and Uncomment Block commands have no corresponding menu items."

- **Comment Block**. "Comments" a line of code in the Code Window. This allows you to change code into text that is ignored when the program runs. It is very useful for explaining what a particular bit of code does in English without having to decipher the code.

- **Uncomment Block**. "Uncomments" a line of code in the Code Window.

The View Menu

"With the View menu," I said, "we're definitely starting to move into some very specific Visual Basic material:"

Before I began to talk about this menu, I had to warn everyone that some of these commands were only active when a running Visual Basic program had been paused.

"What do you mean by a paused program?" Blaine asked.

"Good question," I said. "Everything that we've seen so far today in the IDE has been in design mode. Next week, when we begin to develop the China Shop Project, we'll actually run it. One of the first things I show my students is how to pause a program, so that you can see what's going on behind the scenes. When a program is paused it's stopped in midstream whilst it's still running. Anyone else?"

"When you pause a program," Dave asked, "can you re-start it?" "Indeed you can," I said, "and I'll tell you how when we get to the Run menu."

I waited a moment or two to see if anyone else had any questions. The Code command displays the Code window for the currently selected module. "Remember," I said, "for the duration of our course, the only module we'll be accessing in the IDE is a form module, so selecting this menu will display the Code window for the form."

At this point, I heard the distinct sound of several double-clicks in the lab. "Great," I said, "that's the way we learn, by experimenting!"

"How do you get the form back?" Barbara asked. I glanced at her workstation, and she had the Code window open. However, once the Code Window opens the Form appears to disappear:

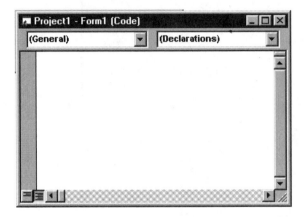

"Don't worry," I said. "Just select Object from the View menu, and the form will be re-displayed."

"The Definition command is dimmed," Linda said. "Do you need to have the Code window open for that to be enabled?"

"That's right, Linda," I said. "If you select text in the Code window, and then select Definition from the View menu, Visual Basic will do its best to display the definition of the selected text, provided it can find it. If it recognizes the text, it will display its definition from the **Object Browser**. If it can't find it, it displays a message notifying you of that fact."

"The Object Browser?" Ward said.

"We're about to get to that," I said. "Let me just quickly tell you that the next menu item, Last Positio<u>n</u>, allows you to move quickly to a previous location in the Code Window. Visual Basic keeps track of the last eight lines that you accessed in the Code Window. Now for the <u>O</u>bject Browser."

Objects and the Object Browser

"First of all," Linda said, "Don't you think you should tell us what an object is before you discuss browsing them?"

"Fair enough," I said. "Every component in Visual Basic is an object, in the same way that I said last week every icon on the desktop is a window. Option buttons, check boxes and labels, all of these are objects that are shipped with Visual Basic. Other software on your PC, such as Microsoft Word, contains objects as well, and when you install this software on your computer, these objects are registered in the Windows Registry."

"In just a bit, we'll see that we can actually include these non-Visual Basic objects in a Visual Basic project. Once these objects are included in our project, we can then use the Object Browser to view their definitions, called **Properties** and **Methods**."

"However," I said, "we won't be including any other objects in the China Shop Project besides the ones shipped with Visual Basic, but we can learn the techniques by using the controls 'out-of-the-box'."

I continued by saying that the next four items, <u>I</u>mmediate Window, Loca<u>l</u>s Window, Wat<u>c</u>h Window, and Call Stac<u>k</u> we would discuss in more detail when we talked about writing code. I decided not to pursue them at this point and everyone agreed that it was probably a good idea.

Organizing the Project

"The next three menu items," I said, "<u>P</u>roject Explorer, Properties <u>W</u>indow, and <u>F</u>orm Layout Window, refer to the three windows we had a quick look at earlier."

Selecting <u>P</u>roject Explorer displays the Project Explorer window, which displays the component pieces of your project. "For the duration of our course," I said, "the only component piece of our project will be just one form. However, if you add an additional form, you'll need to use the Project Explorer to move from one to the other."

The Properties <u>W</u>indow command displays the Properties window for the form or selected control on the form. Each form and control on the form has attributes or characteristics, technically known as properties. "In our next class," I said, "we'll be examining and changing some of the properties of the China Shop form."

"Selecting the <u>F</u>orm Layout Window command displays the Form Layout window, which can be used to change the relative location of the form on the screen," I said

I could see a look of almost universal confusion. "We saw earlier," I continued, "that when we start a new project in Visual Basic, a blank form is displayed within the Project window."

"When we run the program we may want to know where in the screen the program window will appear. The Form Layout window acts as preview of what the screen will look like when you run the program. If you click and drag the outline of the form in the Form Layout window, you can affect the position of the form relative to the screen when your program runs."

Altering the IDE

"Personally," said Jack, "I don't care much for this look and feel. It's hardly what you would call 'what you see is what you get', unlike some other packages."

"Actually," I said, "there is a way to get that 'look and feel'. In fact, it's my preference and it's called a Single Document Interface (SDI). I'm used to it, because that is the look and feel of Visual Basic 4, something I've used for several years."

"Will you show us how to do that?" asked Dave. "Sure," I said. "You can choose it by selecting <u>T</u>ools-<u>O</u>ptions-Advanced from the Main menu, and then selecting <u>S</u>DI Development Environment. If you choose this, you'll need to exit Visual Basic and then re-start it before the changes take place."

"What's the current setting?" Ward asked.

"Multiple Document Interface, or MDI," I replied.

I asked everyone to hold off making any changes to their environment at this point. We still had a lot to cover, and I wanted everyone to be looking at a common interface, at least for today. "You can experiment," I said, "and then choose the environment that is most comfortable for you. Although I should warn you that I'll be using the SDI environment, so if you stick with MDI, your screens may not match mine exactly."

Finishing the View Menu

It was almost time for another break, but I wanted to finish with the <u>V</u>iew menu first.

Property Pa<u>g</u>es refers to User Controls, something that we won't be covering in this introductory course.

Select Toolbo<u>x</u> and the Visual Basic Toolbox is displayed.

In Visual Basic, colors are specified by long, hard to remember numbers. Selecting Color Pal<u>e</u>tte displays, unsurprisingly, a color palette. The displayed color can then be directly selected from the palette, instead of having to specify the number.

The <u>T</u>oolbars menu contains five submenus: Debug, Edit, Form Editor, Standard and <u>C</u>ustomize:

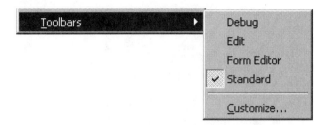

"Visual Basic comes with four built-in toolbars," I said, "each one of which can be either displayed or not displayed by selecting these items."

- **Debug** displays a toolbar with buttons for common debugging tasks.

- **Edit** displays a toolbar with buttons for common editing tasks, which we viewed earlier.

- **Form Editor** displays a toolbar with buttons specific to editing a form.

- **Standard** displays the toolbar that you see when you first start Visual Basic. It's a good idea to have this always present!

- **Customize** displays a Customize dialog box that allows you to customize existing toolbars or even create new ones.

"We can do something similar in Microsoft Word," Barbara said. "Exactly," I agreed. "Most Microsoft products provide similar functionality."

At this point, I suggested that we take a fifteen-minute break before discussing the Project menu.

The Project Menu

When we returned from break, I displayed the Project menu on the classroom projector:

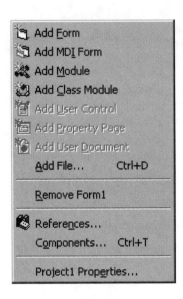

"The Project menu deals with the management of our Visual Basic project," I said.

"One question though," Linda said. "You mentioned earlier today that there was a way to include non-Visual Basic objects in our project. Is this where we do that?"

"Linda, that's a good point; I almost let that get by me."

"Actually," I said, "there are two commands that are used to include other objects in the project, References and Components. In fact, I've just realized that we'll need to use the Components command to include something called the **Common Dialog Control** in the China Shop Project. But I'll lead you through that when we get to that point."

Project Properties

"Project properties apply to the entire project, not just to a particular form or module," I said. I asked the class to click on Project1 Properties to see the following dialog:

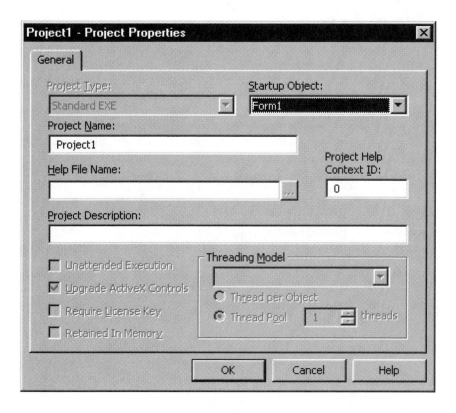

The General Tab

"The version of Visual Basic that we're using, the Working Model, has only the General tab. Other versions have more tabs, but we don't need to worry about them. They're for more advanced work. Even most of the information on the General tab is beyond the introductory nature of this course," I said, "and not something that we'll need to worry about for the China Shop Project. For that reason, plus the fact that we have a lot to cover today, I'll just cover the highlights."

- **Project Type** is the same as the project type you select from the Project Dialog Box when you start Visual Basic.

- Every Visual Basic project requires something called a **Startup Object**. For most cases, and for the China Shop Project, it is the first form added to your project. This selects the form or module it will first start with when the program runs.

- The **Project Name** uniquely identifies your project in the Windows Registry and the Object Browser. "Next week," I said, "we'll change the Project Name to **'China'**."

- Selecting **Help File Name** allows you to specify a Help File for your project. We will not specify one for the China Shop Project.

- **Project Help Context ID** requires an entry in Help File Name.

- **Project Description** specifies the descriptive text that is displayed in the description pane at the bottom of the Object Browser when this project is selected.

The ActiveX check box is disabled in this version of Visual Basic. I told the class that the next five items, Require License Key, Retained in memory, Unattended Execution, Threading Model, Thread Per Object, Thread Pool, and the threads list box were well beyond the introductory nature of our class, and I would not be discussing them today.

The Format Menu

Our look at the Project menu had been quick, since we simply glossed over most of the menu items on it. The Format menu, however, would be a different story.

I directed everyone's attention to the dots on the form, called the Form Grid. "In two weeks," I said, "we'll begin to place controls on the China Shop form, and most of you are going to be very concerned with the exact placement of the controls on your form. Remember the Format menu at that time, because it, in conjunction with the Form Grid, will play an important role in you placing your controls exactly where you want them."

"I'm sorry," Ward said, "but you have used the term several times. What exactly is a control?"

I thought I had mentioned it, but just in case...

"A control is any one of the objects found in the Tool Box," I said, "such as a check box or an option button."

There were no other questions.

"Let's look at the Format menu now:"

The Format Menu

Align

Align contains submenus that allow you to align your controls by some constant, such as the leftmost edge of all the selected controls. As a demonstration, I placed two label controls from the Tool Box on a form, and displayed the form on the classroom projector:

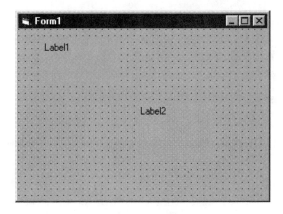

"Don't worry about how to add controls to the form at the moment. We'll cover that in detail later. I'm more interested in you understanding how to align them right now!" I warned the class.

"My IDE doesn't look like that," Linda said. "Your form isn't in a Project Window."

"You're right," I said. "At break, I changed my environment to an SDI. Sorry, I warned you that would happen, I just feel more comfortable with it. If you want your screen to look the same way select Tools-Options-Advanced from the Main menu, and then select SDI Development Environment. Remember that you'll need to restart Visual Basic for this to be realized."

After waiting a few moments for people to make this change, I continued by noting that these controls weren't aligned in any way, neither vertically nor horizontally. "Suppose," I asked, "I want to align these controls? Let's say horizontally. All I need to do is select both of these controls on the form..."

"Hang on a minute," Ward said. "How do you do that?"

"Oops," I said. "Sorry, sometimes you take these things for granted. If you select one control by clicking on it with the mouse, press and **hold** the *Ctrl* key, then select the second control, both controls will be selected."

I then demonstrated that on the classroom projector:

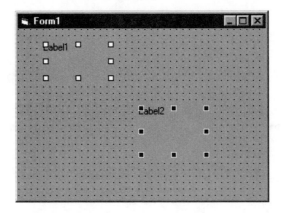

"One of the controls has a blue outline," Kate said, "and the other has a white outline. What's the difference?"

"Remember focus and the active window?" I said. "When you multi-select controls in the Visual Basic IDE, one of the controls is considered to have the focus and is known as the 'active control'. That's the one with the blue outline. By the way, that outline is technically known as **grab handles**. The fact that the other control has white **grab handles** lets us know that it is also selected."

"Selected for what?" Ward asked.

"Selected for whatever action we wish, in this case alignment," I replied. "In fact, there are six alignment commands that you can select once you have multi-selected controls:"

- **Lefts** - Aligns the horizontal position of the selected controls, putting the left-most edges in line with that of the last selected control, which is the one with the blue grab handles.

- **Centers** - Aligns the horizontal position of the selected controls, putting the centers of the controls in line with the center of the active control.

- **Rights** - Aligns the horizontal position of the selected controls, putting the right-most edges in line with that of the active control.

- **Tops** - Aligns the vertical position of the selected controls, putting the tops in line with that of the active control.

- **Middles** - Aligns the vertical position of selected controls, putting the middles in line with the vertical middle of the active control.

- **Bottoms** - Aligns the vertical position of the selected controls, putting the bottoms in line with that of the active control.

- **to Grid** - Aligns the top left of the selected objects to the closest grid point (or dot really).

I then spent some time demonstrating how the different alignment options work. "You won't believe how much time these format options can save you," I said, "if you remember to use them."

Make Same Size

Make Same Size contains submenus for Width, Height and Both. These items give you the ability to quickly make selected controls the same size. "The way to make controls the same size," I said, "is similar to the process with which we use to align them. Multi-select them by selecting one control, then press and hold the *Ctrl* key, then select the next control. Then select a menu item."

"Can you select more than two controls at the same time?" Ward asked. "Yes, you can," I said. "Sorry if I didn't make that clear. You can select as many controls simultaneously as you want."

"I presume," Linda asked, "that these controls are sized the same as the last control selected? Is that right?"

"That's right," I said. "These commands give you the choice of making all the selected controls either the same width, height, or both of the last control selected."

"And that would be the one with the blue grab handles," Kate said.

"Excellent, Kate," I said. "You have it!"

Size to Grid

"I pretty much understand the alignment and size items," Rose said, "but I've been experimenting with Size to Grid, and I simply don't see any changes."

I saw Jack whispering to Rose. Upon seeing me spying them, Jack told me that he had discovered that there is an option in the Tools menu that makes this option the default behavior. Therefore, selecting this item doesn't appear to do a thing.

"Right you are, Jack," I said. "By default, all controls are sized to the grid. That just means that when you place a control on the form, the control's height and width will be automatically adjusted so that its border aligns with the grid."

"And the grid is the dots," Kate said. "That's right," I said.

Horizontal Spacing

Horizontal Spacing contains submenus for Make Equal, Increase, Decrease and Remove. These options give you the ability to quickly vary the horizontal spacing between selected controls. The method to adjust horizontal spacing between controls is similar to the method to align them. Multi-select them, then select a menu item.

- **Make Equal** moves the selected controls so that there is equal space between them using the outermost objects as endpoints. The outermost controls do not move.

- **Increase** increases the horizontal spacing by one grid unit based on the control with focus (which of course is the one with the blue grab handles).

"Speaking of grid units," Linda said. "Is there any way to change the spacing between the dots on the grid?"

"Good question," I said. "Yes, I call that the **grid granularity.** You can change the distance between your grid units by selecting the General tab of the Options menu, something that we'll look at in just a bit."

- **Decrease** decreases horizontal spacing by one grid unit based on the control with focus.

- **Remove** removes the horizontal space between controls so that the controls are aligned with their edges touching based on the control with focus.

Vertical Spacing

Vertical Spacing contains submenus for Make Equal, Increase, Decrease and Remove.

"This menu is identical to the Horizontal Spacing menu, except that it affects the vertical spacing of your selected controls," I said, "so, I'll leave you to experiment on your own with this."

Center In Form

Center In Form contains submenus for Horizontally and Vertically. Selecting this command centers (either horizontally or vertically) selected controls on the central axes of the form.

"Will selecting this command center a single control on the form?" Dave asked. "No," I said. "In fact, if only one control is selected, the Center In Form command is disabled."

- **Horizontally** - Aligns the middle of the selected controls to an imaginary horizontal line in the middle of the form.

- **Vertically** - Aligns the centers of the selected controls to an imaginary vertical line in the center of the form.

Order

"Order contains two submenus, Bring to Front and Send to Back. The Order menu affects the Z-order of the selected controls on a form."

I didn't even need to look at Ward to know his question. "Z-Order is just the third dimension of controls on a form," I said. "It's pretty easy to place one control on top of another. Using <u>B</u>ring to Front you can place a selected control 'on top' of other selected controls. Using <u>S</u>end to Back, you can place a selected control 'underneath' other selected controls."

"Why not just click and drag?" Joe asked. "Using <u>O</u>rder can save you a little work," I said, "particularly if you have a number of controls, and you want just one to be at the top."

"I still don't see the point," Linda said. "Perhaps it's just something I need to work with."

Lock Controls

<u>L</u>ock Controls is the final menu on the F<u>o</u>rmat menu. This command "locks" or freezes all the controls on the form so that you don't accidentally move them.

Again there is a toolbar for this menu: the Form Editor Toolbar...

Remember, use the menu item View-Toolbars-Form Editor to achieve this:

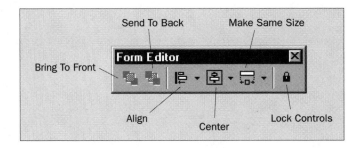

The <u>D</u>ebug Menu

"<u>D</u>ebug is the next menu," I said. "However, we'll be covering this pretty thoroughly a few weeks from now. So we'll hold off on a detailed discussion until then."

The <u>R</u>un Menu

The <u>R</u>un menu contains five submenus: <u>S</u>tart, Start with <u>F</u>ull Compile, Brea<u>k</u>, <u>E</u>nd and <u>R</u>estart:

"Each of these submenus," I said, "pertains to running a program within the IDE and it won't be long before we're running the China Shop Project."

- **Start** - The Start command runs your program.
- **Continue** – This menu item only appears when the program is paused and makes the program continue to run from where it was paused.

"Remember earlier," I asked them, "when I said that you can pause your program? If you pause it, the caption for this command becomes Continue. Select Continue and your program resumes from the point where it was paused."

- **Start With Full Compile** - You compile a program to turn it into an executable file.
- **Break** - This command allows you to pause your program.

"While your program is paused," I said, "Visual Basic is said to be in **break mode**. I'll discuss exactly what you can do while your program is paused in a few weeks."

"On my keyboard," Ward said, "there's a key with the words *Pause* and *Break* on it. Can that key be used also?"

"Yes, Ward." I replied. "You can see that option on the menu, *Ctrl + Break*."

- **End** - This command stops your program.
- **Restart** - When you pause your program, this command restarts your program from the beginning. It can only be selected when Visual Basic is in break mode.

"Remember," I said, "Restart is not the same as Continue. Restart begins your program from the very beginning, whereas Continue resumes your program from the point where it was paused."

The Tools Menu

The Tools menu contains four options: Add Procedure, Procedure Attributes, Menu Editor and Options:

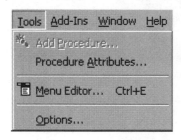

"Everything except the Options submenu is an advanced topic that we will deal with after we have created our prototype, so I'm not covering any of them except that one today."

"We should probably take a break," I told everyone, "because the discussion of the Options submenu may take some time."

Options

When everyone returned a few minutes later, I told them all that the Options menu permits you to change a variety of default settings in the Visual Basic IDE.

"Options that you select in the Options menu," I said, "will still be in force when you start up Visual Basic the next time."

The Options menu contains a dialog box with 6 tabs: Editor, Editor Format, General, Docking, Environment and Advanced:

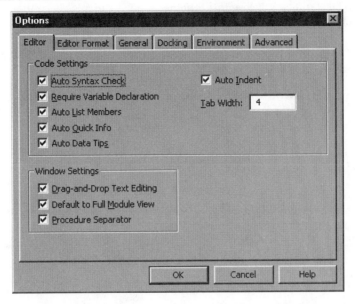

The Editor Tab

The Editor tab contains two sections, one for the Code Settings and one for the Windows Settings.

"Changes that you make here," I said, "apply to the Visual Basic environment, not to a single project. That means when you put Visual Basic to bed after a long night of programming, the next time you start it, these settings will still be in place."

I explained that all of the Code Settings affected the behavior of Visual Basic when you are typing code into the Code window.

- **Auto Syntax Check** - Selecting this box tells Visual Basic that it should automatically verify the Visual Basic syntax of commands that you enter in the Code window.

"In my opinion," I said, "this is an option that should never be turned off."

"So if this is turned on," Barbara said, "any error you enter as you type is flagged in some way by Visual Basic? Why would anyone want to turn that off?"

"Good question," I said. "I wouldn't! Although there are occasions when professional programmers do."

- **Require Variable Declaration** - Determines whether explicit variable declarations are required in modules.

"There you go again with that variable declaration bit," Ward said. "I know those things will be pretty important when we get to them."

I promised everyone that I would discuss variables and how to declare them a little later on in the course. "For now," I told them, "selecting this option adds the `Option Explicit` statement to the General Declarations section of any new module."

"Never, never, never," I said, "turn this option off. It's vitally important that all programmers, beginners included, declare their variables. Selecting this option will force you to do that."

- **Auto List Members** - When this option is selected, Visual Basic will attempt to complete the Visual Basic statement that you are coding.

"Are you kidding?" Linda said. "It does all the work for us?"

"Wait until you see it in action," I said. "You'll love it!"

- **Auto Quick Info** - When this option is selected, Visual Basic will display hints about any Visual Basic functions and their parameters as you enter them in the Code Window. "Like Auto List Members," I said, "you have to see this to believe it."

- **Auto Data Tips** - "This feature is only active in break mode," I said, as I looked at Linda, "and allows you to display the value of a variable in the Code window when you have paused your program. We'll examine this feature a little later in the course."

- **Auto Indent** - I explained that indenting the code you write in Visual Basic makes the code more readable. With this option selected, you can indent a line of code using the *Tab* key and all subsequent lines will start at that same tab location.

- **Tab Width** - This designates the number of characters indented when you press the *Tab* key in the Code window.

I then continued to explain that all of the Window Settings affected the behavior of Visual Basic when you are viewing the Project Explorer window:

- **Drag-and-Drop Text Editing** - Selecting this option allows you to drag and drop elements from the Code window into the Immediate or Watch windows.

"Quite honestly," I said, "I always forget this exists, but it is a time saver. We'll look at the Immediate and Watch windows later in the course, and when we get there, someone remind me to show you how this works."

"Don't worry," Linda said, "I'll remind you."

- **Default to Full Module View** - "In Visual Basic," I said, "code is written and placed into procedures. An event procedure is associated with a particular control and a particular event, such as the `Click` event of a Command Button. By default, Visual Basic displays the code from only one event procedure at a time. We call that **Procedure View**. On occasion, it's convenient to be able to see all of the code that you have written for every control on your form in one big window. That's what **Full Module View** does for you."

- **Procedure Separator** - "The **Procedure Separator** goes hand in hand with **Full Module View**," I said, "by placing a separator bar between the event procedures in that big window I was telling you about. By the way, this option is only available if **Default to Full Module View** is checked."

The Editor Format Tab

"What's the difference between the Editor and the Editor Format tab?" Valerie asked.

"Detail," I said. "The Editor Format tab allows you to really customize the Code window, or the Code Editor as Visual Basic also calls it. I've never touched a single setting in here, but I know some programmers who have fine tuned the look and feel of the Code Editor by adjusting these settings."

"I suggest that you just play around with these settings to get the feel of them!" I said.

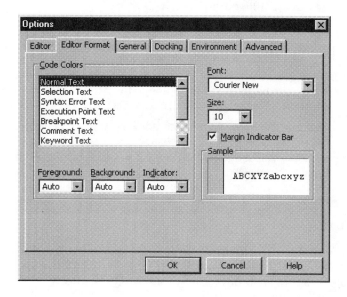

The General Tab

The General tab is used to specify settings, error handling and compile settings for your Visual Basic project:

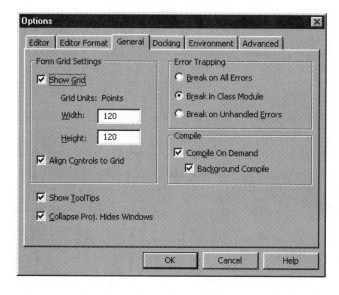

The Form Grid Settings frame specifies the appearance of the form grid. Measurements specified for the grid are in **twips**.

"Did you say twips?" Linda asked.

"Yes," I said, barely able to keep a straight face, "a twip is one twentieth of a printer's point. There are 72 printer points in an inch, so there are 1440 twips in an inch. The great thing about twips is that they are **device independent**. That means that there are 1440 twips to an inch on a 14 inch monitor, on a 17 inch monitor, and also on a piece of paper printed by a laser printer."

- Show Grid - Selecting this option tells Visual Basic to show the form grid at design time.

"So you can turn those dots off?" Rhonda asked.

"If you really want, you can," I said, "but I don't recommend it. You'll see that the form grid is very useful in placing controls on your form."

- Grid Units: Points displays the grid units used for the form. The default is in twips.

- Width determines the width of grid cells or dots on a form. "The larger the number," I said, "the greater the distance between the dots on the grid."

- Height determines the height of grid cells on a form. Again, the larger the number, the greater the distance between dots on the grid.

- Align Controls to Grid. Selecting this option automatically positions the outer edges of controls on grid lines. "If this option isn't selected," I said, "then you can place your controls between the grid lines. Most programmers like the alignment. It makes placement of controls much easier."

The Error Trapping frame allows us to alter what happens when Visual Basic finds an error in our code:

- Break on All Errors. Selecting this option causes Visual Basic to stop for every error it encounters. When we begin to write our own Error Handling code, we don't want this selected.

- **Break in Class Module.** "We won't be talking about class modules during this course," I said, "but selecting this option causes Visual Basic to stop if it encounters an error in a class module as well as in code in our own project."

- **Break on Unhandled Errors.** "This is the one we want, in this class we should have **Break on Unhandled Errors** selected," I said. "Selecting this tells Visual Basic to stop only if it encounters an error for which there is no Error Handler to deal with it. In our next to last class we'll write our very own Error Handler, and we'll want this option set."

"The compile options are fairly straight-forward and I suggest that we leave them set as they are and move on to complete this discussion of our dialog page" I said.

"I think I mentioned ToolTips a little earlier," I said, "when we were discussing the Tool Box. ToolTips provide helpful hints if you allow your mouse to linger over a control in the Visual Basic Tool Box, or over a button on the toolbar. The **Show ToolTips** Check Box allows you to turn the ToolTips on and off."

"I can't see any reason to turn it off," Rose said.

"Neither can I," agreed Jack.

"With **Collapse Proj. Hides Windows** selected," I said, "if you collapse a project in the Project Explorer, your Code window will disappear."

"It doesn't get lost, does it?" Mary asked. "No," I replied, "you can always find it again by bringing the Project Explorer window back into view."

The Docking Tab

A window is docked when it is attached or anchored to other windows or to the IDE. When you move a dockable window, if it is close to any other window, it will attach itself, holding on tight until you tear it away. If the window is 'self-contained' in its own window, it's said to be undocked:

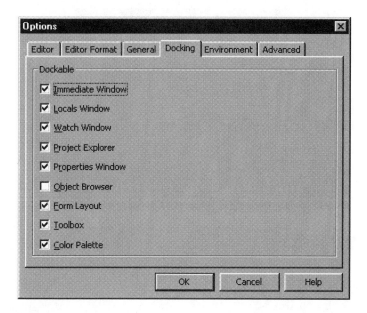

"Personally," I said, "as you know, I prefer an SDI environment and I also undock all of my windows. You'll need to experiment on your own to get the IDE the way you really like."

The Environment Tab

The Environment tab is used to specify startup parameters for the IDE. Changes made here are saved and then loaded every time Visual Basic is started. Most of the options on this dialog are self-explanatory:

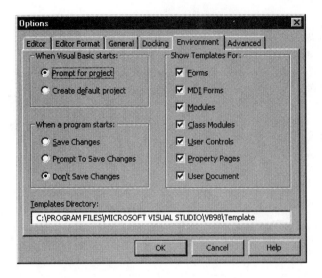

The Advanced Tab

By the time we had reached the **Advanced** tab, Peter suggested that some of the options we had looked at had already been pretty advanced. His statement inspired a few laughs and I told him I had to agree. "That's a testimony to just how much we can customize the Visual Basic environment," I said.

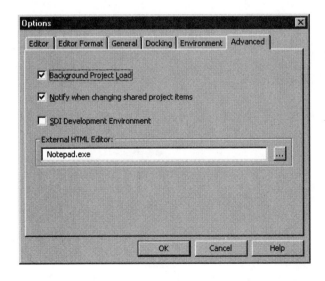

But, for once, we only have three options to discuss:

- **Background Project Load** tells Visual Basic to load your project in the background, thereby returning control to the developer more quickly.

- **Notify when changing shared project items** tells Visual Basic to notify you when you change a 'shared' project item such as a form or module. This option only applies when you have more than one project loaded in the IDE and both projects are sharing an object.

- **SDI Development Environment** changes the development environment from the default Multiple Document Interface (MDI) to the Single Document Interface (SDI). When you select this option, the SDI appears after you exit and then re-enter Visual Basic.

"That's your favorite," said Dave.

"Yes it is," I said. "I just feel more comfortable with it. Again, experiment a bit to see what each one does. Nothing's permanent, so if you don't like the effect you can always change it back."

The Add-Ins Menu

"Add-Ins are programs," I said, "typically written by third parties, which provide additional functionality to your program that Visual Basic does not already possess. For instance, Visual Basic doesn't have a report writer to speak of, but some versions of Visual Basic come shipped with Crystal Reports as an Add-In. The Add-Ins menu allows you to manage any Add-Ins registered on your PC. Although it won't apply to us there are many Add-Ins which can be bought to extend the functionality of Visual Basic."

"The Visual Data Manager and Add-In Manager are both advanced tools, so I'm going to pass them up today."

The Window Menu

"Again, I hate to say things like this, but the Window menu is pretty much standard:"

"One thing I should point out," I said, "is that the Split option is only available when you are working in the Code window."

The Help Menu

The Help menu is unavailable in the Working Model Edition.

The Visual Basic Toolbar

"Just about every toolbar button," I said, "has a corresponding menu item, so it shouldn't take us too long to get through this."

I reminded everyone that when you first start Visual Basic, only the Standard Toolbar is visible. "You can select View-Toolbars from the Visual Basic main menu to see the others," I said. "By default, the Standard Toolbar is docked at the top of the IDE:"

Several of my students were surprised to find that you could move the Standard Toolbar anywhere you wish by dragging and dropping. This is true of the other toolbars as well.

"Don't forget," I said, "you can also customize your own toolbar with the Customize command of the Toolbar menu."

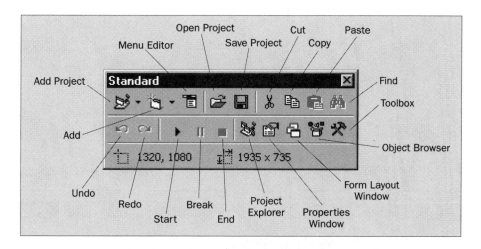

"What do those arrows after the Add Project and Add buttons mean?" Ward asked. I directed everyone's attention to the pull-down arrows on the toolbar.

"Good question, Ward," I said. "Whenever you see an arrow like this, that means that there are more options available."

I clicked on the arrow, and a pull down list was displayed, exposing the rest of the options available when you click on this button:

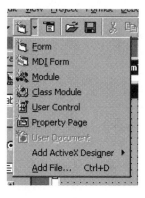

"Don't worry about most of these options, as we are unlikely to be using them," I said.

The Visual Basic Toolbox

I told the class that the Visual Basic Toolbox is a window that contains controls that we will use to design our programs:

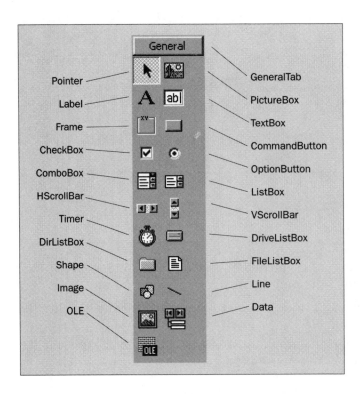

"The Visual Basic default Toolbox contains 21 controls." I said.

"Hold on," said Linda, "I've got all of those controls, but they aren't organized like that!"

"Well, if you remember, the Toolbox is a dockable window. All I've done here is undock the window and resize it to this shape. Remember that the IDE is very easy to customize, and as we go further on, what you look at will begin to differ more and more from what you see as I customize away. Don't worry about the details on the screen, only if you can't find something at all!"

I continued, "We'll discuss most of these controls, *but not all of them*, over the course of the next two weeks."

I directed everyone's attention to the General tab in the Toolbox.

"Some programmers," I said, "especially as their Toolboxes begin to fill with a large number of other controls, categorize their controls by creating additional Toolbox tabs. You can do this by right clicking on the Toolbox. Once you've added a new tab, you can then click and drag your controls and either move or copy them to the new tab."

The Properties Window

We were nearly finished for the day. I just wanted to show the class a **Properties** window. We would leave the details of the **Properties** window for our next class. I displayed the **Properties** window associated with the form that was loaded in the project in my IDE by selecting Propertie<u>s</u> Window from the <u>V</u>iew menu:

"The **Properties** window," I said, "displays properties associated with the form or a control. Properties are attributes that determine the look and behavior of a form or a control on the form."

The Project Window

I displayed the Project window for the project I had loaded on the classroom projector. I had intentionally 'loaded it up' with multiple modules because I wanted everyone to get a feeling for the types of objects than could go into a project, although our China Shop Project would have only a single form.

"The Project window displays the component pieces of a project," I said. "As I mentioned earlier, a Visual Basic project can have multiple modules. The Project window aids you in finding these component pieces. Once you find them, you can double-click on the objects in the project window to select them, and view them in the IDE."

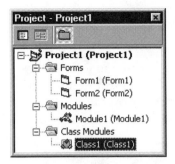

I asked if there were any questions. There were none. This class had been a journey through the IDE, the purpose of which had been to familiarize the class with most of the capabilities of the IDE.

"There are still some areas that we need to cover," I said. "Particularly the <u>D</u>ebug menu, but we'll be looking at that topic in a few weeks."

I dismissed class, telling everyone that next week we would begin to develop the China Shop Project by examining Visual Basic properties, methods and events.

Summary

In this chapter, you were exposed to the 'nitty gritty' of the Visual Basic IDE, covering the Visual Basic Menu, Toolbar and Toolbox. Again, I know there was a tremendous amount of material to assimilate here. However, we couldn't move on until I had taken you on a tour of the IDE. Next chapter, we'll be ready to begin coding the China Shop Project!

We saw that, in Visual Basic, a **project** consists of all the components that make up your program. The project's name and properties are set using the menu item Project – Project1 Properties...

We looked through the Visual Basic menus, which have some similarities with other Microsoft applications, and some items specific to Visual Basic; we also looked at the windows scattered around the IDE.

The View menu brings up the various additional toolbars and windows, for example the Object Browser, that enable you to work with your project.

The Project menu enables you to add forms or modules to your project, and alter the project properties.

The Format menu allows you to size and align the controls on your form to make its appearance more uniform and tidy.

The Options menu item in the Tools menu lets you change various options to suit you, for example whether the Auto Help Info pop-ups are enabled. Certain options in this menu are best left untouched, such as Require Variable Declaration, which can lead to hard-to-spot errors if disabled.

The Toolbox contains the more commonly used controls that you place on your forms.

The Properties window displays the properties for the selected item or control, allowing you to change them for the best operation.

The Project Explorer window lets you see how your project is organized into forms and modules, and allows you to switch to a different form or module to work on it.It's a good idea to become familiar with the interface, just by poking around. I'd definitely recommend spending some time doing just that. Then, you'll feel more comfortable using it and it won't hold you back from learning new things.

Quiz

1. How do you start the IDE?

2. What is the type of Visual Basic project that we are concerned with in this book?

3. Where on the Visual Basic menu is the Print command located?

4. Pretend that you have just fired up Visual Basic. You can't find your Toolbox. Where is it, and what can you do to get it back?

5. While working in Visual Basic, after you've designed your visual interface, you find that you are constantly nudging your controls out of position. How can you prevent this?

6. What menu command of the Format menu aligns selected objects on their left-most edges?

7. What does the Require Variable Declaration option of the Editor Tab of the Options menu do?

8. I mentioned a menu option that I recommend should never be turned off. What is it?

9. Forgive me, but how many twips are there in an inch?

10. What is the name of the window that contains the controls that we will use to design our programs?

11. What is the name of the window that displays properties associated with the form or a control that is currently selected on a form?

12. What window in the IDE is used to see the component pieces of your project?

13. What is the default name for a project in Visual Basic?

Extra Credit – What mathematical term is this?

'What the acorn said when it grew up.'

Chapter 4
Programming is Easy!

In this chapter, follow my computer class as I show them just how easy programming can be in Visual Basic. In today's class, we will begin working with Visual Basic in earnest, with a specific focus on the built-in, or default, behavior of forms and some controls.

We'll begin the chapter by starting the IDE and learning about Visual Basic properties and methods by examining the Visual Basic form – the starting point for the China Shop Project. By the end of today's class, we'll have created and modified the one and only form required for the program.

Less is Best

I began this class with a simple statement: "Less is Best."

Not surprisingly, my statement elicited some strange looks from the students assembled in the computer lab. However, when you teach programming, you become used to this kind of response pretty quickly.

"Visual Basic programming can be very easy," I continued, "provided you don't 'over program'. Many beginners 'over program' their projects, just like new drivers tend to 'over steer' their cars. Whenever you program in Visual Basic, especially when you are just starting out, keep my motto in mind."

"What exactly do you mean by 'over program'?" Kate asked. "Don't you need to program in order for your project to do something?"

"That's exactly my point," I replied. "Beginners always want to begin coding. It is important to understand what your project does with no additional code from you."

"Well, I wouldn't think it could do anything," Ward said. "How can it with no code?"

"Actually, a Visual Basic program with no code can do quite a lot," I said. "Remember, Visual Basic programming is a two-part process. First, we design the visual part of our program, called the **User Interface**. Then we write code."

"Isn't the design of the User Interface just a matter of placing controls on the form?" Linda asked.

"Yes and no," I said. "That's true, but that's not all there is to it. After placing controls on the form, you should pat yourself on the back, and then observe the default behavior of the form and the controls on it."

"What do you mean by default behavior?" Steve asked.

"The form itself, and each control that we place on the form," I said, "comes complete with built-in behavior. You would be amazed at the number of beginners who write code which duplicates, or even defeats this built-in behavior."

"OK," Joe said, "so after observing the default behavior of the form and controls, then we write code?"

"Not quite," I replied. "Then we modify the properties of the form and controls to get them just the way we want them to look."

"And then we write code?" Valerie asked.

"Yes, then we write code," I said. "In today's class, we'll begin the China Shop Project, and examine the default behavior of its form. Then we'll adjust some of its properties according to the design we came up with during the design phase of the Systems Development Life Cycle."

Visual Basic Properties, Methods and Events

I could sense some excitement building in the class when I announced that we would begin working on the China Shop Project.

"First things first," I said. "Let's start Visual Basic."

I asked everyone to start Visual Basic, and select a new Standard EXE project from the Project Dialog box. While the class was doing that, I reminded them that since my personal preference was to work in the Visual Basic IDE with a Single Document Interface (SDI), that's the look that they would be seeing on the classroom projector.

"To avoid confusion," I said, "you might want to do the same. Does anyone remember how to turn on SDI in the IDE?"

"<u>T</u>ools-<u>O</u>ptions-Advanced from the Visual Basic main menu," Linda said. "And then you need to exit Visual Basic, and re-start it to see the effect of the change."

"Good," I said. "You must have been practicing."

"After last week's class," Linda said, "I went home and started practicing, and I haven't stopped since. I have loads of questions for you."

"That's fine, that's how we learn," I said as I took a quick walk around the classroom, and noticed that almost everyone had followed my advice and switched to an SDI interface.

"I've worked with the MDI interface a little bit at work," Dave said, "so I think I'll stay with that."

"Nothing wrong with that," I said. "The idea is to be comfortable with the IDE."

"Everyone at this point," I said, "should have Visual Basic running, with a form displayed. Is everyone OK so far?"

"You've mentioned properties several times so far in this class," Ward said. "Before we get much further, can you give us a definition of a property?"

Visual Basic Properties

"A **property** is an attribute or characteristic of a Visual Basic object," I said. "An object in Visual Basic is most often a form or a control. Properties are to objects what characteristics are to a person. For example, a person has a name, and each object in Visual Basic has a **Name** property. A person can be described by their height, and some objects, such as the form or a command button, have a **Height** property."

"I'm expecting to see the Properties window here," Barbara said, "but I don't see it."

I explained that there are four ways to display the Properties window, all of which require you to select the form first. I told them that to select the form, all they needed to do was to click on it, and preferably on the form's Title bar:

- select Form1 and press the *F4* key
- select Form1 and select <u>V</u>iew-Properties <u>W</u>indow from the main menu
- select Form1 and select the Properties Window button on the Standard Toolbar
- select Form1 in the Project window, right-click the mouse, and then select Prope<u>r</u>ties

I opened the Properties window on my PC, and the following screen was displayed on the classroom projector:

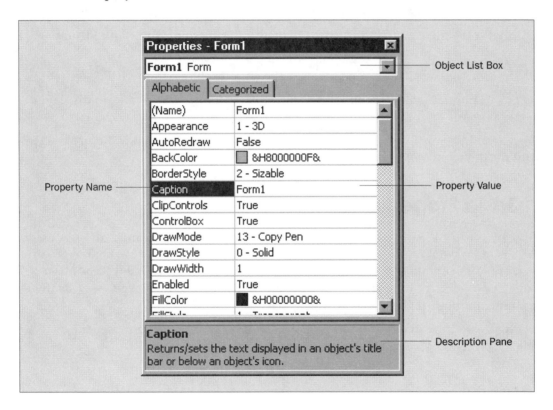

"My Properties window is wider than yours," Mary said. "Should I be worried about that?"

"No," I said. "The Properties window is a standard window. You can re-size it just like any other window to look the way mine does. Notice that it also contains a Close button."

I directed everyone's attention to the most important part of the Properties window, the properties themselves. "Those are properties of what?" Ward asked.

"Properties of the form," I said. "For the moment, don't concern yourselves with the individual property names and values. We'll be getting to those in a minute. Let me take a moment to familiarize you with the layout of the Properties window."

I directed everyone's attention to the **Object List Box**, directly underneath the title bar. "The Object List Box," I said, "lists all of the objects that 'belong' to the selected form, including the form itself."

"I don't see any other objects besides Form1 in the Object List Box," Rhonda said.

"That's because we haven't placed any controls on the Form yet," I replied. "We'll be doing that during our next class."

I continued by saying that directly under the Object list box are two tabs, labeled Alphabetic and Categorized.

"By default," I said, "the Alphabetic tab is selected, which means that the properties are listed alphabetically, with the exception of the Name property which is listed at the very top. If you select the Categorized tab, then the properties are sorted according to categories such as Appearance and Behavior."

I then clicked on the Categorized tab, and the following screen was displayed:

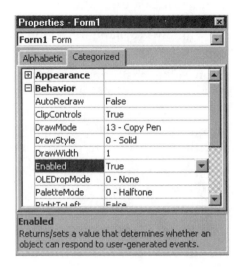

"What do the plus and minus signs mean?" asked Rose.

"The plus sign (+) means that the category is collapsed," I said. "That means there are properties there that you can view, if you expand it by clicking on the plus sign."

I clicked on the plus sign next to the Appearance category and the following screen was displayed:

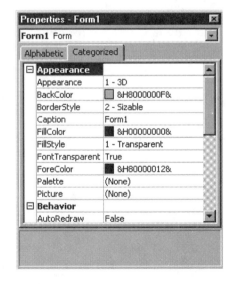

"As you can see," I said, "now we can see the properties that make up the **Appearance** category. The minus sign (-) indicates that the category has already been expanded. In the same way, you can click on the minus sign to collapse the category."
"Do you have a preference for how the properties are displayed?" Peter asked.

"Personally, I prefer to display the list alphabetically," I replied, "but that's because I'm very familiar with them. I think if I were a beginner, I'd prefer to see them categorized."

"The two columns," Ward said. "Are those the property names and their values?"

"Yes, that's right," I said. "The left column is the name of the property, and the right column is the value."

Before moving on, I pointed out that at the bottom of the **Properties** window is a Description Pane, which displays a brief description of the property. I told the class that now I was going to perform a small demonstration.

"I'm going to change properties of the form in the **Properties** window," I said, "so that you can see how changing properties will have an immediate effect on the form."

I collapsed every category in the **Properties** window except for **Position**, and displayed the **Properties** window on the classroom projector:

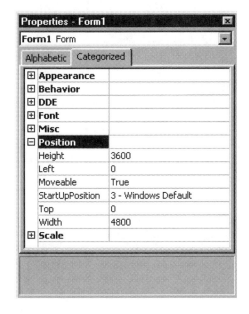

"There are six properties in the Position category," I said. "All of these affect the position of the form relative to the screen."

"What is that number in the Height Property?" Mary asked.

"That's the height of the Form in twips," I said.

"Every time you say that word," Rose said, "I can't help laughing. How many inches would that be?"

I displayed the Windows calculator, and divided 3600 by 1440. "Let's see now," I said. "There are 1440 twips per inch. That works out to exactly two and one half inches."

"What does the Left property mean?" Rhonda asked. I explained that the Left property specifies the distance, in twips, of the form's left border from the left edge of the screen.

"Then the Top property specifies the distance, in twips, of the form's top border from the top of the screen," Barbara said. "That's right," I replied. "We can change the location and dimensions of the form by changing these properties."

To illustrate, I changed the Top property from 1200 to 2500, the form moved down the screen. Then I changed the Left property from 180 to 0. The form moved to the very left edge of the screen.

"I like this," Ward said. "This looks like fun. How many properties of the form are there that we can play with?"

"Probably around 45 or so," I said. "Before you start experimenting, I also want to show you another way to change the position and size of the form. As you would with any window, click and drag the form to move it, or drag the grab handles to re-size it."

Everyone seemed to be having a good time adjusting the properties of the form, and so I gave them a few minutes to experiment.

"I want you to know," I said, "that you are all now programming."

A few students looked up when I said that.

"I wouldn't exactly call this programming," Lou said.

"Sure it is," I said. "It's just not what you thought programming in Visual Basic would be. What you are doing is programming the visual interface to your application. This is the first step in the development of any great Visual Basic program."

"Can't property values be modified through program code?" Dave asked.

"You've been reading ahead, Dave," I said, "but yes, you're right, what you are doing now by adjusting values in the Properties window can also be done while your program is running in code."

"When we begin to develop the China Shop Project," Joe asked, "will we need to change all the properties of the form?"

"No," I said. "That won't be necessary. As you can see, each property has a default value. In most cases, we will just accept that default value. We only need to adjust the properties that are important to us."

"This seems too easy," Chuck said.

"So our next step," Joe said, "would be to place other controls on the form, and then adjust their properties."

"Yes, that's right," I agreed.

"Can I ask a question before we go on?" Linda said. "I was experimenting with some of the other properties. When I click on some of them, a List Box appears."

"That's an excellent point," I said. I displayed the Properties window on the classroom projector and clicked on the Alphabetic tab. Then I clicked on the arrow in the Enabled property next to True:

"Some properties," I said, "have a limited range of acceptable values. In those cases, when you select the property to change it, a list box of valid values will be displayed. For instance, the Enabled property can have one of two values, either True or False."

I asked everyone to select the DrawMode property. "That has 16 possible values," I said.

"What about the BackColor property?" Valerie asked. "What are those hieroglyphics?"

"Good question," I said. I asked everyone to select the BackColor property. I did the same, and the following screen was displayed:

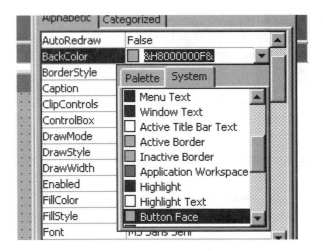

"The BackColor property," I said, "sets the background color of the form. I have to warn you that the color properties are probably the most complicated of all the properties to explain. Fortunately, changing them is pretty easy if you use either the **Palette** or **System** tab. These two tabs are displayed when you select the BackColor property."

"By default," I said, "the **System** tab is selected, and the default setting for BackColor is already selected. For the BackColor property, the system-defined color **Button Face** is selected. **Button Face** refers to the color for Windows buttons specified on the Windows Control Panel. This is the color of all Windows buttons be they in Word, Excel or any other application. This means that you can design your interface to blend in with the other applications as if they were written together."

"So the color associated with **Button Face** on one PC is not necessarily the same color on another PC?" Mary asked. "That's right," I said. "If you want to set an absolute color for BackColor, select the **Palette** tab instead."

I invited the class to do that now. I did the same, and the following screen was displayed:

"You can select a color from the Palette," I said, "and the BackColor of the form will be changed to the exact color you specify."

"But those aren't all of the colors," Valerie said. "What if you want one that isn't displayed?"

"Any time you have any of the various Color properties selected," I said, "you can display the Color Palette by selecting View-Color Palette from the Visual Basic main menu. You can create a custom color and that color will be transferred to the property value."

"Every time I change the BackColor property," Rhonda said, "that number in the BackColor property changes. Can you type that in directly?"

"Yes, you can," I said, "but that's probably not a good idea. Exactly what that number means is a little bit beyond the introductory nature of our course."

"I have another question," Linda said. "Why does the Picture property contain the value (None)?"

"That's another good question," I said. "The short answer is that (None) indicates that no graphic will be displayed, but I like the long answer better."

I displayed the Properties window on the classroom projector, and directed everyone's attention to the Picture property:

"As you can see," I said, "the default value for this property is (None). Do you see those three dots on the button? Whenever you see those three dots, called an **ellipsis**, there is a dialog box available to help do this job. I call the ellipsis an **expression builder.** Sometimes, a property value is long and complicated like a directory path and file name, for example. By including the expression builder with that property, Microsoft has provided you with a way to avoid typing mistakes or plain simple errors."

"What do you mean?" Ward asked.

"Well," I said, "the Picture property of the form designates a graphic file to display as background for the form. Visual Basic needs to know exactly where this file is located. Rather than have us type in a directory and file name, Visual Basic 'builds' it for us with the expression builder."

I clicked on the ellipsis and the following screen was displayed; remember, your display may show a different directory structure from mine.

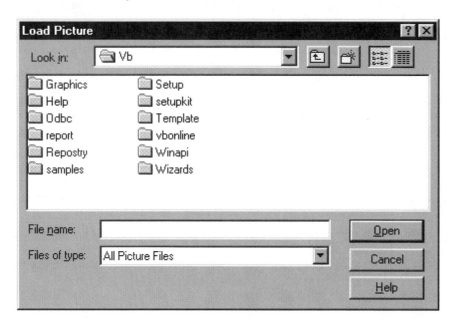

"Now you can use the dialog box to specify a graphics file," I said. I selected **FOREST.BMP** from my **Windows** directory, and the following screen was displayed:

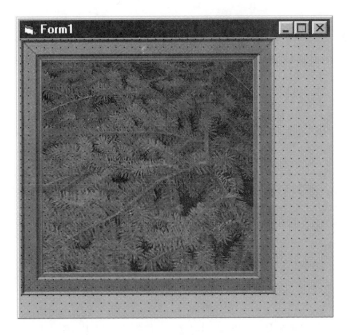

I pointed out that the Picture property now reads (Bitmap). "By the way," I said, "one of the questions I'm asked most is how to set the value of the Picture property back to (None). Just double-click the value to highlight it, and then press the *Delete* key. *Backspace* will not do it."

I asked if anyone had any questions. For the moment, no one did. I thought this would be a good opportunity to let everyone in the class do a formal exercise on their own.

Although the projects for many of the exercises can be found on the CD (in the folder LTP VB 6\Chapter...\Additional Exercises\...), these will only be the more complex ones. Exercises like this one won't be on the CD, so don't worry if you can't find them.

In this exercise, we will explore the Visual Basic Properties window, and change the Name property of our form:

Exercise

Displaying and Modifying the Properties of the Form

1. Start a new Visual Basic **Standard EXE** project.

2. Select the form by clicking on it with the mouse.

3. Once the form is selected, view the **Properties** window by using one of the four methods discussed earlier in today's class. There's only one object in the project so the Object list box at the top of the **Properties** window should read **Form1**.

4. Underneath the Object list box are two tabs, **Alphabetic** and **Categorized**. By default, the **Alphabetic** tab is selected, and the other tab reads **Categorized**. Click on the **Categorized** tab and the arrangement of properties in the window changes. Now the properties are arranged by the following major property categories: **Appearance**, **Behavior**, **DDE**, **Font**, **Misc** (Miscellaneous), **Position** and **Scale**.

5. Look for the **Name** property of the form, which is part of the **Misc** category, instead of at the top of the list in **Alphabetic** view.

6. We are now going to change the value of the **Name** property. Select the **Name** property in the **Properties** window by clicking on it once with your mouse. Once the **Name** property is selected, replace **Form1** with **frmMain**. This change will be accepted either by pressing the *Enter* key or by clicking your mouse on another property.

7. You should notice that the name of the form has changed in the Object list box as well as in the title bar of the **Properties** window. Both should now read **frmMain**:

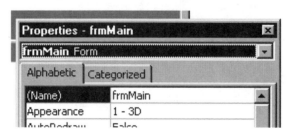

There's a shortcut for navigating through the list of property names in the Properties window. You can quickly scroll to a property by holding down the Shift *and* Ctrl *keys, plus the first letter of the property name you wish to scroll to. Visual Basic will scroll to the first property name beginning with that letter. For example, if you hold down the* Shift, Ctrl *and* M *keys, Visual Basic will scroll to the MaxButton property.*

8. Display the Project Explorer window by pressing the *Ctrl* and *R* keys. The name of the form should change there as well:

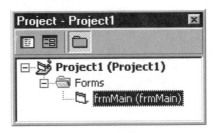

Discussion

The majority of the class seemed to have no problem with our first exercise. Of course, there's always a certain amount of uneasiness the first time you begin working in Visual Basic on your own. But, as I told everyone, you can't hurt anything! If you make a mistake, you can always just start again from the beginning.

Since everyone in the class seemed so comfortable with the first exercise, I asked them to complete another in which they would save the work they had just completed to their hard drive.

"In Visual Basic," I said, "saving your work means both saving a file for your project and one each for every form you have included in the project, and Visual Basic requires a unique name for all of these."

"Is the name of the file the same as the Name property we just changed?" Dave asked.

"No," I said, "the form's Name property, and the name of the file that we save to the hard drive are not the same, although they can be the same if you wish. The Name property is an **internal** name, used whenever we refer to our form in Visual Basic code. The disk file name is an **external** name, used by Windows to load our project and its forms. The same applies to the project itself, which also has a Name property, and an external name with which it is saved. For the China Shop project's one and only form, we'll name the external file **Main.frm**, while the Name property of the form will remain frmMain."

"Why not just make them the same?" Linda asked.

"The Name property of forms and controls," I said, "should be chosen so that the first three characters make it clear what sort of object we're dealing with. That's why we named the Name property of the China Shop form frmMain. External form file names, on the other hand, don't require such a prefix, because they are automatically saved with a filename extension of .frm. So it's really not necessary to name an external form file with the frm prefix."

I continued by explaining that in the following exercise, we would be saving both the project and form file to a subdirectory on the hard disk called \VBFiles\China that we had created the week before.

No one had any questions, and so I distributed this exercise for them to complete.

In this exercise, you will save your project and form files to a subdirectory called \VBFiles\China on your hard disk drive.

Exercise

Saving the China Shop Project

1. The easiest way to save your project and form is by clicking on the Save button on the Toolbar.

2. The first time you save a **new** project the following dialog box will appear:

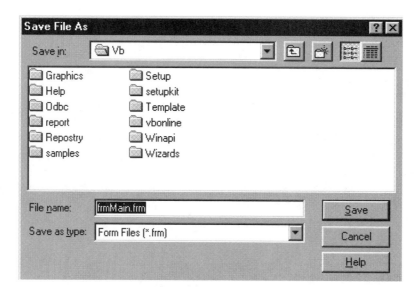

Notice that the dialog box is prompting you to save the form file first. **This is not a mistake**. Visual Basic will first save the form or forms in your project, before the project itself. Also notice that the dialog box is asking you for a disk file name, and the location where it will be saved on your hard disk. The disk file name is located in the text box labeled File name, and the location appears in the text box labeled Save in.

By default, Visual Basic will save your form with the same name as the form's Name property, and save it in the directory where Visual Basic is installed on your PC. We want to name the external form file **Main** and change the location where the form will be saved to the **\VBFiles\China** subdirectory.

3.   Change frmMain to Main in the File name Text Box and change the directory to find our file repository directory:

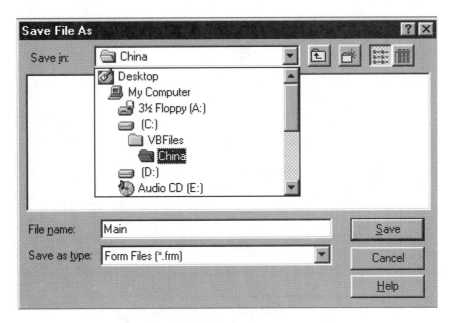

4.   Click on the <u>S</u>ave button to save the form in that directory. There is no need to change anything in the Save as type list box. By default, the form file will be saved with a file extension of .frm.

5.   When you have saved the form, Visual Basic will display another dialog box, prompting you for a project name and location. Notice how Visual Basic presumes that you want to save your project in the same location as your form.

6. A common mistake that beginners make here is to click on the <u>S</u>ave button now, resulting in the project file being saved as Project1. **Don't click on the Save button yet!** You need to change the name of the project from Project1 to China. Do that now, by typing the replacement into the File <u>n</u>ame text box. As was the case when you saved the form, don't change anything in the Save as <u>t</u>ype list box. By default, the project file will be saved with a file extension of **.vbp**:

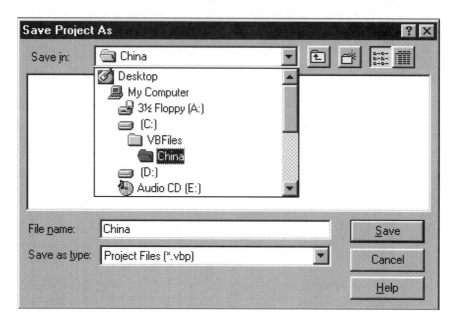

7. Now click on the <u>S</u>ave button to save the project to your directory.

8. The Project Explorer window looks a little different than it did before:

The Project Explorer now shows that the project's Name property is Project1, and its external disk file name is `China.vbp`. The project contains a single form whose Name property is frmMain, and whose external disk file name is `Main.frm`.

9. The final change to the project is to change the project's name to China. Select Project-Project1 Properties from the Visual Basic main menu. Select the General tab and change the Project Name to China:

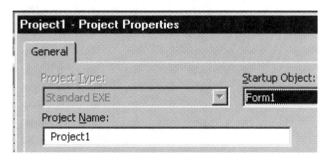

10. Your Project Explorer window should now look like this:

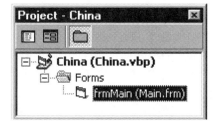

11. Having changed your project's Name property, you now need to save this information to your project file. Click on the Save button on the Toolbar as you did before. This time, because you have already gone through the process of naming and saving both your form and project, Visual Basic saves the changes to your project without prompting you for any information.

Discussion

"Saving projects and forms in Visual Basic the first time," I said, "requires care and attention. Otherwise your project and form end up being saved with meaningless file names such Project1 and

Form1, and saved in the default Visual Basic directory, a place we definitely don't want them. The good news is that once we save the China Shop project and form with the correct names and location, saving them thereafter is a piece of cake."

There had been quite a few problems with this exercise, but most of them were caused by people skipping a step here or there, or being unfamiliar with saving files of any type in Windows. Finally, after a few minutes of walking around the computer lab, I was content that everyone had successfully saved the project and form files.

"I'm a little confused," Valerie said. "I don't remember creating a **Forms** directory, yet one shows up in our Project Explorer window."

I redisplayed the Project Explorer window for the China Shop Project on the classroom projector:

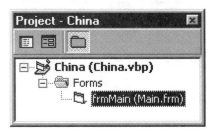

"Oh, I see your confusion," I said. "The word **Forms** in the Project Explorer isn't really a subdirectory, it's the Project Explorer's attempt to categorize the parts of our project. For instance, if we had standard modules in this project, the Project Explorer would show an additional category called **Modules**. If your project window does not display the folder then click the folder icon in the toolbar to make them appear."

I looked for signs of confusion. "Any other questions or comments?" I asked.

"Saving the project the second time around certainly was easier than the first," Ward said. "Is that all there is to it the second time, just click the **Save** icon?"

"That's it," I replied. "That's why it's so important to save the project and form correctly the first time!"

I waited for any additional questions, but there were none.

Running the China Shop Project for the First Time

"OK then," I said, "if there are no more questions, let's run the China Shop Project."

I then asked everyone to click on the Start button on the Toolbar. "That's all we need to do?" Chuck asked. "Just click on the Start button? Shouldn't we compile the program or something?"

"That's a good question, but Visual Basic allows us to quickly test our application within the IDE before we actually compile it. A handy feature, as you will see!" I replied.

"When you start your program," I continued, "a number of things happen in the IDE that let you know that your program is running. First, the caption of Visual Basic's title bar changes; it should display the word [run] somewhere. Secondly, when your program starts to run, the Start button on the Toolbar is dimmed and the Break and End buttons are enabled." Press the End button to return to design mode and finish running the program.

"Finally, the form grid disappears and the form takes on a different look."

"I can see that my program is running," Linda said, "but I wouldn't say it's doing anything. Just about all I can do is minimize, maximize, and close it."

"You can also drag and resize the form, can't you?" I replied. "OK," Linda said, "I'll give you that. Is this its default behavior?"

"Exactly," I said. "That's my point. In a matter of a few minutes, and with a minimum amount of effort, we've designed a working Windows application. Granted, it doesn't do much, but the same application, written in C++ (another programming language) might have taken a week."

"You're kidding," Dave said. "A week to create a program with a single window?"

"Maybe I'm exaggerating a little bit," I said, "but it might take that long the first time round. Nothing is as easy as Visual Basic for rapid development."

I explained that I had an exercise for the class to complete, which would ensure that everyone could find the project and form they had just saved.

In this exercise, you'll exit Visual Basic, so that you can re-load the China Shop Project from your hard drive:

Exercise

Exit and restart Visual Basic and find the China Shop Project

1. Exit Visual Basic by selecting File-Exit from the Visual Basic main menu.

2. Restart Visual Basic.

3. When the New Project dialog box appears, instead of selecting the New tab as we did before, select the Recent tab. This tab displays the list of projects you have recently been working on. The only project listed should be China in its folder, `C:\VBFiles\China`:

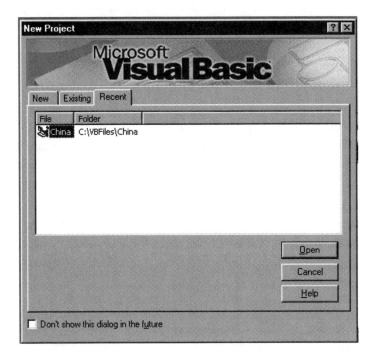

4. Opening the China project is easy. Either double-click on the word China or select it using the mouse and then click the Open button. You don't need to separately load the project and the form, as they will now both appear in the IDE. If your form does not appear then open up the form folder in the project's window and double click on the form icon.

This is also a good place to go to load up the China Shop Project you'll find on the CD. Click on the Existing tab and navigate to the CD drive. The project will be found in \LTP VB6\Chapter...\China Shop, (for Chapter 5 onwards). The project you'll find there is built to the point we got to at the end of the last chapter, ready for the changes you'll make in this one. Of course, it's better to have built your own from scratch, but if anything goes wrong you'll be able to pull out a working project.

Discussion

"This was an exercise that was either going to work or not," I said. "Either you were going to find your China Shop Project listed on the Recent tab, or you wouldn't, in which case, that would mean that something had gone wrong in the save exercise we did before."

Ward immediately had a problem. When he exited Visual Basic, and re-started it, the initial Project dialog box did not appear. After some quick detective work, we discovered that he had mistakenly selected the 'Don't show this dialog in the future' check box the last time he had started Visual Basic. As a result, he was unable to open the China Shop Project in the same way everyone else did.

We found the project by selecting File-Open Project from the Visual Basic main menu. Then we corrected the Option setting that caused the Project dialog box not to be displayed in the first place by selecting Tools-Options-Environment-Prompt for project from the Visual Basic main menu.

I was pleased to find that no one else had any difficulty finding the China Shop Project.

"Successfully saving our project and form in the proper directory," I said, "is simply very important. Now we can move on."

It was time for a well-deserved break. I told everyone that when we returned, we would discuss a few properties of the form, and make changes to the properties of the China Shop form that would begin to shape the look and feel of the program.

"By the way," I said, "next week when we discuss Visual Basic controls and their properties, you'll see that most of the properties we will examine after the break are found in those controls also. That will give us a head start in getting comfortable with the properties of controls."

Properties of the Form

When we returned from break, I told everyone that shortly, they would complete an exercise that would have them changing the properties of the one and only form of the China Shop Project. I displayed the following table on the classroom projector, so that they could have a preview of the changes to come:

Property	Value	Comment
Name	FrmMain	
BorderStyle	1 – Fixed Single	Prevents the user from resizing the form
Caption	The Bullina China Shop	Appears at the top of the form
ControlBox	False	No control box will appear, and neither will minimize, maximize, close or restore buttons
Height	5700	Your value may be different, but don't worry about it
Moveable	False	I don't want the user to move the form
StartUpPosition	2 – Center Screen	Will center form within the screen
Width	8205	Your value may be different, but don't worry about it

"Before we make these changes," I said, "I want to spend a few minutes discussing these properties. Notice that of the approximately fifty or so properties associated with a form, we are only going to change eight."

"Less is best," Linda said. "You took the words right out of my mouth," I replied.

"I thought we already changed the Name property of the form," Dave said. "You're right, Dave," I answered, "but since this table is going to be included in our documentation set, I've included the Name property for completeness. By convention, notice that I've also included the Name property first in the list, and the remaining properties are listed alphabetically."

The Name Property

"I know we've already discussed the Name property," I said, "but I wanted to talk about it a little more formally."

I continued by explaining that the Name property, which I also referred to as the internal name, is the name by which we would refer to the form when we write code that refers to the form.

"We've already changed the default name of the form from Form1 to frmMain," I said. "It is now almost standard practice to name your form and controls according to a convention called **Hungarian Notation,** named after the Hungarian computer scientist Charles Simonyi who developed it."

Naming Conventions

I then distributed a handout with suggestions for naming the common controls that appear in Visual Basic. The first section provided a list of prefixes for all the basic controls that come with Visual Basic:

Control	Prefix
Check Box	Chk
Combo Box	Cbo
Command Button	Cmd
Common Dialog Control	Dlg
Data	Dat
Form	Frm
Frame	Fra
Grid	Grd
Image	Img
Label	Lbl
List Box	Lst
Menu	Mnu
Option Button	Opt
Picture	Pic
Shape	Shp
Text Box	Txt

Timer	Tmr

The second section covered the different variable types used in our Visual Basic code. Although we haven't used these yet, they will come in useful later:

Variable	**Prefix**
Boolean	Bln
Currency	Cur
Double	Dbl
Date & Time	Dat
Long	Lng
Integer	Int
Single	Sng
String	Str
Variant	Var

"In Hungarian Notation," I said, "the name of the object begins with a prefix (usually 3 characters) that describes the object (in our case frm) and the rest of the name should meaningful describe it. For that reason, all of my form names begin with frm. Typically, I give my first form the name Main. Therefore frmMain is the name of the one and only form of the China Shop Project."

"Can a form's Name contain spaces?" Mary asked.

"That's a good question and the answer is no," I replied. "In Visual Basic, the Name property of any object cannot contain spaces. However, remember that the Name property and the external form and project file names are different. In Windows 95 and Windows NT, it is permissible to create a file name with spaces in it. However, the Name property may not have spaces."

The Height and Width Properties

We had previously discussed both the Height and Width properties. They affect the dimensions of the form.

"The values for these properties are displayed in the table as 5700 (about 4") and 8205 (about 5½") respectively," I said. "I want you to feel free to deviate from these exact dimensions if you feel the need. I'm not out to get carbon-copy projects from you all at the end of the course. Those values are just guidelines until you feel comfortable. The important thing is to design your form so that the controls we are going to place on it next week all fit."

The BorderStyle, ControlBox, Moveable Properties

"We're going to change some properties of the form," I said, "that will prevent the user (or the customer) from doing three things:"

- changing the size of the form

- maximizing the form or moving the location of the form

- minimizing or closing the form

Everyone agreed that preventing these actions was important, as we wanted a stable, uniform look to our project. "Fortunately," I told the class, "Visual Basic makes building these safeguards into the program easy. To prevent the user from re-sizing the form, we will set the BorderStyle property of the form to 1 – Fixed Single. To prevent the user from moving the form, we will set the Moveable property to False. However, those Windows Close, Maximize and Minimize buttons are a little more interesting."

I continued by explaining that there are two form properties, MaxButton and MinButton, that can be set to False to prevent the user from maximizing or minimizing the form. And if you try these properties out, you will see that these options are also removed from the Control Box menu. However, we are still left with the Close button.

Another property, the ControlBox property, can also be set to False. This removes the Control Box icon from the form and causes the Maximize, Minimize, and Close buttons to disappear from the form as well. Therefore, if we change the ControlBox property to False, we can take care of all the requirements at the same time.

The StartupPosition Property

"Why didn't you include values for the Left and Top properties?" Blaine asked. "They weren't in the table."

"That's a good point," I said, "but we don't really need to worry about those."

I explained that there's no need to concern ourselves with the location of the form within the screen, because there is a Visual Basic property called StartupPosition, which will center the form right in the middle of the screen. To do this we simply select option 2 - CenterScreen from the list box.

The Caption Property

"Finally," I said, "we'll change the form's caption to display the name of the China Shop by setting the Caption property. This will be displayed in the form's title bar."

I asked if there were any questions and there were none, so I distributed this exercise for the class to complete to make the property changes to the form.

Exercise

Changing the Properties of the China Shop Form

1. Select the form by clicking on it with the mouse.

2. View the Properties window by using one of the four methods discussed in today's class.

3. Find the BorderStyle property in the Properties window, and click once on the value side of the property. A list box will appear offering six possible values for the BorderStyle property. Select 1 - Fixed Single. (Another technique that you can use with a property that contains a list box of multiple values is to double-click on the value side of the window, and the next value in the list will then be displayed. Continue to double-click until the desired value appears.)

4. Change the remainder of the properties according to the table. Remember if you make a mistake, you can just go back and correct the property:

Property	Value	Comment
Name	FrmMain	
BorderStyle	1 – Fixed Single	Prevents the user from resizing the form
Caption	The Bullina China Shop	Appears at the top of the form
ControlBox	False	No control box will appear, and neither will minimize, maximize, close or restore buttons
Height	5700	Your value may be different, but don't worry about it
Moveable	False	I don't want the user to move the form
StartUpPosition	2 – Center Screen	Will center the form within the screen
Width	8205	Your value may be different, but don't worry about it

5. When you have made the remainder of the changes, test the changes that you have made to your project by running the project. Click on the Start button on the Toolbar or select Run-Start from the Visual Basic main menu. Provided Prompt To Save Changes has been selected in Tools-Options-Environment, you should be prompted to save the changes to both the project and form. Answer Yes to the prompt.

6. Verify that the form is centered within the screen when the program begins to run.

7. Verify that there is no ControlBox and no Maximize, Minimize, or Close buttons.

8. Verify that the form cannot be resized.

9. Verify that the form cannot be moved.

10. Verify that the Caption of the form reads The Bullina China Shop.

11. Stop the program by clicking on the End button on the Visual Basic Toolbar.

Discussion

I gave the class about ten minutes to complete this exercise. Everyone agreed that this was the most complicated of our exercises to date, but they also agreed that they felt pretty comfortable doing it and besides, it was fun! Steve remarked that no prompt to save his project had appeared when he ran the program after changing his form properties. A quick trip to his workstation, along with a check of Tools-Options-Environment revealed that Don't Save Changes was selected as a preference for when his project runs.

I must admit that I was glad to see that the students in the class seemed to be pretty pleased with themselves. Although all they had done was change some properties of the form, now they began to see where all of this was leading. Programming is easy, and better yet, they were beginning to realize that it was fun also. They were catching the programming bug!

"It wasn't practical or productive," I said, "to go through each and every property of the form, and explain it in detail. Besides, many of the properties wouldn't mean that much to you now anyway. I recommend you browse through the on-line help or any Visual Basic reference guides you may have and read about some of the other properties of the form and the other objects we will study."

"What's next on the agenda?" Peter asked. "Are we going to start placing objects on the form now?"

"No," I said, "that's for next week. In our closing minutes, I just want to introduce you to Visual Basic methods and events, which form the basis of the code that we will write in the coming weeks."

Visual Basic Methods

"Properties," I said, "are attributes or characteristics of a Visual Basic object. **Methods** are actions that you perform on those objects. If color, number of doors and horsepower are attributes of an automobile, then forward and reverse are methods."

"Methods are used by a programmer to perform an action on an object," I said. "For instance, there is a method called **Move** which can be used to move an object on the screen."

Visual Basic Events

"If we continue with our comparison of Visual Basic objects to automobiles then approaching a red light at a junction could be thought of as an **event**. The ApproachingRedLight event happens to the vehicle and in response it stops," I said.

"The form, and the objects on it, can also recognize and respond to events. An object's type determines the range of events that it can respond to. For instance, a list box is scrollable and has a **Scroll** event. You certainly wouldn't scroll a check box, so check boxes don't have **Scroll** events. Check boxes and list boxes can be clicked on, though, so they both have a **Click** event," I continued.

"For every event that an object can respond to there is an **Event Procedure**. An event procedure is a fragment of code that relates to a particular object and a particular event. You might have a command button called **Command1** that can be clicked on so there would be a '**Command1** gets **Clicked**' event procedure."

"Visual Basic **methods** are placed in these **Event procedures; without them the events would have no way of responding.** Let's go back to our example of the automobile. The ApproachingRedLight event happens but the automobile needs to have a SlowDownAndStop method to be able to respond correctly to this event."

"Who decides what events an object responds to?" Barbara asked.

"Microsoft decided which events an object would be able to respond to when they created the Windows operating system," I said. "For example, most objects in Windows respond to being clicked by the user, but not all. This behavior is a function of the Windows environment."

"So you're saying that to make an object do something," Jack said, "we place code into an event procedure that will be triggered when the user performs an action on the object. The code invokes one of the methods of the object. So, for instance, if we want to move a command button to the bottom of the screen when the user clicks on it, we would code the **Move** method of the command button in the command button's **Click** event."

"That was perfect, Jack," I said. "That's exactly what you would do. Now if this isn't perfectly clear yet for the rest of you, don't worry, it will be soon."

I then started a new Visual Basic project and double-clicked my mouse on the form. This opened up the Visual Basic **Code Window**, which I then displayed on the classroom projector:

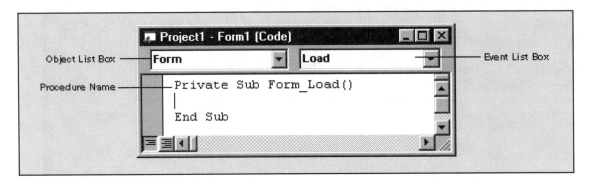

"So that's the code window you've been talking about," Joe said. "Yes, this is the Visual Basic Code Window," I said, "which allows us to place code in an event procedure. As I mentioned, an event procedure is associated with both an object and an event."

I directed everyone's attention to the two list boxes at the top of the code window. "The list box on the left," I said, "is called the **Object List Box**, and the list box on the right is officially known as the **Procedure List Box**, although I prefer to call it the **Event List Box**. The Object List Box contains the name of the form, a general section, plus every control that appears on the form. The Event List Box shows every event that the object selected in the Object List Box can respond to. Notice that the event procedure name is the name of the selected object and the selected event, separated by an underscore (_)."

"What is the line reading **End Sub**?" Joe asked.

"That's the end of the event procedure," I said. "Between that line and the event procedure header is where we place any code that we write for this event procedure."

"How can you see the event procedures for other objects?" Dave asked. "You can display other objects, by clicking on the Object List Box," I said. "At that point, click on the Event List Box and you can display all the events associated with that object."

I clicked on the Event List Box to let everyone see the rest of the events to which the form can respond. The following screen was displayed on the classroom projector:

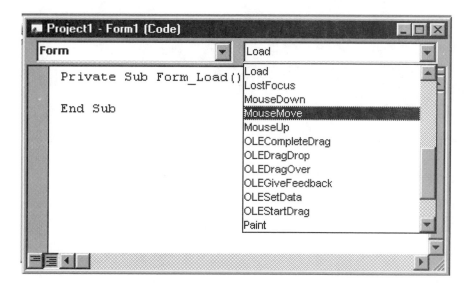

"The form has a number of event procedures," I said, "in which we can place code. As a demonstration, I will place some code in the form's **Click** event procedure."

I found the Click event procedure by scrolling through the list in the Event List Box.

"We'll discuss writing code later in the class," I said. "Right now, I just want to leave you with a feeling of what can be done in code before we finish for the day. I'll demonstrate the Visual Basic **Move** method, which is one of nineteen methods associated with the form. The **Move** method will quickly change the location of the form on the screen."

"Can't we do that by setting the Left and Top properties also?" Valerie asked.

"That's an excellent question," I said. "You're right, you can also move the form by setting the form's Left and Top properties and we'll see in the coming weeks that you can set those properties in code too. This won't be the first time that we'll see that there is a way to achieve the same result by using a method or setting some properties. Given the choice between setting an object's properties, and invoking a method that produces the same result, choose the method. Invoking the method is more efficient, and therefore faster, than setting a property."

I typed some code into the event procedure for the **Click** event of the form, and displayed it on the classroom projector:

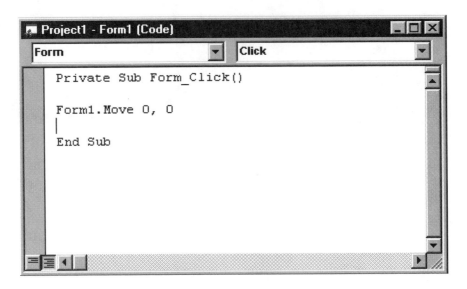

"This code will move the form to the upper left hand corner of the screen when I click on the form," I said. "Do not forget we started a new project to do this and not the China shop project, otherwise it will not work because our form's name in the China project is frmMain not Form1! "

I then ran the program by clicking on the Start button of the Toolbar. When I clicked on the form, the form immediately moved to the upper left-hand corner of the screen.

I waited a few minutes because some of the students had coded this themselves.

"When I entered the code and ran the program," Rhonda said, "the form moved immediately to the upper left-hand corner of the screen and I hadn't even clicked on it."

"Most likely," I said, "that's because you accidentally entered the code into the **Load** event procedure of the form, not the **Click** event. The **Load** event of the form is triggered when the program starts. The **Click** event of the form is triggered when you click on the form. To change it over, just replace the word Load with the word Click in the code."

"Oh, I see, that's what I did," she said. "Now that I got it to work, can you explain what those zeroes mean?"

"Sure," I said, "this line of code:"

```
Form1.Move 0,0
```

"invoked the **Move** event of the form, with the parameters 0,0 which represents the upper left-hand coordinates of the screen."

"Coordinates?" Ward said. "You mean that X and Y stuff in geometry?"

"That's right," I said, "but don't worry, the math in the class doesn't get any more complicated than that."

I assured everyone that we would be discussing methods of the form and controls as they arose during the development of the China Shop project. I asked if there were any questions, but there were none. I told everyone to make sure they had a good night's sleep next Friday night.

"In next week's class," I said, "we'll be completing the China Shop User interface. You'll need to be fresh!"

Summary

In this chapter, you followed my class on a tour of Visual Basic properties and methods. You had your first look at the exercises that will guide you through the China Shop Project.

Along the way, we discussed the default behavior of the Visual Basic form, and at the end of the class, you had a chance to see a Visual Basic method in action.

There are two basic stages to creating a program: designing the user interface, which involves placing controls onto your form and modifying their properties; and writing and checking the code.

Forms and controls are types of **object**. Objects have **properties**, which are characteristics that we can modify, such as their name, or their appearance.

Objects also have **methods**, which are actions that we can perform on them. Methods differ from **events**, which are occurrences that the object will respond to. An **event handler** is a section of code that is executed when an event happens.

When saving a project you first save the forms (using extension .frm), then the project (using the extension .vbp). It's important to remember that forms and projects have two names associated with them; one of these is the name used to refer to it in code (set in

Properties), while the other is its saved name. Don't try to refer to the saved name in code, as it won't be recognized!

The Name property should use Hungarian notation (three letters to indicate the control) and no spaces. Make a habit of this right from the start, because otherwise you'll either have to work with a mix of conventions, or go through and change all your names halfway through (which is dangerous, as it can lead to **orphaned code**).

Quiz

1. What is a Visual Basic property?

2. What is the List Box at the top of the Properties window and what is it for?

3. The Properties window has two tabs that affect the order in which the properties are displayed. What are they called?

4. What property of the form designates a graphic file to display as background for the form?

5. What is the name of the directory in which we save the China Shop Project?

6. Can you name two properties of the form that affect its location within the **Screen** object?

7. Can you name two properties that affect the dimensions of the form?

8. Different objects in Visual Basic share common properties. Can you name one property that every object possesses?

9. What property of the form affects what is displayed in its title bar?

10. What is the property of the form that prevents its Control Box from appearing in the upper left-hand corner of the form?

11. _____ are actions that you can perform on Visual Basic objects.

12. The Visual Basic Code window contains two List Boxes at the top. Can you name them?

13. Can you name one property that can never be changed at run time?

14. How is the **Name** property of a form different than the name specified when the form is saved to disk?

15. Why did we set the **BorderStyle** of the form in the China Shop Project to **1 - Fixed Single**?

16. What function key can be used to bring up the Properties window?

17. How do you turn 'on' the SDI Interface in the IDE?

Extra Credit - How far can a dog run into the woods?

Chapter 5
Building the User Interface

In this chapter, follow my computer class as we complete the interface of the China Shop Project. Along the way, we'll learn more about some of the other Visual Basic controls and their properties.

Completing the User Interface

I began this week by reminding everyone of the tremendous progress we had made during our last class. "In today's class," I told everyone, "we will complete the user interface for the China Shop!"

I reminded everyone that during the design phase of the SDLC, we had developed a sketch of the China Shop Project interface.

"That's not to say that our sketch is the only way we can do it," I said. "In fact, I want to encourage you all to feel free to incorporate some of your own ideas into your program's interface. There are 'many ways to paint a picture'. In designing a Visual Basic interface, don't allow yourself to believe that there is only one 'right' design, or a single 'best' way to code something."

"So are you giving us free reign to deviate from the design sketch?" Linda asked.

"By the end of today's class," I said, "I know we'll design at least one interface that matches the sketch exactly, because that's what I'm going to do. So, if you feel comfortable with the idea, feel free to impart your own style and ideas into the interface, provided that the functionality that we agreed in the design phase remains intact. In other words, you don't have to match the sketch twip for twip. If you want to place a button on the opposite side of the screen, feel free."

The visual aspect of your program is what the user will remember most about your program. It is the most obvious manifestation of your program. It doesn't matter how beautiful, eloquent, or brilliant your program code is; if the user can't interact with the interface you design, then ultimately the program will be considered a failure.

In order to give everyone a perspective on where we were in the development of the China Shop Project, I displayed my 10-step guide for successful Visual Basic development on the classroom projector.

John Smiley's 10-step Guide to Successful Interface Development

1. Develop a Requirements Statement

2. Sketch the user interface on paper

3. Use the Visual Basic IDE to develop the user interface

4. Run the program in Visual Basic

5. Admire your work

6. Observe the default behavior of the interface

7. Modify the interface, if necessary, by changing the properties of the form or controls

8. Run the program in Visual Basic

9. Admire your work

10. Begin coding to enhance the default behavior of the interface

"Looks like we are just about halfway through step 3," Lou said. "That's right," I said, "and we will have completed steps 3 through 9 by the end of today's class."

I took a few moments to emphasize how important it is to work with the default behavior of the Visual Basic forms and controls and to take a steady, measured approach to developing the project. "Even though it seems frivolous," I said, "steps 4, 5, 8 and 9 are crucial to the development of a successful project. You can't have too much positive reinforcement!"

At this point, I asked everyone to start up Visual Basic. It wasn't really necessary, as almost everyone had Visual Basic loaded with the China Shop Project visible in the IDE.

"It's time now," I said, "to take a look at the objects in the Visual Basic Toolbox we will add to our form to complete the user interface. The word Toolbox sounds funny to beginners, but that's exactly what it is. The Toolbox contains controls that we use to build our interface. Remember my analogy of creating a program with building a house. We already have a blueprint for the form (the sketch we created during the design phase of the SDLC), so all we need to do is use the contents of the Toolbox to block out the form in Visual Basic."

I displayed the Visual Basic Toolbox on the classroom projector.

The Visual Basic ToolBox

"This is the Visual Basic default Toolbox," I said.

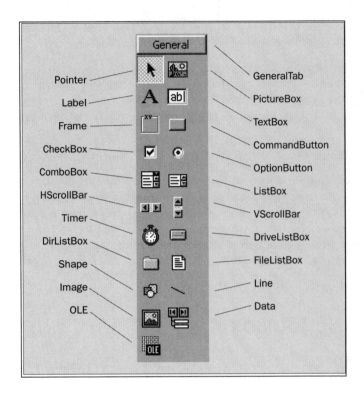

"Why do you call it the default?" Barbara asked. "Well," I said, "this is the appearance of the Toolbox after you first install Visual Basic. It doesn't necessarily look like this each time you see it, because it's possible for you to add other controls to the Visual Basic Toolbox."

"Notice that the Toolbox contains 20 controls," I said, "this excludes the Pointer (the arrow), which is not a control." "I know we've covered this before," Kate said, "but you have used the term control several times. What's the difference between a control and an object?"

"Frequently the terms are used interchangeably, as controls are a type of object. In Visual Basic, a control is an object that you place and position on a form, such as a command button. Most controls contain a visual part, which is drawn on the form. "

"I'm glad you said the word 'most'," Ward said. "During the week, I was experimenting and I placed one of the controls from the Toolbox on a form. When I ran the program, I didn't see it."

"That's right," I agreed. "Most controls are visible when you run your program, but not all. For instance, today we'll place two controls on the China Shop form, the Timer control and the Common Dialog control, which will not be visible when we run the program." I continued by saying that controls have properties, just like the form that we had examined the previous week. These properties affect the appearance and behavior of the controls.

The China Shop Controls

Overview

"Let's take a look at the design sketch for the China Shop interface," I said as I displayed it on the classroom projector:

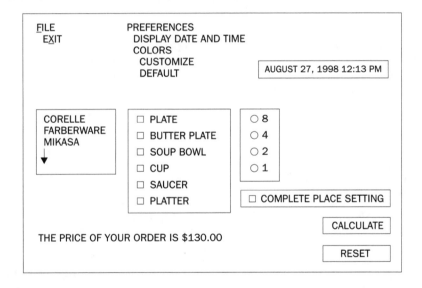

"As you can see, the sketch includes the following Visual Basic components:"

- 1 Form
- 1 Menu
- 1 List Box control
- 2 Label controls
- 2 Command Button controls
- 3 Frame controls
- 4 OptionButton controls
- 7 Check Box controls

"All of the controls that you see on the sketch," I said, "with the exception of the menu, are contained in the default Toolbox. We will also need to add one control, the Common Dialog control, to our Toolbox today in order to complete the interface."

"What about the menu?" Dave asked. "I'm not going to include the menu in the prototype as it doesn't offer any additional core functionality to the application, and core functionality is what the prototype is all about," I replied.

"What is the Common Dialog control used for?" Ward asked. "The Common Dialog control," I said, "displays the standard dialog boxes you see in Windows, such as the Save File dialog box or the Print dialog box. In the China Shop Project, we'll use the Common Dialog control to display the color palette, so that the user can change the color of the form."

"Why isn't the Common Dialog control found in the default Toolbox?" Linda asked. "That's a good question," I said, "and it may be one for Microsoft. Perhaps it's because the Common Dialog control was introduced after the release of the original version of Visual Basic."

"I have a copy of Version 1.0 at home," Lou said, "does that mean I could develop the China Shop project in Version 1.0?"

"Now that's an interesting question," I said. "I can't guarantee it, but I bet you could. Without the Common Dialog control, though, you would have to re-think the method you would use to allow the user to change the color of the China Shop form."

I asked everyone to verify that they had properly retrieved the China Shop Project from the directory on their hard drive, as I distributed this exercise for them to complete (do not forget that if the form does not appear simply open up the form folder in the project window and double click on the form's icon) :

In this exercise, we will add the Common Dialog control to the Visual Basic Toolbox. When you save the China Shop project, the Toolbox setup will also be saved. Therefore, we won't need to do this each time we load the China Shop Project.

If your copy of the China Shop Project has gotten lost or doesn't work, remember that you can load up a 'current' copy of the project (as at the start of the chapter) from the CD. You'll find it in \LTP VB6\Chapter05\China Shop. Note that there aren't separate versions after each exercise, just after each chapter.

Exercise

Add the Common Dialog Control to the Toolbox

1. Select Project-Components from the Visual Basic main menu.

2. Select Microsoft Common Dialog Control from the list of available controls.

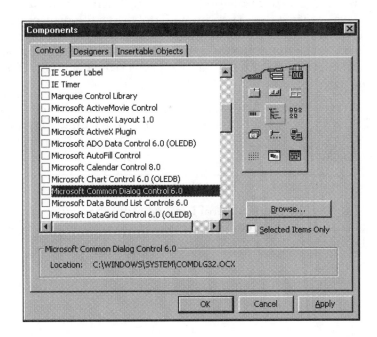

After making sure that the check mark appears next to your new control, click the OK button and the Common Dialog control will be added to your Visual Basic Toolbox.

3. Save the China Shop Project by clicking on the **Save** icon on the Toolbar.

Discussion

"Why did we save the China Shop Project?" Ward asked. "We didn't make any changes to it."

"You're right," I said, "we didn't change the China Shop Project itself. However, by saving the project after we added the Common Dialog control to the Toolbox, we ensured that when we retrieve the project the next time, the icon for the Common Dialog control will still be in the Toolbox."

Linda asked if there was a way to change the contents of the default Toolbox. "For instance," she said, "is there a way to have the Common Dialog control appear in the Toolbox when you start a new project."

I explained that there is. "Create a new project," I said, "then add the Common Dialog control to the Toolbox the way we just did. Then immediately save the project with the name AUTOLOAD in the Visual Basic default directory. Don't forget that when you do that, you'll be prompted to save the form also. Save the file in the default directory as well with the default name of Form1.frm. From then on, when you start a new project, the Common Dialog control will appear in the Toolbox."

"I think it's time," I said, "that we start adding controls from the Toolbox. I think the logical first step is to add the frame controls to the interface of the China Shop Project."

The Frame Control

"The frame control," Blaine said, "isn't that the border we drew on the sketch?"

"That's right," I said, "but the frame control is much more than a border. The frame control is known as a Visual Basic **container control** because it can contain other controls, much as the form contains other controls."

"I'm not sure what you mean by that," Ward said. I explained that experienced programmers like to place controls within frames, because adjusting the properties of the frame will affect all of the controls that are contained within it.

"For instance," I said. "Suppose you place several check boxes within a frame and decide you want to make them all invisible? The check box has a property called `Visible` which, if it's set to `False`, makes it invisible. If you didn't have any frames then, to make all the check boxes invisible, you would need to set all of their `Visible` properties to `False`. However, if all the check boxes are contained within a frame, all you need to do is set the `Visible` property of the frame to `False` to achieve the same result."

Everyone seemed content with that explanation, so I continued by saying that in the China Shop Project we'll use three frame controls; one frame for the china pieces, another for quantity and, finally, one for the Complete Place Setting option.

With no other questions, I distributed this exercise:

In this exercise, we'll add our first control to the China Shop's form. Since the frame control will contain other controls, it makes sense to start our interface design by placing the frame controls identified in our design sketch onto the form first:

Exercise

Adding Frame Controls to the China Shop Form

1. Let's begin by placing the frame that will contain the china pieces on the form. There are two methods to place a control on the form. The first is by double clicking on the frame control icon (that's the one with XY written on a gray square) in the Visual Basic Toolbox. If you are ever unsure what one of the controls in the Toolbox is, just hold your mouse over it and Visual Basic will display ToolTips showing you the name of the control. The other way is to select the frame control icon with one click, then click and drag on the form to draw the frame.

2. After you have double-clicked the frame control, Visual Basic will place it right in the middle of your form, with an arbitrary size. As well as deciding the size for you, Visual Basic has also assigned a name to the control, in this case Frame1, because it is the first frame control placed on the form. Don't worry though, as controls are easy to move once they are on the form by clicking inside the control and dragging. It's also easy to change thedimensions of the control by dragging the size handles that appear along the edges of the control:

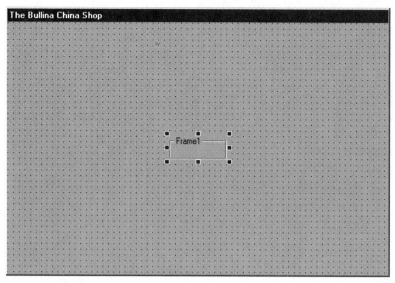

3. Move the frame to the location specified on our design sketch by clicking and dragging on the center of the frame - not the grab handles.

4. Re-size the frame's dimensions according to our design sketch by clicking and dragging on the control's grab handles. When you place your mouse pointer on the grab handles, your mouse pointer will change shape and become a double-headed arrow, as the screen shot below shows:

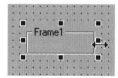

5. Let's use the second technique to add another frame control, for the quantity, to the form. Select the frame control in the Toolbox by clicking on it once. Now position your mouse pointer over the form, at which point it will change shape to 'cross-hairs'. Now click and drag the mouse over the area of the form where you want the control to be placed. As you do so, an outline of the control appears. When the outline is the size that you want, release your mouse button and there it is! Again, notice that a name for the control has been assigned for you, this time **Frame2**, because it is the second frame control placed on the form.

6. The China Shop project requires one last frame control, the one to contain the **Complete Place Setting** option. Use the technique you feel most comfortable with to place the frame control on the form. Your form should look similar to this screen shot:

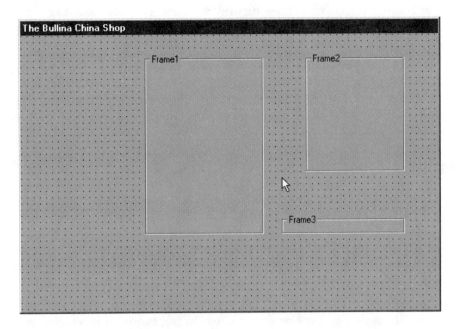

7. Save the China Shop Project by clicking on the **Save** icon on the Toolbar.

Discussion

I took a quick walk around the computer lab, and everyone seemed to being doing fine. I asked members of the class which method of control placement they preferred, and almost universally, they said the double-click method.

"What's your preference?" Linda asked.

"Neither method is right or wrong," I said. "Most beginners feel more comfortable with the double-click method. However, you should practice the alternative method as well, because you'll need to use that when you place controls within the frames we just placed on the form."

I asked if anyone had trouble moving or re-sizing the controls after they had been placed on the form. There were no reports of trouble.

"There's a keyboard alternative to moving and re-sizing the control using a mouse," I said. "You can 'nudge' a control by selecting it with your mouse, then using a combination of the *Ctrl* key plus an arrow key to move it in one direction or another."

"You said you can use the keyboard to re-size controls as well?" Lou asked. "Yes," I said. "Again, select the control with your mouse, then use a combination of the *Shift* key plus an arrow key to either expand or shrink the control." I also pointed out a very important piece of information that if you want to get rid of a control added onto a form then select it and press the *Del* key on the keyboard.

The List Box Control

There were no more questions about the frame control, so we continued by discussing the List Box control. "We'll use the List Box control," I said, "to display the brands of china available for sale in the China Shop. A List Box control eliminates the need for users to type and its inherent functionality means that the user is prevented from making an invalid selection or a spelling mistake. When the user wants to make a selection from the List Box, he or she will click on it with the mouse, resulting in it being highlighted."

"How are items placed in the List Box?" Dave asked. "Items can be placed in the List Box by the programmer either at design time or at run time. In the production version of the China Shop Project, we'll add the items at run time," I replied, "but for speed, we'll add them at design time in the prototype."

"Will we do that by invoking a method?" Barbara asked.

"In the production version, yes," I said. "That's exactly how we'll do it, but we still have some things to learn before we see how that method works."

I continued by explaining that List Box controls occupy a fixed amount of space on the form. Some thought needs to be given in determining how 'high' and how 'wide' to make the List Box. "But it's not really a big deal," I continued. "If the number of items in the List Box exceeds its size, a scrollbar appears automatically which permits the user to scroll through the items in the list. This means that you can use the List Box to display hundreds of items, without using up all of the screen."

"Is there a limit to the number of items you can display?" Joe asked. "Yes," I replied, "but the capacity of the List Box is so large that for almost all purposes it can be considered infinite."

"The size of the list in the List Box is limited to 32KB of data." I added.

"So, how do you decide how big a list box should be?" asked Kate.

"Well," I replied, "initially, we know that there will be only three items in the List Box and none of these items are more than 10 characters in length, so I think we'll be able to display all of them at the same time. And even if the number of items increases later, it will scroll. From a design point of view, I don't recommend making a list box too small, even if it is scrollable. After all, we want the user to be able to see it! For that reason, I always size my list boxes so it displays at least three items."

"To summarize," I said. "Here are some features of the List Box that make it a popular control with the user as well:"

- First, the user does not need to scroll through every item in a list box to make a selection. Although the List Box doesn't accept direct keyboard input, the user can type the first letter of an item in the List Box and it will automatically scroll to the first item beginning with that letter. If the user types that letter again, the List Box scrolls to the next item beginning with that letter and so on. For instance we could have a list box containing the 50 states in the United States. If a user types the letter 'N', 'Nevada' would appear at the top of the list, as it is the first item in the list beginning with 'N'. If the user types 'N' again, then the highlighted entry would change to 'New Jersey', the second item in the list beginning with 'N'.

- Second, the items in a list box can be sorted alphabetically by setting the **Sorted** property to **True**.

There were no other questions, and so I distributed the next exercise:

In this exercise, we'll add a list box to the China Shop's form.

Exercise

Add a List Box Control to the China Shop Form

1. Use one of the two techniques from the previous exercise to place a list box on the form. Be very careful because the list box and the combo box look very similar in the Toolbox. If you are unsure which is which, just hold your mouse over it and Visual Basic will display a ToolTip. Notice that when you place a list box on the form, Visual Basic assigns it the name List1. This name appears as an item in the list box itself. Don't worry about this for the moment as we'll be updating the properties of this control later.

2. Make sure that the list box is in the right place and the right size according to our design sketch, remembering to take into account the contents it will be displaying.

3. Your form should now look similar to this screen shot. Again, don't worry if it doesn't match mine exactly:

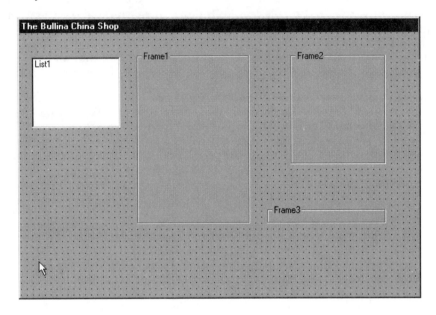

4. Finally, save the China Shop Project by clicking on the **Save** icon on the Toolbar.

Discussion

Again, there were no major problems. A few people had trouble finding the List Box icon and complained that ToolTips were not working, but they just needed to let their mouse pointer linger a little longer over the controls and they appeared. Another student had re-sized his Toolbox, so that only a few controls were displayed. We corrected this problem very easily by expanding the Toolbox as we would a normal window.

The Label Control

"We'll use the Label control to display information to the user," I said, "as there is no way for the user to change the information displayed in one."

We reviewed the sketch of the China Shop interface and determined that we would need two labels: one to display the date and time, and another to display the actual sales quotation.

"How does the information get into a label?" Barbara asked. "The label control," I said, "contains a property called **Caption** which determines what is displayed in the label. Like most properties, that property can be set either at design time or at run time."

With no other questions, I distributed this exercise:

In this exercise, we'll add two labels to the China Shop's form:

Exercise

Adding Label Controls to the China Shop Form

1. Place two labels on the form, using our sketch as a guideline for their location and dimensions. The first label needs to be placed in the upper right-hand corner of the form to display the date and time. The second label needs to be placed in the bottom portion of the form to display the sales quotation. Notice that Visual Basic assigns the names of **Label1** and **Label2** to these controls.

2. Your form should look similar to this screen shot:

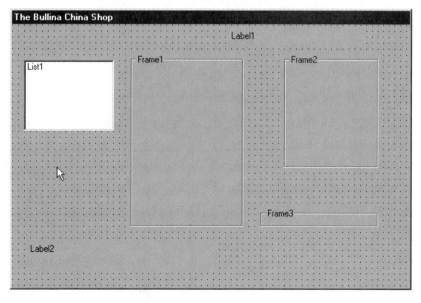

3. Don't forget to save the China Shop Project by clicking on the **Save** icon on the Toolbar.

The Command Button Control

"What's next?" Dave asked. "I'm enjoying this."

I suggested that we place the command buttons on the form next. "You sometimes hear command button called Button controls," I said. "Command buttons are used to initiate some sort of action and because of that, there's usually lots of code in their `Click` event procedure."

I pointed out that when a user clicks on a command button, it changes appearance slightly and appears to have been pressed down. When the user releases the mouse button, the command button reverts back to its normal appearance. "I notice that the command button also displays text," Rhonda said. "Does that mean it has a `Caption` property?"

"Yes, it does," I replied.

I told everyone that by the end of today's class, we would adjust several command button properties. "The `Caption` property will be one," I said, "and the `Default` property the other. If the `Default`

property of the command button is set to `True`, then when the user presses the *Enter* key, Visual Basic treats it the same as if they clicked on the command button. Another property, the `Cancel` property, works in a similar way except it uses the *Esc* key."

Once again we reviewed the sketch of our interface, and determined that we would need two command buttons: one captioned Calculate and the other Reset. We had a little bit of discussion concerning the `Default` and `Cancel` properties and finally decided that if the user presses the *Enter* key, it should be equivalent to clicking on the Calculate button. We also agreed that if the user presses the *Esc* key, it should be equivalent to clicking on the Reset button. I promised that we would make the appropriate property changes before the end of today's class.

With no other questions, I distributed this exercise:

In this exercise, we'll add two command buttons to the China Shop's form:

Exercise

Adding Command Buttons to the China Shop Form

1. Place two Command Button controls on the form, using our sketch as a guideline for their location and dimensions. As has been the case with the other controls we've placed on the form, Visual Basic assigns the names of the controls for us, in this case, Command1 and Command2.

2. Your form should now look similar to this screen shot:

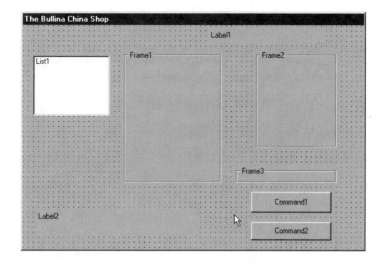

3. Save the China Shop Project by clicking on the Save icon on the Toolbar.

The Check Box Control

I suggested that we next work on the Check Box control. "I've been experimenting with this control a little bit," Ward said, "and it really confuses me."

I explained that I didn't think it was the Check Box control itself that is confusing so much as how check boxes work in unison. "The Check Box control," I said, "allows the user to give a True/False, Yes/No or On/Off answer. The check box will either display a check mark or not. If it does, that indicates a True, Yes or On answer. Without a mark that indicates a False, No or Off answer."

I continued by saying that in Visual Basic terms, when there is a check mark, the control's **Value** property is set to **1**, otherwise it is set to **0**.

"So when the user clicks on a check box," Linda said, " the check mark appears. If they click on it again, the check mark disappears?"

"That's right," I replied, "I call it a **toggle** control. Click it once and it's on. Click it again and it's off."

"What about multiple check boxes?" Dave asked. "Do I remember hearing or seeing something about not being able to select more than one?"

"No," I replied. "That's the option button and we'll be examining that in a moment. Any number of check box controls can be selected at one time." As an example, I displayed a check box group containing four categories of sports on the classroom projector:

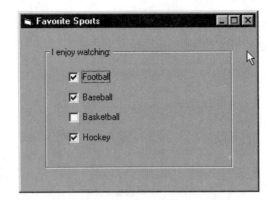

"As you can see," I said, "three of the check boxes are selected." I continued by saying that I thought the check box control was also an ideal way for the customer to select china pieces in the China Shop Project. The customer will need to make six separate Yes/No decisions about pieces. If the customer wants to include an item of china in the price quotation, all he or she needs to do is click on the check box and it will be selected and our program will then know that they've answered 'Yes' to that china item. If the customer changes his or her mind, clicking on the check box again will de-select that item.

"How will our program know that there's a check mark in the check box?" Bob asked. "Later on," I said, "when we start writing code, we'll see that we can examine properties of Visual Basic controls while the program is running. All we'll need to do is examine the **value** property of the check box."

"We have quite a few check boxes," Kate said, "so how will the program know which check box we are examining?"

"Good question," I said. "We'll need to identify that to Visual Basic by specifying the **Name** property of the check box."

I then explained that we were going to place the check box indicating a Complete Place Setting on the form first. The other sets of check boxes were made up of something called a **control array** and I wanted to explain those first before we set them up.

I also cautioned everyone that they were about to see one of the few 'picky' attributes of Visual Basic. Whenever you place a control inside a container control, such as a Frame, you absolutely must use the click and drag technique for control placement, as the double-click method doesn't work.

In this exercise, we'll add one check box to the China Shop's form:

Exercise

Adding a Check Box to the China Shop Form

1. Place a Check Box control on the form within **Frame3**, sizing it roughly according to the screenshot below. It's important that you do not use the double-click method here, because the check box must be explicitly drawn within the frame. You should notice that Visual Basic has automatically given the check box a name of **Check1**, but the name **Check1** will only appear if you draw the control large enough:

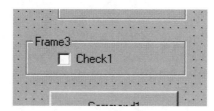

2. It is vitally important that the check box is contained within the frame. To verify this, select the frame and drag it. If it is contained within the frame, the check box will move with it.

3. Save the China Shop Project by clicking on the **Save** icon.

Discussion

I took a quick look around the computer lab to see how everyone was doing. Since most of the students had been double-clicking controls onto the form in the previous exercises, they were a bit unsure using the select-position-draw technique. All in all though, they were doing fine.

"That technique for ensuring that the check box is within the frame is a life saver," Linda said. "I was certain that I had placed it within the frame, but when I moved the frame, the check box didn't move at all!"

I agreed. Whenever you're working with container controls, such as the frame, it's important to make sure that any controls you place within the container control are really in there.

"I wanted to let everyone know," Dave said, "that just for the heck of it, I set the frame's **Visible** property to **False** and not only did the frame disappear when I ran the program, so did the check box. Just the way you said it would."

I knew that our next topic, control arrays, would require the utmost in concentration and so I called for a break.

Control Arrays

After a few minutes we all assembled once more in the computer lab.

"Our next topic is control arrays," I said. "Up until now, every control that you've placed on the China Shop form has had a name of its own and even its very own set of event procedures. Now, we're about to create our first control array."

I continued by explaining that a control array is like a family of controls. When you start a control array, the first control has properties just like an ordinary control. Thereafter, when you add another member to the control array, the new control is created with properties identical to the first one, including the **Name** property. Only one property is different: the **Index** property.

"So in other words," Ward said, "in keeping with the family analogy, all the controls share the same last name, the **Name** property, but have different first names, the **Index** property."

"Ward," I said, "that's a really good explanation."

"What are the advantages of a control array?" Jack said.

"Good question," I said. "The bottom line is that it makes coding much easier. In a control array there is only one set of event procedures that are triggered for all of the members. Remember that an event procedure is executed whenever an event occurs on an object. For example, check boxes respond to being clicked, so when a check box is clicked, its **Click** event triggered. If we have six check boxes representing items and we want to react to the user clicking on each one of them, we need to write code and place it in the **Click** events of all six check boxes."

"Unless," Rose said, "we create the six check boxes as members of a control array, in which case there is only one **Click** event for the entire control array, right?"

"That's perfect, Rose," I said.

I could see that some of the students were still confused. "If there is only one **Click** event procedure for all of those check boxes," Barbara said. "How does our code know which check box has been clicked?"

"By the property that uniquely identifies the member of the control array, does anyone remember what that is?" I said. "The **Index** property," Ward said.

"Very good," I said. "You're absolutely right. Event procedures in a control array are 'aware' of the **Index** property of the member that triggered the event. Using this **Index** property, our code knows which control in the control array triggered the event."

I started to see a little more confidence. "In addition to establishing our check boxes for china items as a control array," I continued, "our option buttons will also form a control array."

"So you can have a control array of any kind of control," Lou said. "That's right," I agreed.

"How is a control array created?" Dave asked.

"The easiest way," I said, "is to place the first member of the control array on the form and select it using your mouse. Select <u>C</u>opy from the Visual Basic <u>E</u>dit menu and then <u>P</u>aste from the same menu. You will then be asked if you wish to create a control array."

At that point, I distributed the following exercise:

In this exercise, we'll place six check box controls on the China Shop's form. This time, however, all six will be members of one control array:

Exercise

Adding a Check Box Control Array

1. Select the Check Box control in the Toolbox and carefully draw it within **Frame1**. Visual Basic will automatically assign it the name, **Check2**. Make sure that you resize it so that you can fit five others within the frame as well.

2. Now we need to add another check box control to **Frame1**, however, this time we won't use the Toolbox. Since we want to create a control array based on the check box already on the form, we can just copy and paste **Check2** instead. Select the **Check2** by clicking on it with your mouse and then select <u>C</u>opy from the <u>E</u>dit menu.

3. This step is extremely important. Select the frame by clicking on one of its borders with your mouse. If you do not properly select the frame, then the second check box will not be contained within the frame.

4. Now select <u>P</u>aste from the <u>E</u>dit menu. You should see the following message:

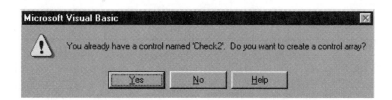

5. Answer <u>Y</u>es and a second check box will be placed within the frame control. Notice how it is also named Check2. You'll need to reposition it, as Visual Basic just places it in the upper left-hand corner of the frame. You should be aware that you don't need to test the frame's containment of the check box as Visual Basic handles that for you when you are creating a control array.

6. Now we need to add the third check box to **Frame1**. This process will be slightly different from placing the second check box since the control array now exists. Therefore, you will not be prompted with the message box again. As you did in step 3, select **Frame1**. Now select <u>E</u>dit-<u>P</u>aste. (You don't need to specify <u>E</u>dit-<u>C</u>opy because a copy of the control is already in the Windows clipboard.) Immediately, Visual Basic will place the third check box into the frame.

7. Add the remaining three check boxes to the frame using the same technique. When you are finished, your form should look similar to this screenshot:

8. Save the China Shop Project.

You can also right-click your mouse to bring up a shortcut menu for Copy and Paste.

Discussion

"I just wanted to comment," Dave said, "that the **Index** properties of the check box controls we just placed within the frame are numbered from 0 to 5."

"Good observation," I said. "The **Index** property is the only property of the check boxes that will be different. As Ward said earlier, the **Index** property is like the first name."

There were no other questions, so we moved on to the OptionButton control.

The OptionButton Control

"Like the Check Box control," I said, "the OptionButton control allows the user to give a True/False, a Yes/No or an On/Off answer. Option buttons are sometimes called 'radio' buttons because they mimic the behavior of old radios, where you pushed a button to select a channel. On a radio with five buttons, one button was always selected, but never more than one."

"The option button is displayed on a form with a caption and a circle next to it, and it is selected when the user clicks their mouse on it. Once selected, the option button displays a small, black circle in it. The difference between an option button and a check box is their group behavior. The user can select **only one** option button in any one group, whereas we saw previously, the user can select any number of check boxes."

"I'm not really certain what you mean by a group," Rhonda said.

"A check box or an option button group," I said, "is a set of check boxes or option buttons bounded by a container, such as a form or a frame. If you have three option buttons in a frame, then there is just one group of option buttons and the user may select only one of them. However, if you have six option buttons on a form where three are contained in Frame1 and three are in Frame2, you have two option button groups."

"That means," Ward asked, "that the user can select one option button within Frame1 and one option button within Frame2?"

"That's right," I said as I displayed the following example on the classroom projector:

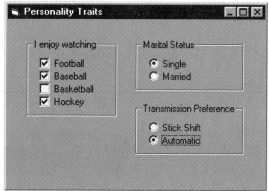

"Here we have a form with three frames," I continued, "with two option button groups and one check box group. Notice the difference in the behavior of the check boxes and the option buttons; more than one check box can be selected at the same time, but only one option button can be selected."

I said that I thought the OptionButton control was a perfect way for the user to specify a quantity selection in the China Shop project. The customer may only select a single quantity selection from four possible values.

"Does the OptionButton have a **value** property," Linda asked, "like the Check Box control?"

"Good question," I said. "Yes it does, but instead of being set to 1 when selected and 0 when deselected, the OptionButton **value** property is set to **True** when selected and **False** when deselected."

As I distributed this exercise, I told everyone that the option buttons we placed on the China Shop form would also be members of a control array:

In this exercise, we'll place four option buttons on the China Shop's form, all of which will be members of one single control array:

Exercise

Adding an OptionButton Control Array

1. We'll start by placing an ordinary OptionButton control in Frame2. As before, please be very careful how you place it within the frame. Visual Basic will automatically name it Option1, which we'll change later. Make sure that you re-size it so that you can fit three others within the frame as well. If you need to re-size the frame control, do that now as well.

2. Now we need to place a second option button in Frame2. Copy and paste the option button already on the form, just as we did with the check boxes. This will alert Visual Basic that we want to create a control array based on that option button.

3. When you select Edit-Paste from the Visual Basic menu, you should see the following message:

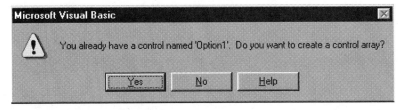

4. Answer Yes and the second option button will be placed in the frame. Notice how it is also named Option1. You'll need to reposition the new control, as Visual Basic just places it in the upper left-hand corner of the frame.

5. Now for the third option button. Select the frame, then select Edit-Paste. (Again, you don't need to specify Edit-Copy because a copy of the control is already in the Windows clipboard.) Immediately, Visual Basic will place the third option button in the frame as part of the control array.

6. Add the final control to the frame using the same technique as in step 5. When you've finished, your form should look similar to this:

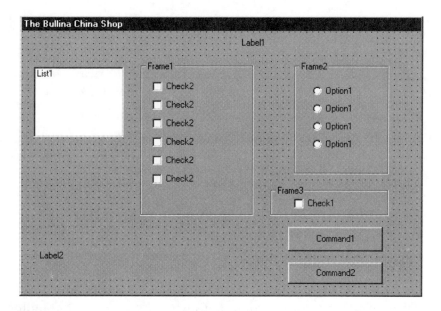

7. Finally, save the China Shop Project.

Discussion

We had been doing pretty well, but quite a few students failed to hit the mark with this exercise. As sharp as they had been at placing check boxes in the frame and properly creating a control array, it was just the opposite here. Several students totally failed to follow the instructions on creating the control array of option buttons and for whatever reason just placed four controls directly from the Toolbox onto the form.

As you can imagine, this took some time to straighten out. However, as I always say, true learning sometimes comes at the expense of frustration. Everyone who had problems understood where they had gone wrong and they were now pretty confident.

Dave again commented on the **Index** properties of the control array, this time noting that the **Index** properties of the option button were numbered from 0 to 3.

"What should we do now?" I asked. "Take a break," Linda said smiling.

"That's not quite what I was thinking of," I said, "Although that is a good idea. Better yet, take a moment and admire your work. You're all doing very well and this interface is shaping up quite nicely. In fact, it won't be long before we are finished."

I told everyone to take a well-earned break. "When you return," I said, "I'll have a surprise for you."

The Image Control

When everyone returned from their break, I told them that I had really wanted to give them a chance to work with either an Image control or Picture Box control, but nothing in our initial interface design had warranted using one.

"However, during the week," I said, "I called Mr. Bullina and ran this idea by him. I told him that I thought it would be a great idea to display a picture of the china pattern as the customer made their brand selection."

This elicited quite a positive response from everyone in the classroom and we quickly decided to add this feature to our interface. "Which control will we be using, the Picture Box or the Image?" Barbara asked.

"Let's discuss that," I replied. "The function of both controls is to display some kind of graphic file."

"What kinds of graphic files?" Dave asked.

I pulled out my Visual Basic reference manual to double check.

"Graphic sources include bitmaps, icons, or metafiles, as well as enhanced metafiles, JPEG, or GIF files. These terms may not mean much to you at the moment but these cover just about every kind of graphic you might want to put into a project," I said.

I warned everyone that my programming abilities far outweighed my artistic ones, but I assured them that in the right hands, Visual Basic is capable of displaying outstanding and powerful graphics.

"There must be something different about the two controls," Ward said, "otherwise there wouldn't be two different controls to display graphics."

"You're right," I replied. "They are different. The Image control is considered a **lightweight** Visual Basic control, whereas the Picture Box control is very much a **heavyweight**. Do you remember our discussion of Window Handles? The Image control is not assigned one, whereas the Picture Box is. In theory, Windows has less work to do when working with an Image control than it does with a Picture Box."

"Give us the bottom line then," Linda said. "What is the advantage of one over the other?"

"When all you need to do is display an image," I said, "then use the Image control. It actually displays graphics faster than a Picture Box. However, there are times you may want to use the Picture Box, because it can do so much more."

"Such as?" Dave asked.

"The Picture Box reacts to three times as many events as the Image control and it can also act as a container control, just like the frame. The Picture Box also has a method called `Print`, which allows you to print the text and graphics held within it."

Considering that all we wanted to do was display a pattern of china, we agreed that the Image control was the correct one to use, so I distributed this exercise:

Exercise

Add an Image Control to the China Shop Form

1. Place an Image control on the form. Since this control did not appear on our original sketch, my suggestion is to place it somewhere under the list box. Unlike the other controls you've placed on the form, there will be no obvious hint as to what Visual Basic has named the control. However, if you check out the control's properties, you'll see that it has been named Image1.

2. Your form should look similar to this screenshot. Again, it doesn't have to match mine exactly:

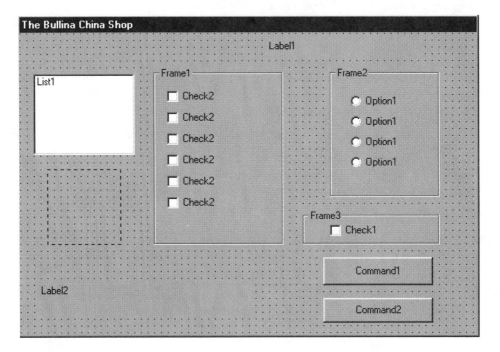

3. Save the China Shop Project.

Discussion

The class did not have any problems with the exercise, nor were there any questions.

"Only two more controls," I said, "and we're done placing controls on the form."

The Common Dialog Control

"The next two controls," I said, "the Common Dialog control and the Timer control, are invisible to the user at run time. However, they are both vitally important to the operation of the China Shop program. We will need to include the Common Dialog control to allow the user to change their preferred colors, while the Timer control is used in order to display the date and time."

I reminded everyone that earlier, we had spent some time adding the Common Dialog control to our Toolbox. I polled the class to ensure that it was still in their Toolboxes and I was glad to find out that everyone still did.

"Great," I said, "let's add the Common Dialog control to the form then. Remember, this control is visible at design time, but invisible at run time."

I distributed this exercise:

Exercise

Adding a Common Dialog Control

1. Add a Common Dialog control to the form. Since the Common Dialog control is invisible at run time, its placement is not very important but you can use the screen shot below as your guide. Visual Basic has named the control CommonDialog1 although there is no obvious clue on the form:

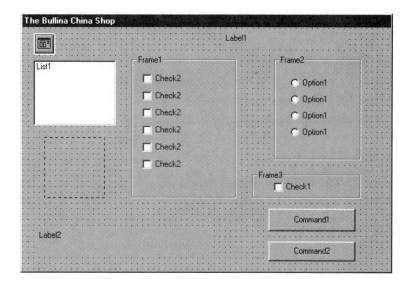

2.   Save the China Shop Project.

The Timer Control

There were no problems placing the Common Dialog control on the form, so we moved immediately to the Timer control.

"Just like the Common Dialog control," I said, "the Timer control is invisible at run time. The Timer control is used to execute code placed in its **Timer** event procedure, at regular intervals, according to the value of its **Interval** property. The **Interval** property determines how often the **Timer** event procedure is triggered, anywhere between 1 millisecond to 64 seconds. The **Interval** property value is expressed in milliseconds, so that a value of 1000 is equal to 1 second. If you wanted to trigger the **Timer** event every tenth of a second, you would set the **Interval** property equal to 100."

I looked for signs of confusion, but there were none. They obviously remembered our earlier lessons. I continued by saying that the uses for the Timer control are virtually limitless. It's a control that is very popular with programmers who write game programs. "In the China Shop Project," I said, "we'll use the Timer control to display a running display of the date and time."

"What do you mean by a running display?" Peter asked.

"I mean a date and time that continuously changes," I said. "Eventually, we'll place code in the **Timer** event procedure to display the date and time. Because the **Timer** event procedure will trigger every second, the minutes and seconds on the display will appear to continuously change."

There were no more questions, and so I distributed this exercise:

Exercise

Adding a Timer Control

1.   Add a Timer control to the form. Since it's invisible at run time, its placement is not crucial. My advice is to place it adjacent to the Common Dialog control. Visual Basic has named it Timer1, although this is not obvious from the form.

2.   Your form should now look similar to this screen:

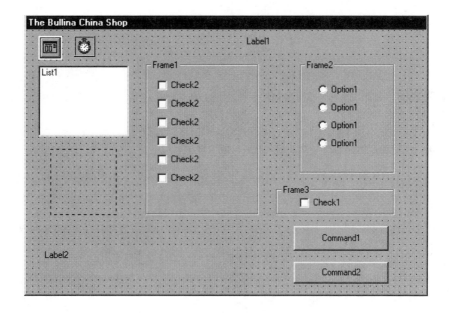

3.   Click on the Save icon on the Toolbar to save the project.

Discussion

"Congratulations," I said, "You've completed the China Shop interface. You definitely deserve a pat on the back and a well-earned break. But we're not done yet!"

I reminded everyone of my 10 steps for successful Visual Basic development, which we had looked at earlier in the class. So far, we had completed the first three steps. We had developed a Requirements Statement and sketched the user interface during our second class meeting. Now we had just completed step 3, which is to use the Visual Basic IDE to develop the user interface. Now it was time for steps 4, 5 and 6. These are to run the program, admire our work, and observe the default behavior of the interface.

Let's Tour the China Shop!

"There's quite a bit of life in this program already," I explained. "Even though we haven't coded anything yet, the form and the controls on it come complete with a lot of built-in behavior. I have an exercise here for you which will ask you to run the program, and observe the default behavior of the controls. Then after that, we will begin to adjust some of the properties of the interface."

Exercise

Let's Run the China Shop Project

1. Test the changes that you have made by running the project. Click on the Start button on the Toolbar or select Run-Start from the main menu.

2. Let's take some time now to examine the China Shop program in action. Visual Basic gives you some clues that you are now in the run time environment. Firstly, notice that the dots in the form grid have disappeared. Secondly, if you look on the Toolbar, you'll notice that the Start button has been disabled, but the Break and End buttons are now active. Finally, notice that the IDE's title bar now says [run] instead of [design].

3. Notice that the list box is now empty. The name of the control, which appears as an item in the design time environment, has now disappeared.

4. Click on the check box in Frame3. When you first click on it, a check mark appears, but if you click again, it disappears. Notice also that you can click on the caption of a check box to select it as well as the check box itself.

5. Click on several of the check boxes in Frame1. Notice that any number of them can be selected.

6. Click on the option buttons in Frame2. Notice that when the form is first displayed, none of them are selected, but as soon as you click on one, it becomes selected. Click on another and it becomes selected, deselecting the previous one as it goes. You should be aware that once an option button that is part of a group has been selected, there is no way to deselect all of them. As with the check boxes, you can also click on an option button's caption to select it.

7. Click on the command buttons. Notice that when you click on either one of the buttons, it appears pressed. When you release the mouse button, it reverts back.

8. Stop the program by clicking on the End button on the Visual Basic Toolbar.

Discussion

Everyone seemed to be admiring their work, and of course, the default behavior of the form and the controls on it. There were no questions about the exercise. Just about everyone expressed some surprise as to how functional the program was already, even Lou, who earlier in the class had been skeptical about default behavior.

I asked if anyone thought there were any changes that needed to be made to their interfaces. Barbara reminded us that we still needed to develop the menu. "That's right," I said, "but, as we have discussed before, that isn't part of the core project functionality, so I'm not going to include it in the prototype. Anything else?"

There were no other suggestions.

"In that case," I said, "I'd like to suggest that we have now completed the first six steps of my 10-step plan for successfully developing a project in Visual Basic. It's time to discuss and complete step 7, which is modifying the interface, by changing the properties of the form or controls. But first, we need to take a break."

Common Properties of the Controls

"OK," I said after we all returned, "it's time to start adjusting some of those properties I was referring to earlier as we placed our controls on the form. Before we start changing properties, though, I think we should discuss them a bit first. Let's begin our discussion by looking at the properties that every control in the China Shop Project possesses. Then we'll look at the unique properties of each control. Let's start now with the most basic of properties, the **Name** property."

Name

"Every object in Visual Basic has a **Name** property," I said. "The **Name** property is the way that Visual Basic identifies an object."

"I know we've gone over this before," Rhonda said, "but the **Name** property is not the same name we specify when we save the project, is it?"

"No, it's not," I said. "In Visual Basic, the **Name** property is the internal name by which Visual Basic identifies every object in your program. When you save your Visual Basic program, you are saving both a project and any forms that you have created, as external disk files on your hard drive. Those names, although they may be the same as the project or form's **Name** property, are not related."

I cautioned everyone never to change the name of a control after writing code for any of the control's event procedures. "If you do that," I said, "you'll **orphan** the code, as I call it, and what that means for a beginner is that your code will appear to have been lost, although there is a way to find it by scrolling through the code window."

"Are there any rules for naming the **Name** property?" Bob asked.

"Yes, there are," I said. "The **Name** property can be up to 40 characters. It must start with a letter. It can contain letters, numbers and the underline character, but it may not contain any other punctuation characters, for example spaces."

I also reminded everyone about the Hungarian notation I had mentioned last week. "Hungarian notation," I said, "suggests that each control be named with a three character prefix that describes the object type, followed by a reasonable description of the object. That's why we set the **Name** property of our China Shop form to **frmMain**. We'll be naming our other controls in the same way."

There were no more questions about the **Name** property, and so we moved on to the **Caption** property.

Caption

"Just about every control in the China Shop project has a **Caption** property," I said. "The form, check box, command button, frame, label, menu and option button all have a **Caption** property. The **Caption** property identifies the object to the user of your program by showing some text on the form to identify it."

The label's caption size is unlimited. For all other controls that have captions, the limit is 255 characters.

"Some students get the **Name** and **Caption** properties confused," I said. "The **Name** property is used to define the object to the program and uses Hungarian notation. The **Caption** property, on the other hand, is used to define the object to the user and has no functional value, " I explained.

I displayed the design time China Shop form on the classroom projector and noted the default captions that were currently being displayed. I also indicated that shortly we would be changing these captions to make them more descriptive.

"As you can see," I said, "each object's caption is displayed in a slightly different way. For instance, the form's caption is displayed in the title bar, whereas the command button's caption is displayed right in the middle of the button."

I reminded everyone that in our second class meeting, we had discussed the concept of a hot key or access key for controls. "You can create an access key for a control," I said, "using a special feature of the `Caption` property. All you need to do is place an ampersand (&) character immediately before the character you wish to identify as the hot key. For instance, to assign the letter O in the caption OK of a command button, you would enter &OK into the `Caption` property. Be careful, however, not to assign the same hot key to more than one control on the same form."

Index

"Every control in the China Shop Project," I said, "has an `Index` property. That's because every object can be a member of a control array. In a control array each member has a unique `Index` property."

"What's the `Index` property for a control that is not a member of a control array?" Kate asked. "Is it zero?"

"No," I replied. "Zero actually identifies the first member of a control array. If the control is not a member of a control array, then the `Index` property is blank."

"I'm glad you told me that," she said, "I thought I should go through all the controls and change the `Index` property to 0."

"Goodness no," I said, "if you do that you'll tell Visual Basic that the control is a member of a control array!"

Dave said, "I was just about to comment that when we created our control arrays for the China Shop Project, the `Index` property of the first member of the control array was automatically assigned a value of 0, the second was 1, etc."

"That's right," I noted. "Visual Basic will assign the `Index` property for you automatically, starting with 0 and working its way up to 32,767. You can change the value if it makes sense for you to do so.

In fact, we're going to do just that for our option button control array, by changing the `Index` property so that it's equal to the quantity the button represents."

ToolTipText

"All controls used in the China Shop Project except the Common Dialog and Timer controls have a `ToolTipText` property," I said. "If you've used Windows 95, Windows 98 or Windows NT for any length of time, you are probably familiar with ToolTips, which are the hints that you receive when you place your mouse over a control."

"Will we be creating ToolTips in the China Shop project?" Mary asked.

"I thought it would be a good idea," I replied. "I don't think you can be too user friendly. Besides, all you need to do is type an entry into the `ToolTipText` property of the control and they're implemented for you automatically."

"`ToolTipText` has nothing to do with those dreaded help files you mentioned, does it?" Bob asked.

"No," I said. "Help files need to be created and compiled using a Help compiler. Enabling ToolTips is just a matter of placing a message in the `ToolTipText` property of the control."

I suggested that at this point, we had exhausted the coverage of the common properties. From here on out, the properties of the controls would be pretty much unique.

Check Box Properties

"There may be some check box properties that will come up later when we discuss coding," I said, "but from a user interface point of view, there are no unique properties of the check box that we need to discuss. For that reason, I'm going to ask you to complete this exercise."

Prior to starting this exercise, it would be a good idea to lock your controls so that you don't accidentally move them out of their location. To do this, select Format-Lock Controls from the Visual Basic menu.

In this exercise, you'll change selected properties for the seven check boxes on the China Shop form:

Exercise

Changing the Properties of the Check Box Controls

1. Bring up the Properties window, by selecting the control and pressing F4.

2. Use the following table to make changes to the check box currently named Check1, which appears inside Frame3:

Property	Value	Comment
Name	ChkCompletePlaceSetting	Hungarian notation
Caption	Complete Place Setting	Provides an identifying caption for the check box
ToolTipText	Check to Select a Complete Place Setting	Provides a ToolTip for this control

3. Use the following table to make changes to the first check box inside Frame1. Don't forget that all the controls in this frame will have the same Name, but different Index properties:

Property	Value	Comment
Name	ChkChinaItem	Hungarian notation

Caption	Plate	Provides an identifying caption for the check box
Index	0	Should already be the value of the property. If not, change it.
ToolTipText	Check to Select a Plate	Provides a ToolTip for this control

4. Use the following table to make changes to the second check box in the frame designated for china items:

Property	Value	Comment
Name	ChkChinaItem	Hungarian notation
Caption	Butter Plate	Provides an identifying caption for the check box
Index	1	Should already be the value of the property. If not, change it.
ToolTipText	Check to Select a Butter Plate	Provides a ToolTip for this control

5. Use the following table to make changes to the third check box:

Property	Value	Comment
Name	ChkChinaItem	Hungarian notation
Caption	Soup Bowl	Provides an identifying caption for the check box
Index	2	Should already be the value of the property. If not, change it.
ToolTipText	Check to Select a Soup Bowl	Provides a ToolTip for this control

6. Use the following table to make changes to the fourth check box:

Property	Value	Comment
Name	ChkChinaItem	Hungarian notation
Caption	Cup	Provides an identifying caption for the check box
Index	3	Should already be the value of the property. If not, change it.
ToolTipText	Check to Select a Cup	Provides a ToolTip for this control

7.   Use the following table to make changes to the fifth check box:

Property	Value	Comment
Name	ChkChinaItem	Hungarian notation
Caption	Saucer	Provides an identifying caption for the check box
Index	4	Should already be the value of the property. If not, change it.
ToolTipText	Check to Select a Saucer	Provides a ToolTip for this control

8.   Use the following table to make changes to the sixth and final check box:

Property	Value	Comment
Name	ChkChinaItem	Hungarian notation
Caption	Platter	Provides an identifying caption for the check box

| Index | 5 | Should already be the value of the property. If not, change it. |
| ToolTipText | Check to Select a Platter. Sorry, only one to a Sales Quotation | Provides a ToolTip for this control |

9.   Save the China Shop Project.

10. Run the program and pay particular attention to the captions of the controls. Also, check to ensure that the ToolTips are displaying properly. Here's a run-time screen shot of how the China Shop form should look with the changes you've made to your Check Box controls:

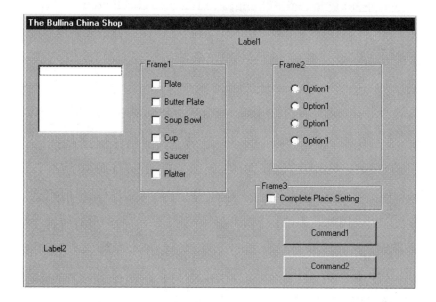

Discussion

This exercise was quite long, so I gave everyone about fifteen minutes to complete it. While they were completing it, a number of students told me they were having trouble changing the properties of the correct control.

"The easiest way to find the control's properties," I said, "is to select the control with your mouse, then bring up the Properties window. Another way of doing this, although somewhat more confusing, is to select the control from the Properties window itself by finding it in the object pull-down list."

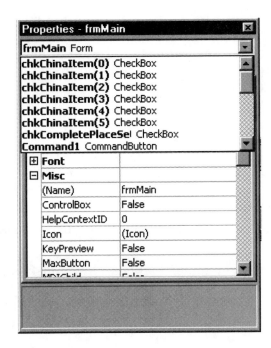

Besides these minor problems, eventually everyone was able to change the check box properties. Now it was time to move on to the command buttons.

Command Button Properties

"The command button," I said, "has two properties we should change in order to make its behavior a little more user friendly to the customer."

Default

"The only control in Visual Basic with a `Default` property is the command button," I said.

"Is that the property of the command button, that if set to `True`, treats the *Enter* key the same as if the user clicked on the command button?" Dave asked. "That's right," I said. "I couldn't have said it better myself!"

"Explain to me why we would want to do that?" Ward asked. I explained that many users of Windows programs are still very keyboard-oriented, and many DOS programs make the *Enter* key a central part of their program. Setting the `Default` property to `True` can provide a comfort level to the customers of the China Shop who are more familiar with DOS programs.

"Also some users," Lou said, "are physically impaired and may not be able to control a mouse. Yet they can still hit the *Enter* key on the keyboard!"

"Good point, Lou," I said.

I noted that only one command button on a form could be designated as the `Default`. We had suggested earlier that the Calculate Command Button should have the `Default` property set to `True`. The customer will then be able to initiate a price calculation by either clicking on the Calculate button or pressing the *Enter* key.

"Are there any guidelines," Valerie asked, "as to which button on the form should be the `Default` button?"

"I say let common sense be your guide," I replied. "Never make a `Default` button something associated with an irretrievable or 'non-correctable' action, such as deleting files. Given a choice, make the `Default` button the most intuitive, safe operation available."

Cancel

"The only control in Visual Basic with a `Cancel` property," I said, "is the command button. The `Cancel` property is similar to the `Default` property. Setting the `Cancel` property of a command button to `True` equates to the press of the *Esc* key to the click of that control. The reasoning behind setting this property to `True` is the same as that for the `Default` property, it can provide a comfort level to those users who are either more comfortable pressing keys or who, for physical reasons, cannot use a mouse."

I pointed out that, as was the case with the Default property, only one command button could be designated as the Cancel command button. We had decided that the Cancel property should be set to True for the Reset command button, which would then reset the controls on the form back so that they would be ready for a fresh price calculation.

There were no more questions, and so I distributed this exercise:

In this exercise, we'll change some of the properties for the two command buttons on the China Shop form:

Exercise

Changing the Properties of the Command Buttons

1. Use the following table to make changes to the command button currently named Command1:

Without code in the click events of the cmdCalculate or cmdReset CommandButtons, it will be impossible to verify either their Default or Cancel behavior at this point.

Property	Value	Comment
Name	cmdCalculate	Hungarian notation
Caption	Calculate	Provides an identifying caption for the command button
Default	True	Makes this command button the Default command button on the form. Its Click event procedure will be triggered if the customer presses the *Enter* key.
ToolTipText	Click to Calculate a Sales Quotation	Provides a ToolTip for this control

2. Use the following table to make changes to the command button currently named Command2:

Property	Value	Comment
Name	cmdReset	Hungarian notation
Cancel	True	Makes this command button the `Cancel` command button on the form. Its `Click` event procedure will be triggered if the customer presses the *Esc* key.
Caption	Reset	Provides an identifying caption for the Command Button
ToolTipText	Click to Begin a new Sales Quotation	Provides a ToolTip for this control

3. Click on the **Save** icon on the Toolbar to save the project.

4. Run the program, paying particular attention to the captions of the command buttons. Also, check to ensure that the ToolTips are displaying properly.

5. Here's a run time screen shot of how the China Shop form should look with the changes you've made to the command buttons:

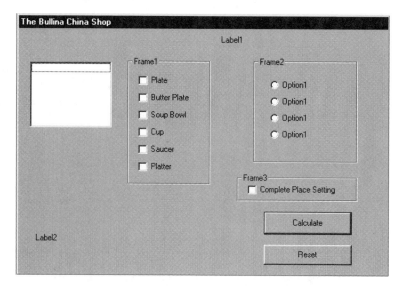

Common Dialog Properties

There were no problems with the previous exercise and so we moved onto a discussion of the Common Dialog control.

"The Common Dialog control is unique among the controls in the China Shop Project," I said. "It's a little unusual in that it displays six different types of dialog boxes for the user to make a variety of selections, such as specifying a file to open or save, change colors or specify printer settings. In the China Shop project, we'll use the Common Dialog control to permit the user to select a color for the background of the China Shop's form. Shortly, in addition to the `Name` property, we'll be changing two of its properties."

"If the Common Dialog control can do all that," Valerie said, "then I would presume it's a little more complicated to work with than the other controls. In other words, I bet you just don't place it on the form and that's it."

"You're right," I agreed. "Because it's multi-faceted, the programmer needs to set its `Flags` property to tell Visual Basic what kind of Common Dialog box to display. Also, there is always the possibility that the user, once presented with a dialog box, will simply change their mind. In order to detect if the user has changed their mind, we need to set the `CancelError` property to `True`, so that Visual Basic will generate a run time error if this happens."

CancelError

"Run time error?" Linda asked. "Won't that make the program bomb?"

"What does Linda mean by bomb?" Rhonda asked.

"In programming," I replied, "when we use the word bomb, we mean that the program just stops running and presents an alarming error message to the user. Not exactly what we want in a program that our client is paying for."

"So you're saying," Steve said, "that we'll intentionally set the `CancelError` property to true in order to generate an error if the user selects the Cancel button?"

"That's right," I said. "We'll set the `CancelError` property to `True`. The alternative is that we just won't know if the user clicked on the Cancel button."

"I'm still a little confused about this," Ward said. "Can you show us?"

"I'll be glad to," I said, as I quickly created a form with a Common Dialog control and a command button. I added some code to display the Color dialog box and to change the background color of the form. I then ran the program and displayed the Color dialog box on the classroom projector:

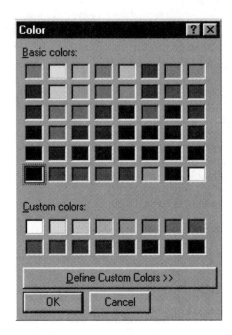

"Do you see the Cancel button on the Color dialog box?" I asked. "Let me select a color."

I selected cyan and the background color of the form immediately changed. I explained that when the user makes a selection from the palette, the numeric value of the color they select is inserted into the Color property of the Common Dialog control. My program then sets the BackColor property of the form equal to that value.

I then stopped the program and ran it again. This time, instead of selecting a color from the palette, I selected the Cancel button instead.

"The color of the form turned black," Rhonda said. "What happened?"

"My program," I said, "not knowing that the user pressed the Cancel key, took the value in the `Color` property of the Common Dialog control and set the `BackColor` property equal to it. Unfortunately, since the user clicked on the Cancel button, the value of the `Color` property of the Common Dialog control was never changed and was still set to its default value of 0."

"Which obviously equates to black," Dave said.

"That's right," I agreed. "Now let me stop the program, and set the `CancelError` property of the Common Dialog control to `True`. This will generate the Visual Basic error."

I made the change, and ran the program again:

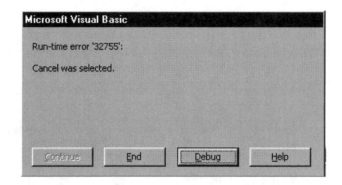

"I thought errors were bad," Ward said.

"Not always," I said. "Given the choice between changing the background color of the China Shop form to black and generating an error, it's preferable to generate an error. We'll see later that we'll be able to detect this error and, because of that, we'll be able to do exactly what the user wanted, which is nothing. In other words, we'll leave the form color the same as it was."

"At this point," Rhonda said, "I'll have to take your word for it. I'm still a little confused."

"The `CancelError` and `Cancel` properties," Chuck said, "are not the same, are they?"

"No," I replied. "`CancelError` is unique to the Common Dialog control. `Cancel` is a property of the command button."

"When will we talk about the code for changing the color of the form?" Steve asked. "We'll begin looking at Visual Basic code next week," I said, "so it won't be long!"

Flags

"You mentioned the `Flags` property earlier," Linda said. "Are you going to discuss that?"

"Sure," I replied. "The `Flags` property is unique to the Common Dialog control. As I mentioned before, the Common Dialog control can be used to display six different dialog boxes, so we use the `Flags` property to set options for the various dialog boxes that we display."

"Such as?" Linda asked.

"In the China Shop Project," I said, "we'll set the `Flags` property equal to 2. This will tell Visual Basic to display the color dialog box along with a section that allows the user to define their own colors."

I made that change to my demonstration program and ran the program:

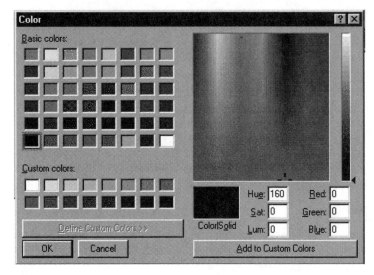

"See the difference?" I said.

Intrinsic Constants

Steve had displayed on-line help for the **Flags** property, and saw a reference to something called an **intrinsic constant**. He asked what it was.

"That's a good question," I said. "In Visual Basic, some properties have values that are so complex and hard to remember that they have been assigned substitute names, called intrinsic constants. Therefore, you can refer to the property value by the intrinsic constant name instead. You'll see that we'll use these intrinsic constant names quite a bit when we start coding."

"What's the intrinsic constant for the value you just entered into the **Flags** property?" Ward asked.

"**cdlCCFullOpen**," I replied.

"Can you enter the name of an intrinsic constant into the Properties window?" Dave asked. "No," I replied, "you can only refer to an intrinsic constant in the code that you write."

There were no more questions, so I distributed this exercise:

Exercise

Changing the Properties of the Common Dialog Control

1. Use the following table to make changes to the Common Dialog control currently named CommonDialog1:

Property	Value	Comment
Name	dlgChina	Hungarian notation
CancelError	True	Generates a Visual Basic error if the user presses the Cancel button
Flags	2	Causes the Custom Colors section in the Color dialog box to display

2. Save the China Shop Project by clicking on the **Save** icon on the Toolbar.

Discussion

We won't see the Common Dialog Control working in our program until the release version, and no-one seemed to have had any problems with the exercise, so we moved onto the properties of our frames.

Frame Properties

"We have a little work to do with our frames, but not much," I said. "All we need to do is change the captions from their default values to something a little more meaningful."

"Are we going to set ToolTips for the frame?" Valerie asked.

After some discussion, everyone agreed that setting ToolTips for the frame would be a bit of an 'overkill', since all of the controls within the frames have their own ToolTips.

In this exercise, we'll change some of the properties for the three frames on the China Shop form, according to the tables below. Be careful that you have selected the frame control and not one of the controls within it:

Exercise

Changing the Properties of the Frames

1. Use the following table to make changes to the frame currently named Frame1:

Property	Value	Comment
Name	fraPieces	Hungarian notation
Caption	China Pieces	Provides an identifying caption for the frame

2. Use the following table to make changes to the Frame currently named Frame2:

Property	Value	Comment
Name	fraQuantity	Hungarian notation
Caption	Quantity	Provides an identifying caption for the frame

3. Use the following table to make changes to the Frame currently named Frame3:

Property	Value	Comment
Name	fraCompletePlaceSetting	Hungarian notation
Caption	Complete Place Setting?	Provides an identifying caption for the frame

4. Save the China Shop Project by clicking on the **Save** icon on the Toolbar.

5. Run the program, paying particular attention to the captions of the frames. Here's a screen shot of how the form should look after you've made these changes to the frame controls:

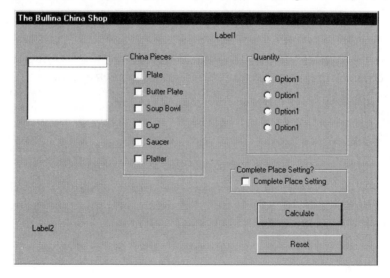

Discussion

"I had some difficulty," Rhonda said, "selecting the frame controls, in order to change their properties. I kept selecting one of the controls within the frame."

"In my experience, Rhonda," I said, "I've had good success by clicking on the borders of the frame. In other words, stay away from the inside. Another method you can use is to display the Properties window and then select the frame from the object pull-down list box."

There were no other questions, and so we moved on to a discussion of the Image control.

Image Control Properties

"There are only two properties of the Image control that we'll be changing," I said. "The **Name** property and the **Stretch** property."

Stretch

"When the customer makes a selection of a brand in the list box," I said, "we'll use the Image control to display a graphics file of the china pattern. Because graphics files come in different dimensions, by default the Image control will re-size to fit the graphic."

"I would think that could wreak havoc on your interface design," Barbara said. "You mean the Image control will change shape to accommodate the graphic?"

"Yes," I said, "and we can't afford to let that happen in the China Shop project. At this point, I'm not sure what the dimensions Mr. Bullina's graphics files are, but we can't afford to have our Image control change shape to accommodate them. Fortunately, there's a property of the Image control called **Stretch**, which if set to **True** causes the reverse to happen. That is, the graphic will change its shape to accommodate the Image control."

"I remember when we changed the **Picture** property of the form last week," Rhonda said. "Will we be changing the **Picture** property of the Image control also?"

"No," I said. "Since there are three possible graphics files to display, depending upon the user's selection in the list box, we'll need to make that determination at run time. We'll use a method of the Image control called **LoadPicture** to specify a graphics file."

There were no other questions or comments, and so I distributed this exercise:

Changing the Properties of the Image Control

1. Use the following table to make changes to the Image control currently named Image1:

Property	Value	Comment
Name	imgChina	Hungarian notation
Stretch	True	Re-sizes the graphic to fit the size of the Image control; otherwise the Image control re-sizes to fit the size of the graphic.

1. Save the China Shop Project by clicking on the Save icon on the Toolbar. Until we write code to load a graphics file into the Image control, there are no obvious changes to the Image control. So, at this time we are unable to check its behavior.

Label Properties

There were no questions or problems with the Image control exercise and so we moved onto the label control. "We'll be changing three properties of our label controls," I said. "The Name, Caption, and AutoSize properties."

I explained that rather than setting a Caption property for the label controls, we would be erasing the default caption already there. "In the exercise," I said, "my instructions call for you to null the caption. That means to erase whatever Caption property is already there."

"I thought we were using the Caption property to display the sales quotation," Rhonda said, "and another to display the date and time. How can we do that if the Caption is empty?"

"We'll assign a caption to the label controls at run time," I said. "But first, we need to erase what's there."

AutoSize

"AutoSize?" Dave said. "Is that similar to the Stretch property of the Image control?"

"In a way," I said, "it's just the opposite."

I explained that the `AutoSize` property tells Visual Basic to re-size the label based on the width of its caption. The captions we will assign to both of the label controls at run time are variable. "For instance," I said, "we'll assign a date and time to Label1's caption property, and a sales quotation to Label2's caption. Depending upon the day of the year and the time of day, the width of Label1's caption can vary by several characters. The width of Label2's caption will vary slightly depending upon the price displayed."

"So this is a formatting nicety?" Linda asked.

"Exactly," I said, "but it's what makes the interface look neater."

I warned everyone that as soon as they set the `AutoSize` property of the label control, it will immediately shrink to apparently nothing. "When you see that happen," I said. "Don't worry about it. Once we assign a value to the caption property, the label will look fine."

"How do we assign a null caption to the label's `Caption` property?" Bob said.

"Good question," I replied. "Select the `Caption`'s property value in the Properties window by double-clicking on it and then press the *backspace* key. That will clear the default entry."

There were no other questions and so I distributed this exercise:

In this exercise, we'll change the `Name`, `Caption` and `AutoSize` properties for the two labels on the China Shop form:

Exercise

Changing the Properties of the Label Controls

1. Use the following table to make changes to the control currently named Label1:

Property	Value	Comment
Name	lblDateAndTime	Hungarian notation
AutoSize	True	To accommodate a date and time which can have different sizes
Caption		Null caption

2.   Use the following table to make changes to the control currently named Label2:

Property	Value	Comment
Name	lblPrice	Hungarian notation
AutoSize	True	To accommodate a date and time which can have different sizes
Caption		Null caption

2.   Save the China Shop Project.

3.   Run your project and ensure that the captions for both labels are now both null.

Discussion

Several students had missed my comments about the size of the label controls shrinking when we set the **AutoSize** property to **True**, and as a result some thought that they had gone horribly wrong after setting the property. "Because we have set the **Caption** property of the labels to null," I said, "Visual Basic automatically re-sized the label control to virtually nothing."

Besides that, there were no other problems with this exercise, so we moved on to the List Box control.

List Box Properties

"We'll only be changing two properties of the list box;" I said, "the **Name** and **ToolTipText** properties. We've seen both of these properties elsewhere, so let's just move on to the exercise."

"Before we do that," Bob said, "Can you tell us how items will be added to the list box?"

"In the prototype's code, we'll use the **AddItem** method of the list box to add the items," I replied. "Eventually we'll do this by reading the items from a disk file maintained by the staff of the China Shop."

Exercise

Changing the Properties of the List Box Control

1.   Use the following table to make changes to the list box control currently named List1:

Property	Value	Comment
Name	lstBrands	Hungarian notation
ToolTipText	Select a Brand of China	Provides a ToolTip for this control

2.   Save the China Shop Project.

3.   Run the program and check that the ToolTips are displaying properly.

OptionButton Properties

There were no problems with the list box exercise, so we moved on to the properties of the OptionButton controls. "There are three properties that we will be changing for the option buttons on our form;" I said, "the **Name**, the **Caption** and the **Index** properties."

I reminded everyone that we had verified the **Index** properties for the members of the control array, a few minutes earlier, in the check box exercise. There, the **Index** properties were assigned sequentially and we had left them like that. "In the next exercise," I said, "we'll be setting the **Index** property equal to the quantity that the appropriate option button represents."

"I'm not sure I understand what you mean," Barbara said. I explained that right now, it was likely that the **Index** property for the first option button in the control array was 0, the second 1 and so on.

"To embody the quantity rules that Mr Bullina provided us with, the first option button will be captioned 8," I said, "and we'll change the **Index** property to **8** also. The second will be captioned 4 and we'll change the **Index** property of that OptionButton to **4**. And we'll repeat this process for the remaining two option buttons."

"I didn't think we could do that," Ward said. "I thought the **Index** property values had to be consecutive."

"No," I said, "not at all. You can make them anything you want."

"I guess my big question is: why would we want to do that?" Dave asked.

I explained that programmers frequently use the **Index** property of a member of a control array to represent some real world attribute of the object. In this case, by using the **Index** property to represent the option button's quantity, it would make the price calculation we would perform for the customer a little easier for us.

"I'll have to take your word on that," Dave said.

"Look at it this way," I said. "If we were to use the default **Index** properties then when we came to coding the quantity calculation the quantity and the index value would be unrelated. Thus, a quantity of 1 would have an index value of 0; a quantity of 2 would have an index value of 1; a quantity of 4 would have an index value of 2; and a quantity of 8 would have an index value of 3. It would be easier for us if the quantity and index had the same value."

"I see what you're getting at now," Dave said.

A few people still looked a bit unsure so I reassured them that when they saw the code that we would begin to write in the coming weeks, the reasoning behind changing the **Index** properties would become clear.

I distributed the following exercise and asked everyone to complete it:

Exercise

Changing the Properties of the OptionButtons

1. Make the following changes to the first (top most) option button currently named Option1 in the Quantity frame. This control, along with the others in this frame, will all have the same name, but different **Index** properties:

Property	Value	Comment
Name	optQuantity	Hungarian notation
Caption	8	Quantity of 8
Index	8	Set the **Index** property equal to the displayed quantity

2. Use the following table to make changes to the second option button in the frame captioned Quantity:

Property	Value	Comment
Name	optQuantity	Hungarian notation
Caption	4	Quantity of 4
Index	4	Set the Index property equal to the displayed quantity

3. Use the following table to make changes to the third option button in the frame captioned Quantity:

Property	Value	Comment
Name	optQuantity	Hungarian notation
Caption	2	Quantity of 2
Index	2	Set the Index property equal to the displayed quantity

4. Use the following table to make changes to the fourth option button in the frame captioned Quantity:

Property	Value	Comment
Name	optQuantity	Hungarian notation
Caption	1	Quantity of 1
Index	1	Set the Index property equal to the displayed quantity

5. Save the China Shop Project.

6. Here's a run time screen shot of how the main form should look with the changes you've made to the OptionButton controls:

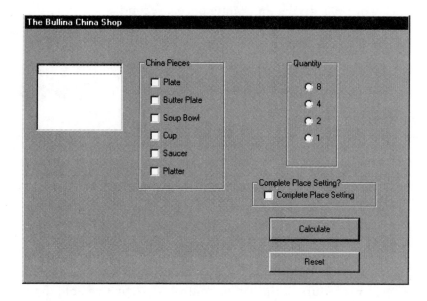

Discussion

There were no questions or problems during this exercise, although I could sense that there still was some confusion about our choice for the **Index** properties. However, it was now time to move on to the Timer control, and I didn't have any misgiving about it because I knew we would be returning to this subject later.

Timer Properties

"We're almost done," I said. "In fact, the Timer is the last control that we have to discuss. We'll be changing only two properties of the Timer control, the **Name** and **Interval** properties."

Interval

"The Timer control," I said, "executes code contained in its **Timer** event procedure at regular intervals according to the value found in its **Interval** property. In other words, the **Interval** property determines how often the **Timer** event procedure is triggered, ranging from 1 millisecond (a thousandth of a second) to 64 seconds. The value in the **Interval** property is expressed in milliseconds, so that a value of 1000 is equal to 1 second. We're going to place code in the `Timer` event procedure to update the date and time continuously. Therefore, an `Interval` property of 1000, giving an update once a second, should do the trick."

There were no questions about the Timer control, so I distributed this exercise:

Exercise

Changing the Properties of the Timer Control

1. Make the following changes to the Timer control:

Property	Value	Comment
Name	tmrChina	Hungarian notation
Interval	1000	Causes the `Timer` event to trigger every second

2. Click on the **Save** icon to save the China Shop Project. Until we write code and place it in the `Timer` event procedure of the Timer control, we won't be able to verify the changes we have just made.

Discussion

Rhonda said that it looked like we were finished with the user interface.

"We're very close to the point where we can pat ourselves on the back and admire our work," I said, "but there is just one more thing to consider, the **tab order** of the controls on the form."

"Tab order?" Mary asked.

Tab Order and the TabIndex Property

"Yes," I said, "the tab order affects the order in which controls receive the focus in a Windows program. In Visual Basic, if the user presses the *Tab* key, the focus moves from the control currently with the focus to the control next in the tab order. For instance, suppose the list box control currently has the focus and the user presses the *Tab* key. If the option button control is next in the tab order, then the option button will receive the focus next."

A brief discussion as to why the user would be pressing the *Tab* key then ensued. Lou reminded everyone of our earlier discussion about the use of the mouse and the need to provide keyboard alternatives. The *Tab* key is a perfect alternative for the user to move from control to control.

I continued by saying that in Visual Basic, tab order is determined by the **TabIndex** property of each control. When the user presses the *Tab* key, the control with the next highest value in its **TabIndex** property receives the focus. When there is no control with a higher value, then the control with the lowest value of all the controls on the form receives the focus.

"What controls on the China Shop form have a **TabIndex** property?" Kate asked. "The check box, command button, frame, label, list box and option buttons all have a **TabIndex** property," I said.

"How important is tab order?" Steve asked. "Some users never press the *Tab* key," I said, "but others, like those we discussed earlier who will press the *Enter* and *Esc* keys, might use the *Tab* key to move from control to control. If the tab order of the program is not in a logical sequence, we'll end up with a few frustrated users.""Another interesting point is that the control with the lowest TabIndex value is also the control that first receives the focus when the form is created at run time." I continued.

"What do you mean by logical sequence?" Rose asked.

"The designer of the program," I said, "should probably sit down with the user and together determine what the logical sequence of events through the program should be. For instance, will the customer select a brand first or a quantity? Once the quantity is selected, does it make sense for the focus to move to the check box items?"

A Surprise Visit

At this point, I noticed that a special guest had arrived. No, it wasn't Bill Gates, but it was the next best person, Joe Bullina.

After I introduced Joe to the class, he thanked them for the magnificent work he had heard they were doing on his system, as he put it.

"Joe," I said, "you're just in time to see the final stages of the China Shop interface being developed and we could use your help here. We are currently working on determining what a logical tab order sequence for the program should be."

Everyone seemed pretty surprised to find that Joe actually knew what I was talking about. They didn't know that he had been outside for the last twenty minutes or so while the concept of the tab order was being discussed. I asked Joe to sit down at my classroom PC. I started the China Shop program and asked him to tab through the controls.

"Hey, I really love what I see here!" he said.

We noted that the current tab order for the controls on the forms was:

- the list box containing the china brands, `lstBrands`
- the Calculate command button, `cmdCalculate`
- the Reset command button, `cmdReset`
- the Complete Place Setting check box, `chkCompletePlaceSetting`
- the Plate check box, `chkChinaItem` (0)
- the Butter Plate check box, `chkChinaItem` (1)
- the Soup Bowl check box, `chkChinaItem` (2)
- the Cup check box, `chkChinaItem` (3)
- the Saucer check box, `chkChinaItem` (4)
- the Platter check box, `chkChinaItem` (5)
- the Quantity 8 option button, `optQuantity` (8)

"I have a question," Ward said. "Why did only the first option button in the control array receive the focus? As soon as Mr. Bullina tabbed off the first option button, the focus moved back to the list box control."

"Ward," I said, "that is an excellent observation. That's the nature of the option button; it's because Visual Basic knows that only one can be selected in a group."

"Joe," I said, turning to Mr. Bullina, "can you come up with an ideal tab order for us?"

Surprisingly, in about a minute or two, he did exactly that. Here is his ideal tab order for the China Shop application:

- the List box containing the China brands, `lstBrands`
- the Complete Place Setting check box, `chkCompletePlaceSetting`
- the Plate check box, `chkChinaItem` (0)
- the Butter Plate check box, `chkChinaItem` (1)
- the Soup Bowl check box, `chkChinaItem` (2)
- the Cup check box, `chkChinaItem` (3)
- the Saucer check box, `chkChinaItem` (4)

- the Platter check box, **chkChinaItem** (5)
- the quantity 8 option button, **optQuantity** (8)
- the Calculate command button, **cmdCalculate**
- the Reset command button, **cmdReset**

"Great work," I said as I turned to the class. "can you see the benefit of having the user directly involved in this process? Of course, it makes perfect sense that the Calculate button should receive the focus after the prerequisite brand, items and quantity have been selected. However, without Joe's help, this might not have been immediately obvious to us."

I quickly came up with an exercise to implement changes to the current **TabIndex** properties of our controls.

"There's one last thing I need to tell everyone," I said, "before we attempt to change the **TabIndex** properties of these controls. Changing the **TabIndex** properties of controls on the form can be tricky at times. When you change the **TabIndex** property of one of the controls, Visual Basic will automatically adjust all of the others as well. It's almost like the old shell game or a game of 'hot potato'. You may find that after changing the **TabIndex** property of one of the controls, as soon as you change the next one, Visual Basic changes all of the others you have just modified. You'll need to be patient and you may need to repeat the process several times to get it right."

Having just explained how 'unforgiving' Visual Basic is when you start changing the tab order; here's an exercise to test out that statement:

Exercise

Changing the TabIndex Properties

1. Use the following table to make changes to the **TabIndex** properties of the controls on the China Shop form. You may want to try changing these properties in reverse order:

Object	TabIndex Value
lstBrands	0
chkCompletePlaceSetting	1
chkChinaItem(0)	2
chkChinaItem(1)	3
chkChinaItem(2)	4
chkChinaItem(3)	5

chkChinaItem(4)	6
chkChinaItem(5)	7
optQuantity(8)	8
optQuantity(4)	9
optQuantity(2)	10
optQuantity(1)	11
cmdCalculate	12
cmdReset	13

2.   Save the China Shop Project.

3.   Run the program and observe the tab order of the controls.

Discussion

"I didn't have any trouble setting the values for the properties," Ward said. I explained that sometimes it's easy and sometimes it's tricky. "Part of that has to do with the original tab order," I said.

"I have a question," Rhonda said. "These tabs are giving me problems. Every time I try to tab through the option buttons the only one I can tab to is the quantity **8** button. What am I doing wrong?"

"That's the behavior I mentioned earlier," I said. "In an option button group, Visual Basic will tab to the button with the lowest **TabIndex** value in the group. When you press the *Tab* key again, Visual Basic moves to the next control in the tab order **outside** the option group."

"I want to thank everyone," Mr. Bullina said, "for the fine job you are doing with this program. I can't wait to get this up and running in my shop." With that, Mr. Bullina excused himself. He had a meeting with an import dealer concerning some china.

Prior to dismissing class, I congratulated everyone myself. After only six weeks, we had completed the China Shop interface. We had come a long way and the fun was just beginning.

"Next week," I said, "we'll begin to write code!"

Summary

Believe it or not, we now have a working user interface. We've come a long way! We've looked at the Visual Basic Toolbox and placed all of the necessary controls on the form of the China

Shop project. We then adjusted the properties of those controls and, like all good developers, we ran the program, admired our work, and prepared to code our program.

We've seen how to add controls to the form, and change their properties. We've also seen the most commonly used controls, such as the Text Box, Frame, and Label controls, and one of the most important, the Command Button control.

Control arrays are made by copying and pasting controls so that each has the same name but a different index number, which you can refer to in the code, and change to suit you. The advantage is that you only need to code one set of event procedures for the whole array.

Some users are more keyboard-oriented, and so it's a good idea to assign common keys, such as the *Enter* and *Esc* keys, to often-used command buttons, using the Default and Cancel properties respectively. It's also worth considering the order the program cycles through the controls when you hit the *Tab* key to make it more intuitive. This is done by setting the TabIndex property of each control. This works best if you assign them in reverse order, because otherwise Visual Basic changes them as you go along. The control that is currently 'in use' is said to have the **focus**.

Quiz

1. Is every control that we will use to build the China Shop Project found in the default Visual Basic Toolbox?

2. How do you add the Common Dialog control to the Visual Basic Toolbox?

3. In Visual Basic, are all controls visible at run time?

4. Where do you find the controls to place on your form?

5. The frame control is a special kind of control called a _____ control.

6. What Visual Basic control is ideal to display a list of items from which the user can select one or more items, but only those items?

7. What control is used primarily to display information to the user?

8. What Visual Basic control is used to initiate some kind of action?

9. The _____ is displayed on a form as a control containing a caption with a circle next to it.

10. Which two controls allow the user to give a True/False or a Yes/No answer?

11. A control array is like a family of controls. It contains members, just like a family. Each member of the control array is created with identical properties (including the `Name` property) exce one, the _____ property.

12. What's the primary difference between the check box and the option button controls?

13. What control will we use in the China Shop Project to display a picture of china patterns?

14. What control will we use in the China Shop Project to display a dialog box permitting the user to change the color of the form?

15. What control will we use in the China Shop Project to display a changing date and time?

16. What property of the controls in the China Shop Project is used to display hints as to their operation?

17. What property of the command button is used to equate the press of the *Enter* key with its `Click` event?

18. What property of the command button is used to equate the press of the *Esc* key with its `Click` event?

19. What is the property of the Image control that tells it to change shape to accommodate the graphic file being loaded into it?

20. What is the property of label that tells Visual Basic to re-size the label based on the 'length' of its `Caption` property?

21. Extra Credit – A man had a flock of 19 sheep. He wanted to give each of his three children a share: half to the eldest, a quarter to the middle one and a fifth to the youngest. He realized that this plan would involve chopping up sheep. What clever way did he come up with to avoid this dilemma?

Chapter 6

A First Look at Coding

In this chapter, we'll examine Visual Basic events in more detail and I'll introduce you to the Visual Basic **debugger**, which is a set of tools that permits you to see what's going on behind the scenes of your program. Most courses treat the debugger as a tool to correct errors instead of treating it as the great learning tool it can be. In my mind, the debugger is like an MRI or CAT Scan, that can allow a programmer (especially the beginner) to see and understand what's going on behind the scenes of their program. Today we'll also write our first piece of code for the China Shop Project.

"I think that you all now have an appreciation," I said, "for the fact that programming in Visual Basic is more than just writing code. After all, we've just spent two weeks working on the visual interface. For those of you who have been waiting anxiously to begin learning how to write code, today is that day."

Events and Event-Driven Programming

"When we write Visual Basic code," I said, "we place that code in event procedures, which are executed when Windows events are triggered. Although we've previously discussed Windows events, I want to take just a little more time to reinforce the concept of an event before we begin writing our first code."

In the Old Days....

"For those of us who programmed in the old days of DOS," Peter said, "it might be a good idea, prior to talking about Windows, to discuss what came before it."

Most of the class agreed, so I told everyone this story.

When I first started programming way back in 1974, procedural programming was really the only way to program. A procedural program tells the computer exactly how to solve a problem, in a step- by-step manner.

"From the programmers' point of view," I said, "this was a wonderful time. You knew what data to expect, where it would be found and in what order it would appear."

I suggested that we compare a procedural program to an old-style grocery store. If a customer wanted to buy a pound of bacon, a dozen eggs and two bananas, they would approach a grocery clerk at a counter and hand over a note with these items written on it. The customer would then wait while the clerk selected those items from the shelves behind the counter.

The clerk would bring the items back to the counter for a quick examination and the items would be rung up. If the customer didn't like the look of the bacon or the color of the bananas, then the clerk would secure replacements. Eventually, the customer would be satisfied and the sale would be finalized. The chain of events for the clerk would look something like this:

- obtain customer's note
- walk down aisle
- obtain bacon in freezer compartment
- walk down aisle
- obtain eggs in freezer compartment
- walk down aisle
- obtain two bananas from fruit bin
- carry items back to counter
- wait for customer to approve the items
- if anything is wrong, repeat appropriate steps
- ring up sale

"From the customer's point of view," I said, "this was very much a procedurally oriented approach with very little room for flexibility. Most customers, given the choice, would prefer to roam the aisles of the grocery store. The customers could then take as little or as much time they needed to shop and could look over the store offerings for themselves. The grocery clerk, on the other hand, enjoyed the predictability of the procedural approach. With no customers behind the counter, the store shelves were always in perfect order. There was less spillage and no pilferage, but of course, there was much less customer satisfaction."

The Modern Approach

Most programmers liked procedural programming. From their point of view, it was much easier to write programs when they knew what input their program would receive. The programmers were able to control how and when that input would be processed. However, as I think you can see from the example of our grocery store, procedural programming has its shortcomings, most notably in terms of efficiency and customer satisfaction.

I suggested that we compare the modern, event-driven approach of Windows programming to a modern self-service grocery store. With this approach, the customer enters the store with the same note detailing the items he or she wishes to purchase. Now, however, the customer can select the package of bacon they want, not the package the clerk selects.

The customer can walk the aisles of the store in any order and if they meet a friend, they can chat a while, without being hurried by anyone. Some customers, instead of composing a note, will just drive up to the modern grocery store, grab a cart and begin walking up and down aisles, picking up items as they go along. In fact, some customers love the freedom of making up their minds as they go along.

With the modern approach, the only thing that the grocery store owner knows for certain is that the customer will appear at the check-out line with items to ring up. Everything else in between is a big unknown. There's no way of knowing whether the customer will start at aisle one and work their way down to aisle ten, or perhaps proceed in the reverse order. Nor is there any reason for the store owner to care. With this new approach to shopping, more customers can be served in less time and with the need for fewer clerks.

"So the bottom line," Linda said, "is that removing the procedural restrictions on the way the customer has to shop resulted in greater customer satisfaction."

"That's right," I agreed. "Of course, it makes managing the grocery store a little more difficult. Removing tight control always does that, but you can't argue that the customer isn't happier this way."

"How does this relate to programming?" Kathy asked.

"The premise behind event-driven programming," I said, "is basically the same as the self-service grocery store. Event-driven programs don't force the user to perform functions in a pre-defined sequence, but instead react to what the user does in the order that the user chooses.

Obviously, event-driven programs need to ensure that all the required data is input, but if the user wants to choose their china items before they specify the china brand, who are we to tell them that they are wrong?"

What's an Event?

"I'm still a bit confused over this concept of events," Ward said. "When do events occur?"

"Events in a Windows program," I said, "occur as the result of one of three things:"

- the user does something to trigger an event
- the OS does something to trigger the event
- an event is triggered through Visual Basic code itself

"There are many Windows events," I said, "but not every object in Visual Basic responds to the same ones. In today's class, I'll discuss the more common events in the Windows environment and of course, we'll start coding the China Shop project."

An Event or an Event Procedure?

"Is an event the same as an event procedure?" Rhonda asked.

"Not quite," I said. "An event is something that happens in the Windows environment and an event procedure is the code that executes when that event takes place. For instance, the `Click` event of command button Command1 happens when the user clicks on it with the mouse. The `Command1_Click` event procedure is triggered as a result of the event happening. I know it sounds like I'm splitting hairs, but the distinction can be important."

I continued by explaining that every object in Visual Basic is pre-programmed to detect and respond to events. For every event to which these objects can react, there is an event procedure **stub** sitting behind the scenes into which the programmer can place code.

"So if the event occurs," Blaine said, "and the programmer hasn't placed any code in the event procedure, what happens? Nothing?"

"That's what most people think," I said, "but the correct answer is that the default behavior of the object occurs regardless of whether or not the programmer has inserted code into the event procedure."

An Example of an Event Procedure Stub

"I think this would make more sense to me if we could look at one of these event procedure stubs," Ward said. "Can we see one?"

I displayed the China Shop Project on the classroom projector, then double-clicked on the Calculate command button and opened up the stub for the `cmdCalculate_Click` event procedure:

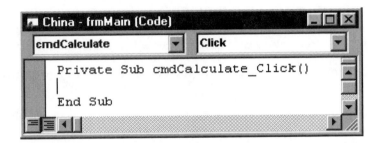

"This is what I mean by an event procedure stub," I said. "Notice the event procedure header that consists of `Private Sub` and the event procedure name, `cmdCalculate_Click()`. The end of the event procedure is marked by the words `End Sub`. There is nothing else in between."

"So an event procedure stub," Ward said, "is just an empty event procedure?"

"You can think of it that way. Notice that there is also a `Click` event procedure for the Reset command button," I said as I selected **cmdReset** from the object list box and displayed its `Click` event procedure.

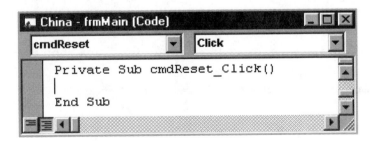

"This event procedure header is just a little different from the other one. How are event procedure names formed?" Bob asked.

I displayed the `click` event procedure for the Reset Command Button:

```
Private Sub cmdReset_Click()

End Sub
```

"Well, first off," I said, "the name of an event procedure is created by Visual Basic. It forms the name by combining the name of the object, an underscore character _ and then the name of the event."

"What does the word `Private` mean?" Rhonda asked. "`Private` refers to the **scope** of the event procedure within the program," I said. I asked everyone to bear with me until we discussed the scope of variables and procedures a little later in the class.

"What about the empty parentheses `()` at the end of the event procedure name?" Linda asked.

"If you see something within the parentheses, that means that the event procedure accepts **arguments**," I said. "An argument is just an additional piece of information forwarded to the event procedure by Windows to allow the procedure to do its job. For example, you might have two numbers which have to be added together."

"Will any event procedures have arguments in the China Shop Project?" Chuck asked. "Yes," I answered. "In fact, you'll see later that we'll write code for the `click` event of the option button control array and our event procedure will be passed a very important argument called `Index`. Can anyone guess what that argument contains?"

"I would guess that it contains the `Index` property of the control array member that triggered the event," Dave said.

"That's quite a guess, Dave," I said, "and you're absolutely right. Windows needs to tell us which member of the array triggered the event, because members of a control array share the same event procedures."

I displayed the `click` event procedure stub for the China Shop Project's control array of option buttons:

```
Private Sub optQuantity_Click(Index As Integer)

End Sub
```

The Events in the China Shop Project

"I will briefly discuss the event procedures for which we will write code in the China Shop Project," I said. "Then we can begin to write some code. Many beginners feel the need to place code in every event procedure in their program and that simply isn't necessary. Remember, for each event in your program, there is default behavior associated with it, as we've already seen with the China Shop Project. It's only necessary to write code to enhance the default behavior of the objects."

I then displayed this chart on the classroom projector:

Object or Control	Name	Event Procedures we will code	Comments
Form	`frmMain`	`Load`	Loads up the china brands
Check Boxes	`chkChinaItem`	`Click`	Will initiate loading of china pattern graphic into Image control
	`chkCompletePlaceSetting`	`Click`	Will initiate selection of all china items
Command Buttons	`cmdCalculate`	`Click`	Initiates price calculation
	`cmdReset`	`Click`	Resets controls to their startup state
Common Dialog	`dlgChina`	None	
Frames	`fraPieces`	None	
	`fraQuantity`	None	
	`fraCompletePlaceSetting`	None	
Image	`imgChina`	None	

Labels	lblDateAndTime	None	
	lblPrice	None	
List Box	lstBrands	Click	Used to display a graphic of a china patter in the Image control
Menu		Click	More on this later
Option Buttons	optQuantity	Click	More on this later
Timer	tmrChina	Timer	Used to display date and time

"This is a list of objects in the China Shop Project," I said, "and a list of the event procedures for those objects which I reckon we will need to code. My guess at this point is that we'll place code in about nine event procedures."

"I don't know about anyone else," Linda said, "but that surprises me. Somehow I though there would be more code in more event procedures."

"See what I mean?" I said. "That's the beginner's inclination. Only write code when necessary."

"Something that I find interesting," Rhonda said, "is that we'll only be writing code that responds to three events, the **Load**, **Click** and **Timer** events."

I suggested that now would be a good time to examine these three events and after that I would give everyone their first exercise of the day.

The Click Event

"In the China Shop Project, five different types of objects will use the **Click** event: the check box, command button, list box, menu and option button. Regardless of the object, this event is triggered when the user presses and then releases a mouse button over the object. It can also be triggered by Visual Basic code."

"Suppose you have a form with several objects," Joe said, "and the user clicks on a command button. Is only the **Click** event of the command button triggered or will the **Click** event of the form also be triggered?"

"That's a good question," I said. "The `Click` event of the command button is triggered. The `Click` event of the form is only triggered when the mouse is clicked over an open area of the form."

"I understand triggering the event by clicking the mouse," Rhonda said, "but I'm confused as to how the `Click` event can be triggered by code."

I thought for a moment, and then gave them this example.

"Think back to last week's discussion of properties," I said. "Do you remember that when the check box is selected, its `Value` property is set to `1`? If we were to set the `Value` property to `1` in our code, that action would trigger the `Click` event of the check box."

There were a few more satisfied smiles around the room, so we moved on to a discussion of the `Load` event.

The Load Event

"In the China Shop Project," I said, "only the form can have a `Load` event, and it only occurs when a form is loaded."

"Does that happen when we run the project?" Valerie asked.

"In the case of the China Shop Project, yes. The form's `Load` event occurs when the project is run."

"What kind of code do you place in the `Load` event procedure?" Dave asked.

"Typically," I said, "any code that is used to set up the display or the environment before the user first sees your interface. Programmers call this **housekeeping** code. In the China Shop Project, we'll place code in the `Load` event procedure that will load the list box with china brands so it is ready before the user first sees the China Shop Project's user interface."

"So the `Load` event procedure takes place before the form becomes visible," Rhonda said. "That's right," I agreed.

The Timer Event

"Only the Timer control reacts to the `Timer` event," I said. "We've already discussed how we'll use this event in the China Shop Project. I think at this point, it makes sense to write some code!"

Writing Code

"The code window is nothing more than an editor," I said, "like Notepad or Word. We use it to write code that becomes part of a procedure, usually (but not always) an event procedure."

I asked everyone to verify that they had properly retrieved the China Shop Project from the directory on their hard drive, as I distributed this exercise for them to complete:

In this exercise, you'll add code to the **Load** event of the China Shop form to add china brands to the **lstBrands** List Box:

Exercise

Let's Bring up the Code Window

1. Run Visual Basic and load the China Shop Project by selecting the Open Project icon on the toolbar. Ensure the form folder in the project window is open and that our form is viewed by double clicking its icon.

2. Double-click on the China Shop form, making sure you don't select one of the controls by accident. The code window will appear:

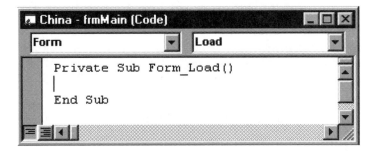

3. We'll use the **AddItem** method to add brands to the list box, so that when the China Shop program begins to run and the **Load** event of the form triggers, the china brands will appear in the list box. To invoke a method in Visual Basic, we need to type the object name, followed by a period and then the method name. Click your mouse pointer on the blank line following the event procedure header and type **lstbrands.** in the code window. As soon as you type the period, Visual Basic should display a list box of the methods of the List Box control:

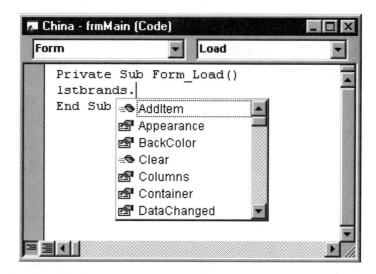

If you don't see the list of methods, select Tools-Options-Editor. Auto List Members must be checked in order for Visual Basic to display this list of methods.

4. Our work here is really easy! The first method displayed in the list box, the **AddItem** method, is the one we want to use. At this point, you can type the method name yourself, use your mouse to select it, or press the *Tab* key and the **AddItem** will be typed for you automatically in the code window:

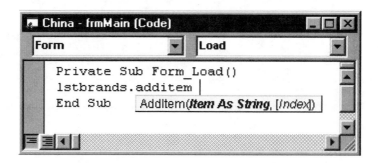

5. The **AddItem** method requires a single argument that tells Visual Basic the item to be added to our List Box control. In this instance, the argument will be enclosed within quotation marks. Complete the line of code by typing a space and **"Corelle",** so that the event procedure looks like this:

```
Private Sub Form_Load()
   lstBrands.AddItem "Corelle"
End Sub
```

6.   Repeat the process for **Faberware** and **Mikasa**:

```
Private Sub Form_Load()
   lstBrands.AddItem "Corelle"
   lstBrands.AddItem "Faberware"
   lstBrands.AddItem "Mikasa"
End Sub
```

7.   Save the China Shop Project.

8.   Run the program and you should see the three china brands in the list box:

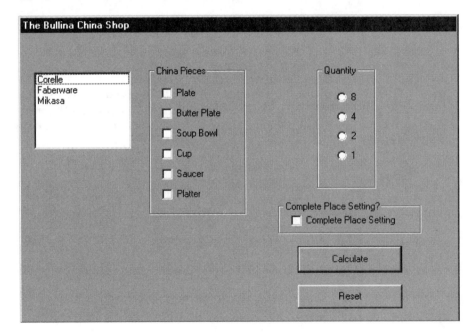

Discussion

The class completed this exercise with very few problems and everyone in the class was more than a little proud of themselves. That's not to say there weren't some anxious moments. After all, this was the first time anyone in the class had coded even a single Visual Basic statement before.

A few people didn't use double quotation marks, and some put a space between **lstBrands** and **AddItem** but these mistakes were quickly and easily resolved.

When everyone was finished, I displayed the following screen on the classroom projector:

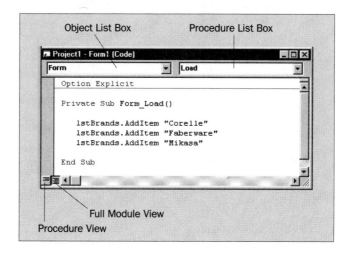

"The code window," I said, "like any ordinary window, has a title bar which displays both the project's name and the name of the form. It also has buttons to minimize, maximize and close itself, and like any other window, the code window can be re-sized."

"How long can the code statements be?" Valerie asked.

"Good question," I said. "A single line of code can be up to 1,023 characters in length and the number of lines in an event procedure is virtually unlimited. That's why you can see both horizontal and vertical scrollbars in the code window."

I directed everyone's attention to the two list boxes directly under the code window's title bar. "The code window contains two list boxes," I said, "the **Object List Box** on the left and the **Procedure List Box** on the right."

"I think we examined these a few weeks ago," Ward said, "and at that time you referred to the Procedure List Box as the Event List Box."

"That's right," I said. "I tend to use the two terms interchangeably, since depending on your perspective, the Procedure List Box also displays all the events to which the object in the Object List Box will respond."

I continued by explaining that when you double-click on an object, the code window's Object List Box will display the name of the object you double-clicked on. "And if it doesn't?" Chuck asked.

"That probably means," I said, "that you didn't double-click on the control you thought you did. That's an important point, because if you double-click on the wrong control, you could wind up placing code in the wrong event procedure. Beginners frequently make that mistake."

I then clicked on the Object List Box:

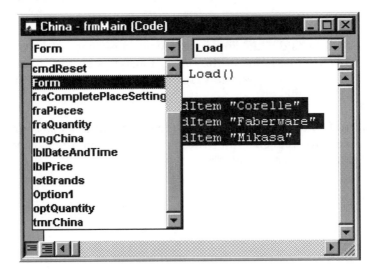

"As you can see," I said, "if you click on the Object List Box, Visual Basic will list all of the objects contained on your form."

I then clicked on the Procedure List Box:

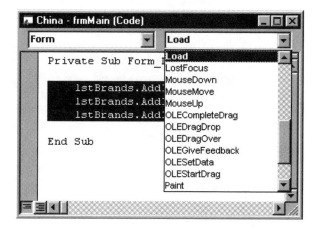

"In a similar way," I said, "if you click on the Procedure List Box, Visual Basic will list all of the events recognized by that object."

"So there's an event procedure stub associated with every event in the Procedure List Box, is that correct?" Lou asked. "That's right," I answered. "As you can see there are a great many events listed here. Don't worry too much about what they all mean as we'll only be using a handful of them."

"Before I move onto comments," I said, "there's one more thing in the Object List Box that I need to show you:"

"At the top of the Object List Box," I said, "you will always see something called (General) displayed. (General) refers to a special section of the form called the Standard Declarations Section. If you now click on the Procedure List Box, you'll see something displayed called (Declarations):"

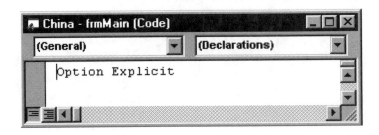

"I'm a little confused," Ward said. "Is (Declarations) the name of an event procedure, and if so, what object is it associated with?"

"Actually," I replied, "it's pretty much the opposite. The General Declarations section, as this is known, is where you place code that is not associated with a particular object."

"So it's a kind of 'catch-all' then?" Dave said. "Will we be placing any code here?"

"Yes," I said. "but that'll be in the next section of this course, when we transfer our prototype to the production release version."

"Now look at the bottom of the code window," I said. "There are two buttons to the left of the horizontal scroll bar. These buttons change the way you view code in the code window. By default, when you view the code window, you only see code associated with the object listed in the Object List Box. This is called **Procedure View**. However, if you click on the right button, **Full Module View** is invoked. Full Module View allows you to see all of the code for your module (in our case the form) in the same code window."

I then clicked on the Full Module button:

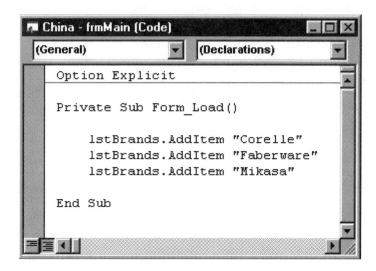

```
China - frmMain [Code]
(General)                    (Declarations)

   Option Explicit

   Private Sub Form_Load()

        lstBrands.AddItem "Corelle"
        lstBrands.AddItem "Faberware"
        lstBrands.AddItem "Mikasa"


   End Sub
```

"Full Module View doesn't look all that different to me," Kathy said.

"Since we have code in only one event procedure," I said, "at this point there isn't much difference between Full Module View and Procedure View. Do you see the phrase **Option Explicit** at the top of the code window? When you see those words, that indicates that the Require Variable Declaration option has been selected from the Tools-Options-Editor menu."

"That's something we definitely want, isn't it?" Chuck asked. "Absolutely," I said, "it will save you a lot of heartache later."

"It looks like we lost the General Declarations section," Ward said. "Full Module View confuses many programmers that way," I said, "and not just beginners. It just appears that way. Actually, **Option Explicit** is in the General Declarations section and you can see that illustrated in the list boxes if you actually click on the word **Option**."

"What's that line in the code window?" Ward asked. "That's the separator bar," I said, "by default that appears between event procedures in Full Module View."

"Some beginners," I said, "become confused by seeing all of the code for every event procedure they have written in one big window. Other beginners, until they become comfortable with the Object and Procedure List Boxes, sometimes believe they have somehow lost the code they have written. Ultimately, the choice of view is up to you."

Kate had a question about our last exercise. "I noticed," she said, "that when you typed the name of the object `lstBrands`, you typed it in lower case. I did the same and Visual Basic changed it automatically to upper and lower case."

"That's an excellent point," I said. "You probably noticed that when we named the objects in the China Shop project, we named them in what I call mixed case, a mixture of upper and lower case letters. Visual Basic maintains a list of all objects in your project and when it sees an object referenced in code it will change the name to match the exact spelling of the object."

"That's convenient," Mary said, "but does it serve any other purpose?"

"It's a great check of your code," I said. "We know that we have named all of our objects in mixed case so if you type the name of an object in an event procedure in lower case, Visual Basic should change it to mixed case."

If the object name remains in lower case, you know one of two things: either you misspelled the object name in the event procedure or the name of the object isn't what you think it is.

There were no other questions, so I said that prior to taking a break, I wanted to talk about Visual Basic program code comments and the line continuation character.

Program Comments

"Program comments are explanatory statements that you can include in the event procedure you are coding in," I said. "Comments are a useful addition to code for three reasons:"

- for ourselves when we come back to maintain or debug the code
- for other programmers who may read the code
- to disable a line of code without deleting it

"All programming languages allow for some version of this. The trick is how to tell Visual Basic that what you are entering in the event procedure is a comment, and not a Visual Basic statement to do something. In Visual Basic, you indicate this by using the special comment character, the apostrophe ('), after which everything on that line is ignored."

I displayed the form Load event procedure we had just written on the classroom projector, this time with comments included:

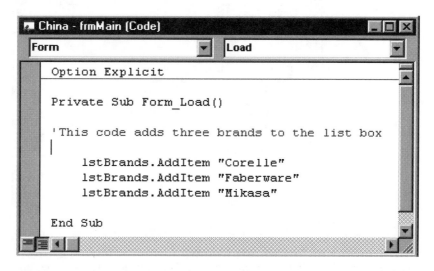

```
China - frmMain (Code)                          _ □ ×

Form                    ▼   Load                    ▼

    Option Explicit

    Private Sub Form_Load()

    'This code adds three brands to the list box

        lstBrands.AddItem "Corelle"
        lstBrands.AddItem "Faberware"
        lstBrands.AddItem "Mikasa"

    End Sub
```

"Notice that the comment is displayed in green," I said. "That's a function of the selections that are set in the Tools-Options-Editor Format menu."

"Is there a standard format for comments?" Rose asked.

"No," I said. "Some programmers include a comment at the top of the event procedure indicating the author of the code, the date the code was written and anything else they might find useful. Some programmers never comment. Myself, I use comments whenever I needed to look up something in the on-line help or one of my reference manuals. I figure that if I needed to look it up, then a comment explaining the code will be helpful the next time I or someone else views the code. Some programmers really make their comments elaborate, by drawing something programmers call a flower box in the code."

I modified the code we had written in the exercise to include a flower box and displayed it on the classroom projector:

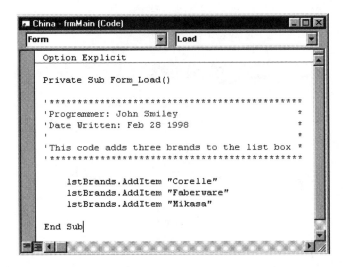

You can also comment a program with the REM statement, which is short for Remark. Begin a line of code with REM and Visual Basic will ignore the rest of the line. I prefer the use of the apostrophe to the REM statement as it is quicker, however, many older programmers still prefer to use REM so be prepared to come across it.

"Can a comment only appear on a line by itself or can it follow a Visual Basic statement?" Dave asked. "Another good question," I said. "Yes, you can place a comment after a Visual Basic statement."

I modified the code and displayed it on the classroom projector:

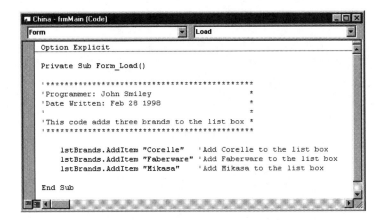

"Will we be adding comments in the exercises we do?" Kathy asked.

"We will only include comments that I consider essential; in other words, no flower boxes! If you want to add your own comments, then do so."

The Continuation Character (_)

As there were no other questions, we moved on to a discussion of the continuation character.

"As I mentioned earlier," I said, "a single line of Visual Basic code can be as many as 1,023 characters long, but for readability purposes, I wouldn't advise you to type beyond the width of the code window. However, as you'll see a little later, some of the code that we need to enter into our event procedures will exceed even that width. When that happens, you have two choices: continue typing or use the Visual Basic continuation character."

"In other words, you just can't break the code up into two lines," Linda said.

"That's right," I said. "Most programming languages are pretty strict as to the format of their code statements and Visual Basic is no exception. For instance, if you split a Visual Basic statement into two separate lines and then run the program, it will display an error message."

I then split the line of code that adds "Corelle" to the list box onto two lines and displayed the code on the classroom projector:

```
Private Sub Form_Load()
    lstBrands.AddItem
    "Corelle"
    lstBrands.AddItem  "Faberware"
    lstBrands.AddItem  "Mikasa"
End Sub
```

When I ran the program, the following error message was displayed:

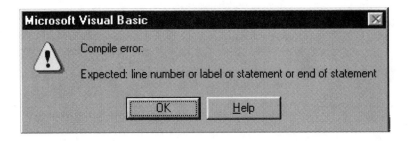

"Another user-friendly error message!" Linda said.

I explained that the answer to our dilemma is to use the continuation character, the underscore character (_).

"By using the continuation character, you can split a Visual Basic statement onto more than one line. Now the code works fine," I said, as I displayed this code on the classroom projector:

```
Private Sub Form_Load()
    lstBrands.AddItem _
    "Corelle"
    lstBrands.AddItem "Faberware"
    lstBrands.AddItem "Mikasa"
End Sub
```

"Is that space between **AddItem** and the continuation character required?" Rhonda asked.

"Excellent question," I said. "The continuation character must be separated from the last word on the line by a space and nothing else can follow the continuation character, not even a comment."

There were no more questions, so I gave the class a ten-minute break.

A Visual Basic Code Overview

When we resumed after break, I told everyone that I wanted to take some time to present a quick overview of the types of Visual Basic code that we would be writing in the coming weeks.

"Whenever possible," I said, "we'll be completing exercises that will ultimately lead to the completion of the China Shop Project. However, we'll also need to complete some exercises just for practice, and so that we don't get confused, we'll save these results to the Practice folder."

"There are three basic code structures that I wish to examine," I said. "First, we'll take a look at **sequence structure**; then **selection structure**; and finally, **loop structure**."

Visual Basic Code is Like a Falling Rock

"By default," I said, "code that we write in event procedures behaves just like a falling rock."

"What do you mean by that?" Steve said, obviously amused.

"In our first exercise today we wrote three separate Visual Basic statements to load china brands to the list box," I said. "Everyone just took it for granted that the first `AddItem` method was executed, followed by the second and finally the third. In other words, the code was executed one line after another. This is what I mean by a falling rock."

"Is there any other way?" asked Ward.

"Yes," I said, "in order to provide decision-making capabilities for your program, this falling rock behavior simply won't do. In order to illustrate the alternatives to the falling rock behavior, I'd like you to complete a series of exercises based on a fictitious collection of restaurants. Pretend, for a few minutes, that these seven restaurants have hired you to display ads for their eateries on a giant display screen in New York's Times Square:"

In this exercise, you'll use a method of the form that we haven't discussed yet called `Print`. The `Print` method allows you to print information on a form, and I believe it is a great learning tool. Pretend that the form is actually the giant display screen...

The completed project for this exercise, and other exercises in this chapter, can be found on the CD in the path \LTP VB6\Chapter06\Additional Exercises, named as indicated. This project is called Joe1.vbp.

Exercise

Eat at Joe's - A Falling Rock

1. Start a new **Standard.EXE** project.

2. Use your Toolbox to place a single command button on the form. Accept the default name that Visual Basic assigns.

3. Double-click on the command button and place the following code into the `Click` event procedure of the command button (OK, so we've strayed a little from the giant display screen idea!):

```
Private Sub Command1_Click()
    Form1.Print "Eat at Joe's"
    Form1.Print "Eat at Tom's"
    Form1.Print "Eat at Kevin's"
    Form1.Print "Eat at Rich's"
    Form1.Print "Eat at Rose's"
    Form1.Print "Eat at Ken's"
    Form1.Print "Eat at Melissa's"
End Sub
```

4. Save the project in `\VBFiles\Practice` with the form name `Ads.frm` and the file with the name `Joe.vbp` and then run the program.

5. Now click on the command button to trigger its `Click` event. The code that we have just placed in that event procedure will execute, one line after another. You should see the restaurant advertisements appear on the form:

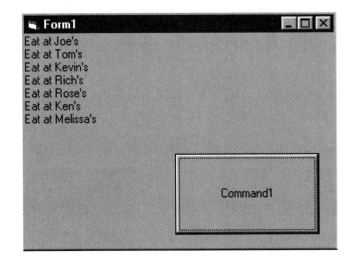

Discussion

No one in the class had any problems with this exercise.

"The four lines of code that we wrote," I said, "represent something known as a **sequence structure**. That just means that the second line of code executes after the first, the third after the second and so on. This is exactly what I meant by falling rock."

"Is everyone OK with the `Print` method?" I asked. "Sure," Rhonda said. "It just prints some text on the form, isn't that right?"

"That's basically it," I said, "Although we'll see as we progress through the next few exercises that the `Print` method can do a little bit more than that."

There were no other questions, so I continued. "Now suppose," I said, "that Joe of Joe's restaurant takes semi-retirement and decides to open only on Sundays. Tom, of Tom's restaurant, hears about this and decides to open only on Mondays. Kevin follows suit and opens Tuesdays, Rich Wednesday, Rose Thursday, Ken Friday and Melissa on Saturdays. To save advertising costs, each owner decides they want to advertise only on the days that their restaurant is actually open. How can we deal with this in our program?"

I gave them a moment or two to think about this. "I suppose," Ward said, "we could always write separate programs for different days of the week. Although I would hope there's a better way than that."

"You're right," I said. "We could write a program for each day of the week, but the ideal would be to have one program that is smart enough to know what day of the week it is and make a decision as to which restaurants to advertise. Fortunately, Visual Basic can know the day of the week and by using something called a **selection structure** we can give our program the capability to make decisions."

The Selection Structure

"Selection structures," I said, "can alter the default (falling rock) behavior of Visual Basic code, but they are a little more complicated to code. The programmer needs to specify conditions for Visual Basic to evaluate, in order for it to make decisions. Coding these conditions requires a little more thought 'up front', than merely coding a plain sequence structure."

In this exercise, we'll modify the program we completed just a few moments ago. We'll use the If statement in conjunction with your PC's date to display the individual restaurant advertising.

On the CD: Joe2.vbp.

Exercise

The If Statement (or Who's Open Today?)

1. Continue working with the Joe.vbp project.

2. Modify the Click event of the command button so that it looks like this:

```
Private Sub Command1_Click()
    If WeekDay(Now) = vbSunday Then Form1.Print "Eat " & _
                    "at Joe's"
    If WeekDay(Now) = vbMonday Then Form1.Print "Eat " & _
                    "at Tom's"
    If WeekDay(Now) = vbTuesday Then Form1.Print "Eat " & _
                    "at Kevin's"
    If WeekDay(Now) = vbWednesday Then Form1.Print "Eat" & _
                    "at Rich's"
    If WeekDay(Now) = vbThursday Then Form1.Print "Eat " & _
                    "at Rose's"
    If WeekDay(Now) = vbFriday Then Form1.Print "Eat " & _
                    "at Ken's"
    If WeekDay(Now) = vbSaturday Then Form1.Print "Eat " & _
                    "at Melissa's"
End Sub
```

3. Save the project and then run it.

4. Click on the command button and, depending on what day it is, you should see one restaurant ad. (Since my course was run on Saturdays, when we ran our project we saw Melissa's ad).

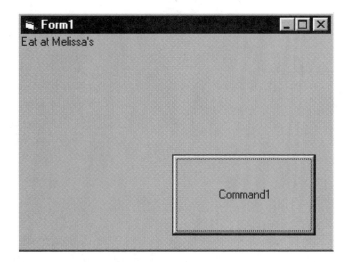

Discussion

Although no one had any trouble completing the exercise, there were still a number of puzzled looks in the classroom.

"I had no idea you could do that," Steve said. I explained that we had modified the program to alter its default behavior. Instead of just printing all seven advertisements on the form, this program determines the day of the week from the date maintained on the user's PC and then prints the advertisement appropriate for that day.

"Is that what that WeekDay statement is?" Dave asked. "That's right," I said. "WeekDay is an example of something called a **function**. We'll learn more about functions after we have completed our prototype. Let's take a look at the code to display Melissa's advertising:"

```
If WeekDay(Now) = vbSaturday Then Form1.Print "Eat " & _
                      "at  Melissa's"
```

"The key to the program," I said, "is the ability of our program to know what day of the week it is. Fortunately, there is a Visual Basic function called Now which interrogates the system date and time on the user's PC.

In Visual Basic, functions return an answer called a **return value**. We then used this return value as an argument to the `WeekDay` function. `WeekDay` examines today's date and determines the day of the week. Then we took the return value of the `WeekDay` function and compared it to the Visual Basic intrinsic constant `vbSaturday`. If the return value of `WeekDay(Now)` equals the value of `vbSaturday`, then we print the advertising message on the form."

"You may be confused at this point," I said, "after all, this is all pretty new to all of you. Hang in there though, because next week we're going to talk about nothing but selection structures."

The third and last programming structure we examined was the **loop structure**.

The Loop Structure

"Loop structures," I said, "allow you to execute portions of your code repetitively without having to write the code more than once."

"Why would we want to do that?" Rhonda asked.

"Let's consider the Automated Teller Machine (ATM)," I said. "When I visit my local ATM, I always find it up and running. After the last customer has finished using the ATM, the program just loops back to the beginning. The program prompts the customer to insert their ATM card to begin a new transaction."

"That's right," Ward agreed. "After I've done with my transaction, it prompts me to remove my card. The next thing it does is display a message to insert the card to begin a new transaction."

"That's the loop structure of the program," I said. "Instead of the program just ending, it continues running."

I suggested that we leave our restaurant advertising business behind and write a program to print the numbers from one to ten on a form. "This will be a pretty tedious exercise," I said, "but I need to show you this method before we see how the loop structure can make our programming work much better."

On the CD: Count1.vbp.

Exercise

Displaying Numbers from 1 to 10 on the Form

1   Start a new **Standard.EXE** project.

2   Use your Toolbox to place a single command button on the form. Accept the default name that Visual Basic assigns.

3   Double-click on the command button and place the following code into its **Click** event procedure:

```
Private Sub Command1_Click()
    Form1.Print 1
    Form1.Print 2
    Form1.Print 3
    Form1.Print 4
    Form1.Print 5
    Form1.Print 6
    Form1.Print 7
    Form1.Print 8
    Form1.Print 9
    Form1.Print 10
End Sub
```

4   Save the form as **Display.frm** and the project as **Count1.vbp** in the **\VBFiles\Practice** subdirectory and run it.

5   Click on the Command1 button and the numbers 1 through 10 will be printed on the form, as the following screen shot shows:

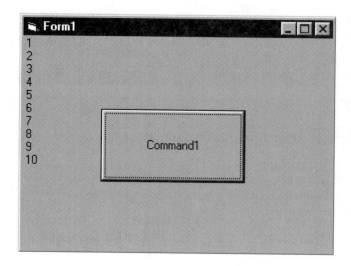

Discussion

Everyone agreed that nothing fancy was going on here. I guess by now, this was 'old hat' to them. All we did was code ten **Print** statements.

"I'd like you to consider," I said, "how you would modify this program to print the numbers from 1 to 10,000?"

"Well," Joe said, "if we follow the same methodology as we used in this program, instead of writing 10 lines of code we're going to have to write 10,000. As Ward said earlier about the restaurant problem, there must be an easier way!"

"Absolutely right," I said. "Instead of coding ten thousand **Print** statements, we'll use a Visual Basic loop structure to repeat the **Print** statement ten thousand times."

"But the number that we print must change each time," Dave said. "How can we handle that?"

"Good question, Dave," I said. "We'll need to use something called a **counter variable** to increment the value we want to print on the form by one each time the **Print** method executes."

I explained that we would cover both the loop structure and variables a little later in the course in much more detail, but for now we'd take a quick glimpse at what we could do.

On the CD: Count2.vbp.

Exercise

Displaying Numbers from 1 to 10,000 - the Loop Structure

1 Start a new Standard EXE project.

2 Place a single command button on the form. Accept the default name that Visual Basic assigns.

3 Double-click on the command button and place the following code into its `Click` event procedure:

```
Private Sub Command1_Click()
    Dim lngCounter As Long        'Declare the counter
                                  'variable
    For lngCounter = 1 To 10000 'Loop structure begins here
        Form1.Cls                 'Clear the form
        Form1.Print lngCounter    'Print a number
    Next lngCounter               'Loop structure ends here
End Sub
```

4 Save the project in the \VBFiles\Practice subdirectory the form as Display2.frm and the project as Count2.vbp then run it.

5 Click on the command button. The numbers 1 through 10,000 print on the form, but this time they will not be listed down the side of the form as they were in the previous exercise. Visual Basic forms are not scrollable and for that reason we are clearing the previously printed number before printing the next. Depending on the speed of your PC, you may or may not see all of the numbers printed. When the program ends, you should see the number 10,000 on your form.

Discussion

I ran the code myself on my classroom PC and it took just under five seconds to run from 1 through to 10,000.

Procedurally, the class had no trouble completing the exercise, but understanding it was something else. I did see some amazement at the speed with which the code counted from 1 to 10,000.

"The first thing we did in this code was to declare a variable," I said, as I displayed this line of code on the classroom projector:

```
Dim lngCounter As Long        'Declare the counter variable
```

"We'll discuss variables and how to declare them a little later in the course," I said.

"For now, think of a variable as just a placeholder in the computer's memory. When we declare a variable, we notify Visual Basic that a variable by that name should be created and placed in memory. Once we had declared the variable, we implemented the Visual Basic loop structure by using this statement:"

```
For lngCounter = 1 To 10000 'Loop structure begins here
```

"A **For...Next** loop," I said, "is a loop structure that causes code within the body of the loop to be executed a definite number of times, something that we want to do in this case because we know the numbers we want to print. There are also other Visual Basic loop structures that will execute code an indefinite number of times."
"Why do that?" Ward asked. "Think back to our ATM example," I said. "The total number of customers who will use the ATM program is not known. A definite type loop doesn't make sense there."

"What part of this code is actually the loop structure?" Peter asked. "The loop structure consists of the four lines of code beginning with the word **For** and ending with the line beginning with the word **Next**. Everything in between is called the **body** of the loop, and it is those statements that are executed the number of times that the **For** line specifies. In this case, a total of 10,000 times."

"How do we know it will execute 10,000 times?" Ward asked. "Is that what the **1 To 10000** tells Visual Basic?"

"That's right," I replied.

"By the way, did you notice the **Cls** method of the form?":

```
Form1.Cls                    'Clear the form
```

"**Cls**," I said, "which I pronounce as clear, is a method of the form that clears it of any numbers previously printed using the **Print** method."

"Why erase a number you just printed?" Chuck said.

"Using the `Print` method of the form," I said, "is a quick way of displaying information on the form, but its one big drawback is that it doesn't scroll. As a result, when you print more than a few lines on the form, numbers begin to 'disappear' off the bottom of the form. However, by clearing the numbers after we display them, we're able to see a running display of the numbers."

"I'm not sure how the numbers are being printed," Barbara said. "Are we printing a variable?"

"Actually," I said, "to be perfectly precise, we're printing the value of a variable. Each time the code within the body of the loop is executed, this statement prints the current value of the variable `lngCounter`":

```
Form1.Print lngCounter    'Print a number
```

"How does the value ever change?" Lou asked.

"Each time the body of the loop is executed," I said, "the value of the variable `lngCounter` is incremented by 1. That's really what the `Next` statement does. Therefore, the first time the loop is executed, the value of `lngCounter` is equal to 1; the second time 2 and so on. Ultimately, the body of the loop executes 10,000 times."

I emphasized that our treatment of the loop structure during this exercise, though perhaps exhausting, wasn't exhaustive. We would talk about loops in much more detail in a future class. I asked if there were any other questions and Chuck indicated that he was still a little uncertain about events and when they occur.

"Your question, Chuck, is perfectly timed," I said. "For the remainder of the class, we're going to look at techniques that give us a behind the scenes look at our program. I have a exercise prepared to show everyone a technique I use to 'visualize' exactly when events occur."

In this exercise, you'll use two new Visual Basic statements to inform you when an event procedure has been triggered.

On the CD: Eview.vbp.

Exercise

Viewing Events as They Take Place

1   Start a new `Standard.EXE` project.

2   Use your Toolbox to place two command buttons on the form, accepting the default names that Visual Basic assigns (Command1 and Command2).

3   Double-click on Command1 and place the following code into its `Click` event procedure:

```
Private Sub Command1_Click()
   MsgBox "Command1 Click event has been triggered"
End Sub
```

4   Save the project in your `Practice` directory the form as `Display3.frm` and the project as `Eview.vbp` and then run it.

5   Click on Command1. A Visual Basic **Message Box** will be displayed informing you that the Command1 Click event has been triggered. You'll need to click on the OK button to clear the message box:

6   We'll use another technique for the second command button; double-click on Command2 and place the following code into its Click event procedure:

```
Private Sub Command2_Click()
   Debug.Print "Command2 Click event has been triggered"
End Sub
```

7   Save `Eview.vbp` again and run your program.

8 Click on Command2 and you should see the Immediate window appear, with a message indicating that the Command2 Click event has been triggered. Click on Command2 again and the message will be repeated. You may want to adjust the size and placement of the Immediate window for easier viewing:

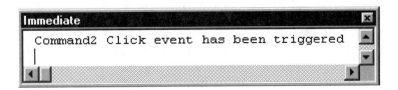

Discussion

I explained that the two techniques that we had employed in this exercise (the MsgBox function and the Print method of the Debug object) are extremely useful whenever you are not sure of the exact timing of a Visual Basic event.

"I use one of these techniques quite often," I said, "to create an event viewer whenever I'm unsure of exactly when an event occurs. By placing these 'sentries' as I call them in an event procedure, you'll know whenever the corresponding event is triggered. Using these sentries, you can answer questions such as: Which event occurs first, the Load event or the Activate event of the form?"

"Do you have a preference?" Linda asked.

"As you can see," I replied, "the MsgBox technique tends to interrupt the program flow a little bit more. The MsgBox function is primarily a tool to communicate with the user of your program, whereas the Print method of the Debug object is strictly a programmer tool."

"When I did the exercise," Valerie said, "I had trouble finding the Immediate window. It was there, I just had to hunt for it."

"That might be a reason to opt for the Message Box technique," I replied. "Of course, if you can't find it at all, you can always select View-Immediate Window. Now let's turn our attention to the Visual Basic debugger."

The Visual Basic Debugger

"When I spoke of the IDE several weeks back," I said, "and we examined the <u>D</u>ebug menu, I promised that we would look at it in greater detail."

"Isn't the debugger a tool for discovering and correcting code errors in your program?" Steve asked. "We haven't written much code at all. Aren't we too early for this?"

"Not at all," I said. "Just as the event viewer can be used to discover what's happening behind the scenes of Visual Basic, the debugger can be used to see what's going on behind the scenes of a perfectly healthy program, not just one with errors. Many courses and books treat the debugger as an afterthought, using it as a tool to uncover problems in programs after they have already been written. I believe the debugger is much more. It's an invaluable learning tool and one you should use frequently as you proceed through the rest of your careers. Whenever you run a program, consider using the techniques that you'll learn in the next few moments to gain a fuller appreciation for how your program really works."

The Debug/Immediate Window

"The debugger isn't one single tool," I said, "but rather a collection of tools. We have already used the `Print` method of the form as a rudimentary debugging tool, enabling us to see the value of a variable as the program was running. In the last exercise, we used the `Print` method again, but this time with a special system object called the `Debug` object. The advantage of using the `Debug` object over the `Form` object is that you aren't using an object (the form) that is part of your user interface to display information about your running program."

I suggested that we modify our code to print the numbers from 1 to 10,000 to the `Debug` object instead of on the `Form` object. One big advantage of the `Debug` object is that it will scroll:

In this exercise, we'll write code that will print the numbers from 1 through 10,000 in the Immediate window.

On the CD: Count2b.vbp.

Exercise

The Immediate Window

1   Load up Count2.vbp **again**.

2   Change the code in the **Click** event procedure so that it looks like this:

```
Private Sub Command1_Click()
    Dim lngCounter As Long        'Declare the counter
                                  'variable
    For lngCounter = 1 To 10000 'Loop structure begins here
       Debug.Print lngCounter     'Output the results to the
                                  'immediate window
    Next lngCounter               'Loop structure ends here
End Sub
```

3   Save Count2.vbp and then run the program.

4   Click on the command button. You should see the numbers 1 through 10,000 displayed in the Immediate window. When the program ends, you'll see that you can scroll up and down in the Immediate window to see some of the 10,000 numbers.

Discussion

"I'm confused," Mary said, "between the Immediate window and the **Debug** object. Are they the same thing?"

"Practically speaking, yes," I said. "The Immediate window is the output 'canvas' for the **Debug** object. You can also enter Visual Basic commands directly into the Immediate window and they will be 'immediately' executed. We'll look at that in more detail in a few minutes."

"How can I clear the contents of the Immediate window?" Dave said. "I tried using a **Debug.Cls** statement?" Dave asked. "Good try," I said. "You can't clear the Immediate window programmatically, although you can select text in the Immediate window and press the *Backspace* key to delete it."

"I just noticed," Linda said, "that although you can scroll in the Immediate window, you can't see all of the numbers that were printed using the **Debug** object's **Print** method. So even the Immediate window has a limit as to how far you can scroll backwards."

Pausing a Visual Basic Program

After acknowledging Linda's excellent point about the limitations of scrolling in the Immediate window, I posed this hypothetical question: Suppose we want to pause our program while it is running?

"Why would we want to do that?" Rhonda asked. "Suppose I told you that if we pause a Visual Basic program," I said, "we can then view the values of object properties and variables in the program."

I could see that some members of the class were pondering that possibility, so I asked everyone to re-run the code to print out the numbers from 1 to 10,000.

"Notice," I said, as I ran the program myself, "that while the program is running, there isn't anything that you can do to interact with it. You can't minimize, maximize, re-size or move the form. You can't click on the close button to stop the program. Neither can you click on the control menu icon and stop it that way either. Try stopping the program by clicking on the End button on the Visual Basic Toolbar. Even that doesn't work! What's happening here?"

"Falling rock behavior?" Dave said.

"Perhaps more like a runaway train," Linda said.

"When we placed code in the command button's `click` event," I said, "to execute the body of the loop 10,000 times, nothing will stop the program before it reaches the end of the event procedure."

"I didn't realize that," Dave said. "You mean when the event procedure starts, it ignores everything else until it ends?"

"Just about," I said. "Let's try an experiment."

I told everyone in the class to run the program again, but this time I asked them to see if they could start another Windows application, such as the Calculator, while the program ran. I gave everyone a few moments to work on this and I did the same on my classroom PC.

"That worked," Rhonda said. "While the program is running, I can run the Calculator. Why is it that we can run another Windows program, but we can't seem to get the attention of our own program?"

"The answer," I said, "is Pre-emptive Multitasking, which we discussed in a previous class. Windows 95 and NT are Pre-emptive Multitasking operating systems, which means that they take steps to ensure that no single program monopolizes the microprocessor. That's why when our program is busy counting from 1 to 10000, Windows still allows us to start up the Calculator."

"Is that a big deal?" Valerie asked. "It can be," I replied. I suggested that there might be times where we want our event procedure to be interruptible by our own program.

"For instance," I said, "suppose you design a program that has two command buttons. One button initiates some kind of long running process involving a loop that may take many minutes, even hours to complete. The other button, when clicked, permits the user to view sales invoices. Now if the user clicks on the first button, you don't want him or her to have to wait hours until the first event procedure ends, before the other button will work."

"However, that could be the case if you have a loop coded in the first event procedure. Fortunately for us, there is a way to tell Visual Basic that you want the event procedure to 'look up' from its work from time to time, and that is by coding a `DoEvents` statement somewhere within the body of the loop."

I asked everyone to make the following change to `Count2.vbp`.

On the CD: Count2c.vbp.

```
Private Sub Command1_Click()
    Dim lngCounter As Long          'Declare the counter
                                    'variable
    For lngCounter = 1 To 10000     'Loop structure begins here
        Debug.Print lngCounter      'Output the results to the
                                    'immediate window

        DoEvents                    'Are there any Windows
                                    'messages
                                    'to process?

    Next lngCounter                 'Loop structure ends here
End Sub
```

Then I asked them to run the program and see if it behaved differently.

"That did the trick," Rose said. "Now I can minimize, maximize, re-size and move the form. It certainly has made a difference!"

"You can also click on the End button on the Toolbar to stop the program," Jack said.

"That's right," I said. "Placing the `DoEvents` statement within the body of the loop instructs your program to check the Windows Message Queue for pending events each time the `DoEvents` statement is encountered. Perhaps most importantly, at least from a debugging point of view, you can also pause your program by clicking on the Break button. Let's look at that Break button now."

The Break Button

"Unlike the End button," I said, "which simply ends your program, the Break button will interrupt your program in midstream. The program can then be re-started by clicking on the Start button, (which becomes the Continue button when the program is paused)."

I asked everyone to run the `Count2.vbp` program again and to pause it shortly after starting it by pressing the Break button.

"If you check the display in the Immediate window," I said, "you'll be able to determine exactly where your program was when you interrupted it. Look at the title bar, as it should indicate that you are now in [break] mode:"

Displaying Values in the Code Window

"While the program is paused," I said, "Visual Basic allows you to view the value of a variable or property in the code window, just by placing your mouse pointer over the code referencing either one."

I invited everyone in the class to view the value of the variable `lngCounter` while their program was paused:

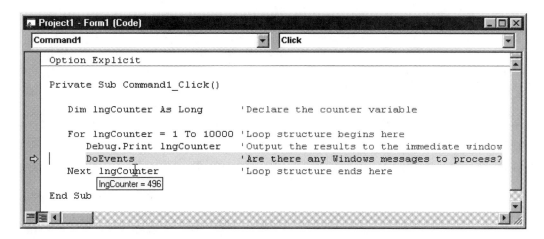

"Here you can see that I stopped the application when the variable was 496," I said.

The Immediate Window

"In addition to viewing the values of variables and properties in the code window while your program is paused," I said, "you can also type Visual Basic commands and statements into the Immediate window. This gives you the ability to interrogate your program while it is paused and even to execute commands to see how they work prior to placing them into event procedures. For instance, after you've paused your program, you can type this command into the Immediate window:"

```
Print lngCounter
```

"This command will display the current value of the variable **lngCounter** in the Immediate window," I said. "You sometimes see the same command abbreviated like this:"

```
? lngCounter
```

"Both commands work in exactly the same way," I said, "and of course, for viewing the values of properties and variables, nothing beats the mouse pointer in the code window."

"You might ask, 'Why use the Immediate window?' The answer is the ability to enter Visual Basic commands that do more than display the value of a variable. For instance, you can type this into the Immediate window when your program is paused:"

```
lngCounter = 1
```

"Entering this statement in the Immediate window sets the value of the variable lngCounter to 1. This causes the program to start counting all over again from 1. Try it yourself if you want."

"I was about to say 'Why bother with the Immediate window?' when you can get information directly out of the code window," Linda said, "but you answered my question."

"You can also change the value of a property using the Immediate window," I said. "Try this one:"

```
Form1.caption = "John's Form"
```

"In fact," I said, "virtually anything you can do in a Visual Basic event procedure can be done in the Immediate window while the program is paused. You probably won't fully realize this benefit until you're in the midst of trying to get some troublesome code to work properly. Then you'll find that being able to pause the program and use the Immediate window like this can be vitally important."

"I tried to type into the Immediate window," Ward said, "but Visual Basic won't let me."

A quick trip to his workstation revealed that he had forgotten to pause the program before trying to type into the Immediate window.

"Now once the program has paused," Rhonda said, "you can start the program again, even if you change the value of a property or a variable?"

"That's right," I said. "You can type anything into the Immediate window while the program is paused and your program should still re-start if you click the start icon. It's also possible to change code in the code window while the program is paused and still re-start the program."

"Do you do that often?" asked Valerie.

"On occasion," I confessed, "I'll have paused my program and realized that a certain piece of code isn't quite right. At that point, rather than stop the program and then correct it, I've just changed it right then and there. Most times Visual Basic will just take the change without balking. If by chance you change something that causes Visual Basic to balk at re-starting the program, it will display a message informing you of the problem."

The Stop Statement

"We've seen," I said, "that you can pause a running program by clicking on the **Break** button or by selecting <u>R</u>un-Brea<u>k</u> from the menu. There is also a keyboard method to do the same thing and that is to press the *Break* key on the keyboard, (although you should note that the *End* key does not perform the same function as the **End** button). There's also a Visual Basic statement that will pause your program, the Visual Basic **Stop** statement."

I asked everyone to make the following change to the **Count2.vbp** program with which we had been experimenting.

 On the CD: Count2d.vbp.

```
Private Sub Command1_Click()
    Dim lngCounter As Long              'Declare the counter
                                        'variable
    For lngCounter = 1 To 10000         'Loop structure begins
                                        'here
        If lngCounter = 500 Then Stop   'Stop when the count
                                        'gets
                                        'to 500
        Debug.Print lngCounter          'Output the results to
                                        'the immediate window
        DoEvents                        'Are there any Windows
                                        'messages to process?
    Next lngCounter                     'Loop structure ends
                                        'here
End Sub
```

"This program will pause as soon as the value of the variable **lngCounter** is equal to 500 by using the **If** statement that we saw earlier. When the program pauses, Visual Basic will display the program's code window with the **Stop** statement highlighted and an arrow in the margin pointing to the paused line of code":

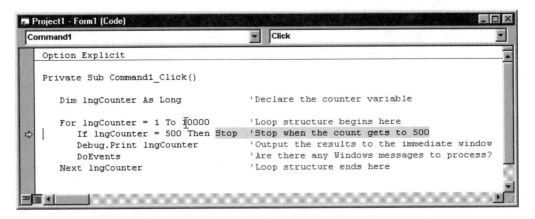

"Interestingly," I said, "the Immediate window displays the value 499, since the program was stopped prior to reaching the line of code that would have printed the value 500."

The Debug Menu

So far, we hadn't really looked at the Debug menu in detail:

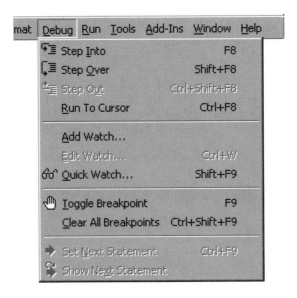

"The <u>D</u>ebug menu," I said, "has several options that are invaluable in seeing behind the scenes of your program as well as in helping you to correct problems with your code."

Step <u>I</u>nto

"I think the Step <u>I</u>nto command is one of the most valuable debugging tools in Visual Basic," I said. "Step <u>I</u>nto, or as I usually call it Step mode, allows you to view the execution of your code one line at a time. As you run your program in Step mode, the Visual Basic code window appears and each line of code that is about to be executed is highlighted."

I suggested that we re-run **Count2.vbp** in Step mode. "Whilst in the design mode either press the *F8* function key," I said, "or select <u>D</u>ebug-Step <u>I</u>nto."

I did so myself and displayed the results on the classroom projector. After the form appeared, I clicked on the command button to begin our count towards 10,000. At that point, the code window appeared and the first line of code in the **Click** event procedure was highlighted:

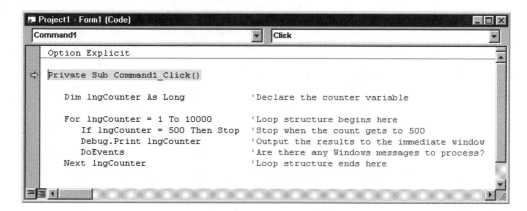

"The important thing to note here," I said, "is that the arrow and the highlight marks the line of code that is *about to be executed*, not the line of code that has been executed."

"Why wasn't the form's **Load** event displayed when we started the program?" Dave said.

"Visual Basic will only step through event procedures which actually contain code," I said. "Since our program contains no code in the **Load** event of the form, its event procedure was never displayed. Once the **Click** event of the command button is triggered, Visual Basic pauses on the first line of the event procedure, the event procedure header. To continue 'stepping through' the program, we must either press the *F8* function key again, or once again select <u>D</u>ebug-Step <u>I</u>nto."

"I noticed that Step mode skipped right by the Dim statement," Barbara said. "Excellent observation," I said. "That's a bit of a quirk in my opinion. The variable declaration was still executed."

As I continued stepping through the program on the classroom projector, we then noticed that Visual Basic paused on this line of code:

```
For lngCounter = 1 To 10000          'Loop structure begins
                                     'here
```

This line of code will causes the loop to count from 1 to 10000.

As we continued stepping through the program, the next four lines of code were executed one after the other:

```
    If lngCounter = 500 Then Stop    'Stop when the count gets
                                     'to 500
    Debug.Print lngCounter           'Output the results to
                                     'the immediate window
    DoEvents                         'Are there any Windows
                                     'messages to process?
Next lngCounter                      'Loop structure ends here
```

Again, I pointed out that in Step mode, the line of code that is highlighted is actually the next line of code that will be executed, not the line that was executed. Therefore, when Visual Basic paused on the line:

```
Debug.Print lngCounter               'Output the results to the
                                     'immediate window
```

nothing had been printed in the Immediate Window yet.

We then saw that after the line:

```
Next lngCounter                      'Loop structure ends here
```

was executed, the program 'jumped' up to the If statement line, which is the first line in the body of the loop. We never saw this line of code:

For lngCounter = 1 To 10000   'Loop structure begins
                                  'here

executed again.

"I really expected that the program would jump back to the `For lngCounter` line," Linda said. "When we cover loops in detail in a few weeks," I said, "we'll discuss possible reasons for this behavior."

I sensed that everyone was enjoying this. I could barely get their attention as I started to cover the next topic.

Run To Cursor

"Stepping through an entire Visual Basic program," I said, "by pressing the *F8* function key can be pretty tiresome. You can always run the program to normal completion after starting in Step mode by pressing *F5* or by selecting Run-Start. But, suppose you don't want to proceed line by line or the program to run to completion. Is there something in between?"

"Actually, there is. Start the program running in Step mode, select a line of code in the event procedure that you want to execute up 'to' and then select Debug-Run To Cursor. This tells Visual Basic to execute the code up to the line in the code window that you have selected. All lines of code up to, but not including that line, will then be executed."

Step Over

"Step Over," I said, "is similar to Step Into, but it differs in the way that code is displayed when one event procedure 'calls' another."

I explained that we hadn't yet seen an example where the code in one event procedure can 'call' or execute code in another procedure.

"Let's say you have two procedures," I said, "procedure A and procedure B. Procedure A contains code which 'calls' procedure B. Suppose you are absolutely certain that the code in procedure B is functioning flawlessly and therefore you have no desire to see it execute line by line. If you select Step Over, the code in procedure A will be displayed line by line. However, when procedure A calls procedure B, the code in procedure B will be executed, but Visual Basic will not display it. The next line of code in procedure A will be displayed instead."

Step Out

"If you are currently running your program in Step mode," I said, "Step Out tells Visual Basic to execute the remaining lines of code in the current event procedure normally. Once the event procedure runs to completion, your program is still in Step mode."

"How is that different from just pressing the Start button?" Linda asked. "The difference," I replied, "is that you are still in Step mode when the event procedure ends."

Set Next Statement

"The other Step commands which we've discussed," I said, "don't affect the way the program executes, just the 'speed' at which they run. With Set Next Statement you can change the order in which your lines of code execute, allowing you to 'skip' or repeat lines of code in an event procedure."

"Can you explain why we would want to do that?" Rhonda asked.

"How about this example," I said. "Suppose you have a program that has been giving you a problem, so you decide to run it in Step mode. While you are interrogating the program, you begin to suspect one line of code as the cause of the problem. So at this point, you could end the program, make the appropriate change to the event procedure (perhaps deleting that line of code), and re-run the program to see if it works."

"However, this is a little 'clunky'. Better yet, while the program is running in Step mode and the code window is open, you can test your theory that this line of code is really the problem by selecting the next line of code after it using your mouse. By selecting Debug-Set Next Statement that line of code will be skipped and you can then verify your theory immediately."

"The great thing about that," Dave said, "is if you're wrong about that line of code, you haven't really altered the event procedure. There's nothing to undo."

"That's right," I agreed, "and if it turns out you are correct, you can then make the change permanent by then deleting the troublesome line of code."

Show Ne_xt Statement

"Programmers frequently become confused," I said, "while running their programs in Step mode."

As you might imagine, this elicited quite a few laughs. "If you want to know the next Visual Basic statement that will be executed in Step mode," I continued, "select _Debug-Show Ne_xt Statement and Visual Basic will highlight it."

We had been working for quite a while and questions were becoming few and far between, a sure sign of fatigue. I called for a ten-minute break and told everyone that when we returned, we would wrap up the topic of the Visual Basic debugger.

The Watch Window

After we returned from break, I said that in addition to the Immediate window, there is another important debugging window called the Watch window.

"The Watch window," I said, "allows you to view **watch expressions**, which I'll show you how to set up shortly. By setting watch expressions, you can view the values of variables and properties just like we did using the `Debug.Print` statement in our code."

"What's the advantage of a watch expression then?" Linda asked.

"Well," I said, "you don't need to make changes to your code as watch expressions are set in the IDE, not in the code. When you run your program, depending upon the **watch type** you have defined, you may see a Watch window like this appear and the value of any defined watch expressions will be displayed:

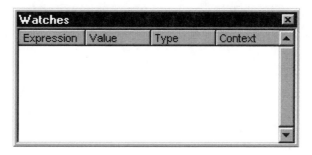

Setting a Watch Expression

As a demonstration of a watch expression, I opened up the code window for the Click event of the `Count2.vbp` project. For demonstration purposes, I decided to modify the code slightly by removing the line of code containing the `Stop` statement. I wanted to show everyone if the event procedure ran without pausing, with a watch, the Watch window would never be displayed.

I also removed the `Debug.Print` statement and, just to be certain that everyone knew that the event procedure had finished, I added a `Msgbox` function to display an `All Done!` message at the end:

```
Private Sub Command1_Click()
    Dim lngCounter As Long          'Declare the counter
                                    'variable
    For lngCounter = 1 To 10000 'Loop structure begins here
        DoEvents                    'Are there any Windows
                                    'messages to process?
    Next lngCounter                 'Loop structure ends here
    Msgbox "All done!"              'Msgbox to denote end of
                                    'procedure
End Sub
```

"There are several ways to set a watch expression," I said. "The easiest way is to set it while you are in the code window."

"There are three references to `lngCounter` in the event procedure," I said. "It's important to choose one that is contained within the body of the loop."

I then selected the reference to `lngCounter` by placing the cursor within the word `lngCounter` that is on the line of code, `Next lngCounter`. "At this point," I said, "you can invoke the Add Watch dialog box in one of three ways:"

- select Debug-Add Watch
- right click on the word and select Add Watch
- select the Watch icon from the Debug Toolbar and right click inside the watch window that appears and choose Add Watch

I selected Add Watch from the Debug menu:

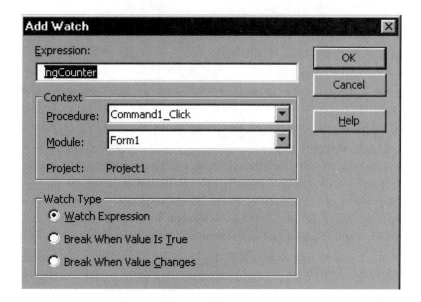

"I know that the Add Watch window can appear to be pretty complicated to beginners," I said, "but it's not really as bad as it looks. At the top of the Add Watch window is a box labeled Expression, this is where the watch expression is specified. Notice that by selecting the variable lngCounter in the code window, the Expression: box should already be filled in."

I explained that the Context section of the Add Watch dialog box had already been completed for us, specifying the Procedure, the Module (in this case Form1), and the Project that the watch expression is set for.

"Since we can specify more than one watch expression at a time," I said, "this information is necessary for Visual Basic to keep track of all of the watch expressions. The Context section is not anything that you need to worry about, since Visual Basic will complete it for you. In fact, if you pre-select your expression in the code window the way we just did, the only choice you need to make is the Watch Type."

I then selected the default watch type of Watch Expression on my classroom PC and clicked on the OK button. After doing so, this Watch window appeared:

"The Watch window is a great source of confusion in itself," I said. "Notice how the Value column specifies <Out of context>. The reason for that is because the program isn't running yet! lngCounter has no value yet, and in fact, before the event procedure is run, it doesn't even exist. The same applies to Type. Since the program isn't running yet, Visual Basic doesn't know what type of variable lngCounter is."

While I ran the program, I reminded everyone that with this type of watch, the program would just run to completion, which is exactly what happened. Five seconds later, a message box announcing the end of the program was displayed:

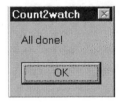

"Beginners find the behavior of this watch type very frustrating," I said. "Like me, they would prefer to see the value of the variable displayed as the program runs, much like the Immediate window displayed the results of our Debug.Print statement, but that's not what happens."

I then ran the program again, but this time I clicked on the Break button shortly after starting it and Visual Basic displayed the Watch window (if your processor is fast then you need to change the loop value in the code from 10000 to something higher to give you time to break the program!):

"Notice," I said, "that the Value column now contains a valid value and the Type column now contains a valid Visual Basic Type of Long (more on that later)."

I continued by saying that pausing a running program yourself, in order to see the value of a watch expression is hardly ideal. "Fortunately," I said, "the vanilla Watch Expression type is not the only type of watch that we can set. For instance, there may be times when we want to pause the program only when the value of an expression becomes equal to a specific value. We can do that by changing our watch type from Watch Expression to Break When Value Is True."

I explained that changing watch types is easy. "You select the watch expression in the Watch window and delete it by pressing the *Delete* key, and then add a new one, just as we did before," I said, "or you can select the watch expression in the Watch window and then select Debug-Edit Watch from the main menu, or right click on the expression in the watch window and select Edit Watch "

I did exactly that on the classroom projector and brought up the Watch window. I decided to have Visual Basic pause our program when the value of lngCounter became equal to 33. To do that, I changed the watch Expression to read, lngCounter = 33:

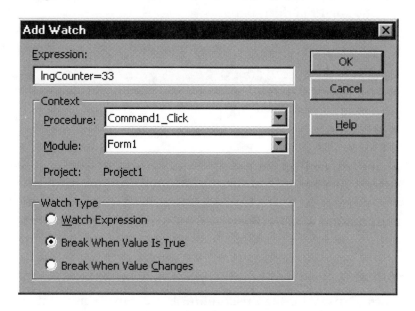

I then changed the Watch Type to Break When Value Is True and ran the program again. This time the program paused when the value of the variable lngCounter became equal to 33:

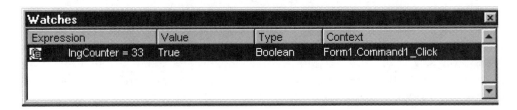

I clicked on the Continue button and the program ran normally to completion without pausing again.

"There are times when you want your program to pause when an expression becomes equal to a certain value," I said. "Similarly, there are times when you want the program to pause if the value of an expression changes at all and the Break When Value Changes watch type does this."

Once again, I selected the watch expression in the Watch window and changed the Watch Type from Break When Value Is True to Break When Value Changes. I changed the Expression back to IngCounter and ran the program:

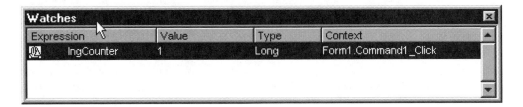

The program immediately paused when the value of IngCounter changed, which occurred the first time the body of the loop executed. "If you continue the program by pressing the Start button," I said, "the program will pause each time the value of the variable changes."

There were no questions on the Watch window, so I deleted the watch expression and continued on with a discussion of breakpoints.

Breakpoints

"The final item to discuss is the **Breakpoint**," I said. I explained that you set a breakpoint in the code window and that it behaves very much like coding a stop statement in your program.

"A breakpoint is not code," I said, "but just a marker on a line of code. When you set a breakpoint in the code window, the line of code is marked in the margin so that when that line is executed, the program pauses.

As was the case with the Stop statement, the line of code is highlighted and an arrow will mark the spot."

"Is there a limit to the number of breakpoints you can have?" Barbara asked.

"No," I said, "You can have multiple breakpoints established at one time. To set a breakpoint, just select a line of code and then use one of the following three methods:"

- press the *F9* key
- select Debug-Toggle Breakpoint
- click in the left margin of the Code window

"When you establish a breakpoint in your program, the line of code is marked in the code window like this," I said:

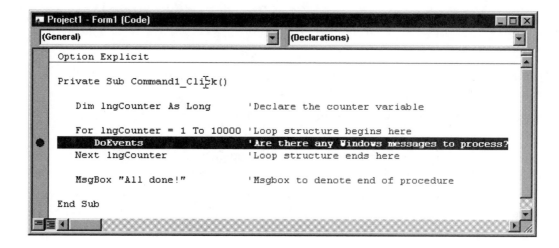

I ran the program and when the **DoEvents** line of code was executed, the program paused (remember the watch expression had been deleted).

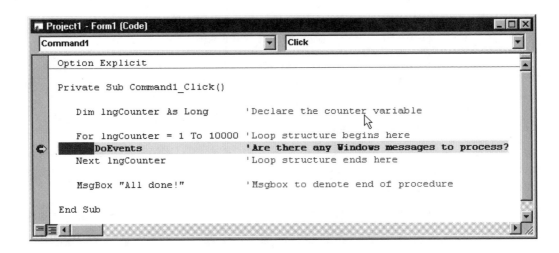

"Notice that the line of code with the breakpoint is highlighted," I said, "and the arrow indicates where the program has paused."

"How can you turn a breakpoint off?" Rhonda asked.

"That's easy!" I said. "Breakpoints can be toggled off and on by selecting *F9* or re-clicking in the margin. There's also a menu option Debug-Clear All Breakpoints that can be used to clear all the breakpoints in your program in one fell swoop."

It had been a pretty exhausting day of code coverage, particularly the latter part of the class where we covered just about everything possible about the topic of debugging. Just before dismissing class, I asked everyone to put these debugging techniques foremost in their minds while writing their programs.

"For instance," I said, "if you call me over about a problem you're having with your program, I will always ask if you've run your program in Step mode first. That's the first step you should take if you're having trouble. I suggest you use Step mode even if you aren't having problems, just to see how your program is really running. For those of you who have told me that the event-driven nature of Windows programs is confusing to you, nothing clears up the confusion like Step mode!"

Summary

In this chapter, we've examined the ideas behind event-driven programming, where your program only has to do something when an event occurs. Everything in between is handled by the operating system. We've also looked at placing code in event handlers, and the use of the Debug window to enable you to see what your code is doing as it happens.

We've looked at some common events, such as the Load event, which takes place when the form loads, but before it is displayed; also the most common event you'll need to code for, which is the Click event.

We spent some time looking at how Visual Basic code behaves like a falling rock, in the sense that it will go through and execute each line, one after the other, unless you include instructions to change this behavior, such as loops or If...Then statements. Without these, your program could never really interact or make decisions based on user input.

I'd like to encourage you at this point to follow through the exercises as they appear in the text. It's much easier to understand how it all works if you can set it up yourself, and get it to work. It's really a case of experience – the more you do something, the more comfortable you'll be with it. The exercises in this chapter demonstrated various aspects of code behavior, and how we can use it to our advantage.

We went on to see how to use the Debug menu options to 'Step' through your code line-by-line, keeping an eye on variables by moving the mouse pointer over them, or by printing them in the Immediate window. You can also set watch expressions to run code either until a value is reached, or while it remains the same. When the appropriate conditions apply, the program pauses. Finally, breakpoints can be set so that the program pauses at a specific line of code. These tools can be very helpful in understanding why something is going wrong, and you should always use Debug methods if your program is not behaving the way it should (or, at least, the way you think it should!).

Quiz

1. When we write Visual Basic code, we place that code in _____ procedures, which are then executed when Windows events are triggered.

2. How are events in a Windows program triggered?

3. What event is triggered when the user presses and then releases a mouse button over an object?

4. What is the full name of the `Click` event of the `Label1` control?

5. True or False: In Visual Basic, different objects or controls can react to the same event?

6. What event occurs when a form is loaded?

7. How many events does the timer react to?

8. What is probably the easiest way to 'open' up the Visual Basic code window?

9. What is the name of the method used to add an item to a list box control?

10. In Visual Basic code, how do you specify a comment?

11. What is the Visual Basic line continuation character?

12. Throughout this chapter, I refer to the default behavior of Visual Basic code as being like _____.

13. What Visual Basic statement did we use to create an event viewer?

14. How do you display the Immediate window in Visual Basic?

15. Can you name three ways to pause your running Visual Basic program?

16. How can you run a Visual Basic program in step mode?

17. Which watch expression type will not pause the program by itself?

18. What kind of watch type causes the program to pause when the value of the expression changes?

Extra Credit – Do they have a 4th of July in England?

Chapter 7
Data

In this chapter, we're going to pick up the pace quite a bit by discussing the concept of computer **data**. Specifically, we'll discuss **variables** and **constants**, the different types of Visual Basic data, and the many operations that can be performed on that data.

Computer Data

"Data can be a very complex topic," I said, "but it's an extremely important one. Failure to understand data can lead to problems with your programs down the line. What you hear today will seem very theoretical in nature but it will be vital for your future careers. Look at it as information that you can tuck into your programming back pocket for future use."

Variables

"When writing Visual Basic programs," I said, "the kind of data that you work with are generally property values. There are times, however, when you need to create something called a **variable**. Last week, we briefly looked at a counter variable, `lngCounter`, that we used to help us execute a loop. Now it's time to examine variables in more detail."

I continued by explaining that variables, as we have already seen, are placeholders in the computer's RAM where we can store temporary information.

"I'm confused as to why you would create a variable in the first place," Barbara said. "Isn't all of the data that we need in our program in some way entered by the user?"

"That's a good question," I said. "Most of the data your program needs will be entered, either by the user, or as we'll see later in the next course, from a disk file. There are times, however, when your program will need to create a variable to hold the result of an intermediate calculation or, as we have seen, to keep track of a count of some kind."

"Variables have a definite lifetime. I analogize variables to a piece of scratch paper that you use when you are adding some numbers together. As soon as you have the result, you crumple the paper and toss it in a trashcan and the same thing applies to variables. When our program is done with them, they are tossed out."

I asked everyone to consider this hypothetical program, which would illustrate the necessity for variables in programs. "Let's say that we need to write a Visual Basic program," I said, "that contains a form with two text boxes, a label and a command button. We want the user of the program to be able to enter two numbers into the text boxes, click on the command button, and get the result of their addition displayed in the label."

I pointed out that the beauty of this program is its flexibility. "We need to design this program to take any two numbers that the user enters and perform the calculation. This program will mark a departure from the examples we've seen so far in this course, where the outcomes were pre-determined. The results produced from this program are dependent on the numbers that the user enters into the text boxes."

I opened up a new Visual Basic project and placed the **two text boxes**, the **label** and the **command button** we required on the form. Then I cleared both the `Text` properties of the text boxes and the `Caption` property of the label, before typing this code into the command button's `Click` event procedure:

```
Private Sub Command1_Click()
    Dim intFirstNumber As Integer
    Dim intSecondNumber As Integer
    intFirstNumber = val(Text1.Text)
    intSecondNumber = val(Text2.Text)
    Label1.Caption = intFirstNumber + intSecondNumber
End Sub
```

I ran the program and typed 1 into the first text box, and 2 into the second. I pressed the command button and the results of the calculation were displayed:

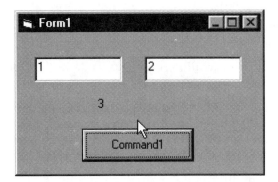

"I have absolutely no idea what that code means," Rhonda said. "At this point, I don't expect you to," I said. "Just hold on, because by the end of today's class, I guarantee that you will be more comfortable with it."

"Can you at least let us know what the code is doing?" Blaine said. "Sure thing!" I said. "The first two lines of code declare two **integer** type variables called `intFirstNumber` and `intSecondNumber` in which we can store the two values that the user enters:"

```
Dim intFirstNumber As Integer
Dim intSecondNumber As Integer
```

"The next two lines of code are a little more complicated," I said. "Don't concern yourself about the use of the `Val(Text1.Text)` statement here. It is all to do with the preparation of the entries that the user made ready for the addition, and I'll be talking about that in more detail later."

"The interesting part of these two lines of code is the use of what's known as a Visual Basic **assignment statement** to store that numeric value in the two variables we had just declared:"

```
intFirstNumber = Val(Text1.Text)
intSecondNumber = Val(Text2.Text)
```

"Finally," I said, "we add the value of the two numeric variables together and assign that result to `Label1`'s `Caption` property:"

```
Label1.Caption = intFirstNumber + intSecondNumber
```

How Do We Create a Variable?

"I understand what a variable is and what it's used for," Rhonda said. "But how do we create one?"

"There's a short story and a long story to your question," I said. "The short story is that in Visual Basic you can create a variable just by referring to it in code, but this is bad practice. The long story is that you should announce to Visual Basic your intention to use a variable in your code by declaring it. This declaration procedure tells the computer the name of the variable, the type of data that the variable will hold, how much space will be required in RAM to store the contents of the variable, and the scope and lifetime of the variable."

"Scope and lifetime?" Dave asked.

"Scope," I said, "means what parts of your program can see the variable, such as other event procedures. Lifetime means how long the variable will exist in RAM. For instance a variable may exist in RAM for as long as the event procedure which it is declared in is running, or while the form that it appears on is loaded or until the program that it appears in ends."

"So let me get this straight," Lou said. "Visual Basic doesn't require you to declare these variables?"

"That's right," I said, "Visual Basic does not require you to declare a variable before first using it; however, everyone thinks that it's extremely foolhardy if you don't declare all of your variables first. Look at this code:"

```
Private Sub Command1_Click()
    intFirstNumber = val(Text1.Text)
    intSecondNumber = val(Text2.Text)
    Label1.Caption = intFirstNumber + intSecondNumber
End Sub
```

"This is perfectly legal according to the rules, provided **Option Explicit** is not in effect. However, writing code in this way can lead to a number of programming errors."

"You've mentioned **Option Explicit** before, haven't you?" Ward asked.

"That's right," I replied. "When I discussed the IDE and spoke about the Editor options of the Tools-Options dialog box, I highly recommended that Require Variable Declaration is always selected. When

that option is in effect, the statement **Option Explicit** will appear in the General Declarations section of any new form you create."

I reminded everyone that all the code we had examined and written so far had been placed in event procedures on a form. "But event procedures," I said, "are not the only place where you can write code and declare variables. You may recall from our discussion of the code window last week that each form has a General Declarations section, where you can place code not associated with a particular event. You can also declare variables there, and in fact, we will do this with the China Shop Project. Now let's look at how we declare variables."

Variable Declaration

"We can declare variables by using four different Visual Basic statements: **Dim**, **Private**, **Public** and **Static**," I explained. "However," I said, "there are rules as to where these statements can and cannot be used."

I distributed the following chart to the class:

Statement	Procedures	General Declarations Section
Dim	YES	YES
Private	NO	YES
Public	NO	YES
Static	YES	NO

Note that the words Private, Public, and Static here are different to the same words used at the start of an event procedure. Here they refer to when we use them before declaring a Variable, not an Event.

"This chart," I said, "shows each of the four variable declaration statements and where these statements can be used. As you can see, the Dim statement can be used in a procedure or in the General Declarations section of a form. Many beginners habitually use Dim to declare a variable anywhere in their project, but as we'll see later, that is not necessarily the correct choice."

"When the chart specifies procedures," Rhonda asked, "do you mean event procedures?"

"In Visual Basic," I said, "it's possible (indeed, we'll do it later on) to create your own procedure, which I call a programmer-written procedure, and place it in a form. As far as Visual Basic is concerned," I said, "an event procedure is really no different to a programmer-written procedure as far as variable declaration rules go."

I continued by saying that we can make some general observations about the four different variable declaration statements:

- The primary difference between the four variable declaration statements is their scope.

- Except for the **Static** statement, the lifetime of variables declared with all four statements is independent of the statement used to declare them. Their lifetime is dependent on where they are declared.

- Variables declared in a procedure cease to exist when the procedure ends. In other words, a variable declared in the **Click** event of a command button 'dies' when Visual Basic encounters the **End Sub** of that event.

- Variables declared in the General Declaration section of a form 'die' when the form is unloaded or the program ends.

"Now let's look at each declaration statement in turn," I said. "As we discuss each one, I'll treat the issues of scope individually."

The Dim Statement

I displayed the syntax for the **Dim** statement on the classroom projector:

Dim variablename [As type]

"Whenever you find a Visual Basic syntax definition like this one," I said, "you know that the words contained within brackets are optional. Therefore, '**As type**' is an optional parameter, but one which, in this case, that you should nearly always include."

"What are the rules for naming a variable?" Steve asked. "Well, there are rules and then there are naming conventions. Here are the Visual Basic rules for naming variables," I said:

- variable names must begin with a letter
- variable names cannot contain periods, otherwise known as fullstops (.)
- variable names can be no longer than 255 characters
- variable names cannot be the same as Visual Basic keywords, such as **Loop** or **If**

"My recommendations go a little further," I said. "Here they are:"

The first three characters of the variable name should describe its data type. For example, we saw **int** used for an integer type variable just a few minutes ago. "Some programmers," I said, "prefer to use a single character to designate the date type of a variable. My recommendation, and also Microsoft's, is to use three characters."

The remainder of the variable name should provide a meaningful description of the variable.

"For example," I said, "earlier we used **intFirstNumber** as a variable used to count something within the body of a loop. Bear in mind that you have 255 characters to describe a variable, but long variable names can be a real pain to type, especially if you're not a quick typist. Every variable you declare with that very illustrative long name will have to be re-typed when you refer to it in code. The bottom line is: make your variable names as meaningful as possible with as few letters as possible."

"Does what you said last week about naming objects in mixed case apply to variables as well?" Dave asked. "That's an excellent point," I said. "Just as I suggested last week that you should always name Visual Basic objects in mixed case, name your variables that way as well."

"The 'As type' parameter," I said, "allows you to specify a data type for the variable you are declaring. Explicitly declaring the data type of a variable using this parameter can save RAM and allows Visual Basic to prevent you from accidentally storing invalid data in a variable."

"What do you mean by that?" Ward asked.

"If, for example, we declare a variable as a numeric type," I said, "and then try to store data other than a number in the variable, Visual Basic will display an error message. If you don't specify a data type when you declare the variable, the variable is declared as a **variant** data type. The variant is a chameleon data type, because it assumes the characteristics of the data that is stored in it."

"That doesn't sound so bad," Joe said. "No," I said, "but a variant consumes much more RAM and can make your program run slower. If you know the type of data that the variable will hold, explicitly declare the variable with that data type."

"Can you give us an example of that?" Rose said.

"Sure," I said, "here's the declaration of a variable as a **long** type. The long type of variable holds large whole numbers which is why we used it last week in the loop structure of our `Count2.vbp`:"

```
Dim lngCounter As Long
```

"So if we had left the `As Long` out of this declaration," Barbara said, "the variable would have been declared as a variant. Is it ever OK to do that?"

"There may be times," I said, "when you are not certain what kind of data your variable will hold, in which case your only choice is to declare it as a variant. By the way, there are two ways of declaring a variable as a variant, either implicitly by not declaring a data type or explicitly by declaring `As Variant`:"

```
Dim varPrice As Variant    'Explicitly declare a variant
Dim varPrice               'Implicitly declare a variant
```

"I'm a little unsure about why you would declare a variant," Kate said. "Can you give us an example?"

"How about this," I said. "Suppose you create a Visual Basic project with a text box and you ask the user a series of questions, such as their name, age, and date of birth. The user must enter the answers into the text box and your intention is to take that answer and store it in a variable. What kind of variable should you declare though? Some of the answers are text, such as the name. The user's age is numeric, but the date of birth is a date. This would be a good reason to declare the variable to hold these responses as a variant data type."

Oops, Don't Do This!

"While we're on the topic of variable declaration," Dave said, "can you declare more than one variable on the same line of code?"

"Yes," I said, "but be careful. Let's look at another variable type, the **integer**, which holds small whole numbers, such as 132 or 2,000."

I wrote the following code and displayed it on the classroom projector:

```
Dim intPrice1, intPrice2, intPrice3 As Integer
```
"Don't declare variables like this!" I said.

I explained that a well-meaning programmer might well believe that they are declaring three integer type variables with this single line statement, but they would be wrong.

"Only the last variable, `intPrice3`, is actually declared as an integer type variable. The other two have no explicit type and therefore end up being declared as variants. Here's the correct syntax:"

```
Dim intPrice1 As Integer
Dim intPrice2 As Integer
Dim intPrice3 As Integer
```

"Or, you can also use this syntax:"

```
Dim intPrice1 As Integer, intPrice2 As Integer, _
                      intPrice3 As Integer
```

"You can also use the colon (:)," I said, "which is the Visual Basic **command separator**. With a colon you can place more than one Visual Basic statement on the same line in the code window:"

```
Dim intValue1 As Integer: Dim invtalue2 As Integer: _
                      Dim intvalue3 As Integer
```

Dim Scope

"I've mentioned scope briefly already," I said. "Variable scope defines which parts of your program can see the variable. Another way to think about it is how far your variable can be

seen from where it is declared. For instance, variables declared with the `Dim` statement in a procedure cannot be seen by any other procedure in your program. Such a variable is said to have **local** scope, or put another way, to be local to the procedure in which it is declared."

"I guess I'm just a little confused," Rhonda said. "Is local scope a good thing or a bad thing?"

"That depends," I replied. "Suppose you place code in the `Click` event of a command button to perform a calculation. You declare a variable in the event procedure to hold the result of that calculation. The variable is local to that procedure. Code in another event procedure cannot see the value of the variable. In fact, when the event procedure ends, the variable and the data contained in it, vanish."

I waited a minute before going on.

"Now suppose," I continued, "you wanted the value in that variable to be accessible from another event procedure. If you declare the variable so that it's local to the event procedure then that is simply impossible."

"OK," she said, "I think I'm beginning to understand. Declaring variables then is more than just typing the word `Dim`."

"How could you make the value of that variable visible to other procedures then?" Dave asked.

"There are several alternatives," I replied. "You could declare the variable in the General Declarations section of the form using the `Dim` statement, then the variable and its value could be seen by any other procedure contained within that form."

"So the `Dim` statement in the General Declaration section of a form is actually local to the form," Bob said. "That's right," I replied. "Variables declared with the `Dim` statement in the General Declarations section of a form can only be seen by procedures in that form."

"I don't want to confuse the issue," I said, "but Microsoft recommends using the Dim statement only within procedures. Although you can use it in the General Declarations section of a form, their recommendation is to use the `Private` statement instead."

"Let me do a little demonstration," I said. I then created a form with a command button and placed the following code in the `Load` event of the form:

```
Private Sub Form_Load()
    Dim intDemo As Integer
    intDemo = 22
End Sub
```

"I declared `intDemo` as an integer type variable," I said, "and because it is declared in an event procedure, it has local scope. The next line is an assignment statement, which assigns the number 22 to the variable `intDemo`:"

```
intDemo = 22
```

"I then placed this code in the Click event of the command button:"

```
Private Sub Command1_Click()
    MsgBox intDemo
End Sub
```

"The intention here is to display the value of the variable intDemo, in a message box."

I clicked on the IDE Start button and ran the program, but when I clicked on the command button, the following error message was displayed on the classroom projector:

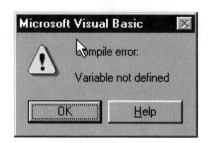

"What happened?" I asked.

"You declared the variable in one event procedure and tried to refer to it in another," Dave said. "You can't do that, because a variable declared in a procedure is local to that procedure and can't be seen outside of it. Besides, when the Load event procedure ended, the variable intDemo died."

"That's perfectly correct," I said. "Now, let's declare the variable intDemo in the General Declarations section of the form instead:"

```
Option Explicit
Private intDemo As Integer
```

"Now let's remove the declaration of the variable in the Load event of the form, so that it looks like this:"

```
Private Sub Form_Load()
    intDemo = 22
End Sub
```

As before, I ran the program and clicked on the command button:

As a rule of thumb, declare your variables with as narrow a scope as possible, run your program and then see what happens. If you determine that you need to broaden the scope of your variables, then you can always do that later.

"OK," Ward said, "explain this to me please."

"Changing the declaration of the variable intDemo," I said, "from the form's Load event procedure to the General Declarations section of the form changed its scope from local to form level. That meant that any procedure on the form could see it, including the Load event procedure of the form and the Click event procedure of the command button."

"Knowing where to declare your variables in order to achieve your programming goals is very important. It takes practice and experience to 'get it right' so don't worry if it doesn't happen overnight," I said.

There were no more questions about the Dim statement.

"Just to repeat," I said, "Microsoft recommends using the Private statement instead of the Dim statement, when declaring local scope variables in the General Declaration section of a form."

The Private Statement

I displayed the syntax for the Private statement on the classroom projector:

Private variablename [As type]

"Notice that the syntax of the Private statement is almost identical to that of the Dim statement," I said. "And not only is the syntax nearly identical, but the usage is too."

"What's the main difference then?" Linda asked.

"If you look at the chart I distributed earlier, you'll see that whereas the `Dim` statement can theoretically be used to declare a variable anywhere within Visual Basic, the `Private` statement cannot be used in a procedure."

Statement	Procedures	General Declarations Section
Dim	YES	YES
Private	NO	YES

"That would mean that `Private` can only be used in the General Declarations section of a form," Rhonda said.

"That's exactly right," I said.

"As far as scope, then," Dave said, "that means that a variable declared using the `Private` statement in the `General Declarations` section of a form will always be form level. Therefore, only procedures on the form will be able to see it."

"Also right," I said. "Now let's move onto the `Public` statement."

The Public Statement

I displayed the syntax for the `Public` statement on the classroom projector:

Public variablename [As type]

"Like the `Private` statement," I said, "the `Public` statement can only be used in the General Declarations section of a form."

"What is the difference, then," asked Dave, "between the `Private` and `Public` statements?"

"In a single word," I said, "**scope**."

"We've already seen that a variable declared as `Private` in the General Declarations section of a form can be seen by procedures only on that form. However," I continued, "a variable declared as `Public` in the General Declarations section of a form can be seen by procedures on other forms (if more that one form is used). The `Public` statement is very useful if your project has multiple forms or a standard module. As this is an advanced topic, I think we'll leave the `Public` statement here and move onto the `Static` declaration."

The Static Statement

"The final variable declaration statement," I said, "is the `Static` statement:"

Static variablename [As type]

"The `Static` statement is the opposite of the `Private` statement," I said, "in that it can only appear in a procedure. You may not use the `Static` statement in the General Declarations section of a form."

"I said earlier, that a variable declared in an event procedure dies when that event procedure ends. Up until now, we haven't seen a variable that can survive the life of the event procedure in which it is declared, but the `Static` statement is the exception to that rule. A variable declared with the `Static` statement will 'live' for as long as your program is running."

I could see some confused faces. "I think I need an example," Ward said.

"For instance," I said, "suppose that you wanted to keep track of the number of times that the user clicks on a command button. You could declare a variable called `intCounter` in the command button's `Click` event procedure and then add 1 to this variable each time the `Click` event is triggered. However, the problem is that each time the command button is clicked, the `Click` event procedure executes but then it ends. When the user clicks on the command button again, the `Click` event is triggered one more time, but the variable is re-declared. As a result, the value of `intCounter` never gets beyond 1. Using the `Static` statement eliminates this problem."

I told the class that I had an exercise for them to complete that would allow them to explore the `Static` variable type:

In this exercise, we'll begin by using a locally declared variable to try to count the number of times that a command button has been clicked. After that fails, we'll use a `Static` variable to solve the problem.

On the CD: Static1.vbp.

Exercise

The Static Variable Type

1. Start a new **standard.EXE** project. Change the **Caption** property of the form to Static Variable Demo.

2. Place a single command button on the form. Accept the default name that Visual Basic assigns.

3. Double-click on the command button and place the following code into its **Click** event procedure:

```
Private Sub Command1_Click()
    Dim intCounter As Integer
    intCounter = intCounter + 1
    Form1.Print intCounter
End Sub
```

4. Save the form and project in your \VBFiles\Practice subdirectory with the names static.frm and static.vbp. Now run the program.

5. Each time you click on the command button, 1 is printed on the form:

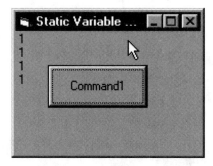

6. Find the Command1_Click event procedure and change the line of code that reads:

```
Dim intCounter as Integer
```

to

```
Static intCounter as Integer
```

On the CD: Static2.vbp.

7.   Run the program again, saving the changes.

8.   Click on the command button repeatedly. Each time you click on it the number printed on the form is incremented by 1:

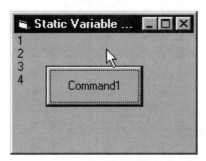

Discussion

"The choice of a variable declaration statement certainly makes a big difference!" I said. "With the **Dim** statement, the value of 1 was continuously printed on the form because the variable **intCounter** was re-declared each time the **Click** event procedure ran. However, when we changed the declaration statement from **Dim** to **Static** the value of the variable **intCounter** was retained, even though the **Click** event procedure ended time and time again."

"Can you explain the middle line of code?" Rhonda asked. "The one that reads:"

```
intCounter = intCounter + 1
```

"Yes," I replied. "This expression may be easier to understand if you read it as 'Add 1 to the current value of intCounter and then assign that result to intCounter'."

"Programmers count by 1 this way," I said.

I asked if there were any questions about **Static** variables.

"I've been thinking about this," Ward said. "Isn't there another way to count the number of times that the command button has been clicked without using a **Static** variable?"

"You're a step ahead of me," I said. "I was just about to mention that. Another way to solve our dilemma with the command button is to use a form level variable. Remember, any variable declared in the General Declaration section of a form will live for as long as the form is loaded."

I wanted to give everyone a chance to work with a form level variable as the mechanics of creating one can be tricky, so I distributed this exercise:

In this exercise, we'll create a form level variable to achieve the same results as before.

On the CD: Mod.vbp.

Exercise

The Module Level Variable

1.   Start a new Standard.EXE project.

2.   Place a single command button on the form. Accept the default name that Visual Basic assigns.

3.   Type the following code into the General Declarations section of the form:

```
Option Explicit
Private m_intCounter As Integer
```

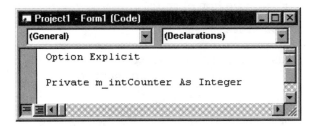

4.   Place the following code into the **Click** event procedure of the command button:

```
Private Sub Command1_Click()
   m_intCounter = m_intCounter + 1
   Form1.Print m_intCounter
End Sub
```

5. Save the program in your **\VBFiles\Practice** subdirectory. The form should be called **mod.frm** and the project, **mod.vbp**. Then run the program.

6. Click on the command button repeatedly. Each time you do so the number printed on the form is incremented by 1.

Discussion

"Notice that we used the **Private** statement to declare the form level variable," I said.

```
Private m_intCounter As Integer
```

"Don't forget that we use the **Private** statement instead of **Dim** in the General Declarations section of a form. The prefix **m** is used to show that this is a form level variable, which is sometimes called a module level variable."

"In addition, we are no longer declaring our variable in the event procedure itself. That's not necessary now, since we've declared it at the form level. Although the variable was declared as **Private**, every procedure on the form can still see it."

"Remember," I said, "you should declare your variables with as narrow a scope as possible."

That statement generated the following discussion.

Where should you Declare a Variable?

"In our last two exercises," I said, "we saw that it's possible to declare a variable in different places within your program and have it produce the same results. Where to declare a variable is one of the most often asked questions that I hear. There are no hard and fast rules but here are some guidelines:"

*   Declare the variable with as limited a scope as necessary. Start by declaring the variable in the event procedure where you will use it. If that doesn't do the trick, expand the scope from there.

- If you know that the variable and its value will need to be accessed from more than one procedure on a form, declare the variable using the **Private** statement in the General Declarations section of the form.

- If you know that the variable and its value will need to be accessed by a procedure on another form, then use the **Public** statement.

Do Variables Need to be Initialized?

Steve remarked that in other programming languages with which he was familiar, a variable is first declared and then its value needs to be **initialized**. He wanted to know if that was true of Visual Basic.

I explained to everyone that the term **initialization** means to assign an initial value to a variable after you declare it.

"You're right, Steve," I said. "In other programming languages that is required, however, it's not necessary in Visual Basic. Visual Basic automatically initializes variables for you, based on the data type of the variable. Variables declared as **numeric** types (for example the long and integer types that we've already looked at) are initialized to 0. Variables declared as **string** types are initialized to a special Visual Basic value called EMPTY. As we'll see in a few moments, there is also a Visual Basic **Date** type. Variables of this type are initialized to December 30, 1899 at 12:00 AM. Finally, there is also a Visual Basic **Boolean** data type; its value is initialized to False."

Visual Basic Data Types

"It's now time," I said, "to take a closer look at the data types in Visual Basic. These are the data types that follow the optional **As** statement in the variable declaration statements."

I reminded everyone that if you choose not to explicitly declare a data type for your variable, the variable is implicitly declared as a variant, a data type that adapts itself to the data entered into it.

"The choice of an appropriate data type for your variable," I said, "can be crucial to the proper operation of your program. As I mentioned earlier, it's only in the rarest of cases that you should declare a variable as a variant. Visual Basic data types have varying RAM requirements, capabilities and operations that you can perform on them."

I displayed this list of data types on the classroom projector:

- boolean
- currency
- date
- double
- integer
- long
- single
- string (fixed and variable length)
- variant

"For the next half hour or so we'll discuss all of these data types in detail. First, though, lets take a quick break so that we can tackle the subject afresh."

Numeric Data Types

After the break, I started to discuss the Visual Basic numeric data types. "You should declare your variable as a numeric data type," I said, "when you will use the variable to store a number which will later be used in a mathematical calculation."

"What about a telephone number or a social security number?" Ward asked.

"A **string** data type is a better choice for them," I said, "because neither one of them will be used in a mathematical calculation."

I continued by saying that Visual Basic has five different numeric data types: **integer**, **long**, **single**, **double** and **currency**.

I then displayed this explanation on the classroom projector:

- Choose integer and long data types to store whole numbers (called integers) such as 23, 45 and 34470.

- Choose single and double data types to store numbers with fractions such as 3.1416, 23.12, 45.22 or 357644.67.

- Currency is a special data type that has a fixed number of decimal places, 4. If you try to store a value with more than 4 decimal places in a currency variable, the extra decimal places will be truncated. For example, 1.2345678 would become 1.2345.

"Now let's take a look at each of these in detail," I said.

Integer

"The integer data type can only hold whole numbers; it can't be used to store a number with a fractional part. The size of the number that you can store in an integer type is also limited; values for the integer data type can range from **-32,768** to **32,767**."

"That means that no value larger than 32,767 or smaller than -32,768 can be placed in an integer data type," I said, "and if you attempt to do so, you'll receive an error message like this:"

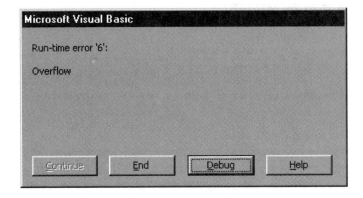

"Why is that?" Bob asked.

"Visual Basic allocates 2 bytes of RAM to store the value of an integer data type and 2 bytes can't hold a range larger than that. As we'll see in just a minute or so, you can use the long data type for larger integer values."

"What happens if you try to store a number with a fractional part in a variable declared as an integer?" Dave asked. "Visual Basic will permit you to do that, but it will chop off the part of the number to the right of the decimal point. So be careful with that."

"Can you give us some examples of where we would want to use the integer type?" Rose asked. "How about the number of employees in a small to medium sized company," I said. "An integer wouldn't be a good choice to store the population of New York, though."

"So declaring all of your numeric variables as an integer will eventually get you into trouble," Linda said. "That's right," I agreed. "Beginners seem to habitually select the integer data type for all of their numeric variables and as you can see, this can mean big trouble for your program."

Long

"Let's get back to the population of the city of New York," I said. "We can use the long data type to store that value. The long data type is really a long integer, the name it is known by in some other programming languages."

I explained that variables declared as long data types consume 4 bytes of RAM, that's why the long data type can hold a greater range of numbers than the integer data type. Values for the long data type can range from **-2,147,483,648** to **2,147,483,647**.

"The bottom line is," I said, "use the long data type when you are storing a whole number that is greater than 32,767 or smaller than -32,768."

At this point I could see that Linda was beginning to look somewhat confused, and was glancing back over her notes. Eventually she asked, "In the code where we counted from 1 to 10,000 using a `For...Next` loop, why did we declare the counter variable as long? Surely, it would have made more sense to declare it as an integer."

"Good point, Linda," I observed. "You are quite right in saying it would be better to declare `lngCounter` as an integer. My excuse is that I used to make the code count up to 100,000, thus, I needed to use a long variable as an integer data type only goes up to 32,767. However, I discovered that with some computers it could take them several hours to count up to 100,000," I admitted sheepishly.

The class laughed.

"Anyway," I continued, "as we'll be using this piece of code many times over the next couple of weeks it was a lot easier to simply remove a zero from the 100,000 rather than change all references to a long variable."

"If you wanted to declare the counter as an integer then your code should look like this," I said as I quickly loaded `Count2.vbp` and changed the code on the projector:

```
Private Sub Command1_Click()
    Dim intCounter As Integer     'Declare the counter
                                  'variable
    For intCounter = 1 To 10000  'Loop structure begins here
        Form1.Cls                 'Clear the form
        Form1.Print intCounter    'Print a number
    Next intCounter               'Loop structure ends here
End Sub
```

Linda was beginning to look smug and I could sense that she had another question.

"The range for a long data type still isn't that large," Linda said. "Suppose you need to store an even greater number?"

"That's when we need to use either the single or double data type," I said.

Single

"The difference between the single and double data types, and the two integer data types is that both the single and double can store something mathematicians call **real** numbers. Real numbers are numbers with fractional parts. Sometimes you hear single and double data types referred to as **floating-point** data types."

I explained that variables declared as single data types consume 4 bytes of RAM. Values for the single data type can range from **-3.402823E38** to **-1.401298E-45** for negative values and from **1.401298E-45** to **3.402823E38** for positive values.

"Unless you're fresh from a math class," I said, "you may be wondering how to read these numbers. These numbers are expressed in a format known as **scientific** or **exponential notation**, which is used to represent very large numbers. For instance, the number 1.0E13 is read as '1 times 10 raised to the 13th power' and would be written as the number 1 followed by 13 zeroes or 10,000,000,000,000."

"That means the upper limit for the single data type is read as, 3.402823 times 10 raised to the 38th power, and can be written as 340,282,300,000,000,000,000,000,000,000,000,000,000. Needless to say, this is a very large number!"

Dave noted that both the long and the single consume the same amount of RAM, yet the single data type holds a much larger range of values. "That's a good point," I said. "In the computer world, floating-point data types such as single and double can hold extraordinarily large values, but they do so at the expense of accuracy. Theoretically, the integer data types are more accurate than the floating-point data types. Also, calculations performed on integer data types are faster than those performed on floating-point numbers."

"It's advisable to use this data type whenever you will be storing a number that contains a fractional part," I said. "Not as obviously, you will also need to use this data type if the value you want to store exceeds the range of the long data type. Don't forget, it's also possible to exceed the limitations of even the single data type."

Double

"Just as the long data type is really a 'bigger' version of the integer," I said, "so the double data type is just a 'bigger' version of the single."

I explained that variables declared as double data types consume 8 bytes of RAM. Values for this data type can range from **-1.79769313486232E308** to **-4.94065645841247E-324** for negative values and from **4.94065645841247E-324** to **1.79769313486232E308** for positive values.

"If you take the upper limit of the single data type," I said, "and add about 270 zeroes, that will give you the upper limit of the double, and I don't have enough room to write that on the board!"

Most of the class believed this would be sufficient for anything they could imagine, so we moved on to a discussion of the currency data type.

Currency

"The final numeric data type is currency," I said. "The currency data type should be used for any operations involving money. The currency type only stores numbers up to 4 decimal places. Any excess decimal places are forgotten."

I explained that variables declared as currency data types consume 2 bytes of RAM. Values for the currency data type can range from **-922,337,203,685,477.5808** to **922,337,203,685,477.5807**.

String Data Types

"Choose the string data type," I said, "when you want to declare a variable that will hold text such as a name, telephone number or social security number. As I mentioned earlier, although your telephone number consists of numbers, these are not numbers that will be used in a mathematical calculation, and so a string data type is more appropriate. Other common examples are zip codes, street numbers and employee ID numbers."

"There are two different string data types, **fixed length** and **variable length**."

I displayed these two string variable declarations on the classroom projector:

```
Dim strVarLengthValue as String         'Declare a Variable
                                         'Length String
Dim strFixedLengthValue as String * 9 'Declares a Fixed
                                         'Length String
                                         'of 9 characters
```

"As you can see," I said, "the difference between the two declarations is the asterisk (*), which is then followed by a number. This number tells Visual Basic how many bytes of RAM to allocate to store the value of the variable. If you don't include the asterisk and the number, Visual Basic knows it's dealing with a Variable Length string data type."

"Practically speaking," Jack asked, "What's the difference between the two?"

"Declare a string as fixed length," I said, "when you are absolutely sure how many characters you will be storing in the variable. Declare a variable as variable length when you can't be certain."

"Can you give us an example of that?" Barbara asked.

"How about our social security number example;" I said, "since it's always the same length, it would make sense to declare it as a fixed length string. On the other hand, if you declared a string variable to store a person's name, it would make sense to declare it as a variable length string."

"Why not just declare everything as a variable length string?" Ward asked.

"Many programmers do just that," I said, "instead of even considering the fixed length string. However, variable length strings require some RAM overhead, 10 bytes. For instance, if you store a 20-character string in a variable declared as a variable length string, the RAM required to store the value is 10+20=30 bytes. By comparison, if you declare the variable as a fixed length string of 20-characters, the total RAM required is just 20 bytes. Declaring all of your strings as variable length strings can quickly add up. However, I'll be honest with you that sometimes it's just faster and easier to declare the variable length string than it is to give some thought to what the actual storage requirement is."

I continued by explaining that a downside of the fixed length string data type is that no more than 65,000 characters can be stored in it.

"Still," I said, "that's a very large string. On the other hand, a variable length string variable can store up to 2 billion characters!"

"Can you clarify for me," asked Ward, "how to assign a value to a string variable? Do you need quotation marks?"

"That's a good question," I said, "and thanks for asking it. You're right, the assignment of a string to a string variable is different from assigning a number to a numeric variable."

I displayed this example on the classroom projector:

```
Dim intDemo as Integer    'Declare an Integer Variable
Dim strDemo as String     'Declare a String Variable
intDemo = 22              'Assign a number
strDemo = "John Smiley"   'Assign a string
```

"Ward's correct," I said, "when assigning a value to a string variable, you must enclose the value within quotation marks. When assigning a number to a numeric variable, you must not enclose it within quotation marks."

I asked if there were any other questions on either numeric or string data types, but there were none, so we continued our discussion.

Other Data Types

"I hate to group the remaining data types into one big 'other' category," I said, "but that's exactly what they are. As a beginner, most of the variables that you will declare will either be numeric data types or string data types."

Boolean

"**Boolean** data types," I said, "are sometimes called **logical** data types. They can have only two values, **True** or **False**."

I displayed this code on the classroom projector:

```
Dim blnMarried As Boolean    'Declare a Boolean Variable
Dim blnRetired As Boolean    'Declare a Boolean Variable
blnMarried = True            'Assign True
blnRetired = False           'Assign False
```

I explained that I had declared two Boolean variables, and then assigned the values True and False to the respective variables.

"Declare a Boolean data type," I said, "when you know that only a True/False or Yes/No value will be stored in it. For example, a variable used to represent marital status or a variable to represent whether a person is retired."

I continued by noting that the treatment of Boolean variables in Visual Basic code is a little different than anything else we've seen before.

"For instance," I said, "you can code an `If` statement to evaluate the 'truth' of a Boolean variable in the following way:"

```
If blnMarried = True Then
```

"Or:"

```
If blnMarried Then
```

"In fact," I said, "those two statements are considered the same by Visual Basic."

"What happened to the word `True` in the second statement?" Barbara asked. "This is a special case with Boolean variables," I said. "If you omit the word `True` or `False` in the comparison statement, Visual Basic assumes the word `True`."

"Earlier," Kate said, "you said that Boolean variables are initialized to `False`."

"I'm not talking about the way the Boolean variable is initialized here," I said. "I mean the way it can be used in a comparison statement."

I continued by explaining that the `False` value is also interesting. I then displayed the following code on the classroom projector:

```
If blnMarried = False Then
```

"You can use that code to evaluate the 'falseness' of a Boolean variable," I said. "But you can also code it like this:"

```
If Not blnMarried Then
```

"Not?" Barbara asked. "That almost sounds like English."

"That's the idea," I said, "Coding `Not blnMarried` is the same as asking Visual Basic if `blnMarried = False`. Again, this is something you can only do with the Boolean variable. We'll examine the `Not` keyword later in today's class."

Date

"**Date** data types, quite simply, are intended to hold dates," I said. "Choose this data type whenever you want to store a date or a time in a variable."

I explained that date data types consume 8 bytes of RAM, which makes them one of the most RAM expensive data types we have examined. Valid values for the date data type can range from **January 1, 100** to **December 31, 9999.**

"What is the advantage of the date type over a string?" Steve asked. "Can't you just store a date in a string variable?"

"The advantage," I said, "is Visual Basic's date arithmetic. When you store a date in a date type variable, you then have access to a variety of Visual Basic's date functions. For instance, if you store today's date in a date variable, and want to know what the date is 180 days from today, you can just add the number 180 to the date variable and display the result."

Variant

"Coincidentally," I said, "by discussing the data types alphabetically, we have saved the default data type for last."

I reminded everyone that if you fail to declare a data type explicitly, a variable is implicitly declared as a variant data type. You can also choose to explicitly declare a variable as a variant. I displayed these two variable declarations on the classroom projector that did exactly the same thing:

```
Dim varValue              'Implicit Variant Declaration
Dim varValue as Variant   'Explicit Variable Declaration
```

"There is a price to pay for declaring a variable as a variant," I said. "16 bytes of RAM. That means if you declare a variable as a variant and store just one character in it, 17 bytes of RAM are consumed."

Not only does the variant consume more RAM than the other data types, but the data held in variants is processed slower than other data types. For instance, you can add the contents of two variant variables provided they contain valid numbers. However, to do this, Visual Basic needs to evaluate the contents of both the variant variables to determine their type, and then internally convert them to one of the numeric data types before performing the calculation.

Property Data Types

"I remember you mentioning that the **Text** property of a text box is actually a string data type," Dave said. "How can we determine what the data type of a property is?"

"That's a good question," I said. "Object properties are really nothing more than the variables declared within the object and as such, each property has its own data type, but the property's declaration is hidden away in the object itself. Fortunately, there is still a way to discover the data type of an object's property and that's to use the **Object Browser**."

I reminded the class that we had briefly discussed the **Object Browser** in our IDE overview class as I displayed the **Object Browser** by pressing the *F2* function key:

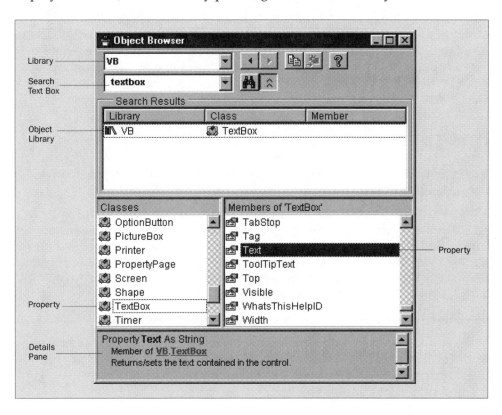

I pointed out that in Visual Basic, objects are members of **Object Libraries**. To find a property for an object using the Object Browser, select VB in the Library list box (the top list box in the Object Browser), then type a search string in the Search text box (we want to know about textboxes) and click on the binoculars.

I did that and then selected TextBox from the Classes list. In the Members list to the right, I selected the Text property and as you can see, the definition of the `Text` property was then displayed in the details pane at the bottom of the Object Browser.

"As you can see," I said, "the `Text` property of the Text Box control is a string data type."

I could see some of the students experimenting with the Object Browser. "Do we need to do this for each property we use?" Rhonda asked.

"I didn't mean to imply that," I replied. "Knowing the data type of an object's property is helpful, but not essential. Some properties are more obvious than others, for instance, the `Enabled` property of a control is intuitively a Boolean data type, since only `True` and `False` appear as options for this property in the Properties window. The point is, other properties may not be so obvious and knowing what the data type of a property is can save you some headache down the road."

Constants

"There is one more Visual Basic entity," I said "that you must choose a data type for when you create it, and that's the **constant**."

"The constant is very much like a variable," I said. "It is a placeholder in RAM that contains a value. Unlike a variable, however, you must assign a value to the constant when you declare it, and once assigned it can never be changed. You declare constants in a manner similar to a variable, and like variables, declaring a data type with the constant is optional. Constants can also be declared anywhere you can declare a variable, that is in a procedure or in the General Declarations section of a form."

"When should you declare and use a constant?" Steve asked.

"Whenever you find yourself using a number in your program, consider using a constant instead. For instance, let's say you are writing a program to process payroll. Let's say that the state tax rate is 1% of gross pay. Somewhere in your program, you are going to need to multiply the gross pay amount by 0.01."

"Now further suppose you perform this calculation in a number of places in your program. What happens if the state tax rate is then increased from 1% to 2%? Because we hard-coded the value into our program, we are going to need to search through every line of code we wrote looking for 0.01, and then change it to 0.02."

"This is where a constant comes in handy. Instead of using the number 0.01 in our calculations, we could declare a constant called STATETAXRATE, assign it the value 0.01 and then use the constant in our calculations instead. Now if the state tax rate changes, we only need to change the declaration statement for the constant to reflect the new value."

"Can we see an example of a constant declaration?" Barbara asked. I displayed this declaration of a constant on the classroom projector:

```
Const STATETAXRATE as Single = .0487
```

"By convention," I said, "constants are named with upper case letters. This makes it easier to pick out constants in your code. Notice that the value of the constant is specified when it is declared."

"I noticed," Ward said, "that the word constant isn't spelled out in the declaration. Is that a mistake?"

"No," I said, "that's correct. In fact, I've seen a number of programmers try to declare a constant by spelling the entire word; that just generates an error."

"To me," Rhonda said, "a constant doesn't seem all that much different from a variable. For instance, in the example with the state tax rate, couldn't you have declared a variable, assigned it a value and then used the variable in all of your calculations?"

"You've raised an interesting point," I said. "There are two benefits to using constants. First and most important, constants take less time for Visual Basic to work with. Therefore, your program runs faster. Secondly, the value of a constant can't be accidentally changed once it's been declared. Many programmers declare variables when they should be declaring constants instead. If you declare a variable, immediately assign it a value, and there is no chance that the value of the variable will ever change, what you have there is a constant, and you should declare it as such."

We had been working for some time and, since there were no more questions, I suggested that we take a break.

Operations on Data

"Since we have discussed Visual Basic's data types," I said, after the break, "it is now time to see how to perform operations on that data."

Arithmetic Operations

I explained that arithmetic operations are performed on data stored in numeric variables, constants or properties as well as with variant data types. However, there is a costly overhead associated with variant data, both in terms of increased RAM requirements and processing speed.

"You can't perform arithmetic operations on any other kind of data," I said. "Otherwise you'll get an error message like this:"

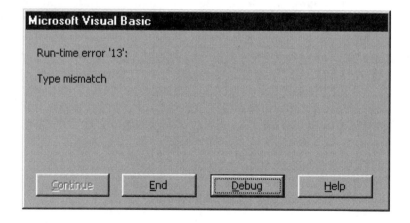

"Now let's look at the various arithmetic operations available in Visual Basic."

The Addition Operator

"The addition operation (+) adds two expressions," I said, as I displayed this example of the addition operation on the classroom projector:

```
intValue1 + intValue2
```

"Notice that I didn't say that it adds two numbers. In Visual Basic, an expression can be a number, a variable, a constant, a property value or any combination of these. In fact, so long as Visual Basic can **evaluate** the expression to a number, the addition operation will work."

"What do you mean when you say evaluate?" Kate asked. "When Visual Basic evaluates an expression," I replied, "it examines the expression. It substitutes actual values for the variables, constants and property values that it sees."

I took a moment to point out that Visual Basic performs operations on only a pair of **operands** at one time. "What's an operand?" Ward asked. "An operand is something that the operator operates on. There's an operand on either side of an arithmetic operator," I said. "No matter how many operators appear in an expression, Visual Basic performs an operation on just two operands at a time."

"That's a little surprising," Rhonda said. "So no matter how fast my PC is, it still performs arithmetic the way I was taught in school; one step at a time."

I continued by explaining that the result of all Visual Basic arithmetic operations must either be assigned to a variable or become an expression in another Visual Basic statement, such as a `MsgBox` statement. I illustrated the use of variables with the operator with this example:

I drew a command button onto a form and placed in its click event the code:

```
Private Sub Command1_Click()
    Dim intValue1 As Integer
    Dim intValue2 As Integer
    Dim intResult As Integer
    intValue1 = 13
    intValue2 = 3
    intResult = intValue1 + intValue2
    MsgBox intResult
End Sub
```

I then ran the program, clicked on the command button and 16 was displayed in a message box.

"This code," I said, "takes the value of the variable `intValue1`, adds it to the value of the variable `intValue2` and then assigns that result to the variable `intResult`. The value of `intResult` is then displayed in a message box using the `MsgBox` statement. We could streamline this code just a bit by using the following code instead:"

```
Private Sub Command1_Click()
   Dim intValue1 As Integer
   Dim intValue2 As Integer
   intValue1 = 13
   intValue2 = 3
   MsgBox intValue1 + intValue2
End Sub
```

I re-ran the program and, once again, 16 was displayed in a message box.

"In both cases," I said, "the addition operation is performed and the answer is displayed in the message box. The end result is the same."

"So why do we need two ways to do the same thing?" Barbara asked. "Well," I replied, "if you use the expression directly, you save on the RAM required to store the results, but you only get to use the result once. To remember the result and use it again, you must use a variable, but that gives you a RAM hit. The choice is yours, depending on the problem you are trying to solve!"

"In both of these examples," Linda said, "you assigned values to variables first and then performed the addition operation on the variables. Can you add the numbers directly?"

"Yes you can," I said, as I displayed this code:

```
Private Sub Command1_Click()
   MsgBox 13 + 3
End Sub
```

I ran the program and achieved the same result, the number 16 appeared in a message box.

The Subtraction Operator

"As you've probably guessed," I said, "the subtraction operator (-) works by subtracting two expressions. Look at this for example:"

```
Private Sub Command1_Click()
    Dim intValue1 As Integer
    Dim intValue2 As Integer
    intValue1 = 13
    intValue2 = 3
    MsgBox intValue1 - intValue2
End Sub
```

I then ran the program and clicked on the command button. As you might expect, this time the number 10 was displayed in a message box.

The Multiplication Operator

"The multiplication operator (*) multiplies two expressions," I said.

"Now this is a little different than what I used in school," Mary said. "We used the letter x to denote multiplication."

"I did as well," I said, "but, for historical reasons, the computer uses the asterisk, and except for that, everything is as you would expect:"

```
Private Sub Command1_Click()
    Dim intValue1 As Integer
    Dim intValue2 As Integer
    intValue1 = 13
    intValue2 = 3
    Msgbox intValue1 * intValue2
End Sub
```

When I ran this program and clicked on the command button, the number 39 was displayed in a message box.

The Integer Division Operator

"In Visual Basic," I said, "there are two division operations: integer division and floating-point division."

"Integers, those are the whole numbers, right?" Barbara asked. "That's right," I said, "integers are numbers without fractional parts. Integer division results in an answer that is a whole number."

"Is the answer rounded up or down?" Linda asked. "Neither I'm afraid," I replied, "there isn't any rounding. This is what I call guillotine math, the fractional part is just chopped off and forgotten."

"Floating-point division returns a result with a fractional part then," Dave said. "That's right," I answered.

"Can you give us a quick example?" Ward asked.

I thought for a moment and then said, "Seven divided by two returns a result of three if you use integer division. Seven divided by two returns a result of three and a half if you use floating-point division."

"Why use integer division in the first place?" Steve asked. "Don't we want to be as accurate as possible?"

"Now that's a very good question," I said. "However, sometimes we don't need to be that accurate. Prior to coding a division operation, ask yourself if the fractional part of your answer is significant. If the answer is 'No' then use integer division, as integer division is up to one hundred times faster than floating-point division."

I continued by explaining that using the back-slash (\) specifies integer division, while the forward-slash (/) specifies floating-point division.

"The following code illustrates the use of integer division," I said:

```
Private Sub Command1_Click()
    Dim intValue1 As Integer
    Dim intValue2 As Integer
    intValue1 = 7
    intValue2 = 2
    Msgbox intValue1 \ intValue2
End Sub
```

I ran the program, clicked on the command button and the number 3 was displayed in a message box.

"We all know that 7 divided by 2 is 3.5," I said, "but integer division returns a result of 3."

"In other words," Rose said, "it discards the remainder."

"That's a good point," I said. "I want you to keep that remainder in mind, because in a few minutes, I'll show you a Visual Basic operation that keeps the remainder and discards everything else!"

The Floating-Point Division Operator

I continued with our discussion of division by saying that floating-point division is the type of division we are all familiar with. I displayed the following code illustrating the use of floating-point division operator (/) on the classroom projector:

```
Private Sub Command1_Click()
    Dim intValue1 As Integer
    Dim intValue2 As Integer
    intValue1 = 7
    intValue2 = 2
    Msgbox intValue1 / intValue2
End Sub
```

This time when I ran the program and clicked on the command button, the number 3.5 was displayed in a message box.

The Mod Operator

"A few moments ago Rose mentioned the remainder that we lose when we perform integer division. You can think of the **Mod** operation as the reverse. It retains the remainder and discards the rest. For instance, 7 divided by 2 is 3, with a remainder of 1, therefore 7 mod 2 is 1. It's that simple, really."

"What's the symbol for the **Mod** operation?" Ward asked.

"There's no special symbol as there are with the arithmetic operations," I said. "You actually use the word **Mod**. Let me show you:"

```
Private Sub Command1_Click()
    Dim intValue1 As Integer
    Dim intValue2 As Integer
    intValue1 = 7
    intValue2 = 2
    MsgBox intValue1 Mod intValue2
End Sub
```

I ran the program and clicked on the command button. The number 1 was displayed in a message box.

"I think I'm OK with the mechanics of the Mod operation," Rhonda said. "I just can't understand why you would ever want to do this. Can you give us an example?"

"The usefulness of the **Mod** operation," I said, "is not as obvious as some of the other arithmetic operators. Probably the main reason that I've used the **Mod** operation in my work is the fact that when the result of the **Mod** operation is zero, you know that the first expression is exactly divisible by the second expression. Look at this line of code for example:"

```
100 Mod 10
```

"This produces a result of 0, because 100 is divisible by 10 exactly, there is no remainder."

"Sometimes there are operations within our programs that we want to perform at certain intervals," I said. "For instance, in last week's class we used a loop to count from 1 to 10,000. In that code, we displayed every number on the form as it was counted, but because the form doesn't scroll the numbers just flew by. Of course, our other choice was to display no numbers at all. Again, hardly an ideal solution. Might it not be a good idea to display every 10th number or every 100th number? Using the **Mod** operation, we can do exactly that. All we need to do is take advantage of the exactly divisible characteristic I just mentioned."

I displayed the following code on the classroom projector:

```
Private Sub Command1_Click()
    Dim lngCounter As Long
    For lngCounter = 1 To 10000
        If lngCounter Mod 1000 = 0 Then
            Form1.Print lngCounter
        End If
    Next lngCounter
End Sub
```

I ran the program and clicked on the command button. The form looked like this:

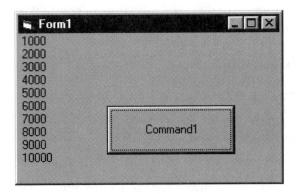

"You're going to have to explain this to me," Ward said. "I think this went right over my head."

"Sure, Ward," I said. "The key to this program are these three lines of code:"

```
If lngCounter Mod 1000 = 0 Then
    Form1.Print lngCounter
End If
```

"In the If statement," I said, "we Mod the value of the counter variable lngCounter by 1000. If the remainder is 0, the counter variable is exactly divisible by 1000 and the value of lngCounter is printed on the form. Of course, 999 times out of 1000, the result of the Mod operation is something other than 0 and we don't print the value of lngCounter."

"It can't be that easy," Ward said.

"It really is," I replied. "If we wanted to print every 500th number, we would simply change the code to look like this:"

```
If lngCounter Mod 500 = 0 Then
```

"One more arithmetic operator to discuss before break," I said.

The Exponentiation Operator

"Math phobics beware," I said. "It's time to talk about exponentiation. The exponentiation operation (^) raises a number to the power of the exponent. Take 2 ^ 8 for example, this notation means, raise 2 to the power of 8, where 8 is the exponent. When you raise a number to the power of an exponent, you multiply that number by itself the number of times specified by the exponent. In this instance, that means you multiply 2 by itself 8 times, like this:"

$2 * 2 * 2 * 2 * 2 * 2 * 2 * 2 = 256$

"The exponentiation operation is typically used in complex scientific and mathematical formulas. Fortunately, a lot of those are included as ready-made Visual Basic functions. Let's see how we would code this in Visual Basic:"

```
Private Sub Command1_Click()
    Dim intValue1 As Integer
    Dim intValue2 As Integer
    intValue1 = 2
    intValue2 = 8
    MsgBox intValue1 ^ intValue2
End Sub
```

I ran the program, clicked on the command button and got the expected answer of 256.

"Where is the character for exponentiation located on the keyboard?" Rhonda asked. "It appears on the key with the number 6," I said.

I asked if there were any questions, but there were none. As promised, I asked everyone to take a break. I told them that when they returned we would resume with a coverage of the order of operations.

Order of Operations

"I mentioned earlier that Visual Basic, when it evaluates an expression containing more than one operation, performs each operation one at a time. The natural question then," I said, "is how it decides which operation to perform first."

"I would think it would perform the operations left to right," Barbara said. "I think that's how a person does it."

"However," I said, "that's not how Visual Basic would perform the operations. Visual Basic follows a set of mathematical rules, known as the **order of operations**, that governs the order in which it performs these operations. A knowledge of the order of operations is crucial if you want your program to actually execute the way you intend."

I displayed this code on the classroom projector and before running it, I asked everyone in the class to perform the calculation themselves:

```
Private Sub Command1_Click()
    MsgBox 3 + 6 + 9 / 3
End Sub
```

I received a number of different responses. A couple said 12, quite a few said 6 and a number of students said that the answer would depend on when you performed the division.

I ran the program, clicked on the command button, and got the following message box:

"It looks as though Visual Basic performed the division first," Dave said.

"You're right, Dave," I said. "Visual Basic broke the expression into three separate operations:"

1. 3 + 6

2. + 9

3. / 3

"Following the rules of mathematics, Visual Basic decided to perform the third operation, the division, first," I said. "The order of operations is determined by the following rules:"

- operations in parentheses ( ) are performed first
- then any exponentiation operations
- then any multiplication or division operations are performed, depending upon which one appears furthest left in the expression
- then any addition or subtraction operations are performed, depending upon which one appears first in the expression

"What does all that mean?" Rhonda asked.

"Here's what happens," I said, "when Visual Basic examines an expression, it looks to see if there are any operations within parentheses first. When it finds an operation or another expression inside parentheses, it performs everything within the parentheses first."

"Once all of the operations within parentheses are out of the way, Visual Basic then looks for operations involving exponentiation and performs them. If there is more than one exponentiation operation, it starts from the left and works its way to the right."

"Next, Visual Basic looks for operations involving multiplication or division and performs them. It treats them the same as far as the order of executing them is concerned. If it finds more than one, it performs the operations starting at the left side of the expression and works its way to the right."

"Finally, Visual Basic then looks for operations involving addition or subtraction and performs them. It performs them starting at the left side of the expression and working its way to the right."

"Can you relate that to the code example?" Kathy asked.

"Sure," I said. "Visual Basic first looked for parentheses in our code example. Finding none, it then looked for an exponentiation operator, but found none of those either. Next, it looked for multiplication or division operations. It found just the single division operation, which it performed."

"It then looked for addition or subtraction. Since there were two addition operations it performed the additions, from left to right, 3 plus 6 first, then the addition of 9 plus 3. If we take this step by step, here are the results of the intermediate operations:"

- Step 1 : 3 + 6 + 9 / 3
- Step 2 : 3 + 6 + 3
- Step 3 : 9 + 3
- Step 4 : 12

"I hope this example shows everyone how important it is to compose the expressions you use carefully. For instance," I said, "suppose we had intended that Visual Basic compute the average of 3, 6 and 9 with this code. Relying on the answer that Visual Basic came up with would be a big mistake!"

"You're right," Rose said, "but how could we form the expression to have Visual Basic compute the average of 3, 6 and 9?"

"Use parentheses," Jack suggested. "That's right," I said, and I modified the code to show this and displayed it on the classroom projector:

```
Private Sub Command1_Click()
   MsgBox (3 + 6 + 9) / 3
End Sub
```

Now when I ran the program and clicked on the command button, the following message box appeared:

"This time," I said, "because of the parentheses, Visual Basic performed both sets of addition operations prior to the division. Step by step, it looks like this:"

- Step 1 : (3 + 6 + 9) / 3
- Step 2 : (9 + 9) /3
- Step 3 : 18 / 3
- Step 4 : 6

Comparison Operators

"I was talking to a programmer friend of mine," Ward said, "and she mentioned something called comparison operators. Will you be explaining those as well?"

"Yes, I will," I replied. "Comparison operators compare two expressions and return a result of **True** or **False**. Here are the six comparison operators:"

Symbol	Explanation
=	Equal to
<>	Not equal to
>	Greater than
>=	Greater than or equal to
<	Less than
<=	Less than or equal to

"We'll only discuss the most common comparison operator today: the equals sign (=)," I said.

"Isn't the equals sign the way we assign a value to a variable?" Barbara asked. "You're right," I said. "The equals sign is used in two ways in Visual Basic. As we've already seen it can be used to assign values to properties and variables, but it can also be used as a comparison operator to evaluate the truth of this statement:"

```
If intValue = 22
```

"So the result of this example with either be **True** or **False** depending upon the current value of **intValue**?" Dave said. "That's exactly right," I replied. "The duality of the equal sign in Visual Basic is sometimes confusing for the beginner. Let me display some code which uses the equal sign both ways in the same event procedure:"

```
Private Sub Command1_Click()
   Dim intValue As Integer
   intValue = 22
   If intValue = 22 Then
      MsgBox "The value of the variable is 22"
   End If
End Sub
```

I ran the program, clicked on the command button and the following message box was displayed:

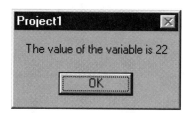

"In this example," I said, "since the value of the variable **intValue** is 22, the expression evaluates to **True** and the message box is displayed. Now let's modify the program slightly to this:"

```
Private Sub Command1_Click()
   Dim intValue As Integer
   intValue = 22
   MsgBox intValue = 22
End Sub
```

I ran the program again, clicked on the command button and the following message box appeared:

"We've displayed the result of the comparison operation directly here, haven't we?" Kate said.

"Yes," I replied, "we've displayed the result of the comparison of `intValue` and the value 22. Since they are equal, `True` was displayed in the message box."

Logical Operators

"In Visual Basic," I said, "there are three logical operators: `And`, `Or` and `Not`. Logical operators return a `True` or `False` value as the result of performing their operations on an expression. Logical operators can be confusing for the beginner, primarily because of the necessity to understand the 'trueness' or 'falseness' of expressions. Let's take a look at these operators individually."

The And Operator

"An `And` operation," I said, "is true only if both the two expressions being evaluated are true."

"Can you relate this to a real-world situation?" Ward asked.

"I'll do my best," I replied. "How about this? On Wednesday morning, your best friend invites you to lunch on Friday. However, you have two problems that prevent you from giving her an unconditional acceptance. First, you and your boss haven't been on the best of terms lately, and you don't want to wind up taking an extra long lunch which you know will happen if you go out with her. Therefore, you know that you can go to lunch with your friend only if your boss happens to be out of the office on Friday."

"Second, you're short of cash and it's your turn to pay! However, Friday is payday and cash won't be a problem if the direct deposit of your paycheck comes through that morning, something that is 50-50 at best. Ultimately, you tell your friend that you will call her around 11 a.m. on Friday to let her know for sure."

I explained that we can express this dilemma in the form of two expressions joined with the `And` operator. "You can go to lunch with your friend if your boss is out of the office on Friday `And` if your paycheck gets into your bank account by 11 a.m. on Friday morning." I said.

"In other words, both expressions, 'Boss out of office?' and 'Money in Account?' must be true for the entire statement to be evaluated as **True**."

"On Friday morning," I said, "you arrive at the office. Your boss calls in to say she has the flu and won't be in until Monday. Therefore, the first expression now evaluates to **True**."

"The morning drags as lunch time gets closer and closer. For the moment, the expression that must be **True** in order for you to go to lunch with your friend still evaluates to **False**. The right-hand side expression, 'money in your bank account' is **False**, because at your last check, the direct deposit still hasn't been made to your account, and $1.38 won't buy you and your friend much of a lunch. Let's express this dilemma in the form of something called a **truth table**, which looks like this:"

Expression 1	And	Expression 2	Statement
True	And	True	True
True	And	False	False
False	And	True	False
False	And	False	False

"A truth table," I said, "shows you the four possible outcomes for the **And** operator. There is only one way that the entire statement can be **True**, which is if both expression 1 and expression 2 are **True**. However, there are three ways for the entire statement to be considered **False**."

"I don't like those odds," Kate said.

"Can you express that in terms of the boss and the money?" Rhonda said. I took a moment to work up this table and then displayed it on the classroom projector. The current situation is highlighted in bold:

Boss Out	And	Money in Bank	Go to Lunch
True	And	True	True
True	And	**False**	**False**
False	And	True	False
False	And	False	False

"That's better," Steve said. "This is beginning to make sense to me now."

"However, as of 10:30," I said, "there's no lunch date. At 10:55, you call the bank and your direct deposit has made it, which means the second expression now also evaluates to **True**. Since the first expression evaluated to **True** when your boss called in sick, the entire statement now evaluates to **True**. You and your friend can now go off to lunch:"

Boss Out	And	Money in Bank	Go to Lunch
True	**And**	**True**	**True**
True	And	False	False
False	And	True	False
False	And	False	False

"How about an example of the **And** statement using Visual Basic code?" Dave asked.

I thought for a moment, then created a form with the now familiar single command button and placed this code in the **Click** event procedure:

```
Private Sub Command1_Click()
    Dim intValue As Integer
    Dim strName As String
    intValue = 13
    strName = "Smith"
    If strName = "Smith" And intValue = 14 Then
        MsgBox "Both are True"
    Else
        MsgBox "One or more are false"
    End If
End Sub
```

I then ran the program, clicked on the command button and this message box appeared:

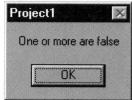

"In this expression," I said, "the left-hand side expression is **True**, but the right-hand side expression is **False**, because the value of **intValue** is 13. Therefore, the **And** operation evaluates to **False** (**True And False** evaluate to **False**)."

I then changed the code by assigning the value 14 to the variable `intValue`. When I re-ran the program, Visual Basic displayed this message box:

"Now the `And` operation evaluates to `True`," I said, "because `True And True` equals `True`."

The Or Operator

"If you're comfortable with the `And` operation," I said, "then I don't think you'll have any trouble with the `Or` operation. In an `Or` operation, the entire statement evaluates to `True` if **either** the left expression or the right expression is true."

I displayed a truth table representing the `Or` operation on the projector:

Expression 1	Or	Expression 2	Statement
True	Or	True	True
True	Or	False	True
False	Or	True	True
False	Or	False	False

"Notice," I said, "that with the `Or` operation, once again we have four possible outcomes. In this case, however, three out of four result in the statement evaluating to `True`. In fact, with the `Or` operation, there is only one way for it to evaluate to `False` and that is if both expressions are `False`."

"Can you give us another real world hypothetical for the Or operation, although I think it will be hard for you to top that last one," Linda said, laughing.

I thought for a moment. "OK," I said, "let's try this one. It's Friday morning. While dressing for work, you receive a phone call from an early morning radio show. The radio station is running a contest. If the month of your birthday ends in 'r' **or** the last digit of your license plate is 4, you will be the lucky winner of $10,000!"

"Sounds great to me!" Ward said.

"Let's see how the `Or` operation works here," I said. "Now, according to the rules of the contest, you will win the $10,000 if **either** of these two expressions are `True`. Unlike the lunch date problem, where you needed both expressions to be **True** to get to lunch, with an **Or** operation you only need one."

A quick poll of the class revealed that 4 out of the 18 students would win. Of course, since I had made up the hypothetical example, I won as well!

As I had done before, I displayed the truth table, modified to reflect our unique problem:

Birthday Month ends in 'r'	Or	Last Digit of License Plate is '4'	Win $10, 000
True	Or	True	True
True	Or	False	True
False	Or	True	True
False	Or	False	False

I then took the previous code example and modified it by changing the **And** operator to **Or**:

```
Private Sub Command1_Click()
    Dim intValue As Integer
    Dim strName As String
    intValue = 13
    strName = "Smith"
    If strName = "Smith" Or intValue = 14 Then
        MsgBox "One or more are True"
    Else
        MsgBox "Both are false"
    End If
End Sub
```

I ran the program and this message box was displayed:

Mistakes with the Or Operator

Everyone seemed pretty clear on the use of the **And** and **Or** operators. Now I wanted to show them a mistake many beginners make with the **Or** operator. I displayed the following code on the classroom projector:

```
Private Sub Command1_Click()
   Dim intValue As Integer
   intValue = 13
   If intValue = 9 Or 12 Then
      MsgBox "intValue is either 9 or 12"
   Else
      MsgBox "intvalue is not 9 or 12"
   End If
End Sub
```

Before running the program, I asked everyone in the class what they thought this code would do.

"Since the value of `intValue` is neither 9 nor 12," Rhonda said, "that's what the program will tell us."

I ran the program and clicked on the command button. Visual Basic displayed this message box:

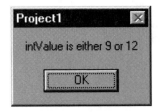

"That's not correct," Ward said. "The program is saying that the value of `intValue` is either 9 or 12, but it's actually 13."

"The `Or` operator can also be used to perform something called a **bitwise comparison** on the numbers 9 and 12. Strange as it seems," I said, "the result of the operation is actually the number 13. This is why the 'erroneous' message was displayed. Ultimately, the problem here was we coded the statement the way we would say it in English.

"Remember, Visual Basic code is English-like, but it's not English. We didn't really have two valid expressions here, because we didn't repeat the name of the variable `intValue` in the right-hand expression. The following statement is the problem:"

```
If intValue = 9 Or 12 Then
```

"It should be this:"

```
If intValue = 9 Or intValue = 12 Then
```

I changed the code, re-ran the program and this time we got the result we expected:

The Not Operator

"The **Not** operator is also known as an **unary** operator," I said. "That means it operates on just a single expression, not a pair of expressions like the **And** and **Or** operators we just examined."

"The **Not** operator is used as a negation," I continued. "In other words, it evaluates the expression, takes the result and then returns the opposite value. So if the expression evaluates to **True**, the **Not** operator returns a **False**. If the expression evaluates to **False**, the **Not** operator returns a **True**."

"Why in the world would you want to do that?" Rhonda asked. "One common reason to use the **Not** operator," I said, "is to simplify some code."

I created a Visual Basic project with a single command button and placed this code in its **Click** event:

```
Private Sub Command1_Click()
    Dim intValue As Integer
    intValue = 13
    MsgBox intValue = 13
End Sub
```

"Can anyone tell me what will happen when we run this code?" I asked. Dave suggested that a message box would be displayed with the word True in it.

"That's right," I said."Since the value of **intValue** is 13, Visual Basic will evaluate the expression **intValue = 13** as **True**."

I then ran the program and clicked on the command button. As Dave had predicted, a message box was displayed with the word True in it. I then changed the line of code that displays the message box to this:

```
MsgBox Not intValue = 13
```

"Now what will happen?" I asked. Dave answered that he thought a message box with the word False would be displayed.

"Can you tell us why?" I replied.

"Because," he said, "the expression intValue = 13 will evaluate to True. The Not of True is False."

"Excellent," I said, as I ran the program. Dave was right; a message box was displayed with the word False in it. "To do the same thing without the Not operator we would have to write the following, much more unintuitive code:"

```
MsgBox intValue < 13 Or intValue > 13
```

"Is that all there is to the Not operator then?" Barbara asked.

"Basically, yes," I said. "There is another interesting use for it. It's been a while since you've done an exercise, why don't you all complete this one."

In this exercise, you'll apply the Not operator to a Boolean property - the Enabled property.

On the CD: Not.vbp.

Exercise

The Not Operator

1.   Start a new Standard.EXE project.

2.   Place a command button and a label control on the form, accepting the default names for both controls.

3.   Double-click on the command button and place the following code into its Click event procedure:

```
Private Sub Command1_Click()
   Label1.Visible = Not Label1.Visible
End Sub
```

4. Save the project in your **\VBFiles\Practice** subdirectory. Save the form as **Not.frm** and the project as **Not.vbp**. Run the program.

5. Click on the command button and the label control disappears. Click on the command button again and the label becomes visible once more.

Discussion

"By using the **Not** operator," I said, "we were able to create what amounts to a toggle switch in the **Click** event procedure of the command button."

"Initially, the label control was visible. When the command button is clicked, we take the current value of the **Visible** property (either **True** or **False**) and **Not** it. If it's **True**, we set it equal to **False**. If it's **False**, we set it equal to **True**."

How Not to use Not

Everyone seemed content with their understanding of the **Not** operator, but before I moved on, I took a few moments to emphasize that the **Not** operator should only be used with expressions that evaluate to **True** or **False**.

"Here's a mistake that many beginners make with the **Not** operator," I said:

```
Private Sub Command1_Click()
   Dim intValue As Integer
   intValue = 10
   If intValue Not 10 Then
      MsgBox "Intvalue is not equal to 10"
   Else
      MsgBox "intValue is equal to 10"
   End If
End Sub
```

I asked everyone to consider what this code was attempting to do. "It looks to me," Rose said, "as if you are asking Visual Basic to determine if the value of the variable **intValue** is **Not** equal to 10. Since the value is 10, the program should tell us that."

I then ran the program, clicked on the command button and Visual Basic displayed the following message box:

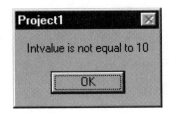

"Let me guess," Linda said. "Bitwise operations!"

"That's right," I said. "From an English point of view, this code makes perfect sense. Don't forget, the **Not** operator is a logical operator, not a comparison operator. Using the **Not** operator on an expression that results in anything other than **True** or **False** will give you incorrect results. Linda is right. The **Not** operation in this case performed a bitwise operation."

"Are we going to use bitwise operations in this class?" Rhonda asked.

"No," I replied. "Bitwise operations are very much an advanced topic."

"How could we code this to determine if the value of **intValue** is not 10?" Rhonda asked.

"Use a comparison operator," I said, as I displayed the modified code on the classroom projector:

```
If intValue <> 10 Then
    MsgBox "Intvalue is not equal to 10"
Else
    MsgBox "intValue is equal to 10"
End If
```

I asked if there were any more questions. There were none, so I dismissed the class.

I told everyone that next week we would take a more detailed look at selection structures in Visual Basic and, of course, apply that to the China Shop Project. And that would result in a completed prototype, ready for Joe's approval.

Summary

This was quite an exhaustive look at the use of data in Visual Basic. In this chapter, we learned about the importance of variables in Visual Basic. We learned about when, where and how to use them, and also about the different types of variable that we can use. In addition we discovered how we can use a variety of operations to manipulate the data contained in those variables.

Variables define an area in RAM to hold information. Each variable has a **scope** (what parts of a program can view the variable) and a **lifetime** (they can be re-initialized when the procedure is re-run, or they can be constructed to retain their data even when the procedure has finished running). Variables should always be declared and, indeed, the use of `Option Explicit` in your code forces you to declare them.

Declaring variables can be done in one of four ways, depending on the scope, position, and lifetime of the variable:

Dim is used within a procedure, and its scope is only within this procedure.

Static is used within a procedure when the variable has to retain its value, rather than being re-initialized.

Private is used in the General Declarations section, and its scope is all the objects on that form **only**.

Public is used in the General Declarations section, and its scope is **all** forms and objects.

It's a good idea to keep your variables as small in scope as you can, only making the odd variable of wider scope when you need to. Similarly, if you know the **data type** of your variable, you should declare it as such, because variant-type variables consume more memory.

Data types come in 5 categories:

- `Boolean`: True or False
- `Numeric`: Numbers only.
- `Date`: Dates and times.
- `String`: A set of characters, treated as text, even if it holds a number. These can be set to a fixed length and, if you know that your string will always be one

length (e.g. a social security number or zip code), you should declare its length to save memory.

- **Variant**: Can take all data types, but is slower and uses more memory.

A **constant** is like a 'fixed variable' (if that isn't too much like a contradiction in terms!), but is declared using the Const keyword. Constants should be named in capital letters so they stand out in your code.

Finally, we took a look at mathematical and comparison **operators**, which act on variables or statements and give a result. An example of a mathematical operator is the plus sign. Multiple operators are treated in a defined order: operations in parentheses first, followed by multiplication and division, and finally addition and subtraction. Otherwise it performs actions from left to right.

An example of a comparison operator is the word **Not**, which returns the opposite value of a Boolean variable **only**; True becomes False, and vice versa. An important point is to realize that this is not the same as the comparison operator <>, which means 'is not equal to'.

Hopefully, you should now be familiar, if not totally comfortable, with the ways we can manipulate data in Visual Basic Programs. Next, we'll see how selection structures can be used to allow your program to make decisions based on user input and other conditions.

Quiz

1. _____ are placeholders stored in the computer's memory.

2. What's the most common keyword used to declare a variable in an event procedure?

3. If you don't specify a specific variable data type when you declare it, then the variable is set up as something called a _____ data type.

4. What's wrong with the following code?

```
Dim intPrice1, intPrice2, intPrice3 as Integer
```

5. What's unusual about the static type variable in Visual Basic?

6. Must variables be declared in Visual Basic?

7. There are five Visual Basic numeric data types. Can you name them all?

8. Which two numeric data types only deal with whole numbers?

9. What's the upper limit for an integer data type?

10. Name the data types that permit you to store fractions.

11. What's the difference in the following two declarations?

```
Dim strValue1 as String
Dim strValue2 as String * 9
```

12. What two values can a Boolean data type contain?

13. What are the valid ranges for a date data type?

14. What's the operator symbol for exponentiation?

15. What's the difference between the / and \ division operators?

16. What does the Mod operator do?

17. Based on the order of operations, in the absence of parentheses, what operation is performed first, subtraction or multiplication?

18. What logical operation is true only if both the left and right expressions are true?

19. What logical operation is false only if both the left and right expressions are false?

Extra Credit – If you had only one match and entered a darkened room in which there was a kerosene lamp, an oil burner, and a wood-burning stove, which would you light first?

Chapter 8
Selection Structures

In programming, one of the most important capabilities your program must have is the ability to adapt to the conditions that are encountered during run time. In this chapter, we'll continue to follow my Visual Basic class as we examine selection structures, specifically, the `If` statement and the `Select...Case` statement.

I arrived in the classroom a little later than usual, and found a little bit of a commotion.

"What's wrong?" I asked, noting that there was a group of people surrounding Rose and Jack.

"As you know," Jack said, "we're both engineers by trade and work for the same company. Our company's biggest account is overseeing the construction of a new cruise ship in the United Kingdom. Anyway, it seems that the construction is way ahead of schedule, and yesterday our supervisor told us that we're being called away to participate in the sea trials. So you see, this will probably be our last class!"

"I'm most disappointed," Rose said, "because I had hoped to finish the coding for the China Shop Project before we left, but there's no way we'll be near to that point today."

I explained to both of them that we would all be sorry not to have them present all through the project, but we hoped they could return in time to see the release version of the China Shop Project implemented in Mr Bullina's store.

"As for as the China Shop Project," I said. "I have a surprise for you. By the end of today's class, we'll have coded a complete working prototype of the China Shop Project."

While the obvious shock of my last statement subsided, I began the final class of the prototyping of the China Shop Project.

Falling Rock Behavior

I began by reminded everyone of my analogy about the execution sequence of Visual Basic code being like the behavior of a falling rock.

"In the absence of other instructions," I said, "Visual Basic begins execution of the code in an event procedure from the first line of code and executes each line through to the **End Sub** statement without interruption."

I explained that although that behavior may be fine sometimes, it isn't in all cases.

"For example," I said, "suppose you want to perform a calculation, but the calculation varies depending upon a set of conditions that the program encounters at run time. A program that is as inflexible as a rock dropped from your hand cannot possess this capability."

"In the China Shop project, for example, we will be multiplying the price by the quantity but the quantity can vary depending upon which option button the user selects. Fortunately for us, Visual Basic gives you the ability to vary the way your program behaves based on pre-defined conditions. I know that we've already done some experimentation with this falling rock behavior, but I want to give you a chance to work with a series of exercises which will enable you to observe this behavior and then alter it."

In this exercise, we'll place a text box and a command button on the form. We'll then place code in the **Click** event procedure of the command button to print the contents of the **Text** property onto the form. We'll see that whatever we enter into the text box will be printed on the form. In a later exercise, we'll use a **selection structure** to print only numbers that appear in the text box on the form.

On the CD: Select.vbp.

Exercise

Everything entered into the Text Box is displayed.

1. Start a new **standard.EXE** project. Change the form's **Caption** property to **Falling Rock Behavior**.

2. Place a text box and a command button on the form. Accept both the default names that Visual Basic assigns.

3. Select the **Text** property of the text box in the Properties window and clear it by pressing the Backspace key.

4. Double-click on the command button and place the following code into its **Click** event procedure:

```
Private Sub Command1_Click()
    Form1.Print Text1.Text
    Text1.Text = " "
    Text1.SetFocus
End Sub
```

5. Save the project in your **\VBFiles\Practice** subdirectory. Save the form as **Select.frm** and the project as **Select.vbp**. Run the program.

6. Enter some text into the text box and then click on the command button. Whatever you type in the text box will be printed on the form, the text box will be cleared and ready for your next entry. Type some more text into the text box and click on the command button. The new text in the text box will be printed on the form as well:

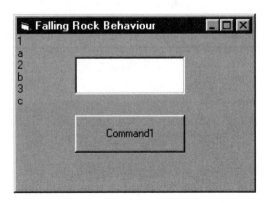

Discussion

I asked if there were any questions. "There are a couple of things I don't understand," Ward said. "What's the purpose behind assigning two quotation marks to the **Text** property of the text box, and what is going on with the **SetFocus** statement?"

"Let's take this from the top. The following line of code just prints the contents of the text box on the form," I said.

```
Form1.Print Text1.Text
```

"We've seen this before, and I don't think anyone had any trouble with that. Now, Ward, here's the line of code you had a question about:"

```
Text1.Text = ""
```

"This line of code," I said, "clears the contents of the text box control by setting its **Text** property equal to an empty string **""**. This is similar to what we did in the Properties window before we ran the program, except this time we are doing it in program code."

"Does that mean the properties you can change in the Properties window at design time can also be changed at run time with code?" Steve asked.

"In general that's true," I said, "with a few exceptions, such as the **Name** property."

"What about that next line of code?" Rhonda asked. "I don't understand what's going on there."

I displayed it on the classroom projector:

```
Text1.SetFocus
```

"After the user has entered something in the text box," I said, "and clicks on the command button, focus is shifted to the command button. When our code prints the contents of the text box onto the form, the focus is still on the command button. And since it's reasonable to believe that the user might want to enter some more text into the text box, as a courtesy, we then use the **SetFocus** method of the text box to set the focus back to the text box. Now the user can just start typing again."

How Can We Improve Upon This?

"This code has quite a few deficiencies." I said. "For instance, suppose the user doesn't enter anything into the text box but clicks on the command button? The code assumes that something has been entered into the text box and then prints it on the form."

To show what I meant, I ran the program again and clicked on the command button several times when the text box was empty of text:

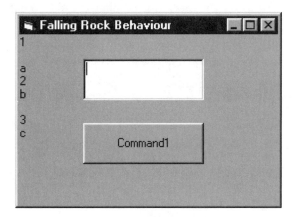

"Do we really want to print 'nothing' on the form?" I asked. "Probably not. As is the case with event-driven programming, we have at least a couple of choices here. We can disable the command button until an entry has been made in the text box, or we can place code in the `click` event procedure of the command button to see if the text box is empty. If it is, then we can display a message informing the user that they need to enter something in the text box in order to print it on the form."

"Which of those two alternatives is the best?" Jack asked. "Best is relative," I said, "but I think that the second alternative is probably the easiest, since all we need to do is code an `If` statement."

"You make that sound so simple!" Ward exclaimed, and he was right, so I apologized. Nothing is simple when you're a beginner, at least not until you've done it once or twice.

If...Then

"I know that we looked at the **If...Then** statement a few weeks ago," I said, "but I think we need to look at it in more detail now."

"Programmers," I continued, "use the **If...Then** statement to **conditionally** execute one or more statements. Conditionally means that lines of code may or may not be executed, depending upon conditions found by your program at the time it runs."

"There are several ways to code the **If...Then** statement. I call the first way the **single-line** style," I said, as I displayed the following syntax on the classroom projector:

```
If some condition is true Then execute a statement
```

"There is also a **multi-line** style." I said, as I displayed its syntax on the classroom projector:

```
If some condition is true Then
    execute a statement or statements
End If
```

"Notice that with the multi-line style, you must code an **End If** statement," I said.

"Another point is that the execution statements must appear after the word **Then** on a line or lines of their own. With the single-line method you can execute only a single statement if the condition being tested is true, and it must appear on the same line as the word **Then**."

"So if you need to execute more than one statement," Dave said, "you must use the multi-line method."

"This syntax is picky!" Rhonda said.

"Don't worry too much about this," I said. "After a while, the syntax will be second nature to you. In fact, what many beginners do rather than be confused by the dual nature of the **If** statement, is code everything using the multi-line style, even where there is just a single line of code to execute if the condition is true."

I gave them a moment to take that in.

"I notice that neither of these styles use **Else**," Steve commented. "Actually," I said, "**Else** is a variation of the basic **If...Then** statement and we'll look at it shortly."

"In the syntax," Rhonda said, "what's a **condition**?"

"A condition is any Visual Basic expression that evaluates to a true or false value," I replied. "OK," she replied, "just like those expressions we looked at last week with the comparison and logical operations."

"So you're saying that if a condition evaluates to True," Valerie said, "then all of the statements following the word **Then** are executed."

"That's right," I said. "Don't forget, there can be any number of statements executed if the condition is true. Typically, these statements appear as separate lines of code following the word **Then**."

"What if the condition evaluates to False?" Ward asked. "All of the statements following the word **Then** are bypassed," I replied.

"I think this would make more sense to me if you could give us an example," Rhonda said.

I created a new project with a single command button and placed the following code into its **Click** event procedure:

```
Private Sub Command1_Click()
    Dim intValue As Integer
    intValue = 22
    If intValue = 22 Then MsgBox "The variable is 22"
End Sub
```

"Here's an example of the single-line syntax," I said. "Notice that there is a single statement following the word **Then** which appears on the same line. Also, notice there is no **End If** statement in the code."

I then ran the program, clicked on the command button and predictably, the message box appeared, displaying its message.

"You mentioned that some programmers use the multi-line style, even though it's not required," Dave said. "Could you show us that here?"

"And could you explain why we would want to do that again?" Ward asked.

"Some programmers," I said, "believe that using the multi-line style even when it's not required enhances the readability of their code. In addition, they don't need to remember when to use the single-line and when to use the multi-line. They just always use the multi-line style!"

I changed the code slightly and displayed it:

```
Private Sub Command1_Click()
    Dim intValue As Integer
    intValue = 22
    If intValue = 22 Then
        MsgBox "The variable is 22"
    End If
End Sub
```

I ran the program, clicked on the command button and received the same result.

"OK," Linda said, "I understand better now and I think you're right. Using the multi-line style does seem to make the If statement stand out more. Is that why you indented the code?"

"Yes," I replied. "Programmers routinely indent their code to make it more readable, particularly If…Then statements. Of course, indenting has no effect on the execution of your code, although…"

"Although what?" Steve asked. "Hiring managers look for good coding habits such as these," I said.

"Are you saying that not indenting your code can affect whether you are hired for a programming position?" Steve repeated. "It could have a negative impact," I said, "in the same way that failing to properly comment your code can have an impact."

"Getting back to the code," I said, "Suppose that we change the assignment statement so that the value of IntValue is 23, what will happen then?"

"Nothing," Dave answered. "We only have code in place to execute if the condition intValue = 22 is true."

"Nothing appears to happen," I said. "In fact the condition is evaluated but returns a value of False, so the program skips to the line following the words **End If**, which is of course the **End Sub**."

I continued by saying that if you need to execute more than one statement when the condition evaluates to true, you must use the multi-line syntax. I quickly added a text box to the project and then modified the code in the command button's **Click** event procedure to execute a second statement if the condition evaluates to true:

```
If intValue = 22 Then
    MsgBox "The variable is 22"
    Text1.SetFocus
End If
```

There were no more questions. I reminded everyone that now that we understood this technique, we could enhance the last exercise to handle the problem of the empty text box:

In this exercise, we'll modify the code from our previous attempt at the problem, so that if the user doesn't make an entry in the text box, a message box will be displayed instructing the user that this is not allowed.

On the CD: Select2.vbp.

Exercise

Using If...Then to Check for an Empty Text Box

1. Continue working with the project from the last exercise, **Select.vbp**.

2. Modify the **Click** event procedure of the command button so that it looks like this:

```
Private Sub Command1_Click()
    If Text1.Text = "" Then
        MsgBox "You must make an entry in the Textbox"
        Text1.SetFocus
        Exit Sub
    End If
```

```
    Form1.Print Text1.Text
    Text1.Text = ""
    Text1.SetFocus
End Sub
```

3. Save the project and then run it.

4. Enter some text into the text box and then click on the command button. As in the previous exercise, whatever text you enter into the text box will be printed on the form.

5. Now click on the command button when the text box is empty. A message box will be displayed warning you that that is not allowed:

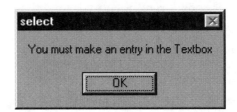

Discussion

"I think I understand what's going on here," Ward said, "but what is the purpose of the Exit Sub statement?"

"Good question," I said. "Let me ask you this. If the user makes no entry in the text box and we display an error message, what should happen next?"

There was silence.

"We've displayed the error message," I said, "and we've set the focus back to the text box. We then need to bypass the rest of the code in the event procedure and wait for the user to type something into the text box."

```
Exit Sub
```

"This line of code ensures that the rest of the code in the event procedure is not executed. It ends the event procedure right there and then."

"Do you mean that nothing after the word **Exit Sub** is executed?" Barbara asked.

"That's right," I said. "As soon as Visual Basic sees the **Exit Sub** statement, the event procedure is terminated. Without the **Exit Sub** statement we would fall right into the statements to print the contents of the text box on the form."

"Couldn't we have placed the **If** statement after that other code?" Rhonda asked.

"What's that expression about closing the barn door after the horse is gone?" I said. "If we placed the **If** statement after the **Print** statement, we would print the contents of the empty text box and then we would perform the **If** test to see if it was empty!"

After a moment or two, Rhonda readily agreed that this wouldn't make any sense at all. The **If...Then** statement was exactly where it belonged, at the beginning of the event procedure.

If...Then...Else

"There must be a more eloquent way of writing this code," Dave said. "Isn't the use of an **Exit** statement such as **Exit Sub** frowned upon?"

"You're right," I said, "there is a more eloquent way of writing this code, and it will free us from having to code an **Exit** statement in our event procedure."

I continued by explaining that with the **If...Then** statement we had just examined, we tell Visual Basic to execute one or more statements if a condition is true, but we don't say what to do if the condition is false. "The **If...Then...Else** statement," I said, "allows you to specify one or more statements to execute if the condition is false."

I displayed the syntax for the **If...Then...Else** statement:

```
If some condition is true Then
    execute a statement or statements
ElseIf some other condition is true Then
    execute a statement or statements
Else
    execute a statement or statements
End If
```

"You can't use that! You never mentioned anything about **ElseIf**," Dave said jokingly.

"**ElseIf** is an optional statement;" I said. "It's really just another **If** statement. You can have as many **ElseIf** statements as you need to express the condition or conditions for which you are testing, or you can have none at all."

"This looks like it can get pretty complicated," Ward said. "We really have three variations on the **If** statement, don't we? How do you decide which one to use?"

"You're right," I said. "There really are three 'flavors' of the **If** statement and the differences can be very subtle:"

- The first flavor, the simple **If…Then** statement, specifies code to execute for a true condition, but no code for the false condition.

- The second flavor, the **If…Then…Else** statement, specifies code for both the true and false conditions.

- Finally, the **ElseIf** statement allows you to specify multiple true and false conditions.

I suggested that we take the code from the previous exercise and modify it to include statements to execute if the condition is false.

On the CD: Select3.vbp.

Exercise

The If…Then…Else Statement

1. Continue working with the **Select.vbp** project.

2. Modify the **Click** event procedure of the command button so that it looks like this:

```
Private Sub Command1_Click()
    If Text1.Text = "" Then
        MsgBox "You must make an entry in the textbox"
    Else
        Form1.Print Text1.Text
        Text1.Text = ""
    End If
    Text1.SetFocus
End Sub
```

3.   Save the project and then run it.

4.   Notice how the behavior of the program hasn't changed.

Discussion

"So the behavior of the program hasn't changed a bit here," Ward said, "although we did change the code."

"That's right," I said, "but the code is a bit more eloquent."

"How so?" Steve asked.

I asked everyone to compare the previous code with the new code. "We have one less line," Steve said, "is that what makes it more eloquent?"

"That's part of it," I said. "I think you would also have to agree that the code is much more readable now. We explicitly state what code will be executed if the condition is true and what code will be executed if the condition is false. Nothing is left to the imagination."

"I notice," Dave said, "that in the previous version we repeated the line Text1.SetFocus twice; now that line of code is entirely outside of the If...Then...Else structure. I presume that's because we SetFocus to the text box regardless of whether the condition evaluates to true or false?"

"That's an excellent observation," I said. "Sometimes, if programmers have code that is to be executed regardless of whether the condition is true or false, they accidentally write code that executes it twice, which is what we had to do in the first exercise."

I displayed the old 'bad' solution on the classroom projector and highlighted the repeated code:

```
Private Sub Command1_Click()
    If Text1.Text = "" Then
        MsgBox "You must make an entry in the Textbox"
        Text1.SetFocus
        Exit Sub
    End If
    Form1.Print Text1.Text
    Text1.Text = ""
    Text1.SetFocus
End Sub
```

"Does everyone understand why this code is not as 'good' as the other code?" I asked.

Everyone seemed OK with the concept.

If...Then...ElseIf

"Can you give us an example of some code with an ElseIf option?" Joe asked.

After thinking for a few moments, I said, "To make this all a little more understandable, let's use pseudocode to illustrate an ElseIf statement. You may remember that I mentioned pseudocode very early in the course. Remember that pseudocode is just a tool that programmers use to express a complex problem. It's not Visual Basic code, so don't try to type what you see here into a code window!"

I displayed this pseudocode on the classroom projector:

Pseudocode is just a way of expressing a complex statement in English, prior to coding it in an actual programming language. This is not unlike the wording we used in our Requirements Statement.

There is an employee

If the employee's age is 62 or greater then

   he must be retired

ElseIf the employee's age is 61 then

　　he has 1 year until retirement

ElseIf the employee's age is 60 then

　　he has 2 years until retirement

ElseIf the employee's age is 59 then

　　he has 3 years until retirement

Else

　　he has a really long time to go

End If

I suggested that we take a crack at coding this, but I warned everyone that this code would be intentionally a bit unwieldy. "In the next exercise," I said, "we'll refine this code by using another selection structure called the `Select…Case` statement."

 On the CD: Retire.vbp.

Exercise

The If...Then...ElseIf Statement

1. Start a new Standard.EXE project. Change the form's Caption property to Selection Structures.

2. Place a text box and a command button on the form. Accept the default names that Visual Basic assigns.

3. Select the Text property of the text box in the Properties window and clear it by pressing the Backspace key.

4. Double-click on the command button and place the following code into its `Click` event procedure:

```
Private Sub Command1_Click()
   If Text1.Text = "" Then
      MsgBox "You must make an entry in the textbox"
   ElseIf Val(Text1.Text) > 61 Then
      Form1.Cls
      Form1.Print Text1.Text & " - You must be retired"
   ElseIf Val(Text1.Text) = 61 Then
      Form1.Cls
      Form1.Print Text1.Text & " - You have 1 year " & _
                              "until retirement"
ElseIf Val(Text1.Text) = 60 Then
      Form1.Cls
      Form1.Print Text1.Text & " - You have 2 years " & _
                              "until Retirement"
   ElseIf Val(Text1.Text) = 59 Then
      Form1.Cls
      Form1.Print Text1.Text & " - You have 3 years " & _
                              "until retirement"
   Else
      Form1.Cls
      Form1.Print Text1.Text & " - You have a long " & _
                              "time until retirement"
   End If
   Text1.Text = ""
   Text1.SetFocus
End Sub
```

5. Save the project in your **\VBFiles\Practice** subdirectory. Save the form as **Retire.frm** and the project as **Retire.vbp**.

6. Type 62, 61, 60 and 59 into the text box and press the command button after each entry. All of the various messages should be displayed on the form, and if you try clicking the comand button with nothing in the text box, you will receive an error message. Enter the number 40 and your form should look like this:

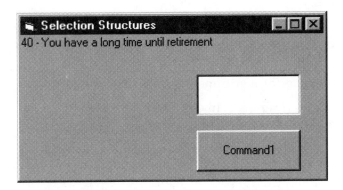

Discussion

There was probably more code in this exercise than in any of the others, and many of the students became confused and lost their places. About 15 minutes later, though, everyone had successfully completed it.

"I don't think we've ever written that much code," Rhonda said. "I think you're right," I replied. "When you have code that executes based on a variety of conditions, your code will 'balloon' and it's something that just can't be helped. This code, though lengthy, is still manageable. Suppose we had a requirement to print a different message for every possible age between 1 and 100! That would make the code a great deal less manageable."

I displayed the first two lines of code on the classroom projector:

```
If Text1.Text = "" Then
    MsgBox "You must make an entry in the textbox"
```

"What we're doing here," I said, "is checking to ensure that the user has made an entry in the text box, which is exactly what we did in the previous exercise. Now the next line of code may have given you some cause for concern:"

```
ElseIf Val(Text1.Text) > 61 Then
```

"I see that we're using the **val** function here," Linda said, "I don't recall having discussed it before."

"That's right," I answered. "The **val** function converts a string data type into a numeric data type. We're using it here to convert the user's entry in the text box to a number."

"Why is using the `Val` function necessary?" Steve asked.

I reminded everyone that each property has a data type of its own and the `Text` property of the text box is a string data type.

"It's not possible to perform arithmetic on a string," Ward said. "Isn't that right?"

"That's exactly right," I replied. "In order to perform any arithmetic on a string data type, we must first convert the string to a numeric data type, and that's what the `Val` function does."

I continued by explaining that the next line of code uses the concatenation character, `&`.

```
Form1.Print Text1.Text & " - You must be retired"
```

The ampersand, technically called the concatenation character, joins the string " - You must be retired" with the `Text` property in the text box. So if the number 62 has been entered into the text box, the form displays the following message: 62 - You must be retired

"Using the concatenation character," I said, "enables us to create a much more descriptive message. No matter what age the user enters into the text box, that age is printed on the form, joined with an appropriate descriptive message."

"Can we get back to the code?" Ward said.

"Sure," I said. "After we convert the entry in the text box to a numeric data type, if that value is greater than 61, we clear the form, and then print the user's age, joined with the string '- You must be retired' on the form."

"What does `Form1.Cls` do again?" Steve asked. "The `Cls` method of the form," I said, "deletes any text we had put on the form before."

"What if the user's age is not greater than 61?" Kate asked. "Then our code falls into the next `ElseIf` statement," I said. "Remember the falling rock behavior of code:"

```
ElseIf Val(Text1.Text) = 61 Then
   Form1.Cls
   Form1.Print Text1.Text & " - You have 1 year " & _
                        "until retirement"
```

"This code also converts the value in the **Text** property to a numeric date type," I said, "and then determines if it is equal to 61. If it is, then we execute the two statements following the word **Then**, once again clearing the form and printing an appropriate message. Now, if the entry in the text box is not equal to 61, we fall into the next **ElseIf** section, to determine if the age is 60:"

```
ElseIf Val(Text1.Text) = 60 Then
   Form1.Cls
   Form1.Print Text1.Text & " - You have 2 years " & _
                        "until retirement"
```

"I'm OK with this," Linda said. "This is basically the same as the code to determine if the age is 61. If it is, we print a slightly different message."

"That's right," I agreed, "and we can say the same thing about this section of code, which checks to see if the user's age is 59:"

```
ElseIf Val(Text1.Text) = 59 Then
   Form1.Cls
   Form1.Print Text1.Text & " - You have 3 years " & _
                        "until retirement"
```

"Can you imagine," I said, "if we had to write a section of code for every age from 59 on down. Fortunately, we take care of all of those possibilities with the **Else** statement:"

```
Else
   Form1.Cls
   Form1.Print Text1.Text & " - You have a long " & _
                        "time until retirement"
End If
```

"By using the **Else** statement," I said, "we specify all of the remaining ages into one big category and print a generic message about having a long time until retirement."

I asked if there were any questions. "We didn't cover the two lines of code outside of the **If…Then…Else** structure," Rhonda said. "Good point," I replied. "These two lines of code are executed regardless of the age that the user enters into the text box:"

```
Text1.Text = ""
Text1.SetFocus
```

"I just wanted to mention," Linda said, "that I ran this code in step mode and it really cleared up some of the confusion I was having with it."

I agreed and explained that beginners should probably be running every piece of code they write in step mode to see what's going on behind the scenes of their program.

Select...Case

"I think that we've done the best that we can using the If...Then structure," I said. "Suppose we're asked to modify the program to do something like this?"

I displayed the modified requirements on the classroom projector:

There is an employee

If the employee's age is 62 or greater then

    he must be retired

ElseIf the employee's age is 61 then

    he has 1 year until retirement

ElseIf the employee's age is 60 then

    he has 2 years until retirement

ElseIf the employee's age is 59 then

    he has 3 years until retirement

ElseIf the employee's age is between 50 and 59

    he has a short time to go

ElseIf the employee's age is between 40 and 49

    he has some time to go

ElseIf the employee's age is between 25 and 39

    he has a pretty long time to go

ElseIf the employee's age is between 18 and 24

    he has a really long time to go

Else he should be in school

End If

"That will complicate the program quite a bit," I said. "Are we up to an `If...Then...Else` statement with eight alternatives?"

"That's a lot of `ElseIf` statements," Ward said.

"The more alternatives we have in an `If...Then...Else` statement," I said, "the harder the program is to write, read and modify, and it's more likely that we'll make a mistake when we write it. There is an alternative to the `If...Then...Else` statement called the `Select...Case` statement which can be a godsend when your program must evaluate many alternatives."

I displayed the syntax for the `Select...Case` statement on the classroom projector:

```
Select Case testexpression
    [Case expressionlist1
        [statementblock-1]]
    [Case expressionlist2
        [statementblock-2]]
        .
        .
    [Case Else
        [statementblock-n]]
End Select
```

"Rather than trying to dryly explain this," I said, "let me display an example of the `Select...Case` statement on the classroom projector. This is the first statement in a `Select...Case` structure:"

```
Select Case intValue
```

"As you can see, the `Select...Case` statement begins with the words `Select Case` followed by what is known as the **test expression.** There can only ever be one of these expressions, and it must return either a number or a string. In this example, I am testing a variable called `intValue`:"

```
Case 1
    Msgbox "intValue is equal to 1"
```

"This code instructs Visual Basic to display a message if the value of the variable is equal to 1. What makes the `Select...Case` structure so powerful is the ability to easily specify multiple conditions such as this:"

```
Case 2,3
   Msgbox "intValue is either 2 or 3"
```

"Here," I explained, "the comma is read as an implied **Or**."

"Look how easily a range of values can be specified:"

```
Case 4 to 8
   MsgBox "intValue is in the range 4 through 8"
```

"Or this way:"

```
Case is > 45
   Msgbox "intValue is greater than 45"
```

"Why is the **is** in that code?" Linda asked.

"You are not allowed to repeat the name of the test expression in a **Case** expression," I replied. "In other words, you can't repeat the word **intValue** anywhere in a **Case** expression. You need to use the keyword **is** in the comparison instead. You can read it as **Case intValue > 45**, but you must only use the word **is** in the code."

"Finally, how about this code?" I continued:

```
Case 1 To 3,5,9 To 13, Is > 100
   Msgbox "Wow!"
   Msgbox "This is great!"
```

"This type of multiple condition testing," I said, "can be very unwieldy if you try to do the same thing with an **If...Then...Else** structure."

"It looks to me," Rhonda said, "like the **Select...Case** statement is just perfect. Why bother using the **If...Then...Else** statement at all?"

"Remember," I said, "with the **Select...Case** statement you are limited to a single test expression, which means you have to formulate your case expressions around that limitation. The **If...Then...Else** statement gives you a lot more freedom to formulate your selections, but perhaps less power."

"In the syntax you displayed on the projector," Dave said, "there was a **Case Else** statement. What does that do?"

"The **Case Else** statement is optional," I said. "It's used as a catchall just like an **ElseIf**."

```
Case Else
   Msgbox "Nothing was True"
```

"Suppose you have several `Case` expressions that evaluate to true?" Barbara asked. "Are all the tests done or does Visual Basic stop after the first true one, like the `If` statement?"

"That's a good question," I said. "Once a `Case` expression evaluates to true, all of the remaining `Case` expressions are skipped. Therefore, if you have more than one `Case` expression which can evaluate to true, the first one in the list is the one that will have its code executed."

We had been working for a long time without a break. I suggested that we complete one more exercise before taking a break.

On the CD: Retire2.vbp.

Exercise
The Select...Case Statement

1. Continue working with the `Retire.vbp` project.

2. Modify the `Click` event procedure of the command button so that it looks like this:

```
Private Sub Command1_Click()
   If Text1.Text = "" Then
      MsgBox "You must make an entry in the textbox"
      Text1.SetFocus
      Exit Sub
   End If
   Select Case Val(Text1.Text)
      Case Is > 61
         Form1.Cls
         Form1.Print Text1.Text & " - You must be retired"
      Case 61
         Form1.Cls
         Form1.Print Text1.Text & " - You have 1 " & _
                        "year until retirement"
      Case 60
```

```
         Form1.Cls
         Form1.Print Text1.Text & " - You have 2 " & _
                     "years until retirement"
      Case 59
         Form1.Cls
         Form1.Print Text1.Text & " - You have 3 " & _
                     "years until retirement"
      Case 50 To 58
         Form1.Cls
         Form1.Print Text1.Text & " - You have a " & _
                     "short time to go"
      Case 40 To 49
         Form1.Cls
         Form1.Print Text1.Text & " - You have " & _
                     "some time to go"
      Case 25 To 39
         Form1.Cls
         Form1.Print Text1.Text & " - You have a " & _
                     "pretty long time to go"
      Case 18 To 24
         Form1.Cls
         Form1.Print Text1.Text & " - You have a " & _
                     "long time to go
      Case Else
         Form1.Cls
         Form1.Print Text1.Text & " - You should " & _
                     "be in school"
   End Select

   Text1.Text = ""
   Text1.SetFocus
End Sub
```

3. Save the project and then run it.

4. As was the case with the previous exercise, as you enter different retirement ages into the text box, various retirement messages will be displayed on the form.

Discussion

"Most programmers find the Select…Case statement to be pretty straightforward," I said.

"I noticed that we included the test for an empty text box outside the Select…Case statement," Dave said.

"That's right," I said, as I displayed the code on the classroom projector:

```
If Text1.Text = "" Then
   MsgBox "You must make an entry in the textbox"
   Exit Sub
End If
```

"Do you remember that I said that we could specify only a single test expression using the `Select Case` statement? That means that within the `Select...Case` structure we can't specify a test expression for both an empty text box and a specific value."

"As we coded the test expression like this:"

```
Select Case Val(Text1.Text)
```

"we needed a separate `If...Then` test for the empty text box. As we did before, we convert the string data type of the `Text` property of the text box to a numeric value using the `Val` function."

```
Case 61
```

"This line of code is pretty straightforward," I said. "Here we're checking whether the value entered into the text box is 61. The next few lines of code perform the same check for the ages 60 and 59."

```
Case 50 To 58
```

"This line of code illustrates how easily you can check for a range of values entered into the text box using the `Select...Case` structure. The next three series of ranges operate in the same manner, the only thing that changes is the message displayed."

"Finally," I said, "here's the catchall `Else` case:"

```
Case Else
   Form1.Cls
   Form1.Print Text1.Text & " - You should be in school"
```

"If none of the other `Case` expressions evaluates to True," I said, " - You should be in school is displayed."

"So the presumption here," Linda said, "is that if we get this far in the code, the age is less than 18?"

"That's right." I said. "Now before you say it, Linda, I know we could have coded a `Case` expression to say exactly that, such as this for example:"

```
Case Is < 18
```

"but I wanted to give everyone a chance to work with the **Case Else** statement. Finally, beginners frequently forget this all-important line!"

```
End Select
```

"When a Case expression evaluates to True and its statement or statements are executed," I continued, "Visual Basic execution resumes with the line of code following the **End Select** statement."

I concluded by asking everyone to look at the code after the **End Select** statement. This code is executed regardless of the evaluation of the individual **Case** expressions:

```
Text1.Text = ""
Text1.SetFocus
```

I asked if there were any questions. There were none, so I called for a break.

"When we come back from break," I said, "we'll begin coding the China Shop Project."

The China Shop Project

"We now know enough about Visual Basic to put the basic code structure into our prototype. With the skills we have amassed we can now code the project. It won't have all the bells and whistles our Requirements Statement asked for, but it should at least produce a usable quote." I explained.

"Let's take a moment to review where we are with the project," I said, "since it's been a couple of weeks since we last worked with it. Our user interface is basically in place now. The menu must be added of course, but we'll leave that to the advanced course. When we start the program, the list box is loaded with three brands of china. Clicking on the option buttons and check boxes triggers the default behavior of these controls, but nothing more. Clicking on the Calculate and Reset buttons has no effect on the program."

"How far can we get with this today?" Rhonda asked.

"We'll write code for the **Click** event procedures of the Calculate and Reset command buttons," I said. "You mean we can actually calculate a price today?" Ward asked.

"That's right," I said. "First, though, we need to place some code in the **Click** event procedure of the option button control array."

I reminded everyone that to calculate a sales quotation for the China Shop application, our program needs three pieces of information: a brand of china, a quantity and one or more china items.

"I believe it will make our job of calculating a price a little easier," I said, "if we store the customer's quantity selection in a form-level variable for later use in our computations. We can use the **Click** event procedure of the **optQuantity** option button array to do that:"

Exercise

Coding the Click Event of the optQuantity Array

1.   Load up the China Shop Project.

2.   Place the following code in the General Declarations section of the form. This statement will declare a form-level variable called **m_intQuantity**:

```
Option Explicit
Private m_intQuantity as Integer
```

3.   Place the following code into the **Click** event procedure of the **optQuantity** option button control array:

```
Private Sub optQuantity_Click(Index As Integer)
   m_intQuantity = Index
End Sub
```

4.   Save the China Shop Project

5.   The addition of this code will have no obvious impact on your program, but you should run the program anyway to ensure that it still runs without errors.

Discussion

"I was able to complete this," Rhonda said, "but I must confess I'm totally lost. What's going on here?"

"I suspect you're not the only one having trouble with this one," I said. I made sure that everyone realized that the code in this event procedure would be executed whenever **any** of the option buttons in the option button group was clicked, and that we had used **Private** to declare the variable as we were declaring a form level variable.

"I'm OK with that," Steve said, "and I remember that a form-level variable such as **m_intQuantity** is visible from any event procedure on the form, but I don't understand why we're setting the variable equal to something called **Index**."

```
Private Sub optQuantity_Click(Index As Integer)
   m_intQuantity = Index
End Sub
```

"Remember," I said, "every option button in the option button group is a member of a control array. Each member of a control array shares the same event procedure. So for the four option buttons in this option button group, there is only **one** Click event procedure executed whenever **any** of the option buttons are clicked."

"If that's the case," Joe asked, "how does our program know which option button has been pressed?"

"Exactly!" I said. "That's the information that the Index parameter provides the Click event procedure. Do you remember that when we set the properties for the option buttons we assigned each one an Index property equal to the quantity that it represents? When an option button is pressed, the Index parameter is passed to the Click event procedure."

"It's almost like a messenger of sorts," Dave said. "That's right," I said, "but there is one problem with this scenario. When the customer selects a quantity by clicking on the option button, it may be some time before they're ready to request a price calculation. We're working in an event-driven programming world and we don't know if they've made a selection of their brand or china items. Remember, as soon as the Click event procedure ends, we lose the quantity they selected.

"We need a way of 'remembering' the quantity the customer has selected, and we remember it by using a variable to store their selected quantity. So as soon as the customer clicks on an option button, we immediately take the Index parameter and assign its value to the form-level variable m_intQuantity."

"That makes sense," Ward said. "You're saying that if the customer selects the option button for a quantity of 8, then Visual Basic passes to the Click event procedure an Index property equal to 8."

"That's right!" I said. "Once we have the customer's desired quantity stored in the variable m_intQuantity, that value is known by all of the event procedures on the form. Later on we'll see that becomes very important to the Click event procedure of the cmdCalculate command button."

"I just wanted to let everyone know," Kate said, "that if you run your program in step mode, you'll get a beautiful view of the assignment of the variable being made."

Kate's point was excellent. The code we had just added had no obvious impact on our program, and the only way to see its effect was to use step mode to view it.

"That's a great point, Kate. By running our program in step mode," I said, "we'll be able to see the assignment of **Index** parameter to **m_intQuantity** as it takes place."

I then ran the program in step mode by selecting Debug-Step Into. I reminded everyone that we could move through the program line by line by pressing *F8*. The first thing we saw was the **Form_Load** event procedure executing as the china brands were added to the list box:

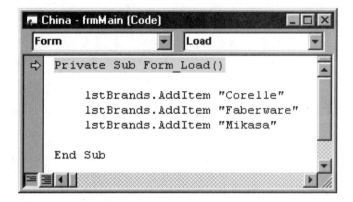

I pressed *F8* until each item in the list box was loaded and the China Shop form was displayed. I then clicked on the option button for a quantity of 8. This then brought up the code window for the **Click** event procedure of the option button control array. When I placed my mouse pointer over the **Index** parameter of the **Click** event procedure, I was able to show everyone that its value was 8:

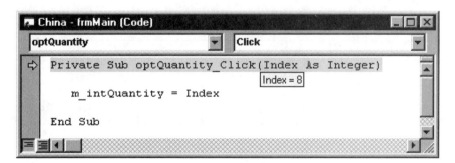

"That's neat," Rhonda said, "but I just placed my mouse pointer on **m_intQuantity** and its value is still 0."

I placed my mouse pointer over the variable **m_intQuantity** in the code window and we saw that the value of the variable was still set to its initial value of 0:

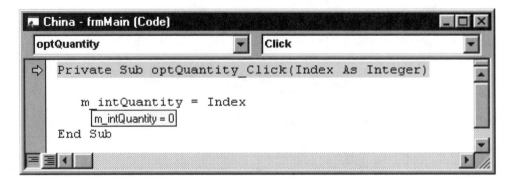

"That's a good point," I said. "The reason is that in step mode, the line of code highlighted is the code that is **about to be executed**, not the code that **has been executed**. In other words, the assignment of the **Index** property to **m_intQuantity** hasn't taken place yet. That will happen with the next press of *F8*."

I pressed the *F8* key and Visual Basic executed the assignment statement. As I had done before, I placed my mouse pointer over the variable **m_intQuantity** in the code window:

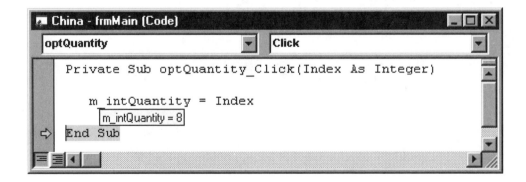

"Now our form-level variable m_intQuantity has been assigned the value 8," I said.

I decided it would be a good idea to demonstrate the Immediate window as well. I selected View-Immediate Window (you can also use the *Ctrl* and *G* key combination).

"Why did you bring up the Immediate window?" Dave asked. "I just wanted to show you," I said, "that you can also use the Immediate window to display program values while your program is paused or while running in step mode."

"Oh I see," Ward said, "we can see what the value of m_intQuantity is another way."

"That's right," I said. "Plus we can also see what the value of Index is."

I then typed the following two statements into the Immediate window:

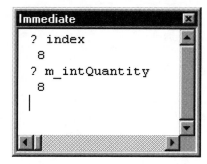

"Remember, the question mark is a short-cut key for the Print command," I said.

"I didn't realize how much," Barbara said, "step mode and the Immediate window could help me understand what is actually going on in the program, I think I'll use it all of the time now."

I then reminded everyone that part of our requirements for the China Shop Project was to provide a Complete Place Setting check box, which when selected, would automatically select all of the individual china items:

Exercise

Coding the chkCompletePlaceSetting CheckBox

1. Load up the China Shop Project.

2. Place the following code into the Click event procedure of the chkCompletePlaceSetting check box:

```
Private Sub chkCompletePlaceSetting_Click()
    If chkCompletePlaceSetting.Value = 1 Then
        chkChinaItem(0).Value = 1
        chkChinaItem(1).Value = 1
        chkChinaItem(2).Value = 1
        chkChinaItem(3).Value = 1
        chkChinaItem(4).Value = 1
    End If
    If chkCompletePlaceSetting.Value = 0 Then
        chkChinaItem(0).Value = 0
        chkChinaItem(1).Value = 0
        chkChinaItem(2).Value = 0
        chkChinaItem(3).Value = 0
        chkChinaItem(4).Value = 0
    End If
End Sub
```

3. Save the China Shop Project.

4. Run the program and click on the **Complete Place Setting** check box. All of the china items (except for the platter) will automatically be selected:

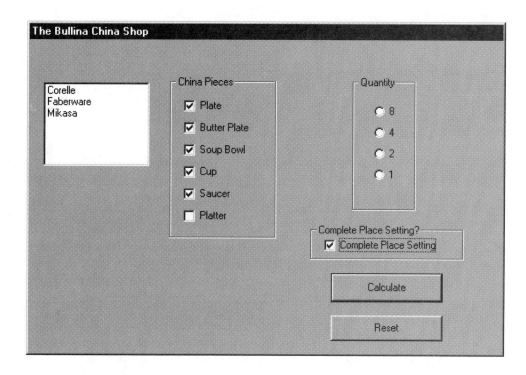

5. Click on the **Complete Place Setting** check box again. This time all of the china items (except for the platter) will automatically be de-selected.

Discussion

"What's confused me here," Linda said, "is understanding when this event procedure takes place. Does it take place before or after the check mark appears or disappears in the check box?"

"That's a good question," I said. "This event procedure executes after the check mark appears or disappears. You're absolutely right, that is one of the keys to understanding what is going on in this exercise."

I continued by explaining that the first thing we do in this code is check to see if the `Value` property of the **Complete Place Setting**'s check box is equal to 1:

```
If chkCompletePlaceSetting.Value = 1 Then
```

"If it is," I said, "that tells us two things. First, the check box previously had no check mark, and secondly, the customer has just placed a check mark in the check box. We should now place check marks in the five check boxes that comprise a Complete Place Setting (i.e., all of the items except for the platter), by setting their **Value** properties to 1:"

```
chkChinaItem(0).Value = 1
chkChinaItem(1).Value = 1
chkChinaItem(2).Value = 1
chkChinaItem(3).Value = 1
chkChinaItem(4).Value = 1
```

"Now we check to see if the **Value** property of the Complete Place Setting's check box is equal to 0:" I said.

```
If chkCompletePlaceSetting.Value = 0 Then
```

"If it is," I said, "that tells us two things. First, the check box previously had a check mark, and secondly, the customer has just removed it. We should now remove the check marks in the five check boxes that comprise a Complete Place Setting, by setting their **Value** properties to 0:"

```
chkChinaItem(0).Value = 0
chkChinaItem(1).Value = 0
chkChinaItem(2).Value = 0
chkChinaItem(3).Value = 0
chkChinaItem(4).Value = 0
```

"What are those numbers in parentheses following the name of the check box?" Rhonda asked.

"Those numbers," I said "represent the **Index** properties of the individual **chkChinaItem** control array members and are necessary to identify individual members of a control array. Referring to members of a control array in code can be confusing for beginners and a common mistake is:"

```
chkChinaItem.Value(0) = 1    'Don't do this!
```

"However," I said, "all this will get you is an error when you code it. Remember, place the **Index** number after the control name, not the property."

Since there were no more questions about this event procedure, I told everyone that it was now time to move onto the 'bread and butter' of the program, the `Click` event procedure of the Calculate button:

Coding the Click Event of the Calculate Button

1. Load up the China Shop Project.

2. Place the following code into the Click event procedure of the cmdCalculate command button:

```
Private Sub cmdCalculate_Click()
'Declare our variables
   Dim curTotalPrice As Currency
   Dim curBowlPrice As Currency
   Dim curButterPlatePrice As Currency
   Dim curCupPrice As Currency
   Dim curPlatePrice As Currency
   Dim curPlatterPrice As Currency
   Dim curSaucerPrice As Currency
'Has the customer selected a brand of china?
   If lstBrands.Text = "" Then
      MsgBox "You must select a China brand"
      Exit Sub
   End If
'Has the customer selected one or more china items?
   If chkChinaItem(0).Value = 0 And _
         chkChinaItem(1).Value = 0 And _
         chkChinaItem(2).Value = 0 And _
         chkChinaItem(3).Value = 0 And _
         chkChinaItem(4).Value = 0 And _
         chkChinaItem(5).Value = 0 Then
      MsgBox "You must select one or more china items"
      Exit Sub
   End If
'Has the customer selected a quantity?
   If optQuantity(8).Value = False And _
         optQuantity(4).Value = False And _
         optQuantity(2).Value = False And _
         optQuantity(1).Value = False Then
```

```
         MsgBox "You must select a quantity"
         Exit Sub
      End If
'If the customer has selected a platter
'warn them that there is only 1 permitted per sales
'quotation
   If chkChinaItem(5).Value = 1 And m_intQuantity > 1 Then
         MsgBox "Customer is limited to 1 platter per " & _
               "order." & vbCrLf & _
               "Adjusting price accordingly"
   End If
'All the pieces are here, let's calculate a price
'Assign prices to each item
   Select Case lstBrands.Text
      Case "Mikasa"
         If chkChinaItem(0).Value = 1 Then _
               curPlatePrice = 25
         If chkChinaItem(1).Value = 1 Then _
               curButterPlatePrice = 10
         If chkChinaItem(2).Value = 1 Then _
               curBowlPrice = 10
         If chkChinaItem(3).Value = 1 Then _
               curCupPrice = 5
         If chkChinaItem(4).Value = 1 Then _
               curSaucerPrice = 5
         If chkChinaItem(5).Value = 1 Then _
               curPlatterPrice = 50
      Case "Faberware"
         If chkChinaItem(0).Value = 1 Then _
               curPlatePrice = 10
         If chkChinaItem(1).Value = 1 Then _
               curButterPlatePrice = 3
         If chkChinaItem(2).Value = 1 Then _
               curBowlPrice = 5
          If chkChinaItem(3).Value = 1 Then _
               curCupPrice = 3
         If chkChinaItem(4).Value = 1 Then _
               curSaucerPrice = 3
         If chkChinaItem(5).Value = 1 Then _
               curPlatterPrice = 13
      Case "Corelle"
         If chkChinaItem(0).Value = 1 Then _
               curPlatePrice = 4
```

```
        If chkChinaItem(1).Value = 1 Then _
              curButterPlatePrice = 1
        If chkChinaItem(2).Value = 1 Then _
              curBowlPrice = 2
        If chkChinaItem(3).Value = 1 Then _
              curCupPrice = 1
        If chkChinaItem(4).Value = 1 Then _
              curSaucerPrice = 1
        If chkChinaItem(5).Value = 1 Then _
              curPlatterPrice = 5
   End Select
'Add the prices together and multiply by the quantity to
'calculate a grand total
   curTotalPrice = (((curBowlPrice + curButterPlatePrice _
         + curCupPrice + curPlatePrice + curSaucerPrice) _
         * m_intQuantity) + curPlatterPrice)
'If the price is greater than 0, display the price and
'make the label visible
   If curTotalPrice > 0 Then
      lblPrice.Caption = "The price of your order is " & _
              curTotalPrice
      lblPrice.Visible = True
   End If
End Sub
```

3. Save the China Shop Project.

4. Run the program. Select Mikasa as your choice of china brand, 2 for quantity and select
    Plate, Butter Plate and Soup Bowl as your china items. If you now click on the Calculate
    command button, a calculated price of 90 should be displayed:

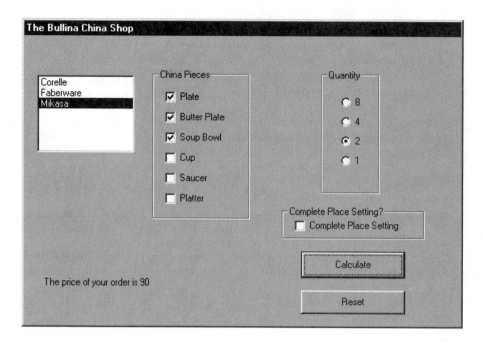

Discussion

It took about 15 minutes for us to complete this exercise. As I had warned the class, there was quite a bit of typing to do, and some of the students made some typos entering the code. After they were all finished, I began my explanation by saying that the code in the `cmdCalculate` event procedure is the bread and butter of our program. Without a correct price calculation, our project is worthless.

"The first thing we did here was to declare variables that are required for the price calculation. It's good programming practice," I said "to declare variables at the 'top' of the event procedure. Also, as a courtesy to others who may read your code, it's a good idea to insert a comment, like the one we have here, indicating exactly what is going on in the program."

```
'Declare our variables
   Dim curTotalPrice As Currency
   Dim curBowlPrice As Currency
   Dim curButterPlatePrice As Currency
   Dim curCupPrice As Currency
```

```
Dim curPlatePrice As Currency
Dim curPlatterPrice As Currency
Dim curSaucerPrice As Currency
```

"What exactly will these be used for?" Dave asked.

"We'll calculate a total price," I said, "by calculating subtotal prices for each of the individual items and adding them together. The variable `curTotalPrice` is used to hold the grand total and the other variables represent the prices of each item."

"That makes a lot of sense to me," Rhonda said.

"Before we can calculate a price," I said, "we need to ensure that we have the following three pieces of information:"

- a brand of china

- one or more china items

- a quantity

"This section of code ensures that the customer has made a selection in the list box by checking the `Text` property of the list box," I said.

```
'Has the customer selected a brand of china?
  If lstBrands.Text = "" Then
     MsgBox "You must select a China brand"
     Exit Sub
  End If
```

"When the customer makes a selection of an item in the list box, the `Text` property of the list box is set to the item that they select."

"So if the customer selects Mikasa in the list box," Valerie said, "the `Text` property of the list box is then assigned the value `Mikasa`?"

"I can see that," Ward said excitedly. "I just ran the program in step mode and used the Immediate window to display the `Text` property of the list box."

"Great, now you're getting the idea," I said. "If the customer has made no selection in the list box, the `Text` property will contain an empty string."

"Is this the only technique we could use here to determine that the customer hasn't made a selection in the list box?" Steve asked.

"Actually, there are several," I said. "In programming, there are frequently a number of ways to solve a problem and one method is not necessarily better than any other. For instance, we could also have used the Len function to determine if the length of the text property of the list box was greater than 0. There's also a ListIndex property of the list box, which is equal to -1 until an item is selected. Here's an example of how we might have used it:"

```
    If lstBrands.Text = -1 Then
        MsgBox "You must select a China brand"
        Exit Sub
End If
```

"I get the idea," Steve said. "I guess the important thing is to ensure that the technique you use works and it works all the time."

"You hit the nail on the head there!" I said. "Ultimately, regardless of how we code this, if no item in the list box is selected, we display a message to the customer and then exit the event procedure using the Exit Sub statement."

"Now let's examine the code to determine if the customer has made at least one selection of a china item," I said.

```
'Has the customer selected one or more china items?
    If chkChinaItem(0).Value = 0 And _
            chkChinaItem(1).Value = 0 And _
            chkChinaItem(2).Value = 0 And _
            chkChinaItem(3).Value = 0 And _
            chkChinaItem(4).Value = 0 And _
            chkChinaItem(5).Value = 0 Then
        MsgBox "You must select one or more china items"
        Exit Sub
End If
```

"This code," I said, "checks the Value property of each member of the chkChinaItem check box control array to ensure that the customer has selected at least one item. Notice the use of the And operator here."

"That means for the entire statement to be considered true," Barbara said, "none of the china items can be selected, is that right?"

"Yes," I replied. "If the customer hasn't selected at least one item, then we display a warning message to the customer and we exit the event procedure using the `Exit Sub` statement."

I displayed the code that checks that the customer has selected a quantity:

```
'Has the customer selected a quantity?
   If optQuantity(8).Value = False And _
         optQuantity(4).Value = False And _
         optQuantity(2).Value = False And _
         optQuantity(1).Value = False Then
      MsgBox "You must select a quantity"
      Exit Sub
End If
```

"If the `Value` property of all four option buttons is `False`, we know that the customer has yet to make a quantity selection," I said.

"I noticed that in this case, you are comparing the `Value` property of the option button to the Boolean value, `False`," Mary said. "With the check box, you checked for a `Value` property of `0`. Why is that?"

"The `Value` property of a check box is an integer data type," I replied, "whereas the `Value` property of an option button is a Boolean data type."

"How would we know that?" Rose asked.

"I bet by checking the Object Browser," Jack said.

"That's right, Jack," I said. "At this point, we now know that we have all the ingredients necessary to calculate a price, but there's one more section of code we need to execute before we get to the actual price calculation."

```
'If the customer has selected a platter
'warn them that there is only 1 permitted per sales
'quotation
   If chkChinaItem(5).Value = 1 And m_intQuantity > 1 Then
      MsgBox "Customer is limited to 1 platter " & _
            "per order." & vbCrLf & _
            "Adjusting price accordingly"
   End If
```

"Remember," I said, "Mr. Bullina has restricted the purchase of platters to one per customer. Handling that in the calculation isn't a problem, but we really should tell the customer about the limitation and that's what this code does."

"Why are we checking element 5 of the check box control array?" Steve asked. "That's the check box item for Platter," I said.

"Have we needed **vbCrLf** before?" Barbara asked. "I think I've mentioned this before," I said. I ran the program and selected Misaka, the Platter as an item and a quantity of 4. Then I clicked on the Calculate button and the following message box was displayed:

"**vbCrLf** is one of several **intrinsic constants**," I said. "It's used here is to break the message in the message box into more than one line."

"That's right," Barbara said. "I remember you mentioning **intrinsic constants** before."

"How do you decide what to do now?" Rhonda exclaimed. "This is the part of coding that really confuses me!"

"What we need to do now is come up with an **algorithm**," I said. "What's an algorithm?" Steve asked.

"An algorithm is just a method to solve a problem," I said. "My children are learning algorithms in school now, although they call them word problems. As I tell all of my programming students, determine how to solve a problem using paper and pencil first.

Once it works on paper, then the hard part is out of the way and you can translate your algorithm into Visual Basic code."

"You make it sound easy," Ward said. "What's the algorithm here?"

"First," I countered, "tell me what the problem is. What do we need to do?"

"Calculate a price," Ward answered. "Very good, Ward," I said, "but that's only one half of the equation. Now how exactly do we calculate the price?"

"Determine the brand of china that the customer has selected, determine the quantity the customer has selected and for each item of china the customer has selected, multiply the price by the quantity," Ward replied after thinking for a moment. "That sounds like a pretty good algorithm to me!" I said.

"It can't be that easy," Barbara said.

"Let's try to translate Ward's algorithm into Visual Basic terms now," I said. "How do we know what brand the customer has selected?"

"By examining the list box," Linda said.

"'What's in the list box?" I asked.

"The **Text** property of the list box," Steve answered.

"Excellent," I said. "How do we know what quantity the customer has selected?"

"By the option button that's selected," Kathy said. "That's true," I said, "but what happens when the customer clicks on one of the option buttons?"

"We store the value of the **Index** property in the variable **m_intQuantity**," Dave said, "and that value represents the quantity the customer selected."

"Great," I said. "Now what about the items of china the customer has selected. How can we determine which items the customer has selected?"

"By examining the check box controls," Ward answered. "If the check box has a check mark in it, I mean if the **Value** property is equal to 1, the customer wants that item to be included in their price quotation."

"All of this is excellent," I said. "Now how will we 'look up' the prices for the individual china items?"

While everyone was considering this, I displayed this code on the classroom projector:

```
'All the pieces are here, let's calculate a price
'Assign prices to each item
   Select Case lstBrands.Text
      Case "Mikasa"
         If chkChinaItem(0).Value = 1 Then _
               curPlatePrice = 25
         If chkChinaItem(1).Value = 1 Then _
               curButterPlatePrice = 10
         If chkChinaItem(2).Value = 1 Then _
               curBowlPrice = 10
         If chkChinaItem(3).Value = 1 Then _
               curCupPrice = 5
         If chkChinaItem(4).Value = 1 Then _
               curSaucerPrice = 5
         If chkChinaItem(5).Value = 1 Then _
```

```
                        curPlatterPrice = 50
        Case "Faberware"
            If chkChinaItem(0).Value = 1 Then _
                    curPlatePrice = 10
            If chkChinaItem(1).Value = 1 Then _
                    curButterPlatePrice = 3
            If chkChinaItem(2).Value = 1 Then _
                    curBowlPrice = 5
            If chkChinaItem(3).Value = 1 Then _
                    curCupPrice = 3
            If chkChinaItem(4).Value = 1 Then _
                    curSaucerPrice = 3
            If chkChinaItem(5).Value = 1 Then _
                    curPlatterPrice = 13
        Case "Corelle"
            If chkChinaItem(0).Value = 1 Then _
                    curPlatePrice = 4
            If chkChinaItem(1).Value = 1 Then _
                    curButterPlatePrice = 1
            If chkChinaItem(2).Value = 1 Then _
                    curBowlPrice = 2
            If chkChinaItem(3).Value = 1 Then _
                    curCupPrice = 1
            If chkChinaItem(4).Value = 1 Then _
                    curSaucerPrice = 1
            If chkChinaItem(5).Value = 1 Then _
                    curPlatterPrice = 5
    End Select
```

"Can anyone explain what's going on in this code?" I asked.

"It looks to me," Dave said, "that we are using a Select...Case statement to determine the brand of china that the customer selected. Within the Select...Case structure, we appear to be checking each check box in the chkChinaItem control array to determine what items the customer has selected. If the customer has selected the item, we assign a price to that item's price variable."

"That's an excellent analysis," I said. "In fact, that's exactly what we are doing."

I explained that in the beginning of the event procedure, we had declared six variables to serve as price variables for each of the individual items of china. "For instance," I said, "curPlatePrice is the variable that we'll use to hold the price for the plate, curBowlPrice is the variable to hold the price for the soup bowl, and so on."

"One thing bothers me about this code," Linda said. "Didn't we promise Mr. Bullina that we would look up china prices from a text file?"

"Good point," I replied, "and you are right. Including prices as we have done here, in an event procedure, is a bad idea in a commercial program. However, it is a quick and dirty way to get the program to work, and for our prototype, that's all we need. However, before we produce the release version of the code, the topic of the next part of the course, we'll have to fix this!"

"Let's examine the hypothetical question I asked you to test in the exercise," I continued. "The customer selects Mikasa for the brand, a quantity of 2, and selects a plate, butter plate and soup bowl. What will be the values of the price variables?"

"Let's see," Linda said. "`curPlatePrice` will be equal to 25, `curBowlPrice` will be equal to 10 and `curButterPlatePrice` will equal 10, `curCupPrice` will equal ..."

She hesitated.

"Excellent so far," I said. "But why the hesitation?"

"I'm not sure what the value of `curCupPrice` will be, since the customer hasn't selected it," she said.

"No need to worry," I assured here. "We've explicitly declared `curCupPrice` as a currency type variable, so it was automatically initialized with a value of 0. Since the customer hasn't selected a cup, we never assign a value to `curCupPrice` and it retains its initial value of 0."

"In that case," she continued, "`curCupPrice` is 0, `curSaucerPrice` is 0 and `curPlatterPrice` is 0."

"That's perfect," I said. "Now that we have the individual prices we need to calculate the grand total:"

```
'Add the prices together and multiply by the quantity to
'calculate a grand total
    curTotalPrice = (((curBowlPrice + curButterPlatePrice _
        + curCupPrice + curPlatePrice + curSaucerPrice) _
        * m_intQuantity) + curPlatterPrice)
```

"Any idea what is happening here?" I asked.

"It looks like we are taking the value of all the prices, except for the platter, and adding them together. Then we multiply that sum by the value of the variable `m_intQuantity`, which is the customer's selected quantity. Then we add on the price of the platter to give the total price and assign that value to the variable `curTotalPrice`," Barbara said.

"Great!" I said. "I couldn't have said it any better myself."

"Why is the price for the platter not multiplied by `m_intQuantity`?" Rhonda asked. "Don't forget, there is a limit of one platter per customer," I replied.

There were no more questions. Everyone seemed to understand the calculation of the sales quotation, but we still had one more piece of code in the event procedure to discuss:

```
'If the price is greater than 0, display the price and
'make the label visible
   If curTotalPrice > 0 Then
      lblPrice.Caption = "The price of your order is " & _
               curTotalPrice
      lblPrice.Visible = True
   End If
```

"This is the code that displays the sales quotation price," I said.

I reminded everyone that earlier in the course we had decided to make the label control invisible until we displayed the price. "For that reason," I said, "we use an If...Then statement to determine if the value of the variable curTotalPrice is greater than 0. If it is, we then assign the value of the variable curTotalPrice to the Caption of the label and then make the label control visible."

"Let's move on to the final exercise in today's class:" I said.

Exercise

Coding the cmdReset Command Button

1. Load up the China Shop Project.

2. Place the following code into the Click event procedure of the cmdReset command button:

```
Private Sub cmdReset_Click()
    lstBrands.ListIndex = -1
    chkChinaItem(0).Value = 0
    chkChinaItem(1).Value = 0
    chkChinaItem(2).Value = 0
    chkChinaItem(3).Value = 0
    chkChinaItem(4).Value = 0
    chkChinaItem(5).Value = 0
    optQuantity(8).Value = False
    optQuantity(4).Value = False
    optQuantity(2).Value = False
    optQuantity(1).Value = False
    chkCompletePlaceSetting.Value = 0
    lblPrice.Visible = False
End Sub
```

3.   Save the China Shop Project.

4.   Run the program. Select a brand of china, a quantity, some items and then press the Calculate command button. If you now press the Reset command button, all the selections will be cleared.

Discussion

"The following line of code deselects the china brand in the list box by setting the ListIndex property of the list box to –1:"

```
lstBrands.ListIndex = -1
```

I explained that the ListIndex property of the list box contains the number of the item selected in the list box, where the first item is 0, the second item is 1 and so on. "Setting this property to -1 deselects the item in the list box," I said.

"This next section of code deselects all of the china items," I explained.

```
chkChinaItem(0).Value = 0
chkChinaItem(1).Value = 0
chkChinaItem(2).Value = 0
chkChinaItem(3).Value = 0
chkChinaItem(4).Value = 0
chkChinaItem(5).Value = 0
```

"And this code deselects each option button," I said.

```
optQuantity(8).Value = False
optQuantity(4).Value = False
optQuantity(2).Value = False
optQuantity(1).Value = False
```

"Next we remove the check mark in the Complete Place Setting check box," I continued.

```
chkCompletePlaceSetting.Value = 0
```

"And finally, the lblPrice label is made invisible again:"

```
lblPrice.Visible = False
```

There were no questions about this code and no more material to cover in this lesson as we had just finished the last event procedure required to complete the prototype.

However, now comes the moment of truth when you have to unveil your work to the customer! As I had known we would finish the coding today, I had arranged for Joe to make another surprise visit.

Reviewing the Prototype

"So now we have a working prototype, the next step is to get the customer's opinion on what we have done so far!" I said.

"And about time too!" Joe Bullina exclaimed, as he walked into the classroom with a smile on his face.

Everyone seemed very excited about showing off the prototype, so after the 'hellos', I sat Joe down in front of a computer and ran the application. Joe spent a few moments playing with the interface, selecting options and calculating prices, while everyone in the class crowded behind him in dead silence.

"Well, I don't know what to say," Joe finally said, "it's fantastic!"

Everyone let out a big gasp. Obviously, they were all as tense as I was.

"So when can I have it installed in the store?" he asked, "I don't think the computer is ready yet. My nephew is still organizing it for me!"

"Well," I replied, "you won't be able to have it for a good few weeks yet! You see, it's not finished!"

"I don't understand!" Joe exclaimed. "It does everything I wanted it to do...you can select your options...calculate a price...what more do you have to do?"

"What you are looking at," piped up Linda, "is a prototype of your application. We have designed it just to show you how things will look in the real version, but to do it quickly, we have cut some corners."

"What kind of corners?" Joe asked suspiciously.

"Well, for instance," Ward began, "you can't easily change the prices of your china and you can only run the application on a computer with Visual Basic installed."

"And we haven't put the menus or the customize options in yet!" added Barbara.

"Oh, yes," said Joe, "I remember those from the Requirements Statement! Well, in that case, I'll leave you to get on with it! Let me know how things are going, won't you John?"

I assured Joe that I'd keep him up to date on the project and thanked him for coming in to see us.

"Well, there you have it!" I exclaimed, when I got back from showing Joe out of the classroom, "Joe seemed to like what we have done so far, and has given us the green light to continue!"

"But did you notice how excited he got when he saw the prototype?" Kate added.

"Yes," said Linda, "he really was excited. In fact, I thought he might take a computer with the application back to the store today if we hadn't stopped him."

"That's right, and it was only the Requirements Statement that stopped him from rushing ahead with a program that was only half complete!" I continued. "The value of the Requirements Statement isn't only to make sure that everyone is okay with what should be in the project at the start, but also to keep everyone on the right track as the project progresses!"

With that final statement, I dismissed the class, telling them that next week, we would begin the real job of turning the prototype into a production-ready application.

Summary

In this chapter, we examined selection structures and how they are used to vary the way our program behaves based on conditions found at run-time. We have seen that there are several types of selection structure and how each is best utilized.

We've also come to a significant point in our project – the working prototype. This is a very important stage in the development process, because all the key working parts of the program are in place. From this point onwards, we'll be adding functionality and code to turn our prototype into a professional-level program. Let's just take a look at what this chapter taught us.

Remember the falling rock? We've seen how we can use selection structures to change this behavior, starting with the plain **If...Then** statement. If a certain condition that you supply is true, then the following lines of code are executed. The statement can be expanded to include alternative instructions for the case that the condition is false, using the **Else** keyword, and even further with a set of **ElseIf** keywords.

After a certain number of ElseIfs, your code will begin to look cumbersome. At this point, it's more elegant to use the **Select Case** structure. Always remember to include the **End Select** (or, in the case of If...Then statements, the **End If** line); otherwise, Visual Basic will complain that it doesn't know where your statement ends. You'll get a compile error when you try to run the program.

Quiz

1. Can you name a common Visual Basic selection structure discussed in this chapter?

2. There are two syntaxes for the **If...Then** statement. What are they?

3. When isn't an **End If** statement required in an **If...Then** statement?

4. What does the statement **Form1.Cls** do?

5. What's an alternative to the **If...Then...Else** statement which is useful when there are many alternatives to evaluate?

6. Pretend that we have a text box on a form with the name **txtNumber**. The number 23 is in the text box. What will the following code do when the user clicks on the form?

```
Private Sub Form_Click()
    Select Case txtNumber.Text
        Case 23
            MsgBox "DO RE MI"
        Case 10 To 25
            MsgBox "FA SO LA"
        Case Is < 30
            MsgBox "TI DO"
    End Select
End Sub
```

7. What will this code do when the **Command1** button is clicked?

```
Private Sub Command1_Click()
    If "X" = "x" Then
        MsgBox "I like to swim"
    Else
        MsgBox "I like to ski"
    End If
End Sub
```

8. What selection structure is very useful when you are only testing for a single expression?

9. When do you need to use the keyword **Is** in a **Select Case** statement?

10. What's the function of `Case Else` in a `Select` statement?

11. What will be the output of this code?

```
Private Sub cmdOK_Click()
    Dim intValue As Integer
    intValue = 13
    If intValue = 13 Then
        MsgBox "Yes"
    End If
End Sub
```

12. What will be the output of this code?

```
Private Sub cmdOK_Click()
    Dim intValue As Integer
    intValue = 13
    If intValue = 12 Then
        MsgBox "Moe"
    Else
        MsgBox "Larry"
    End If
End Sub
```

13. What will be the output of this code?

```
Private Sub cmdOK_Click()
    Dim intValue As Integer
    intValue = 13
    If intValue > 14 Or intValue < 13 Then
        MsgBox "Yes"
    Else
        MsgBox "No"
    End If
End Sub
```

14. What will be the output of this code?

```
Private Sub cmdOK_Click()
    Dim intValue As Integer
    intValue = 13
    If intValue > 17 Or intValue < 14 Then
       MsgBox "Yes"
    Else
       MsgBox "No"
    End If
End Sub
```

15. What will be the output of this code?

```
Private Sub cmdOK_Click()
    Dim intValue As Integer
    intValue = 13
    If intValue > 10 And intValue < 13 Then
       MsgBox "Yes"
    Else
       MsgBox "No"
    End If
End Sub
```

16. What will be the output of this code?

```
Dim intValue As Integer
    intValue = 13
    If intValue > 11 Then
       If intValue = 13 Then
          MsgBox "Yes"
       Else
          MsgBox "No"
       End If
    End If
End Sub
```

17. What will be the output of this code?

```
Private Sub cmdOK_Click()
    Dim intValue As Integer
    intValue = 13
    Select Case intValue
        Case 12
            MsgBox "Moe"
        Case 13
            MsgBox "Larry"
        Case 14
            MsgBox "Curly"
    End Select
End Sub
```

18. What will be the output of this code?

```
Private Sub cmdOK_Click()
    Dim intValue As Integer
    intValue = 13
    Select Case intValue
        Case 11
            MsgBox "Moe"
        Case 12
            MsgBox "Larry"
        Case Else
            MsgBox "Curly"
    End Select
End Sub
```

Extra Credit – How many birthdays does the average person have?

Chapter 9
Loops

In this chapter, we'll discuss the various types of loop structures available in Visual Basic. Loop processing can give your program tremendous power.

Why Loops?

"A few weeks ago we took a brief look at loops," I said. "In today's class, we'll examine the loop structures available in Visual Basic in much more detail."

I continued by explaining that a loop structure allows the programmer to repeat the execution of a section of code without having to re-type it. The ability to have portions of your program repeat can give it enormous power to do many types of operations that would otherwise be impossible.

"For instance," I said, "in a few weeks, we'll see that in Visual Basic we can read records from a disk file using the Visual Basic **Input** statement. What would happen if you needed to read all of the records in a one million record file and you had to individually code one million **Input** statements? The Visual Basic loop structure makes it possible to read every record in the file with just a few lines of code."

"Some loops," I said, "are designed to execute code a definite number of times, such as the code we saw earlier in the course that counted from 1 to 10,000."

"Wasn't that the **For...Next** loop?" Linda asked.

"That's right," I said. "Other loops are less definite in nature, meaning that when you write your program, you can't be sure how many times the loop will need to be executed. For instance, let's use that example of the disk file again. If your program needs to read all of the records in a disk file, you never know ahead of time how many records are in that file, neither should you need to. In fact, the disk file could be empty! This type of programming problem requires you to use an 'indefinite' type of loop to read all of the records in the file, regardless of how many records are in it. There are two loop structures that can do this type of indefinite looping: the **Do...While** and the **Do...Until**."

I suggested that before we look at the newer loop structures we should revise the **For...Next** loop structure.

The For...Next Loop

As I said this, I displayed its syntax on the overhead projector:

```
For loop counter = start To end [Step increment]
    statements
Next loop counter
```

"The **For...Next** loop," I said, "is executed a definite number of times determined by the start and end parameters of the loop counter."

"Do you remember the looping example we used before? Let's take another look at it now! Load up **Count2.vbp** from your **\VBFiles\Practice** subdirectory (or from the CD) and check out the code in the command button's click event:"

```
Private Sub Command1_Click()
    Dim lngCounter As Long        'Declare the counter variable
    For lngCounter = 1 To 10000   'Loop structure begins here
        Form1.Cls                 'Clear a form
        Form1.Print lngCounter    'Print a number
    Next lngCounter               'Loop structure ends here
End Sub
```

I suggested that everyone should run the program in step mode while I described what was happening with the code.

"Most beginners believe that the first step in coding a **For...Next** loop is the first line of the loop statement, the **For** line," I said. "However, prior to that, you need to declare a **loop counter variable** as a numeric variable."

```
Dim lngCounter As Long
```

"The loop counter is an ordinary variable," I said, "and so it should be declared like just like any other. You can name the loop counter variable anything you want, but typically, I name mine **intCounter** or **lngCounter** to reflect its use in the program."

```
For lngCounter = 1 To 10000
```

"This is the first statement in a **For...Next** loop. It provides Visual Basic with a wealth of information. It identifies the loop counter variable, and it specifies the **start** parameter as 1 and the **end** parameter as 10,000. It also initializes the value of **lngCounter** to 1."

"Does this mean that the loop will execute 10,000 times?" Peter asked.

"Yes, that's exactly what it means!" I said.

I ran the program in step mode and displayed it on the classroom projector. I clicked on the command button and my code window looked like this:

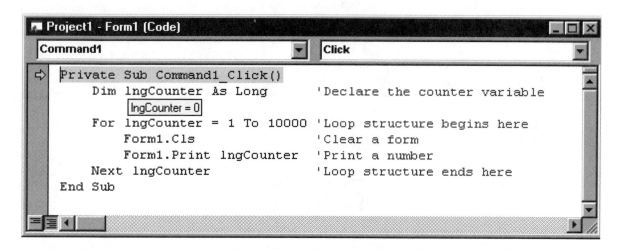

"Notice the value for the variable **lngCounter**," I said as I placed my mouse pointer over the word **lngCounter** in the code window. "The current value of the variable **lngCounter** is 0. When the **For** line is executed the value of **lngCounter** will be set to 1."

I pressed *F8* until the line of code beginning with the word **For** was executed. Then I held my mouse pointer over the word **lngCounter** again:

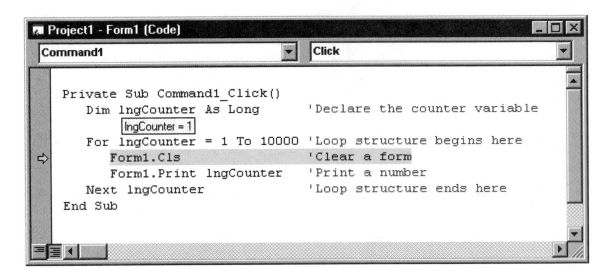

"This time," I said, "the value is 1, indicating that the loop counter variable has been initialized by the **For...Next** loop."

I continued to run the program by pressing *F8*. The value of the loop counter was incremented by one each time the loop was executed.

"What statement is it that actually does the incrementation?" Kate asked.

"It's actually the **Next** statement," I said. "**Next** marks the end of the loop structure. Between the line beginning with the word **For** and the line beginning with the word **Next** is the **body** of the loop. Now, before any of the code inside the body of the loop is executed, the value of the counter variable is compared to the end parameter. As long as the value of the counter variable has not exceeded the end parameter, the code inside the body of the loop will be executed."

"In the syntax you displayed on the projector," Barbara said, "there's a **step** parameter. Why didn't we code one?"

"The step parameter is optional," I said, "and if you don't specify one the step parameter is presumed to be 1."

"What does the step parameter do?" Lou asked.

"It tells Visual Basic how much to increment or decrement the loop counter variable after each iteration or repetition of the loop," I explained. "We could also have coded the `For` statement like this:"

```
For lngCounter = 1 To 10000 Step 1
```

Variations on the For...Next Theme

I pointed out that the `For...Next` loop in `Count2.vbp` was a pretty 'vanilla' version of what the `For...Next` loop can do.

"By this I mean that you can code the step parameter of a `For...Next` loop so that the value of the counter variable decreases instead of increasing. The start parameter doesn't need to be 1; it doesn't even have to be a positive number."

I explained that you can simulate real-world situations more accurately if you get a little creative with the parameters of a `For...Next` loop.

"For instance," I said, "suppose you own a hotel, and the floors in the hotel are numbered from 2 to 20. Let's pretend that your hotel has three elevators. Elevator #1 stops at all the floors, Elevator #2 stops only at the even numbered floors and Elevator #3 stops only at the odd numbered floors. Now suppose we wanted to write a `For...Next` loop that prints the floor numbers that Elevator #1 stops at. In this exercise, we'll find out how to do exactly that."

Exercise

A More Complex For...Next Loop

1. Start a new `Standard.EXE` project. Place a command button in the center of the form. Change the form's `Caption` property to the For...Next loop.

2. Place the following code in the command button's `Click` event procedure:

```
Private Sub Command1_Click()
    Dim intCounter As Integer
    For intCounter = 2 To 20
        Form1.Print intCounter
    Next intCounter
End Sub
```

3. Save the project in your **\VBFiles\Practice** subdirectory. Save the form as **Hotel1.frm** and the project as **Hotel1.vbp**.

4. Run the program and click on the command button. Your form should look like this:

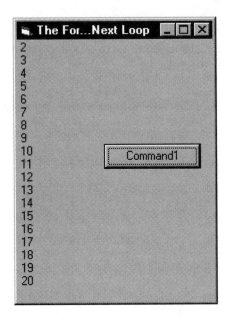

Discussion

"Where's the first floor?" Kathy asked.

"Remember, the floors are numbered from 2 to 20," Mary said.

"That's right," I said. "Now let's work on Elevator #2, that's the one that stops only at the even numbered floors. Any ideas on how to code a **For...Next** loop to print the floors where it makes its stops?"

There was some hesitation. After a minute or so, Dave suggested that a **For...Next** loop with a start parameter of 2, an end parameter of 20 and a step parameter of 2, would probably work.

Exercise
Modifying the For Loop to Handle Even Floors

1. Now modify the code in the **Click** event procedure so that it looks like this:

```
Private Sub Command1_Click()
    Dim intCounter As Integer
    For intCounter = 2 To 20 Step 2
        Form1.Print intCounter
    Next intCounter
End Sub
```

2. Save the project in your **\VBFiles\Practice** subdirectory as **Hotel2.vbp**. Run the program and click on the command button:

Discussion

"Well done, Dave," Rhonda said, obviously impressed.

"What about Elevator #3, the one that stops only at odd numbered floors?" I said.

Linda suggested that a **For...Next** loop with a start parameter of 3, an end parameter of 20 and a step parameter of 2 would be the way to go.

Exercise

Modifying the For Loop to Handle Odd Floors

1. Modify the code again, so that it looks like this:

```
Private Sub Command1_Click()
```

```
      Dim intCounter As Integer
      For intCounter = 3 To 20 Step 2
          Form1.Print intCounter
      Next intCounter
End Sub
```

2. Save the project in your **\VBFiles\Practice** subdirectory as **Hotel3.vbp**. Run the program and click on the command button:

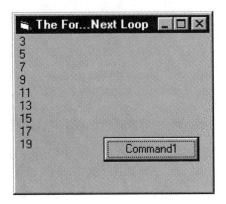

Discussion

"Why not use an end parameter of 19?" Barbara asked.

"That would also work," I said.

I continued by saying that all three of the loop's parameters (start, end, and step) don't need to be numerical literals; they can be any Visual Basic expression, such as a variable or a constant.

Exercise

Modifying the For Loop to Work with Constants

1. Now let's modify the code we wrote to print all of the floor numbers, Hotel1.vbp to this:

```
Option Explicit
   Const BOTTOM_FLOOR As Integer = 2
   Const TOP_FLOOR As Integer = 20
   Dim intCounter As Integer
Private Sub Command1_Click()
   For intCounter = BOTTOM_FLOOR To TOP_FLOOR
      Form1.Print intCounter
   Next intCounter
End Sub
```

2. Save the project as **Hotel4.vbp** in your **\VBFiles\Practice** subdirectory. Run the project. It works exactly the same as **Hotel1.vbp**:

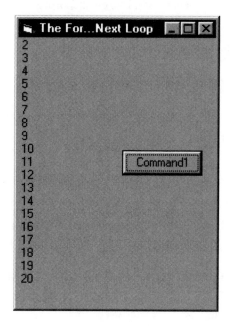

Discussion

"Does everyone see what I'm doing here?" I asked.

"The names **BOTTOM_FLOOR** and **TOP_FLOOR** are constants that you have declared," Linda said, "and you are using them in place of numeric literals for parameters in the **For...Next** loop."

"That's excellent," I said. "See how using constants like this can make your code more readable."

"Suppose," I continued, "we want to print the floors of the hotel backwards. We can do that also, but we must be careful. Let's take a look at this code:"

Exercise

Displaying the Floors Backwards

1. Modify your existing code to look like that shown below (don't forget to delete all the code in the **General Declarations** section) and then save the project in your **\VBFiles\Practice** subdirectory as **Hotel5.vbp**:

```
Private Sub Command1_Click()
    Dim intCounter As Integer
    For intCounter = 20 To 2
        Form1.Print intCounter
    Next intCounter
End Sub
```

2. Run the program and click on the command button.

Discussion

"Nothing's happening," Rhonda said.

Rhonda was correct. Nothing appeared to be happening, at least nothing was displayed on the form. We decided to run the program in step mode to see what was really happening. We clicked on the command button. The **For** line of the **For...Next** loop executed and then the program immediately jumped to the **End Sub** line, and the event procedure ended.

"What happened?" I asked.

No one had a solution. I suggested that since the start parameter of the counter variable (20), was already greater than the end parameter (2) at the beginning of the loop, the body of the loop was never executed, and the **For...Next** loop was exited.

"I would have thought," Dave said, "that Visual Basic would have executed the body of the loop at least once."

"There are some types of loops," I said, "where that is the case. However, in a `For...Next` loop, the comparison of the loop counter variable to the end parameter is done before the body of the loop is ever executed. In a few moments, we'll examine another type of Visual Basic loop structure that executes the body of the loop first and then evaluates whether it should terminate."

"So how do we make this loop count backwards?" Rhonda asked.

"I think we need to specify a step parameter with a negative number, such as –1." Barbara said.

"You're absolutely right," I affirmed.

Exercise

Displaying the Floors Backwards Correctly

1. Change the `For` line of code to this:

```
For intCounter = 20 To 2 Step -1
```

2. Save the project as `Hotel5.vbp` once more. Run the program and the click on the command button. The form should look like this:

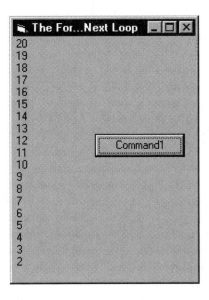

"Remember to be very careful when you compose the **For** line in a **For...Next** loop," I said.

"If there are no more questions, let's take our first break," I said. "When we return, we'll examine the indefinite kinds of Visual Basic loops."

Do...Loops

After resuming from break, I began a discussion of what I term the indefinite kinds of loops, known as Do...Loops.

I displayed the syntax for the **Do...Loop** on the classroom projector:

```
Do [[While | Until] condition]
    [statements]
    [Exit Do]
    [statements]
Loop
```

"Or you can use this syntax," I said:

```
Do
    [statements]
    [Exit Do]
    [statements]
Loop [[While | Until] condition]
```

"This looks really confusing to me," Joe said.

I explained that the syntax for the **Do...Loop** appears confusing because there are four variations of the **Do...Loop**.

I continued by saying that just like the **For...Next** Loop structure, the **Do...Loop** structure allows you to repeat the execution of a section of code without having to re-type it. However, the end point for the **Do...Loop** is not nearly as definite as for the **For...Next** loop.

"In the **For...Next** loop," I said, "we code a definite start and end parameter for the counter variable, plus an optional step parameter. That's what I mean by the definitive nature of the **For...Next** loop. With a **Do...Loop**, there is no built-in counter variable. Instead, we need to specify a condition in the **loop control statement** (the line that begins with the word **Do**) that is tested each time the loop is executed."

"What kind of conditions do you specify in these loops?" Ward asked.

"Any expression or condition that evaluates to a true or false value," I said, "much like the comparison operations that we saw earlier in the course."

I warned everyone that it's very possible to code a `Do...Loop` that never ends, something called an **endless loop**.

"Coding an endless loop in a `For...Next` loop is next to impossible," I said, "because the counter variable is automatically incremented, and its value will eventually reach the end parameter of the loop. However, in a `Do...Loop`, the responsibility for ending the loop is up to the programmer, and sometimes a beginner can forget that."

"Are we going to discuss all four variations of the `Do...Loop`?" Dave asked.

"Yes we are," I replied. "Each variation has its own advantages and peculiarities, and I think it's important to understand all four variations."

Do While...Loop

I suggested that we begin with the `Do While...Loop`. I displayed its syntax on the classroom projector:

```
Do While condition
    statements
    Exit Do
    statements
Loop
```

"Notice," I said, "that this loop structure begins with the words `Do While`, and ends with the word `Loop`. Everything in between is the body of the loop. In a `Do While...Loop`, the body of the loop is executed while the condition is true."

"What this means is that the body of the loop may not necessarily execute even once," I said, looking at Dave who had made a similar point earlier. "Before the body of the loop is executed, the condition is evaluated. If the condition evaluates to false immediately, the body of the loop is never executed. That's an important consideration if you are deciding what kind of loop structure to employ in order to solve a problem."

At this point, I suggested that we complete an exercise to illustrate the `Do While...Loop`.

Exercise

The Do While...Loop

1. Start a new Visual Basic `Standard.EXE` project.

2. Place a command button on the form. Accept the default name that Visual Basic assigns. Change the `Caption` property of the form to The Do While...Loop.

3. Double-click on the command button. Write the following code in the `Click` event procedure of the command button:

```
Private Sub Command1_Click()
    Dim intValue As Integer
    intValue = 1
    Do While intValue < 5
        Form1.Print intValue
        intValue = intValue + 1
    Loop
End Sub
```

4. Save the project in your `\VBFiles\Practice` subdirectory. Save the form as `Wloop1.frm` and the project as `Wloop1.vbp`. Now run the program.

5. Click on the command button. The numbers 1, 2, 3, and 4 will be printed on the form:

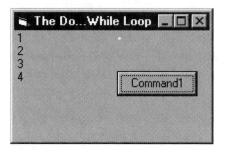

Discussion

"One of the nice things about working with the `Do While...Loop`," I told everyone, "is that it is somewhat intuitive. In this case, the loop prints the value of the variable `intValue` on the form, while the value of `intValue` is less than 5."

"The variable `intValue`," Dave said, "reminds me of the counter variable from the `For...Next` loop."

"You're right about that," I said. "While there is no formal counter variable in a `Do...Loop`, as there is in a `For...Next` loop, in effect, we created our own counter variable here. Unlike the `For...Next` loop, we were responsible for its initialization and incrementation. For instance, this line of code initialized the value of the variable used in our condition statement:"

```
intValue = 1
```

"This line of code incremented its value by 1," I continued:

```
intValue = intValue + 1
```

"Notice that this incrementation must be done **within** the body of the loop. Many beginners place this code outside the loop and that can cause an endless loop to occur."

"I have a question about the loop execution," Joe said. "Why didn't the number 5 print on the form?"

"And what makes this loop end?" Ward asked.

I explained that as long as the value of `intValue` is less than 5, the body of the loop executes.

"As soon as the value of `intValue` reached 5," I said, "the loop structure was exited."

"This loop lacked some of those indefinite traits I told you `Do...Loops` exhibit," I said. "Here's a exercise for you to complete that has a true indefinite characteristic to it."

Exercise

An Indefinite Version of the Do While...Loop

In this exercise, we'll create a loop structure that prints numbers on the form. However, the numbers will only be printed if the user chooses to continue.

1. Start a new **Standard.EXE** project. Change the form's **Caption** property to The Indefinite Loop.

2. Place a command button on the form. Accept the default name that Visual Basic assigns.

3. Double-click on the command button and place the following code into its **Click** event procedure:

```
Private Sub Command1_Click()
    Dim intValue As Integer
    Dim strContinue As String
    strContinue = "YES"
    intValue = 1
    Do While UCASE$(strContinue) = "YES"
        Form1.Print intValue
        intValue = intValue + 1
        strContinue = InputBox("Should I continue?", _
              "The Indefinite Loop", "Yes")
    Loop
    MsgBox "All Done!"
End Sub
```

4. Save the project in your **\VBFiles\Practice** subdirectory. Save the form as **Indefinite_Do_Loop.frm** and the project as **Indefinite_Do_Loop.vbp**. Run the program.

5. Click on the command button. The program will print the number 1 on the form and then ask you if you want to continue:

6. Answer **Yes** by clicking on the **OK** button. The number 2 will be printed on the form, followed by the same question. Numbers will continue to be printed on the form as long as you answer yes.

7. Answer **No** or click on the **Cancel** button. A goodbye message will be displayed and the program will end:

Discussion

"This code was an example of the indefinite type of `Do...Loop`," I explained. "When we wrote this code, we had no idea how many numbers the user would want to print on the form. You see, that's the beauty of this type of loop. This program will run forever, but can be ended at any time if the user wants to. Is this the kind of `Do...Loop` that always executes at least once?"

"I think so," Steve said, "because the number 1 is displayed prior to the user being asked whether they want to continue."

"Excellent Steve," I said. "Even if the user immediately answers **No**, the number 1 has already been printed on the form. We'll see in a minute how easy it is to change that behavior. Let's take a closer look at this code now."

I continued by saying that, as we had done in the previous exercise, the first thing we did was to declare the variables we would need to use in the event procedure.

466 Learn to Program with Visual Basic 6

"The key to this loop finally ending," I said, "is not the value of the counter variable reaching some pre-determined limit, but a variable, the value of which, the user will provide for us. Therefore, in addition to declaring the variable **intCounter**, which we use to keep track of the numbers we will print on the form, we also need to declare **strContinue**. This variable contains the user's response to the question 'Should I continue?' Notice that we declare **strContinue** as a string data type:"

```
Dim strContinue As String
```

"What are we doing with the next line of code?" Kate asked.

```
strContinue = "YES"
```

"In order to assure that our loop executes at least once," I said, "we need to store the value **YES** in the variable **strContinue**. In my old days of COBOL programming, we used to call this **priming** the variable."

"I don't understand," Steve said.

"Take a look at the first line of the loop statement," I said.

```
Do While UCASE$(strContinue) = "YES"
```

"Remember," I said, "we are instructing Visual Basic to execute the body of the loop as long as the value of **strContinue** is equal to **YES**. When we declare the variable **strContinue**, it is initialized as an empty string. If we don't store the value **YES** in **strContinue**, the body of the loop will never execute at all, because our loop statement instructs Visual Basic to execute the body of the loop *while* **strContinue** = **"YES"**."

"I don't think we've covered the **UCASE$**," Linda said. "How does it work?"

"You're right," I agreed. "**UCASE$** is a function that takes a string and returns the value of that string converted to upper case characters. The condition comparison we perform is always done in upper case, whatever combination of upper and lower case characters is entered in response to the question 'Should I continue?'"

"Is there an advantage in performing an upper case comparison?" Valerie asked.

"Yes, there is," I said. "Did you realize, that the user can enter the word YES in eight different ways. Converting the user's response to all upper case means that we need only perform the comparison one way."

"What do you mean eight different ways?" asked Barbara.

"Each letter of yes can be either upper or lower case," I explained. "If you were to write out all the different combinations you would find there were eight different ways of writing the word 'Yes'."

"That makes sense," Ward said. "Is there a significance to the dollar sign?"

"Whenever you see a dollar sign in a function," I said, "that means that the function returns a string value."

"We've seen these next two lines of code before," I continued.

```
Form1.Print intValue
intValue = intValue + 1
```

"Here we print the number on the form and increment the value of `intValue` by 1. This line of code will be new to you:"

```
strContinue = InputBox("Should I continue?", _
     "The Indefinite Loop", "Yes")
```

"What is going on here?" Barbara asked.

"The `InputBox` function permits you to quickly and easily obtain a response from the user," I replied. "In this instance, we use it to display the question 'Should I continue?'"

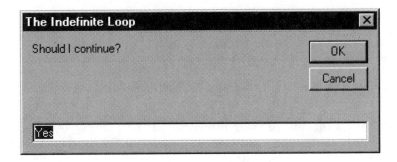

"That looks like a message box with a text box on it," Rhonda said.

"That's a pretty accurate description," I said. "Notice that the input box has a title, a prompt, two buttons labeled OK and Cancel, and, as Rhonda mentioned, a text box, in this case with the word Yes already in it."

"What's the syntax for the InputBox function?" Dave asked.

"The InputBox function has seven parameters in all," I said, "but the first three are the most important to us, a **prompt** (`"Should I continue?"`), a **title** for the input box (`"The Indefinite Loop"`) and a **default response** (`"Yes"`)."

"What does the default response specify?" Valerie asked.

"That's the value that appears in the text box," I said. "Specifying a default response can save the user some typing. In our exercise, if the user wishes to continue printing numbers on the form, all they need to do is click on the OK button or press the *Enter* key."

"So this loop continues until the user answers, no?" Ward asked.

"Not exactly," I said. "The loop continues until the user answers something other than Yes or if they click on the Cancel button."

Prior to moving on, I repeated that one of the biggest mistakes beginners make with the Do...Loop family is to forget to include code within the body of the loop that enables the loop to end.

"For instance," I said, "I've seen beginners place the InputBox statement before or after the loop, but not within the body of the loop where it belongs. Once the loop starts to execute, the InputBox function is never executed. As a result, there's no opportunity for the user to instruct the program to stop."

Do...Loop While

When we began our discussion of loops in today's class, I mentioned that there are four variations of the Do...Loop structure. With the Do While...Loop, the words Do While are coded at the top of the loop and the word Loop is coded at the bottom. Everything in between is the body of the loop.

"The location of the word While is significant," I said. "Coming as it does **before** the body of the loop, that means that the condition statement for the loop is evaluated prior to the body of the loop executing. Therefore, it's possible that the body of the loop will never execute. We're about to examine the cousin of the Do While...Loop, the Do...Loop While. The only difference between the two is that the Do...Loop While always executes at least once."

I suggested that we complete an exercise in which we would code one more Do While...Loop and then change it to the Do...Loop While variation.

Exercise

The Do...Loop While vs. the Do While...Loop

In this exercise, we'll place two command buttons on the form. We'll then place code in the Click event procedure of Command1 that implements a Do While...Loop structure, while in the Click event procedure of Command2, we'll place code that implements a Do...Loop While structure.

1. Start a new Standard.EXE project.

2. Place two command buttons on the form and accept both default names.

3. Double-click on Command1 and place the following code into its Click event procedure:

```
Private Sub Command1_Click()
    Dim intValue As Integer
    intValue = 5
    Do While intValue < 5
        Form1.Print intValue
        intValue = intValue + 1
    Loop
End Sub
```

4. Double-click on Command2 and place the following code into its Click event procedure:

```
Private Sub Command2_Click()
   Dim intValue As Integer
   intValue = 5
   Do
      Form1.Print intValue
      intValue = intValue + 1
   Loop While intValue < 5
End Sub
```

5.   Save the form as `Wloop2.frm` and the project as `Wloop2.vbp` in your `\VBFiles\Practice` subdirectory. Run the program.

6.   Click on Command1: Oops! Nothing appears on the form!

7.   However, if you click on Command2, the number 5 appears.

Discussion

"Can anyone tell me what's going on here?" I asked.

"Despite the fact that the code was basically the same in both command buttons," Dave said, "the code for `Command2` printed the number 5 on the form because the body of the loop was executed *before* the evaluation of the test condition. Since the test condition of the loop in `Command1` was evaluated prior to executing the loop, nothing was printed."

"That's an excellent analysis," I said. "As the test condition for `Command1` is *true* – intValue is equal to 5 – the code goes straight to the end sub without running the body of the loop. For `Command2`, the loop runs before the test is made, so the `Print` command gets executed first."

I asked if there were any questions about the `Do...While` family of loops. There were none, so we moved onto the `Do...Until` family of loops.

Do Until...Loop

"It looks to me as though the difference between the `Do...While` family and the `Do...Until` family may be largely a matter of semantics," Linda suggested.

"You're quite right," I said. "The problems you can solve using the `Do...While` family can also be solved using the `Do...Until` family. With the `Do...While` family, the body of the loop is executed **while** a condition is true. With the `Do...Until` family, the loop is executed **until** a condition becomes true."

I pointed out that the location of the word `Until` is just as significant in the `Do...Until` family as the word `While` is in the `Do...While` family.

I suggested that to illustrate the difference between the two loop families, we should take our earlier project, `Wloop1.vbp` and simply change the word `While` to `Until`.

Exercise

The Do Until...Loop

1. Load up `Wloop1.vbp` from your `\VBFiles\Practice` subdirectory.

2. Bring up the code window for the command button and change the highlighted lines of code:

```
Private Sub Command1_Click()
    Dim intValue As Integer
    intValue = 1
    Do Until intValue < 5
        Form1.Print intValue
        intValue = intValue + 1
    Loop
End Sub
```

3. Save the project in your `\VBFiles\Practice` subdirectory. Save the form as `Uloop1.frm` and the project as `Uloop1.vbp`. Now run the program.

4. Click on the command button. Nothing appears on the form.

Discussion

"What's happened here?" I said. "It seems that nothing has."

"I think I can explain what happened," Dave said. "The condition, `intValue <5`, was already true when the loop began execution. As a result, the body of the loop never executed."

"Very good, Dave," I said. "Now let's take a look at this code in step mode:"

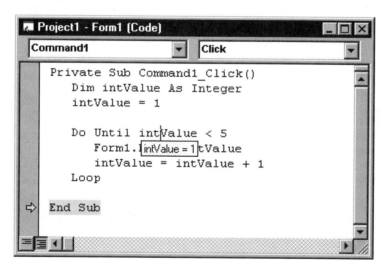

```
Project1 - Form1 (Code)                          _ □ ×
Command1                  ▼   Click                ▼
    Private Sub Command1_Click()                    ▲
       Dim intValue As Integer
       intValue = 1

⇨  |   Do Until intValue < 5
          Form1.│intValue = 1│tValue
          intValue = intValue + 1
       Loop

    End Sub                                         ▼
```

When I displayed the value of **intValue** in the code window, everyone saw immediately what had happened.

"We told Visual Basic to execute the **Do Until...Loop** until the value of **intValue** was less than 5," I said. "The **Do Until...Loop** evaluates the loop condition before executing the loop, so since the value of **intValue** started at 1, the body of the loop was never executed and the event procedure ended."

```
Project1 - Form1 (Code)                          _ □ ×
Command1                  ▼   Click                ▼
    Private Sub Command1_Click()                    ▲
       Dim intValue As Integer
       intValue = 1

       Do Until int│Value < 5
          Form1.│intValue = 1│tValue
          intValue = intValue + 1
       Loop

⇨   End Sub                                         ▼
```

"Who would have thought that one little word could make such a difference?" Rhonda said.

"It certainly can make a difference," I said, "that's why we must be careful how we choose to code our loops. However, with five methods of coding loops available to us, we should be able to find one that suits our needs."

"It would seem to me that you should be able to convert a `Do...While` into a `Do...Until`, and vice versa," Kathy said.

"Yes," I said. "As we said earlier, it's frequently just a matter of semantics. For instance, these two statements will generate the same results."

```
Do While intValue < 5
Do Until intValue > 4
```

"The bottom line," I said, "is to use the right tool for the job. Where there appear to be methods or techniques that appear to produce identical results, double-check their operation and make sure you really understand how they work. In other words, test, test, test!"

Do...Loop Until

I told everyone there was just one more variation of the `Do...Loop` to discuss, the `Do...Loop Until`.

"The `Do...Loop Until` is very similar to the `Do...Loop While` we examined just a little while ago," I explained. "As with the `Do...Loop While`, the location of the word `Loop` is significant. The `Do...Loop Until` will be executed at least once, something that is not guaranteed by the `Do Until...Loop`, as we saw in the previous exercise. In the `Do...Loop Until` variation, the body of the loop is executed before the condition is evaluated. If the condition immediately evaluates to true, the body of the loop is still executed once."

Exercise
The Do...Loop Until

1. Continue working with the project from the previous exercise, `Uloop1.vbp`.

2. Modify the highlighted lines of code in the `Click` event procedure of the command button:

```
Private Sub Command1_Click()
    Dim intValue As Integer
    intValue = 1
```

```
    Do
        Form1.Print intValue
        intValue = intValue + 1
    Loop Until intValue < 5
End Sub
```

3. Save the project in your \VBFiles\Practice subdirectory. Save the form as Uloop2.frm and the project as Uloop2.vbp. Now run the program.

4. Click on the command button. The number 1 will be printed on the form.

Discussion

"Can anyone tell me the difference between this program and the one from the previous exercise?" I asked.

"I think I can," Ward said. "In this program, even though the value of intValue was already less than 5, the loop still executed because of the location of the Until statement. That's why 1 was printed on the form in this program. In the previous exercise, the body of the loop was never executed."

"You're right on the mark, Ward," I said. "We've been working for a long time and have now finished with our treatment of loops. Ordinarily, I would dismiss class for the day, but I want you all to take a quick break. When you return I'll have a surprise for you."

Mr. Bullina Pays a Surprise Visit

When my students returned from break, they found our client, Joe Bullina, present in the classroom. Unknown to them, I had visited Joe during the course of the week and had shown him the great progress the class had made with the project.

"I've got to tell you," Joe Bullina said, "I'm most impressed with the progress you've made with the program in such a short time. In fact, when Mr. Smiley showed it to me earlier this week, I liked it so much that I tried to talk him into installing the program right then and there in my China Shop. John cautioned me to be patient though, as you still have some work to do with it."

I could see that the students in the class were just about to burst with pride.

"As I'm sure Mr. Smiley told you," Joe Bullina said, "several weeks ago he called to ask me what I thought of the idea of displaying pictures of the china brand when the customer made a selection. I thought it was a great idea and I immediately set out to get some pictures of the china we sell. I'm pleased to say I have them here with me today."

"I've placed the three files, `Corelle.gif`, `Faberware.gif`, and `Mikasa.gif` in your `\VBFiles\China` subdirectory," I announced.

 These three files are on the CD, in the `Chapter09\China Shop` folder.

At this point, I distributed this exercise:

Exercise
Loading the Image Control

In this exercise, we'll modify the China Shop Project to load graphic files into the `Picture` property of the image control when a china brand in the list box is selected. We'll place code in the `Click` event procedure of the `lstBrands` list box to do this.

1. Load up the China Shop Project.

2. Ensure that the following three files have been copied from the CD into your `\VBFiles\China` subdirectory: `Corelle.gif`, `Faberware.gif,` and `Mikasa.gif`.

3. In the `Click` event procedure of the `lstBrands` list box, place the following code:

```
Private Sub lstBrands_Click()
   If lstBrands.ListIndex = -1 Then Exit Sub
   imgChina.Picture = LoadPicture("C:\VBFiles\China\" & _
        lstBrands.Text & ".gif")
End Sub
```

4. Save the China Shop Project.

5. Run the program and select a brand of china in the list box. When you do, you should see the corresponding china pattern appear in the image control:

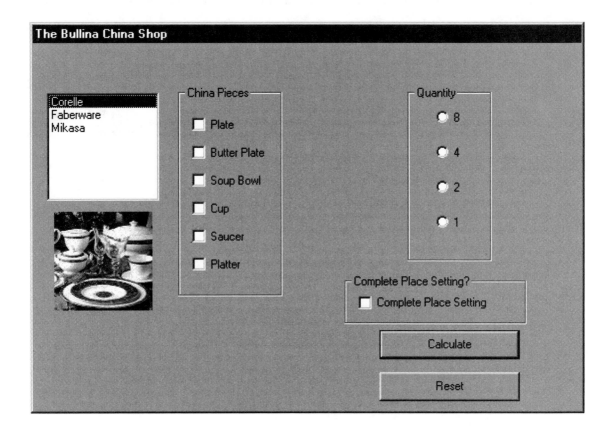

Discussion

"I think the customers will really love the graphics," Mr. Bullina said. "I'd love to take this program back to the shop with me. I could always give my nephew a call, and ask him to rush my PC order. Are you sure you won't change your mind?"

"We don't want to rush things," I said. "We want to deliver a program that both you, and we, can be proud of."

I also reminded Joe Bullina of the need to adhere strictly to the SDLC that we had discussed the first day that I met with him. Joe reluctantly agreed, but he was still very excited as he bid everyone goodbye on his way back to the china shop. "See you all in a few weeks," he said.

"Before we all forget the code we've just written," I said, "let's discuss it. When the customer selects a china brand in the list box, their selection is stored in the **Text** property of the list box control. We can use that **Text** property to determine the appropriate graphic file to load into the **Picture** property of our image control. That's what this line of code does:"

```
imgChina.Picture = LoadPicture("C:\VBFiles\China\" & _
    lstBrands.Text & ".gif")
```

"It's important to note here," I continued, "that in order for this process to work, the name of the graphics file for the china brand must match the name of the brand that is selected in the list box. As long as that is the case, we can use the **LoadPicture** function of the image control to load the graphics file into the **Picture** property of the image control. The graphic file will then be displayed in what, prior to that, is an empty image control. We use the ampersand character to join the name of the **Text** property of the list box control to the directory path of the China Shop. We then join the file name extension for the graphics file, **.gif**, to the end of that string."

I could see that several people were confused.

"For instance," I said, "if the customer selects Mikasa as their brand, the **Text** property of the list box control contains **Mikasa**. Let's translate this line of code as Visual Basic would."

```
imgChina.Picture = LoadPicture("C:\VBFiles\China\" & _
     "Mikasa" & ".gif")
```

This becomes:

```
imgChina.Picture = LoadPicture("C:\VBFiles\China\Mikasa" & _
     ".gif")
```

which becomes:

```
imgChina.Picture = LoadPicture("C:\VBFiles\China\Mikasa.gif")
```

"Did that help?" I asked.

I could see that it had.

"What does the line of code before we load the **Picture** property of the image control do?" Dave asked.

```
If lstBrands.ListIndex = -1 Then Exit Sub
```

"Good question," I said. "Before loading the **Picture** property of the image control, we need to account for the possibility that the **Click** event of the list box could be triggered with no china brand selected. Our program will bomb if we attempt to execute the **LoadPicture** function with nothing in the **Text** property of the image control. That's why we check to see if the **ListIndex** property of the list box control is -1. That means no brand has been selected, so we need to exit the event procedure."

"How can the **Click** event of the list box control be triggered when no item has been selected?" Barbara asked. "I thought that was one of the benefits of the list box control."

"Another good question," I said. "Do you remember earlier in the course, I said that an event can be triggered in three ways? One way is by some user action, such as clicking on an item in the list box, another is by the operating system and, finally, through Visual Basic code. The following code that we placed in the **cmdReset** command button will trigger the **Click** event of the list box."

```
lstBrands.ListIndex = -1
```

"If a selection has been made in the list box," I explained, "then setting the **ListIndex** property to -1 will trigger the **Click** event of the list box."

I invited everyone to run the program in step mode. When we clicked on the **cmdReset** command button, the **Click** event of the list box control was triggered.

"There is an extra line of code we need to add to the **cmdReset** button," I warned everyone. "So let's do today's final exercise."

Exercise
The cmdReset Button Revisited

1. Load up the China Shop Project (if it's not already loaded).

2. Modify the code in the `Click` event procedure of the `cmdReset` button so that it looks like this:

    ```
    chkCompletePlaceSetting.Value = 0
    lblPrice.Visible = False
    ImgChina.Picture = LoadPicture()
    End Sub
    ```

3. Save the China Shop Project.

4. Run the program. Pressing the Reset button will now clear the image control.

Discussion

The line of code we added simply clears out any pictures we were displaying in the image control when the `cmdReset` button is clicked.

It had been a long class. I could see that everyone was feeling proud of the product they were producing week by week. In addition, I could also see that they were pretty worn out; it had been an intense session. Prior to dismissing them, I told everyone that in our next class, we would be doing some work with strings.

Summary

In this chapter, we discussed how loop processing can make our lives a lot easier by saving us from unnecessary repetitive typing. There are several types of loop statement and the key is to know when it is appropriate to use the relevant type.

Here's a reminder of some of the different loops we discussed:

- **For...Next** Loops: these execute a definite number of times. The number of times that the loop runs is determined by the range of values set in the loop counter.

- **Do...While** loops: these execute <u>while</u> a specified condition is true.

- **Do...Until** loops: these execute <u>until</u> a specified condition is true.

We have also modified the China Shop Project so that the appropriate graphic image is loaded into the frame to display an image of each type of China.

In the next chapter, we'll take a look at strings, and at how to manipulate them.

Quiz

1. What does a loop do?

2. There are five types of loop structures. Can you name them?

3. What is the syntax for the `For...Next` Loop?

4. Which of the following three parameters of the `For...Next` loop is optional – *start*, *end* or *step*?

5. What is the default value for *step*?

6. Can the step parameter be a negative number?

7. True or False: The *start*, *end*, and *step* parameters must be specified as a numeric literal.

8. In the following `For...Next` loop, what is the initial value of the counter?

```
Dim lngCounter As Long
For lngCounter = 22 To 400
    Debug.Print lngCounter
Next lngcounter
```

9. In the following `For...Next` loop, what is the end value of the counter?

```
Dim lngCounter As Long
For lngCounter = 22 To 400
    Debug.Print lngCounter
Next lngcounter
```

10. In the following `For...Next` loop, what is the step value?

```
Dim lngCounter As Long
For lngCounter = 22 To 400
    Debug.Print lngCounter
Next lngcounter
```

11. What will be the output of this code?

```
Private Sub Command1_Click()
    Dim lngcounter As Long
    For lngcounter = 1 To 10 Step 3
        Debug.Print lngcounter
    Next lngcounter
End Sub
```

12. What will be the output of this code?

```
Private Sub Command1_Click()
    Dim lngCounter As Long
    Dim lngStart As Long
    Dim lngStop As Long
    Dim lngStep As Long
    lngStart = 50
    lngStop = 500
    lngStep = 100
    For lngCounter = lngStart To lngStop Step lngStep
        Debug.Print lngCounter
    Next lngCounter
End Sub
```

13. What will be the output of this code?

```
Private Sub Command1_Click()
    Dim lngCounter As Long
    For lngCounter = 50 To 14 - 1
        Debug.Print lngCounter
    Next lngCounter
End Sub
```

14. What will be the output of this code?

```
Private Sub Command1_Click()
    Dim lngCounter As Long
    For lngCounter = 50 To 14 Step -10
        Debug.Print lngCounter
    Next lngCounter
End Sub
```

15. What is the only place that an **Exit For** statement can be coded?

16. True or False: In a **Do...Loop While** the body of the loop will be executed at least once.

17. True or False: In a **Do Until...Loop** the body of the loop will be executed at least once.

18. What will be the output of this loop?

```
Private Sub cmdOK_Click()
    Dim intValue As Integer
    intValue = 5
    Do While intValue < 9
        Form1.Print intValue
        intValue = intValue + 1
    Loop
End Sub
```

19. What will be the output of this loop?

```
Private Sub cmdOK_Click()
    Dim intValue As Integer
    intValue = 5
    Do
        Form1.Print intValue
        intValue = intValue + 1
    Loop Until intValue > 13
End Sub
```

Extra Credit – Some months have 30 days, some have 31 days; how many have 28 days?

Chapter 10
String Manipulation

In the last chapter, we looked at loop structures which, combined with our knowledge of selection structures, allow us to write powerful programs that display decision-making capabilities. In this chapter, you'll follow my class as we turn our attention to working with strings and manipulating them. By the end, you should be familiar with the various string manipulation operations that can be performed with Visual Basic.

What Exactly is a String?

I began this week's class by telling everyone that I had good news.

"I heard from Rose and Jack via email," I said, "and they told me that they had arrived safely in the United Kingdom, and hoped to wrap up their work in time to get back for the implementation of the China Shop Project. They told me to pass their best wishes on to everyone."

I continued by saying that, in today's class, we would be taking a close look at the string data type.

"The string data type," I said, "is just one of the many Visual Basic data types, but a working knowledge of this data type is very important to your ability to create powerful programs."

"To refresh your memory," I said, "a string is just a series of characters such as your name, or your address, or even your social security number. User entries in a text box are strings. Fields in a record read from a disk file may be string data."

"Being able to work with string data and knowing how to manipulate it, in my opinion, is so important that we'll be spending our entire class session on the topic. Not only is working with strings important for itself, but the process of working with strings strengthens your programming skills. After today's class, I dare say you'll be amazed at some of the algorithmic processes we come up with to manipulate string data."

String Concatenation

"We've already spent some time working with numerical arithmetic," I said. "Today, you'll see that it's possible to perform similar 'arithmetic' on strings."

"String arithmetic!" Rhonda exclaimed.

"That's right," I said. "The string equivalent of number arithmetic is called **string concatenation**, and you've already had a chance to see it in action. Concatenation is defined in Webster's dictionary as a verb that means 'to link together in a series or chain'. In Visual Basic, concatenation means to join two strings together, like railroad cars are joined to a locomotive."

I reminded everyone that we had already used string concatenation in the China Shop Project; the code for the Click event procedure of the Calculate command button employed it. I displayed this code on the classroom projector:

```
If curTotalPrice > 0 Then
    lblPrice.Caption = "The price of your order is " & _
        curTotalPrice
    lblPrice.Visible = True
End If
```

"In Visual Basic," I continued, "there are actually two operators that perform string concatenation, the plus (+) operator and the ampersand (&) operator. Microsoft recommends using the & operator instead of the + operator."

"Why is that?" Joe asked.

"The interesting thing about the & operator is that it can be used to concatenate a string with a non-string data type, such as a number or even a date," I explained. "The & is much more forgiving of the data types it is asked to join, whereas the + operator works only with actually string data. What this means is that if you try to concatenate a string with something you believe is a string (but isn't really) using the + operator, your program can bomb."

"Can you give us an example of that?" Barbara asked.

I thought for a minute, then created a project with a command button and typed in the following code:

```
Private Sub Command1_Click()
    Dim datValue As Date
    Dim strValue as String
    strValue = "Today's date is "
    datValue = Date
    MsgBox strValue + datValue
End Sub
```

I then ran the program and clicked on the command button. The following error was displayed:

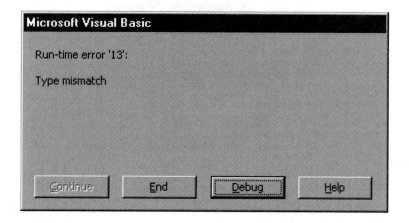

"What happened?" Rhonda asked.

"We attempted to concatenate the string value of the variable **strValue** with the data value of the variable **datValue**," I said. "Visual Basic bombed because the + operator requires that both expressions in the concatenation be of the string data type. Because the variable **datValue** was declared as a date data type, the concatenation operation failed with a **Type mismatch** error."

"Nasty," Linda said. "So the rule of thumb is what, don't use the + operator?"

"That's the Microsoft recommendation," I said. "Now let's change the + operator to the & operator and see what happens."

```
Private Sub Command1_Click()
    Dim datValue As Date
    Dim strValue as String
    strValue = "Today's date is "
    datValue = Date
    MsgBox strValue & datValue
End Sub
```

I then ran the program and clicked on the command button. The following screen was displayed:

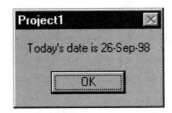

"Does everyone see the difference?" I asked.

"OK," Kathy said, "I'm convinced. I won't use the + operator. Can you give us another example of concatenation?"

I cited this example:

"There are two text boxes on a form. One text box is for the user to enter their first name, and the other for the user to enter their last name." I said. "Using string concatenation, join the first name and the last name, and print the full name on the form."

"I don't even know where to start with that one!" exclaimed Kate. "In that case," I replied, "let's go through this exercise:"

Exercise

Adding Strings

1. Start a new **Standard.EXE** project, and change the form's **caption** property to read String Concatenation.

2. Place a command button on the form and accept the default name that Visual Basic assigns.

3. Place two text boxes on the form.

4. Change the relevant **Name** properties of the text boxes to **txtFirstName** and **txtLastName** respectively.

5. Clear the **Text** properties of the two text boxes, by selecting the **Text** property of the text box in the Properties window and pressing *Backspace*.

6. Double-click on the command button, and place the following code into its **Click** event procedure:

```
Private Sub Command1_Click()
   If txtFirstName.Text = "" Then
      MsgBox "First name must be entered"
      txtFirstName.SetFocus
      Exit Sub
   ElseIf txtLastName.Text = "" Then
      MsgBox "Last name must be entered"
      txtLastName.SetFocus
      Exit Sub
   End If
   Form1.Print "Your full name is " & _
         txtFirstName.Text & txtLastName.Text
End Sub
```

7. Save the project in your **\VBFiles\Practice** subdirectory. Save the form as **Names.frm** and the project as **Names.vbp**. Now run the program.

8. Type your first name into the first text box and your last name into the second text box. Now click on the command button. The program will print your full name on the form. But wait, there's something wrong! What is it?

Discussion

"I see a problem," Ward said. "There's no space between the first and last name. It all ran together."

"Absolutely right," I said, as I ran the program myself.

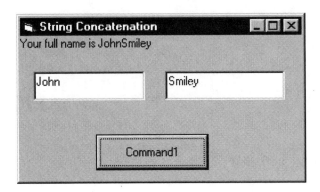

I explained that the code we had entered contained a common error that many beginners make when performing string concatenation.

"Before I address the mistake in the code, though," I said, "let's make sure we understand what's happening here."

I continued by explaining that the code contained some of the elements that we had seen in the last few classes.

"Notice how we use an **If...Then...Else** statement to determine if either the first name or last name text box is empty," I said.

```
If txtFirstName.Text = "" Then
```

"This type of data validation is extremely important," I said. "As your coding prowess increases, you must try to anticipate the kinds of mistakes the user will make. In this case, we are anticipating the possibility that the user won't enter a first name or last name in the text boxes prior to clicking on the command button."

"The double quotation marks," Blaine said. "Is that how we check for an empty text box?"

"Yes, it's one way," I said. "Here, we are checking the `Text` property of each text box for an empty string, by comparing it to a pair of quotation marks with no space in between. If the `Text` property of either `txtFirstName` or `txtLastName` is empty, we display a warning message (always make them pleasant!). Then, as a courtesy to the user, we set the focus back to the empty text box using the `SetFocus` method. Finally, we exit the `Click` event procedure by using the `Exit Sub` statement."

"Does everyone understand why we exit the event procedure if one of the text boxes is empty?" I asked.

"Yes," Lou said. "If both text boxes are not empty, we could conceivably print part of the name. It makes sense not to print any of the name at all if a part of it is missing."

"That's right," I said. "If the user supplies us with the first name, but not the last name, why bother printing just the first name? On the other hand, why bother printing just the last name if the user doesn't supply us with the first name?"

I continued by examining these two lines of code.

```
Form1.Print "Your full name is " & txtFirstName.Text & txtLastName.Text
```

"These two lines perform the actual string concatenation," I said. "Notice the use of the `&` operator. Unfortunately, this code also contains the 'mistake' I alluded to earlier."

I continued by pointing out that this code contains two `&` operators.

"There are actually two separate concatenations taking place here. First, the string literal `'Your full name is'` is concatenated with the `Text` property of the `txtFirstName` text box. Then that 'joined' string is concatenated with the `Text` property of the `txtLastName` text box. By the way," I said, "just like the numeric operations that we discussed earlier, if there are multiple string operators in an expression, the operations are performed left to right."

I waited for questions, but there were none.

"Finally," I said, "provided we have data in both text boxes, we print the entire joined string on the form using the **Print** method of the form. Most beginners expect that if we enter John into the first text box and Smiley into the second, that this string will be printed."

Your full name is John Smiley

"Certainly," I said, "that's what we intended to do here. However, computer programs do exactly what you tell them to do and, unfortunately, that's not what we told the program to do."

I asked everyone to count the number of spaces in the string that was actually printed on the form.

"There are four spaces," I said.

- One space between the words Your and Full
- One space between the words Full and Name
- One space between the words Name and is
- One space between the words is and JohnSmiley

"Now count the number of spaces in the string we actually wanted to print," I said. "You should count five spaces."

- One space between the words Your and Full
- One space between the words Full and Name
- One space between the words Name and is
- One space between the words is and John
- One space between the words John and Smiley

"What was missing?" I asked.

"The space between John and Smiley," Peter said. "But how can we insert a space there?"

"That's the trick," I said. "How to insert a space between the first and last names. There are actually several ways to do it and we'll learn one right now in this exercise."

Exercise

Correcting the String Concatenation

1. Load up the **Names.vbp** project from the **\VBFiles\Practice** subdirectory.

2. Modify the **click** event procedure of the command button so that it looks like this:

```
Private Sub Command1_Click()
   If txtFirstName.Text = "" Then
      MsgBox "First name must be completed"
      txtFirstName.SetFocus
      Exit Sub
   ElseIf txtLastName.Text = "" Then
      MsgBox "Last name must be completed"
      txtLastName.SetFocus
      Exit Sub
   End If
   Form1.Print "Your full name is " & txtFirstName.Text _
         & " " & txtLastName.Text
End Sub
```

3. Save the project as **Names2.vbp** and the form as **Names2.frm**. Then run the program.

4. Enter your first name in the first text box and your last name into the second. Now click on the command button. The program will then print your full name on the form, this time with a space between your first and last name.

Discussion

I ran the program myself, and the following screen was displayed on the classroom projector:

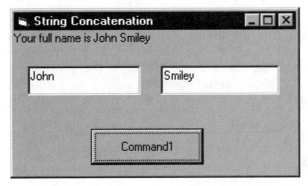

"This is much better," I said. "Can anyone tell me the difference between this code and the code from the previous exercise that didn't work?"

"In this exercise," Kate said, "there were actually three concatenations performed and one of them was the concatenation of a space between the first and last names."

```
Form1.Print "Your full name is " & txtFirstName.Text & " " &
txtLastName.Text
```

"Perfect!" I exclaimed.

We've Joined Strings, Now Let's Break Them Apart

I could sense that everyone was feeling pretty confident with string concatenation.

"OK," I said, "now that we've joined strings together, let's look at how we can take strings apart."

To say that I was greeted with some very perplexed looks would be an understatement.

"Take strings apart?" Ward asked. "Why would we ever want to do that?"

"Sometimes," I said, "you might find yourself forced to work with strings that are not necessarily in the format you need. For instance, several years ago, I received a call from a potential client. She had just purchased a huge list of names from a mailing list company for a mass direct marketing campaign."

"Everything was fine until the client finally examined the data on the diskette, and realized that the city, state, and zip code were all contained within a single 'field' in the record. This was a problem because the client wanted to target the mailing by zip code, and with only a single address field on the diskette, the client's database program couldn't do the sort. This meant that, potentially, she would have to sort over 20,000 mailing labels by hand."

"What happened?" Mary asked.

"Ultimately," I said, "I wrote a program to pull the zip code portion of the address away from the rest of the address."

"In other words," Peter said, "you broke the address string apart."

"That's exactly right," I said, "and I did that using the techniques which I'm about to show you here."

I suggested that we now complete an exercise in which we would enter a full name into a text box, and ask Visual Basic to separate the first and last name portions.

Exercise

Pulling Strings Apart

1. Start a new **Standard.EXE** project.

2. Change the **Caption** property of the form to Pulling Strings Apart.

3. Place a command button on the form. Accept the default name that Visual Basic assigns.

4. Place a text box on the form, change its **Name** property to **txtFullName** and clear its **Text** property.

5. Double-click on the command button and place the following code into its **Click** event procedure:

```
Private Sub Command1_Click()
    Dim intLengthOfString As Integer
    Dim intWheresTheSpace As Integer
    Dim strFullName As String
    Dim strFirstName As String
    Dim strLastName As String
    If txtFullName.Text = "" Then
        MsgBox "Your full name must be entered"
        txtFullName.SetFocus
        Exit Sub
    End If
    strFullName = txtFullName.Text
    intLengthOfString = Len(strFullName)
    intWheresTheSpace = InStr(strFullName, " ")
    If intWheresTheSpace = 0 Then
        MsgBox "Please enter your full name with a space" _
```

```
                & vbCrLf _
              & "between your first name and last name"
      txtFullName.SetFocus
      Exit Sub
   End If
   strFirstName = Left$(strFullName, intWheresTheSpace - 1)
   strLastName = Right$(strFullName, intLengthOfString - intWheresTheSpace)
   Form1.Print "Your first name is: " & strFirstName
   Form1.Print "Your last name is: " & strLastName
End Sub
```

6.   Save the project in your \VBFIles\Practice subdirectory. Save the form as FName.frm and the project as String_Magic.vbp. Now run the program.

7.   Enter your full name in the text box, separating the first and last names with a space. Now click on the command button. The program will print your first name and last name on the form.

Discussion

I immediately ran the program and the form looked like this:

"I don't know about anyone else," Rhonda said, "but I'm pretty confused about this one."

"This exercise illustrates what I call the blindfold nature of programming."

"Blindfold?" Valerie asked.

"My full name," I said, "including the space between first and last names, contains 11 characters. Linda's full name contains 16 characters."

"And your point is?" Linda asked.

"My point," I said, "is that it's impossible to know ahead of time the exact construction of the full name that the user will enter into the text box. That's what I mean by the blindfold nature of programming. We have to devise a technique, an algorithm, that allows us to deduce the first and the last name from any entry made in the text box."

"How do we go about doing that?" Blaine asked.

"The first step," I said, "is to take an inventory of the things we do know, even before the user makes an entry in the text box."

"Such as?" Joe said.

"How about the full name," Dave suggested. "We know that the user will enter their full name into the text box and then click on the command button."

"Good," I said. "That is a definite 'given'. Now can anyone tell me the characteristics of what we call a full name?"

This seemed to stymie everyone a bit.

"How about this?" I said. "A full name is really just two words separated by a space."

I continued by explaining that this process of looking at what you know, what you don't know, and then determining how to solve the problem is called developing an algorithm.

"Developing an algorithm to solve a problem," I said, "may be the single hardest thing to do in all of programming. After all, syntax can be looked up and there are many sources of information on techniques. Unfortunately though, no one can teach you how to develop an algorithm to solve a problem. I can give you guidelines and show you some examples, but learning how to solve a problem, and not necessarily problems involving a computer, takes different people different amounts of time to develop. There is good news, however. Most of the hard algorithms have already been developed for us."

"Where do we find these algorithms?" Rhonda asked.

"On-line help, Visual Basic books, Visual Basic magazines," I replied. "You really can't read too much! Some of the topics you come across may seem difficult to begin with, but the more contact you have with new ideas and programming techniques, the better your skills will become."

"Can you explain the algorithm you used to solve this problem?" Valerie said. "And may I ask where you found it?"

"I developed this algorithm on my own," I said, "and it probably took me several hours to work it out. But as I recall, it was loads of fun working it out."

I displayed the algorithm on the classroom projector.

Problem: The user has entered his or her full name into a text box. Determine the user's first name and last name.

Assumptions:

1. The user types his or her full name into the txtFullName text box

2. The first name begins in position 1 of the txtFullName text box

3. There is a space between the first and last name in the full name text box

4. The first character of the last name appears one character after the space

5. The user has typed 'John Smiley' into the txtFullName text box

The Algorithm:

Step 1: Determine the length of the full name (11 characters)

Step 2: Determine the position of the space character (position 5). To the left of the space character is the first name.

Step 3: Determine the length of the first name, which is equal to the location of the space less 1 (5 - 1 = 4)

Step 4: To the right of the space character is the last name. The length of the last name is the length of the full name less the position where the space was located (11 - 5 = 6)

"If you think this is cryptic," I said, "Let me ask you this question. How would you describe your methodology to solve a Cryptogram or a Crossword puzzle to someone who has never worked on one before? That would be pretty problematic. Just give this a chance and be patient with yourself if you don't understand it the first time through."

"The first thing I do when developing an algorithm," I said, "is to assume a certain set of conditions. Such as the user entering my full name into the text box. Working with a concrete example makes developing and solving the problem much easier. Something else I do is to draw the interface on a sheet of paper. I also draw boxes on the paper to represent the values of variables and properties. While developing this algorithm, I drew a box on a sheet of paper to represent the text box, and then wrote my name in it. Then I took a minute to note the characteristics that I mentioned in my algorithm, and eventually I developed the full algorithm."

"I think you left out a few hours of pain and suffering here," Linda said jokingly.

"Not really," I said. "As I mentioned earlier, once you get involved in the process of developing an algorithm, it really can be a lot of fun. However, understanding and working with someone else's algorithm can be difficult at first. If you feel overwhelmed with the notion of an algorithm, just relax. As we proceed through the rest of the course, you'll see most of the common algorithms that you'll need to be productive programmers."

It was time to explain the code in the exercise in detail.

"The first thing we did, as usual," I said, "was to declare the variables we will need in the event procedure."

```
Dim intLengthOfString As Integer
Dim intWheresTheSpace As Integer
Dim strFullName As String
Dim strFirstName As String
Dim strLastName As String
```

"We'll discuss these variables as we encounter them in the remainder of this code," I said.

I continued by saying that, after declaring these variables, we checked to ensure that the user has entered something into the text box:

```
If txtFullName.Text = "" Then
    MsgBox "Your full name must be entered"
    txtFullName.SetFocus
    Exit Sub
End If
```

"At this point," I said, "we aren't testing for a valid full name. We just want to make sure the text box isn't empty. If it is, we display a message to the user and set the focus to the text box. The test for a valid full name is a little more complicated, and we'll get to that in a moment."

So far, so good. No one seemed to be having any problems.

"Now," I said, "if the user has entered something into the text box, the next thing we do is take the **Text** property of the **txtFullName** text box and assign it to the variable **strFullName**."

```
strFullName = txtFullName.Text
```

"I noticed," Dave said, "when I was completing the exercise, that we use this variable in several string operations later on in the code. Could we have worked with the **Text** property directly?"

"That's a good question," I said. "The answer is that your program will run faster if you work with a variable value in code, rather than work directly with the value of a property. If you find yourself using a property value several times in a procedure, it makes a lot of sense to assign the value of the property to a variable, and then use the variable throughout the remainder of the procedure. It's like using a reference book in a library; if you find yourself needing to return to the library to look something up on a regular basis, it's probably worth getting a copy at home."

I continued by explaining that once we assigned the **Text** property of **txtFullName** to the variable **strFullName**, we then used the **Len** function to determine the length of **strFullName**.

```
intLengthOfString = Len(strFullName)
```

"By the way," I said, "this satisfies step 1 of our algorithm, which is to determine the length of the full name that the user enters into the text box."

"Have we seen this function before?" Kate asked.

"No," I answered. "The **Len** function returns a value equal to the length of the string specified as its argument. In this code, we then take this value and assign it to the variable **intLengthOfString**. By the way, note the descriptive variable name. It makes the code much easier to follow."

"Let's presume," I said, "that the user has entered 'John Smiley' into the text box. What will the value of the variable **intLengthOfString** be?"

"Eleven," Mary said.

She was correct and I began to discuss the next line of code:

```
intWheresTheSpace = InStr(strFullName, " ")
```

"This line of code," I said, "fulfills the second step of our algorithm, which is to determine the location of the space in the full name that the user entered into the text box. In order to do that, we use the Visual Basic **InStr** function, which returns a value equal to the beginning position of one string within another. In other words, the **InStr** function searches for one string within another string, and here we're using it to search for a space character, " ", within the string **strFullName**. We take the return value of the **InStr** function and assign it to the variable **intWheresTheSpace**."

"I'm still a little confused," Ward said.

"Maybe this will help," I said, as I showed her the help file for the **InStr** function, which contains the following syntax:

```
InStr([start, ]string1, string2[, compare])
```
"That doesn't help much," Ward said, smiling.

"The `InStr` function," I said, "is an example of a Visual Basic function that has optional arguments. Only two arguments, the string to search for and the string to be searched, are required. However, if you wish, you can specify all four arguments."

I explained that the first argument, **start**, is optional and is used to specify the start position in **string1**, which is the string that you want to search in. By default, `InStr` begins searching at the first character position of string1. However, if you wanted to start searching from character position 2, for instance, you would specify a start argument of 2.

"The second argument, **string1**, is the string to be searched," I said. "This argument is required. In our code, string1 is the variable `strFullName`, which contains the `Text` property of `txtFullName`. The third argument, **string2** is also required. String2 is the string to search **for** in string1. In our code, string2 is the space character."

"And that's specified by a pair of quotation marks with a space in between," Ward said. "I think I understand a little better now."

"The fourth and final argument, **compare**," I said, "specifies the type of comparison `InStr` should perform while searching for string2 in string1. There are two possible values for this argument, 0 (binary) or 1 (textual)."

"I'm almost afraid to ask what the differences are," Joe said.

A quirk of Visual Basic is that if you specify a comparison value, you must also specify a starting position argument.

"A **binary** comparison," I said, "is a case-sensitive search and a **textual** comparison is case-insensitive. By default, the comparison type for `InStr` is binary. With a binary comparison, the upper case letter **A** is considered different to the lower case letter **a**. Remember our discussion of the ASCII code? These two characters have different ASCII values. With a textual comparison, however, the letter A and the letter a are considered to match."

"Suppose," Kathy asked, "string2 is found in string1 more than once?"

"That's a good question," I said. "If the string you are searching contains more than one instance of the string you are searching for, `InStr` stops after the first occurrence. In other words, the location of the first instance is returned. This is important to remember if you attempt to use the `InStr` function to search for more than one occurrence of a string within another string."

"How can you get around that limitation?" Dave asked.

"Later on," I said, "we'll see that there's another technique that can be used to find the next occurrence. However, that technique is not nearly as easy to use as `InStr`."

"Suppose string2 isn't found in string1?" Chuck asked.

"Then the return value will be 0," I replied, "and that's the reason for the next bit of code."

```
If intWheresTheSpace = 0 Then
    MsgBox "Please enter your full name with a space" _
        & vbCrLf _
        & "between your first name and last name"
    txtFullName.SetFocus
    Exit Sub
End If
```

"This code," I said, "checks the value of the variable `intWheresTheSpace` to determine if the user has entered a valid full name into the text box. If the value of `intWheresTheSpace` is 0, we know that the `InStr` function found no space in `strFullName`, and that the user's entry in the text box does not meet our criteria for a valid full name. If that's the case, we display a message box with a warning message and exit the event procedure."

"In other words," Lou said, "if `intWheresTheSpace` is 0, there's no space in the variable `strFullName`."

"That's right," I said. "By the way, take note of the way we concatenate the intrinsic constant `vbCrLf` to the message we are displaying in the message box. This causes the message to the user to be neatly formatted on two lines."

As a demonstration, I ran the program, entered a string in the text box that did not contain a space, and then clicked on the command button:

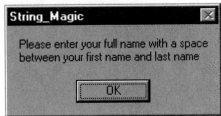

"OK," I said. "Let's review where we are so far. At this point in our code, we now have the user's entry in the variable `strFullName`. We also know the position, within that variable, of the space character. Those are the two pieces of information that we need to extract the first and last names."

"I know you mentioned this while you were discussing the algorithm," Rhonda said. "But can you explain it to us again."

"Sure," I said. "In general terms, we know that the first name portion of the full name entered in the text box lies to the left of the space character. We also know that the first character of the first name starts at position 1. Because of that, we can deduce that the length of the first name is equal to the location of the space character less 1; or to express it another way, `intWheresTheSpace - 1`. Therefore, if the user entered John Smiley in the text box the length of the first name is 4, which is equal to value of `intWheresTheSpace - 1`."

"Knowing the length of the first name," I said, "fulfills step 3 of our algorithm and also allows us to extract the first name from the `strFullName` variable. We do that by using the `Left$` function."

You will also see references to the Left function in Visual Basic. The Left function is virtually identical to the Left$ function. The difference is that the Left$ function returns a string value, whereas the Left function returns a variant value.

I explained that the `Left$` function returns a string of characters from the left side of a string.

"The `Left$` function" I said, "requires two arguments. The first argument is a string or an expression containing a string. The second argument is the number of characters to return from the **left** side of the first argument. Since we know that the first name's length is equal to the location of the space character - 1, we can then code this statement."

```
strFirstName = Left$(strFullName, intWheresTheSpace - 1)
```

"`intWheresTheSpace -1` is evaluated by Visual Basic as 4," I reminded everyone.

I displayed the Visual Basic 'translation' on the classroom projector:

```
strFirstName = Left$("John Smiley", 4)
```

"So when this code executes," Kate said, "the value `John` is assigned to the variable `strFirstName`."

"The final step in the puzzle," I said, "is to extract the last name from the full name. This is a little more complicated than extracting the first name. Before we go on, let's review what we know and what we don't know. The last name portion of the full name lies to the right of the space character. We know that the location of the space character in the variable strFullName is at position 5. Also, we can deduce that the length of the last name is the length of the full name minus the position where the space character is located."

"How did you deduce that?" Ward asked.

"Pencil and paper," I said. "Remember, I draw everything. Maybe deduce isn't the correct term. When I wrote my name on the paper, I just experimented with it, and I more or less discovered this one."

"Based on that," Rhonda said, "we now know that the length of your last name, 'Smiley', is 6."

"That's right," I said. "The length of my full name is 11 and the space character is found at position 5. Now 11 less 5 is 6. We'll see in a moment that knowing the length of the last name is crucial to being able to extract it."

I waited for questions, but so far everyone was holding on.

"We can extract the last name portion of the full name in a manner similar to the way we extracted the first name," I continued. "However, this time we use the Right$ function, not the Left$ function. The Right$ function returns a string of characters from the right side of a string. Like the Left$ function, the Right$ function requires two arguments. The first argument is a string or an expression containing a string. The second argument is the number of characters to return from the **right** side of the first argument. Since we know that the last name's length is equal to the length of the full name minus the location of the space character, we can code this statement."

> You will also see references to the Right function in Visual Basic. The Right function is virtually identical to the Right$ function. The difference is that the Right$ function returns a string value, whereas the Right function returns a variant value.

```
strLastName = Right$(strFullName, intLengthOfString - intWheresTheSpace)
```

"Where intLengthOfString - intWheresTheSpace is evaluated by Visual Basic as 6," I explained.

I displayed the Visual Basic 'translation' on the classroom projector.

```
strLastName = Right$("John Smiley", 6)
```

"So when this code executes," I said, "the value Smiley is assigned to the variable strLastName."

"We now have both pieces of the puzzle," I said, "the first name and the last name! The next two lines of code just print the values of the variables `strFirstName` and `strLastName` on the form."

```
Form1.Print "Your first name is: " & strFirstName
Form1.Print "Your last name is: " & strLastName
```

I asked if there were any questions.

"I think I understand what we've done," Barbara said, "but until I've had a chance to work with these functions myself, I'm going to be uncomfortable with them."

"That's true of most of what we'll learn in this course," I said. "That's why I'm so glad you all have the chance to work on the China Shop Project."

We had been working for some time, and I asked the class to take a break.

After returning from break, I told everyone that we were not finished with our treatment of strings.

"Earlier, I said that you can't use the `InStr` function to locate more than one occurrence of a string within another string, and I mentioned that there was another technique we could use. I want to illustrate that in our next exercise, where you'll write your own version of a search and replace function.

Exercise

The Mid$ Function (or Your own Search and Replace!)

1. Start a new `Standard.EXE` project. Change the default form's `Caption` property to Search and Replace.

2. Place a command button on the form. Change its `Caption` property from Command1 to Search and Replace.

3. Change the **Caption** property of the form to Search and Replace.

4. Now place three text boxes on the form and clear their **Text** properties.

5. Change the **Name** property of the first text box to **txtSource**. Place a label control next to the text box and change its **Caption** property to Source.

6. Change the **Name** property of the second text box to **txtSearchFor**. Place a label control next to the second text box and change its **Caption** property to Search For.

7. Change the **Name** property of the third text box to **txtReplaceWith**. Place a label control next to the **txtReplaceWith** text box and change its **Caption** property to Replace With. If you run the application now, your form should look similar to this:

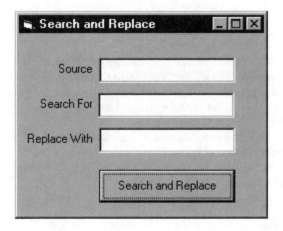

8. Change the **MaxLength** properties of both **txtSearchFor** and **txtReplaceWith** to 1. This will ensure that not more than one character is entered into either text box.

9. Double-click on the command button, and place the following code into its **Click** event procedure:

```
Private Sub Command1_Click()
    Dim intLengthOfSource As Integer
    Dim intLengthOfSearchfor As Integer
    Dim intCounter As Integer
    Dim strSource As String
```

```
Dim strSearchFor As String
Dim strReplaceWith As String
Dim strPiece As String
If txtSource.Text = "" Then
   MsgBox "A string to be searched must be entered"
   txtSource.SetFocus
   Exit Sub
ElseIf txtSearchFor.Text = "" Then
   MsgBox "A search character must be entered"
   txtSearchFor.SetFocus
   Exit Sub
ElseIf txtReplaceWith.Text = "" Then
   MsgBox "A replacement character must be entered"
   txtReplaceWith.SetFocus
   Exit Sub
End If
strSource = txtSource.Text
strSearchFor = txtSearchFor.Text
strReplaceWith = txtReplaceWith.Text
intLengthOfSource = Len(strSource)
intLengthOfSearchfor = Len(strSearchFor)
For intCounter = 1 To intLengthOfSource _
      Step intLengthOfSearchfor
   strPiece = Mid$(strSource, intCounter, _
      intLengthOfSearchfor)
   If strPiece = strSearchFor Then
      Mid$(strSource, intCounter, _
         intLengthOfSearchfor) =  strReplaceWith
   End If
Next intCounter
Form1.Print "The replacement string is: " & _
      strSource
End Sub
```

10. Save the project in your \VBFiles\Practice subdirectory. Save the form as Titanic.frm and the project as Search.vbp. Now run the program.

11. Type Titanic into the Source text box.

12. Enter the character t into the Search for text box.

13. Enter the character * into the Replace with text box.

14. Click on the command button. What is printed on the form?

Discussion

"I thought the other exercise was confusing," Rhonda said. "This one is much worse!"

"This exercise is more complicated than the previous one," I said. "However, after we've gone through the code step by step, you will all understand what's going on in the program. You'll also have a real appreciation for how the Find and Replace functions."

"You mean this is how Find and Replace works in Word?" Joe asked.

"Not far from it," I said. "I don't want to mislead you though, this code has some deficiencies. I didn't ask you to set the **MaxLength** properties of those two text boxes for nothing. This code works best when it needs to search for a single character and replace it with a single character. Feel free to see how it behaves with more than one character to search for, and more than one character to replace. The important thing about this exercise isn't so much writing a perfect Search and Replace program, but to see the power that the ability to manipulate strings can give your program."

I continued by saying that, once again, this code illustrates the blindfold nature of programming.

"Just as we saw in the previous exercise," I said, "there are pieces of data that we don't know when we write the program, and pieces of data that only become known to our program when the program runs. Unfortunately, just about everything in this exercise amounts to an unknown at the time we code it. We have absolutely no idea what the user may enter in all three of the text boxes. At least in the previous exercise, we knew the format to expect in the text box. Here, we're totally in the dark. Who can tell me what the first step in solving a problem like this should be."

"I bet I can guess," Kate said. "Develop an algorithm!"

"Perfect, Kate," I said as I displayed this algorithm on the classroom projector:

> **Problem**: Search for a character within a string and replace that character, when found, with a replacement character.

Assumptions:

1. The user will enter a string to search through in a text box. It can be any length.

2. The user will enter a single character to search for in a second text box.

3. The user will enter a character to replace with the found character in a third text box.

The Algorithm

Assume the source string is 'Titanic'

Assume the search string is 't'

Assume the replacement string is '*'

Step 1: Determine the length of the source string (7 characters)

Step 2: Determine the length of the search string (1 character)

Step 3: Use the Mid$ function to 'move' through the source string in increments of the length of the search string (1) looking for the search string until the end of the source string is reached

Step 4: If the search string is found, replace the found string with the replacement string

Step 5: If the search string is not found, continue with the next character in the string

I could see plenty of confusion, so I suggested that we begin with a discussion of the code.

"As usual," I said, "the first thing we did was to declare the variables we will need in the event procedure."

I displayed the first two variable declarations on the classroom projector:

```
Dim intLengthOfSource As Integer
Dim intLengthOfSearchfor As Integer
```

"These two variables will be assigned the length of the `Text` properties of the `txtSource` and `txtSearchFor` text boxes," I said. "`intLengthOfSource` contains the length of the string to be searched and `intLengthOfSearchfor` contains the length of the string to search for."

"The next variable declaration declares a loop control variable that we will use in a `For...Next` loop," I explained.

```
Dim intCounter As Integer
```

"One of the reasons the code in this exercise is more difficult to follow than the code in the previous one is that we need to use a loop structure in order to examine the source string character by character."

"The next three variable declarations contain the `Text` property values of the three text boxes," I said. "Remember, it's best to work with variable values instead of property values in code."

```
Dim strSource As String
Dim strSearchFor As String
Dim strReplaceWith As String
```

"What is that next variable declaration?" Steve asked.

```
Dim strPiece As String
```

"Do you remember how we assigned the return value of the `Left$` and `Right$` functions to a variable in the previous exercise?" I asked. "We're using this variable, `strPiece`, in a similar way with the `Mid$` function. However, the `Mid$` function doesn't return the left or right portions of a string, but can return a piece of a string from anywhere within another string. In this code, `strPiece` is the variable we will use to store the 'piece' of the string extracted by the `Mid$` function."

Everyone was pretty comfortable with the next section of code. It was the same type of text box validation that we had performed in previous exercises:

```
If txtSource.Text = "" Then
   MsgBox "A string to be searched must be entered"
   txtSource.SetFocus
   Exit Sub
ElseIf txtSearchFor.Text = "" Then
   MsgBox "A search character must be entered"
   txtSearchFor.SetFocus
   Exit Sub
ElseIf txtReplaceWith.Text = "" Then
   MsgBox "A replacement character must be entered"
   txtReplaceWith.SetFocus
   Exit Sub
End If
```

"We want to be sure," I said, "that the user has entered something into all three text boxes. The `If...ElseIf` statement is ideal for checking this."

"I meant to ask you this while I was completing the exercise," Barbara said. "Why did we set the `MaxLength` property to 1?"

"The `MaxLength` property of the text box can be used to restrict the number of characters entered into a text box," I replied. "We wanted to restrict the replacement string to 1 character, and this is the easiest way to do that."

I then explained that, after checking to ensure we have all of the information we need from the user, we assign the `Text` property of each text box to a variable:

```
strSource = txtSource.Text
strSearchFor = txtSearchFor.Text
strReplaceWith = txtReplaceWith.Text
```

"Since our algorithm indicates that we need to determine the length of the `strSource`, `strSearchFor`, and `strReplaceWith` strings, we do that with the next three lines of code:"

```
intLengthOfSource = Len(strSource)
intLengthOfSearchFor = Len(strSearchFor)
intLengthOfReplaceWith = Len(strReplaceWith)
```

Everyone seemed comfortable with this code, as we had used the `Len` function in the previous exercise.

"Before we look at the next section of code," I said, "I want to try to reproduce for you the methodology I followed when I was trying to develop this algorithm on paper."

I asked everyone in the class to take a piece of paper and look away from their monitors for a few minutes.

"OK now," I said. "Follow along with me and let's see what happens."

1. Write the source string on a sheet of paper. In our case 'Titanic'.

2. Take your pen or pencil and use it to advance through your source string, examining each character.

3. As you advance through the characters in the source string, mark each character you examine with an arrow.

4. If the character you examine in the source string does not match your search string (a 't') then write the examined character underneath the source string.

5. If the character you examine in the source string matches the search character (a 't'), then write the replacement string character (an '*') underneath the source string.

"This process is a repetitive one; that's just perfect for a Visual Basic loop," I said.

I performed this process myself. Here's an illustration of what I did on the classroom whiteboard:

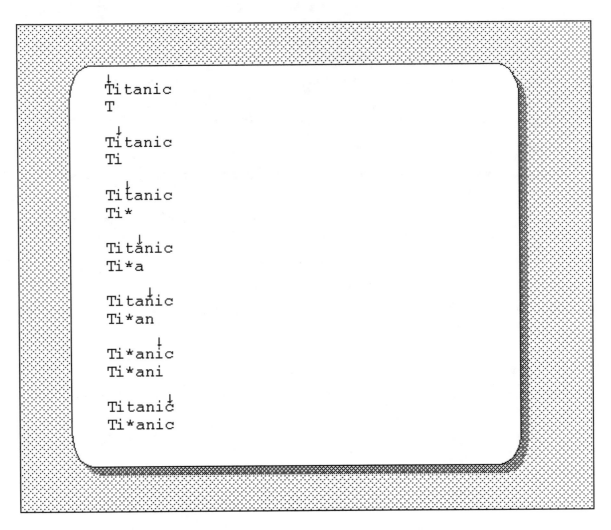

"Starting at the first character of a string," I said, "and moving one character at a time to the right until we reach the end of the string, is something that we can simulate in code using a Visual Basic loop structure. The examination of each character in a string can be done by using the **Mid$** function."

Here's the first line of the loop structure:

```
For intcounter = 1 To intLengthOfSource Step intLengthOfSearchfor
```

"Using the **For...Next** loop," I said "is very convenient, since we have definite start and end parameters for the loop. The start parameter will represent the first character in the string, and end parameter is the last character position of the string, which just so happens to be stored in the variable **intLengthOfSource**."

"Why did we specify the **Step** parameter as the length of the search string?" Dave asked. "Why not just make it 1?"

"You're right," I said. "We could have just accepted the default value of 1 for the **Step** parameter and it would have worked fine, since the replacement string is only one character in length. Looking down the road, which as programmers is something we should always do, we need to build in the capability of searching for a string that is more than just a single character. If you want to experiment with using replacement strings longer than one character, remember to set the **MaxLength** property of **txtReplaceWith** back to its default value of 0."

"What do you mean by 'looking down the road'?" Ward asked.

"I mean," I replied, "that we want this program to eventually be able to search for, and replace, any number of characters, just like Microsoft Word does."

"This line of code," I told everyone, "allows us to move through our string, character by character, just like our pen or pencil did on paper. However, that capability is not enough. Alone, that would be like moving your pen or pencil over the letters of the string on paper without taking the time to examine them individually. We must be able to determine if we have found the search string we are looking for, and that's what these next few lines of code do."

```
strPiece = Mid$(strSource, intCounter, intLengthOfSearchfor)
```

"During each iteration of the loop," I said, "this line uses the **Mid$** function to progressively extract the characters in the source string, in this case one by one and then stores the return value in the variable **strPiece**. Once we have isolated the characters in the variable **strPiece**, then it's just a matter of a simple **If** test to determine if we've found the character or characters that we're looking for, by comparing the value of **strPiece** with the value of **strSearchFor**."

```
      If strPiece = strSearchFor Then
```

"If this statement evaluates to true," I said, "then we know we've found the character or characters that we're looking for. At this point, we can use a cousin of the **Mid$** function called the **Mid** statement that permits us to make a quick and easy replacement."

```
      Mid(strSource, intCounter, intLengthOfSearchfor) = strReplaceWith
   End If
```

"I'm a little confused with the syntax of the **Mid$** function and the **Mid** statement," Barbara said. "Can you explain those in a little more detail?"

"The **Mid$** function accepts three arguments," I said. "The string to search, the starting position at which to start the search and the length of the string to extract or return. Provided all of these arguments are valid, then a character or characters will be returned. Let's examine what Visual Basic does with this statement the first time through the loop."

```
      strPiece = Mid$(strSource, intCounter, intLengthOfSearchfor)
```

I displayed the 'translation' of this code on the classroom projector:

```
strPiece = Mid$("Titanic", 1, 1)
```

"OK, that makes more sense," Rhonda said. "**strSource** is easy, that's just the string to search. **intCounter** is the loop control variable, which is equal to 1 the first time through the loop and **intLengthOfSearchfor** is 1 because that's the length of the string we're searching for."

"That's a great analysis," I said. "Now what about the second time through the loop?"

"Each time the loop is executed," Dave said, "the value of **intCounter** is incremented by 1, so the start argument of the **Mid$** function will also be incremented by 1."

"Absolutely correct," I said.

I then displayed the translation of the **Mid$** statement through the next five iterations of the loop:

```
strPiece = Mid$("Titanic", 2,1)
strPiece = Mid$("Titanic", 3,1)
strPiece = Mid$("Titanic", 4,1)
strPiece = Mid$("Titanic", 5,1)
strPiece = Mid$("Titanic", 6,1)
```

"As you can see," I said, "each iteration through the loop results in a different character being extracted and assigned to the variable strPiece. In essence, what we've done with this For...Next loop is simulate the action of the pen and paper process of examining the source string character by character."

"We've been able to simulate the mechanics of examining the source string character by character," I said. "Now what about the replacement process? Remember that, if the character we examine is not the character we are looking for, we just repeat that character under the source string. If the character is the one we are looking for, we write the replacement character under the source string. This next section of code is crucial:"

```
If strPiece = strSearchFor Then
    Mid(strSource, intCounter, intLengthOfSearchfor) = strReplaceWith
End If
```

"The Mid statement is a real life saver," I said, "because it enables you to take a string and replace a character or characters within that string. In conjunction with the If statement we examined just a little earlier, if we determine that we have found the character we are looking for in the source string, it's a simple matter of using the Mid statement to make the replacement with the value of strReplaceWith."

"The Mid statement, not to be confused with the Mid$ function, accepts four arguments," I said. "The string to modify, the starting position at which to start the replacement, the number of characters to replace, and the replacement string."

I continued by pointing out that the only time, in our hypothetical example, that the If statement evaluates to true is on the third character of the source string, when the lower case t is found in the source string. At that point, this statement:

```
Mid(strSource, intCounter, intLengthOfSearchfor) = strReplaceWith
```

is read by Visual Basic as:

```
Mid("Titanic", 3, 1) = "*"
```

"What this tells Visual Basic," I said, "is to replace character position 3 in **strSource** with an asterisk."

I looked around the room for signs of confusion, but it appeared that everyone was OK with the explanation.

"I notice," Dave said, "that only the lower case **t** was replaced in the source string. I suppose we could make this program case-insensitive as well, couldn't we?"

"Yes, we can," I said.

I reminded everyone that in last week's class, we had used the **UCASE$** function to make the return value of an **InputBox** statement upper case.

"To make this code case-insensitive all we need to do is change one line of code, and that's in the body of our loop," I explained. "Change your code so that it looks like this."

```
For intcounter = 1 To intLengthOfSource Step intLengthOfSearchfor
    strPiece = Mid$(strSource, intCounter, _
          intLengthOfSearchfor)

    If UCASE$(strPiece) = UCASE$(strSearchFor) Then
        Mid(strSource, intCounter, intLengthOfSearchfor) = strReplaceWith
    End If
```

I ran the program again:

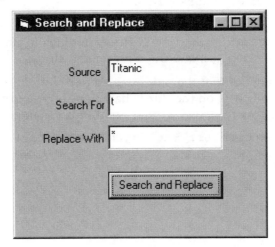

"That did the trick," I said. "Now every t, regardless of case, has been replaced with an asterisk."

It had been another intensive class and I began to dismiss everyone for the day.

"I'm a little disappointed," Rhonda said. "We haven't touched the China Shop project today."

"This is the last week that we won't work on it," I said. "Next week, we'll examine reading and writing disk files in Visual Basic. We'll also be modifying the China Shop Project to load both brands and inventory prices from a disk file."

Summary

In this chapter, we examined string manipulation in detail. In particular, we saw that:

- A **string** is a series of characters.

- **String concatenation** allows us to manipulate strings, putting multiple series of characters together in a meaningful way.

- We can also manipulate strings by breaking them apart using built-in Visual Basic functions.

- We can use Visual Basic to find particular characters in strings, and particular positions in strings.

Strings are an integral part of programming in Visual Basic and so having a sound working knowledge in how to manipulate them will stand us in good stead for future programming.

In the next chapter, we'll be considering how to send and retrieve data to and from disk files, and how to print information using Visual Basic.

Quiz

1. What does string concatenation mean?

2. What are the two concatenation operators?

3. Which concatenation operator is preferred by Microsoft?

4. What will the following code display?

```
Private Sub command1_click()
    Dim strValue1 As String
    Dim strValue2 As String
    Dim strValue3 As String
    Dim strValue4 As String
    strValue1 = "Eat"
    strValue2 = "at"
    strValue3 = "Joe's"
    strValue4 = "Diner"
    Form1.Print strValue1 & strValue2 & strValue3 & _
            strValue4
End Sub
```

5. There's a problem with the code from question 4. What would be one way to correct it?

6. True or False: Strings can be 'broken apart' and 'isolated' as well as joined together.

7. What does the Len function do?

8. What does the function InStr do?

9. What does a return value of 0 from the InStr function indicate?

10. How many arguments of the function InStr are optional?

11. If you provide the InStr function with a comparison argument, do you need to provide any other arguments to the function?

12. What technique can you use to have a message appear in a message box with more than one line?

13. What's an algorithm?

14. What does the function Left$ do?

15. What does the function Right$ do?

16. What does the Mid$ function do?

17. What's the difference between the Mid$ function and the Mid function?

18. What function can be used to 'convert' a string to upper case?

19. What will the value of strValue be after this code runs?

```
strValue = UCase("Who doesn't love Visual Basic")
```

Extra Credit – A farmer had 17 sheep. All but 9 died. How many did he have left?

Chapter 11
Disk Files and Printer Operations

The ability to read data from and write to disk files is an important programming skill. In this chapter, you'll follow my class as they learn how to perform these disk operations, and also learn how to direct output to a printer.

I began by informing everyone that the topics for today's class would be disk files and printer operations.

"I thought that disk file operations had pretty much gone the way of the dinosaur," Dave said, "I hardly ever see file operations mentioned anywhere in the books that I pick up. Everything seems to point you in the direction of using databases. Besides, I didn't even know you could print within Visual Basic, I thought you needed to use Crystal Reports."

"Your observations," I said, "are right on the mark. Disk file operations and the ability to print from within Visual Basic may be two of its biggest secrets. More advanced programmers choose to use databases to store data from their programs, and Crystal Reports is probably the reporting tool of choice for most programmers. Both of those topics are beyond the level of this introductory course, but disk files and printer operations are a perfect fit for the beginner programmer. The skills you learn today, as we read and write files, and direct output to the printer, will not be wasted. They'll form an important foundation when you graduate to database processing and writing more advanced reports."

Disk File Operations

"Let's take a look at disk file operations first," I said.

I continued by explaining that working with disk files, though not as prevalent as it once was, is still a viable way of saving data from within your program.

"You can also read data from a disk file into your program," I said. "Don't forget, part of our China Shop Requirements Statement indicates that we will read inventory data into our program from a disk file. Specifically, data that we will use to load china brands into the 1stBrands list box, and the inventory pricing data necessary to calculate a sales quotation. Right now, that data is included in our program code. After today's class, the China Shop Project will read the brands data from a disk file!"

"Are disk file operations like this done much in the real world?" Kathy asked.

"That's a hard question to answer," I said. "Perhaps not so much for newer applications, which tend to rely on interacting with modern databases like Microsoft's Access. However, I believe there is a huge inventory of existing DOS Basic programs that were written long before the advent of PC database packages. Some of these programs are still running today, and still reading and writing disk files."

"It's not uncommon for me to have a student or two enroll in my class because of a desire or need to convert one of these programs into Visual Basic. You never know when you might be hired to convert one of these old programs to Visual Basic, and an understanding of disk file operations can be the difference between getting the job and losing it to someone else."

Writing Data to a Disk File

"What types of operations do you think we can perform on a disk file?" I asked.

"Writing records to a file and reading records from a file," Valerie suggested. "That's basically correct," I said, "but let's also add **append** to that list."

"Append?" Blaine asked. "Append means to write to the end of an already existing file," I said. "We'll get to that operation in a few minutes. Let's first examine writing records to a disk file. This isn't difficult, but it does require that you perform three steps in this order:"

1.　You open the file to which you wish to write records by the Open statement.

2.　You write records to that file using the Write # statement.

3. You close the file you have opened using the Close Statement.

"That doesn't seem very difficult at all," Joe said.

"The process isn't very difficult," I said. "Probably the most complicated part is learning the syntax of the Open Statement. Let's examine that first."

The Open Statement

I displayed the syntax for the Open statement on the classroom projector:

```
Open pathname For mode As [#]filenumber
```

"Let's look at each one of these parameters one by one," I said.

- The **pathname** is the full name, including the directory, of the file to which you wish to write.

- The **mode** specifies how the file is to be opened. The five modes are Input, Append, Output, Binary, and Random. I explained that in our introductory class, we would only use Input, Output, and Append.

- Input mode is used to read data from a file. If you specify Input mode, the file must already exist. You cannot write records to a file opened for Input mode.

- Output mode is used to write data to a file. If you specify Output mode, Visual Basic will create the file for you. If the file already exists, it will be overwritten and its previous contents lost. You cannot read records from a file opened for Output mode.

- Append mode tells Visual Basic that we want to write records to the end of the file referenced in the Open statement. However, if for some reason Visual Basic cannot find that file in the location specified, it will create the file for us. Any records we write to the file will be added to the newly created file.

"Now let's discuss the **file number** parameter," I said. "When you open a file in Visual Basic, from that point forward, you must refer to that file by a file number instead of by its name."

"It's a bit quirky," I said, "but that's how it works in Visual Basic and that's what the file number parameter refers to."

"What number do we use?" Barbara asked. "Do we need to pick a special number?"

"Actually," I said, "you can use any number you want. The file number parameter can range from 1 to 511. Ordinarily, you would specify 1 for the first file opened in your program, 2 for the second, and so on."

I continued by explaining that some programs may open a large number of files.

"Keeping track of the next available file number can be a real pain," I said. "For that reason, Visual Basic provides a function called `FreeFile`, which returns a value representing the next available file number."

"So, if the last file number you used was 5," Dave said, "the return value of `FreeFile` would be 6?"

"Exactly," I said. "It's a very handy function to use, especially as I said, if your program opens many files."

"That's just about it for the syntax. Why don't I show you an example of an `Open` statement now."

```
Open "C:\VBFILES\PRACTICE\GRADES.TXT" For Append As #1
```

"Uh-oh," Blaine said jokingly, "you're not going to display our grades, are you?"

"Don't worry," I said, "everyone in this class is well on their way to earning an A. The file you see referenced here contains the grades from my summer course in Systems Analysis, but the names have been changed to protect the innocent!"

I continued by explaining that this open statement was instructing Visual Basic to open a file named GRADES.TXT, located in the subdirectory C:\VBFILES\PRACTICE for Append mode as file number 1.

"I just noticed the hash sign," Dave said. "Is it required?"

"No, it's not," I said, "but I like to use it because it makes any file operations in my code stand out."

"How exactly do we write data to the file?" Barbara asked. "Is that part of the Open statement?"

"No," I said. "Writing data to a file requires a separate Visual Basic statement, the Write # statement. Before I discuss it though, I'd like to quickly review disk files."

I explained that there are many types of disk files on a PC, but the type we are interested in are specifically data files.

"A typical data file contains records," I said, "and each record in the file usually contains one or more **fields** of data. For instance, I'm sure there are data files at this university which contain information about students. Each record might, for example, be comprised of fields representing the student's name, address, telephone number, and other pertinent information."

The Write # Statement

"The Write # statement", I said, "allows you to write fields of data as discrete pieces of data which a program can then read into a Visual Basic program, again as discrete pieces of data. These fields and records are stored in a format known as an **ASCII delimited format.**"

"There's that ASCII word again," Lou said.

"Don't be intimidated by it," I said. "You sometimes hear the word **comma delimited** as well. This means that the record is written to the file, with each field separated by commas, and with non-numeric data enclosed within quotation marks. Additionally, each record appears on a separate line within the file. For instance, take a look at this code:"

```
Open "C:\VBFILES\PRACTICE\DEMO1.TXT" For Output As #1
Write #1, "John Smith", 100
Write #1, "Joe Jones", 99
Close #1
```

"This code", I said, "consists of an `Open` statement, two `Write #` statements and a `Close` statement. The `Open` statement just opens a file called `Demo1` for `Output` in the `\VBFILES\PRACTICE` subdirectory. We'll talk about the `Close` statement in a few minutes. The first `Write #` statement will write the string `John Smith`, followed by a comma, and then the number 100, to the file designated as file number 1. After the first `Write #` statement is executed, a new line in the file is begun and the string `Joe Jones` is written to it, followed by a comma and then by the number 99. This process will then be repeated as long as `Write #` statements are executed. When the file is closed, an invisible **End Of File marker** (sometimes called an **EOF**) is placed at the end of the last record."

I quickly created a new project, placed this code in a command button and ran the program. I then used Notepad to view the file:

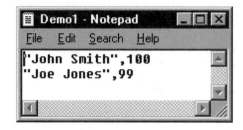

I asked if there were any questions about the `Write #` statement.

The Close Statement

"I do have a question, but not directly about the `Write` statement." Barbara said. "First, you said that you would discuss the `Close` statement. Secondly, you said that an invisible `End Of File` marker is placed at the end of the file when you close it. Can you elaborate on those a little bit?"

"Let's tackle the invisible `End Of File` marker first," I said. "This marker is automatically placed at the end of a file when the file is closed. Now, how a file gets closed is another story. Technically, the programmer should close an open file by referencing its file number, the way we did in the previous code example. For instance, this statement closes the file opened as file #1:"

```
Close #1
```

"You can also choose not to reference a file number and close every open file in your program, by writing this:"

`Close`

"However, I must caution you to use this statement carefully. Beginners sometimes accidentally close files that they are still working with by using this form of the `Close` statement," I said.

"Closing an open file is the last operation you should perform on your file," I said. "If for some reason, you forget to close a file that you have opened for `Write` or `Append` mode, the potential exists that all of the data you have written will be lost."

"Wow, that's severe," Steve said.

"Very severe," I agreed. "I can assure you, if you make that mistake once, you won't forget to close a file ever again."

I then told the class a story about a COBOL program that I had written many years ago that was intended to write output records to a mainframe disk file.

"This program," I said, "ran for hours and hours, and after it finished, I anxiously reviewed the contents of the output file, only to find that it was empty. After scouring through my code for several days trying to determine what was wrong, making minor modifications, and then running and re-running the program, I suddenly realized that my program had no `Close` statement! With no `Close` statement, the data that my program had been writing to the output disk file was never saved. Needless to say, I have never forgotten to code a `Close` statement since!"

"So other programming languages besides Visual Basic have `Close` statements?" Rhonda asked.

"Goodness, yes!" I said. "Just about everything that we're learning in this course applies equally to the other major programming languages such as C, C++, and Java. All of our fundamentals, such as selection structures, loops, string manipulation, and print and file operations are available in other programming languages too."

"That's great news," Steve said. "Does that mean that after this course I can apply what I've learned here to C and C++?"

"Yes," I said. "Some of the language is even identical. Some of the particulars of the language might vary a little bit, but you'll find that the basics are the same."

"I have a pretty far-fetched question," Joe said. "Is there any way to see the EOF?"

"That's not far-fetched at all," I said. "Curiosity is the sign of a good programmer. Unfortunately, with the tools available here in the classroom, we can't see the EOF. Notepad certainly won't do it. Just remember that the EOF is really nothing special. It's just a character that the operating system uses to identify where a file ends."

There were no more questions.

"What we need now is an exercise that will give you an opportunity to create your own disk file," I said.

Exercise

Create an Output Disk File

1. Start a new `Standard.EXE` project.

2. Place two text boxes on the form.

3. Change the `Name` properties of the text boxes to `txtName` and `txtGrade` respectively.

4. Clear the `Text` properties of the two text boxes.

5. Place a command button on the form using your toolbox and accept the default name.

6. Double-click on the command button, and place the following code into its `Click` event procedure:

```
Private Sub Command1_Click()
    If txtName.Text = "" Then
        MsgBox "Name must be entered"
        txtName.SetFocus
        Exit Sub
    ElseIf txtGrade.Text = "" Then
        MsgBox "Grade must be entered"
        txtGrade.SetFocus
        Exit Sub
    End If
    Open "C:\VBFILES\PRACTICE\L3EXAM1.TXT" For Append As #1
    Write #1, UCASE$(txtName.Text), Val(txtGrade.Text)
    txtName.Text = ""
    txtGrade.Text = ""
    txtName.SetFocus
    Close #1
End Sub
```

7. Save the project in your \VBFiles\Practice subdirectory. Save the form as Grades.frm and the project as Grades.vbp. Run the program.

8. Add the first record to the disk file now by typing **Tom** into the first text box and **95** into the second. Then click on the command button, and the record will be written to the file L3EXAM1 in the \VBFILES\PRACTICE subdirectory of your hard disk.

9. Using the following table, enter the remaining five students' names and grades into your disk file. Don't forget to click on the command button after each entry.

Name	Grade
Tom	95
Kevin	70
Melissa	100
John	85
Mary	85
Sue	65

10. End your program and use Notepad to examine the file. It should look like this:

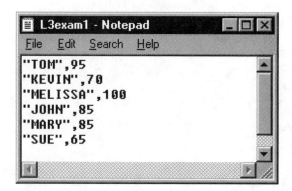

Discussion

There were no major problems with this exercise.

"I have a couple of questions," Linda said.

"First, remember that I'm a DOS user at heart. Anyway, while I was entering the information into the text boxes, out of habit I would press the *Enter* key and of course, nothing happened. Only when I clicked the command button would the new record be added to the file. I was hoping that there is a way that pressing the *Enter* key would trigger the `Click` event of the command button."

"That's a good idea," Rhonda said. "That would make data entry easier. I seem to recall discussing something like that when we talked about properties of the command button earlier in the course."

"You're right Rhonda," I said. "You can set the `Default` property of the command button to `True`, in which case, pressing the *Enter* key does trigger the `Click` event of the command button. That would produce the behavior that Linda is looking for."

"OK, second question," She said. "I know I must have done something wrong. When I ran the program and began to type the student's name into the first text box, I noticed that the focus wasn't on the text box, but on the command button instead."

"You must have placed the command button on the form before your text boxes," I said. "The initial *Tab* order of your controls on the form is determined by the order in which you place them on the form. The exercise was written so that you placed the text boxes on the form first, then the command button. When you started your program, the focus should have been on the first text box you placed on the form."

"Say no more," Linda said. "That's exactly what I did. I guess as I was used to placing a command button on the form first, that's exactly what I did. So that's why the command button received the focus first."

"That's right," I said. "Don't forget, you can always change the *Tab* order of your controls by changing the `TabIndex` properties of your controls."

"Do you need to code a `Close` statement after each `Write` statement?" Barbara asked. "That's not the technique you used in your earlier example, where you opened a file, wrote two records to it, and then closed it."

"That's a good question," I said. "Writing data to a disk file is relatively easy, but it does require that we give some thought as to how we want to code it. In this exercise, each time the user wanted to add another record to the file, they clicked on the command button. This action triggered the `Click` event procedure of the command button, in which we opened the file, wrote a record to that file and then closed it."

"By now you should be getting the idea that event procedures are really mini-programs of their own. When you click on the command button, its `Click` event procedure is started, the code within it is executed, and then the event procedure ends."

"We really don't have much choice as to opening and closing the file within the event procedure. In order to write a record to the file, we must open the file first. After writing the record to the file we have no choice but to immediately close the file at that point, since the event procedure is about to end."

After thinking for a moment, I suggested that another alternative would be to open the file in the `Load` event of the form and write records each time the command button is clicked. Then close the file in the `FormUnload` event of the form, which is triggered when the form is unloaded.

"I'm not a big fan of using a technique like that," I said. "I like to code the `Open` and `Close` statements in the same procedure that the records are being written in. With this scenario, there's always the possibility that the user will start the program, enter some records, and then, for whatever reason, not end the program for some time thereafter. What happens if there's a power failure or their computer is accidentally turned off? All of their work could be lost."

I suggested that we should take a closer look at the code.

"This first section of code," I said, "performs validation on the `txtName` and `txtGrade` text boxes, the same type of validation that we performed on the text boxes in the exercises we did last week."

```
If txtName.Text = "" Then
   MsgBox "Name must be entered"
   txtName.SetFocus
   Exit Sub
ElseIf txtGrade.Text = "" Then
   MsgBox "Grade must be entered"
   txtGrade.SetFocus
   Exit Sub
End If
```

"When writing data to a disk file," I said, "validation is more important than ever. Disk files are by their nature, permanent, and the output your program produces may be input to another program. The last thing we want to do is write incomplete or inaccurate data to a disk file."

"If you don't mention **GIGO** here," Kate said, "you'll be the first computer teacher I've had who hasn't."

"GIGO?" Ward asked.

"That's right," I said. "GIGO stands for **Garbage In, Garbage Out**. It basically means that, if you allow bad data to get into a file, sooner or later that data will be output from a program with potentially embarrassing results."

I continued by explaining that this next line of code opens the file `L3EXAM1.TXT` for `Append` mode in the `\VBFILES\PRACTICE` subdirectory:

```
Open "C:\VBFILES\PRACTICE\L3EXAM1.TXT" For Append As #1
```

"Remember, Append mode says that if this file does not exist in the specified directory, then Visual Basic should create it for us," I said. "If the file does exist in the specified directory, then Visual Basic should add the records we write to the end of the file."

"Can you help me?" Bob said. "I'm confused by the next line of code after the Open statement."

"Yes, that would be the Write statement," I said as I displayed it on the classroom projector:

```
Write #1, UCASE$(txtName.Text), Val(txtGrade.Text)
```

"This line of code," I said, "is the code that writes the record to the file. The syntax is pretty simple, just the word Write, followed by the number of the file we opened previously with the Open statement, and then one or more expressions representing the fields that we wish to write in the record. In this instance, both expressions are just the Text properties of the two text boxes."

"That's not what's confusing me," Bob said. "I'm confused by the UCASE$ and Val functions. Why are we using those here?"

"We discussed the UCASE$ function briefly last week in our class on string manipulation," I said. "Here we are using it to convert the name that the user types into the txtName text box to upper case. Converting text like this, so that the name is capitalized in the disk file, is a personal decision. I like the consistency it provides, in that all the names in the disk file are in the same format. Besides, I don't want names that are all in lower case letters. When those names eventually are output, they will look horribly sloppy."

"What about the Val function?" Chuck asked.

"If we had coded the Write statement like this, without the Val function," I said, "Visual Basic would have written the grades to the file as a string instead of as a number."

```
Write #1, UCASE$(txtName), txtGrade.Text
```

"Is that a big deal?" Dave asked.

"It could be," I answered. "If we later write a program to read the data in this file and then attempt to perform arithmetic on the grades, we'll encounter an error. The `Val` function takes the string data in the text box and converts it to a numeric data type, as long as the text box contains a valid number."

"So, if we didn't use the `Val` function," Ward asked, "the numbers would have been written to the file with quotation marks around them?"

"That's right," I said.

I then removed the `Val` function from the code, re-ran the program, re-entered all the grades, and then displayed the updated file using Notepad:

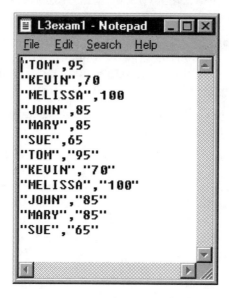

"Do you see the difference?" I asked. "Now the 'new' grades have quotation marks around them, indicating they have been written to the file as string data."

"I guess," Dave said, "that we could always use the `Val` function to convert the string data to a number when we read the file?"

"That's a good point," I said. "That would work too. Remember our GIGO principle though. If the data is a number, write it to the file as a number. There's no guarantee that you will be the programmer who writes the code to read the file. Plus, even if you are, there's no guarantee that you'll remember."

I continued by displaying this section of code:

```
txtName.Text = ""
txtGrade.Text = ""
txtName.SetFocus
```

Follow my advice and close each file as soon as you are done with it. Explicitly closing files in this way leads to less trouble down the line.

"All we're doing here," I said, "is clearing the entries in the text boxes and setting the focus to the first text box. This is just a courtesy to the user. Finally, this line of code may be the most crucial line of code in the program!"

```
Close #1
```

I asked if there were any more questions about writing data to a disk file. There were none, and so we moved on to a discussion of reading data from a disk file.

Reading Data from a Disk File

"The basic process of reading data from a disk file," I said, "is the same as writing data. Personally, I think it's even easier. Again, it requires three steps":

1. Open the file from which you wish to read records by using the Open statement.

2. Read records from that file using the Input# statement.

3. Close the file you have opened using the Close statement.

"Is this Open statement the same as the one we used to write records to a file?" Kathy asked.

"It's the same statement," I said, "except to read records from a file we specify Input mode."

"And the Close statement is the same one too?" Ward asked.

"Yes," I said. "The Open statement is similar to the one we used to write records and the Close statement is identical. The only thing we do differently, when we read records from a disk file, is to code an Input# statement instead of a Write# statement."

The Input# Statement

"The Input# statement is in essence the reverse of the Write# statement we used in the previous exercise. The Write# statement writes data to a disk file and the Input# statement reads data from a disk file."

"I understand where the data goes when we write to a file," Ward said, "but where does the data from the file go when we read it?"

"We'll read the data into variables," I said. "When we discuss variable arrays in a few weeks, you'll see that they are ideal structures into which to read data from a disk file."

I displayed the syntax of the Input# on the classroom projector:

```
Input #1, strName, intGrade
```

"This syntax is pretty simple," I said. "The important thing is to declare appropriate variables to 'hold' the data that you read from the file. Here's an exercise to read the data from the file we created in the last exercise."

In this exercise, you'll read the file you created in the previous exercise, so be sure it can be found in your \VBFILES\PRACTICE subdirectory (it's also among the files you can download from the CD, in the Chapter 11 folder).

Exercise

Reading Records from a Disk File

1. Start a new `Standard.EXE` project.

2. Place a command button on the form and accept the default name that Visual Basic assigns.

3. Double-click on the command button and place the following code into its `Click` event procedure:

```
Private Sub Command1_Click()
    Dim strName As String
    Dim intGrade As Integer
    Open "C:\VBFILES\PRACTICE\L3EXAM1.TXT" For Input As #1
    Do While Not EOF(1)
        Input #1, strName, intGrade
        Form1.Print strName, intGrade
    Loop
    Close #1
End Sub
```

4. Save the project in your `\VBFiles\Practice` subdirectory. Save the forms as `Grades2.frm` and the project as `Grades2.vbp`.

5. Before you run the program, make sure that you delete the 6 illustrative 'all string' records from the `txt` file if you followed along with the `Val` discussion. Now run the program.

6. Click on the command button. The program will print the six records you wrote to the disk file `\VBFILES\PRACTICE\L3EXAM1.TXT` in the previous exercise.

Discussion

I ran the program myself and the form looked like this:

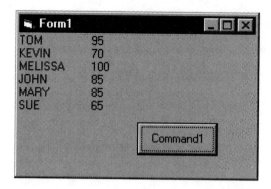

"That really was pretty easy," Ward said.

"Let's look at the code now," I said. "As usual, we start out by declaring any variables we will need to use in our event procedure."

```
Dim strName As String
Dim intGrade As Integer
```

"These two lines of code declare the two variables, `strName` and `intGrade` into which the `Input#` statement will load the data it reads," I explained.

"The next line of code opens the file `L3EXAM1.TXT` for `Input` mode in the `\VBFILES\PRACTICE` subdirectory," I said.

```
Open "C:\VBFILES\PRACTICE\L3EXAM1.TXT" For Input As #1
```

"Notice that this time we open the file for `Input` mode. Again, notice that we use the number 1 as our file number."

I waited for questions before continuing.

"This line of code," I said, "requires special attention."

```
Do While Not EOF(1)
```

"We know that this file contains 6 records," I said, "but the number of records in a disk file will vary. The `Do While...Loop` structure is a perfect way to read records in a file. All we need to do is tell Visual Basic to begin reading the records in the file and continue to read them until it reaches the `EOF` marker. Because Visual Basic can detect this **End Of File** marker, we code our loop in so that it continues to read records from a disk file until it encounters the `EOF`. Once Visual Basic finds it, we know that there are no more records to read from the file and we end the loop. Does that make sense to everyone?"

"It does," Steve said, "but I think I'll run this program in step mode to make sure I understand it."

"Great idea," I said.

I gave everyone a moment to run the exercise in step mode, and then continued with the next line of code.

"There are two lines of code in the body of the loop," I said, "and this is the first."

```
Input #1, strName, intGrade
```

"This line of code uses the `Input#` statement to read two fields from the disk file into the variables `strName` and `intGrade`. Once the data has been read into these variables, then we use the `Print` method of the form to print their values on the form."

```
Form1.Print strName, intGrade
```

"The loop statement just repeats until we reach the `EOF`."

```
Loop
```

"And finally, this line of code closes the opened file," I explained.

```
Close #1
```

There were no questions, so I suggested that we use our newly acquired file skills to modify the China Shop Project so that it can load the china brands in the `lstBrands` list box from a disk file. I reminded everyone that currently we had the following code in the `Load` event of the China Shop form:

```
Private Sub Form_Load()
    lstBrands.AddItem "Corelle"
    lstBrands.AddItem "Faberware"
    lstBrands.AddItem "Mikasa"
End Sub
```

Exercise

Reading Data into the lstBrands List Box

1. Load up the China Shop Project (if you're loading the version from the CD files, make sure you use the project files in the Chapter 11 folder).

2. Use Notepad to create a file called BRANDS.TXT containing the following three records. Make sure that the brands are enclosed within quotation marks, as this screen shows:

3. Save this file in the \VBFILES\CHINA subdirectory (again, don't forget that you can get this file from the CD-provided files).

4. Find the Form_Load event of frmMain and erase the code that is already there.

5. Replace it with the following:

```
Private Sub Form_Load()
   Dim strBrand As String
   Open "C:\VBFILES\CHINA\BRANDS.TXT" For Input As #1
   Do While Not EOF(1)             ' Loop until end of file.
      Input #1, strBrand
      lstBrands.AddItem strBrand
   Loop
   Close #1    ' Close file.
End Sub
```

6. Save the China Shop Project by clicking on the Save icon.

7. Run the program. Once again, the items will appear in the list box, but this time the brands are loaded from the disk file instead.

Discussion

In spite of the ease with which everyone completed the exercise, I didn't think it would hurt to go over the code in detail, especially after I had to remind one or two students to save the file in their China subdirectory.

"Is the code that we see here," Linda asked, "pretty much a blueprint for reading any kind of file?"

"That's right," I said. "Declare a variable or variables for each one of the fields in the record, open the file, create a loop to read the records until the EOF is reached and then close the file. Of course, what you do with the data once you have read it is up to you. In our case, we just load the data into a list box."

I continued by saying that since the BRANDS.TXT file contains only a single field, we only need to declare one variable, strBrand, to hold the contents of the records as we read them.

```
Dim strBrand As String
```

"This line of code opens the file BRANDS.TXT for Input."

```
Open "C:\VBFILES\CHINA\BRANDS.TXT" For Input As #1
```

"This next section of code," I said, "sets up a loop structure to read BRANDS.TXT until EOF is reached. This line reads the single field of the file into the variable strBrand."

```
Input #1, strBrand
```

"Then this line of code uses the AddItem method of the list box to load the value of the variable into the list box."

```
lstBrands.AddItem strBrand
```

"Finally, this line of code closes the file."

```
Close #1      ' Close file.
```

I asked if there were any questions, but there were none.

"We have one more topic to discuss today," I said. "Let's take a break, and when we return from our break, we'll discuss printer operations."

Printer Operations

"As I mentioned earlier in the class," I said, "using the Visual Basic printer operations to generate output to a printer seems to be mostly overlooked these days. Having taught Visual Basic almost since Version 1, I can tell you that later versions of Visual Basic provide alternatives to the techniques I'll be showing you today. In fact, many experienced Visual Basic programmers don't even know these techniques exist and information about them isn't even included in the help files that come with the full versions of Visual Basic."

"What do programmers use instead of the Visual Basic print techniques?" Dave asked.

"Some versions of Visual Basic," I said, "now come with a package called Crystal Reports, which is a wonderful report writer that you can use right from within Visual Basic. Crystal Reports allows you to create beautiful reports very quickly and pretty easily."

"Then why don't we just use Crystal Reports?" Rhonda asked.

"There are several reasons," I said, "why you should learn how to generate your own reports and direct them to the printer using Visual Basic, and not a third party tool:"

- Crystal Reports is not supplied with all versions of Visual Basic, for example the Working Model.

- No matter what version of Visual Basic you use, you can always be sure that the techniques I show you today will be available to you.

- In the past, when I've demonstrated these print techniques, many students have actually preferred creating their own reports using Visual Basic techniques to creating them using Crystal Reports.

- Knowing how to create your own reports in Visual Basic is a sound, fundamental technique to include in your programmer's bag of tricks.

The Printer Object

"We've already seen a system object in this course, the `Debug` object," I said. "Printer operations in Visual Basic require us to use another system object called the `Printer` object."

"What's the purpose of a system object anyway?" Dave asked.

"A system object provides the **device independence** that we so often hear about when Windows is described. As programmers, we often need to interact with the PC's screen, for instance. We don't want to be concerned with the idiosyncrasies of the user's particular monitor. Because Visual Basic communicates with the PC's monitor via the `Screen` object, we don't need to worry about the monitor's dot pitch, or the number of horizontal and vertical pixels on the screen. The same applies to printer operations. Our program will communicate with the `Printer` object, and we'll rely on Windows to worry about the particularities of the user's printer. You'll see that using the `Printer` object to output a report in Visual Basic is very similar to using the `Print` method to print to the form. In fact, we will use the `Print` method of the `Printer` object."

I continued by saying that the output generated via the `Printer` object will, by default, be sent to the user's default printer.

"What about the printer selection dialog box that's displayed in other Windows programs, such as Microsoft Word? Is there a way to display that in our programs also, prior to printing a report from our program?" Dave asked.

"Yes, by placing a Common Dialog control in your project and then using its `ShowPrinter` method, you can display that very same dialog box," I replied.

"Are you saying," Kathy asked, "that if we're comfortable printing to the form, our transition to using the `Printer` object to generate printed reports will be pretty seamless?"

"The two processes are nearly identical," I said, "but there is a subtle difference. When you use the `Print` method of the form, output is immediately printed on the form. When you use the `Printer` object's `Print` method, the line you print is not immediately printed. Rather, Windows 'queues' the output of the individual `Print` statements until you explicitly tell Visual Basic that you want the printer to begin printing. You do that by invoking the `EndDoc` method of the `Printer` object."

"This really does sound easy," Barbara said. "I somehow thought it would be a lot harder."

"Everything's easy when you know how to do it," I said. "Let's see how easy it is by completing this exercise."

Exercise

Sending Output to the Printer

1. Start a new `Standard.EXE` project.

2. Place a command button on the form and accept its default name.

3. Double-click on the command button and place the following code in its `Click` event procedure:

```
Private Sub Command1_Click()
    Printer.Print "The Bullina China Shop"
    Printer.Print "253 Melrose Drive"
    Printer.Print "West Chester, PA. 19077"
    Printer.Print
    Printer.Print
    Printer.Print
    Printer.Print "Dear Mrs. Jones,"
    Printer.Print
    Printer.Print "I want to take this opportunity to thank you for your " _
```

```
            ;"recent purchase of fine china at my shop."
        Printer.Print
        Printer.Print "Should you have any other needs in the future, please " _
            ; "do  not hesitate to contact me."
        Printer.Print
        Printer.Print "Sincerely"
        Printer.Print
        Printer.Print "Joseph Bullina"
        Printer.EndDoc

End Sub
```

4. Save the project in your \VBFiles\Practice directory. Save the form as Letter.frm and the project as Letter.vbp. Now run the program.

5. Now click on the command button. A letter will be output to your default printer.

Discussion

In just a matter of a few minutes, we had 16 letters printed on the classroom printer.

I explained that the code in the exercise was really just a series of Print method statements, using the Printer object where previously we had used the Form object.

"The only statement we haven't seen before," I said, "is the EndDoc method."

Printer.EndDoc

"This line of code," I said, "tells Visual Basic to actually print all of the lines of text it has been queuing as a result of the previous Print method statements."

"Are you saying that if you forget to code the EndDoc method, nothing prints?" Rhonda asked.

"Yes," I replied, "nothing will print. As you can imagine, that can be pretty frustrating."

"What about the multiple lines of code that just read Printer.Print — what's going on there?" Steve asked.

"The `Print` method with no expression following it," I said, "outputs a blank line to the printer."

"That whole process was really easy," Joe said. "You were right," Rhonda said, "if you can print to the form, you can print with a printer."

"Printing in Visual Basic is easier than people would believe, but there's more to it than meets the eye. Sending a letter to the user's printer isn't very difficult. Sending a complex columnar report of several hundred pages with headings, page numbers, control breaks, subtotals, and grand totals is another matter." I added.

"Let me guess," Dave said. "In that case, we use Crystal Reports!"

"Not necessarily," I said. "All of that can be done in Visual Basic, but using a powerful report writer makes the process much easier. Let's take a look at how we would do that now."

Exercise

Directing Fancier Output to the Printer

1.   Start a new `Standard.EXE` project.

2.   Place a text box on the form.

3.   Change the `Name` property to `txtName`.

4.   Clear the `Text` property of the text box.

5.   Place a command button on the form and accept the default name that Visual Basic assigns.

6.   Double-click on the command button and place the following code into its `Click` event procedure:

```
Private Sub Command1_Click()
   Dim strFontName As String
   Dim sngFontSize As Single
   If txtName = "" Then
      MsgBox "You must type a name in the text box"
   Else
      Printer.Print Tab(40); "The Bullina China Shop"
      Printer.Print Tab(40); "253 Melrose Drive"
      Printer.Print Tab(40); "West Chester, PA. 19077"
      Printer.Print Tab(40); Format(Date, "Long Date")
      Printer.Print
      Printer.Print
      Printer.Print
      Printer.Print "Dear " & txtName.Text & ","
      Printer.Print
      Printer.Print "I want to take this opportunity " _
         ;"to thank you for your recent purchase of fine china at " _
         ;"my shop."
      Printer.Print
      Printer.Print "Should you have any other needs in, " _
         ;"the future please do not hesitate to contact me."
      Printer.Print
      Printer.Print "Sincerely"
      Printer.Print
      strFontName= Printer.FontName
      sngFontSize = Printer.FontSize
      Printer.FontName = "Script"
      Printer.FontSize = "36"
      Printer.Font.Bold = True
      Printer.Print "Joseph Bullina"
      Printer.Font.Bold = False
      Printer.FontName = strFontName
      Printer.FontSize = sngFontSize
      Printer.EndDoc
   End If
   txtName.Text = ""
   txtName.SetFocus
End Sub
```

7. Save the project in your \VBFiles\Practice subdirectory. Save the form as Letter2.frm and the project as Letter2.vbp. Now run the program.

8. Enter your name into the text box and click on the command button. A custom letter will be output to your default printer.

Discussion

I ran the code myself, and produced a much more visually attractive letter than the letter from the previous exercise. I could see that the students were pleased with their results as well.

I explained that as usual, we declared the variables we needed for use in the event procedure first:

```
Dim strFontName As String
Dim sngFontSize As Single
```

"Whenever I change any of the `Printer` object properties," I said, "I always save the original values, so that I can easily set them back if they are changed. Since we'll be changing both the font name and size in this code, I use these variables to hold those original values."

"How did you know to declare `strFontName` as a string and `sngFontSize` as a single?" Steve asked.

"Some programmers," I said, "would be inclined to declare these variables as variant data types because they don't know the correct data type for the `Printer`'s `FontName` and `FontSize` properties. However, I used the **Object Browser** to check the data types for these `Printer` object properties. Remember, declaring a variable as a variant is not as efficient as declaring it properly. When in doubt, check the **Object Browser**."

"I know you've mentioned this before," Rhonda said, "but how do we get to the **Object Browser**?"

"Select **O**bject Browser from the **V**iew menu or just press the *F2* function key," I replied.

I gave everyone an opportunity to check the **Object Browser** for the `Printer` object. Here's a screenshot showing the details for the `FontSize` object property:

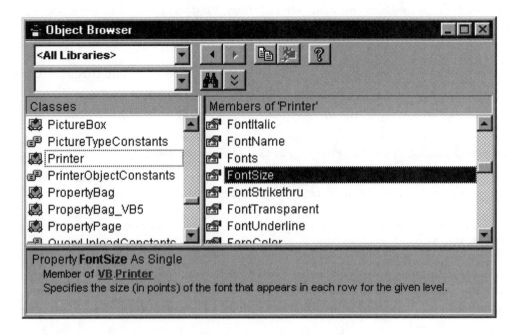

"Notice," I said, "that in the bottom pane of the object browser window it tells you that FontSize is declared As Single."

There was plenty of quiet nodding, so I guessed that I had made my point.

"Okay, let's get back to our code."

"These two lines of code," I said, "perform validation on the text box to ensure that the user has entered something."

```
If txtName = "" Then
   MsgBox "You must type a Name in the Text box"
```

"The next three lines of code are similar to the code from the previous exercise," I said, "but with the inclusion of Tab."

```
Printer.Print Tab(40); "The Bullina China Shop"
Printer.Print Tab(40); "253 Melrose Drive"
Printer.Print Tab(40); "West Chester, PA. 19077"
```

"What's the function of the word Tab here?" Joe asked.

"The Tab parameter, when used in conjunction with the Print method, permits you to specify the character position on either the form or printer where you want the output to be printed," I replied. "In this case, we're telling Visual Basic to print the name and address of Mr. Bullina's shop at character position 40 on the printer."

"Is the semicolon required?" Steve asked.

"Yes, it is," I said, "although in later versions of Visual Basic, if you forget to type it in, Visual Basic will do it for you."

I explained that this next line of code prints the current date, again at character position 40:

```
Printer.Print Tab(40); Format(Date, "Long Date")
```

"Here," I said "we're using the Format function to print the current date in a Long Date format, which would take the form of November 7, 1997."

"In Visual Basic," I said, "the Format function allows you to dress up your display or output a bit. You can choose from a series of pre-defined formats, for example the Long Date, or you can specify a custom format of your own. The Format function requires two arguments. The first argument is the expression to be formatted and the second argument is either a standard format or custom format."

"What is Date here?" Rhonda asked.

"Date is the current system date on the user's PC," I said.

"How is that different from Now," Mary asked, "which we are using in the Timer event of the Timer control to display the date and time on the user's PC."

"Date doesn't display the time,' I explained. "Now displays both date and time."

```
Printer.Print "Dear " & txtName.Text & ","
```

"This line of code," I said, "takes the value of the Text property of the txtName text box, concatenates it to the string "Dear ", and then concatenates that string to a comma. This concatenation forms the salutation of our letter."

Everyone was comfortable with what was going on here, since we had covered the concept of string concatenation the previous week when we discussed string manipulation.

"The next section of code," I said, "is identical to the code from the previous exercise and just prints the body of the letter. These two lines of code take the current values of the `FontName` and `FontSize` properties of the `Printer` object and store them in the variables `strFontName` and `sngFontSize`. This way, we can easily restore these properties to their original values before exiting the event procedure."

```
strFontName = Printer.FontName
sngFontSize = Printer.FontSize
```

"These next three lines of code change the `Printer` object's `FontName` property to `Script`, the `FontSize` property to `36`, and its `Bold` property to `True`."

```
Printer.FontName = "Script"
Printer.FontSize = "36"
Printer.Font.Bold = True
```

I pointed out that the `Bold` property is actually part of an object hierarchy that includes the `Printer` object and the `Font` object of the printer. I didn't expect everyone to grasp this concept immediately, so when I saw some confused looks, I told everyone not to worry.

"As soon as these `Printer` properties are set," I said, "whatever output is set to the printer using the `Print` method will be printed as a bold, 36 point, Script font, in this case, Joe Bullina's name."

"What would happen if for some reason the Script font is not installed on the user's computer?" Dave asked.

"What do you mean by that, Dave?" Rhonda asked.

I warned everyone that it's possible to specify a printer attribute, such as a font or a size, that is not installed on the user's PC or that the user's printer does not support. If that happens, Visual Basic will do its best to come up with a suitable substitute for the one you've specified.

"By the way," I said, "that warning applies not only to `Printer` properties, but also `Font` properties in any of the other Visual Basic objects, such as a text box or label. If the font is not installed on the user's PC, Visual Basic will make a substitution for you."

I continued by saying that once we print Joe Bullina's name, we then set the `Printer` object's `FontName` and `FontSize` properties back to their original settings and turn the `Printer`'s `Bold` property to `False`, or off.

```
Printer.Font.Bold = False
Printer.FontName = strFontName
Printer.FontSize = sngFontSize
```

"That's the code," I said. "Are there any questions about this exercise?"

There were none. Before dismissing class for the day, I told everyone to get plenty of rest prior to our next class.

"Next week," I said, "we'll be very busy enhancing the look and feel of the China Shop Project, by adding menus."

Summary

In this chapter, we examined file and printer operations. Specifically, we saw that:

- **Open** statements define the file that we want to write records to
- **Write #** statements allow you to write data to a file
- **Close** statements – surprisingly! – close a file that we've been writing data to
- **Input #** statements let us read data from a file

We learned the simple GIGO principle, which in this case amounts to: always make sure that the data you write to a file is in the correct format. If you think you're working with one kind of data, but you're actually getting another, you will get strange and unusable results.

You now know how to use disk files to read and write simple data and how to print directly to the default printer.

In the next chapter, we will continue to enhance our China Shop program's interface by adding some neat, functional menu choices that let the user adapt the interface to their own requirements.

Quiz

1. What Visual Basic statement is used to prepare a disk file to be read from or written to?

2. Which Visual Basic statement allows you to write data to an opened file?

3. What are the three steps necessary in order to write data to a disk file?

4. What modes of the Open statement can be used to write data to a disk file?

5. What are the valid ranges of file numbers?

6. If you had a file opened with a file number of 1, what code would you use to close it?

7. What code would you write to close every open file in your program?

8. What are the three steps necessary in order to read data from a disk file?

9. What modes of the Open statement can be used to read data from a disk file?

10. What statement is used to read data from an open disk file?

11. What function can be used to return the next available file number?

12. What is EOF?

13. In order to send output to the printer, you must use the special Visual Basic object called the _____.

14. What will this code do?

```
Printer.Print "I love"
Printer.Print "Visual Basic"
```

15. What will this code do?

```
Printer.Print "I love Visual Basic"
Printer.EndDoc
```

16. What is the Tab parameter of the Print method used for?

Extra Credit – Divide 30 by 1/2 and add 10. What is the answer?

Chapter 12
Finishing the User Interface

In this chapter, we'll finish building the user interface of the China Shop Project. By the end of this chapter it will begin to look and behave like a high powered Visual Basic program. Follow my class as we learn how to create a Visual Basic menu structure for the China Shop Project.

Where Are We Now?

I began the class by asking everyone to tell me where they thought we stood with the China Shop Project. After a few minutes, the consensus was that the China Shop Project was functional, but fell short of the Requirements Statement we had developed during our first two weeks of the course. In comparing the Requirements Statement to the current state of the program, we noted the following deficiencies:

1. There is no menu structure.

2. There is no way for the user to turn the display of the system date and time on or off.

3. Since there is no way for the user to turn off or turn on the display of the system date and time, this preference is not being saved to the Windows Registry.

4. There is no way for the customer to change the colors of the form.

5. Since the color of the main form cannot be changed, the user's color preference is not being saved to the Windows Registry.

6. Although we are reading china brands from a disk file, inventory prices are still hard coded, and not being read from a disk file.

7.   There is no way to gracefully exit the program and doing so should require the use of a password.

"During today's class," I said, "we'll take care of the deficiencies numbered 1, 2, 4 and 7. We'll handle number 6 next week when we discuss arrays. Numbers 3 and 5 will be corrected in our last class. Let's discuss how to develop a Visual Basic menu today."

Drop-Down Menus

"In Visual Basic," I said, "there are two types of menus: **drop-down menus** and **pop-up menus**."

In order to demonstrate exactly what I meant by a drop-down menu, I asked everyone to click on the <u>P</u>roject menu. I did the same and the screen looked like this:

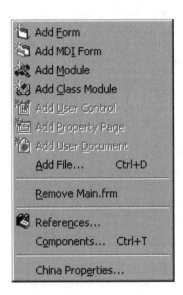

"A drop-down menu," I said, "is just a standard Windows menu. A pop-up menu, however, is something some of you may not be familiar with."

As an example of a pop-up menu, I asked everyone to open up the code window and to 'right-click' the mouse within the code window. I did the same and the following menu was displayed:

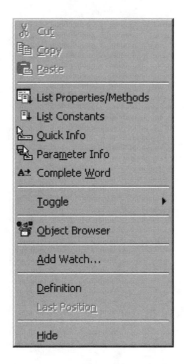

"In Windows 95 and Windows NT," I said, "a right-click of the mouse displays a pop-up menu, also called a **shortcut menu**, sometimes also called a **context menu**. The term **context menu** applies because the exact pop-up menu displayed varies depending upon where you right-click with the mouse."

"So if I right-click on the form," Ward said, "the pop-up menu I see will be different from the one I see if I right-click in the code window?"

"That's right," Rhonda said. "When I right-click on the form, I do see a different pop-up menu:"

"Also," I said, "You'll get a still-different menu if you right-click when the mouse pointer is over a control on the form:"

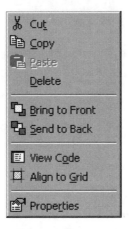

"Will we learn how to create pop-up menus?" Barbara asked.

"Yes, we will," I said. "In fact, before the end of today's class, we'll have added both types of menu to the China Shop Project."

A First Look at the Menu Editor

"So far, whenever we have wanted to add a visual control to our interface, we have gone to the toolbox to find it. However, one thing that always confuses beginners," I said, "is that there isn't a menu control in the toolbox."

"So how do we get one?" asked Barbara.

"The menu, while considered a control in Visual Basic, is not placed on the form, but is instead attached to it by using the Menu Editor," I replied.
"So how do we get to that then?" Steve asked.

"Well, there are several ways," I said, "and each method requires that the form be visible in the IDE. Here are the three methods to access the Menu Editor."

- Select Tools-Menu Editor

- Click on the Menu Editor icon on the toolbar

- Press Ctrl and E

"I think you forgot one," Rhonda said. "If you right-click on the form, the Menu Editor is one of the choices on the pop-up menu."

"Right you are, Rhonda," I said.

I then selected the Menu Editor from the toolbar:

"The Menu Editor," I said, "is divided into two sections. The top section, the **Properties window** contains the properties for the currently selected menu item. The bottom section, called the **Menu Control List Box**, displays the items that are contained on the menu. When you select a menu item in the menu control list box, that item's properties are displayed in the Properties window."

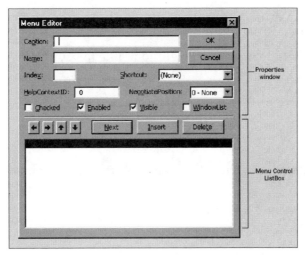

"Each form in a project can have only one menu control," I said, "but you can have as many menu items as you like, adding them to your form one at a time. Each menu item has properties that you specify in the Properties window portion of the **Menu Editor**. And as each menu item is added, that menu item then appears in the menu control list box."

"Can you have submenus in a Visual Basic menu?" Blaine asked.

"Yes, you can," I said. "I'll show you how shortly."

"Suppose you make a mistake while making an entry in the **Menu Editor**?" Dave asked.

"It's easy to correct any mistakes you might make," I said, "even after closing the **Menu Editor**. For instance, you can add menu items that you forgot, you can delete menu items that you no longer need and you can rearrange the menu structure any way you want."

"Can the properties of the menu items be modified at run time, like the properties of some of the other controls we've examined?" Joe asked.

"Good question," I said, "and the answer is yes. Most times you'll use the **Menu Editor** to specify menu item properties, but you can also set them at run time, in fact, we'll do that a little later in the China Shop project. Now let's take a closer look at the menu control properties that we'll be using."

Menu Control Properties

"Let's look at each of the menu control properties in turn." I said.

Caption

"Each menu item in a drop-down menu," I said, "has a caption. This caption identifies the menu item to the user."

I then displayed what the main menu will look like for our China Shop Project on the classroom projector:

"Both <u>F</u>ile and <u>P</u>references are top-level menu items of the China Shop's main menu," I said.

"What's a top-level menu?" Rhonda asked.

"Well," I said, "there are top-level menu items and submenu items. A top-level menu is the menu item that you see displayed on the menu bar."

I pointed out that the letter F in the caption File and the letter P in the caption Preferences were underlined.

"Can anyone tell me what the underline in the caption signifies?" I asked.

"That's the **hot key**," Steve said.

"Yes," I agreed, "that's the **access key**, sometimes called the hot key."

"How do you specify an access key for a menu item?" Chuck asked.

"The access key," I said, "is specified when you type the menu's caption into the Caption property of the Menu Editor. For instance, to designate the letter F as the access key for the File menu item, you need to type an ampersand (&) directly in front of the letter F."

I brought up the Menu Editor on the classroom projector and did exactly that:

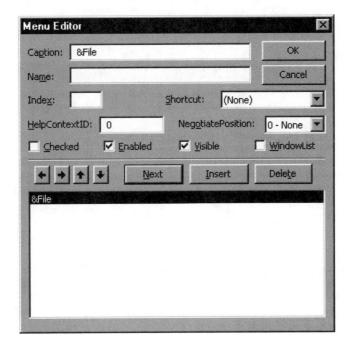

"Suppose you don't want the access key to be the first character of the caption, is there a way to make the access key something other than the first character?" Steve asked.

"Yes there is," I replied. "The access key can be any character in the caption. Just place the ampersand in front of the character you want to designate as the access key. For instance, Microsoft standards suggest that the access key for the Exit submenu item of the File menu should be the lower case letter x. To designate that letter as the access key, specify the Caption as E&xit."

"What about the **separator bar**, how do we specify that in Visual Basic?" Linda asked.

"You use a hyphen (-) when you want to create a separator bar between menu items," I explained.

"What's a separator bar?" Mary asked.

"A separator bar is a bar, or an underline that divides menu items in a menu," I said. "It's used to make a group of menu items stand out from another group."

I started up Microsoft Word and displayed the File menu on the classroom projector.

"The File menu in Microsoft Word," I said, "has several separator bars. The first one appears between Close and Save."

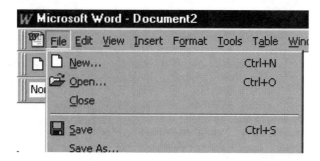

Name

"Each menu item is an object just like any other object in Visual Basic," I said, "and therefore must have a unique Name property, used to identify it to Visual Basic. Just like other controls in Visual Basic, it is possible to write code that manipulates the menu item's properties so, as with the other controls, you need to establish a sound naming convention for your menu items. Microsoft standards suggest that menu item names should begin with the prefix mnu. Of course, as with other controls, the rest of the name should convey the meaning and use of the menu item. By convention, for example, the name for the top-level menu item File is mnuFile."

"What about submenu names?" Dave asked. "How should they be named?"

"Microsoft," I said, "recommends including the name of the **parent** menu item in the submenu's name. For example, the submenu Exit of the top-level menu File is commonly named mnuFileExit."

"You said that each menu item must have a unique name. Does that apply to separator bars also?" Kathy asked.

"Yes, it does." I said. "Each separator bar must have a unique name. I typically name my first separator bar mnuDash1, the second mnuDash2 and so on."

Checked

"If you select the Checked property," I said, "then a check mark will appear next to the menu item when the program runs. You frequently see this property used to remind the user of the options they have selected in their program. For instance, in the Microsoft Word View menu, if the user has chosen to display the ruler, a check mark appears next to that menu item."

Once again, I displayed Word on the classroom projector and directed the class' attention to the View menu:

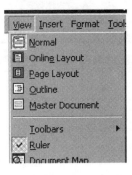

"Because I have chosen to display the <u>R</u>uler in Word," I said, "that menu item has a check mark next to it. By default, the <u>C</u>hecked property is not selected, however we will use this property to let the user know which Date and Time display preference they have chosen."

The Navigation Buttons

"After adjusting the properties for the first menu item on your menu," I said, "what you do next depends on whether there are more menu items to place in your menu structure. If you have more menu items to enter, either click on the *Enter* key or click on the <u>N</u>ext button. Many beginners press the OK button which will save the menu structure, but will also close the Menu Editor."

"So you should only click on the OK button when you have finished entering your menu items," Linda said.

"That's right," I said. "If you have more menu items to enter, click on the <u>N</u>ext button."

After entering the first menu item for the China Shop Project, I clicked on the <u>N</u>ext button and the Menu Editor looked like this:

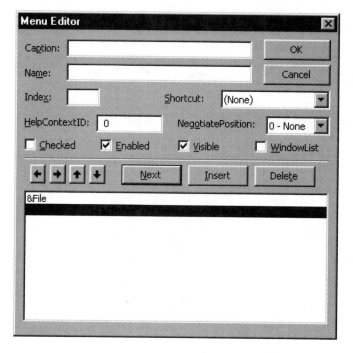

"Notice how the Properties window is empty and the selected menu item in the menu control's list box is blank," I said. "This tells us that the Menu Editor is ready for us to add our next menu item in the menu control."

I explained that the up and down arrows are used to reposition existing menu items in the menu hierarchy. I could see that Ward was confused.

"Suppose," I said, "you accidentally place the Preferences top-level menu 'ahead of' the File top-level menu item. All you need to do is select Preferences in the list box and press the down arrow. Preferences will then be moved after File in the hierarchy."

"What if you need to modify the property of a menu item?" Joe asked.

"Use your mouse to select the menu item in the list box," I said, "and the properties for that menu item will appear in the Properties window."

"That doesn't sound too bad," Barbara said.

"What do the right and left arrows do?" Rhonda asked.

"The right arrow is used to create submenus," I said. "If you select a menu item and then click on the right arrow, that menu item then becomes a submenu of the one above it. The menu item will also be indented in the menu control list box."

At this point, I added both a separator bar and the Exit submenu to the menu. The Menu Editor now looked like this:

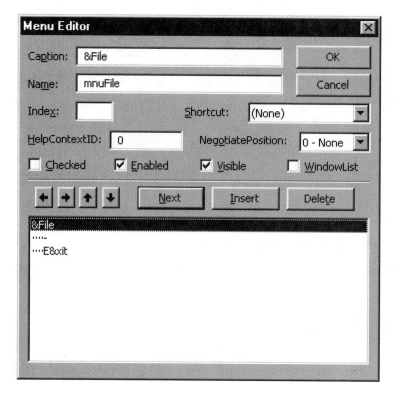

"E**x**it is now a submenu of **F**ile," I said. "Notice how E**x**it is indented in the menu control list box."

"I see that the separator bar appears to be a submenu as well," said Dave.

"That's an excellent observation Dave," I said. "Separator bars cannot be top-level menu items. They can only be submenu items."

"What about the left arrow?" Rhonda asked.

"The left arrow does just the opposite of the right arrow," I said. "If you have a menu item that is currently a submenu, you can select it, click on the left arrow and it will become a top-level menu item."

"Just out of curiosity," Dave said, "how many levels of submenus can we have?"

"You can have a total of five submenus 'nested' from the top-level menu item," I replied, "or if you want to think of it in this way, a total of six menu levels."

Next

"I've been playing with the Menu Editor a bit," Steve said, "and I'm confused about the function of the Next button."

"It's easy to confuse the Next button with the down arrow," I said. "The down arrow moves the selected menu item down one level in the menu hierarchy, but the Next button performs two functions. You can use it instead of using your mouse to select menu items in the menu control list box. In addition, clicking on the Next button when the last menu item in the menu control list box is selected tells Visual Basic that you want to create a new menu item. I should also mention that the Next button is the default button of the Menu Editor. Pressing the *Enter* key is the same as clicking the Next button."

An alternative to using the Next button is to use the mouse to directly select a menu item.

Insert

"When you click on the Insert button," I said, "you insert a new menu item directly **above** the currently selected menu item in the menu control list box."

Delete

"The Delete button deletes the currently selected menu item in the menu control list box," I said. "Be very careful when using the Delete button, as there is no Undo capability in the Menu Editor."

Cancel

The discussion of the Delete button led us quite naturally to a discussion of the Cancel button.

"You can always press the Cancel button, but that will cancel all of the work you have done during the Menu Editor session."

"That means, that if we have added five menu items during the session and press the Cancel button, none of them will be saved." Linda said.

"That's right," I said, "so be very careful when clicking on that Cancel button."

OK

"Selecting the OK button closes the Menu Editor and saves your changes," I explained. "Once the Menu Editor is closed, you will be able to see the menu structure on your form and even select items in the menu, both at design-time and at run-time. Of course, until you place code in the Click event procedures of the menu items, nothing will happen if you click on them."

I clicked on the OK button myself. The China Shop project and its partially completed menu were displayed:

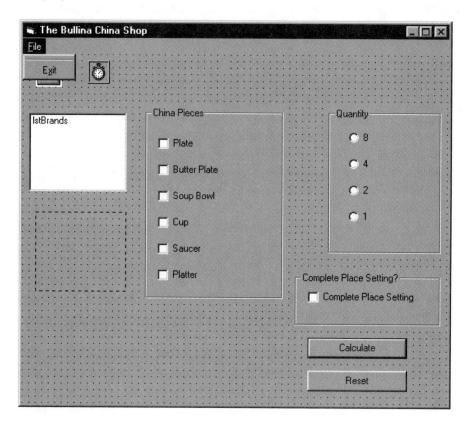

"I'm surprised that you can see the submenu at design-time," Peter said.

"That's a great feature," I said, "because it allows you to verify the look and feel of your menu without having to run your program."

"If you close the Menu Editor, can you go back into it to modify your menu?" Rhonda asked.

"Yes," I replied. "Just select your form and open the Menu Editor as usual. Your existing menu structure will be there for you to modify any way you want."

"I believe you said there is only one event procedure associated with the menu control, the Click event procedure," Barbara said. "Is there only one Click event procedure for the entire menu or does each menu item have its own one?"

"Good question," I said. "Every menu item reacts to its own click event, therefore each menu item, top-level or submenu, has its own Click event procedure."

"How and where do we place the code for the Click event procedure?" Rhonda asked.

"There are two ways to add the code to the Click event procedure," I said. "Probably the easiest way is to click on the menu item in design-mode. That will open up the code window for the Click event procedure of that particular menu item. You can also find the event procedure for the menu item by opening up the code window as you normally would and then selecting it using the object list box and procedure list box of the code window."

There were no more questions about the Menu Editor, so I suggested that at this point it would be a good idea for everyone to begin coding the menu for the China Shop Project on their own.

Exercise

Create the Menu for the China Shop Project

1. Load up the China Shop Project.

2. Select the form by clicking on it with the mouse. Remember that you won't be able to open the Menu Editor if the form is not both displayed and selected.

3. Open the Menu Editor by selecting <u>T</u>ools-<u>M</u>enu Editor, by selecting the Menu Editor icon on the toolbar, by right-clicking on the form and selecting <u>M</u>enu Editor, or by pressing *Ctrl* and *E*.

4. With the Menu Editor open, enter &File as the Ca<u>p</u>tion property. This caption will designate the letter F as the access key for this menu item.

5. Either press the *Tab* key to move to the Na<u>m</u>e property or use your mouse to select it. **Do Not Press Enter.** Pressing *Enter* is the same as clicking on the <u>N</u>ext button and this action will add this menu item to the menu hierarchy before you've had a chance to complete the Na<u>m</u>e property.

6. Enter mnuFile in the Na<u>m</u>e property.

7. Since we have no more properties to designate for this menu item, press *Enter*. The menu item will be added to the menu control list box and an empty Properties window will appear for you to enter the next menu item:

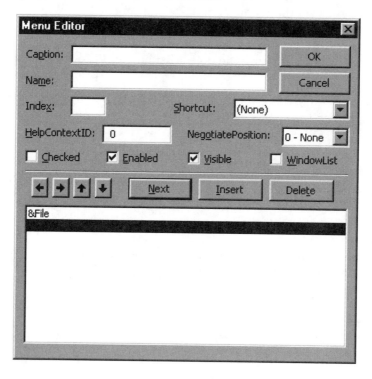

8.   The next menu item we'll add is a separator bar. Enter a hyphen (-) as the Caption property.

9.   Either press the *Tab* key to move to the Name property or use your mouse to select it. Enter mnuDash1 in the Name property.

10. Before we add the next menu item, we need to make the separator bar a submenu of the File menu. Select '-' in the menu control list box and then click on the right arrow. This will indent the separator bar and make it subordinate to the File menu item directly above it:

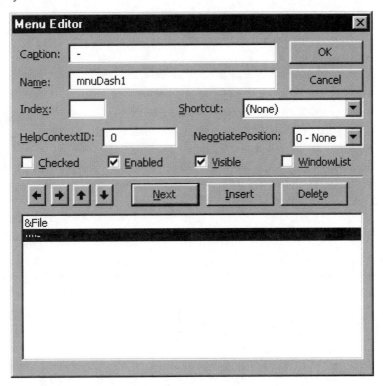

11. Click on the Next button to tell Visual Basic that you want to add a new menu item. An empty Properties window will appear. Notice how Visual Basic has automatically indented this menu item for you:

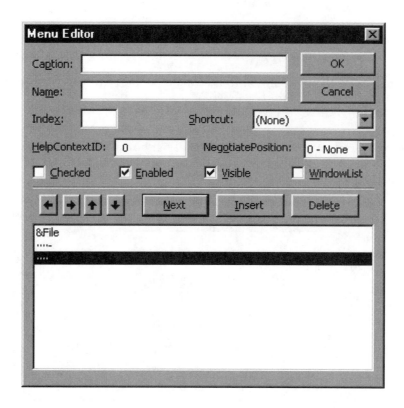

Note that if you click the Next button, Visual Basic automatically indents the next menu item to the level of the last item you entered. This can be time-saving, but sometimes it isn't what we want. Click on the left arrow to un-indent it to a top level menu item. By coincidence, clicking on a blank item doesn't offer this auto-indenting and saves you having to do this.

12. Enter E&xit in the Caption property. This caption will designate the letter x as the access key for this menu item.

13. Either press the *Tab* key to move to the Name property or use your mouse to select it. Enter mnuFileExit in the Name property:

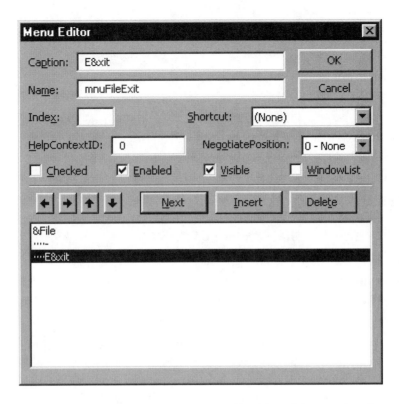

14. Do **not** press *Enter* as this is the last menu item we will add in this exercise. Instead, click on the OK button to save your changes and close the Menu Editor.

15. Save the China Shop Project by clicking on the Save icon.

16. Now run the program. You should have a menu with one top-level menu called File. If you click on the File menu item, you should see the Exit submenu:

You might also want to experiment with the access keys. At this point of course, clicking on the menu items doesn't do anything, but don't worry, we'll get to that in just a few moments.

Discussion

I told everyone that I decided to break the process of creating the China Shop menu into two exercises in order to give me a chance to check on everyone's progress and to make sure there were no major problems. As there were none we moved onto the next exercise:

Exercise

Completing the China Shop Menu

1. Stop the China Shop Project by clicking on the End button on the toolbar.

2. Select the form by clicking on it with the mouse. Remember that you won't be able to open the Menu Editor if the form is not both displayed and selected.

3. Open the Menu Editor.

4. When you open the Menu Editor you'll see the existing menu structure. The first menu item, File, will most likely already be selected in the menu control list box.

5. To add a new menu item, you'll either need to use the Next button to scroll past the three existing menu items in the menu control list box or use your mouse to select a blank menu item directly after the last one. Either way, an empty Properties window will appear.

6. Enter &Preferences as the Caption property. This will designate the letter P as the access key for this menu item.

7. Either press the *Tab* key to move to the Name property or use your mouse to select it. **Remember don't press Enter**.

8. Enter mnuPreferences as the Name property.

9. We have no more properties to designate for this menu item so press *Enter*. The menu item will be added to the menu control list box and an empty Properties window will appear for you to enter the next menu item. You should now have four menu items.

10. Add the fifth menu item, the Date and Time On submenu of the <u>P</u>references menu, by entering Date and Time On in the Ca<u>p</u>tion property. For this menu item, we will **not** designate an access key.

11. Press the *Tab* key to move to the Na<u>m</u>e property and enter mnuPreferencesDateandTimeOn in the Na<u>m</u>e property.

12. Date and Time On is a submenu of the <u>P</u>references menu so we need to indent it in the menu control list box. Select Date and Time On in the menu control list box and then click on the right arrow. This will indent the menu item and make it a submenu of the top-level <u>P</u>references menu item directly above it. Your menu hierarchy, as represented in the menu control list box, should be identical to this:

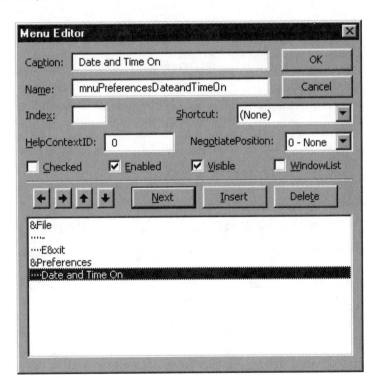

13. On your own, complete the remainder of the menu using the following table as your guide. Included in the table are the menu items we've already completed. Note that both Custom and Default are submenus of a submenu (Custom is a submenu of Colors which is a submenu of Preferences). Therefore, you'll need to indent these menu items twice.

Caption	Name	Submenu ?	Parent
&File	mnuFile	No	
-	mnuDash1	No	
E&xit	mnuFileExit	Yes	mnuFile
&Preferences	mnuPreferences	No	
Date and Time On	mnuPreferencesDateAndTimeOn	Yes	mnuPreferences
Date and Time Off	mnuPreferencesDateAndTimeOff	Yes	mnuPreferences
&Colors	mnuPreferencesColors	Yes	mnuPreferences
Custom	mnuColorsCustom	Yes	mnuColors
Default	mnuColorsDefault	Yes	mnuColors

14. When you have finished, your menu hierarchy should be identical to this screen. If anything is wrong, just select the menu item in the menu control list box and correct it:

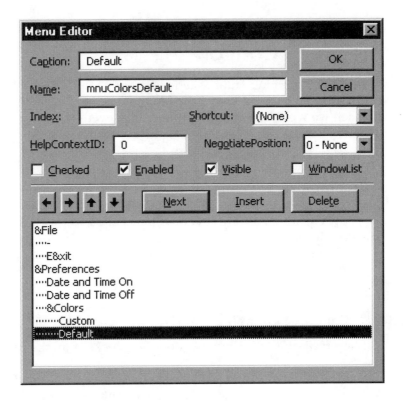

15. Click on the OK button to save your changes and close the Menu Editor.

16. Save the China Shop Project.

17. Run the program to verify the menu structure. Again, at this point, if you click on the menu items nothing happens, but it won't be long before we add code to fix that.

Discussion

As with the last exercise, there were very few problems, just a couple of typos here and there. It was time to move on to placing code in the Click event procedures of the menu items to make them functional.

Coding the Menu Control

It had been a pretty busy morning and I asked everyone to take a ten minute break. When they returned, I said that we would spend the remainder of the class completing a series of exercises in which we would place code in the Click event procedures of the menu items.

"Before we start to code the Click event procedures," I said, "we need to declare two form-level variables."

"We've already declared one of those, if I remember rightly," Kate said.

"That's right," I said. "We added a form-level variable called m_intQuantity a few weeks ago. Now we need to declare two additional form-level variables; one to hold the user's color preference and the other to hold the user's date and time display preference."

Exercise

Declaring Two Form-Level Variables

1. If the China Shop project is still running, stop it by clicking on the End button.

2. Double-click on the form to bring up the code window and find the General Declarations section of the form. It should already contain our first form-level variable declaration.

3. Enter the following code after the variable declaration for m_intQuantity:

```
Private m_intQuantity As Integer
Private m_lngBackColor As Long
Private m_blnDateDisplay As Boolean
```

4. Save the China Shop Project.

Discussion

"I know we've covered this," Ward said, "but what does the m prefix signify?"

"The m prefix signifies that this is a variable declared in the General Declarations section of a form module," I said.

I waited for more questions but there were none.

"We'll see shortly how these variables are used," I said, "but first, let's code the `Click` event procedure of the E<u>x</u>it menu item."

I then distributed the following exercise:

Exercise

Add Code to the Click Event Procedure of mnuFileExit

1. Make sure that the China Shop program is not running.

2. In design mode, click on the form's <u>F</u>ile - E<u>x</u>it menu item and the code window for the `Click` event procedure of `mnuFileExit` will open.

3. Place the following code in the `Click` event procedure of `mnuFileExit`:

```
Private Sub mnuFileExit_Click()
   Dim varResponse As Variant
   varResponse = InputBox("Enter a password in " & _
          "order to exit the program", "Exit the Program?")
   If varResponse = "061883" Then
      MsgBox "Thank you for using the China Shop Program!"
      Unload Me
   Else
      MsgBox "The password is not correct!"
   End If
End Sub
```

4. Save the China Shop Project.

5. Run the program and select <u>F</u>ile-E<u>x</u>it from the China Shop's menu. A dialog box will be displayed prompting you for a password:

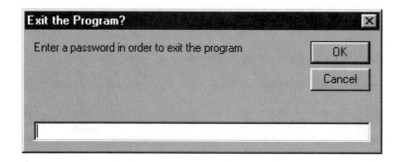

6.   Enter an incorrect password; this can be anything except 061883. A message will be displayed telling you that the password is incorrect:

7.   Enter the correct password, 061883, and a message will be displayed thanking you for using the China Shop program. The program will then end.

Discussion

In contrast to the last few exercises, there were quite a few questions at the conclusion of this one.

"In this exercise," I said, "we placed code in the Click event procedure of the Exit submenu which will prompt the user for a password and provided the correct password is entered, end the program. Prompting for a password is a good idea, particularly in a kiosk-style application, where invariably a user will either accidentally or intentionally try to exit the program."

I continued by explaining that there were two new Visual Basic statements introduced in this code, the Unload statement and the InputBox function.

"Let's examine the InputBox function first," I said. "The InputBox function is similar to a MsgBox function in that it displays a quick and dirty dialog box, containing an OK and a Cancel button. Unlike the MsgBox function, which is used only to display a message, the InputBox function has the ability to accept a response from the user, via a text box. The user's entry in the text box is then returned to the event procedure that called it and the result is usually stored in a variable."

"Is that why we declared the variable varResponse?" Ward asked.

```
Dim varResponse As Variant
```

"Yes," I replied, "the user can enter anything they want into the text box, so it makes sense to declare the variable to hold their response as a variant."

I continued by saying that this line of code is the line that triggers the display of the InputBox:

```
varResponse = InputBox("Enter a password in " & _
        "order to exit the program", "Exit the Program?")
```

"The InputBox function can have up to seven arguments, we used just two of them here. The first argument is the **prompt** that is displayed in the dialog box and the second is the **title** displayed in the dialog box."

"What happens after the user makes an entry in the text box and presses the *Enter* key?" Blaine asked.

"At that point," I answered, "whatever entry the user makes is returned to the variable varResponse. We then use an If statement to determine if the password they have entered is correct."

```
If varResponse = "061883" Then
    MsgBox "Thank you for using the China Shop Program!"
    Unload Me
Else
    MsgBox "The Password is not correct"
End If
```

"In this case, we're looking for the value 061883 as the correct password," I said. "If the value of varResponse is equal to that, then we display a message thanking the user for using the China Shop Program and then use the `Unload Me` statement to unload our form. When the last open form in a Visual Basic project is unloaded, the program ends. If the password the user entered is incorrect, we display a message telling them that they have entered an incorrect password and the event procedure ends."

"`Unload Me`?" Rhonda asked.

"The `Unload` statement is used to unload a form," I explained. "You could have written this instead:"

```
Unload frmMain
```

"However," I said, "you see the `Unload Me` syntax quite a bit and for that reason I wanted to show it to you here. `Me` here represents the form of our China Shop Project, `frmMain`. I can guarantee that you'll see `Me` sometime in the future when you're reading other programmer's code. Programmers love shortcuts and `Me` is shorter and quicker to type than an actual form name."

I concluded our discussion of the `InputBox` by stating that it does have some disadvantages.

- You can only use the `InputBox` function to accept a single piece of information from the user. For instance, you can ask the user to provide their name using an `InputBox`, but you cannot use it to accept both their name and age at the same time.

- You cannot perform validation on the entry the user makes in the text box until the user presses the *Enter* key and their entry is stored in the variable you have declared to hold the return value of the function. This is in contrast to the validation capability that exists by using the `KeyPress` event of the text box control.

- There is no `PasswordChar` property of the `InputBox` as there is with the text box control. The `PasswordChar` property of the text box control allows you to echo back a character, such as an asterisk, while the user is making an entry in the text box. The `InputBox` has no such capability.

"If you ask the user to enter a password," I said, "as we do here, anyone looking over their shoulder will see the password as they enter it into the `InputBox`."

"What's the alternative to using the `InputBox` function?" Dave asked.

"You could add another form to your project, that had one or more text boxes on it, in addition to a couple of command buttons and simulate the behavior of the `InputBox`. With your own form, you can overcome the deficiencies of the `InputBox`. As you can imagine, some programmers simply don't bother. It's easier to use the `InputBox` function."

I asked if there were any other questions.

"Isn't embedding the password in the code like this a bad idea?" Linda asked. "Suppose Mr. Bullina wants to change the password after we've installed the program in the shop?"

"You're right," I said. "Embedding the password in code like this isn't the greatest idea. I want to keep things as simple as possible for now. We could certainly think of alternatives to this, such as creating another disk file containing the password, but that would be one more file for the China Shop staff to manage. Let's agree to look at this as a future enhancement. I'm sure Mr. Bullina will want us to review how the program is working after a few months of operation as part of Phase 6 of the SDLC."

"What's the significance of the password?" Rhonda asked.

"A little mystery is a good thing," I said.

I then distributed this exercise:

Exercise

Add Code to the Timer Event Procedure of tmrChina

1. Make sure that the China Shop program is not running.

2. Double-click on the Timer control and place the following code into its `Timer` event procedure:

```
Private Sub tmrChina_Timer()
   lblDateAndTime.Caption = Now
End Sub
```

3. Save the China Shop Project.

4. Run the program. The date and time should be displayed in the label control's caption in the upper right hand portion of the China Shop form.

Discussion

I ran the program myself and, sure enough, the date and time were now displayed:

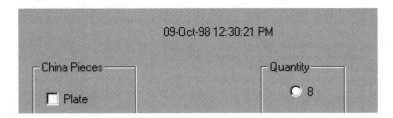

"I don't see a date and time," Ward said.

I took a quick walk over to Ward's workstation and we discovered that he had not set the `Interval` property of the Timer control when he placed it on the form.

"By default," I said, "the `Interval` property of the Timer control is 0, which means that the `Timer` event is never triggered. When we placed the Timer control on the form, we set it to 1000, which equates to one second."

"Can you explain this code?" Lou asked.

"Sure," I replied. "This single line of code takes the value of the system variable `Now`, which is your PC's date and time, and assigns it to the `Caption` property of the label control `lblDateAndTime`."

```
lblDateAndTime.Caption = Now
```

"What makes the date and time display change?" Steve said.

"Because we set the `Interval` property of the Timer control to 1000," I said, "the `Timer` event is triggered every second. Each time it's triggered, the code in the `Timer` event procedure assigns the current value of `Now` to the label's `Caption`. "

I waited for questions, but there were none.

"Now that we have the date and time displayed," I said, "we'll add code to the menu items that determine whether the user wants the date and time to be displayed."

Exercise
The Click Event Procedure of mnuPreferencesDateAndTimeOff

1. Make sure that the China Shop program is not running.

2. Click on the Date and Time Off menu item and the code window for its Click event procedure will open.

3. Enter the following code into the Click event procedure of mnuPreferencesDateAndTimeOff:

```
Private Sub mnuPreferencesDateAndTimeOff_Click()
    mnuPreferencesDateAndTimeOff.Checked = True
    mnuPreferencesDateAndTimeOn.Checked = False
    tmrChina.Enabled = False
    lblDateAndTime.Visible = False
    m_blnDateDisplay = False
End Sub
```

4. Save the China Shop Project.

5. Run the program. Select Preferences-Date and Time Off from the menu. When you do, the date and time will no longer be displayed. In addition, a check mark will be displayed next to the menu item in the Preferences menu. Unfortunately, selecting Preferences-Date and Time On will not re-display the date and time (not until you complete the next exercise anyway)!

Discussion

Many of the students seemed impressed with the bells and whistles we were adding to the China Shop Project. We only had one problem with the exercise. Several students accidentally placed the code in the mnuPreferencesDateAndTimeOn Click event procedure instead of mnuPreferencesDateAndTimeOff. A quick matter of a cut and paste took care of that problem.

I ran the program myself and selected Date and Time Off from the Preferences menu:

As promised, there was no longer a date and time display, but perhaps most impressive to everyone was the check mark next to **Date and Time Off** alerting the user to that fact.

"The first thing we did here was to update the Checked properties of mnuPreferencesDateAndTimeOff and mnuPreferencesDateAndTimeOn. Remember, if the Checked property of a menu item is set to True, that menu item will have a check mark displayed next to its Caption. When the users decide they do not want the date and time displayed, it makes sense to place a check mark next to the **Date and Time Off** menu item. We also remove the check mark from the **Date and Time On** menu item by setting its Checked property to False."

```
mnuPreferencesDateAndTimeOff.Checked = True
mnuPreferencesDateAndTimeOn.Checked = False
```

"Now we need to stop the display of the date and time," I said. "There were a number of ways we could have chosen to do this. We could have made the label control that displays the date and time invisible. We could have disabled the Timer control. We could also have set the Interval property of the Timer control to 0. The cleanest way, from my point of view, is to disable the Timer control and then make the label control invisible."

```
tmrChina.Enabled = False
lblDateAndTime.Visible = False
```

"By setting the Enabled property of the Timer control to False," I said, "we stop the Timer event from triggering, which prevents the code in the event procedure from executing. Now if we stop here, we will have stopped the date and time display from changing, but it would still be visible. For that reason, we must also make the label control invisible by setting its Visible property to False."

"Why didn't we just make the label control invisible and not worry about the Timer control?" Steve asked.

"It wouldn't be a great use of our system resources to have the `Timer` event triggering unnecessarily every second," I replied.

I waited for questions, but there were none.

"Finally," I said, "we set the form-level variable `m_blnDateDisplay` to `False`."

```
m_blnDateDisplay = False
```

"We'll see the importance of this variable later," I said. "It will be used by the `Load` event of the form to determine the initial setting of the date and time display, and also when we save the user's preferences to the Windows Registry."

"Now let's code the other related menu option:"

Exercise
Coding mnuPreferencesDateAndTimeOn's Click Event Procedure

1. Make sure that the China Shop program is not running.

2. Click on the Date and Time On menu item, the code window for its `Click` event procedure will open.

3. Enter the following code into the `Click` event procedure of `mnuPreferencesDateAndTimeOn`:

```
Private Sub mnuPreferencesDateAndTimeOn_Click()
    mnuPreferencesDateAndTimeOff.Checked = False
    mnuPreferencesDateAndTimeOn.Checked = True
    tmrChina.Enabled = True
    lblDateAndTime.Visible = True
    m_blnDateDisplay = True
End Sub
```

4. Save the China Shop Project.

5. Run the program and select Preferences-Date and Time Off from the menu to turn off the display of the date and time.

6. Now select Preferences-Date and Time On. When you do, the date and time will be displayed again. In addition, a check mark will be displayed next to Date and Time On.

Discussion

Again, everyone seemed to be pretty impressed with the progress they were making enhancing the user interface.

"I'm confused! Why, when we started the program, was the date and time still being displayed? At the end of the previous exercise, we had turned it off. Why didn't the program remember that?" Rhonda asked.

"In short," I answered, "because we haven't built that functionality into the program yet. Eventually, we'll save the value of the variable m_blnDateDisplay to the Windows Registry. Until then, our program isn't smart enough to remember the user's preferred settings when it starts up, but I guarantee we'll take care of that in our last class. For now though, our program will start up with the date and time displayed."

Rhonda and the rest of the class seemed satisfied with that explanation.

"This code," I continued, "is very similar to the code that turns off the display of the date and time. As we did with the code in the mnuPreferencesDateAndTimeOff event procedure, we update the Checked properties of mnuPreferencesDateAndTimeOff and mnuPreferencesDateAndTimeOn. This time, however, we want to place a check mark next to the Date and Time On caption and take the check mark off the Date and Time Off menu item."

```
mnuPreferencesDateAndTimeOff.Checked = False
mnuPreferencesDateAndTimeOn.Checked = True
```

"We had previously turned off the display of the date and time by disabling the Timer control and making the lblDateAndTime label control invisible, so we reverse those settings with this code," I explained.

```
tmrChina.Enabled = True
lblDateAndTime.Visible = True
```

"Finally, we set the form-level variable m_blnDateDisplay to True."

```
m_blnDateDisplay = True
```

I asked if there were any more questions about the menu items pertaining to the date and time display. There were none, so we began to discuss changing colors. I distributed the following exercise:

Exercise

The Click Event Procedure of mnuColorsCustom

1. Make sure that the China Shop program is not running.

2. Select <u>P</u>references-<u>C</u>olors-Custom and the code window for the Click event procedure of mnuColorsCustom will open.

3. Enter the following code into the Click event procedure of mnuColorsCustom:

```
Private Sub mnuColorsCustom_Click()
    dlgChina.ShowColor
    frmMain.BackColor = dlgChina.Color
    m_lngBackColor = frmMain.BackColor
End Sub
```

4. Save the China Shop Project.

5. Run the program. Select <u>P</u>references-<u>C</u>olors-Custom from the menu and the Color dialog box will be displayed. Select a color and click on the OK Button. The background color of the form will change.

Discussion

I immediately ran the program myself and selected <u>P</u>references-<u>C</u>olors-Custom from the main menu. The following dialog box was displayed:

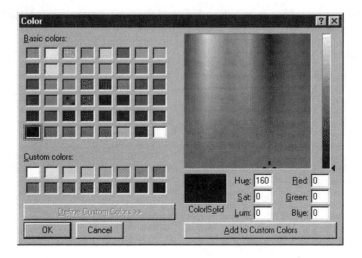

I selected one of the colors from the Color dialog box and the color of the form changed.

"Let's take a look at this code," I said. "This line of code is all it takes to display the Color dialog box of our Common Dialog control."

```
dlgChina.ShowColor
```

"The ShowColor method of the Common Dialog control, displays the Color dialog box," I explained. "Once the user has made a selection of a color and clicked on the OK button, that color selection is stored as a hexadecimal number in the Common Dialog's control Color property. At that point, all we need to do is set the BackColor property of the form equal to the Color property of the Common Dialog control."

```
frmMain.BackColor = dlgChina.Color
```

"Finally, we set the form-level variable m_lngBackColor equal to the new value of the BackColor property of the form."

```
m_lngBackColor = frmMain.BackColor
```

We'll store the value of m_lngBackColor in the Windows Registry and we'll read this value when our program starts up so that the user's preferred color will be displayed when the form loads.

"So at this point, if we change the color of the form, stop the program and then run it again, the color will go back to that that drab gray," Ward stated.

"That's right," I said. "Not until we save the user's preferred m_lngBackColor value in the Windows Registry and then write code to read that value when the program starts up, will the user's preferred color be saved."

"What happens if the user clicks the Cancel button instead of the OK button?" Joe asked. "I just did that and an error message was displayed."

"That's an excellent point, Joe," I said.

I reminded everyone that quite a few weeks ago, we changed the CancelError property of the Common Dialog to True. "This causes an error to be generated whenever the user selects the Cancel button of the Color dialog box," I explained.

I then selected <u>C</u>olors-Custom and clicked on the Cancel button on the Color dialog box. The following screen was displayed:

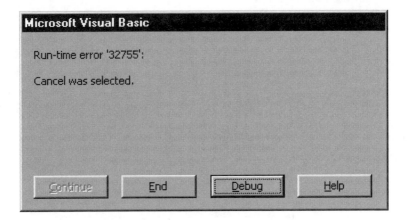

As a demonstration, I stopped the program and changed the CancelError property of the Common Dialog control to False. I then ran the program, selected <u>C</u>olors-Custom and clicked on the Cancel button in the Color dialog box. This time no error was generated, but the color of the China Shop form changed to black!

"We'll take care of the error message in two weeks, when we discuss error handling in Visual Basic," I explained.

I then changed the CancelError property of the Common Dialog control back to True.

"We have one more menu item to add code to," I said, "the <u>C</u>olors-Default menu item which will change the color of the form back to its default color."

Exercise

The Click Event Procedure of mnuColorsDefault

1. Make sure that the China Shop program is not running.

2. Click on <u>P</u>references-<u>C</u>olors-Default and the code window for the Click event procedure of mnuColorsDefault will open.

3.   Enter the following code into the `Click` event procedure of `mnuColorsDefault`:

```
Private Sub mnuColorsDefault_Click()
    frmMain.BackColor = &H8000000F
    m_lngBackColor = frmMain.BackColor
End Sub
```

4.   Save the China Shop Project.

5.   Run the program. Select Preferences-Colors-Custom and change the color of the form.

6.   Now select Preferences-Colors-Default. When you do, the background color of the form will change back to its default color.

Discussion

Again, everyone seemed to be excited about the enhancements they were making to the user interface of the China Shop Project. I explained that changing the color of the form back to its default value was just due to a single line of code:

```
frmMain.BackColor = &H8000000F
```

"What is that strange number?" Rhonda asked.

"That is a hexadecimal number," I said. "Hexadecimal is just another number system like binary or decimal. You can recognize a hexadecimal number in Visual Basic as it will be preceded by "&H". The number tells Visual Basic to set the `BackColor` property of the form back to the default color. We then set the value of the variable `m_lngBackColor` equal to the `BackColor` property of the form."

```
m_lngBackColor = frmMain.BackColor
```

I explained that we would eventually make use of this form-level variable to load the user's preferred color when we load the China Shop form. At this point, there were no more questions, so we took a break.

"When you come back from the break, we'll create a pop-up menu and spend a few minutes discussing Visual Basic's `MsgBox` function," I said.

Pop-Up Menus

I began our discussion of **pop-up menus** after everyone returned from break.

"The menus that we have created so far today, have all been of the drop-down variety," I said. "As I mentioned earlier though, there is another type of Visual Basic menu called the pop-up menu. The pop-up menu is a type of floating menu that is displayed over the form. By convention, pop-up menus are displayed when the user clicks on the right mouse button. You can vary the pop-up menu displayed, depending upon where the mouse pointer is located over the form when the right mouse button is clicked. For this reason, pop-up menus are sometimes called **context menus**."

I explained that many users habitually right-click their mouse buttons, looking for context sensitive help or shortcuts. Most times, but not always, the menu items that appear on a pop-up menu also appear on the program's menu bar. Pop-up menus provide a shortcut to the user, reducing the number of clicks necessary to navigate to a deeply nested menu item.

"Displaying a pop-up menu in Visual Basic isn't difficult at all, you just use the `PopupMenu` method to display the menu," I explained.

I displayed the syntax for the `PopupMenu` method on the classroom projector:

```
object.PopupMenu menuname
```

"What does `object` refer to here?" Steve asked.

"`object`," I said, "is the name of the form upon which you wish to display the menu item and `menuname` is the name of the menu item you wish to display. For instance to display the `mnuPreferences` menu item in the China Shop Project as a pop-up menu, the syntax could be:"

```
frmMain.PopupMenu mnuPreferences
```

If you leave off the object `frmMain`, Visual Basic will assume the current form.

"If you pop-up a top-level menu, will the submenus also be displayed?" Dave asked.

"Yes, they will," I said. "In fact, that's exactly what we'll do in the next exercise."

"Where do we place the code to display the pop-up menu?" Kathy asked.

"Code to display a pop-up menu is usually placed in the MouseUp event of a form or a control. Since virtually every object in Visual Basic has a MouseUp event, this gives you the ability to display multiple pop-up menus in your program, depending upon where the mouse pointer is when the right-mouse button is clicked. For instance, in the China Shop Project we could display a pop-up menu when the right mouse button is clicked over the form, another when clicked over the Check Box control array and still another when clicked over the list box."

Exercise

Creating a Pop-Up Menu in the China Shop Project

1. Make sure that the China Shop program is not running.

2. Double-click on the form to open up the code window. Carefully find the MouseUp event of the form by selecting **Form** in the object list box and **MouseUp** in the procedure list box:

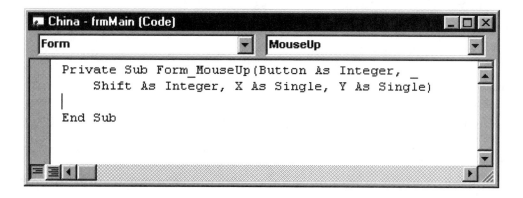

3. Enter the following code into the MouseUp event of the form:

```
Private Sub Form_MouseUp(Button As Integer, _
      Shift As Integer, X As Single, Y As Single)
   If Button = vbRightButton Then
      PopupMenu mnuPreferences
   End If
End Sub
```

4. Save the China Shop Project.

5. Run the program. Click the right mouse button over an open area of the form. Be careful not to click on the empty image control. The Preferences menu will appear as a pop-up menu, exactly where you right-clicked the mouse. If you wish, change some of the preferences.

Discussion

A few students had problems running the program after they'd finished coding it.

"I right-clicked the mouse, but I didn't get a pop-up menu to display," Ward said.

A quick trip to his workstation revealed that he was not clicking over the form, but actually clicking over one of the controls on the form.

"Remember that we placed the code in the MouseUp event of the Form. If you right-click the mouse over one of the other objects on the form, that object's MouseUp event will be triggered, not the form's MouseUp event."

"What is the significance of vbRightButton?" Steve asked.

"The MouseUp event procedure is passed a parameter telling you which mouse button the user clicked. vbRightButton is a Visual Basic **intrinsic constant.** It's equal to the number 2, which is the number passed to the MouseUp event procedure when the user clicks the right mouse button."

"We use an If statement to determine if the right mouse button has been pressed and if it has we invoke the PopUpMenu method of the form," I explained.

```
If Button = vbRightButton Then
   PopupMenu mnuPreferences
End If
```

I asked if there were any questions, but there weren't any.

"We have one more topic to cover today. We're going to spend a few minutes taking a more in-depth look at the MsgBox function," I said.

More on the MsgBox Function

I started my discussion of the MsgBox function by saying that although we had used it quite a bit throughout the course, we really had only scratched the surface of what it can do.

"For instance, every message box that we've displayed so far has had only one button. We can actually display as many as three buttons with the MsgBox function and use the return value of the MsgBox function to determine which button the user clicked."

"I thought all the MsgBox function could do was display a message and an OK button," said Barbara.

The Return Value of the MsgBox Function

"The message box can display as many as three buttons and a title. Here's the syntax for the MsgBox function:"

```
MsgBox (prompt[, buttons] [, title])
```

"Only the **prompt** argument is required," I explained. "The **buttons** and **title** arguments are optional. Let's practice using the MsgBox function."

Exercise
Using the MsgBox Function

1. Create a new Standard.EXE project.

2. Place a command button on the form. Type the following code in its Click event procedure:

```
MsgBox "I love Visual Basic"
```

3. Save the program in your VBFILES\PRACTICE folder. Save the form as
    MsgBox_Trials.frm and the project as MsgBox_Trials.vbp. We'll amend this project in
    the next few examples.

As the code in these examples is minimal, and as we change it so often, we haven't
included these examples on the CD.

4. Run the program and click on the command button:

"The title of the message box defaults to the project name, Project1, because I didn't specify
a title argument," I explained. "Now let's add a title argument."

5. Modify the code to look like this:

```
MsgBox "I love Visual Basic",,"Programming is Fun"
```

6. Save the project. Now run the project again and click on the command button:

"Does everyone see the effect of coding the title argument?" I asked. "Now I have a title of my own choosing."

"I see that, but what is that extra comma for?" Rhonda asked.

"Good question," I said. "The syntax of the MsgBox function calls for the buttons argument to appear between the prompt argument and the title argument. In Visual Basic procedures and functions, optional arguments always appear last in the argument list, following the required arguments. It's OK not to specify any optional arguments, but if you specify optional argument #2 for instance, you either need to specify optional argument #1 or place a comma there as a placeholder."

"So the comma is acting as a placeholder for the buttons argument." Rhonda observed.

"Excellent," I said. "That's right. In fact, during our last week of class, I'll show you how to write your own procedures and functions and specify optional arguments of your own."

I continued by explaining that the buttons argument is a number, which is calculated by adding four other numbers together.

"The first number," I said, "represents the buttons that you want to display in the message box. The second number represents the kind of icon you wish to display. The third number represents the button that is to be the default button. The final number represents the message box's **modality**."

"Here are the possible values for each one of the four numbers," I said:

Intrinsic Constant	Value	Description
vbOKOnly	0	Display OK button only
vbOKCancel	1	Display OK and Cancel buttons
vbAbortRetryIgnore	2	Display the Abort, Retry and Ignore buttons

vbYesNoCancel	3	Display Yes, No and Cancel buttons
vbYesNo	4	Display Yes and No buttons
vbRetryCancel	5	Display Retry and Cancel buttons
vbCritical	16	Display Critical Message icon
vbQuestion	32	Display Query Message icon
vbExclamation	48	Display Warning Message icon
vbInformation	64	Display Information Message icon
vbDefaultButton1	0	First button is default
vbDefaultButton2	256	Second button is default
vbDefaultButton3	512	Third button is default
vbApplicationModal	0	The user must respond to the message box before continuing work in the current application
vbSystemModal	4096	All applications are suspended until the user responds to the message box

"Notice that the table is made up of four distinct sections," I said.

"The buttons argument is the sum of the values from each one of these four sections. The buttons argument is almost like an à la carte menu at your favorite restaurant. You pick a value from each section, add them up and specify that value as the buttons argument for the MsgBox function."

I waited for this to sink in.

"Suppose," I continued, "you wanted to display a message box that had **Abort**, **Retry** and **Ignore** buttons, with a Critical Message icon, where the **Retry** button, the second button, is the default and you wanted the message box to be system modal. There are actually two ways of coding that; by using the values from the table, or by specifying the intrinsic constants from the table."

I displayed the following graphic on the classroom projector:

Condition	Intrinsic Constant	Value
Abort,Retry,Ignore buttons	`vbAbortRetryIgnore`	2
Critical Message Icon	`vbCritical`	16
Button #2 is default	`vbDefaultButton2`	256
System Modal	`vbSystemModal`	4096
Total		**4370**

"Notice that I am displaying a value from each one of the four sections and then adding up those values," I explained. "If I then specify `4370` as the buttons value for my `MsgBox` function, I'll display a message box with exactly those characteristics I desired."

"Is that it?" Barbara asked. "You just add up the numbers?"

"That's right," I replied.

Exercise

Pushing the MsgBox Function to the Edge

1.   Modify the code in your current `MsgBox_Trials` project to look like this:

```
MsgBox "I love Visual Basic",4370,"Programming is Fun"
```

2.   Now re-run the program and click on the command button:

3. Click on any of the buttons to close the message box.

Discussion

I explained that I could alternatively have coded it like this, using intrinsic constants:

```
MsgBox "I love VisualBasic", vbAbortRetryIgnore + _
     vbCritical + vbDefaultButton2 + vbSystemModal, _
     "Programming is Fun"
```

"You can add the values like that?" Ward asked.

"Yes," I said, "the buttons argument is looking for any expression that evaluates to a number. Adding Visual Basic intrinsic constants is perfectly fine."

"Why is it that even though we displayed three buttons, we didn't have to set up a variable to handle the return value?" Dave asked.

"That's an excellent question," I said. "In Visual Basic, you have the option of discarding the return value when you call a function. The bottom line is that if you do not place parentheses around the argument list, you tell Visual Basic you are not interested in the return value."

I quickly changed the code to look like this:

```
MsgBox ("I love VisualBasic", vbAbortRetryIgnore + _
     vbCritical + vbDefaultButton2 + vbSystemModal, _
     "Programming is Fun")
```

"By placing parentheses around the argument list, we're telling Visual Basic that we are interested in the return value from this function," I explained. "If we don't use the return value in an expression, then Visual Basic will flag this statement as a syntax error."

Even before I could run the code, Visual Basic had generated the following error:

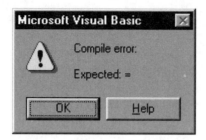

"Visual Basic," I said, "is telling us that we need to use the return value from this function in an expression or to store the return value in a variable."

Exercise

Pushing the MsgBox Function to the Edge with a Variable

1. Modify the `MsgBox_Trials` code again, so that it looks like this:

```
Private Sub Command1_Click()
Dim varValue As Variant
    varValue = MsgBox("I love VisualBasic", _
           vbAbortRetryIgnore + vbCritical + _
           vbDefaultButton2 + vbSystemModal, _
           "Programming is Fun")
    Debug.Print varValue
End Sub
```

2. Re-run the project. Click on the Abort button when the message box is displayed. The number 3 will be displayed in the Immediate window.

Discussion

"What's the number 3 for?" Rhonda asked.

"That's the return value from the `MsgBox` function," I replied. "That means that the Abort key had been clicked by the user."

"Is there a list of possible return values from the MsgBox function?" Dave asked.

"Yes there is," I said as I displayed the list on the classroom projector:

Constant	Value	Description
VbOK	1	OK
VbCancel	2	Cancel
VbAbort	3	Abort
VbRetry	4	Retry
VbIgnore	5	Ignore
VbYes	6	Yes
VbNo	7	No

I asked if there were any more questions, but there were none. Prior to dismissing class, I told everyone that next week's class would be pretty intense as we would be examining variable arrays.

Summary

In this chapter, we spent some time enhancing the visual interface of our China Project. In the process, we discussed creating drop-down menus using the Visual Basic Menu Editor and coding a pop-up menu in the code window. We also learned more about the MsgBox function and how to adapt it to fit a particular function.

Specifically, we covered:

- Using the Visual Basic Menu Editor to construct drop-down menu items
- Adding Captions, Names, and Shortcuts to the menu items that we built
- Using the Menu Editor's navigation buttons to change the location and seniority of menu items
- Creating Pop-Up Menus
- How to create customized message boxes

The user interface is an important part of your application. A user likes to feel like the application knows what it's doing. Even if you think that you will be the only person to use your program, you'll find that it's a lot nicer to have something that behaves like a well-polished application at your fingertips – even more so if you know that you've created it yourself!

In the next chapter we're going to take a look at arrays, and see how they can help us in our programming.

Quiz

1. In Visual Basic, there are two types of menus. Can you name both of them?

2. True or False: The Menu Editor can be invoked by using the *Ctrl* + *M* key combination.

3. If you wanted to create a menu option named File where the access key is *Alt* + *F*, how should the caption read?

4. If you wanted to create a menu option named Exit where the access key is *Alt* + *X*, how should the caption read?

5. Can more than one menu option have the same shortcut key?

6. How do you create a separator bar for a menu?

7. True or False: A menu option specified as a separator bar does not require an entry for name.

8. What events does the menu control respond to?

9. What does the 'checked' property of a menu item do?

10. Can you have more than one Pop-Up Menu displayed at any given moment?

11. True or False: In order for a Pop-Up Menu to appear, the menu item must be designed using the menu editor.

12. To how many levels can a menu be nested?

13. How do you bring up the code window for a menu item?

14. What is the function of the Insert button in the Menu Editor?

15. Can a menu item have the same name as another?

Extra Credit – If an electric train is traveling Northwest at 80 MPH, and there is a Southwest breeze of 15 MPH, in which direction does the smoke from the train blow?

Chapter 13
Arrays

In this chapter, we'll see how array processing can make long, tedious programming chores easier to handle.

I began the next class by telling everyone that today would be devoted to **variable arrays**.

"Is a variable array different to a control array?" Rhonda asked.

"Yes," I replied. "A control array is a collection of controls that are placed on a form. A variable array is a collection of variables, stored in RAM, with the same name, each of which is uniquely identified by a **subscript.** (You may see this referred to as an **index**. I prefer to keep the term 'subscript' because 'index' has many other meanings, and they're easily confused). Each variable in the collection is said to be an **element** of the array. In the world of programming, solutions to certain kinds of programming problems lend themselves quite nicely to the use of variable arrays, which we'll refer to as arrays from here on in."

Why Do We Need Arrays?

"Last Wednesday evening I gave a midterm examination to my Database Administration class," I explained. "I want to write a program to calculate the class average for the midterm examination. Let's keep it simple by pretending that I have only six students in the class. Does anyone have any ideas as to how we should begin to write the program?"

"I guess one way to do it would be to create a form with six text boxes and a command button," Rhonda suggested. "You could then enter the grades into the six text boxes and when you click on the command button, we could display the average of the six grades."

"That would work," I said. "I term that the brute force method. Now suppose I told you that my Database Management class really has 150 students. Now what?"

"I think we need to find a better approach," Rhonda replied. "I don't think we want to place 150 text boxes on a form!"

"That better approach is through the use of arrays," I said. "However, before we start to discuss arrays in detail, I first want to give you an understanding of how tedious programming would be without them. Let's code the brute force method in this exercise:"

Exercise

Brute Force - Life without Arrays

1. Start a new **Standard.EXE** project.

2. Place six text boxes on the form.

3. Place a command button on the form and accept the default name that Visual Basic assigns.

4. Change the **Name** properties of the six text boxes to **txtGrade1**, **txtGrade2**, **txtGrade3**, **txtGrade4**, **txtGrade5** and **txtGrade6**.

5. Clear the **Text** properties of the six text boxes.

6. Double-click on the command button and place the following code into its **Click** event procedure:

```
Private Sub Command1_Click()
   Dim sngAverage As Single
   Dim intGrade1 As Integer
   Dim intGrade2 As Integer
   Dim intGrade3 As Integer
   Dim intGrade4 As Integer
   Dim intGrade5 As Integer
   Dim intGrade6 As Integer
   If txtGrade1.Text = "" Or txtGrade2.Text = "" Or _
         txtGrade3.Text = "" Or txtGrade4.Text = "" Or _
         txtGrade5.Text = "" Or txtGrade6.Text = "" Then
      MsgBox "You must fill in all 6 grades"
      Exit Sub
   End If
```

```
    intGrade1 = txtGrade1.Text
    intGrade2 = txtGrade2.Text
    intGrade3 = txtGrade3.Text
    intGrade4 = txtGrade4.Text
    intGrade5 = txtGrade5.Text
    intGrade6 = txtGrade6.Text
    sngAverage = (intGrade1 + intGrade2 + intGrade3 + _
          intGrade4 + intGrade5 + intGrade6) / 6
    Form1.Print "The class average is " & sngAverage

End Sub
```

7. Save the project in your **\VBFiles\Practice** subdirectory. Save the form as **average.frm** and the project as **midterm.vbp**. Now run the program.

8. Enter the following grades into the six text boxes: 90, 91, 80, 77, 100 and 44. Then click on the command button. The average 80.33334 will be printed on the form.

Discussion

Everyone agreed that the code in this exercise did what every good program must do, it worked. Beyond that, it had been an extremely tedious exercise to code.

"Let's take a look at the code now," I said. "As usual, the first thing we do is to declare any variables that we will need to use in the event procedure."

```
Dim sngAverage As Single
Dim intGrade1 As Integer
Dim intGrade2 As Integer
Dim intGrade3 As Integer
Dim intGrade4 As Integer
Dim intGrade5 As Integer
Dim intGrade6 As Integer
```

"I mentioned earlier in the course that it's a good practice to perform arithmetic operations on variable values, not property values," I reminded them. "That's why we have declared a variable to hold the **Text** property of each one of the six text boxes. In addition, we have also declared a variable to hold the result of our calculation."

"Single, that's a data type with a fractional part, isn't it?" Blaine asked.

"That's right," I answered. "We want to calculate the average as precisely as possible so we need to declare a variable that can handle fractions."

I explained that in the next section of code, we do the same type of validation we've been performing on text boxes throughout the course to ensure that a grade has been entered into each text box:

```
If txtGrade1.Text = "" Or txtGrade2.Text = "" Or _
      txtGrade3.Text = "" Or txtGrade4.Text = "" Or _
      txtGrade5.Text = "" Or txtGrade6.Text = "" Then
   MsgBox "You must fill in all 6 grades"
   Exit Sub
End If
```

"This next section of code takes the `Text` property of each text box and assigns that value to a variable," I explained.

```
intGrade1 = txtGrade1.Text
intGrade2 = txtGrade2.Text
intGrade3 = txtGrade3.Text
intGrade4 = txtGrade4.Text
intGrade5 = txtGrade5.Text
intGrade6 = txtGrade6.Text
```

"Here's the bread and butter of the code," I continued, "the calculation of the average. We calculate the class average by adding the values of the six variables and then dividing by six. The result of that calculation is stored in the variable `sngAverage`."

```
sngAverage = (intGrade1 + intGrade2 + intGrade3 + intGrade4 _
      + intGrade5 + intGrade6) / 6
```

"Finally, we print the result on the form, concatenating the value of the variable to the message," I added.

```
Form1.Print "The class average is " & sngAverage
```

"I think you're all pretty comfortable with this code," I said. "There's really nothing here we haven't seen before."

I then made a startling suggestion.

"Let's modify this code to calculate the class average for a class with 500 students."

"I know you're kidding," Joe said.

"Well, I am...and then again I'm not. Suppose we really did have that problem to solve? Could we do it?" I asked.

Everyone agreed that modifying the code in this exercise to calculate the class average for 500 students would be a nightmare.

"For one thing," Kate said, "we would need 500 text boxes and 500 variables to store the values of the **Text** properties."

"We can't fit that many text boxes on a single form," Barbara said.

"Plus we would need to change the **Name** properties of 500 text boxes and clear the **Text** properties of 500 text boxes," Chuck added.

What's an Array?

"All of your points are excellent ones," I said. "You now understand the type of problem that lends itself to array processing. An array can make this problem much easier to solve."

"Is an array a separate data type, like an integer or a single?" Peter asked.

"Many beginners make the mistake of thinking of an array as a separate data type," I said, "but they're just a special implementation of a regular data type. For instance, there are integer arrays, string arrays and even date arrays. In the past, some of my students have warmed to the hotel analogy."

"The hotel analogy?" Rhonda asked.

"That's right," I said. "Start out by thinking of an ordinary variable as a placeholder in RAM with a single floor. An array, on the other hand, is a placeholder in RAM with more than one floor and each floor has a floor number, just like a hotel."

"I'm not much of an artist, but here goes," I replied:

		5	44
		4	100
		3	77
		2	80
		1	91
90		0	90
intGrade			intGrades

"Let's stick with the previous example of six midterm grades," I said. "On the left, we have an ordinary integer variable called `intGrade`. On the right, we have an array of integer variables called `intGrades`. As you can see, the variable on the left can hold only one value at one time and it contains the first midterm grade. However, the array on the right contains all 6 midterm grades."

"What are those numbers to the left of the grades?" Barbara asked.

"In keeping with the hotel analogy," I said. "Those are the floor numbers, or in computer terms, the subscripts. The subscript uniquely identifies the element within the array."

"Why does the first floor begin with 0?" Ward said. "Let me guess, that's the basement?"

"As we've seen throughout the course," I replied, "many numbers in the computer world begin with 0. An array is no different. By default, the first floor of an array begins with the number 0."

"The bottom element is technically called the **lower bound** of the array and the top element is called the **upper bound** of the array," I explained.

I told everyone that it is possible to number the elements of an array so that they begin with 1 instead of 0.

"We all know about the `Option Explicit` statement," I said. "As it turns out, there is another `Option` statement that can be placed in the General Declarations section called `Option`

Base. The `Option Base` statement is used to specify the lower bound of an array. If you code the following statement in the General Declarations section, all arrays declared on that form will be numbered starting at 1."

```
Option Base 1
```

Declaring an Array

"How do you declare an array; is it different to declaring an ordinary variable?" Steve asked.

"There are actually two ways of declaring an array," I replied. "You can declare an array as a **static array** or as a **dynamic array**. Dynamic arrays are a little more complicated than static arrays and we'll cover them a little later in today's class."

"The word static in static array means **unchanging**," I explained. "Once you declare a static array, there is no way to change the lower or upper bounds of the array. That is, the number of elements in a static array can never change."

"Declaring a static array isn't much different to declaring an ordinary variable," I continued, "you just need to let Visual Basic know up front how many elements the array will contain. Here's the array declaration for `intGrades`:"

```
Dim intGrades(5) as Integer
```

"What's that number in the parentheses?" Ward asked. "Is that the number of elements in the array?"

"No," I replied, "that's what most beginners think at first. The number in parentheses is the upper bound, or top floor, of the array. If the array is numbered beginning from 0, then the lower bound of the array is 0, with an upper bound of 5, and there will be a total of 6 elements in this array."

"Some programmers prefer the certainty of knowing the upper and lower bound of an array declaration when they see it," I continued. "For that reason, they choose to explicitly code both the lower bound and the upper bound of an array when they declare it."

I then displayed this array declaration:

```
Dim intGrades(0 to 5) as Integer
```

"This declaration explicitly tells Visual Basic to declare an integer array, where the lower bound is 0 and the upper bound is 5," I said.

"Now take a look at this declaration," I continued:

```
Dim intEmployeeNumbers (1001 to 3000) as Integer
```

"Using your hotel analogy the starting floor number is numbered 1001 and the top floor is number 3000," Mary observed.

"Very good," I said. "What you have here is an array with a lower bound of 1001 and an upper bound of 3000, for a total of 2000 elements."

"Why would you number the elements in an array like that?" Barbara asked.

"Programmers frequently number arrays to represent real-world conditions," I replied. "Suppose you want to create an array to hold employee information in your company and you want to use the subscript of the array to represent employee ID numbers. Further, suppose that the valid employee ID numbers at your company are 1001 to 3000. It makes sense to number the array elements starting at 1001 and ending at 3000. Numbering the elements in the array like that can make working with the array elements much easier when you start referring to them in code. For instance, if Joe Smith has an employee ID number of 1129, you know that the information about him is stored in array element 1129."

"To make things simpler we shall only use arrays with a lower bound of zero in the rest of this course," I explained, "but of course you can use any lower bound you wish when you write your own code."

"What happens if you declare an array like we just did and then in code you try to refer to an element that doesn't exist?" Dave asked.

"You'll receive the following error message," I answered. I took a minute or two to quickly reproduce Dave's question in Visual Basic and then I ran the program:

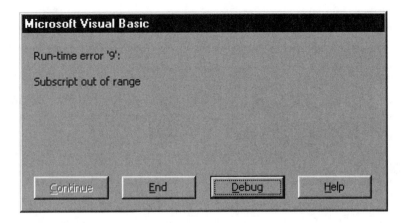

I waited for questions, but there were no more. I think everyone, for the moment anyway, felt pretty comfortable with declaring a static array.

Referring to Elements of an Array

As there were no more questions about declaring arrays, it was time to move onto the subject of working with them in code.

"Just as it's important to be able to refer to an ordinary variable in code, it's equally important that we be able to refer to a particular element in an array. We do this by using the array name with the subscript written within parentheses. For example, we would use this code to refer to the element of **intGrades** that contains the midterm grade of 80:"

```
intGrades(2)
```

"Can you assign values to an element of an array in the same way?" Steve asked.

"Yes you can," I replied. "Again, just use the subscript of the array within parentheses. Use this syntax to assign the value 80 to subscript 2 of the array **intGrades**:"

```
intGrades(2) = 80
```

I pointed out that you are not restricted to using numeric literals when referring to subscripts of an array.

"You can use any expression within the parentheses, as long as the expression evaluates to a valid subscript number." I explained. "For instance, provided the value of intCounter is a valid subscript number, this is a valid assignment statement:"

```
intGrades(intCounter) = 80
```

"I have a exercise for you to do which will give you a chance to use an array to perform the same average calculation we did in the last exercise:"

Exercise

Our First Look at Arrays

1. Start a new Standard.EXE project.

2. Place a command button on the form and accept the default name that Visual Basic assigns.

3. Double-click on the command button and place the following code into its Click event procedure:

```
Private Sub Command1_Click()
    Dim intGrades(5) As Integer
    Dim intGradeCounter As Integer
    Dim intTotal As Integer
    Dim sngAverage As Single
    intGrades(0) = 90
    intGrades(1) = 91
    intGrades(2) = 80
    intGrades(3) = 77
    intGrades(4) = 100
    intGrades(5) = 44
    For intGradeCounter = 0 To 5
        Form1.Print intGrades(intGradeCounter)
        intTotal = intTotal + intGrades(intGradeCounter)
    Next
    sngAverage = (intTotal / intGradeCounter)
    Form1.Print "The class average is " & sngAverage
End Sub
```

4. Save the project in your \VBFiles\Practice subdirectory. Save the form as average2.frm and the project as midterm2.vbp. Now run the program.

5.   Click on the command button. The numbers 90, 91, 80, 77, 100 and 44 will be printed on the form, along with the average 80.33334:

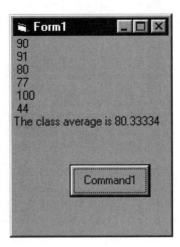

Discussion

"As usual," I said, "we declare any variables that we will need to use in the event procedure. This line of code declares a static array called **intGrades** consisting of 6 elements, where the lower bound is 0 and the upper bound is 5:"

```
Dim intGrades(5) As Integer
```

"We now declare our variables. **intGradeCounter** is a loop counter variable, and **intTotal** and **sngAverage** are used to calculate the class average," I explained.

```
Dim intGradeCounter As Integer
Dim intTotal As Integer
Dim sngAverage As Single
```

"The next six lines of code load the elements of the **intGrades** array," I said.

```
intGrades(0) = 90
intGrades(1) = 91
intGrades(2) = 80
intGrades(3) = 77
intGrades(4) = 100
intGrades(5) = 44
```

"At this point," I continued, "we now have an array with six elements loaded. We can now use the following **For...Next** loop technique to print each element of the array on the form and add the values to the variable **intTotal**:"

```
For intGradeCounter = 0 To 5
   Form1.Print intGrades(intGradeCounter)
   intTotal = intTotal + intGrades(intGradeCounter)
Next
```

"Within the body of the loop, we use the **Print** method of the form to print the value of the array element," I explained. "Notice that the loop counter variable is used to specify the subscript of the array element to print."

```
Form1.Print intGrades(intGradeCounter)
```

"After we have printed the value of the array element, we add it to the value of the variable **intTotal**," I continued. "**intTotal** thus maintains a running total of the array elements we have printed on the form."

```
intTotal = intTotal + intGrades(intGradeCounter)
```

I explained that the first time through the loop, this statement was interpreted by Visual Basic as this:

```
intTotal = intTotal + intGrades(0)
```

This can also be written as this:

```
intTotal = 0 + 90
```

The second time through the loop, it was interpreted by Visual Basic as:

```
intTotal = intTotal + intGrades(1)
```

or:

```
intTotal = 90 + 91
```

This was repeated until all the elements of the array had been processed.

"This line of code calculates the average once the loop processing has ended," I explained. "Remember that `intTotal` is the running total of all the scores and `intGradeCounter` is a loop counter variable that counts the number of grades."

```
sngAverage = (intTotal / intGradeCounter)
```

This line of code prints the class average on the form:

```
Form1.Print "The class average is " & sngAverage
```

"Something is bothering me," Dave said. "The calculation of the class average works, but I don't quite understand why. The class average is equal to the sum of the grades divided by the number of grades entered. In this case, 6. Isn't the value of `intGradeCounter` at the end of the loop equal to 5?"

"That's a good question," I said, "but you're forgetting about the behavior of the `For…Next` loop. After the iteration of the loop where the final grade is printed, the `Next` statement causes the value of `intGradeCounter` to be incremented by 1. At that point, its value becomes 6. The `For` statement then compares the value of `intGradeCounter` to the end parameter of the loop, which is 5, and because it is greater, the loop ends."

That seemed to satisfy Dave.

"I understand what is happening here. My only question is why we would use this technique to load the elements of an array." Steve said.

"That's a good question, Steve. The reason is because programmers frequently declare arrays to hold information of a reference variety," I replied. "For instance, you might declare an array in your program to hold the fifty United States or the twelve months of the year or the thirteen branches of your company. Once this data is present in your program, you can use array processing to access it quickly."

"So data loaded into an array in this manner would most likely be used for the convenience of the programmer," Chuck observed.

"That's right," I agreed. "Let's take a look at another method to load the elements of an array that is similar to the one we just looked at in this exercise."

The Array Function

There were no more questions, so I moved on to the topic of loading values into an array.

"In the last exercise, the values of the array were entered by the programmer, but that is not always the case," I explained. "The array can be loaded from a file for example; a technique we'll use later today in the China Shop Project."

> We won't be able to use the Array function when we begin working with multi-dimensional arrays. The Array function can only be used to load elements into a one-dimensional array.

"Another technique, using the **Array** function, does the same job as the more 'wordy' example in the last exercise, but it's much more compact."

Exercise

Using the Array Function

1. Start a new **Standard.EXE** project.

2. Place a command button on the form and accept the default name that Visual Basic assigns.

3. Double-click on the command button and place the following code into its **Click** event procedure:

```
Private Sub Command1_Click()
    Dim varGrades As Variant
    Dim intGradeCounter As Integer
    Dim intTotal As Integer
    Dim sngAverage As Single
    varGrades = Array(90, 91, 80, 77, 44, 100)
```

```
    For intGradeCounter = 0 To 5
        Form1.Print varGrades(intGradeCounter)
        intTotal = intTotal + varGrades(intGradeCounter)
    Next
    sngAverage = (intTotal / intGradeCounter)
    Form1.Print "The class average is " & sngAverage
End Sub
```

4. Save the project in your \VBFiles\Practice subdirectory. Save the form as average3.frm and midterm3.vbp. Now run the program.

5. Click on the command button. The numbers 90, 91, 80, 77, 100 and 44 will be printed on the form, along with the average 80.33334:

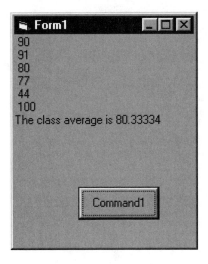

Discussion

"Using the Array function, I streamlined the process of adding elements to our array," I explained.

"We didn't declare the variable varGrades as an array, but as a variant variable instead," Dave commented.

"That's an excellent observation," I said. "The Array function essentially transforms a variant variable into an array. The Array function only works with a variable of a variant data type."

"So that means if you use the **Array** function, you can't declare the variable as an array ahead of time?" Rhonda asked.

"Yes," I replied, "that's why in the previous exercise, our array was declared like this:"

```
Dim intGrades(5) As Integer
```

"But in this exercise we used this instead:"

```
Dim varGrades As Variant
```

I continued by saying that the code in this exercise was virtually identical to the code from the previous exercise, with the exception of the way we declared and loaded the array elements.

"The array, is declared and loaded through a single Visual Basic statement, the **Array** function," I explained:

```
varGrades = Array(90, 91, 80, 77, 44, 100)
```

"How does Visual Basic know what to make the lower and upper bounds of the array?" Barbara asked.

"Visual Basic can tell by the number of arguments supplied to the **Array** function and by the **Option Base**, which we know is 0 by default. So with an **Option Base** of 0, and 6 arguments passed to the **Array** function, the lower bound is 0 and the upper bound is 5."

We had been working for some time, so I suggested that we take a break.

"When we resume after break, we'll look at dynamic arrays," I told them.

Dynamic Arrays

"I mentioned earlier, that in addition to the static arrays we've just been looking at, there's another type of array called a dynamic array," I said. "The word dynamic means **to change**. The lower and upper bounds of a dynamic array can change during the running of your program. Because of that, we need to declare a dynamic array differently to a static array."

"Why would you declare a dynamic array? Don't you always know the lower and upper bounds of your array ahead of time? Why would it change while the program is running?" Ward asked.

"Let's go back to our example of 500 grades," I replied. "We don't always know ahead of time the number of students who have actually taken the midterm. There may be 500 students enrolled in the course, but not all 500 may show up. The dynamic array is the perfect way to handle this situation. Here's how we would declare `intGrades` as a dynamic array:"

```
Dim intGrades()
```

"To declare a dynamic array, you place an empty set of parentheses at the end of the array name."

"How many elements are there in this array?" Kate asked.

"Right now, none," I replied. "With a dynamic array, at some point later in your program, you need to use a `ReDim` statement to provide Visual Basic with that information."

```
ReDim intGrades(0 to 5)
```

"So with a dynamic array," Linda said, "the process is to declare the array with an empty set of parentheses, then later declare it as you would a static array."

"That's right," I said. "In fact, with a dynamic array, you can use the `ReDim` statement as many times as you want within your program. You can declare an upper bound of 10, for instance and then use a `ReDim` statement to change the upper bound to 50 if you need to."

"What happens to the data already present in the array when you use the `ReDim` statement?" Linda asked.

"That's an excellent question," I replied. "Ordinarily, if you use the `ReDim` statement, any data already present in the array will be lost. Fortunately, there's an optional parameter of the `ReDim` statement that permits any data already in the array to be saved and that's the `Preserve` parameter."

```
ReDim Preserve intGrades(0 to 5)
```

I continued our discussion of dynamic arrays by saying that they are extremely handy for file processing.

"In fact," I said, "shortly, we'll use array processing to read the inventory prices into our China Shop program in order to calculate the customer's sales quotation. I have a exercise here which will illustrate the use of array processing in reading data from a disk file."

Exercise

Adding Elements to an Array from a Disk File

1. Use Notepad to create a file called L5EXAM1.txt in your \VBFiles\Practice subdirectory that contains the data you see in the following screen shot:

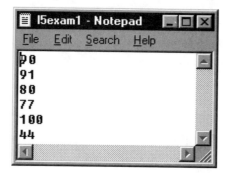

Notice that the file contains six records and each record contains a single numeric value representing a midterm grade.

2. Start a new **standard.EXE** project.

3. Place a command button on the form and accept the default name that Visual Basic assigns.

4. Double-click on the command button and place the following code into its **Click** event procedure:

```
Private Sub Command1_Click()
   Dim intGrades() As Integer
   Dim intGradeCounter As Integer
   Dim intTotal As Integer
   Dim sngAverage As Single
   Open "C:\VBFILES\PRACTICE\L5EXAM1.TXT" For Input As #1
   Do While Not EOF(1)
      ReDim Preserve intGrades(intGradeCounter)
      Input #1, intGrades(intGradeCounter)
      intGradeCounter = intGradeCounter + 1
   Loop
   Close #1
   For intGradeCounter = LBound(intGrades) To UBound(intGrades)
      Form1.Print intGrades(intGradeCounter)
      intTotal = intTotal + intGrades(intGradeCounter)
   Next
   sngAverage = (intTotal / intGradeCounter)
   Form1.Print "The class average is " & sngAverage
End Sub
```

5. Save the project in your \VBFiles\Practice subdirectory. Save the form as average4.frm and the form as midterm4.vbp. Now run the program.

6. Click on the command button. The numbers 90, 91, 80, 77, 100 and 44 will be printed on the form, along with the average 80.33334:

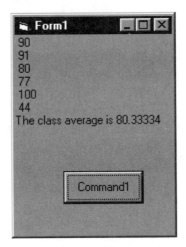

Discussion

I ran the program myself, and the midterm grades and the class average were displayed on the form.

"Different program, same result," I said. "You may recognize some of this code from our previous exercise on file processing, the difference being that we have declared and loaded a dynamic array."

I continued by explaining that as usual, the first thing we do is declare the variables that we will need to use in the event procedure. Notice the empty parentheses following the name of the array which indicates to Visual Basic that intGrades is a dynamic array:

```
Dim intGrades() As Integer
```

"The next three lines of code," I continued, "declare the same variables that we've used in the last few exercises. intGradeCounter is declared as a loop counter variable. intTotal is a variable that will contain the sum of the values of the array and sngAverage is a variable that will contain the calculated class average."

```
Dim intGradeCounter As Integer
Dim intTotal As Integer
Dim sngAverage As Single
```

"The next line of code opens the disk file L5EXAM1.TXT for input," I explained.

```
Open "C:\VBFILES\PRACTICE\L5EXAM1.TXT" For Input As #1
```

"This next section of code," I stated, "sets up a loop structure that reads each record in the disk file into an element of the dynamic array:"

```
Do While Not EOF(1)
    ReDim Preserve intGrades(intGradeCounter)
    Input #1, intGrades(intGradeCounter)
    intGradeCounter = intGradeCounter + 1
Loop
```

I reminded everyone that the Do While statement tells Visual Basic to execute the statements in the body of the loop as long as we don't read the invisible EOF marker found after the last record in our file:

```
Do While Not EOF(1)
```

I then directed everyone's attention to the lines of code within the body of the loop:

```
ReDim Preserve intGrades(intGradeCounter)
```

"As we initially declared the array `intGrades` as a dynamic array we need to use the `ReDim` statement to re-size the array each time the body of the loop is executed," I explained. "Each time the body of the loop is executed, the array's size is increased by one, because the value of the loop counter variable `intGradeCounter` is being incremented by one. We use the `Preserve` parameter because we don't want to lose any data already present in the array."

I displayed this sketch on the classroom projector to illustrate how our dynamic array expands each time the body of the loop is executed:

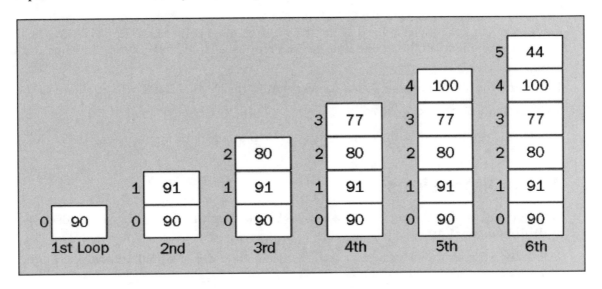

The following statement is similar to the code we saw in one of our previous exercises. Remember that the `Input` statement reads a record from the open file into a variable. Here, the record is being read into an element of the `intGrades` array and the subscript is determined by the value of the variable `intGradeCounter`."

```
Input #1, intGrades(intGradeCounter)
```

"In fact, it is this next statement that increments the value of `intGradeCounter` by 1," I continued.

```
intGradeCounter = intGradeCounter + 1
```

"To summarize," I said, "within the loop we ReDim or re-declare the size of the array, we then read a record into the next element of the array and then increment the value of the variable intGradeCounter by 1."

"We've seen this next line of code before - all it does is close the file we opened earlier," I explained:

```
Close #1
```

The following section of code prints each grade on the form and keeps a running total of the grades:

```
For intGradeCounter = LBound(intGrades) To UBound(intGrades)
   Form1.Print intGrades(intGradeCounter)
   intTotal = intTotal + intGrades(intGradeCounter)
Next
```

"LBound returns the lower bound of an array and UBound returns the upper bound of an array," I explained. "Both LBound and UBound require a single argument, the name of the array."

Therefore, the above code sets up a loop structure that Visual Basic will evaluate as this:

```
For intGradeCounter = 0 To 5
```

"We've all seen the rest of the code before, so I won't waste time discussing it," I added.

Array Dimensions

We were making good progress on what can be a difficult topic, so I began to discuss **multidimensional** arrays.

"All of the arrays that we've seen so far, have been one-dimensional arrays," I explained.

"Dare I ask the difference?" said Kathy tentatively.

"Let's use Notepad, to see the difference. In Notepad, one-dimensional arrays appear as a single column of data. Two-dimensional arrays appear as rows and columns of data. For instance..." I said, as I displayed this file on the classroom projector:

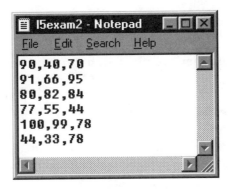

"This is a two-dimensional text file," I explained. "This file contains not only the original grades we've worked with today, but two other grades as well, the final examination and research paper grade also."

"You mean then, that the first column of numbers are scores from the midterm, the second column the final examination and the third column the research paper?" Ward asked.

"That's right," I replied. "And each row represents one student."

I explained that instead of using a two-dimensional array to represent this data, we could have used three distinct single-dimensional arrays, with each column of numbers assigned to a one-dimensional array. In fact, we will do exactly that in the China Shop Project.

"Using a series of one-dimensional arrays, instead of a single multidimensional array can improve your program's performance," I explained.

"You mentioned the word multidimensional when you began this section and you just said it again. Does that mean you can have more than two dimensions in an array?" Joe asked.

"Yes, you can," I answered. "You can create 3- or 4-dimensional arrays. In fact, Visual Basic allows you to declare up to 60 dimensions in an array!"

I explained that Visual Basic gives you the ability to represent any real world object with an array, but anything more than a 3-dimensional array is difficult for most people to visualize.

"Can you give us an example of a three-dimensional array?" Kathy asked.

"The classic example," I said, "is that of a farm, where crops are kept track of not only by the row and column where they are planted, but by the field as well. For instance, consider a farm that is divided into ten separate fields and where each field is made up of one hundred rows and columns. A three-dimensional array, where one dimension represents the field, the second dimension the row and the third dimension represents the columns would work quite well in this case."

There is a practical memory limit as to how many dimensions an array can store. Adding dimensions to an array will geometrically increase the storage requirements for an array.

I could see that some of the students were getting tense.

"Don't worry," I told everyone, "we'll restrict our discussion today to two-dimensional arrays. However, our discussion of arrays with two dimensions can easily be applied to an array with three or more dimensions."

I continued by explaining that the declaration for a multidimensional array is slightly different from the declaration for a one-dimensional array.

"With a multidimensional array, you need to declare an upper bound for each dimension of the array," I explained. "Here's the declaration for the file we just viewed in Notepad that contains a midterm, final and research grade for six students."

```
Dim intGrade(5, 2) As Integer
```

"When you see a comma like this, right away you should know that you are seeing the declaration for a two-dimensional array. In this instance, the first dimension of the array has an upper bound of 5 and the second dimension has an upper bound of 2. Therefore, with an Option Base of 0, the first dimension would contain 6 elements and the second dimension, 3. To calculate the total number of elements in the array, you just multiply those two numbers. So we have 18 elements in total in this file."

I continued by saying that just as the declaration for a multidimensional array is different from that of a one-dimensional array, so too is the way we refer to elements within the array.

"One-dimensional arrays are referenced by using a single subscript," I said. "Two-dimensional arrays are referenced by using two subscripts. For instance, to reference the research paper grade for the second student, we would use this notation:"

```
intGrades(1,2)
```

I suggested that now would be a great time for an exercise to get their feet wet with a two-dimensional array:

Exercise

A Two-Dimensional Static Array

1. Use Notepad to create a file called **L5EXAM2.txt** in your **\VBFILES\PRACTICE** subdirectory, that contains the data you see in the following screen shot. Notice that the file contains six records and each record contains three numeric values separated by commas representing a midterm, final examination and research paper grade.

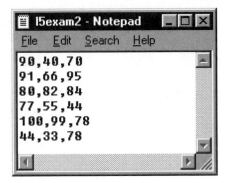

2. Start a new **standard.EXE** project.

3. Use your toolbox to place a command button on the form. Accept the default name that Visual Basic assigns.

4. Double-click on the command button and place the following code into its **Click** event procedure:

```
Private Sub Command1_Click()
    Dim intGrades(5, 2) As Integer
    Dim intRow As Integer
    Dim intCol As Integer
    Open "C:\VBFILES\PRACTICE\L5EXAM2.TXT" For Input As #1
    For intRow = LBound(intGrades, 1) To UBound(intGrades, 1)
        For intCol = LBound(intGrades, 2) To _
            UBound(intGrades, 2)
            Input #1, intGrades(intRow, intCol)
        Next intCol
    Next intRow
    Close #1
    For intRow = LBound(intGrades, 1) To UBound(intGrades, 1)
        For intCol = LBound(intGrades, 2) To _
            UBound(intGrades, 2)
            Form1.Print intGrades(intRow, intCol)
        Next intCol
    Next intRow
End Sub
```

5. Save the project in you **\VBFiles\Practice** subdirectory. Save the form as **average5.frm** and the project as **midterm5.vbp**. Now run the program.

6. Click on the command button. The grades from the file will be printed on the form.

Discussion

I immediately ran the program and the following screen was displayed on the classroom projector:

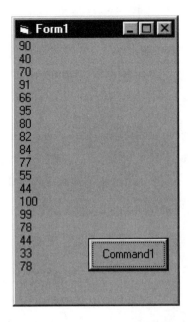

"Not very pretty, is it?" I said. "However, the important thing is that we successfully read the data from the disk file into the elements of our two-dimension array and we can access each element of the array. We'll pretty it up a little bit later, so that we display rows and columns of data. Now let's take a closer look at the code."

"That first line of code, is that the declaration for the two-dimensional array?" Ward asked.

"Yes," I replied. "As we are reading row and column data from a file, it makes sense to declare a two-dimensional static array. Don't forget we could also have declared three one-dimensional arrays."

```
Dim intGrades(5, 2) As Integer
```

"What are those next two variable declarations?" Joe asked. "At this point, I'm used to seeing a declaration for `intCounter`."

```
Dim intRow As Integer
Dim intCol As Integer
```

I explained that since we will be loading data into a two-dimensional array, we needed to use **nested** `For...Next` loops to keep track of our current position in the array. Instead of the single loop counter variable, `intCounter`, we need a loop counter variable for each of the inner and outer loops, `intRow` and `intCol`.

"I don't think we've come across nested loops before," Ward said.

"Don't worry," I said, "I'll cover the nested loops in detail when we get there."

I continued by pointing out that the next line of code is virtually identical to the code in the previous exercise:

```
Open "C:\VBFILES\PRACTICE\L5EXAM2.TXT" For Input As #1
```

"These next five lines contain the nested `For...Next` loops," I explained.

```
For intRow = LBound(intGrades, 1) To UBound(intGrades, 1)
   For intCol = LBound(intGrades, 2) To UBound(intGrades, 2)
      Input #1, intGrades(intRow, intCol)
   Next intCol
Next intRow
```

"Notice that a nested loop is just a loop within another loop," I continued. "Don't worry if this looks a little difficult to you right now, let's run the program in step mode to fully understand what's going on here."

"Let's look at the body of the loop first," I said, "amazingly, that's this single line of code:"

```
Input #1, intGrades(intRow, intCol)
```

"This line of code will execute 18 times," I explained, "which makes perfect sense because it happens to be the total number of elements declared in our array and the total number of grades in the file. By using nested `For...Next` loops, we can vary the values of `intRow` and `intCol` to place the grades read from the disk file into the correct rows and columns, in other words the subscript, of our array. Ultimately, we want to set up nested `For...Next` loops that Visual Basic evaluates to this:"

```
For intRow = 0 To 5
   For intCol = 0 To 2
      Input #1, intGrades(intRow, intCol)
   Next intCol
Next intRow
```

"The first loop in this code, is also known as the **outer loop** and you may be able to see that we will use it to process the records in the file," I continued. "That's why its start parameter is 0 and its end parameter is 5. The second loop, also known as the **inner loop**, will process the fields in the file. That's why its start parameter is 0 and its end parameter is 2."

"If that's how we want the loop to be evaluated by Visual Basic, what is this business with `LBound` and `UBound`?" Ward asked.

I explained that in the first `For` statement, `intRow` is a counter variable that we will use to loop through the row component of the array.

"We've seen the `LBound` function before, but not quite the way it is here," I said. "Remember that the `LBound` function returns the lower bound of an array. However, with multidimensional arrays, you need to specify the number of the dimension whose lower bound you want to know."

```
LBound(intGrades, 1)
```

"Therefore the statement returns the lower bound of the first dimension of our array. As it turns out, the lower bound of both dimensions of our array is 0."

I explained that the `UBound` function works in the same way. Therefore, this code returns the upper bound of the first dimension of our array, in this case 5.

```
UBound(intGrades, 1)
```

Therefore, Visual Basic interprets the first `For` line of code to read:

```
For intRow = 0 to 5
```

"OK, so far so good," Ward said. "What about the second `For` loop?"

"No problem," I replied. "The second loop looks like this:"

```
For intCol = LBound(intGrades, 2) To UBound(intGrades, 2)
```

"This code works in exactly the same way that the previous `For` line did, except here we're dealing with the second dimension of the array," I explained. "Therefore, this line returns a value of 0:"

```
LBound(intGrades, 2)
```

"Whereas this line returns a value of 2," I continued:

```
UBound(intGrades, 2)
```

"And so Visual Basic interprets the second `For` line of code to read this," I explained:

```
For intCol = 0 To 2
```

"Now let's take a look at the code inside the inner most **For...Next** loop," I said.

```
Input #1, intGrade(intRow, intCol)
```

"Because we're loading values into a two-dimensional array, we need to specify **two** subscripts when referring to array elements, which is why we need both variables **intRow** and **intCol** in the **Input** statement," I explained.

"I'm confused by this **Input** statement," Joe said. "Since we have three fields in each record, shouldn't we have three variables in the argument list of the **Input** statement?"

"That's a good question Joe," I said. "With the **Input** statement, you have the choice of reading as many fields at one time as you want. Knowing there are three fields per record, you can use the **Input** statement with three variables. You can also choose to read the data one field at a time and that's what we did here."

Again, I emphasized that the body of the loop is executed 18 times and I verified that by running the code in step mode one more time. Here I've illustrated some of the results I saw:

Statement	intRow	intCol	intGrades	Value of intGrades
For **intRow** = 0 to 5	0	0	0,0	
For **intCol** = 0 to 2	0	0	0,0	
Input #1, intGrade(0,1)	**0**	**0**	**0,0**	**90**
Next intCol	0	1	0,1	

Input #1, intGrade(0,2)	0	1	0,1	40
Next intCol	0	2	0,2	
Input #1, intGrade(0,3)	0	2	0,2	70
Next intCol	0	2	0,2	
Next intRow	1	2	1,2	
For intCol = 0 to 2	1	0	1,0	
Input #1, intGrade(1,0)	1	0	1,0	91

"There's really quite a bit of code executing here, but don't forget, the most important line of code is this one:"

```
Input #1, intGrade(intRow, intCol)
```

"It assigns values to the correct elements of our array. This line of code is executed 18 times, but only needs to be coded once."

I waited for questions. There were none.

"Once we've processed the records in the file," I said, "this line of code closes our open file:"

```
Close #1
```

"Now that we have the data in our two-dimensional array, the next step is to print it out," I continued.

I continued by saying that the next five lines of code are virtually identical to the first set of nested For...Next loops, except that the code in the body of the loop is used to print the grades on the form.

```
For intRow = LBound(intGrades, 1) To UBound(intGrades, 1)
   For intCol = LBound(intGrades, 2) To UBound(intGrades, 2)
      Form1.Print intGrades(intRow, intCol)
   Next intCol
Next intRow
```

Again, we ran the program in step mode to see how the code in this section was processing.

I asked if there were any questions, but there were none. I told everyone that if they were still confused by the code they saw here, they weren't alone. Working with multidimensional arrays requires patience and practice, and the more you work with them, the more comfortable you'll become.

"My only question," Kathy said, "is when to use an array."

"You need experience to determine when your program can benefit from an array," I explained. "I tell my students that beginner programmers never know when to use an array and experienced programmers are always looking for an excuse to use them."

It was now time for a break. I told everyone that when they returned, we would modify the China Shop Project to incorporate some array processing of our own.

Modifying the China Shop Project

"In our last two exercises of the day we will modify the China Shop Project to incorporate array processing," I told them.

Exercise

Modify the China Shop Project to Load Up an Array

1. Use Notepad to create a file called `prices.txt` according to the following screen shot:

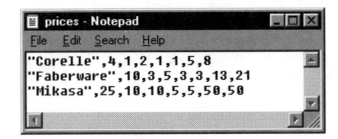

2. Save this file in the **\VBFiles\China** subdirectory.

3. Load up the China Shop Project.

4. You need to declare several form-level dynamic arrays in the General Declarations section of the form. Since these are dynamic arrays, don't forget to add the closing parentheses. You should notice that you have three variables already declared there. Now add the code that's highlighted below:

```
Option Explicit
Private m_intQuantity As Integer
Private m_lngBackColor As Long
Private m_blnDateDisplay As Boolean
Private m_curBowlPrice() As Integer
Private m_curButterPlatePrice() As Integer
Private m_curCupPrice() As Integer
Private m_curPlatePrice() As Integer
Private m_curPlatterPrice() As Integer
Private m_curSaucerPrice() As Integer
Private m_curCompletePrice() As Integer
```

5. Find the **Form_Load** event of **frmMain** and erase the code that is already present there.

6. Add the following code instead:

```
Private Sub Form_Load()
   Dim strBrand As String
   Dim intCounter As Integer
   Open "C:\VBFILES\CHINA\PRICES.TXT" For Input As #1
   Do While Not EOF(1)
      ReDim Preserve m_curBowlPrice(intCounter)
      ReDim Preserve m_curButterPlatePrice(intCounter)
```

```
            ReDim Preserve m_curCupPrice(intCounter)
            ReDim Preserve m_curPlatePrice(intCounter)
            ReDim Preserve m_curPlatterPrice(intCounter)
            ReDim Preserve m_curSaucerPrice(intCounter)
            ReDim Preserve m_curCompletePrice(intCounter)
            Input #1, strBrand, _
                m_curPlatePrice(intCounter), _
                m_curButterPlatePrice(intCounter), _
                m_curBowlPrice(intCounter), _
                m_curCupPrice(intCounter), _
                m_curSaucerPrice(intCounter), _
                m_curPlatterPrice(intCounter), _
                m_curCompletePrice(intCounter)
            lstBrands.AddItem strBrand
            intCounter = intCounter + 1
        Loop
        Close #1
End Sub
```

7. Click on the Save icon to save the China Shop Project.

8. Run the program. At this point, you won't notice any difference in the program. We still need to change the code in the **Click** event procedure of the **cmdCalculate** command button to utilize the prices loaded in the array to calculate the customer's sales quotation. We'll do that in the next exercise.

Discussion

"The purpose of this exercise, was to eliminate the 'hard coding' of the china inventory prices into our program and to load them into an array for later processing instead. In the next exercise, we'll modify the code in the **Click** event procedure of **cmdCalculate** to read prices from that array."

"I understand why we're loading the prices from a file, but why load them into an array, why not just an ordinary variable?" Rhonda asked.

"Loading prices into a dynamic array, provides the most flexibility for our program," I replied. "This allows the china shop to offer another brand of china for sale without us having to change the code. That can make you very popular with a client believe me. To offer another brand of china for sale, all the staff of the china shop need to do is add another brand and prices to the **prices.txt** file."

"I noticed that we are no longer reading the **brands.txt** file and that it appears we are loading the list box by using the **prices.txt** file," Linda commented.

"That's right," I said. "It doesn't make sense to maintain two files when one will do. Our program will read the first field of the **prices.txt** file and load the china brands into the list box using that field."

"Our code will actually load the data from the file into seven separate one-dimensional arrays," I explained. "We'll establish a separate array for each china item and each element in the array will represent a different china brand. Element 0 will be the brand associated with the first record in the file, in this case Corelle, element 1 the second brand, i.e. Faberware, and element 2, Mikasa."

"Why not use a two-dimensional array?" Dave asked.

"Two reasons really," I said, "the first reason is that a one-dimensional array will give us the flexibility that we need. Secondly, for beginners, arrays are difficult enough to deal with, without taxing you with a two-dimensional array when a one-dimensional array will do."

"The first thing we did in the exercise, was to use Notepad to create the **prices.txt** file," I continued. "This is the file that the staff will modify when they wish to update inventory prices. Let's review the format of the input file."

I explained that there is a record for each brand of china in the China Shop's inventory.

"The first field in the record," I said, "is a string consisting of the china brand, followed by seven numeric fields representing the price for a plate, butter plate, bowl, cup, saucer and platter of that brand. The final field represents the discounted complete place setting price. Remember that the seven numeric fields will be loaded into separate arrays. The string field will be used to populate the **lstBrands** list box."

"I had forgotten about that discount price," Linda said.

"I almost did myself," I said, "we didn't calculate a discounted price in the previous version of the code."

"After creating the file `prices.txt`," I added, "I then asked you to declare seven form-level dynamic arrays in the General Declarations section of the form."

```
Private m_curBowlPrice() As Integer
Private m_curButterPlatePrice() As Integer
Private m_curCupPrice() As Integer
Private m_curPlatePrice() As Integer
Private m_curPlatterPrice() As Integer
Private m_curSaucerPrice() As Integer
Private m_curCompletePrice() As Integer
```

"I noticed, that some of you almost forgot to code that empty set of parentheses at the end of the declaration," I continued. "Don't forget that's what tells Visual Basic that it is dealing with a dynamic array."

"Why did we declare the dynamic arrays at the form module level?" Dave asked. "Aren't all of the calculations using those variables performed in the `Click` event procedure of `cmdCalculate`?"

"You raise a good point," I said. "The reason I asked you to declare them at the form level is that I can foresee the possibility that we might want to access the values in these arrays from another event procedure sometime in the future. In fact, during our last week of class, we'll do exactly that."

I suggested that we look at the revised code in the `Click` event procedure of `cmdCalculate`.

I began by saying that as usual, the first thing we do is declare any variables that we'll need to use in the event procedure:

```
Dim strBrand As String
Dim intCounter As Integer
```

"`strBrand` is the variable into which we read the first field (the brand of china) of `prices.txt` and `intCounter` is a loop counter variable which will be used to specify the subscript numbers of the elements we load to our arrays," I explained.

I waited for questions but there were none.

"This line of code opens the file `PRICES.TXT` for `Input`," I said:

```
Open "C:\VBFILES\CHINA\PRICES.TXT" For Input As #1
```

I explained that the next line of code initiates a Do While...Loop that will repeat until the invisible EOF marker of prices.txt is encountered:

```
Do While Not EOF(1)
```

"Within the body of the loop," I continued, "we coded seven ReDim Preserve statements:"

```
ReDim Preserve m_curBowlPrice(intCounter)
ReDim Preserve m_curButterPlatePrice(intCounter)
ReDim Preserve m_curCupPrice(intCounter)
ReDim Preserve m_curPlatePrice(intCounter)
ReDim Preserve m_curPlatterPrice(intCounter)
ReDim Preserve m_curSaucerPrice(intCounter)
ReDim Preserve m_curCompletePrice(intCounter)
```

I reminded everyone that the ReDim statement 're-declares' the boundaries of our dynamic arrays.

"As we've seen before in other exercises," I said, "each time the body of the loop is executed, the upper bound of these arrays is increased by one. The next line of code is the Input statement that reads the eight fields in the disk file into the variable strBrand and the seven dynamic arrays. The value of the counter variable intCounter is used to specify the subscript."

```
Input #1, strBrand, _
      m_curPlatePrice(intCounter), _
      m_curButterPlatePrice(intCounter), _
      m_curBowlPrice(intCounter), _
      m_curCupPrice(intCounter), _
      m_curSaucerPrice(intCounter), _
      m_curPlatterPrice(intCounter), _
      m_curCompletePrice(intCounter)
      lstBrands.AddItem strBrand
```

"The next line of code increments the counter variable intCounter by 1," I explained:

```
intCounter = intCounter + 1
```

"And this line of code closes the prices.txt file:"

```
Close #1
```

I noticed a few students using the Immediate window to display the values of the various elements of the arrays and I praised them for it. I then told everyone that in our final exercise of the day, we would modify the code in the Click event procedure of the cmdCalculate command button to calculate a sales quotation for our customer using the arrays.

Exercise

Calculating Prices Based on Our Arrays

1. Continue working with the China Shop Project.

2. Delete the existing code in the Click event procedure of cmdCalculate, and replace it with the code shown below (you can cut and paste this code from the cmdCalulate Code.txt file supplied with the CD in the Chapter 13 folder):

```
Private Sub cmdCalculate_Click()
'Declare our variables
   Dim curTotalPrice As Currency
   Dim curBowlPrice As Currency
   Dim curButterPlatePrice As Currency
   Dim curCupPrice As Currency
   Dim curPlatePrice As Currency
   Dim curPlatterPrice As Currency
   Dim curSaucerPrice As Currency
   Dim curCompletePrice As Currency
   Dim intSubscript As Integer
'Has the customer selected a brand of china?
   If lstBrands.Text = "" Then
      MsgBox "You must select a China brand"
      Exit Sub
   End If
'Has the customer selected one or more china items?
   If chkChinaItem(0).Value = 0 And _
         chkChinaItem(1).Value = 0 And _
         chkChinaItem(2).Value = 0 And _
         chkChinaItem(3).Value = 0 And _
         chkChinaItem(4).Value = 0 And _
         chkChinaItem(5).Value = 0 Then
      MsgBox "You must select one or more china items"
      Exit Sub
```

```
   End If
'Has the customer selected a quantity?
  If optQuantity(8).Value = False And _
       optQuantity(4).Value = False And _
       optQuantity(2).Value = False And _
       optQuantity(1).Value = False Then
    MsgBox "You must select a quantity"
    Exit Sub
  End If
'If the customer has selected a platter
'warn them that there is only 1 permitted per sales
'quotation
  If chkChinaItem(5).Value = 1 And m_intQuantity > 1 Then
    MsgBox "Customer is limited to 1 Platter per order" & _
         vbCrLf & "Adjusting price accordingly"
  End If
'All the pieces are here, let's calculate a price
'Calculate subtotal prices by item
  intSubscript = lstBrands.ListIndex
  curBowlPrice = m_curBowlPrice(intSubscript) * _
       chkChinaItem(2).Value
  curButterPlatePrice = m_curButterPlatePrice(intSubscript) _
       * _
       chkChinaItem(1).Value
  curCompletePrice = m_curCompletePrice(intSubscript)
  curCupPrice = m_curCupPrice(intSubscript) * _
       chkChinaItem(3).Value
  curPlatePrice = m_curPlatePrice(intSubscript) * _
       chkChinaItem(0).Value
  curPlatterPrice = m_curPlatterPrice(intSubscript) * _
       chkChinaItem(5).Value
  curSaucerPrice = m_curSaucerPrice(intSubscript) * _
       chkChinaItem(4).Value
  If chkChinaItem(0).Value = 1 And _
       chkChinaItem(1).Value = 1 And _
       chkChinaItem(2).Value = 1 And _
       chkChinaItem(3).Value = 1 And _
       chkChinaItem(4).Value = 1 Then
    MsgBox "Price includes a Complete Place Setting Discount"
    curTotalPrice = (curCompletePrice * m_intQuantity) + _
         curPlatterPrice
  Else
    curTotalPrice = (((curBowlPrice + curButterPlatePrice _
       + _
         curCupPrice + curPlatePrice + curSaucerPrice) * _
         m_intQuantity) + curPlatterPrice)
```

```
      End If
'If the price is greater than 0, display the price and
'make the label visible
   If curTotalPrice > 0 Then
      lblPrice.Caption = "The price of your order is " & _
            Format(curTotalPrice, "$##,###.00")
      lblPrice.Visible = True
   End If
End Sub
```

3. Save the China Shop Project.

4. Run the program. Select Mikasa as your choice of china brand, select 2 for quantity and select Plate, Butter Plate and Soup Bowl as your china items. Then click on the Calculate command button. A calculated price of 90 should be displayed.

Discussion

The final exercise of the day was not without its difficulties. The code was pretty tedious to enter and because some of the code remained the same, and some of it needed to be changed, it became confusing at times. However, all in all, the exercise went pretty smoothly and after about fifteen minutes, everyone had completed it.

"The purpose of this exercise," I said, "was to remove the prices that had been hard-coded into the program and instead use the prices in the arrays which we loaded into the project in the last exercise. As was the case in the previous version of the code, we'll calculate subtotals for the various items of china selected by the customer and then add them together to arrive at the grand total sales quotation. Obviously, what will complicate matters here is the fact that we'll be 'looking up' the prices for the items in the appropriate array and calculating a discount for a complete place setting. Let's look at the code now, much of which is identical to what was in this event procedure before we modified it, so we won't need to cover it all."

I continued by explaining that as usual, the first thing we do is declare any variables that we'll need to use in our event procedure:

```
Dim curCompletePrice As Currency
Dim intSubscript As Integer
```

"Only curCompletePrice and intSubscript are new declarations," I explained. "The other variables remain from the previous version of this code. The variable curCompletePrice will hold the subtotal value for a complete place setting, if the program detects that one has been selected. intSubscript is a variable that we will use to 'look up' the correct price in the appropriate price array. Its value will be equal to the ListIndex property of the lstBrands list box. If the customer selects Corelle for instance, the value of this variable will be set to 0 and element 0 of the seven price arrays will be accessed to determine the subtotal prices for the various china items."

"Since each of our seven arrays has three different elements, based on the brand of china, we need to know the brand that the customer has selected in order to 'look up' the correct price in the arrays," I continued. "The elements in our array are numbered 0, 1 and 2; where 0 is equal to Corelle, 1 is Faberware and 2 is Mikasa. That is also the same order that these brands appear in the list box. In fact, that order is by design, since both the list box items and the arrays were loaded from the same records in the `prices.txt` disk file. The bottom line is that we can use the `ListIndex` property of the list box to lookup prices in the seven arrays, because the `ListIndex` property is equal to 0 when the customer selects Corelle, 1 when Faberware is selected and 2 when it's Mikasa."

"Would this code work even if the records in the file weren't sorted alphabetically?" Linda asked.

"Yes, it would," I replied, "since both the list box and the arrays are loaded from the same record. The only thing that could cause us a problem here is if the records were not sorted alphabetically and the `Sorted` property of the list box was set to `True`. If that were the case, the `ListIndex` property and the element number in the arrays would not match, and we would look up the wrong values in the array."

I waited for questions, but I think everyone was satisfied with my explanation.

"Therefore we assign the value of the `ListIndex` property to the variable `intSubscript`," I explained.

```
intSubscript = lstBrands.ListIndex
```
"This next section of code," I continued, "looks pretty complicated, but it isn't really. What we're doing here is calculating the individual subtotal prices for each item of china. We take the price of the item in the array and multiply it by the `Value` property of its Check Box. For instance, let's look at the calculation for the soup bowl subtotal:"

```
curBowlPrice = m_curBowlPrice(intSubscript) * _
    chkChinaItem(2).Value
```

"Let's pretend that the customer has selected Mikasa as their brand of choice," I said. "If they have, then the `ListIndex` property of the `lstBrands` list box is equal to 2. We then assign the number 2 to the value of the variable `intSubscript`. The value of element #2 of the array `m_curBowlPrice` is equal to 10."

"How do you know that?" Ward asked.

"That's the price that is found in the `prices.txt` file," I replied. "It's also the value that I've recorded in our documentation for the Mikasa soup bowl."

"Now if the customer has indicated a desire for the soup bowl by selecting that Check Box, then the `Value` property of `chkChinaItem(2)` will be equal to 1," I continued. "10 multiplied by 1 is 10. Therefore, the value of `curBowlPrice` will be 10. If the customer has decided against the purchase of a soup bowl, then the `Value` property of `chkChinaItem(2)` will be equal to 0. Anything multiplied by 0 is 0 and so the value of `curBowlPrice` will be 0. We then perform this same calculation for the remaining six subtotal variables: `curButterPlatePrice`, `curCompletePrice`, `curCupPrice`, `curPlatePrice`, `curPlatterPrice` and `curSaucerPrice`."

```
curButterPlatePrice = m_curButterPlatePrice(intSubscript) * _
    chkChinaItem(1).Value
curCompletePrice = m_curCompletePrice(intSubscript)
curCupPrice = m_curCupPrice(intSubscript) * _
    chkChinaItem(3).Value
curPlatePrice = m_curPlatePrice(intSubscript) * _
    chkChinaItem(0).Value
curPlatterPrice = m_curPlatterPrice(intSubscript) * _
    chkChinaItem(5).Value
curSaucerPrice = m_curSaucerPrice(intSubscript) * _
    chkChinaItem(4).Value
```

"I noticed, that the calculation for `curCompletePrice` is different from the others," Kate said.

"Good observation," I responded. "Although there is a Check Box to indicate a **Complete Place Setting**, we won't multiply the `Value` property of its Check Box by the price in the `m_curCompletePrice` array. Instead, we'll use an `If` test to determine if the complete place setting price should be used in the calculation of the grand total."

I could see some students were confused here and I asked them to hold on.

"In this version of the code," I said, "we use an `If...Else` statement to determine if the Plate, Butter Plate, Soup Bowl, Cup and Saucer Check Boxes have been selected."

```
If chkChinaItem(0).Value = 1 And _
     chkChinaItem(1).Value = 1 And _
     chkChinaItem(2).Value = 1 And _
     chkChinaItem(3).Value = 1 And _
     chkChinaItem(4).Value = 1 Then
  MsgBox "Price includes a Complete Place Setting Discount"
```

I continued by saying that because there is a discount for a complete place setting selection, we have two different price calculations that can be performed here.

```
curTotalPrice = (curCompletePrice * m_intQuantity) + _
     curPlatterPrice
```

"We take the value of `curCompletePrice`, multiply it by the value of `m_intQuantity`, which contains the customer's selected quantity, and then add the value of `curPlatterPrice` to that."

I reminded the class that if the customer had not made a selection of a platter, the value of `curPlatterPrice` would be 0.

"Does everyone understand what is going on here," I asked. There were mostly affirmative nods, but I thought an example here was in order.

"Suppose a customer selects the Mikasa brand, a quantity of 4 and checks the Complete Place Setting Check Box, but doesn't want a platter. "

"Let's substitute the `m_intQuantity` with its value, 4," I suggested. "Let's replace the `curCompletePrice` with its value, which for Mikasa is 50. The value for `curPlatterPrice` is 0, since the customer hasn't selected a platter. So our line of code which performs the calculation becomes this:"

```
curTotalPrice = (50 * 4) + 0
```

"Taking this a step further, the calculation becomes this," I said:

```
curTotalPrice = (200) + 0
```

"So the calculated price is 200," I announced.

I then ran the program and displayed the results on the classroom projector. Several students asked me to run the program in step mode, which I thought was a great idea.

I explained that the discounted complete place setting calculation is slightly simpler than the alternative, where we add all of the subtotal prices together to arrive at a grand total. This code is identical to the calculation we had performed before so I did not discuss it.

I continued by explaining that the following code was virtually identical to the previous version, with the exception of the line with the **Format** function:

```
If curTotalPrice > 0 Then
    lblPrice.Caption = "The price of your order is " & _
        Format(curTotalPrice, "$##,###.00")
    lblPrice.Visible = True
End If
```

"Here, we improved upon the display of the price," I explained, "by using the **Format** function to display a currency format."

"I think we're just about ready to deliver this program to the china shop," Kate said.

"Just about," I agreed. "We don't have very much left to do. In fact, it's nearly time to contact Joe Bullina to schedule a delivery date and time for the program! Next week, we'll look at error handling in Visual Basic and take care of the problem with the Common Dialog Control that occurs when the user presses the Cancel button. Then, in our last week of class, we'll discuss saving the user's preferences to the Windows Registry and finally wrap up by looking at some code optimization techniques."

I dismissed class for the day and I told everyone that during the evening I would be placing a shore-to-ship call to Rose and Jack to see how they were coming along with the ocean tests on their company's new ocean liner.

Summary

In this chapter, I daresay you learned just about everything you've always wanted to know about array processing, and more. In particular we learnt about the various types of array, both static and dynamic and also about array dimensions. Arrays are a frequent source of confusion for new programmers and I hope our coverage of them will make your future work with them easier.

Specifically, we saw:

- Why arrays are useful in making our code easier to write and use

- Different types of arrays: static, dynamic, one- and two-dimensional

- How arrays can reduce the amount of hard-coding we have in our China Shop project: this means that when prices change we don't need to change the Visual Basic Code –- we only need to amend the prices stored in the disk file

In the next chapter, we'll explore some of the common errors that can occur in Visual Basic programming, and look at how to make allowances for problems that might occur when our programs run.

Quiz

1. What's the difference between an 'ordinary' variable and an array variable?

2. What's the difference between a static array and a dynamic array?

3. What statement is used to 'refine' the number of elements to be stored in a dynamic array?

4. What does this code do?

```
Dim intValue(0) as Integer
```

5. What does this code do?

```
Dim strValue() as String
```

6. What's wrong with this declaration?

```
Private intQuizScore(10000) As Integer
```

7. What is the default Lower Bound value for arrays?

8. Here is an array declaration. With an Option Base of 0, how many elements does this contain?

```
Dim intArray(100)
```

9. With an Option Base of 1, how many elements does this array contain?

```
Dim intArray(100)
```

10. Suppose you have an array that contains 100 employee names. Now you decide you need 101. What statement should you use to resize the array to 101, yet still retain the original 100 names? Option Base is 1.

11. What does this code do?

```
Dim intQuizScore(2 to 5) As Integer
```

12. What does this code do?

```
Dim intQuizScore(4,5) As Integer
```

13. What does this code do?

```
Dim intQuizScore(4 to 6,5) As Integer
```

14. What does this code do?

```
Dim intQuizScore(4,5) As Integer
Form1.Print Lbound(intQuizScore,1)
```

15. What does this code do?

```
Dim intQuizScore(4,5) As Integer
Form1.Print Ubound(intQuizScore,2)
```

Extra Credit – What are the holes numbered on the IBM Executive Golf Course in New York State?

Chapter 14
Error Handling

In this chapter, you'll follow my university class as I show them how to avoid some of the common beginner mistakes. Just in case some of those errors escape you, I'll also show you how to detect and handle the errors that slip through your defenses.

Common Beginner Errors

I began our penultimate class by telling everyone that my shore to ship call to Jack and Rose had gone well and that they had said they would be back in time for next Saturday's class. Both would be returning to the United States on the maiden voyage of the ocean liner that they had helped engineer.

"Talk about following through with the SDLC," Dave said. "They helped design the ship, now they're participating in the implementation, and feedback and maintenance phases."

"That's a good point," I said. "We'll be doing the same thing next week when we deliver the China Shop Project to Joe Bullina."

As a programming teacher, it's always tempting to show my students examples of bad code early in a class. However, after many years of teaching, I have learnt that there's a danger in illustrating bad code or code that contains errors too early in the class.

"I always wait," I said, "until we've established a strong foundation in good coding techniques, before discussing the types of errors you can make which can ruin your programming reputation. We'll be spending today's class examining the common errors that beginners make and then finish up by insulating the China Shop Project for those same errors."

Dim X, Y, Z as Integer

"This is one of the most common errors I see," I said:

```
Dim intValue1, intValue2, intValue3 As Integer
```

"Can anyone tell me what's going on with this statement?" I asked.

"It looks like you are declaring three integer type variables," Steve volunteered.

"Exactly," I agreed, "that's what it looks like were are doing and in some other programming languages, that's exactly what would happen. However, in Visual Basic, that's not what happens. In Visual Basic, this statement results in three variables being declared, but only `intValue3` is declared as an integer type. Both `intValue1` and `intValue2` are declared as variants."

"Are you sure?" Peter asked. "I've even seen that same type of declaration in some Visual Basic books."

I assured Peter that this was indeed the case.

"If you want to declare more than one variable," I continued, "you can use the 'brute force' method and declare one variable to one line of code:"

```
Dim intValue1 As Integer
Dim intValue2 As Integer
Dim intValue3 As Integer
```

"Or you can use this syntax:"

```
Dim intValue1 as Integer, intValue2 as Integer, _
    intValue3 As Integer
```

Forgetting to Increment a Counter

I continued by explaining that many of the programming tasks we had examined during the course depend heavily upon declaring, incrementing and examining a counter variable somewhere within a program.

"Counter variables," I explained, "are variables that you declare to do exactly that: count something. For example, last week we wrote code that added elements to an array from a disk file."

I gave everyone a chance to refer back to the exercise.

"In order to calculate the correct average," I said, "we must know the number of grades that have been entered. In order to keep track of this number, we declared a variable called `intGradeCounter`. If we had forgotten to increment this counter variable, a number of problems could result."

I displayed the code on the classroom projector and highlighted the line where we incremented the counter variable `intGradeCounter`:

```
Private Sub Command1_Click()
    Dim intGrades() As Integer
    Dim intGradeCounter As Integer
    Dim intTotal As Integer
Dim sngAverage As Single
Open "C:\VBFILES\PRACTICE\L5EXAM2.TXT" For Input As #1

Do While Not EOF(1)
    ReDim Preserve intGrades(intGradeCounter)
    Input #1, intGrades(intGradeCounter)
    intGradeCounter = intGradeCounter + 1
Loop
Close #1
For intGradeCounter = LBound(intGrades) To UBound(intGrades)
    Form1.Print intGrades(intGradeCounter)
    intTotal = intTotal + intGrades(intGradeCounter)
Next
sngAverage = (intTotal / intGradeCounter)
Form1.Print "The class average is " & sngAverage
End Sub
```

"Notice the highlighted code," I said. "I can't tell you the number of times that beginners forget to declare and increment a counter variable."

Forgetting to Add to an Accumulator

"An **accumulator**," I said, "is not much different from a counter variable. Not to overstate the obvious, but we use the counter variable to count something, like test grades or the number of employees in a company. The accumulator variable is declared to hold the sum of something, such as the total of all the grades or the total value of all employee salaries in the company."

"At work," Barbara said, "I've heard accumulator variables referred to as data **buckets** by some of the programmers."

"That term brings back some pleasant early memories of programming in COBOL," I chuckled. "We used to call accumulators data buckets as well."

"Last week, we wrote code to add together the individual midterm grades, then divide that total by the number of grades and print the average on the form. In that code, we declared an accumulator variable called **intTotal** and, every time the user entered another grade, we added the grade to this accumulator value. If we had forgotten to add the grade to the accumulator variable, we would have printed an incorrect average on the form."

"And there goes our reputation!" Rhonda said.

"That's right," I agreed. "It doesn't take many mistakes of that type to tarnish it."

I displayed the code on the classroom projector and highlighted the area of code where we added the grade to the accumulator variable.

```
For intGradeCounter = 0 To 5
    Form1.Print intGrades(intGradeCounter)
    intTotal = intTotal + intGrades(intGradeCounter)
Next
```

"Forgetting to add to the accumulator variable is a very common type of Visual Basic error," I explained.

"What kind of error would this generate?" Ward asked.

"The program would run," I said, "but most likely the program would display an average of 0. Something bound to greatly upset the professor of the class."

Forgetting to Open a File

"The next six errors that we'll discuss," I said, "all deal with file operations. The first error is a very common one for beginners; forgetting to open a disk file before attempting to read from it or write to it. A few weeks ago, we wrote code and placed it in the Click event procedure of the command button to write records to a disk file in our practice directory."

I displayed the code on the classroom projector and highlighted the area of code where we opened the disk file to which we would write records:

```
Private Sub Command1_Click()
    If txtName.Text = "" Then
        MsgBox "Name must be entered"
        txtName.SetFocus
        Exit Sub
    ElseIf txtGrade.Text = "" Then
        MsgBox "Grade must be entered"
        txtGrade.SetFocus
        Exit Sub
    End If
    Open "C:\VBFILES\PRACTICE\L3EXAM1.TXT" For Append As #1
    Write #1, UCASE$(txtName.Text), Val(txtGrade.Text)
    txtName.Text = ""
```

```
    txtGrade.Text = ""
    txtName.SetFocus
    Close #1
End Sub
```

"Let's see what happens if I delete the **Open** statement from the code and then try to write records to file #1 using the **Write** statement," I suggested.

I did exactly that, ran the program and clicked on the command button. The following message was displayed:

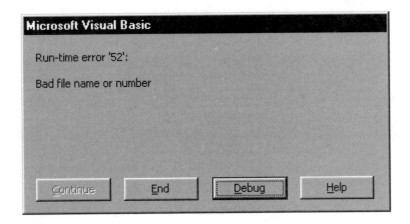

"Run-time error '52' is generated when you try to write to a file that you haven't opened," I explained.

"What should we do now?" Kate asked.

"Notice that the Continue button is not enabled, but there may be occasions where the error generated is minor enough that you can click on the Continue button and resume the program," I explained. "If you click on the End button, the program will just end and that isn't a great deal of help. If you click on the Help button, you'll get some pretty useless information about minimizing and maximizing a form. The action to take here is to click on the Debug button. When you do, Visual Basic will display the Code window and highlight the line of code where the error occurred."

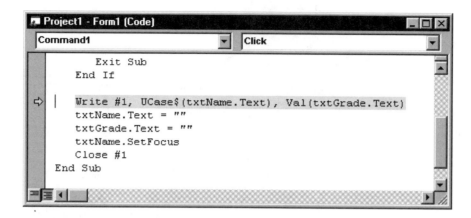

"That seems pretty useful. Is there a list of error codes and what they mean?" Barbara asked.

"That's a good question," I replied. "One of the purposes of today's class is to show you the common errors that you may encounter and so you'll develop a list of error codes during the course of the day. However, you can also bring up Visual Basic 6 Help and search the Index for run-time errors, codes and then Trappable Errors. Unfortunately, if you're running the Working Model Edition of Visual Basic, you don't have access to the help files that come with the full edition."

Then I displayed a screenshot of the trappable error codes and descriptions that are available in the full versions of Visual Basic:

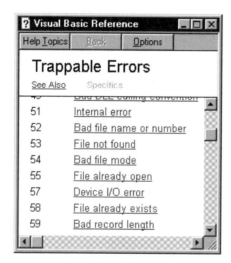

"At this point," I continued, "click on the error message, and a pretty well-written description of the error code and what it means will be displayed."

Opening a File That's Already Open

"Another fairly common error for a beginner," I said, "is to open a file that's already been opened in your program. Once you open a file, you should either read records from it or write records to it, and then close it as soon as possible. If you issue an **Open** statement for a disk file and then, before closing it, issue another **Open** statement for the same file, you'll create an error."

"Can we see the error code that this mistake generates?" Ward asked.

I wrote some code that contained the following two **Open** statements back to back:

```
Open "C:\VBFILES\PRACTICE\L3EXAM1.TXT " For Append As #1
Open "C:\VBFILES\PRACTICE\L3EXAM1.TXT " For Append As #1
```

When I ran the program, the following error message was displayed:

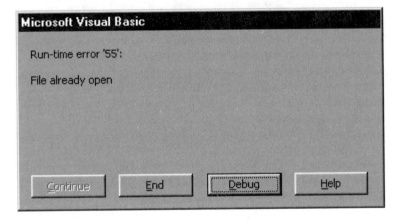

"Well," Ward said, "there isn't much doubt about that error message. It's very descriptive."

Forgetting to Close a File

"I know we covered this a few weeks back, but suppose you forget to close a disk file? Does that cause problems?" Rhonda asked.

"Yes," I replied. "Forgetting to close a file is another typical error for the beginner. Forgetting to close a file can have some disastrous results for your program, especially if you are writing records to a file."

I reminded everyone that we had used the **Write** statement to write records to a disk file during our class on file processing.

"It may surprise you to know," I said, "that just because a program issues a **Write** statement, that does not mean that the data is immediately written to the open file. The operating system typically **buffers** write requests."

"What exactly does that mean?" Kate asked.

"It means that Windows, in an effort to speed up overall program performance, will write records in batches," I explained. "For instance, suppose that you are writing several thousand records to a disk file. Rather than writing this data one record at a time, Windows may choose to write ten records at a time, twenty, perhaps more. The problem comes if your program just ends without issuing the **Close** statement. You may have records in the disk buffer that haven't been written yet."

"So you won't lose all of the data you've written," Linda said. "Just some of it."

"That's always a possibility," I said. "The bottom line is that it's a bad idea to forget to code the **Close** statement."

Reading Beyond the End of the File

"Another common error," I said, "is for your program to try to read beyond the invisible EOF marker at the end of the file. Whenever you are reading records from a disk file, you must check for the hidden EOF marker that is found after the last record in the file."

I displayed the code from our previous exercise on the classroom projector and highlighted the area of code where we checked for the EOF marker:

```
Private Sub Command1_Click()
   Dim strName As String
   Dim intGrade As Integer
   Open "C:\VBFILES\PRACTICE\L3EXAM1.TXT" For Input As #1
   Do While Not EOF(1)
   Input #1, strName, intGrade
   Form1.Print strName, intGrade
   Loop
   Close #1
End Sub
```

"The `Do While...Loop` that you see here is the best way to read a disk file," I remarked. "How can you go wrong here? Forget to check for the EOF marker. I've also seen beginners use all sorts of structures to read a disk file, such as a `For...Next` loop. In order to show you the kind of error you'll receive if you attempt to read a record past the EOF, let me change the code to look like this."

```
Private Sub Command1_Click()
   Dim strName As String
   Dim intGrade As Integer
   Dim intCounter As Integer
   Open "C:\VBFILES\PRACTICE\L3EXAM1.TXT" For Input As #1
   For intCounter = 1 To 10000
      Input #1, strName, intGrade
      Form1.Print strName, intGrade
   Next
   Close #1
End Sub
```

"Here, I've intentionally coded a `For...Next` loop that I know will read beyond the EOF marker in our file," I explained.

I then ran the program and clicked on the command button. The following message was displayed.

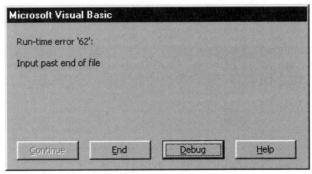

"Another illustrative error message," Barbara said. "No doubt about that one. Why would anyone use a **For...Next** loop to read a disk file?"

"People make mistakes," I replied. "Or perhaps they just haven't been taught the proper techniques. I've had beginners tell me that they thought they would just specify a large number for the end parameter of the **For...Next** loop and figured the program would just stop when it got to the last record. Of course, we know that it won't."

"Hey, I'm having a good time today," Ward said. "Looking at mistakes other people make is fun. Is this all we're going to do today?"

"No," I answered, "we'll examine the China Shop Project and modify it slightly to try to insulate it from errors over which we have no control."

Writing to a File Opened for Input

"Another typical error," I said, "is to try to write records to a file you opened for **Input**. You can only read records from a file opened for **Input**. In the same way, you cannot read records from a file opened for **Output** or **Append**. Let's go back to our code from chapter 11, **Grades.vbp**."

I displayed the code on the classroom projector and highlighted the area of code necessary to open the file for **Append** mode:

```
Private Sub Command1_Click()
    If txtName.Text = "" Then
       MsgBox "Name must be entered"
       txtName.SetFocus
       Exit Sub
    ElseIf txtGrade.Text = "" Then
       MsgBox "Grade must be entered"
       txtGrade.SetFocus
       Exit Sub
    End If
    Open "C:\VBFILES\PRACTICE\L3EXAM1.TXT" For Append As #1
    Write #1, UCASE$(txtName.Text), Val(txtGrade.Text)
    txtName.Text = ""

    txtGrade.Text = ""
    txtName.SetFocus
    Close #1
End Sub
```

"Let's see what happens, if I change the word **Append** to **Input**," I suggested.

```
Open "C:\VBFILES\PRACTICE\L3EXAM1.TXT" For Input As #1
```

I changed the code, ran the program and clicked on the command button. The following error message was displayed:

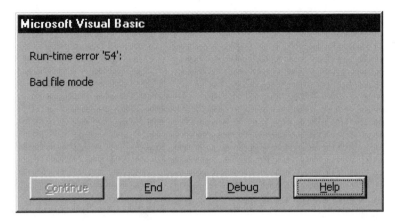

"You'll receive this error message whenever the mode of your Open statement doesn't make sense with the read or write statements that follow it," I explained.

At this point, I asked everyone to take a break. I told them that we were finished discussing the most blatant mistakes a beginner could make.

"When you return," I said, "we'll begin to look at the subtle types of errors that can really drive you crazy."

Your Program Doesn't Read Any Records

"Nothing is more frustrating for a beginner," I said, resuming after break, "than having your code read records from a disk file, but apparently not find any in the file, even though you know for certain that there are records there. Let's take a look at the code from chapter 11 again, Grades2.vbp, and see the type of mistake that can lead to this problem."

Once again, I displayed the code on the classroom projector and highlighted the line of code that is crucial to reading records from the disk file:

```
Private Sub Command1_Click()
   Dim strName As String
   Dim intGrade As Integer
   Open "C:\VBFILES\PRACTICE\L3EXAM1.TXT" For Input As #1
```

```
   Do While Not EOF(1)
       Input #1, strName, intGrade
       Form1.Print strName, intGrade
   Loop
   Close #1
End Sub
```

"How can you mess this up?" Ward asked.

"Like this," I said. "I've seen programmers, and not just beginners, leave the word Not out of their code."

```
Do While EOF(1)
```

"As soon as the Do...Loop begins to execute, Visual Basic recognizes that the record it is reading is not the special EOF and the loop immediately terminates. The file closes and the event procedure is exited. As a result, no records are read from the file!"

"So Visual Basic reads this statement, as Do the loop While EOF. Since we are not immediately at EOF, the loop never executes," Valerie commented. "That's right," I said. "Let's remove the word Not from the Do...Loop statement and see what happens."

I then changed the code and ran the program, this time in step mode to illustrate slowly what was happening. Sure enough, that's exactly what happened. As soon as Visual Basic encountered the first statement of the Do...Loop, the loop was terminated. The body of the loop was never executed and no records were read.

"Take my advice and don't vary from our Do...While method of reading records from a disk file," I suggested." It's a style that works well and you can't go wrong using it."

What If the File You Are Reading is Missing or Empty?

"Something just occurred to me," Dave said, "What happens if the disk file you want to read either doesn't exist or the file is there, but it's empty?"

"That's a good question," I said. "A missing file is much more of a problem than a file that is there, but which has no records. A little later in today's class we'll discuss and deal with the possibility of a missing prices.txt file."

I continued by saying that not too many beginners ponder these two possibilities.

"Programmers, and not just beginners, sometimes wear rose-colored glasses," I said.

"How could a file be missing?" Ward asked.

"Well," I replied, "the user could erase it by accident. Some files are created by other programs; perhaps the other program didn't run."

As a demonstration, I used Windows Explorer to rename the file **L3EXAM1.txt** to **L3EXAM1.bak**.

"OK," I said, "I've just renamed the disk file that the program requires. Let's see what happens when we run the program."

I then ran the original version of the program and clicked on the command button. The following error message was displayed:

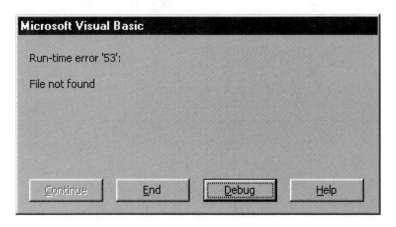

"That must be a frightening error message for the user when they receive it. How can we program for this possibility?" Blaine asked.

"Later on," I said, "we'll see that it's possible to intercept these frightening non-user friendly error messages and replace them with a message box that is a little more soothing. Most importantly, instead of the program just stopping, we can have our program continue on."

"I understand how the file can be missing and that we'll write code to handle the error later on," Ward said. "But what about an empty file? I didn't think it was possible to have a file with no records."

"Yes, it's possible," I said. "In fact, it's quite easy to do using Notepad."

I then started up Notepad and without adding any records to the file, immediately saved it as **L3EXAM1.txt**.

"We now have an empty **L3EXAM1.txt** file," I said.

I then ran the code and clicked on the command button. Nothing appeared to happen. I clicked on the command button again. Still nothing was displayed on the form.

"The program didn't bomb," Peter said.

"That's right. The program didn't bomb because the code immediately encountered the hidden EOF marker," I explained. "You need to consider what will happen to your program if the file you are reading is empty."

"What do you mean?" Barbara asked.

"Well, if the file is present, but empty, and your code assumes that there will be records in the file and then attempts to perform some processing based on that assumption, you could have some problems," I explained. "You should always check to see if the file is empty, and if it is, display a message to that effect. It would certainly have made this situation a little more user friendly, if we had displayed a message like that."

"Depending upon the program," I continued, "the effects of an empty file can be as mild as they were here, where we simply didn't display any data on the form, or the effects could be more severe. For instance, in last week's code that read test grades into an array from a disk file, summed the total of the test grades, divided that total by the number of grades, and printed that calculated average on the form."

I displayed the code on the classroom projector:

```
Private Sub Command1_Click()
    Dim intGrades() As Integer
    Dim intGradeCounter As Integer
    Dim intTotal As Integer
    Dim sngAverage As Single
    Open "C:\VBFILES\PRACTICE\L5EXAM2.TXT" For Input As #1
    Do While Not EOF(1)
        ReDim Preserve intGrades(intGradeCounter)
        Input #1, intGrades(intGradeCounter)
        intGradeCounter = intGradeCounter + 1
    Loop
    Close #1
    For intGradeCounter = LBound(intGrades) To UBound(intGrades)
        Form1.Print intGrades(intGradeCounter)
        intTotal = intTotal + intGrades(intGradeCounter)
    Next
    sngAverage = (intTotal / intGradeCounter)
    Form1.Print "The class average is " & sngAverage
End Sub
```

"What happens to our program if L5EXAM2.TXT is empty?" I asked the class.

No one was really quite sure. I went into Windows Explorer and created a new L5EXAM2.TXT file with no records. I then ran the program and clicked on the command button. The following error message was displayed:

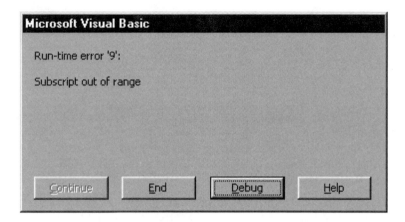

"Another nasty message, is that what they mean when they say a program bombed?" Joe asked.

"That's a bomb all right," I said. "The problem with this code is that it assumed there would always be data in the array. This program bombed when our code attempted to determine the lower bound of our array because we had declared a dynamic array. There were no records in the file, so the dynamic array was never allocated."

"I guess the bottom line is never to assume anything in programming," Steve said.

"This error isn't really our fault," Ward said. "After all, who would have thought that the file would be empty?"

"You're right, but it's not a matter of fault, it's a matter of reputation," I replied. "Programs that bomb leave a bad taste in the user's mouth and that can translate into lost referrals. When you write a program, you need to consider all of the things that could go wrong, things that, as you pointed out, are not necessarily your fault."

"That's what makes error handling so difficult. As a programmer, you spend a lot of time developing your program and test it as you go along. In testing their programs, most programmers never make data entry mistakes. In addition, when you test code designed to read records in a file, the file is always present and there are always records in it. But you see, you really need to be thinking about how you will handle errors like this as you develop your program."

Reading Too Many or Too Few Fields From a Disk File

"Another frustrating type of problem," I continued "is when you read records from a file and get the data into your program, only to discover that it doesn't seem to be in the right place."

"What do you mean?" Rhonda asked.

"For instance," I answered, "let's say you have a file with three fields in each record. You write code to open the file, read the data into three variables and then perform some kind of processing. Somehow, it appears that the data from field 1 is in the variable declared for field 2. However, sometimes it appears in the variable declared for field 3. I term this 'skewed' data."

"That happened to me last week when I was working on the code for the China Shop Project," Kate said. "I finally figured out that I left a field out of my `Input` statement."

"You hit the nail on the head there, Kate," I said. "If your `Input` statement doesn't match up perfectly with the number of fields in the record, you'll have this problem. Remember that the `Input` statement doesn't read records. It reads fields in a file."

"Do you think you could give us an example of this?" Steve asked. "I'm still not sure I understand the problem."

I thought for a moment and then gave this example.

"Suppose we have a file called `Cities.txt`, which contains 10 records. Each record contains three fields representing a city, state and zip code. That gives us a total of 30 fields in the file."

I took a minute to create the file in Notepad, saving it as Cities.txt in the `VBFiles\Practice` folder.

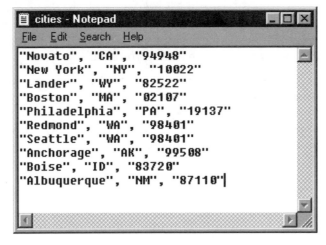

"We can use this code," I continued, "to read the data from the file and print it in neat columns:"

```
Private Sub Command1_Click()
   Dim strCity As String
   Dim strState As String
   Dim strZipCode As String
   Open "C:\VBFILES\PRACTICE\CITIES.TXT" For Input As #1
   Form1.Print "City", "State", "Zip Code"
   Form1.Print "----", "-----", "--------"
   Form1.Print
   Do While Not EOF(1)
      Input #1, strCity, strState, strZipCode
      Form1.Print strCity, strState, strZipCode
   Loop
   Close #1
End Sub
```

I quickly created a project, placed the above code in the Click event procedure of a command button and ran the program. The following results were displayed on the form:

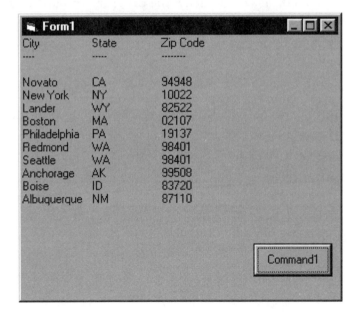

"In an ideal world," I said, "you open the file, declare a placeholder variable for each field in the record and then code an `Input` statement to read the fields in the file within a `Do...Loop`. However, this can be a lot more difficult than it appears here. Suppose next year, after successfully completing this course, you are hired by a big company and asked to write a program to read data from a data file that contains not three fields but three hundred and thirty three!"

"With a file that large, you wouldn't be able to use Notepad to view the fields in the file. You would be at the mercy of a specification sheet, which would list the number of fields in the record, their location and their data type."

"That sounds like we have a mistake brewing here," Rhonda said.

"That's right," I agreed. "With so many `Input` arguments to code, it's easy to make a mistake. You can forget to include an argument for one of the fields or declare a placeholder variable with the wrong data type. What if the program that produces the file is modified to include an additional field, giving it 334 fields, but no one bothers to tell you?"

"If any of these things happens, won't the program just bomb?" Kathy asked.

"Not necessarily," I replied. "If you're lucky, the program will bomb and the problem will become evident to you."

"What do you mean if we're lucky the program will bomb?" Rhonda asked. "Isn't that the last thing we want to happen?"

"If we have miscoded the `Input` statement and the program doesn't bomb, we have a potential disaster in the making," I explained. "The program will be working with incorrect data in the placeholder variables. There's no telling what it might do. That's what I mean."

"Can you give us an example of this?" Mary asked.

"Let's say," I suggested "that someone modifies our `Cities.txt` disk file, by including a country code and doesn't tell us."

I modified the file using Notepad and displayed it on the classroom projector.

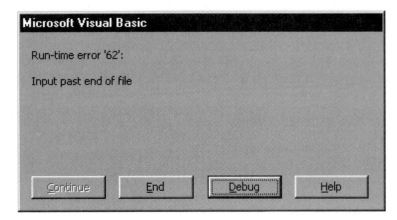

"Any guesses as to what will happen when we run our program against this file?" I asked.

"I think that instead of displaying 10 records, we'll display 13," Dave said.

"I think the program will bomb," Steve suggested.

"My guess is that the program will still display 10 records," Ward said, "but the data will be in the wrong place."

"Let's see," I said as I ran the program with the modified cities.txt file. The following error message was displayed:

"Well," I said, "looks like Steve was right."

"What happened?" Rhonda asked.

"Don't think of the file as a collection of records. I think it's easier to understand if you think of the file as a collection of fields. Our `Input` statement contained three placeholder variables in its argument list. Each time the `Input` statement was executed, we read three fields. The argument list exactly matched the number of fields in the disk file record, so it took us exactly 10 executions of the `Input` statement to read all 30 fields in the file."

I waited for questions, but there were none.

"After we changed the file structure, it's a 'given' that the data we are reading is going to be wrong," I explained. "Why does the program bomb, though? There are now 40 fields in the file. With each execution of the `Input` statement, the program reads 3 fields. After the first execution of the `Input` statement, for instance, it has read the first three fields of the first record. After the second execution, it has read the fourth field of the first record and the first two of the second. After the third execution, it has read the third and fourth field of the second record, and the first field of the third record."

"I think we get the idea," Linda said.

"My point is," I continued, "that after the thirteenth execution of the `Input` statement, the program has read 39 fields. With only one field remaining in the file, the next execution of the `Input` statement causes the program to read beyond the EOF marker, and it bombs."

"I think I understand why the program bombed," Kathy said. "Is there any way that this program wouldn't blow up?"

"It could happen," I said. "For instance, since our `Input` statement contains three placeholder variables, if our incorrectly formatted input file contained a total number of fields that was a multiple of 3, the program would run successfully to completion. Suppose I delete the last record in the file. That will give us 9 records. What is 9 multiplied by 4?"

"36," Dave replied. "A multiple of 3. So you're saying the program won't bomb this time because it will believe it is reading 12 records of 3 fields each, when in reality it's reading a file containing 9 records of 4 fields each."

"That's right," I said. "Wait until you see the results!"

I then used Notepad to delete the last record of the file and the following results were printed on the form:

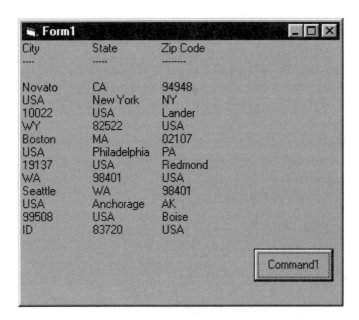

"Now I see what you mean by the data being skewed," Blaine said.

"So was it just luck that allowed this code to run without bombing?" Ward asked.

"Yes," I replied. "Bad luck. This program ran successfully to completion with no obvious sign, aside from the printed results on the form, that the program was not operating properly. If this had been a real-world program, one in which there was no output to alert the user that something was wrong, a program like this could run without anyone noticing the incorrect results."

"What can you do about something like this?" Ward asked.

"For this kind of error, there isn't much you can do, except to enforce strict validation on the data that you read into your program," I answered. "That's why I had termed this one of the most frustrating types of errors to try to uncover and correct. Good design, specifications, documentation and most important of all communication, will go a long way toward preventing this type of error."

Division by Zero

I continued by stating that in the computer world, division by zero is a big 'no-no'.

"What's 12 divided by 1?" I asked.

"12," Mary replied.

"Now what about 12 divided by 1/2?" I continued.

After a moment's hesitation, Dave answered, "24."

"Correct," I said.

There were some puzzled faces.

"I know I've caught you math phobics on that one," I said. "A number, divided by a number smaller than one, always results in an answer larger than the original number."

"I believe in using math terms," Ward said, "you mean to say that when we divide by a number smaller than one, we take the **reciprocal** and multiply by it. In other words, 12 divided by 1/2 becomes 12 multiplied by 2."

I then displayed the following chart on the board:

Number 1	Divided by	Number 2	Answer
12	/	1	12
12	/	1/2	24
12	/	1/3	36
12	/	1/4	72
12	/	1/10	120
12	/	1/100	1200
12	/	1/1000	12000

I told them that as the **divisor** (Number 2) approaches zero, the answer becomes larger and larger. In fact, it becomes an infinite number.

"For that reason," I continued, "dividing a number by 0 in your computer program will simply cause your program to bomb. This will happen in whatever computer language you program."

I then displayed the following code on the classroom projector, placed it in a command button and ran the program.

```
Form1.Print 12 /0
```

The following error message was displayed:

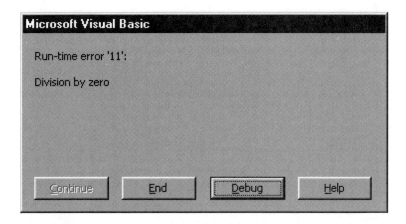

I explained that most beginners aren't aware of the problem of division by zero and their immediate response is that they will never intentionally divide by zero.

"That's what I was going to say," Ward said.

"Exactly what everyone says," I continued. "This error is more likely to occur when you use a property value or an uninitialized variable value. Take a look at this":

```
Form1.Print Text1.Text / intCounter
```

"If the value of intCounter here has never been incremented then your program will bomb," I explained.

"This seems like something that you can check for with an If statement," Barbara suggested.

I explained that all of the run-time errors that we had examined can be detected by our program pretty easily by using If...Then...Else statements.

"However," I said, "these errors can be detected and handled even easier by using **error handling** routines. That's what we'll look at when we come back from break."

Error Handling

After break, I told everyone that we had intentionally caused programs to bomb during the first part of our class. Now we would be looking at ways of handling those errors in such a way that our programs just don't stop in mid-stream.

"Nothing can ruin your reputation faster," I said, "than having a customer mention to someone else that he loves your program, except that it bombs once in a while."

I explained that it isn't always possible to code a program that will never encounter an error. For instance, you might write a program, based on a customer's request, that reads data from a disk file of their choosing.

"Suppose," I said, "the customer tells your program that the disk file is on a diskette, but then forgets to insert the diskette? Your program bombs."

"That generates an error?" Ward asked. "In Word, a warning message is displayed."

"That's exactly the point," I replied. "The programmer who coded Microsoft Word intercepts the error message generated by Windows and replaces a more user-friendly message for the Windows error message. Most important, though, Word continues running instead of unceremoniously bombing."

"Not in my experience," joked Steve, "but I guess it's harder to handle every error in a complicated application like that."

"Can we do that in our programs? I mean, intercept these errors?" Barbara asked.

"Yes we can," I said. "It's possible to code in such a way that those nasty Visual Basic error messages are replaced with soothing, user friendly ones that appear as warning messages instead and that can be great for your reputation."

Let's begin our look at error handlers by intentionally coding a division by zero operation in the next exercise, to make the program bomb.

Exercise

Intentionally Generating an Error

1. Start a new **Standard.EXE** project.

2. Place a command button on the form. Accept the default name that Visual Basic assigns.

3. Double-click on the command button and place the following code into its **Click** event procedure:

```
Private Sub Command1_Click()
    Dim intValue1 As Integer
    Dim intValue2 As Integer
    intValue1 = 12
    Form1.Print intValue1 / intValue2
End Sub
```

4.   Save your project in your \VBFiles\Practice subdirectory. Save the form as Error.frm and the project as Error.vbp. Now run the program.

5.   The program will bomb with a Division by zero run-time error:

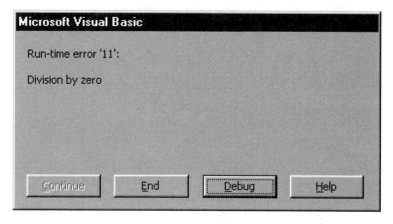

Discussion

There weren't any questions about the exercise. Everyone understood what had happened. Our program had divided the value of the variable intValue1 by the uninitialized variable intValue2 (which therefore had a value of 0) and the program had bombed.

Everyone seemed eager to see what we could do to intercept this error code, so I distributed the following exercise:

Exercise
Your First Error Handler

1.   Now use the File menu to save Error.vbp from the previous exercise, saving the form as Error2.frm and the project as Error2.vbp. Now continue to work with Error2.vbp.

2.   Change the code in the Click event procedure of the command button so that it looks like this. New code that you should type in has been highlighted:

```
Private Sub Command1_Click()
    On Error GoTo ICanDealWithThis
    Dim intValue1 As Integer
    Dim intValue2 As Integer
    intValue1 = 12
    Form1.Print intValue1 / intValue2
    Exit Sub
ICanDealWithThis:
    MsgBox "Error Number:" & Err.Number & vbCrLf & _
        Err.Description
    Resume Next
End Sub
```

3.   Save the project again and then run the program.

4.   Click on the command button. This time the program doesn't bomb. A message box of our own is displayed with the error number and description, but the program continues to run.

Discussion

After I ran the program, the following screen was displayed on the classroom projector:

"This code isn't much different from the code from the first **Error.vbp** exercise," I explained. "However, notice that once the message box is displayed and the OK button is clicked, the program keeps running. There's the difference."

"So what we've done here," Dave said, "is substitute our error message for Visual Basic's and keep the program alive."

"Yes," I agreed. "We can get even fancier than this with the way we handled it, so much so that the user may not even realize a potentially fatal error occurred."

I suggested that we take a look at how the code works.

"What we've done here," I continued, "is to enable a Visual Basic **error handler**."

I explained that an error handler must be coded in each procedure in which you want the ability to intercept an error the way we did here. Once coded, if an error (any error at all) occurs in that procedure, Visual Basic will then skip right to that coded error handler and execute the code it finds there.

"Suppose no error occurs in the procedure?" Barbara asked.

"If no error occurs in the procedure, then Visual Basic will execute the code as normal," I explained. "Well, that's almost true. We also need to place an **Exit Sub** statement before the error handler code, otherwise the error handler code will be executed."

I could see that the last statement had confused some of the class.

"Hang on," I said, "I'll get to that in a minute – first let's look at the line of code that enables the error handler."

```
On Error GoTo ICanDealWithThis
```

"I'm not sure," Ward said, "but didn't I hear somewhere that **GoTo** is something you shouldn't code in your program?"

"Good point," I said, "with one exception, and this is it. In Visual Basic, you must use the **GoTo** statement to enable an error handler."

"What is **ICanDealWithThis**?" Joe asked.

I explained that **ICanDealWithThis** is the name of a Visual Basic **label**.

"That's not a label control," I said. "In Basic, a label was like a section name in your code procedure almost like a bookmark in Microsoft Word. You hardly ever see it used anymore, except of course with an error handler. In Visual Basic, you designate a label in code by entering the name in your procedure, followed by a colon (:)." I displayed our error handler label on the classroom projector.

```
ICanDealWithThis:
```

I explained that the code following the label name is the actual code of the error handler, that's the code which is executed if an error occurs in the procedure.

"Can you name the label anything?" Peter asked. "Yes," I replied, "anything you want. Just make sure that the name that follows the **GoTo** statement is repeated later as a label in the procedure.""Must the error handler label and code appear at the end of the procedure?" Mary asked. "That's the best location for it," I responded. "By convention, that's where you'll find it."

There were no more immediate questions, so I suggested that we look at the code within the error handler now.

"I want you to notice," I continued, "that immediately before the error handler label, we have coded an **Exit Sub** statement."

```
    Exit Sub
ICanDealWithThis:
   MsgBox "Error Number:" & Err.Number & vbCrLf & Err.Description
   Resume Next
```

"You must always code an **Exit Sub** immediately in front of the error handler label," I explained. "Without an **Exit Sub**, because of the falling rock behavior of Visual Basic code, Visual Basic would eventually execute the code in the error handler anyway. **Exit Sub** is a way of skipping the error handler code and ending the procedure."

"What's going on in that **MsgBox** statement?" Steve asked.

I explained that we are displaying the **Number** and **Description** properties of something called the **Err** object in the message box. The **Err** object is created or instantiated whenever a Visual Basic error occurs. Because it's an object, just like a form or a control, we have access to it and can display its property values in a message box.

"Is the **Err** object only instantiated if we code an error handler?" Dave asked.

"No, it's instantiated regardless," I replied. "In fact, that's where those nasty Visual Basic error messages get their information."

"I think I'm a little confused here. Can we run this program in step mode?" Linda asked.

"Good idea," I said, and I did as she requested. We saw that as soon as the line to perform division by zero was executed, Visual Basic jumped immediately to the **MsgBox** statement within the error handler code.

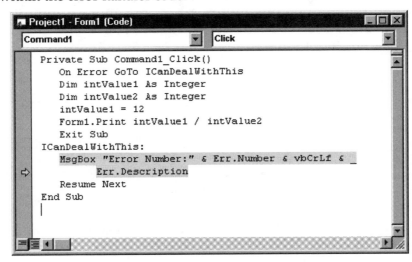

The program displayed the message box informing us of the error (to which I answered OK), and then executed the `Resume Next` statement.

Then the program jumped back up to the line following the division by zero line.

"Wait a minute," Ward said, "what's that `Resume Next` statement?"

Resume Next

I explained that once Visual Basic jumps to the code in your error handler, you have several choices as to what to do at that point.

"In this code," I said, "all we did was to display the number and description of the `Err` object in a message box. If we did nothing else, the program would reach the `End Sub` statement in the procedure and the procedure would end."

I continued by saying that in an error handler, after you react to the error, you can do one of three things:

- You can end the program by coding an `Exit Sub` statement within the error handler or just let the program reach the `End Sub`.

- You can instruct Visual Basic to continue running the program at the same line of code that caused the error to begin with. You do this by coding a `Resume` statement.

- You can instruct Visual Basic to resume running the program from the next line of code following the one that caused the error. You do that by coding a `Resume Next` statement.

"The second one sounds like a really bad idea to me. Why go back to the line of code that generated the error?" Joe asked.

"That's a good point," I agreed, "however, it's possible that the condition that caused the error may have been corrected, perhaps in response to a message that you displayed to the user. For instance, remember my earlier example of the user who tells our program that there is a file on a diskette in the diskette drive, but then forgets to insert the diskette? A user friendly message asking them to insert the floppy, followed by a `Resume` statement will do the trick!"

I continued by explaining that the decision as to how to proceed after the code in the error handler has been executed is influenced by the likelihood that either the program or the user can somehow correct the problem that caused the error in the first place.

"In this exercise," I said, "there's absolutely no sense in continuing execution with the same line of code because there's no way that the expression will ever result in anything other than division by zero. Coding a `Resume` statement can be very dangerous. If, for whatever reason, your program or the user cannot resolve the error, you've essentially created what I call an **endless error**."

"So, `Resume Next` is the way to go then?" Dave asked.

I explained that you couldn't just code the `Resume Next` statement in a vacuum. Since `Resume Next` essentially skips the line of code that generated the error, if that line of code was crucial to the successful completion of the procedure, this can cause disastrous results as well.

"The bottom line," I continued, "is that you've got to carefully consider your error handler strategy in light of the types of conditions you might encounter."

"You mean you can take different actions at different times?" Barbara asked.

"That's right," I said, "you can check the number property of the `Err` object and take different corrective action based on the error that triggered the error handler."

Exercise
Select...Case in the Error Handler

1. Now save the project under a different name again, saving `Error2.frm` as `Error3.frm`, and `Error2.vbp` as `Error3.vbp`.

2. Working with `Error3.vbp`, Change the code in the `Click` event procedure of the command button so that it looks like this:

```
Private Sub Command1_Click()
    On Error GoTo ICanDealWithThis
    Dim intValue1 As Integer
    Dim intValue2 As Integer
    intValue1 = 12
    Form1.Print intValue1 / intValue2
    Exit Sub
ICanDealWithThis:
    Select Case Err.Number
        Case 11
            MsgBox "Division by Zero"
        Case Else
            MsgBox "Error Number:" & Err.Number & vbCrLf & _
                Err.Description
    End Select
    Resume Next
End Sub
```

3. Save the project again. Now run the program.

4. Click on the command button. This time the program displays a customized error message and continues to run.

Discussion

I immediately ran the program and the following message box was displayed:

"This code isn't much different from that in the previous exercise, with the exception of the **Select Case** statement," I explained.

I added that using the **Select Case** statement to examine the **Number** property of the **Err** object gives your program tremendous flexibility.

"Is that basically what you do, code a **Case** statement for each possible error?" Joe asked.

"That's what some programmers do," I replied. "Others just create one for the errors they feel are likely to occur."

"What do you do?" Ward asked.

"I let experience be my guide," I answered. "As you begin to write more and more programs, you develop a feel for the types of errors that could occur and when. Those are the ones I include in my error handler."

"Something just occurred to me," Dave said. "You said you need to code an error handler in every procedure...that could mean a lot of **Case** statements in your project."

"That's not exactly right Dave," I said. "What I said was that you need an error handler in every procedure in which you want to catch errors."

"So you don't necessarily code an error handler in every procedure?" he responded.

I explained that you would see instances of both extremes, that is, no error handling at all and error handlers coded in every procedure.

"But what do you do?" Ward asked again.

"I use my experience," I replied. "I code error handlers in procedures that historically have produced errors, such as procedures where I'm reading or writing files."

"Can you tell us what's going on with the `Case Else` statement?" Barbara asked.

I reminded everyone that `Case Else` is the 'catchall' of the `Select Case` statement. That is, if none of the other `Case` statements are found to be true, then the statements in the `Case Else` clause are executed.

"In this instance, if we encounter an error that we're not expecting, we display the error number and description," I explained.

There were no more questions, so it was time to turn our attention to error handling in the China Shop Project.

Error Handling in the China Shop Project

"We'll code error handlers in two procedures of our China Shop Project, the `Click` event procedure of `mnuColorCustomize` and the `Load` event procedure of the form."

I loaded up the China Shop Project, ran it and then selected <u>P</u>references-<u>C</u>olors-Custom from the menu. Instead of selecting a color from the palette, however, I clicked on the Cancel button. The following error message was displayed:

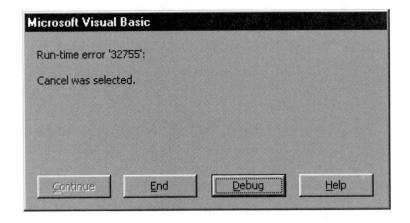

"That's right," Rhonda said. "I forgot about that. If you select Cancel, instead of a color, the program bombs. Why is that happening?"

I explained that earlier we had changed the `CancelError` property of the Common Dialog control to `True`, because if the user clicked on the Cancel button, our form was being changed to black.

"We decided that we wanted to be able to detect the user clicking on the Cancel button and the way we did that was to change the `CancelError` property to `True`," I continued. "Unfortunately, at the time we didn't have enough knowledge to write an error handler to deal with this error. Now we're ready."

Exercise
Coding an Error Handler in the China Shop Project

1. Load up the China Shop Project.

2. Change the code in the `mnuColorsCustom_Click` event procedure so that it looks like this:

```
Private Sub mnuColorsCustom_Click()
    On Error GoTo ICanHandleThis
    dlgChina.ShowColor
    frmMain.BackColor = dlgChina.Color
    m_lngBackColor = frmMain.BackColor
    Exit Sub
ICanHandleThis:
    Select Case Err.Number
        Case 32755
            MsgBox "Color change canceled"
            Exit Sub
        Case Else
            MsgBox "Unexpected error has occurred" & vbCrLf _
                & "Contact a member of staff"
    End Select
End Sub
```

3. Save the China Shop Project.

4. Run the program. Select <u>P</u>references-<u>C</u>olors-Custom from the menu. When the Color dialog box appears, select the Cancel button. This time the program displays a message informing the user that their color change has been canceled.

Discussion

I'm not sure if it was fatigue, but several students made errors in this exercise. Two students forgot to code the `Exit Sub` statement right above the error handler and generated endless loops in the procedure. After we resolved these minor problems, everyone seemed to be impressed with their first error handler.

"All we did here," I explained, "was to use a `Select...Case` statement to look for the number of an error we know is a distinct possibility in this procedure. And just in case, we coded a `Case...Else` statement, asking the user to contact a member of staff if any other error is encountered."

I waited for questions, but there were none.

"We have one more error handler to code, before we can call it a day," I continued. "That's the error handler for the `Load` event procedure of the form. Can anyone tell me why I think it's a good idea to code an error handler in that procedure?"

"The disk file access, I would think," Chuck answered.

"Right you are," I said. "Any time you have a procedure that works with disk files, you should code an error handler."

I explained that the most likely error to occur in the `Load` event procedure of the form would be if the input file `prices.txt` was missing.

"There's really nothing we can do if this happens," I explained, "beyond displaying a user friendly message to the China Shop staff and ending the program. However, that message will prevent the program from bombing and destroying our reputation."

In this exercise, we'll temporarily rename the file `prices.txt` to `oprices.txt`. Then we'll run the program. The program won't find the file when it starts up so the program will bomb. We'll then add an error handler to deal with the missing file. When we run the program, our new error handler will gracefully handle the missing file. Finally, we'll rename `oprices.txt` to `prices.txt`.

Exercise
Code an Error Handler in the Form_Load Event Procedure

1. If the China Shop project is running, stop it by clicking on the End button on the Toolbar.

2. Use Explorer to rename `prices.txt` as `oprices.txt` (remember, `prices.txt` should be in your `VBFiles\China` folder. If it's not, you can find a copy in the CD-provided files for this chapter.)

3. Run the program. The file that the Load event procedure requires is missing so the program will bomb with the following message:

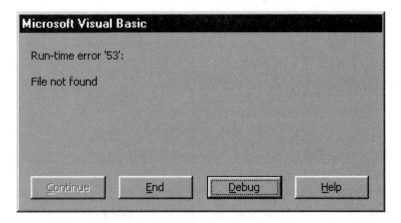

4. Click on the End button to stop the program.

5. Enter the following code in the Form_Load event procedure. The changed code is highlighted:

```
Private Sub Form_Load()
    On Error GoTo ICanHandleThis
    Dim strBrand As String
    Dim intCounter As Integer
    Open "C:\VBFILES\CHINA\PRICES.TXT" For Input As #1
    Do While Not EOF(1) ' Loop until end of file.
        ReDim Preserve m_curBowlPrice(intCounter)
        ReDim Preserve m_curButterPlatePrice(intCounter)
        ReDim Preserve m_curCupPrice(intCounter)
        ReDim Preserve m_curPlatePrice(intCounter)
        ReDim Preserve m_curPlatterPrice(intCounter)
        ReDim Preserve m_curSaucerPrice(intCounter)
        ReDim Preserve m_curCompletePrice(intCounter)
            Input #1, strBrand, _
                m_curPlatePrice(intCounter), _
                m_curButterPlatePrice(intCounter), _
                m_curBowlPrice(intCounter), _
                m_curCupPrice(intCounter), _
                m_curSaucerPrice(intCounter), _
                m_curPlatterPrice(intCounter), _
```

```
                m_curCompletePrice(intCounter)
        lstBrands.AddItem strBrand
        intCounter = intCounter + 1
    Loop
    Close #1
    Exit Sub
ICanHandleThis:
    Select Case Err.Number
        Case 53                     'File not found
            MsgBox "A file required by the " & _
                   "China Shop program " & vbCrLf & _
                   "is missing. Please ensure that " & vbCrLf & _
                   "PRICES.TXT is in " & vbCrLf & _
                   "the China Shop directory " & vbCrLf & _
                   "on the computer's hard drive"
            Unload frmMain
            Exit Sub
        Case Else
            MsgBox "Unexpected error has occurred" & _
                   vbCrLf & "Contact John Smiley"
            Unload frmMain
            Exit Sub
    End Select
End Sub
```

6. Save the China Shop Project.

7. Run the program. This time, instead of bombing with a File not found error, the program will display a user-friendly message indicating that the input file cannot be found:

8. Click on OK. The program will gracefully end.

9. Use Explorer to rename `oprices.txt` back to `prices.txt`.

10. Run the program. This time the program runs normally.

Discussion

There were no obvious problems as the class completed this exercise.

"I see that if we couldn't find the input file," Linda said, "we unloaded the form, which just ends the program. But why are we ending the program if we encounter any other kind of error?"

"It's partly a defense mechanism," I replied. "I can't anticipate any other kind of error occurring here and since the `Load` event procedure of the form is so important, I'm reluctant to let the program go any further if we encounter any other error at all. I just prefer to display a message asking the user to contact us and to end the program."

There were no other questions.

"Next week will be a bittersweet class for us," I continued, "as we finish up the China Shop Project and the course. Don't forget, if you wish, you can travel to the China Shop with me and participate in the installation of the program."

Summary

This chapter was designed to give you an idea about errors. We've actually covered two different types of errors here: the common mistakes made by beginning programmers, and the kind of error that is not caused by a programming mistake.

Everyone makes mistakes when they start programming. Never let this discourage you. It's a case of experience. When you first learn a new thing, it's strange and awkward; as you become more familiar with it, you'll make less mistakes. Sometimes it looks like a program should work a certain way, when it actually interprets it a different way. Let's take a simple example.

When you're using a combo box, and you change the selected item in the box by clicking on the list, what event is that? Sounds like a `Change` event if you're not familiar with the way combo boxes work. But it's not; it's a `Click` event. Once you know that, you won't keep making that mistake.

The other type of error is the kind you have to try to foresee; the possibility that the divisor of an operation will be zero; the possibility that a disk file you require is not on the drive; and so on. If you can foresee it, you can code an error handler. A lot of the time, all an error handler does is replace a Windows error message with a fluffier design of your own. But you can also code a handler so it recognizes that there was an error, logs it, and lets the program continue.

You have to remember that you can't always code for every eventuality. You could put handlers in for everything you can think of, just in case, but your code would be mostly error handlers! You should definitely put an error handler in when you're working with disk access, though.

In the final chapter of this book, we're going to complete the China Shop project: among the enhancements we'll add is some code that makes it easier for the user to save and retrieve their customized settings (their chosen background color, for example).

Quiz

1. The Err object has six properties. What is the property that contains the error code that was last generated by your application?

2. What is wrong with this code? Telling me that division by 0 is wrong, or noting the use of the Visual Basic GoTo are not what I'm looking for either.

```
Public Sub Division()
    On Error GoTo ErrorHandler
    Print 12 / 0
    Exit Sub
ErrorHandle:
    Msgbox Str(Err.Number) & ": " & Err.Description, , "Error"
Exit Sub
```

3. In this code, what is the function of the Exit Sub before the label?

```
Public Sub Division()
    On Error GoTo ErrorHandler
    Print 12 / 0
Exit Sub
ErrorHandler:
    Msgbox Str(Err.Number) & ": " & Err.Description, , "Error"
End Sub
```

4. There are three variations on the Resume statement found in an error handler. Don't worry, I'll only ask you about two. What is the difference between Resume and Resume Next?

5. What's wrong with this piece of code?

```
Private Function Divide(ByVal dOne As Double, _
        ByVal dTwo As Double) As Double
    Divide = dOne / dTwo
End Function
```

6. What's wrong with this code?

```
Private Function Divide(ByVal dOne As Double, _
        ByVal dTwo As Double) As Double
    On Error GoTo Divide_Err:
    Divide = dOne / dTwo
Divide_Err:
    Resume
End Function
```

7. What happens if you type the following statement into the Immediate window pane?

```
? sMyValue
```

8. What's the purpose of a counter?

9. What's the purpose of an accumulator, and how is it different from a counter?

10. What error code is generated when you perform a read or write operation on a file that hasn't been opened?

11. What error code is generated when you attempt to read past the EOF marker in a disk file?

12. The key to error handling in Visual Basic is to first _____ an error handler in the procedure.

13. What follows the keyword GoTo?

14. What is the property of the CommonDialog control that enables your program to 'intercept' an error if the user presses the Cancel button?

15. True or False: An instance of the Err object is created when an error occurs in a procedure only when the procedure has an enabled error handler.

Extra Credit – If a plane crashes on the border between two states, where are the survivors buried?

Chapter 15
Customizing Your Application

In this, our final chapter, we'll follow my class as we complete the China Shop Project, and then deliver and install the application in the China Shop.

"When do we deliver the program?" Ward asked.

"I have some exciting news," I said. "At the end of last week's class, I told you that we would be delivering the program to the China Shop today. During the week, Joe Bullina called me and told me he was having a huge ribbon cutting ceremony for the program today, including food and music."

It seemed to me, from the looks on their faces, that everyone would be making the trip to the China Shop. "It's a shame, but it doesn't look like Rose and Jack will make it. Has anyone heard from them?" Mary asked.

"They called me from their ship two nights ago," I replied. "They said the weather was frigid and they had spoken to the Captain who assured them they would be in New York harbor early this morning, a few hours ahead of schedule. I expect them to be here before the end of class."

"Will the delivery and installation of the China Shop program wrap up the SDLC?" Linda asked. "Just about," I said. "Phase 5, which is the **Implementation** phase, will definitely begin today and conclude during the course of the week. Phase 6, which is **Audit and Maintenance**, will actually begin today as well."

I waited for more questions.

"In today's class, we'll be covering areas related to the customization of the China Shop program," I explained. "First, there are a few items from our Requirements Statement that we haven't yet implemented in the program; specifically, saving the user's preferences to the Windows Registry. Secondly, in the last part of today's class, I want to discuss streamlining our code."

Writing to the Windows Registry

"I always thought that writing to the Windows Registry was dangerous," Kate said.

"Yes," Kathy agreed. "Can't you corrupt the Registry database when writing to it?"

I explained that the Windows Registry is just a database that Windows uses to store and track information necessary for the operation of your computer.

"Writing to the Windows Registry is perfectly safe, provided you use the functions provided by Visual Basic to write to and read from the Registry," I explained. "But for those of you who feel squeamish about it, I'll also show you how to back up the Registry prior to working with it."

I continued by explaining that the benefits of using the Windows Registry to record information for later use in your program are immeasurable.

"What types of information do you record in the Registry?" Kate asked.

"I use the Registry to store information that must be maintained from one session of the program to another," I replied. "For instance, some programs record the user's preferences for Window size and location, and the Registry is a perfect place to store that information. If you use Microsoft Word, you'll notice that it records the last few files that you accessed. That information is stored in the Registry as well. Options for grammar checking, spell checking, etc., are all stored in the Registry."

"Does anyone remember what we said we'd use the Registry for in the China Shop Project?" I asked.

"Information about the user's preference for colors, and the date and time display," Blaine answered.

GetSetting and SaveSetting

"That's correct," I said. "I think you'll find that writing to, and reading from, the Windows Registry is amazingly easy. Two Visual Basic statements allow you to do this. The `GetSetting` function reads from the Registry, and the `SaveSetting` statement writes to the Registry. Let's take a look at the `SaveSetting` statement first."

I displayed the syntax for the `SaveSetting` statement on the classroom projector:

```
SaveSetting appname, section, key, setting
```

"I know this looks a little confusing," I said, "but let me try to de-mystify it for you."

"Remember that the Windows Registry is just a database, and a database is very much like a file which is composed of records and fields," I continued. "The entries that you store in the Registry in Visual Basic are really nothing more than records. However, since they are records stored in a database, we need to provide just a little bit more information than the value that we want to store in the Registry. We also need to supply an **appname**, **section,** and **key**."

I waited for questions, but there were none.

"That's what the first three arguments to the `SaveSetting` statement are," I said. "For instance, we'll write the user's preferred color to the Registry with an **appname** of `"BULLINACHINA"`, a section of `"STARTUP"`, and a key of `"BackColor""`.

"What's the **setting** argument?" Ward asked. "The **setting** argument is the actual value that we are saving to the Registry," I replied.

"Can we name the appname, section, and key as anything we want?" Linda asked. "Yes," I replied, "but of course, as with all of our naming conventions, pick something that's meaningful."

"Are all the arguments required?" Blaine asked. "Yes, you must use all four," I responded.

I explained that once you've decided what to call your registry entry, that is, you've determined the first three arguments, the rest is easy.

"At that point," I continued, "all you need to do is issue the `SaveSetting` statement, specify the appname, section, and key arguments you've decided upon, and provide a value. Visual Basic does the rest for you, finding and opening the Windows Registry, creating the record in the Registry if one does not exist, or updating the existing record if it is already there."

"Are you saying that if an entry already exists with that key combination, then Visual Basic will update it; and if the entry is not there, then Visual Basic creates it?" Dave asked.

"That's right," I said. "I told you it was easy."

I displayed this example on the classroom projector:

```
SaveSetting "MyApp","STARTUP", "Left", 50
```

"This code," I explained, "will create an entry with the value 50 in the Windows Registry with the appname MyApp, the section STARTUP, and a key of Left. If that combination of appname, section, and key already exists, then the value 50 will overlay the value already present."

I told the class that, at this point, the logical step to take was to complete an exercise to write to the Windows Registry.

"You did mention that we should backup the Registry before we do anything to it. Are you going to show us how to do that before this next step then?" Rhonda said.

"You're right," I said, "I almost forgot. I just happen to have an exercise that will lead you through that process."

Exercise

Backing Up the Windows Registry

1.   Click on the Windows Start button.

2.   Click on Run.

3.   Type regedit into the text box and click on the OK button.

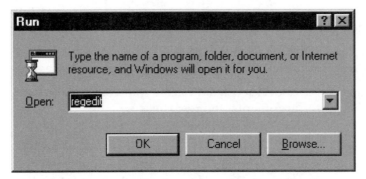

4.   The Windows Registry Editor will appear:

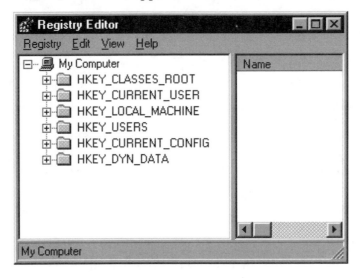

5. Select <u>R</u>egistry-<u>E</u>xport Registry File from the menu:

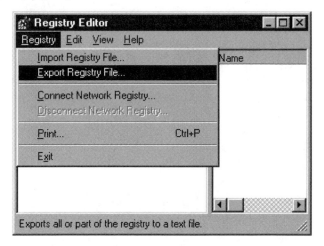

6. A dialog box will appear asking you to specify the name for the Registry backup. I usually name my Registry backup files according to the date I backed it up. For instance, since today was October 5, 1998, I named the Registry backup 100598. The extension `.reg` will automatically be added to the file.

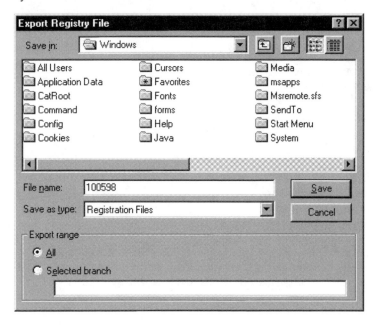

7. Click on the <u>S</u>ave button and a backup of the Registry will be saved for you.

Discussion

"Backing up the Registry, as you can see, is pretty easy," I explained. "Restoring the Registry, if you need to do that, is a little more complicated, and I'm not going to get into that here. The important thing is that you now have peace of mind that, if something does happen to your Registry, there is a way to restore it. Believe me, if anything corrupts your Registry it won't be anything I teach you here today."

Everyone seemed content that they knew how to backup the Registry.

"In this next exercise," I continued, "we'll use the **SaveSetting** statement to save the user's preferences to the Registry."

In this exercise, we'll place code in the China Shop Project to write the user's preferred color preference and date and time display to the Windows Registry.

Exercise

Write to the Windows Registry

1. Load up the China Shop Project.

2. Modify the **mnuColorsCustom_Click** event procedure so that it looks like this:

```
Private Sub mnuColorsCustom_Click()
    On Error GoTo ICanHandleThis
    dlgChina.ShowColor
    frmMain.BackColor = dlgChina.Color
    m_lngBackColor = frmMain.BackColor
    SaveSetting "BULLINACHINA", "STARTUP", "BackColor", _
        m_lngBackColor
    Exit Sub
ICanHandleThis:
    Select Case Err.Number
        Case 32755
            MsgBox "Color change canceled"
            Exit Sub
        Case Else
            MsgBox "Unexpected error has occurred" & vbCrLf & _
            "Contact a member of the China Shop staff"
    End Select
End Sub
```

3. Find the `mnuColorsDefault_Click` event procedure. Change it so that it looks like this:

```
Private Sub mnuColorsDefault_Click()
    frmMain.BackColor = &H8000000F
    m_lngBackColor = frmMain.BackColor
    SaveSetting "BULLINACHINA", "STARTUP", "BackColor", _
        m_lngBackColor
End Sub
```

4. Modify the `mnuPreferencesDateAndTimeOff_Click` event procedure so that it looks like this:

```
Private Sub mnuPreferencesDateAndTimeOff_Click()
    mnuPreferencesDateAndTimeOff.Checked = True
    mnuPreferencesDateAndTimeOn.Checked = False
    tmrChina.Enabled = False
    lblDateAndTime.Visible = False
    m_blnDateDisplay = False
    SaveSetting "BULLINACHINA", "STARTUP", "DateDisplay", _
        m_blnDateDisplay
End Sub
```

5. Find the `mnuPreferencesDateAndTimeOn_Click` event procedure and change it so that it looks like this:

```
Private Sub mnuPreferencesDateAndTimeOn_Click()
    mnuPreferencesDateAndTimeOff.Checked = False
    mnuPreferencesDateAndTimeOn.Checked = True
    tmrChina.Enabled = True
    lblDateAndTime.Visible = True
    m_blnDateDisplay = True
    SaveSetting "BULLINACHINA", "STARTUP", "DateDisplay", _
        m_blnDateDisplay
End Sub
```

6. Save the China Shop Project by clicking on the Save icon on the Toolbar.

7. Run the program. Select Preferences-Colors-Custom from the main menu. When the Color dialog box appears, select your favorite color, and then click on the OK button. The background color of the form will change.

8. Select Preferences-Date and Time Off to toggle the display of the date and time off.

9. End the program by selecting File-Exit from the main menu. Don't forget to enter the correct password (061883)!

10. Run the program again. Did the program remember the changes you made to the color of the form and the date and time display?

Discussion

"Something's wrong," Ward said. "My settings weren't saved. After I started the China Shop program again, my colors were still the default, and the date and time was displayed."

"Actually," I said, "you haven't done anything wrong. The answer to step 10 of the exercise is that the program didn't remember the changes you made to the color and date and time preference. Who can tell me why that's the case?"

"We haven't written any code yet to read those settings when the program starts up," Dave replied.

"That's right," I said. "We need to place code in the Load event procedure of the form to read these preferences from the Window Registry, and we'll do that shortly. Before we do that though, let's take a quick look at the code that we wrote to save the user's preferences to the Windows Registry, to make sure that everyone understands what is happening here."

I suggested that we examine the Click event procedure of mnuColorsCustom first.

"All but one line of this code was in the event procedure already," I explained.

```
SaveSetting "BULLINACHINA", "STARTUP", "BackColor", m_lngBackColor
```

"This line of code saves the value of m_lngBackColor to the Windows Registry," I continued. "Don't forget that the value of the BackColor property of the form has been assigned to the form-level variable m_lngBackColor."

"Is there a way to verify that this setting was actually saved in the Registry?" Steve asked.

Using RegEdit

"Yes, there is," I said. "Again, we'll use the Registry Editor to verify that the setting has been written."

I started up the Registry Editor:

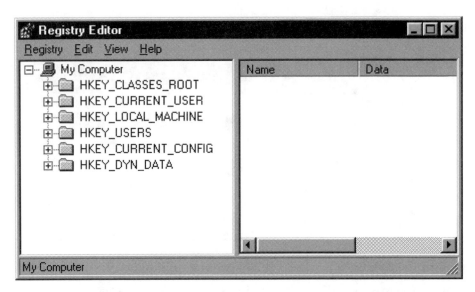

"Navigating through the Registry can be pretty tedious, and of course you never want to change any values that you see here," I explained. "That's why I use the Find dialog to search for my Registry entries. You can either select Edit-Find or press *Ctrl +F* to bring up the Find dialog box."

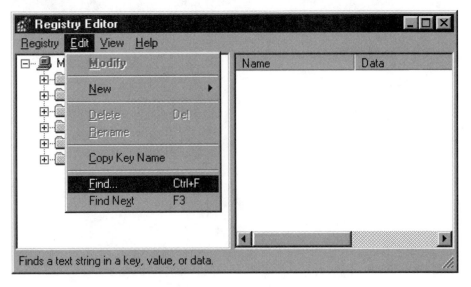

After the Find dialog box appeared, I entered the word BULLINACHINA into the Find what: text box:

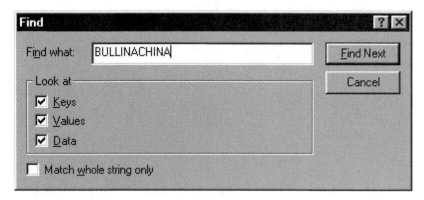

"Searching for the appname is probably easiest," I continued.

After a delay of many seconds, the following screen was displayed:

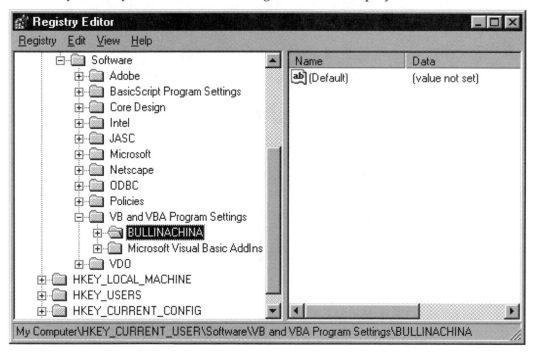

"There's our **BULLINACHINA** entry in the Registry," I said.

I then expanded the **BULLINACHINA** folder and the **STARTUP** folder was revealed:

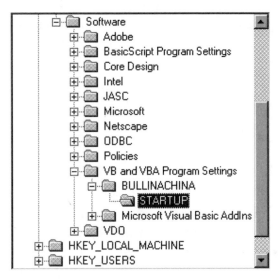

Finally, after expanding the **STARTUP** folder, we were able to see that both of our entries had been stored in the Windows Registry:

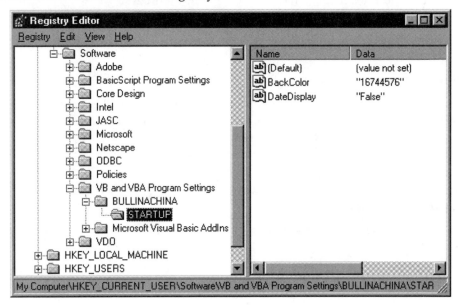

"As you can see," I said, "in the right-hand window are our two keys: BackColor with a value of 16744576, and DateDisplay with a value of False. These are the values that were created when I chose my custom color and turned off the data and time. So they were definitely saved in the Registry when I closed the China Shop project down."

"Don't change any values you see in the Registry," I instructed everyone. "Changing Registry values can cause your system not to come 'up' the next time you start your PC."

Everyone was successful in finding the values that had been written to the Registry during the exercise.

"So that's the Registry," Ward said. "I always thought it was this big, mysterious, hidden thing."

"Don't underestimate it," I said nervously. "We've just seen a part of it."

We continued by looking at the code for the `mnuColorsDefault_Click` event procedure.

"This code," I explained, "is very similar to the code in the `Click` event procedure of `mnuColorsCustom`. The value of the `BackColor` property of the form has been assigned to the form-level variable `m_lngBackColor`. In our new line of code the value of `m_lngBackColor` is saved to the Windows Registry."

```
SaveSetting "BULLINACHINA", "STARTUP", "BackColor", m_lngBackColor
```

"Really, then," Linda observed, "the code to save to the Registry is the same in both procedures."

"Yes," I agreed. "The actual code to save to the Registry is the same whether the user selects a custom color or a default color."

I waited for questions, but there were none.

"Let's look at the code to save the user's preferences for date and time display," I continued, "by examining the code in `mnuPreferencesDateAndTimeOff`. This code is very similar to the code we saw in the other two procedures. Basically, we set the value of the form-level variable, then use the `SaveSetting` statement to save it to the registry."

```
m_blnDateDisplay = False
SaveSetting "BULLINACHINA", "STARTUP", "DateDisplay", _
     m_blnDateDisplay
```

"Here's the code for `mnuPreferencesDateAndTimeOn`," I explained. "It's nearly identical."

```
m_blnDateDisplay = True
SaveSetting "BULLINACHINA", "STARTUP", "DateDisplay", _
     m_blnDateDisplay
```

I asked if there were any questions about saving to the Registry. There were none, and so we moved on to a discussion of reading from the Registry.

Reading from the Windows Registry

"We just saw how relatively easy it is to write to the Windows Registry," I said. "I think you'll find it just as easy to read from the Registry using the corresponding `GetSetting` function. Just as writing to the Registry has some 'quirks', reading from the Registry has some quirks of its own. For instance, when writing to the Registry, if no record exists for the appname, section, and key combination, then a new record is created in the Registry. If the Registry record already exists, then its value is updated."

"Suppose you attempt to read from the Registry, and the Registry combination of appname, section, and key isn't found, what happens?" I asked.

"Just a guess," Dave said. "A Visual Basic error?"

"Not quite," I replied, "something called a **zero length string** is returned."

"That sounds like it can be nasty," Chuck said.

"It can be if you're not expecting it," I explained. "Fortunately, we'll see in just a bit that, when using the `GetSetting` function to read the Registry, you can specify a default value to be used in case the Registry record you seek is not found. Let's look at the `GetSetting` function now."

I displayed the syntax of the `GetSetting` function on the classroom projector.

```
GetSetting(appname, section, key[, default])
```
"It looks like the first three arguments are identical to the `SaveSetting` statement," Barbara stated. "I guess the difference is the fourth argument."

"That's right," I said. "The first three arguments determine the entry that you are looking for in the Registry and these three arguments are identical to the arguments for the `SaveSetting`. For the `GetSetting` function, the fourth argument is the optional default value to be used if the Registry entry cannot be found."

"How does that default value work?" Valerie asked.

"To understand how the default value works," I explained, "just realize that since `GetSetting` is a function, it returns a value. Therefore, you need to use the return value in an expression, as in the example below."

I displayed this example syntax on the classroom projector:

```
Myval = GetSetting("MyApp", "STARTUP","Left", "25")
```

"Here `Myval` is a variable declared to hold the return value from the `GetSetting` function," I said. "I think you understand the first three arguments. The last argument is the default value, which is returned from the function call if the combination of appname, section, and key are not found in the Registry."

"So, in this example, if the Registry entry was not found, the value `25` would be assigned to the variable `Myval`." Blaine said.

"That's right," I said.

"The default argument is optional, what happens if you don't specify it?" Ward asked.

"If you don't specify a default value," I explained, "a zero length string is returned, which can really wreak havoc with your code if you use it somewhere. For instance, if you assign a zero length string to the `BackColor` of the form, you'll receive a Visual Basic run-time error. Take my advice and always code a default value when using the `GetSetting` function."

"Will we use default arguments in the China Shop Project?" Kate asked.

"Yes, we will," I replied. "When we read the `BackColor` key from the Registry, we'll specify a default value of `&H8000000F`, which is the same value as the default color of the form and a default value of `True` for the `DateDisplay` key."

In this exercise, we'll place code in the `Load` event procedure of the form to read the Registry entries we wrote in our earlier exercise:

Exercise
Reading from the Windows Registry

1. Load up the China Shop Project.

2. Find the `Load` event procedure of the form. Modify it so that it looks like this:

```
Private Sub Form_Load()
   Dim strBrand As String
   Dim intCounter As Integer
   m_blnDateDisplay = GetSetting("BULLINACHINA", "STARTUP", _
        "DateDisplay", True)
   If m_blnDateDisplay Then
      Call mnuPreferencesDateAndTimeOn_Click
```

```
        Else
        Call mnuPreferencesDateAndTimeOff_Click
    End If
    m_lngBackColor = GetSetting("BULLINACHINA", "STARTUP", _
            "BackColor", &H8000000F)
    frmMain.BackColor = m_lngBackColor
    Open "C:\VBFILES\CHINA\PRICES.TXT" For Input As #1
    Do While Not EOF(1)  ' Loop until end of file.
        ReDim Preserve m_curBowlPrice(intCounter)
        ReDim Preserve m_curButterPlatePrice(intCounter)
        ReDim Preserve m_curCupPrice(intCounter)
        ReDim Preserve m_curPlatePrice(intCounter)
        ReDim Preserve m_curPlatterPrice(intCounter)
        ReDim Preserve m_curSaucerPrice(intCounter)
        ReDim Preserve m_curCompletePrice(intCounter)

        Input #1, strBrand, _
                m_curPlatePrice(intCounter), _
                m_curButterPlatePrice(intCounter), _
                m_curBowlPrice(intCounter), _
                m_curCupPrice(intCounter), _
                m_curSaucerPrice(intCounter), _
                m_curPlatterPrice(intCounter), _
                m_curCompletePrice(intCounter)
                lstBrands.AddItem strBrand
        intCounter = intCounter + 1
    Loop
    Close #1
End Sub
```

3. Save the China Shop Project.

4. Run the program. When the program starts up, the changes you made to the form's background color, and to the date and time display in the previous exercise will be restored.

Discussion

"This looks and feels like a Windows program now," Linda said, obviously proud of herself.

"Congratulations," I said, "this completes the China Shop Project. We have fulfilled all of the requirements we agreed to in our written Requirements Statement with Joe Bullina.

All we'll do in the second half of the class is to optimize our code a little bit, but as far as Joe Bullina is concerned, it's time for him to pop the champagne! Let's look at the code now."

"This line of code," I said, "uses the `GetSetting` function to find the `DateDisplay` key in the Windows Registry. Notice that we have specified a default value of `True` in case the entry is not found."

```
m_blnDateDisplay = GetSetting("BULLINACHINA", "STARTUP", _
      "DateDisplay", True)
```

"I know the default parameter works," Rhonda admitted. "I accidentally used the appname of `CHINA` instead of `BULLINACHINA`. The key combination wasn't found, so my date and time weren't displayed, and my form was that bland gray color."

"Why isn't the default value `True` enclosed within quotation marks?" Mary asked.

"Good question," I said. "`m_blnDateDisplay` is defined as a Boolean variable, so if we put quotation marks around the word `True`, we would be telling Visual Basic to assign a string to `m_blnDateDisplay`, not a Boolean value."

I continued by explaining that once we read the value of the `DateDisplay` key from the Windows Registry, its value is assigned to the `m_blnDateDisplay` form-level variable.

"At this point," I said, "we have read the value for the user's preference for date and time from the Windows Registry. Now we have to do something with it. That's what this next section of code does."

```
If m_blnDateDisplay Then
    Call mnuPreferencesDateAndTimeOn_Click
Else
    Call mnuPreferencesDateAndTimeOff_Click
End If
```

"This code really confused me," Ward said. "What's going on here?"

"We're checking the value of the variable `m_blnDateDisplay` for a `True` value," I explained. "If the value is equal to `True`, meaning the user prefers to see the date and time, then we call the `mnuPreferencesDateAndTimeOn_Click` event procedure. If the value is `False`, then we call the `mnuPreferencesDateAndTimeOff_Click` event procedure."

"I don't see the words `True` or `False` in the `If` statement," Barbara said. "Are they implied somehow?"

"Yes, you're right," I replied. "When comparing Boolean variables like this in an `If` statement, the comparison to `True` is implied. The longer version of the code would look like this":

```
If m_blnDateDisplay = True Then
```

"I think this version is a little more readable," Ward said. "Your choice," I responded. "I just wanted you to see this style, because you see it a lot."

"I'm also confused about the word `Call`," Barbara said.

"It's not fair, using new terms on the last day of class!" Kate teased.

"`Call`?" Ward said. "That is a new one. I don't remember seeing that before."

"We're going to see it quite a bit before today's class is over," I said. "Do you remember what the code in the `Click` event procedure of `mnuPreferencesDateAndTimeOn` does?"

```
Private Sub mnuPreferencesDateAndTimeOn_Click()
   mnuPreferencesDateAndTimeOff.Checked = False
   mnuPreferencesDateAndTimeOn.Checked = True
   tmrChina.Enabled = True
   lblDateAndTime.Visible = True
   m_blnDateDisplay = True
   SaveSetting "BULLINACHINA", "STARTUP", "DateDisplay", _
         m_blnDateDisplay
End Sub
```

"Let's see," Dave said as he looked at the code on the classroom projector. "This code places a check mark on the menu item Date and Time On, removes the check mark on the menu item Date and Time Off, enables the Timer control, and makes the date and time label visible."

"That's right," I said. "And all of those actions seem pretty reasonable to execute when you start up the project and the user's preference is to display the date and time. But how would you feel having to code all of that into the `Load` event procedure of the form, when a single line `Call` statement can save you the trouble."

"Are you saying that using the `Call` statement here executes the code in the `Click` event procedure of `mnuPreferencesDateAndTimeOn`?" Linda asked.

"That's exactly what it does," I replied.

"So, by calling the code in the `mnuPreferencesDateAndTimeOn_Click` event procedure we saved ourselves some typing. Is that right?" Barbara asked.

"Yes," I replied. "Along with the burden of retyping it, we also eliminated the possibility that we would make a mistake when entering the same code in the Load event procedure of the form. Plus, and this is a big benefit, if we decide we want to do something else when the user tells our program to display the date and time such as displaying a confirming message box, we only need to change the code in one place. Procedures that call the code won't have to change."

"That sounds like the Dynamic Link Library or DLLs you discussed in our first class or so," Dave commented.

"Good memory, Dave," I said. "It does sound much like that. We'll discuss calling procedures quite a bit today."

"I had no idea you could call other procedures like this," Rhonda said. "How often do you really need to repeat code like this?"

I explained that it could happen pretty frequently.

"Let's finish up our review of this code, and then we'll take a break and discuss the Call statement some more."

```
m_lngBackColor = GetSetting("BULLINACHINA", "STARTUP", _
        "BackColor", &H8000000F)
```

"This line of code uses the GetSetting function to find the BackColor key in the Windows Registry. Notice here that we have specified a default value of &H8000000F in case the entry is not found. Notice also, that since &H8000000F is a long integer value, we don't enclose it within quotation marks. Once the GetSetting function is executed, the value of m_lngBackColor is assigned the value found in the Registry."

"Finally," I continued, "this line of code assigns that value to the BackColor property of frmMain: "

```
frmMain.BackColor = m_lngBackColor
```

I asked if there were any more questions, but there were none.

"I want to congratulate all of you on completing your first application," I said. "At this point, the China Shop Project is now complete."

"From our point of view, anyway!" Dave said.

"You're right," I agreed. "There's still some work to be done. We should give the program a thorough test before heading off to the China Shop to deliver and install the program. Plus, we still have training to conduct with the sales staff at the China Shop."

"When is Mr. Bullina expecting us?" Kathy asked.

"At about 3 p.m." I said as I checked the classroom clock. "Let's see, it's about 12.30 now. Take a quick break, and when we return, we'll discuss some optimization techniques. Then we'll then pack up and head off to the China Shop."

As the rest of the class headed off in the direction of the vending machines, I took a quick peek out the windows of the classroom towards the parking lot. No sign of Rose and Jack yet.

Optimizing Visual Basic Code

Everyone was so excited at the prospect of delivering the China Shop Project to Mr. Bullina that they quickly returned to the classroom. After checking the parking lot for Rose and Jack, I had taken the opportunity to give Joe Bullina a call to confirm that all was ready for our arrival.

"Our final topic for the course," I said upon returning to the classroom, "is optimizing the code that we write."

"What exactly is **code optimization** anyway?" Bob asked.

"From our point of view," I said, "there are two types of code optimization. Optimization that you perform to make your program code more readable, and therefore easier to maintain, and optimization that you perform to make your program run more quickly and efficiently."

User-Written Procedures

"Virtually all of the code that we've written to date," I continued, "with the exception of some form-level variables, has been placed in an event procedure. We know that event procedures are executed when the event that they are associated with is triggered in the Windows environment. For instance, if the user clicks on the `Command1` command button, the `Command1_Click` event procedure is executed, along with any code that has been placed in it. In the last exercise you saw, for the first time, you could call one event procedure from another. It's also possible to write a procedure of your own which you can then call from another procedure."

"Are you talking about creating our own event procedures?" Bob asked.

"No," I replied, "not event procedures. I'm talking about creating stand-alone procedures. These procedures are not associated with any particular event. On their own, they would never execute. However, they can be executed if we call them from another procedure."

"There's that 'call' word again," Ward said. "So there's no way for these procedures to execute unless an event procedure is triggered that calls them?"

"That's right," I replied.

"Why bother writing your own procedures?" Linda asked. "Are they really necessary?"

"No. After all, we've really completed the China Shop Project without creating a single procedure of our own. Nevertheless, writing your own procedures can make your code neater and more readable. The real payback comes in reducing the amount of duplicated code."

"For instance, in the last exercise, we saw that we were inclined to write the same code in the `Load` event procedure of the form that's already present in the `Click` event procedures of `mnuPreferencesDateAndTimeOn` and `mnuPreferencesDateAndTimeOff`."

"But we didn't duplicate it," Linda said. "We called the `Click` event procedures to execute their code."

"You're right," I agreed. "However, the next logical step would be to take any code that we execute from multiple locations within our program and place it in a single procedure of its own."

"Such as the code in the `Click` event procedures of those menu items?" Linda asked.

"The code in those event procedures would be candidates, yes" I replied. "Another reason to write your own procedures is **modularity**. In theory, the code in a procedure, either an event procedure or one of your own, should perform only one process. If you find that you have code in an event procedure which is performing multiple processes, that's a good reason to take that code and place it in a procedure of its own."

"Can you give us an example of that?" Kate asked.

"How about the `Load` event procedure of the China Shop form?" I replied. "Right now, you could argue that the code in that event procedure is performing more than one process. We're reading the Windows Registry, opening a disk file, loading the `lstBrands` list box, and loading the elements of an array. That sounds like four processes to me."

"So we should take that code," Dave said, "and turn it into separate procedures."

"That's a possibility," I said. "Remember now, we're talking about optimization here. Our project is complete and the program works. We don't need to do any of this, but the payback in making our program easier to read and maintain can be great."

"Where do you place the procedures that you've written?" Barbara asked.

"The subprocedures that we'll write today will all go in the General Declarations section of our form," I replied. "If we had more than one form we'd have to place them in the General Declarations section of what's called a standard module."

I suggested that at this point, we should examine how to write our own subprocedures.

Writing Our Own Subprocedures

"A subprocedure is just code that executes and does not return a value to the calling procedure," I explained. "I have a series of exercises for you to complete that I hope will show you just how easy it is to create and write your own subprocedures."

I then distributed the following exercise:

Exercise

Creating Our Own Subprocedure

1.   Start a new **Standard.EXE** project.

2.   Place a command button on the form. Accept the default name that Visual Basic assigns.

3.   We will now create a subprocedure of our own called **DisplayAnswer**. Double-click on the command button to open the code window.

   You must have the code window open in order to create a subprocedure of your own.

4.   Select Tools-Add Procedure from the Visual Basic menu.

5.   A dialog box will appear. Complete the entries according to the screenshot below:

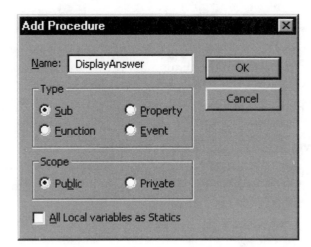

6. Click on the OK button and the code window for the subprocedure **DisplayAnswer** will appear:

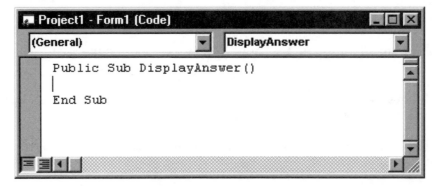

7. Click your mouse between the subprocedure name and the line **End Sub**.

8. Enter the following code:

```
Public Sub DisplayAnswer()
Dim intX As Integer
Dim intY As Integer
intX = 9
intY = 13
Form1.Print intX + intY
End Sub
```

9. Double-click on the command button and place the following code into its `Click` event procedure:

```
Private Sub Command1_Click()
   Call DisplayAnswer
End Sub
```

10. Save the project in your `\VBFiles\Practice` subdirectory. Save the form as `Sub1.frm` and the project as `SubPro.vbp`. Now run the program.

11. Click on the command button. The number **22** will be printed on the form.

Discussion

"Congratulations!" I said. "You've written your first subprocedure."

"Is that all there is to it?" Rhonda asked. "I thought it would be more complicated than that."

"That's all," I replied. "Our first subprocedure wasn't bad at all. All we did was place some code in the subprocedure called `DisplayAnswer` and coded a `Call` statement in the `Click` event procedure of our command button. When we clicked on the command button, the `Click` event called the subprocedure that we had written separately."

"When we named and defined the procedure, why did we place an empty set of parentheses after the procedure name?" Mary asked.

"That tells Visual Basic that the procedure has no arguments," I explained. "That mean that we don't want to pass it any extra information when we call it – we just want it to run its code as it stands."

"When I first created the procedure," Valerie said, "I misspelled it, so that when I called it, the procedure I called wasn't found. However, it was easy enough to go back and change the name of the procedure in the code window."

"I think I mentioned this tip earlier," I said, "but if I didn't, here goes again. Define all of your procedure names in mixed case, as we did here. Then, when you reference the procedure name in your code, type it in lower case. If Visual Basic doesn't change the name of the procedure to mixed case for you, then you know that something's wrong somewhere. Either you have spelled the procedure name incorrectly, or the procedure wasn't defined with the name you think it is."

"That's right, I remember you saying that." Valerie commented. "I should have noticed that when I coded the `Call` statement that the name wasn't changed to mixed case. I typed it in lower case and it stayed that way."

"Do we need to use the word `Call` when we call our procedure?" Kate asked.

"No," I replied, "using `Call` is optional, although I prefer to use it. We could have coded our call statement like this:"

DisplayAnswer

"The reason I prefer to use the word `Call`," I continued, "is that it quickly signals to me, and to anyone else reading my code, that the procedure I am calling is one of my own."

"What about naming conventions for the procedures you write?" Barbara asked.

"Good question," I said.

I then displayed these Microsoft Recommendations on the classroom projector:

- The procedure name should use mixed case and be as long as necessary to describe its purpose.
- For frequently used or long terms, standard abbreviations are recommended to help keep name lengths reasonable.

I waited a moment and then asked if there were any questions. There were none. I checked the classroom clock. It was about 1:30. I was about to move onto the China Shop Project modifications that we were about to make when I became aware of a distraction in the classroom.

"Rose and Jack," I said. "Welcome back. It's good to see you. We were getting worried about you."

"You didn't tell anyone about our surprise, did you?" Rose asked.

"You swore me to secrecy," I said, "and I keep a secret better than anyone I know."

"What secret?" Rhonda asked.

"The strangest thing happened on our cruise to New York," Jack said. "There we were, eating a late dinner on Thursday night. It was about 11:30, just short of midnight when this incredible urge came over us…"

"Well, what happened?" Blaine asked

"We made our way to the bridge of the ship," Rose explained, "looking for the captain. He wasn't there, and so we asked the first officer to get him out of his cabin."

"Go on," Lou said excitedly, "this is getting interesting. Don't tell me you noticed something on the horizon?"

"After he came to the bridge," Jack continued, "for some reason, something caught his eye, and he ordered half speed on the engines. And then…"

"And then what?" Mary asked anxiously.

"Then he married us," Rose replied. "Right there on the bridge of the ship."

"I didn't think sea captains still did that," Ward said.

"So that's the big surprise!" Valerie said. "Congratulations. You've decided to spend your honeymoon in the China Shop. You two are dedicated!"

"John has been keeping us apprised of the developments with the project," Rose explained. "And of course, we took our laptops along. We're right on pace...well just about on pace, with the course. I don't think we've missed a beat."

"Well, Rose and Jack," I said, "I'm glad that you're both with us today. With you two in attendance today, we can put a nice close on the project we started 16 weeks ago. How about if we make a few enhancements to the China Shop Project before we deliver it?"

Subprocedures in the China Shop Project

"The enhancements I have in mind," I said, "are not really code enhancements. However, I thought it would be a good idea if we moved some of the code we've already written into separate procedures. This will make our code more modular and if we should modify the program in the future, it will be easier to change."

In this exercise, we'll take the code in the **Load** event procedure of the form and place it into two separate procedures:

Exercise

Coding the China Shop Project Subprocedures

1. Load up the China Shop Project.

2. We will now create a subprocedure called **ReadTheRegistry**. Remember that you must have the code window open in order to create a subprocedure of your own.

3. Select <u>T</u>ools-Add <u>P</u>rocedure from the menu.

4. A dialog box will be displayed. Complete the entries according to the screenshot below:

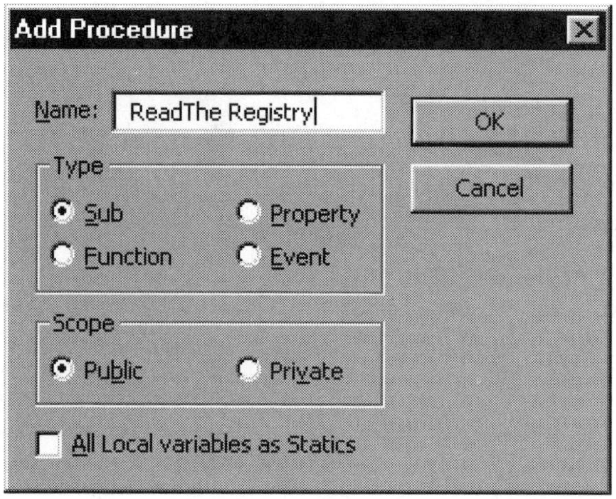

5. Click on the OK button and the code window for the subprocedure `ReadTheRegistry` will appear.

6. Enter the following code between the subprocedure name and the line `End Sub`. You may recognize this as code that currently exists in the `Load` event procedure of the form. Don't worry about that for now. You'll erase this code from the `Load` event procedure shortly:

```
Public Sub ReadTheRegistry()
    m_blnDateDisplay = GetSetting("BULLINACHINA", "STARTUP", _
        "DateDisplay", False)
    m_lngBackColor = GetSetting("BULLINACHINA", "STARTUP", _
        "BackColor", &H8000000F)
End Sub
```

7. We will now create a subprocedure called `ReadPrices`. Remember that you must have the code window open in order to create a subprocedure of your own.

8. Select Tools-Add Procedure from the Visual Basic menu.

9. A dialog box will be displayed. Complete the entries according to the screenshot below:

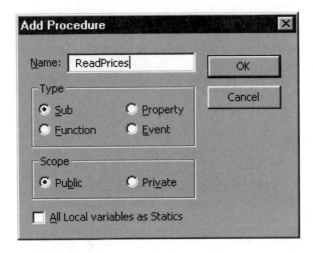

10. Click on the OK button and the code window for the subprocedure ReadPrices will appear.

11. Enter the following code between the subprocedure name and the line End Sub. You may recognize this as code that currently exists in the Load event procedure of the form. If you wish, copy this code from the Load event procedure of the form and paste it to this subprocedure:

```
Public Sub ReadPrices()
    On Error GoTo ICanHandleThis
    Dim strBrand As String
    Dim intCounter As Integer
    Open "C:\VBFILES\CHINA\PRICES.TXT" For Input As #1
    Do While Not EOF(1) ' Loop until end of file.
        ReDim Preserve m_curBowlPrice(intCounter)
        ReDim Preserve m_curButterPlatePrice(intCounter)
        ReDim Preserve m_curCupPrice(intCounter)
        ReDim Preserve m_curPlatePrice(intCounter)
        ReDim Preserve m_curPlatterPrice(intCounter)
        ReDim Preserve m_curSaucerPrice(intCounter)
        ReDim Preserve m_curCompletePrice(intCounter)

        Input #1, strBrand, _
            m_curPlatePrice(intCounter), _
            m_curButterPlatePrice(intCounter), _
            m_curBowlPrice(intCounter), _
```

```
               m_curCupPrice(intCounter), _
               m_curSaucerPrice(intCounter), _
               m_curPlatterPrice(intCounter), _
               m_curCompletePrice(intCounter)
        lstBrands.AddItem strBrand
        intCounter = intCounter + 1
   Loop
   Close #1
   Exit Sub
ICanHandleThis:
   Select Case Err.Number
      Case 53              'File not found
         MsgBox "A file required by the " & _
                "China Shop program " & vbCrLf & _
                "is missing. Please ensure that " & vbCrLf & _
                "PRICES.TXT is in " & vbCrLf & _
                "the China Shop directory " & vbCrLf & _
                "on the computer's hard drive"

         Unload frmMain
         Exit Sub
      Case Else
         MsgBox "Unexpected error has occurred" & vbCrLf & _
                "Contact John Smiley"
         Unload frmMain
         Exit Sub
   End Select
End Sub
```

12. Most of the code in the **Form_Load** event procedure of the form has been moved to subprocedures. Erase the existing code from the **Form Load** event and replace it with the following code instead:

```
Private Sub Form_Load()
   Call ReadTheRegistry
   Call ReadPrices
   If m_blnDateDisplay Then
      Call mnuPreferencesDateAndTimeOn_Click
   Else
      Call mnuPreferencesDateAndTimeOff_Click
   End If
   frmMain.BackColor = m_lngBackColor
End Sub
```

13. Save the China Shop Project.

14. Run the program. Verify that the program runs and behaves as it did before. In particular, make sure that the list box of china items is loaded at startup, along with the user's preferences.

Discussion

"All we did in this exercise," I explained, "was to take code out of the **Load** event procedure of the China Shop form and place it into two subprocedures of our own."

"Why did we do that again?" Rhonda asked.

"The **Load** event procedure of the form had lost its modular characteristics," I replied. "There was code in there which was reading the Registry, loading the list box, and loading pricing data into our arrays. It made sense to take the code and separate it into distinct procedures. One big benefit of doing this will be maintainability of the program. For instance, if we decide to store another value in the Windows Registry and need to modify the code to read it at startup, we only have one place to go, the **ReadTheRegistry** subprocedure."

"Isn't it another benefit that now the code in those procedures is available from every procedure in our project?" Dave asked. "So that if we want to read the Registry to obtain the most current user preferences, we can just code a call to **ReadTheRegistry**."

"That's a great point, Dave," I said.

"I think everyone is eager to get to the China Shop," I continued. "For the last time, are there any questions?"

There were none.

"I want to thank everyone," I said, "for an excellent class. I can't ever remember enjoying a class more. I can't think of a better group of people I could have spent 4 months of Saturdays with than you."

"Don't get melancholy on us now," Linda said. "You know we'll all be back next term to take your Intermediate Visual Basic course. Besides, we still have some work to do. Shouldn't we be heading out to the China Shop now?"

"Absolutely," I replied, "I told Joe Bullina we would be there about 3 p.m."

"How are we going to work this?" Dave asked. "We have 19 different versions of the China Shop Project. After all, you encouraged us to be creative. We don't have 19 carbon copies of the same program. Which one are we going to install in the China Shop?"

Testing the Program

"When I spoke to Joe Bullina earlier in the week," I explained, "I told him that we had 19 different versions of the program. I guess because he's in a customer service business, he's reluctant to hurt anyone's feelings. He asked that prior to showing up at the China Shop today, we'd somehow pick one of the programs as the one we want to install. So here's what I'm going to ask you to do."

"I want everyone to take a few moments to test their programs and then take a quick walk around the classroom. Then we'll take a ballot and vote for our top three projects. The project that receives the most first place votes will be the program that we install at the China Shop. I'm going to remove my project from eligibility. This is your project and one of you deserves to have the place of honor in the China Shop."

"Can you give us some guidelines on testing our programs?" Linda asked.

"That's a good point," I said. "At a minimum, the program must work, that is, calculate the prices correctly. You also want to ensure that the flexibility we designed into the program as far as being able to change prices and add additional brands of china works."

"I would think that most of the real bugs have been discovered by now," Valerie commented.

"I'm not sure we can say that with 100% certainty," I said. "There's always the possibility that something has slipped through our fingers. However, I must say that I'm fairly confident that this program is bug free. Obviously, the more complicated the program, the less certain you can feel."

"How should we test the price calculations?" Rhonda asked. "Is it possible to test each and every combination?"

"You're right," I said. "There are quite a few possible price combinations. I do scenario testing. I write down several scenarios on a piece of paper. For instance, John Smith comes in and selects Mikasa, a platter, a plate and a cup, with a quantity of 2. Then I calculate the prices manually and run the program to see if the calculated price is the one you expected."

"I did something similar," Chuck said, "except that I used Excel to develop a spreadsheet of possible scenarios, then ran my program and tested as many as I could."

"That's a good idea. You might want to try that as well," I suggested.

Everyone then spent the next fifteen minutes or so testing their projects one last time, playfully reviewing everyone else's project and voting for their top three projects. As I collected the ballots and tallied the totals, I asked everyone to give me a disk with a copy of their project as well. I also provided everyone with a map to the China Shop.

"Class is officially dismissed for today," I said. "See you at the China Shop and drive safely."

I called Dave aside. Dave had volunteered to coordinate the installation of Visual Basic on the China Shop's PC, along with the installation of the program itself. I handed Dave the installation CD-ROM for Visual Basic, along with the project that had received the most first place votes.

"If patterns hold true," I said, "I'll end up being the last one at the shop. Would you mind installing these?"

"Not at all," he said, as he glanced at the student's name on the disk and smiled. "I'll take care of this. See you there."

We Meet at the China Shop

As I had predicted, no sooner was I out the door of the classroom than a former student of mine approached me with a problem. Half an hour later, I was finally on my way and, as I am not the world's fastest driver, I arrived nearly an hour late at the China Shop.

As I arrived there, I could tell from the lack of available parking places that quite a bit of fanfare was taking place. When I walked in the door, I was met by an incredible amount of activity. The place was packed with students and customers. There was a buffet table of food set up in the corner, and balloons and streamers hung from the ceiling.

Joe Bullina caught sight of me.

"John, this program is great," he said excitedly. "I can't believe what a great job your students did with this. Everyone loves it. The customers love it. The sales staff loves it. I love it. Here, have a sandwich."

Amidst the hullabaloo, I glanced towards the middle of the shop and there on a kiosk in the middle of the sales floor, was a computer running the China Shop program. Rhonda was standing in front of the computer, training the sales staff.

"Well, Joe," I said, "you really know how to celebrate the computer age."

"Rhonda's been proudly demonstrating her version of the program to the sales staff now for the last ten minutes," Joe explained. "They haven't gotten up yet. They can't help but play with it. She really did a great job with it."

Joe shouted across the room. "Come on Midge, give the customers a chance to use the program."

I wandered over to the kiosk and caught Rhonda's eye.

"I'm flabbergasted that the class voted for my version of the project," Rhonda said. "To say that this has made my week is an understatement. More like my year. I'm just so honored that someone with absolutely no programming background like me could actually write a program like this. And I've got to tell you, I felt like I asked so many stupid questions during the course…"

"Rhonda," I interrupted, "you know what I say, the only stupid question is the question you don't ask. Your questions were always good ones. They were probably questions that some of the other students were dying to ask. By the way, when I put this course together, I had someone just like you in mind."

"Really?" she said. "You know I really enjoyed the course very much. You should consider taking those notes of yours and writing a book."

"Maybe I'll do that someday," I told her.

Joe Bullina motioned to a lively looking couple at the buffet table to come over.

"I met this couple about an hour ago," he said directing his attention to the man and woman who must have been in their 80's. "Apparently they saw my ad in the paper about our Celebration Sale. This is Rita and Gil."

Joe told me that when he explained to the couple that the shop would be implementing a new computer system within the hour they had insisted on being the first customers to use it.

"John and his programming class developed this new system," Joe said as he uprooted Midge from in front of the computer.

"Oh really, our son teaches computers also," Rita said as she sat down on a chair Joe Bullina brought over for her.

"And he's very good," Gil added. "Well," Joe said, "I'm extremely honored to have you be the first customers to use our new computer system."

"Gil has promised to buy me new china for our anniversary," Rita explained. "63 years on November 23rd."

"Congratulations!" Joe said. Gil sat down beside Rita and the two of them began to use the system.

"Gil," Linda said, "you seem to be pretty good with that mouse. Have you used a PC before?"

"I used computers quite a bit while I was working," Gil explained, "but I've been retired for over twenty years. We didn't have personal computers when I worked. However, I've gotten pretty good with them in my retirement."

"These two both look familiar to me," Linda whispered. "Have we seen them at the University?"

"I don't think so. I've had senior citizens in my classes, but not these two. You're right though, they do look very familiar to me," I said smiling. I took out a notepad and made notes of Rita and Gil's session in front of the China Shop program. I began to chat with some of the other students, as I continued to observe them at the kiosk. After a few minutes, Rita and Gil got up from their chairs, and made their way to the counter at the front of the store.

"The system worked as designed," I told the assembled class. "The customers used the system to make some selections on the screen. After making a decision, they proceeded to the counter and purchased their china."

Another customer took their place in front of the kiosk. Linda, sensing that he was having some difficulty, came over to assist him. I heard Linda ask his name (Bill, I believe). As Linda proceeded to help him, I called as many of my students over as I could gather around the PC. Some of them were still eating the sandwiches that Joe Bullina had provided. By now, there was a crowd gathered around Linda and the man with the thick head of black hair.

"I want to thank Dave for installing both Visual Basic and Rhonda's version of the China Shop Project on the kiosk PC," I said. "By installing the software on the kiosk PC, we have begun phase 5 of the SDLC, the **Implementation** phase. Installation, fine tuning, and training are all part of this phase."

Joe Bullina happened to be right next to me at the time. I turned to him and said that this phase would last for at least the next week.

"Pairs of students have volunteered to be 'on site' to make observations and assist with any problems that might come up," I explained. "They volunteered even before they knew what a good party you throw. They'll also be showing your sales staff how to update your inventory prices."

"It's comforting to know that they'll be here," he said. "I'll need to order more sandwiches! What are those notes that you are taking?"

"Even though we're now in the midst of phase 5 of the SDLC," I replied, "we can proceed concurrently with phase 6 which is **Feedback and Maintenance**."
"Feedback and maintenance?" Joe asked.

"We want to make sure that the program is behaving according to the Requirements Statement we gave you when we agreed to write the program for you," I explained. "A big part of this phase is just observing the system to see how it's being used."

"And how it's being admired," Joe Bullina added.

"Positive feedback is a wonderful thing," I said smiling.

"What about program maintenance?" Joe asked.

"The maintenance phase handles any change to the program that are necessitated by governmental regulations, changes in business rules, or just changes that you decide you want to make to the program," I replied.

"After seeing the great work you've done on the project," he said, "I'm sure I'll have more work for your class."

"Sadly, though," I said, "this is the end of our introductory course. But many, if not all, of these students will be signed up for my intermediate programming course starting in five weeks."

Joe seemed happy with that idea, and went with Bill to the counter who made a surprise purchase of china for his daughter.

"He looked very familiar to me also," Linda said. "What is it about this place? By the way, can I see your notes from Rita and Gil's session at the kiosk?"

"Here they are," I said, as I handed her my notes. "In fact, based on my initial observation, I think I already know what the first change to the program will be. We've got to make the font size larger for our customers over 40!"

1. Rita sits down at the computer.

2. Rita wants Mikasa china, so she clicks on Mikasa in the list box. The Mikasa pattern appears in the Image control.

3. Rita wants a complete place setting so she clicks on the Complete Place Setting Check Box. Five check marks appear for the china items comprising a complete place setting.

4. Rita clicks on the Calculate command button.

5. A message box displays a warning that she has not yet picked a quantity. The bell that sounds when the message box displays startles her.

6. Rita clicks on the OK button to make the message box go away.

7. Rita selects a quantity of 8 by clicking on the Option Button labeled 8.

8. Rita clicks on the Calculate command button.

9. A message box displays a message that the calculated price reflects a discount for a complete place setting. I think both Rita and Gil are puzzled as to what this message means. Rita clicks on the OK button to make the message box go away.

10. The order price of $400 is displayed in the lower left-hand corner of the form.

11. Gil takes over and clicks on the Reset command button. All of the controls are reset.

12. Gil is having trouble seeing the display, so he changes the color from the default gray to cyan by using the main menu of the form. A larger font here would be a good idea.

13. Gil believes they are 'running late' for a movie that they want to see. He turns the display of the date and time on using the form's menu. Now he knows they are late!

14. Gil thinks the price of Mikasa is too expensive and clicks on Faberware in the list box.

15. Gil doesn't think they need a complete place setting. He selects the Plate, Cup, Saucer and a Platter.

16. Gil thinks they only need 4 of each. He clicks on the Option Button labeled 4.

17. Gil only wants one platter, but is confused because there is no place to specify a quantity for just the platter.

18. Gil clicks on the Calculate command button.

19. A message box is displayed saying that he is limited to a quantity of one platter. He clicks on the OK button to make the message box go away.

20. The order price of $77 is displayed in the lower left-hand corner of the form.

21.   They get up to go to the counter to make their purchase. Their final selection will forever remain their, and my, secret.

"Interesting observations," Linda said. "I can see we still need to do some work."

"Joe," I said, turning to Mr Bullina a final time, "on behalf of the class, I want to thank you for a wonderful opportunity. I'm sure we'll be in touch."

I shout across the room, "I've got to take off now. Everyone please be mindful of your coverage schedules and, if you have any problems, you all know where to find me. I hope to see you in five weeks."

Summary

Congratulations! You've finished the class, and completed and implemented the China Shop Project. I hope you felt the excitement of delivering and installing the China Shop Project as much as the students in my class did, because you were a big part of it. However, don't let this be the end of your learning.

At this point, you should feel confident enough to tackle a variety of programs. I hope that by following my introductory computer programming class, you've seen how real-world applications are developed.

That's not to say that all projects go as smoothly as this one did; neither does every client meet us on delivery day with sandwiches, balloons, and streamers. You can expect your share of mistakes, misinterpretations, and misunderstandings along the way. Nevertheless, it's always exciting, and if you love it as I do, it's always fun.

As I close, I just want to give you a few words of advice.

Firstly, remember that in programming there's rarely a single 'correct' solution.

Secondly, always be your own best friend. Inevitably, while trying to work through a solution, there will be frustrating moments. Never doubt yourself, and never get 'down' on yourself.

Finally, remember that there is always more to learn. The world of programming is an endless series of free learning seminars. All you need to do is open up a manual, read a help file, surf the Internet, or even pick up a copy of your favorite book, and you are well on your way. You can never know it all, let alone master it all. But always try to move in that direction. Good luck and I hope to see you in another Visual Basic class some day!

Quiz

1. How can you back up the Windows Registry?

2. What function is used to read an entry from the Windows Registry?

3. What happens if you use the GetSetting function to read an entry from the Windows Registry that doesn't exist?

4. How many arguments does the SaveSetting statement require?

5. What happens if you call the SaveSetting function, and an entry already exists for that AppName, Section, and Key?

6. What is a user-written procedure?

7. What is the difference between a subprocedure and a function?

8. What is the syntax to 'call' a user-written subprocedure called CalculatePrice with no arguments?

9. Is the word 'call' mandatory when calling a subprocedure or function?

10. The following code contains a user written subprocedure called 'Bell', and a call to that subprocedure. What will be the output of the code?

```
Sub Bell()
   Dim x As Integer
   x = 22
   MsgBox "The value of x is " & x
End Sub

Private Sub Command1_Click()
   Call Bell
End Sub
```

Extra Credit – Two people were playing checkers. They played five games, and each won the same number of games. There were no ties. Explain this.

Appendix A

Answers to Quiz Questions

Here are the answers to the quiz questions for each chapter. Make sure you understand why the answers are what they are, especially if you got any wrong the first time around. But it's not a test, so don't feel bad if you didn't get them all right.

Chapter 1

1. In Chapter 1, I compare writing a program to what activity?

Building a house

2. When I enter the store to meet with the China Shop owner for the first time, how many people are in the store?

Ten to fifteen

3. What does SDLC stand for?

Systems Development Life Cycle

4. What are the six phases of the SDLC?

1. The Preliminary Investigation phase

2. The Analysis phase

3. The Design phase

4. The Development phase

5. The Implementation phase

6. The Maintenance phase

5. What is typically the shortest phase of the SDLC?

The Preliminary Investigation phase

6. What is the purpose of the SDLC's Preliminary Investigation phase?

The Preliminary Investigation is intended to verify the problem or deficiency, or to pass judgment on the new requirement

7. After the Preliminary Investigation of the SDLC is completed, a go or no-go decision is made.

There are three factors, typically called 'constraints', which result in a go or no-go decision. Can you name them?

Technical, Time and Budgetary

8. The second phase of the SDLC, the **Analysis Phase**, is sometimes called the...

Data Gathering phase

9. What takes place in the Analysis phase of the SDLC?

During the Analysis phase of the SDLC, the problem, deficiency or new requirement is studied in detail

10. How many brands of china does the China Shop sell?

Three - Mikasa, Corelle and Faberware

11. How many components did my Visual Basic class design during the Design phase of the SDLC?

Four - Input, Output, Processing and File

12. During the Design phase of the SDLC, what component does the analyst or designer typically start with?

Output design

13. What is a Requirements Statement?

The Requirements Statement forms the basis of our agreement with our client. The detail is sufficient for a Visual Basic programmer to begin coding

14. What is the definition of computer processing?

The conversion of inputs to outputs

15. What is a computer record?

A computer record is an electronic representation of something - usually a person, place or thing

16. What is the purpose of the Systems Development Life Cycle (SDLC)?

The SDLC is a methodology that has been developed to ensure that systems are developed in a methodical, logical and step-by-step approach

17. Can you name the end result, or deliverable, from the first phase of the SDLC, the Preliminary Investigation?

Either a willingness to proceed further with the project, or the decision to 'call it quits'

18. Which of the following, a flowchart or pseudo-code, is a graphical depiction of the processing logic of your computer program?

Flowchart

19. What is Joe's biggest requirement for the application that we are writing for him?

That it is simple

Extra Credit – The following number is the only one of its kind. What's so special about it?

8,549,176,320

It's the only one where the numerals appear in alphabetical order

Chapter 2

1. Approximately how many bytes are in a kilobyte?

1000

2. What does the term **volatile** mean when we speak of RAM?

Since RAM is stored and refreshed electrically, when the computer is turned off or when power to the computer is lost, the contents of RAM will disappear

3. How many bits are in a byte?

Eight (8)

4. How many possible values can a bit have?

Two. One (1) or Zero (0)

5. Place these terms in order from least to greatest: Megabyte, Kilobyte, Terabyte, Gigabyte

Kilobyte

Megabyte

Gigabyte

Terabyte

6. What's the difference between operating systems and application programs?

Operating systems are programs that manage the computer's resources. Application programs are practical programs that are of much more interest to end users. Application programs run with the assistance of operating systems

7. True or False: Visual Basic can be used to create both operating systems and application programs.

False. Programs such as Assembler, C or C++ are used to write operating systems. Visual Basic is used to write application programs only

8. What does RAM stand for?

Random Access Memory

9. True or False: Computers are capable of running only one operating system.

False. Most computers are capable of running more than operating system

10. What does DOS stand for?

Disk Operating System

11. Where do application programs need to be loaded before they can be run?

Into RAM

12. What are three characteristics of DOS that Windows improved upon?

DOS is a character-based interface

DOS cannot take advantage of the modern PC's abundant RAM. It ignores anything over a Megabyte

DOS is single tasking

13. What did Windows replace DOS's character-based interface with?

A graphical user interface (GUI)

14. There are two kinds of multi-tasking. Can you name both?

Non-preemptive and pre-emptive multitasking. Programs running under a non-preemptive operating system must be specially written to cooperate in multitasking by yielding control of the microprocessor at frequent intervals. Pre-emptive multitasking differs from non-preemptive multitasking in that the operating system decides when a task will no longer have control of the microprocessor, and simply takes it away

15. True or False: Dynamic Link Libraries (or DLL's) are a characteristic of DOS programs.

False. Only Windows programs use Dynamic Link Libraries.

16. Each window in the Windows environment is uniquely identified by a Windows _____.

Handle

Extra Credit - How many of each animal did Moses take aboard the Ark with him?

Moses did not make the Ark trip. It was Noah!

Chapter 3

1. How do you start the IDE?

Trick question. You don't need to start the IDE. It's just there

2. What is the type of Visual Basic project that we are concerned with in this book?

The Standard.EXE project

3. Where on the Visual Basic menu is the Print command located?

On the File menu

4. Pretend that you have just fired up VB. You can't find your Toolbox. Where is it, and what can you do to get it back?

Since the Toolbox is a window, it's very possible that you have closed it. You can get it back by selecting View-Toolbox from the main menu.

5. While working in VISUAL BASIC, after you've designed your visual interface, you find that you are constantly nudging your controls out of position. How can you prevent this?

You can lock your controls once you are pleased with their locations. Do this either by selecting Lock Controls from the Format menu, or selecting the Lock Button on the Form Toolbar.

6. What menu command of the Format menu aligns selected objects on their left-most edges?

Align – Lefts

7. What does the Require Variable Declaration option of the Editor Tab of the Options menu do?

Selecting this option inserts Option Explicit in the General Declarations section of any new module.

8. I mentioned a menu option that I recommend should never be turned off. What is it?

Require Variable Declaration

9. Forgive me, but how many twips are there in an inch?

A twip is one twentieth of a printer's point. There are 72 printer points in an inch, so there are 1440 twips in an inch.

10. What is the name of the window that contains the controls that we will use to design our programs?

The Toolbox

11. What is the name of the window that displays properties associated with the form or a control that is currently selected on a form?

The Properties window

12. What window in the IDE is used to see the component pieces of your project?

The Project Explorer

13. What is the default name for a project in Visual Basic?

Project1

Extra Credit – What mathematical term is this?

'What the acorn said when it grew up.'

Geometry (as in 'Gee, I'm a tree!')

Chapter 4

1. What is a Visual Basic property?

A property is an attribute or characteristic of a Visual Basic object

2. What is the List Box at the top of the Properties Window and what is it for?

It's the Object ListBox, which lists all of the objects that belong to the form

3. The Properties Window contains two tabs that affect the order in which the properties are displayed. What are the names of the two tabs?

Alphabetic and Categorized

4. What property of the form designates a graphic file to display as background for the form?

The Picture Property

5. What is the name of the directory in which we save the China Shop Project?

\VBFILES\CHINA

6. Can you name two properties of the form that affect its location within the `Screen` object?

Top and Left

7. Can you name two properties that affect the dimensions of the form?

Height and Width

8. In general, different objects in Visual Basic share common properties. Can you name one property that every object possesses?

The Name property

9 What property of the Form affects what is displayed in the Form's Title Bar?

The Caption property

10. What is the property of the Form that prevents the Form's Control Box from appearing in the upper left hand corner of the form?

The ControlBox property.

11. _____ are actions that you can perform on Visual Basic objects.

Methods

12. The Visual Basic Code Window contains two ListBoxes at the top. Can you name them?

The Object ListBox and the Event ListBox.

13. Can you name one property that can never be changed at run time?

The Name property

14. How is the Name property of a form different from the name specified when the form is saved to disk?

The Name property is the way you refer to the control in your VISUAL BASIC Code. The name of the form that is saved to disk is used by your operating system to load the form into memory for use by your project. They are two different animals

15. Why did we set the `BorderStyle` of the form in the China Shop Project to `1 - Fixed Single?`

We didn't want customers to be able to move or resize the form

16. How do you turn 'on' the SDI Interface in the IDE?

Tools-Options-Advanced from the main menu

Extra Credit – How far can a dog run into the woods?

Halfway. After that, the dog is running out of the woods

Chapter 5

1. Is every control that we will use to build the China Shop project found in the default Visual Basic ToolBox?

No – the Common Dialog control needs to be added

2. How do you add the CommonDialog Control to the Visual Basic ToolBox?

Select Project-Components from the Visual Basic Main Menu

3. In Visual Basic, are all controls visible at run time?

No – The Common Dialog Control and the Timer Control are invisible at run time

4. Where do you find the controls to place on your form?

In the Visual Basic ToolBox

5. The Frame control is a special kind of control called a _____ control?

Container

6. What Visual Basic control is ideal to display a list of items from which the user can select one or more items, but only those items?

The ListBox control.

7. What control is used primarily to display information to the user?

The Label control

8. What Visual Basic controls are used to initiate some kind of action?

The Command Button control.

9. The _____ is displayed on a form as a control containing a caption with a circle next to it.

The OptionButton Control

10. Which two controls allow the user to give a True/False or a Yes/No answer?

The CheckBox Control and the Option Button Control.

11. A control array is like a family of controls. It contains members, just like a family. Each member of the control array is created with identical properties (including the **Name** property) except for one, the _____ property.

Index

12. What's the primary difference between the check box and the option button controls?

Both allow the user to give a True/False or a Yes/No answer. The difference between the two controls is their behavior in groups. A user can select only one OptionButton control in a group, whereas they can select any number of CheckBoxes in a group

13. What control will we use in the China Shop project to display a picture of china patterns?

The Image Control

14. What control will we use in the China Shop project to display a dialog box permitting the user to change the color of the form?

The Common Dialog control

15. What control will we use in the China Shop project to display a changing date and time?

The Timer Control

16. What property of the controls in the China Shop project is used to display hints as to their operation?

The ToolTipText property

17. What property of the Command Button is used to equate the press of the Enter key with its Click event?

The Default property

18. What property of the Command Button is used to equate the press of the Esc key with its Click event?

The Cancel property

19. What is the property of the Image control that tells it to change shape to accommodate the graphic file being loaded into it?

The Stretch property

20. What is the property of the Label control that tells Visual Basic to re-size the label based on the 'width' of its Caption property?

The AutoSize property

Extra Credit – A man had a flock of 19 sheep. He wanted to give each of his three children a share: half to the eldest, a quarter to the middle one, and a fifth to the youngest. He realized that this plan would involve chopping up sheep. What clever way did he come up with to avoid this dilemma?

To avoid chopping up sheep, he borrowed an extra sheep from one of his friends. Now he had 20 sheep all together. He gave 10 sheep (half) to the eldest child, 5 (a quarter) to the middle one, and 4 (a fifth) to the youngest. Then he gave the sheep he had borrowed back to his friend.

Chapter 6

1. When we write Visual Basic code, we place that code in _____ Procedures, which are then executed when Windows events are triggered.

Event

2. How are events in a Windows program triggered?

1. The user does something to trigger the event

2. The Operating System does something to trigger the event

3. The event is triggered through Visual Basic code

3. What event is triggered when the user presses and then releases a mouse button over an object?

The Click event

4. What is the full name of the `Click` event of the `Label1` control?

Label1_Click

5. True or False: In Visual Basic, different objects or controls can react to the same event?

True. For instance, both the Form and the Command Button react to the click event.

6. What event occurs when a form is loaded?

The Load event

7. How many events does the Timer control react to?

Only one – appropriately enough, the Timer Event

8. What is probably the easiest way to open up the Visual Basic Code Window?

Double click on the form or an object on the form

9. What is the name of the method used to add an item to a list box control?

The AddItem method

10. In Visual Basic code, how do you specify a comment?

Type an apostrophe ('). As soon as Visual Basic sees an apostrophe, it ignores the rest of the line of code

11. What is the Visual Basic line continuation character?

The underscore (_)

12. Throughout the chapter, I refer to the default behavior of Visual Basic code as
_____

A falling rock

13. What Visual Basic statement did we use in the chapter to create an 'Event Viewer'?

The Debug.Print statement

14. How do you display the Immediate window in Visual Basic?

With the program 'paused', press Ctrl+G

15. Can you name three ways to pause your running Visual Basic program?

The Pause button on the Visual Basic ToolBar

The Run-Break option of the main menu

The Break Key on the keyboard

16. How can you run a Visual Basic program in step mode?

Press Function Key [F8]

Select Debug-Step Into from the Visual Basic main menu

17. Which watch expression type will not pause the program by itself?

The vanilla 'Watch Expression' type

18. What kind of watch type causes the program to pause when the value of the expression changes?

Break When Value Changes

Extra Credit – Do they have a 4th of July in England?

Yes, they have one everywhere!

Chapter 7

1. _____ are placeholders stored in the Computer's memory.

Variables

2. What's the most common keyword used to declare a variable in an event procedure?

Dim

3. If you don't specify a specific variable data type when you declare it, then the variable is set up as something called a _____ data type.

Variant

4. What's wrong with the following code?

```
Dim intPrice1, intPrice2, intPrice3 as Integer
```
If the programmer intended to declare three Integer type variables, that's not going to happen. The first two variables, because a data type is not specified, are declared as Variant type variables Only the last variable is declared as an Integer type

5. What's unusual about the static type variable in Visual Basic?

Its value is retained as long as the program is running.

6. Must variables be declared in Visual Basic?

Unfortunately, variable declaration is not required unless Option Explicit is specified in the General Declarations section of the module

7. There are five Visual Basic numeric data types. Can you name them all?

Integer, Long, Single, Double, and Currency

8. Which two numeric data types only deal with whole numbers?

Integer and Long

9. What's the upper limit for an integer data type?

32,767

10. Name the data types that permit you to store fractions.

Single, Double, and Currency

11. What's the difference in the following two declarations?

```
Dim strValue1 as String
Dim strValue2 as String * 9
```
The first declaration is a variable length string, and the second is a fixed length string of 9 characters. The rule of thumb is, if you are sure of the length of the string, declare it as a fixed length string.

12. What two values can a Boolean data type contain?

True or False

13. What are the valid ranges for a date data type?

The valid ranges are:

January 1, 100 to December 31, 9999

14. What's the operator symbol for exponentiation?

^

15. What's the difference between the / and \ division operators?

/ is the Floating Point Division operator. Its result is a number with a fractional part.

\ is the Integer Division operator. Its result is a whole number.

16. What does the Mod operator do?

It returns a value equal to the remainder of a division operation.

17. Based on the Order of Operations, in the absence of parentheses, what operation is performed first, subtraction or multiplication?

Multiplication

18. What logical operation is true only if both the left and right expressions are true?

The AND operation.

19. What logical operation is false only if both the left and right expressions are false?

The OR Operation

Extra Credit – If you had only one match and entered a room in which there was a kerosene lamp, and oil burner, and a wood-burning stove, which would you light first?

The match.

Chapter 8

1. Can you name a common Visual Basic selection structure discussed in this chapter?

The If...Then statement

The Select...Case Statement

2. There are two syntaxes for the `If…Then` statement. What are they?

The single line syntax and the multiple-line syntax

3. When isn't an `End If` statement required in an `If…Then` statement?

When the If statement and the Then statement begin and end on the same line

When the Then statement consists of a single statement

4. What does the statement `Form1.Cls` do?

It clears the form of the output of any previous Print statements.

5. What's an alternative to the `If...Then...Else` statement which is useful when there are many alternatives to evaluate?

The Select...Case Statement

6. Pretend that we have a text box on a form with the name `txtNumber`. The number 23 is in the text box. What will the following code do when the user clicks on the form?

```
Private Sub Form_click()
  Select Case txtNumber.Text
    Case 23
      MsgBox "DO RE MI"
    Case 10 To 25
      MsgBox "FA SO LA"
    Case Is < 30
      MsgBox "TI DO"
  End Select
End Sub
```

A MsgBox with the message "DO RE MI" will be displayed. Most people think that all 3 message boxes will be displayed, but you must remember, that in a Select Case statement, when a true condition is encountered, the structure is exited.

7. What will this code do when the `Command1` button is clicked?

```
Private Sub Command1_click()
  If "X" = "x" Then
    MsgBox "I like to swim"
  Else
    MsgBox "I like to ski"
  End If
End Sub
```

A MsgBox will be displayed with the message "I like to ski"

8. What selection structure is very useful when you are only testing for a single expression.

Select Case

9. When do you need to use the keyword "`Is`" in a `Select Case` statement?

When you are using a comparison operator in the test condition

10. What's the function of `Case Else` in a `Select` Statement?

It's a "catchall". If none of the other Case conditions evaluate to True, then the code after the Case Else is executed.

11. What will be the output of this code?

```
Private Sub cmdOK_Click()
  Dim intValue As Integer
    intValue = 13
  If intValue = 13 Then
    MsgBox "Yes"
  End If
End Sub
```

Yes

12. What will be the output of this code?

```
Private Sub cmdOK_Click()
  Dim intValue As Integer
    intValue = 13
  If intValue = 12 Then
    MsgBox "Moe"
  Else
    MsgBox "Larry"
  End If
End Sub
```

Larry

13. What will be the output of this code?

```
Private Sub cmdOK_Click()
  Dim intValue As Integer
  intValue = 13
  If intValue > 14 Or intValue < 13
    MsgBox "Yes"
  Else
    MsgBox "No"
  End If
End Sub
```

No

14. What will be the output of this code?

```
Private Sub cmdOK_Click()
  Dim intValue As Integer
    intValue = 13
  If intValue > 17 Or intValue < 14 Then
    MsgBox "Yes"
  Else
    MsgBox "No"
  End If
End Sub
```

Yes

15. What will be the output of this code?

```
Private Sub cmdOK_Click()
  Dim intValue As Integer
    intValue = 13
  If intValue > 10 And intValue < 13 Then
    MsgBox "Yes"
  Else
    MsgBox "No"
  End If
End Sub
```

No

16. What will be the output of this code?

```
Dim intValue As Integer
  intValue = 13
  If intValue > 11 Then
    If intValue = 13 Then
      MsgBox "Yes"
    Else
      MsgBox "No"
    End If
  End If
End Sub
```

No

17. What will be the output of this code?

```
Private Sub cmdOK_Click()
  Dim intValue As Integer
  intValue = 13
  Select Case intValue
    Case 12
      MsgBox "Moe"
    Case 13
      MsgBox "Larry"
    Case 14
      MsgBox "Curly"
  End Select
End Sub
```

Larry

18. What will be the output of this code?

```
Private Sub cmdOK_Click()
  Dim intValue As Integer
  intValue = 13
  Select Case intValue
    Case 11
      MsgBox "Moe"
    Case 12
      MsgBox "Larry"
    Case Else
      MsgBox "Curly"
  End Select
End Sub
```

Curly

Extra Credit – How many birthdays does the average person have?

One. Do you know anyone with two birthdays?

Chapter 9

1. What does a loop do?

Loop structures allow you to execute a line or lines of code repeatedly without having to type those lines over and over again

2. There are five types of loop structures. Can you name them?

For...Next

Do While...Loop

Do...Loop While

Do...Loop Until

For Each...Next

3. What is the syntax for the For...Next Loop?

For counter = start To end [step increment]

   statements

Next Counter

4. Which of the following three parameters of the For...Next loop is optional – Start, End or Step?

Step

5. What is the default value for Step?

Positive One

6. Can the Step parameter be a negative number?

Yes.

7. True or False: The Start, End, and Step parameters must be specified as a numeric literal

False. These parameters can be specified as a Visual Basic expression, which can really be anything ranging from a variable, a constant, to a combination of variables, constants, and numeric literals

8. In the following For...Next loop, what is the initial value of the counter?

```
Dim lngCounter as Long
  For lngCounter 22 to 400
  Debug.Print lngCounter
Next lngCounter
```

22

9. In the following For...Next loop, what is the end value of the counter?

```
Dim lngCounter As Long
   For lngCounter 22 to 400
   Debug.Print lngCounter
Next lngcounter
```

400

10. In the following For...Next loop, what is the step value?

```
Dim lngCounter As Long
For lngCounter 22 to 400
   Debug.Print lngCounter
Next lngCounter
```

It's presumed to be +1

11. What will be the output of this code?

```
Private Sub Command1_Click()
   Dim lngCounter As Long
   For lngCounter = 1 To 10 Step 3
      Debug.Print lngCounter
   Next lngCounter
End Sub
```

The numbers 1,4,7 and 10 will be printed in the Debug window

12. What will be the output of this code?

```
Private Sub Command1_Click()
   Dim lngCounter As Long
   Dim lngStart As Long
   Dim lngStop As Long
   Dim lngStep As Long
   lngStart = 50
   lngStop = 500
   lngStep = 100
   For lngCounter = lngStart To lngStop Step lngStep
      Debug.Print lngCounter
   Next lngCounter
End Sub
```

Surprise. Yes, as I mentioned in the chapter, the start, end, and step values can be specified as a number, or an expression such as a variable or constant.

The numbers 50, 150, 250, 350, and 450 will be printed in the Debug window

13. What will be the output of this code?

```
Private Sub Command1_Click()
  Dim lngCounter As Long
  For lngCounter = 50 To 14 - 1
    Debug.Print lngCounter
  Next lngCounter
End Sub
```

Nothing. It's a trick question. A lot of people read that "- 1" as a negative step value, but it's really part of the expression "14 -1" or 13. Since 50 is already greater than the end point of 13, and since the step is presumed to be a positive one, the loop never executes.

14. What will be the output of this code?

```
Private Sub Command1_Click()
  Dim lngCounter As Long
  For lngCounter = 50 To 14 Step -10
    Debug.Print lngCounter
  Next lngCounter
End Sub
```

This time you've got it. That minus sign really is a negative step.

The numbers 50, 40, 30 and 20 will be printed in the Debug window.

15. What is the only place that an Exit For statement can be coded?

Within the body of a For...Next loop.

16. True or False: In a Do While...Loop the body of the loop will be executed at least once.

True

17. True or False: In a Do Until...Loop the body of the loop will executed at least once.

False.

18. What will be the output of this loop?

```vb
Private Sub cmdOK_Click()
  Dim intValue As Integer
  intValue = 5
  Do While intValue < 9
    Form1.Print intValue
    intValue = intValue + 1
  Loop
End Sub
```

The numbers 5,6,7 and 8.

19. What will be the output of this loop?

```vb
Private Sub cmdOK_Click()
  Dim intValue As Integer
  intValue = 5
  Do
    Form1.Print intValue
    intValue = intValue + 1
  Loop Until intValue > 13
End Sub
```

5,6,7,8,9,10,11,12,13

Extra Credit – Some months have 30 days, some have 31 days, how many have 28 days?

All of them!

Chapter 10

1. What does string concatenation mean?

"Concatenation" means to join two strings together

2. What are the two concatenation operators?

The ampersand(&) and

The plus(+) sign

3. Which concatenation operator is preferred by Microsoft?

The & is preferred because it eliminates the need to do data type conversion

4. What will the following code display?

```
Private Sub Command1_Click()
Dim strValue1 As String
Dim strValue2 As String
Dim strValue3 As String
Dim strValue4 As String
strValue1 = "Eat"
strValue2 = "at"
strValue3 = "Joe's"
strValue4 = "Diner"
Form1.Print strValue1 & strValue2 & strValue3 & strValue4
End Sub
```

EatatJoe'sDiner

5. There's a problem with the code from question 5. What would be one way to correct it?

```
Private Sub Command1_Click()
Dim strValue1 As String
Dim strValue2 As String
Dim strValue3 As String
Dim strValue4 As String
strValue1 = "Eat "
strValue2 = "at "
strValue3 = "Joe's "
strValue4 = "Diner "
Form1.Print strValue1 & strValue2 & strValue3 & strValue4
End Sub
```

6. True or False: Strings can be "broken apart" and "isolated" as well as joined together.

Wow, you would really have to have been asleep when you read this chapter to get this wrong. The answer of course is True, and there are three Visual Basic functions that allow you to do this – Left\$, Mid\$, and Right\$.

7. What does the Len function do?

The Len function returns an integer value equal to the length of a string provided as the argument.

8. What does the function InStr do?

The InStr function returns an integer value equal to the beginning position of one string within another. In other words, it searches for a character or characters within a string.

9. What does a return value of 0 from the Instr function indicate?

That no "match" of the search string within the string searched was found.

10. How many arguments of the function Instr are optional?

2 arguments are optional---the first argument, which specifies the starting location, and the fourth argument, which specifies the comparison type.

11. If you provide the Instr function with a comparison argument, do you need to provide any other arguments to the function?

Yes. Arguments 2 and 3, which represent the string to be searched, and the string to search for, respectively, must always be supplied. However, if you supply an argument for comparison, you must supply an argument for the starting position within the string to be searched.

12. What technique can you use to have a message appear in a message box with more than one line?

Concatenate a carriage return and a line feed character to a string, then concatenate a string to the carriage return and the line feed.

13. What's an algorithm?

An algorithm is a plan for solving a problem, usually itemized step by step, and drawing upon the information that is known at coding time and the information that will be gathered at run time.

14. What does the function Left$ do?

The **Left$** function returns a specified number of characters from the left side of a string.

15. What does the function Right$ do?

The Right$ function returns a specified number of characters from the right side of a string.

16. What does the Mid$ function do?

The Mid$ function returns a specified number of characters from a string, and is not restricted to working from one "side" of the string or another.

17. What's the difference between the Mid$ function and the Mid function?

The difference is in the data type of the return value. The Mid$ function returns a string data type, whereas the Mid function returns a variant data type.

18. What function can be used to "convert" a string to upper case?

The UCase function

19. What will the value of `strValue` be after this code runs?

```
Dim strValue as String
strValue = LCase("Who doesn't love Visual Basic")
```
strValue will be equal to "who doesn't love visual basic"

Extra Credit – A farmer had 17 sheep. All but 9 died. How many did he have left?

9!

Chapter 11

1. What Visual Basic statement is used to prepare a disk file to be read from or written to?

The Open statement

2. Which Visual Basic statement allows you to write data to an opened file?

Write#

3. What are the three steps necessary in order to write data to a disk file?

Open the file using the Open Statement

Write data to the file using the Write# statement

Close the File using the Close Statement

4. What modes of the `Open` statement can be used to write data to a disk file?

Append and Output

5. What are the valid ranges of file numbers?

1 to 511. Ordinarily, you start with 1 for the first file opened in your program, 2 for the second, etc.

6. If you had a file opened with a file number of 1, what code would you use to close it?

```
Close #1
```
7. What code would you write to close every open file in your program?

```
Close
```

8. What are the three steps necessary in order to read data from a disk file?

Open the file using the Open Statement

Read data from the file using the Input# statement

Close the File using the Close Statement

9. What modes of the Open statement can be used to read data from a disk file?

Only one – Input

10. What statement is used to read data from an open disk file?

Input#

11. What function can be used to return the next available file number?

The Freefile function

12. What is EOF?

EOF is really just a special character in a disk file that tells programs there is no more data beyond this point.

13. In order to send output to the printer, you must use the special Visual Basic object called the _____

The Printer Object

14. What will this code do?

```
Printer.Print "I love"
Printer.Print "Visual Basic"
```
Most people would say it would print "I love" and then "Visual Basic" on two different lines of the printer paper. However, without an EndDoc, this output will never be sent to the printer

15. What will this code do?

```
Printer.Print "I love Visual Basic"
Printer.Enddoc
```
Send the Print the statement "I love Visual Basic" on the PC's attached default printer

16. What is the Tab parameter of the Print method used for?

It directs output to a particular location on the Form or Printer

Extra Credit – Divide 30 by 1/2 and add 10. What is the answer?

70!

Chapter 12

1. In Visual Basic, there are two types of menus. Can you name Can you name both of them?

Drop Down and PopUp. If you're a stickler, there's also something called a Dynamic menu, but we don't cover those in the course.

2. True or False: The Menu Editor can be invoked by using the `Ctrl+M` key combination.

False. Ctrl+E

3. If you wanted to create a menu option named File where the access key is `Alt + F`, how should the caption read?

&File

4. If you wanted to create a menu option named Exit where the access key is `Alt + X`, how should the caption read?

E&xit

5. Can more than 1 menu option have the same shortcut key?

No

6. How do you create a separator bar for a menu?

Create a menu option whose caption is the dash(-)

7. True or False: A menu option specified as a separator bar does not require an entry for name.

False

8. What events does the menu control respond to?

Only the click event

9. What does the "checked" property of a menu item do?

Clicking on this property, or setting it to True in code, causes a tick, or check mark to appear besides the menu item. This is great for lists of options.

10. Can you have more than one PopUp Menu displayed at any given moment?

No

11. True or False: In order for a PopUp Menu to appear, the menu item must be designed using the menu editor.

True

12. To how many levels can a menu be nested?

5 levels below the top level.

13. How do you bring up the code window for a menu item?

Single-click on the item on the form at design time, or bring up the code window in the normal way, and search for the menu item in the object list box.

14. What is the function of the Insert button in the Menu Editor?

It allows you to insert a menu item between two others.

15. Can a menu item have the same name as another?

Only if it's a member of a control array.

Extra Credit – If an electric train is traveling Northwest at 80 MPH, and there is a Southwest breeze of 15 MPH, in which direction does the smoke from the train blow?

Electric trains don't have smoke!

Chapter 13

1. What's the difference between an "ordinary" variable and an array variable?

An "ordinary" variable is capable of having only one value. An array variable is a variable that can contain multiple values.

2. What's the difference between a static array and a dynamic array?

A static array is declared with a fixed amount of elements. A dynamic array is declared with a variable amount of elements.

3. What statement is used to 'refine' the number of elements to be stored in a dynamic array?

The ReDim statement

4. What does this code do?

```
Dim intValue(0) as Integer
```

It declares intValue as an Integer array with a Lower Bound of 0 and an Upper Bound of 0. Exactly one element

5. What does this code do?

```
Dim strValue() as String
```

It declares strValue as a dynamic String array. Until a ReDim is executed, this array has no size, and cannot have a value assigned to any of its elements

6. What's wrong with this declaration?

```
Private intQuizScore(10000) As Integer
```

Nothing, provided all of the elements will be used. Over-allocating the size of an array because you don't know how many elements it will hold is not a good idea. It wastes precious memory.

7. What is the default Lower Bound value for arrays?

The default Lower Bound value is 0. This can be changed by placing the statement

```
Option Base 1
```

in the General Declarations section of a Form, Standard, or Class Module.

8. Here is an array declaration. With an Option Base of 0, how many elements does this contain?

```
Dim IntArray(100)
```

The answer is 101. The number in parenthesis is the "Upper Bound" of the array. With an Option Base of 0, the "Lower Bound" is 0, and with an "Upper Bound" of 100, the number of elements is 101.

9. With an Option Base of 1, how many elements does this array contain?

```
Dim IntArray(100)
```

The answer is 100. The number in parenthesis is the "Upper Bound" of the array. With an Option Base of 1, the "Lower Bound" is 1, and with an "Upper Bound" of 100, the number of elements is 100.

10. Suppose you have an array that contains 100 employee names. Now you decide you need 101. What statement should you use to resize the array to 101, yet still retain the original 100 names. Option Base is 1.

Redim Preserve IntArray(101)

11. What does this code do?

```
Dim intQuizScore(2 To 5) As Integer
```
This code declares a Static array called intQuizScore with a Lower Bound of 2 and an Upper Bound of 5, for a total of 4 elements.

12. What does this code do?

```
Dim intQuizScore(4,5) As Integer
```
This code declares a two dimensional Static array called intQuizScore with a first dimension Upper Bound of 4, and a second dimension Upper Bound of 5. With an option base of 0, both Lower Bounds would be 0, for a total of 30 elements. (0 to 4 is 5 elements, 0 to 5 is 6 elements – 5 multiplied by 6 is 30 total elements)

13. What does this code do?

```
Dim intQuizScore(4 to 6,5) As Integer
```
It declares a two dimensional Static array called intQuizScore with a first dimension Lower Bound of 4, an Upper Bound of 6, and a second dimension Upper Bound of 5. With an option base of 0, the Lower Bound of the second dimension would be 0, for a total of 18 elements. (4 to 6 is 3 elements, 0 to 5 is 6 elements – 3 multiplied by 6 is 18 total elements)

14. What does this code do?

```
Dim intQuizScore(3,4 to 6,5) As Integer
```
This code declares a three dimensional Static array called intQuizScore with a first dimension Upper Bound of 3, a second dimension Lower Bound of 4, and an Upper Bound of 6, and a second dimension Upper Bound of 5. With an option base of 0, the Lower Bound of the first and third dimensions would be 0, for a total of 72 elements. (0 to 3 is 4 elements, 4 to 6 is 3 elements, 0 to 5 is 6 elements – 4 multiplied by 3 multiplied by 6 is 72 total elements)

15. What does this code do?

```
Dim intQuizScore(3,4 to 6,5) As Integer

Form1.print Lbound(intQuizScore,1)
```
It prints the value of the Lower Bound of the first dimension of array intQuizScore, or the value 0.

Extra Credit – What are the holes numbered on the IBM Executive Golf Course in New York State?

0 to 17

Chapter 14

1. The `Err` object has six properties. What is the property that contains the error code that was last generated by your application?

Err.Number

2. What is wrong with this code? Telling me that division by 0 is wrong, or noting the use of the Visual Basic `GoTo` are not what I'm looking for either.

```
Public Sub Division()
   On Error GoTo ErrorHandler
   Print 12 / 0
Exit Sub

ErrorHandle:
   Msgbox Str(Err.Number) & ": " & Err.Description, , "Error"
Exit Sub
```

The name of the Label for the Error Handler is spelled incorrectly. The Error Handler will never be invoked.

3. In this code, what is the function of the `Exit Sub` before the label?

```
Public Sub Division()
   On Error GoTo ErrorHandler
   Print 12 / 0
   On Error Goto 0
Exit Sub
ErrorHandler:
   Msgbox Str(Err.Number) & ": " & Err.Description, , "Error"
   On Error GoTo 0
End Sub
```

Exit Sub before the Error handler ensures that if the program encounters no error, the Error handler will not accidentally be invoked.

4. There are three variations on the `Resume` statement found in an error handler. Don't worry, I'll only ask you about two. What is the difference between `Resume` and `Resume Next`?

Resume Next causes the program, after executing the instructions in the Error handler, to resume execution of the program after the line that generated the error. Resume causes the program, after executing the instructions in the Error handler, to attempt to execute the line of code that caused the Error handler to be invoked in the first place.

5. What's wrong with this piece of code?

```
Private Function Divide(ByVal dOne As Double, ByVal dTwo As Double) As
    Double
    Divide = dOne / dTwo
End Function
```

Trick question – sorry. Nothing is really wrong with it, but it has no error handling to check for a divide by zero.

6. What's wrong with this code?

```
Private Function Divide(ByVal dOne As Double, ByVal dTwo As Double) As
    Double
    On Error GoTo Divide_Err:
    Divide = dOne / dTwo
    Divide_Err:
    Resume
End Function
```

You might think that we have error checking to cope with the divide by zero, but Resume just resumes execution at the line that caused the error. So this will just loop forever.

7. What happens if you type the following statement into the Immediate window pane?

```
? sMyValue
```

This is the same as typing Print sMyValue. The value of the variable sMyValue will be displayed in the Immediate window.

8. What's the purpose of a counter?

In a Visual Basic program, a counter is a variable that is normally incremented by 1. It is usually declared in order to count something – records read, entries made, etc.

9. What's the purpose of an accumulator, and how is it different from a counter?

An accumulator is not much different from a counter. Both the counter and accumulator are variables that are declared to count something. The difference is that a counter typically is incremented by 1, whereas an accumulator usually has a more substantial value added to it.

10. What error code is generated when you perform a read or write operation on a file that hasn't been opened?

Run-time error '52'---Bad file name or number

11. What error code is generated when you attempt to read past the EOF marker in a disk file?

Run-time error '62' – Input past end of file

12. The key to error handling in Visual Basic is to first _____ an error handler in the procedure.

Enable

13. What follows the keyword `GoTo`?

A Visual Basic label

14. What is the property of the CommonDialog control that enables your program to 'intercept' an error if the user presses the `Cancel` button?

The CancelError property

15. True or False: An instance of the `Err` object is created when an error occurs in a procedure only when the procedure has an enabled error handler.

False. Regardless of whether you have enabled an error handler, when an error occurs in your procedure, an instance of the Err object is created.

Extra Credit – If a plane crashes on the border between two states, where are the survivors buried?

Why would you want to bury the survivors?

Chapter 15

1. How can you back up the Windows Registry?

Select Registry-Export Registry File from RegEdit's Main menu

2. What function is used to read an entry from the Windows Registry?

GetSetting

3. What happens if you use the `GetSetting` function to read an entry from the Windows registry that doesn't exist?

If the entry cannot be found, if a default value has been specified, then that value will be used as for the return value of the function. If no default value has been specified, then "" will be used as the return value. Not specifying a default value can cause your program to "bomb".

4. How many arguments does the **SaveSetting** statement require?

Four. Appname, Section, Key and Setting.

5. What happens if you call the **SaveSetting** function, and an entry already exists for that **AppName, Section** and **Key**?

The Value is updated.

6. What is a user-written procedure?

A user-written procedure is code that is not associated with an object, and therefore is not executed as part of a triggered event.

7. What is the difference between a subprocedure and a function?

A function returns a value to the calling procedure and a sub procedure returns no value.

8. What is the syntax to "call" a user-written subprocedure called '**CalculatePrice**' with no arguments?

Call CalculatePrice

9. Is the word "call" mandatory when calling a subprocedure or function?

No, it's optional. Many programmers use it because it alerts them to the fact that they are calling a user-written procedure.

10. The following code contains a user written subprocedure called '**Bell**', and a call to that subprocedure. What will be the output of the code?

```
Sub Bell()
  Dim x As Integer
  x = 22
  MsgBox "The value of x is " & x
End Sub

Private Sub Command1_Click()
  Call Bell
End Sub
```

A message box with the message "The value of x is 22" will be displayed.

Extra Credit – Two people were playing checkers. They played five games, and each won the same number of games. There were no ties. Explain this.

They weren't playing each other.

Appendix B

Hungarian Notation

Having a naming convention for your controls and objects makes it a lot easier for you to remember what you're working with. The prefixes here are called Hungarian Notation, having been first used by the Hungarian Charles Simonyi.

Control	Prefix
Check Box	chk
Combo Box	cbo
Command Button	cmd
Common Dialog Control	dlg
Data	dat
Form	frm
Frame	fra
Grid	grd
Image	img
Label	lbl
List Box	lst
Menu	mnu
Option Button	opt
Picture	pic
Shape	shp
Text Box	txt
Timer	tmr

It's also a good idea to label your variables in the same way, so that you can see at a glance what data type a variable uses, even if you declared it somewhere else.

Variable	Prefix
Boolean	`bln`
Currency	`cur`
Double	`dbl`
Date & Time	`dat`
Long	`lng`
Integer	`int`
Single	`sng`
String	`str`
Variant	`var`

Index

Index

Index

Index

Index

Index

Index

Index

Index

Index

Index

Now That You're Ready...

For weeks, maybe months even, you ate, drank, and breathed Visual Basic. Now you feel like your life is somehow over. You were tantalized into believing that life could be rosier with VB, but with no direction, you've been plunged into the abyss of depression once more. "How can this be?" you ask. But nobody listens. Heck, even I'm getting sick of listening to you.

But then you realize. You're not on the road to oblivion. You're on an Active Path. So get off your backside and *Get Active*. Go to `www.activepath.com` and take the ultimate test. If you fail, huge monsters from two blocks away will suck on your toes in a disgusting manner.

But if you pass, having been equipped for the struggle by the ineffable wisdom of the great Simelius, you shall have attained the rank of Initiate, ready to progress along the great Path, as described by the ancestors. You shall be paraded in the streets in front of many, who shall bow, and cry out in admiration, "Long live the great Programmer, who shall ever increase in power."

And you'll get a T-shirt worthy of such an achievement. It's not over; no, not by a long way. I haven't finished with you. Why, you haven't even cried out for mercy yet.

activepath

activepath

If you enjoyed this book, and

you're interested in other titles

by Active Path, why not drop in

to our web site at:

www.activepath.com

Support • Sample Code • New Titles • News

activepath

Active Path writes books for you. Any suggestions, or ideas about how you want information presented in your ideal book will be studied by our team. Your comments are always valued at Active Path.

Free phone in USA 800-873-9769
Fax (312) 397 8990

UK Tel. (0121) 706 6826   Fax   (0121) 706 2967

———— Computer Book Publishers ————

NB. If you post the bounce back card below in the UK, please send it to:
Active Path Ltd. 30 Lincoln Road, Birmingham, B27 6PA

NO POSTAGE
NECESSARY
IF MAILED
IN THE
UNITED STATES

BUSINESS REPLY MAIL
FIRST CLASS MAIL   PERMIT#64   CHICAGO, IL

POSTAGE WILL BE PAID BY ADDRESSEE

WROX PRESS
1512 NORTH FREMONT
SUITE 103
CHICAGO IL 60622-2567